The West

Encounters and Transformations

Volume C: From the French Revolution to the Present

Fourth Edition

Brian Levack

University of Texas at Austin

Edward Muir

Northwestern University

Meredith Veldman

Louisiana State University

PEARSON

Boston   Columbus   Indianapolis   New York   San Francisco   Upper Saddle River
Amsterdam   Cape Town   Dubai   London   Madrid   Milan   Munich   Paris   Montréal   Toronto
Delhi   Mexico City   São Paulo   Sydney   Hong Kong   Seoul   Singapore   Taipei   Tokyo

Editor-in-Chief: Dickson Musslewhite
Executive Editor: Jeff Lasser
Editorial Project Manager: Rob DeGeorge
Director of Marketing: Brandy Dawson
Executive Marketing Manager: Wendy Albert
Marketing Assistant: Stephanie Toronidis
Production Project Manager: Mirella Signoretto
Senior Managing Editor: Ann Marie McCarthy
Senior Operations Supervisor: Mary Ann Gloriande
Senior Art Director: Maria Lange
Text Design: Red Kite Project
Cover Design: Maria Lange/Red Kite Project

Manager, Visual Research & Permissions: Beth Brenzel
Editorial Assistant: Maureen Diana
Cover Illustration: Gregor Mendel, by Paul Chung /
 © INTERFOTO / Alamy
Media Director: Brian Hyland
Media Project Manager: Claudine Bellanton
Program Manager: Emily Tamburri
Media Editor: Thomas Scalzo
Composition/Full-Service Project Management: S4Carlisle
 Publishing Services
Printer/Binder: LSC Communications
Cover Printer: LSC Communications

This book was set in Minion Pro Regular 10.5/13

Credits and acknowledgments borrowed from other sources and reproduced, with permission, in this textbook appear on page C-1 or on the appropriate page within the text.

Library of Congress Cataloging-in-Publication Data
Levack, Brian P.
 The West : encounters & transformations / Brian Levack, Edward Muir, Meredith Veldman. — Fourth edition, Combined volume.
  pages cm
 Includes bibliographical references and index.
 ISBN-13: 978-0-205-94715-7 (paperback : combined volume : alkaline paper)
 ISBN-10: 0-205-94715-8 (paperback : combined volume : alkaline paper) 1. Civilization, Western—History—Textbooks.
 I. Muir, Edward. II. Veldman, Meredith. III. Title.
 CB245.W455 2013
 909'.09821—dc23

2013004227

Combined Volume	Volume 1	Volume 2
ISBN 10: 0-205-94715-8	ISBN 10: 0-205-94859-6	ISBN 10: 0-205-94858-8
ISBN 13: 978-0-205-94715-7	ISBN 13: 978-0-205-94859-8	ISBN 13: 978-0-205-94858-1
Instructor's Review Copy	Volume 1 A La Carte	Volume 2 A La Carte
ISBN 10: 0-205-97274-8	ISBN 10: 0-205-94921-5	ISBN 10: 0-205-94922-3
ISBN 13: 978-0-205-97274-6	ISBN 13: 978-0-205-94921-2	ISBN 13: 978-0-205-94922-9
Volume A	Volume B	Volume C
ISBN 10: 0-205-98768-0	ISBN 10: 0-205-98769-9	ISBN 10: 0-205-98770-2
ISBN 13: 978-0-205-98768-9	ISBN 13: 978-0-205-98769-6	ISBN 13: 978-0-205-98770-2

8 17

BRIEF CONTENTS

CONTENTS

Each chapter concludes with the following: Making Connections, Taking It Further, Chapter Review, and Time Line.

MAPS

DOCUMENTS

Note: The following documents are referenced in the margins of the text and are available at **www.myhistorylab.com**. Document titles bearing a red speaker are available with audio.

Engage your students
beyond the classroom . . .

. . . with **MyHistoryLab** and
THE WEST: Encounters and Transformations, Fourth Edition

Would your students get more out of their introductory history course if you could engage them with history *beyond* the classroom? Would class discussion go farther if they were reading and writing more, working with primary sources, studying maps, and mastering key topics . . . *before* class meetings begin?

If your answer to these questions is yes, then it's time to consider how MyHistoryLab can help you meet these challenges. MyHistoryLab offers immersive content, tools, and experiences to engage students and help them succeed, enabling you to craft a better learning experience for them in your introductory survey course.

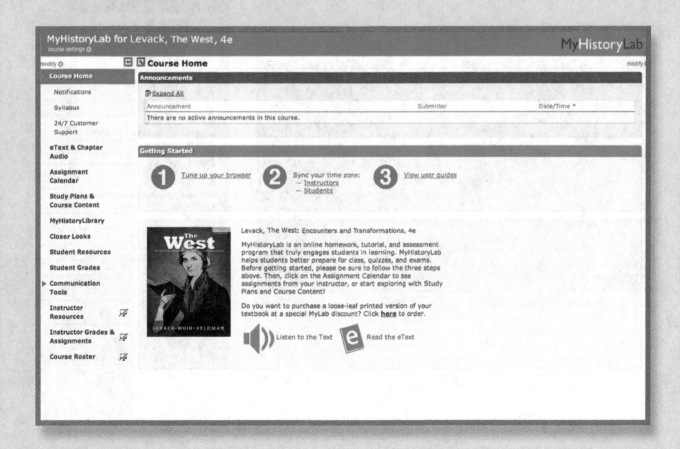

Prepare students on key topics with the MyHistoryLab Video Series

Are your introductory history students ready and eager to contend with a college textbook narrative? If not, help them get up-to-speed with the new MyHistoryLab Video Series: Key Topics in Western Civilization. Correlated to the chapters of *The West*, each video unit reviews key topics of the period, readying students to get the most from the text narrative. These engaging videos feature seasoned historians reviewing the pivotal stories of our past, in a lively format designed to demonstrate the power of historical narrative.

Drive your students into primary sources with the new MyHistoryLibrary

Now your students can read more than 200 of the most commonly assigned primary source documents, specially formatted in Pearson's powerful new eText. Students also have the option of listening to each reading in the accompanying Chapter Audio. Either way, students may access the text or the audio with various devices anytime they have access to the Internet.

Immerse your students in a powerful eText deeply integrated with MyHistoryLab

ntroductory survey teachers have long struggled to get students engaged in traditional textbooks. Now Pearson's MyHistoryLab offers a deeply immersive eText that transforms how students experience history. With a new pedagogically-driven design, it highlights a clear learning path through the material and offers a visually stunning learning experience in print or on a screen. With the Pearson eText, students can transition directly to MyHistoryLab resources such as primary source documents, videos, and Closer Look features. At last, history students can experience the eText they have been waiting for—one that comes alive on the screen.

Key Supplements and Customer Support

Annotated Instructor's eText

Contained within MyHistoryLab, the *Annotated Instructor's eText* for your Pearson textbook leverages the powerful Pearson eText platform to make it easier than ever for you to access subject-specific resources for class preparation. The *AI eText* serves as the hub for all instructor resources, with chapter-by-chapter links to PowerPoint slides, content from the Instructor's Manual, and *MyHistoryLab's* ClassPrep engine, which contains a wealth of history content organized for classroom use.

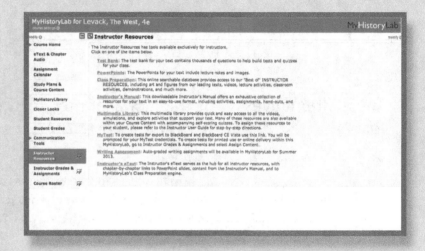

Instructor's Manual

The Instructor's Manual for *The West: Encounters and Transformations* contains learning objectives, a list of important themes discussed in the chapter, an overview of the Different Voices feature in the chapter, an annotated chapter outline with summaries of each section's content, suggestions for class activities, discussion questions, and suggestions for additional print and online resources for instructors. At the end of each chapter, MyHistoryLab Media Assignments catalog all of the MyHistoryLab resources for the chapter. The Instructor's Manual also contains a MyHistoryLab syllabus and suggestions for integrating MyHistoryLab into your course.

PowerPoint Presentations

Strong PowerPoint presentations make lectures more engaging for students. Correlated to the chapters of *The West*, each presentation includes a full lecture outline and a wealth of images, maps, and time lines from the textbook.

MyTest Test Bank

Containing a diverse set of multiple-choice, short-answer, and essay questions, the MyTest test bank supports a variety of assessment strategies. The large pool of multiple choice questions for each chapter includes factual, conceptual, and analytical questions, so that instructors may assess students on basic information as well as critical thinking.

Customer Support

Our dedicated team of local Pearson representatives will work with you not only to choose course materials but also to integrate them into your class and assess their effectiveness. Moreover, live support for MyHistoryLab users, both educators and students, is available 24/7.

Provide choices for your students through a variety of formats and price points

These alternatives to the traditional printed textbook are available for *THE WEST: Encounters and Transformations,* Fourth Edition.

>>> **MyHistoryLab with eTextbook** offers a full digital version of the print book and is readable on iOS and Android tablets. Students can get access to **MyHistoryLab** with the print book or save even more by purchasing on-line access at **www.myhistorylab.com**.

>>> **Books a la Carte** is a convenient, three-hole-punched, loose-leaf version of the traditional text at a discounted price—allowing students to carry only what they need to class. The Books a la Carte edition is also available with **MyHistoryLab** access.

>>> **Black & White Printed Textbook,** a discounted alternative, contains all the same content of the traditional text, rendered without color. To ensure full editorial integrity, some maps and illustrations in the Black & White edition have been redrawn. The Black & White edition is also available with **MyHistoryLab** access.

>>> **CourseSmart eTextbooks** offer the same content as the printed text in a convenient online format—with highlighting, online search, and printing capabilities. Learn more at **www.coursesmart.com**. **The CourseSmart eTextbook** is also available with **MyHistoryLab** access.

>>> **Pearson Custom Library** helps instructors build the perfect course solution. For enrollments of at least 25, create your own textbook by combining chapters from best-selling Pearson textbooks and reading selections. To begin building your custom text, visit **www.pearsoncustomlibrary.com**.

PREFACE

We wrote this textbook to answer questions about the identity of the civilization in which we live. Journalists, politicians, and scholars often refer to our civilization, its political ideologies, its economic systems, and its cultures as "Western" without fully considering what that label means and why it might be appropriate. The classification of our civilization as Western has become particularly problematic in the age of globalization. The creation of international markets, the rapid dissemination of ideas on a global scale, and the transmission of popular culture from one country to another often make it difficult to distinguish what is Western from what is not. *The West: Encounters and Transformations* offers students a history of Western civilization in which these issues of Western identity are given prominence. Our goal is neither to idealize nor to indict that civilization, but to describe its main characteristics in different historical periods.

The West: Encounters and Transformations gives careful consideration to two basic questions. The first is, how did the definition of the West change over time? In what ways did its boundaries shift and how did the distinguishing characteristics of its cultures change? The second question is, by what means did the West—and the idea of the West—develop? We argue that the West is the product of a series of cultural encounters that occurred both outside and within its geographical boundaries. We explore these encounters and the transformations they produced by detailing the political, social, religious, and cultural history of the regions that have been, at one time or another, a part of the West.

Defining the West

What is the West? How did it come into being? How has it developed throughout history? Many textbooks take for granted which regions or peoples of the globe constitute the West. They treat the history of the West as a somewhat expanded version of European history. While not disputing the centrality of Europe to any definition of the West, we contend that the West is not only a geographical realm with ever-shifting boundaries, but also a cultural realm, an area of cultural influence extending beyond the geographical and political boundaries of Europe. We so strongly believe in this notion that we have written the introductory essay "What Is the West?" to encourage students to think about their understanding of Western civilization and to guide their understanding of each chapter. Many of the features of what we call Western civilization originated in regions that are not geographically part of Europe (such as North Africa and the Middle East), while ever since the fifteenth century various social, ethnic, and political groups from non-European regions (such as North and South America, eastern Russia, Australia, New Zealand, and South Africa) have identified themselves, in one way or another, with the West. Throughout the text, we devote considerable attention to the boundaries of the West and show how borderlines between cultures have been created, especially in eastern and southeastern Europe.

Considered as a geographical and cultural realm, *the West* is a term of recent origin, and the civilization to which it refers did not become clearly defined until the eleventh century, especially during the Crusades, when western European Christians developed a distinct cultural identity. Before that time we can only talk about the powerful forces that created the West, especially the dynamic interaction of the civilizations of western Europe, the Byzantine Empire, and the Muslim world.

Over the centuries Western civilization has acquired many salient characteristics. These include two of the world's great legal systems (civil law and common law), three of the world's monotheistic religions (Judaism, Christianity, and Islam), certain political and social philosophies, forms of political organization (such as the modern bureaucratic state and democracy), methods of scientific inquiry, systems of economic organization (such as industrial capitalism), and distinctive styles of art, architecture, and music. At times one or more of these characteristics has served as a primary source of Western identity: Christianity in the Middle Ages, science and rationalism during the Enlightenment, industrialization in the nineteenth and twentieth centuries, and a defense of individual liberty and democracy in the late twentieth century. These sources of Western identity, however, have always been challenged and contested, both when they were coming into prominence and when they appeared to be most triumphant. Western culture has never been monolithic; even today references to the West imply a wide range of meanings.

Cultural Encounters

The definition of the West is closely related to the central theme of our book, which is the process of cultural encounters. Throughout *The West: Encounters and Transformations,* we examine the West as a product of a series of cultural encounters both outside the West and within it. We show that the West originated and developed through a continuous process of inclusion and exclusion resulting from a series of encounters among and within different groups. These encounters can be described in a general sense as external, internal, or ideological.

External Encounters

External encounters took place between peoples of different civilizations. Before the emergence of the West as a clearly defined entity, external encounters occurred between such diverse peoples as Greeks and Phoenicians, Macedonians and Egyptians, and Romans and Celts. After the eleventh century, external encounters between Western and non-Western peoples occurred mainly during periods of European exploration, expansion, and imperialism. In the sixteenth and seventeenth centuries, for example, a series of external encounters took place between Europeans on the one hand and Africans, Asians, and the indigenous people of the Americas on the other. Two chapters of *The West: Encounters and Transformations* (Chapters 13 and 18) and a large section of a third (Chapter 24) explore these external encounters in depth and discuss how they affected Western and non-Western civilizations alike.

Internal Encounters

Our discussion of encounters also includes similar interactions between different social groups *within* Western countries. These internal encounters often took place between dominant and subordinate groups, such as between lords and peasants, rulers and subjects, men and women, factory owners and workers, masters and slaves. Encounters between those who were educated and those who were illiterate, which recurred frequently throughout Western history, also fall into this category. Encounters just as often took place between different religious and political groups, such as between Christians and Jews, Catholics and Protestants, and royal absolutists and republicans.

Ideological Encounters

Ideological encounters involve interaction between comprehensive systems of thought, most notably religious doctrines, political philosophies, and scientific theories about the nature of the world. These ideological conflicts usually arose out of internal encounters, when various groups within Western societies subscribed to different theories of government or rival religious faiths. The encounters between Christianity and polytheism in the early Middle Ages, between liberalism and conservatism in the nineteenth century, and between fascism and communism in the twentieth century were ideological encounters. Some ideological encounters had an external dimension, such as when the forces of Islam and Christianity came into conflict during the Crusades and when the Cold War developed between Soviet communism and Western democracy in the second half of the twentieth century.

* * *

The West: Encounters and Transformations illuminates the variety of these encounters and clarifies their effects. By their very nature encounters are interactive, but they have taken different forms: They have been violent or peaceful, coercive or cooperative. Some have resulted in the imposition of Western ideas on areas outside the geographical boundaries of the West or the perpetuation of the dominant culture within Western societies. More often than not, however, encounters have resulted in a more reciprocal process of exchange in which both Western and non-Western cultures, or the values of both dominant and subordinate groups, have undergone significant transformation. Our book not only identifies these encounters, but also discusses their significance by returning periodically to the issue of Western identity.

Coverage

The West: Encounters and Transformations offers both comprehensive coverage of political, social, and cultural history and a broader coverage of the West and the world.

Comprehensive Coverage

Our goal throughout the text has been to provide comprehensive coverage of political, social, and cultural history and to include significant coverage of religious and military history as well. Political history defines the basic structure of the book, and some chapters, such as those on Hellenistic civilization, the age of confessional divisions, absolutism and state building, the French Revolution, and the coming of mass politics, include sustained political narratives. Because we understand the West to be a cultural as well as a geographical realm, we give a prominent position to cultural history. Thus, we include rich sections on Hellenistic philosophy and literature, the cultural environment of the Italian Renaissance, the creation of a new political culture at the time of the French Revolution, and the atmosphere of cultural despair and desire that prevailed in Europe after World War I. We also devote special attention to religious history, including the history of Islam as well as that of Christianity and Judaism. Unlike many other textbooks, our coverage of religion continues into the modern period. *The West: Encounters and Transformations* also provides extensive coverage of the history of women and gender. Wherever possible the history of women is integrated into the broader social, cultural, and political history of the period. But there are also separate sections on women in our chapters on classical Greece, the Renaissance, the Reformation, the Enlightenment, the Industrial Revolution, World War I, World War II, and the postwar era.

The West and the World

Our book provides broad geographical coverage. Because the West is the product of a series of encounters, the external areas with which the West interacted are of major importance. Three chapters deal specifically with the West and the world.

- Chapter 13, "The West and the World: The Significance of Global Encounters, 1450–1650"
- Chapter 18, "The West and the World: Empire, Trade, and War, 1650–1815"
- Chapter 24, "The West and the World: Cultural Crisis and the New Imperialism, 1870–1914"

These chapters present substantial material on sub-Saharan Africa, Latin America, the Middle East, India, and East Asia. Our text is also distinctive in its coverage of eastern Europe and the Muslim world, areas that have often been considered outside the boundaries of the West. These regions were arenas within which significant cultural encounters took place. Finally, we include material on the United States and Australia, both of which have become part of the West. We recognize that most American college and university students have the opportunity to study American history as a separate subject, but treatment of the United States as a Western nation provides a different perspective from that usually given in courses on American history. For example, this book treats America's revolution as one of four Atlantic revolutions, its national unification in the nineteenth century as part of a broader western European development, its pattern of industrialization as related to that of Britain, and its central role in the Cold War as part of an ideological encounter that was global in scope.

What's New to This Edition?

This edition of *The West: Encounters and Transformations* has been revised to reflect the latest developments in historical research and has added a host of new features to assist student learning. The most significant pedagogical innovation has been the seamless integration of documents, maps, videos, illustrations, and other resources from MyHistoryLab into the textbook. A new pedagogically driven design highlights a clear learning path through the material and offers a visually stunning learning experience in print or on a screen. With the Pearson eText, students can transition directly to MyHistoryLab resources such as primary source documents, videos, and maps.

Additionally, questions have been added to the captions of all the maps. The list of Suggested Readings has been revised and updated, and many of the terms in the Glossary have been edited to improve student comprehension.

Specific changes in the contents of this edition are as follows:

- Chapter 20 includes a new illustration that highlights the militancy of the *sans-culottes* and includes new material on the Republic of Virtue. The Closer Look in MyHistoryLab on the execution of Louis XVI supplements the discussion of this event in the text and in the "Justice in History" feature.
- Chapter 21 includes new material on industrialization in Europe and an illustration of the Stockton and Darlington Railway. It also refers the student to a new map of English Railways in MyHistoryLab.
- Chapter 22 clarifies the doctrine of liberalism and includes excerpts from John Stuart Mill and David Ricardo to support the description of this new ideology. Inclusion of the Chartist People's Petition of 1838 helps explain why Britain did not experience a revolution in 1848.
- Chapter 23 includes a new map of the United Kingdom in 1910. The section titled "The Irish Identity Conflict" has been completely rewritten, incorporating new material. The section on "Russia: Revolution and Reaction" has been revised to reflect the emphasis in scholarship on nationalist upheaval within the Russian Empire and adds a discussion on the tsarist policy of Russification.
- Chapter 24 strengthens and reorganizes the section titled "The Birth of Modernism."
- Chapter 25 includes a new map on the Eastern Front that identifies the national regions of Poland, the Baltics, Ukraine, Caucasus, East Prussia, and Galicia. It adds new sub-sections titled "A War of Movement" and "Germany and the East" to reflect current research on the Eastern Front and the German occupation of Russian territories. Another new sub-section, "A Very Different Battle," deals with the influenza pandemic. The discussion of the October Revolution has also been expanded.
- Chapter 26 has been extensively reorganized to make discussions more coherent, to improve "teachability," and to take into account recent research. It adds new sub-sections titled "NEP and Nationalities" and "From Lenin to Stalin." The substantially revised section on the Irish Revolution includes new material.
- Chapter 27 includes a new section titled "The Wars Within the War" that takes into account the most recent research on the Holocaust and the Eastern Front. The section titled "The Decisive Front" has been extensively revised and includes new material.
- Chapter 28 incorporates new material in the section titled "Devastation, Death, and DPs."
- Chapter 29 adds a new sub-section, "The Turn to Terrorism," in the section on "Economic Stagnation and Political

Change: The 1970s and 1980s." It also extensively revises and adds new material to the sections "Islam and the West" and "The European Union." This chapter also brings the story of Russia under Putin up-to-date.

Features and Pedagogical Aids

In writing this textbook we have endeavored to keep both the student reader and the classroom instructor in mind at all times. The text includes the following features and pedagogical aids, all of which are intended to support the themes of the book.

"What Is the West?"

The West: Encounters and Transformations begins with an essay to engage students in the task of defining the West and to introduce them to the notion of cultural encounters. "What Is the West?" guides students through the text by providing a framework for understanding how the West was shaped. Structured around the six questions of What? When? Where? Who? How? and Why?, this framework encourages students to think about their understanding of Western civilization. The essay serves as a blueprint for using this textbook.

"Encounters and Transformations"

These features, which appear in about half the chapters, illustrate the main theme of the book by identifying specific encounters and showing how they led to significant transformations in the cultures of the West. These features show, for example, how camels enabled encounters among nomadic tribes of Arabia, which led to the rapid spread of Islam; how the Mayans' interpretation of Christian symbols transformed European Christianity into a hybrid religion; how the importation of chocolate from the New World to Europe changed Western consumption patterns and the rhythms of the Atlantic economy; and how Picasso's encounter with African art contributed to the transformation of modernism. Each of these essays concludes with questions for discussion.

"Justice in History"

Found in every chapter, this feature presents a historically significant trial or episode in which different notions of justice (or injustice) were debated and resolved. The "Justice in History" features illustrate cultural encounters within communities as they try to determine the fate of individuals from all walks of life. Many famous trials dealt with conflicts over basic religious, philosophical, or political values, such as those of Socrates, Jesus, Joan of Arc, Martin Luther, Charles I, Galileo, and Adolf Eichmann. Other "Justice in History" features show how judicial institutions, such as the ordeal, the Inquisition, and revolutionary tribunals, handled adversarial situations in different societies. These essays, therefore, illustrate the way in which the basic values of the West have evolved through attempts to resolve disputes and conflict.

Each "Justice in History" feature includes two pedagogical aids. "For Discussion" helps students explore the historical significance of the episode just examined. These questions can be used in classroom discussion or as student essay topics. "Taking It Further" provides the student with a few references that can be consulted in connection with a research project.

"Different Voices"

Each chapter contains a feature consisting of two primary source documents that present different and often opposing views regarding a particular person, event, or development. An introduction to the documents provides the necessary historical context, identifies the authors of the documents, and suggests the different perspectives they take. A set of questions for discussion follows the two documents.

Questions for Discussion

This edition of *The West: Encounters and Transformations* offers many opportunities for students to address a variety of questions in each chapter.

- The main question that the chapter addresses appears after the introduction to each chapter.
- Each of the major sections of the chapter begins with the main question that the section addresses. These questions also appear at the bottom of the first page of the chapter under the "Learning Objectives" heading and are repeated in the Chapter Review at the end of the chapter.
- At the end of each chapter a set of questions under the heading "Making Connections" asks the student to think about some of the more specific issues discussed in the chapter.
- Each Encounters and Transformations, Justice in History, and Different Voices feature is followed by a set of questions under the heading "For Discussion."
- The caption for each map includes a question related to the map for which the text of the chapter provides an answer.

Maps and Illustrations

Artwork is a key component of our book. We recognize that many students often lack a strong familiarity with geography, and so we have taken great care to develop maps that help sharpen their geographic skills. Complementing the book's standard map program, we include maps focusing on areas outside the borders of Western civilization. More than 300 images of fine art and photos tell the story of Western civilization and help students visualize the past: the way people lived, the events that shaped their lives, and how they viewed the world around them.

Chronologies

Each chapter includes a varying number of chronologies in time line format that list the events relating to a particular topic discussed in the text. Chronologies present the sequence of events and can be helpful for purposes of review.

Key Terms and Glossary

We have sought to create a work that is accessible to students with little prior knowledge of the basic facts of Western history or geography. Throughout the book we have explained difficult concepts at length. For example, we present in-depth explanations of the concepts of Zoroastrianism, Neoplatonism, Renaissance humanism, the various Protestant denominations of the sixteenth century, capitalism, seventeenth-century absolutism, nineteenth-century liberalism and nationalism, fascism, and modernism. We have identified these concepts as key terms by printing them in bold in the narrative and defining them in the margins of the book. All key terms are listed in alphabetical order, together with their definitions, in the Glossary at the end of the book.

Suggested Readings

An annotated list of suggested readings for all the chapters appears at the end of the book. The items listed there are not scholarly works for the benefit of the instructor, but suggestions for students who wish to explore a topic in greater depth or to write a research paper. References to books or articles relevant to the subject of the "Justice in History" feature appear at the end of each feature under the heading "Taking It Further."

Chapter Reviews

At the end of each chapter, a Chapter Review revisits the questions that accompany each section heading and summarizes key concepts within the section that address these questions.

Time Lines

A time line at the end of each chapter lists important events discussed within the chapter.

A Note About Dates and Transliterations

In keeping with current academic practice, *The West: Encounters and Transformations* uses B.C.E. (before the common era) and C.E. (common era) to designate dates. We also follow the most current and widely accepted English transliterations of Arabic. *Qur'an*, for example, is used for *Koran*; *Muslim* is used for *Moslem*. Chinese words appearing in the text for the first time are written in pinyin, followed by the older Wade-Giles system in parentheses.

Acknowledgments

We are grateful to Jeff Lasser for guiding us through the long process of preparing the fourth edition and Rob DeGeorge for his help in selecting the illustrations and preparing the manuscript for publication.

We would like to thank the following reviewers for their helpful suggestions: Frank Biletz, Loyola University, Chicago; Julian Bourg, Boston College; Jace Crouch, Oakland University; Stephanie Annette Finley-Croswhite, Old Dominion University; Nichole Gotschall, Columbia Southern University; Derrick Griffey, Gadsden State Community College; Erik Heinrichs, Bridgewater State University; Carol Herringer, Wright State University; Stephanie Lamphere, Sierra College; Alison Williams Lewin, Saint Joseph's University; Erik Lindseth, Indiana University; Michael Martin, Fort Lewis College; Lindsey McNellis, University of Central Florida; Patricia O'Neill, Central Oregon Community College; Karen Sonnelitter, Purdue University; Tamrala Swafford, Columbia Southern University; Tom Ward, Spring Hill College; Bradley Woodworth, University of New Haven; and Terry Young, Patrick Henry Community College.

We would also like to thank the following friends and colleagues for their valuable advice and suggestions: Gabor Agoston, Catherine Clinton, Catherine Evtuhov, Wojciech Falkowski, Benjamin Frommer, Andrzej Kaminski, Adam Kozuchowski, Christopher Lazarski, David Lindenfeld, Suzanne Marchand, John McNeill, John Merriman, James Miller, Daria Nalecz, Karl Roider, Steven Ross, and Mark Steinberg. Finally, we wish to thank Graham Nichols for his telecommunications assistance and expertise.

ABOUT THE AUTHORS

Brian Levack grew up in a family of teachers in the New York metropolitan area. From his father, a professor of French history, he acquired a love for studying the past, and he knew from an early age that he too would become a historian. He received his B.A. from Fordham University in 1965 and his Ph.D. from Yale in 1970. In graduate school he became fascinated by the history of the law and the interaction between law and politics, interests that he has maintained throughout his career. In 1969 he joined the history department of the University of Texas at Austin, where he is now the John Green Regents Professor in History. The winner of several teaching awards, Levack teaches a wide variety of courses on British and European history, legal history, and the history of witchcraft. For eight years he served as the chair of his department, a rewarding but challenging assignment that made it difficult for him to devote as much time as he wished to his teaching and scholarship. His books include *The Civil Lawyers in England, 1603–1641: A Political Study* (1973), *The Formation of the British State: England, Scotland and the Union, 1603–1707* (1987), *The Witch-Hunt in Early Modern Europe* (3rd edition, 2006), and *Witch-Hunting in Scotland: Law, Politics, and Religion* (2008).

His study of the development of beliefs about witchcraft in Europe over the course of many centuries gave him the idea of writing a textbook on Western civilization that would illustrate a broader set of encounters between different cultures, societies, and ideologies. While writing the book, Levack and his two sons built a house on property that he and his wife, Nancy, own in the Texas hill country. He found that the two projects presented similar challenges: It was easy to draw up the design, but far more difficult to execute it. When not teaching, writing, or doing carpentry work, Levack runs along the jogging trails of Austin and has recently discovered the pleasures of scuba diving.

Edward Muir grew up in the foothills of the Wasatch Mountains in Utah, close to the Emigration Trail along which wagon trains of Mormon pioneers and California-bound settlers made their way westward. As a child he loved to explore the broken-down wagons and abandoned household goods left at the side of the trail and from that acquired a fascination with the past. Besides the material remains of the past, he grew up with stories of his Mormon pioneer ancestors and an appreciation for how the past continued to influence the present. During the turbulent 1960s, he became interested in Renaissance Italy as a period and place that had been formative for Western civilization. His biggest challenge was finding the time to explore yet another new corner of Italy and its restaurants.

Muir received his Ph.D. from Rutgers University, where he specialized in the Italian Renaissance and did archival research in Venice and Florence, Italy. He is now the Clarence L. Ver Steeg Professor in the Arts and Sciences at Northwestern University and former chair of the history department. At Northwestern he has won several teaching awards. His books include *Civic Ritual in Renaissance Venice* (1981), *Mad Blood Stirring: Vendetta in Renaissance Italy* (1993 and 1998), *Ritual in Early Modern Europe* (1997 and 2005), and *The Culture Wars of the Late Renaissance: Skeptics, Libertines, and Opera* (2007). His books have also been published in Italian.

Some years ago Muir began to experiment with the use of historical trials in teaching and discovered that students loved them. From that experience he decided to write this textbook, which employs trials as a central feature. He lives beside Lake Michigan in Evanston, Illinois. His twin passions are skiing in the Rocky Mountains and rooting for the Chicago Cubs, who manage every summer to demonstrate that winning isn't everything.

Meredith Veldman grew up in the western suburbs of Chicago, where she learned to love winter and the Cubs—which might explain her preference for all things improbable and impractical. Certainly that preference is what attracted her to the study of history, filled as it is with impractical people doing the most improbable things. Veldman majored in history at Calvin College in Grand Rapids, Michigan, and then earned a Ph.D. in modern European history, with a concentration in nineteenth- and twentieth-century Britain, from Northwestern University in 1988.

As an associate professor of history at Louisiana State University, Veldman teaches courses in nineteenth- and twentieth-century British history and twentieth-century Europe, as well as the second half of "Western Civ." In her many semesters in the Western Civ. classroom, Veldman tried a number of different textbooks but found herself increasingly dissatisfied. She wanted a text that would convey to beginning students at least some of the complexities and ambiguities of historical interpretation, introduce them to the exciting work being done in cultural history, and, most important, tell a good story. The search for this textbook led her to accept the offer Levack and Muir made to join them in writing *The West: Encounters and Transformations*.

An award-winning teacher, Veldman is also the author of *Fantasy, the Bomb, and the Greening of Britain: Romantic Protest, 1945–1980* (1994) and *Margaret Thatcher: Shaping the New Conservatism* (2014). She and her family ride out the hurricanes in Baton Rouge, Louisiana. She remains a Cubs fan and she misses snow.

What Is the West?

Many of the people who influence public opinion—politicians, teachers, clergy, journalists, and television commentators—refer to "Western values," "the West," and "Western civilization." They often use these terms as if they do not require explanation. But what do these terms mean? The West has always been an arena within which different cultures, religions, values, and philosophies have interacted; any definition of the West will inevitably arouse controversy.

The definition of the West has always been disputed. Note the difference in the following two poems, the first by Rudyard Kipling (1865–1936), an ardent promoter of European imperialism who wrote "The Ballad of East and West" at the height of the British Empire:

> OH, East is East, and West is West, and never the twain shall meet,
> Till Earth and Sky stand presently at God's great Judgment Seat. . . .

The second, "East/West Poem," is by a Chinese-American living in Hawaii, Wing Tek Lum (1946–), who expresses the confusion caused by terms that designate both cultural traits and directions around the globe:

> O
> East is East
> and
> West is West.
> but
> I never did
> understand
> why
> in Geography class
> the East was west
> and
> the West was east
> and that no
> one ever
> cared
> about the difference.

This textbook cares about the difference. It also shows that East and West have, in contrast to Kipling's view, often "met." These encounters created the idea of the East and the West and helped identify the ever shifting borders between the two.

The Shifting Borders of the West

The most basic definition of the West is of a place. Western civilization is now typically thought to comprise the regions of Europe, the Americas, Australia, and New Zealand. However, this is a contemporary definition of the West. The inclusion of these places in the West is the result of a long history of European expansion through colonization and conquest.

This textbook begins about 10,000 years ago in what is now Iraq; the final chapter returns to discuss the Iraq War, but in the meantime the Mesopotamian region is only occasionally a concern for Western history. The history of the West begins with the domestication of animals, the cultivation of the first crops, and the establishment of long-distance trading networks in the Tigris, Euphrates, and Nile River valleys. Cities, kingdoms, and empires in those valleys gave birth to the first civilizations in the West. By about 500 B.C.E., the civilizations that were the cultural ancestors of the modern West had spread from southwestern Asia and north Africa to include the entire Mediterranean basin—areas influenced by Egyptian, Hebrew, Greek, and Roman thought, art, law, and religion. The resulting Greco-Roman culture created the most enduring foundation of the West. By the first century C.E. the Roman Empire drew the map of what historians consider the heartland of the West: most of western and southern Europe, the coastlands of the Mediterranean Sea, and the Middle East.

For many centuries, these ancient foundations defined the borders of the West. During the last century, however, the West came to be less about geography than about culture, identity, and technology. When Japan, an Asian country, accepted

human rights and democracy after World War II, did it become part of the West? Most Japanese might not think they have adopted "Western" values, but the thriving capitalism and stable democracy of this traditional Asian country that was never colonized by a European power complicates the idea of what is the West. Or consider the Republic of South Africa, which the white minority—people descended from European immigrants—ruled until 1994. The oppressive white regime violated human rights, rejected full legal equality for all citizens, and jailed or murdered those who questioned the government. Only when democratic elections open to blacks replaced that government did South Africa fully embrace what the rest of the West would consider Western values. To what degree was South Africa part of the West before and after these developments?

Or how about Russia? Russia long saw itself as a Christian country with cultural, economic, and political ties with the rest of Europe. The Russians have intermittently identified with their Western neighbors, especially during the reign of Peter the Great (1682–1725), but their neighbors were not always sure about the Russians. After the Mongol invasions of the thirteenth and fourteenth centuries much of Russia was isolated from the rest of the West, and during the Cold War from 1949 to 1989 Western democracies considered communist Russia an enemy. When was Russia "Western" and when not?

Thus, when we talk about where the West is, we are almost always talking about the Mediterranean basin and much of Europe (and later, the Americas). But we will also show that countries that border "the West," and even countries far from it, might be considered Western in many aspects as well.

THE TEMPLE OF HERA AT PAESTUM, ITALY Greek colonists in Italy built this temple in the sixth century B.C.E. Greek ideas and artistic styles spread throughout the ancient world, both from Greek colonists, such as those at Paestum, and from other peoples who imitated the Greeks.

WHERE IS THE WEST? The shifting borders of the West have moved many times throughout history, but they have always included the areas shown in this satellite photo. These include Europe, north Africa, and the Middle East.

Changing Identities Within the West

In addition to being a place, the West is the birthplace of Western civilization, a civilization that encompasses a cultural history—a tradition stretching back thousands of years to the ancient world. Over this long period the civilization we now identify as Western gradually took shape. The many characteristics that identify it emerged over this time: forms of governments, economic systems, and methods of scientific inquiry, as well as religions, languages, literature, and art.

Throughout the development of Western civilization, the ways in which people identified themselves changed as well. People in the ancient world had no such idea of the common identity of the West, only of being members of a tribe, citizens of a town, or subjects of an empire. But with the spread of Christianity and Islam between the first and seventh centuries, the notion of a distinct civilization in these "Western" lands subtly changed. People came to identify themselves less as subjects of a particular empire and more as members of a community of faith—whether that community comprised followers of Judaism, Christianity, or Islam. These communities of faith drew lines of inclusion and exclusion that still exist today. Starting about 1,600 years ago, Christian monarchs and clergy began to obliterate polytheism (the worship of many gods) and marginalize Jews. From 1,000 to 500 years ago, Christian authorities fought to expel Muslims from Europe. Europeans developed definitions of the West that did not include Islamic communities, even though Muslims continued to live in Europe, and Europeans traded and interacted with the Muslim world. The Islamic countries themselves erected their own barriers, seeing themselves in opposition to the Christian West, even as they continued to look back to the common cultural origins in the ancient world that they shared with Jews and Christians.

MARINER'S COMPASS The mariner's compass was a navigational device intended for use primarily at sea. The compass originated in China; once adopted by Europeans, it enabled them to embark on long ocean voyages around the world.

During the Renaissance in the fifteenth century, these ancient cultural origins became an alternative to religious affiliation for thinking about the identity of the West. From this Renaissance historical perspective Jews, Christians, and Muslims descended from the cultures of the ancient Egyptians, Hebrews, Greeks, and Romans. Despite their differences, the followers of these religions shared a history. In fact, in the late Renaissance a number of Jewish and Christian thinkers imagined the possibility of rediscovering the single universal religion that they thought must have once been practiced in the ancient world. If they could just recapture that religion, they could restore the unity they imagined had once prevailed in the West.

The definition of the West has also changed as a result of European colonialism, which began about 500 years ago. When European powers assembled large overseas empires, they introduced Western languages, religions, technologies, and cultures to many distant places in the world, making Western identity a transportable concept. In some of these colonized areas—such as North America, Argentina, Australia, and New Zealand—the European newcomers so outnumbered the indigenous people that these regions became as much a part of the West as Britain, France, and Spain. In other European colonies, especially on the Asian continent, Western cultures failed to exercise similar levels of influence.

As a result of colonialism Western culture sometimes merged with other cultures, and in the process, both were changed. Brazil, a South American country inhabited by large numbers of indigenous peoples, the descendants of African slaves, and European settlers, epitomizes the complexity of what defines the West. In Brazil, almost everyone speaks a Western language (Portuguese), practices a Western religion (Christianity), and participates in Western political and economic institutions (democracy and capitalism). Yet in Brazil all of these features of Western civilization have become part of a distinctive culture in which indigenous, African, and European elements have been blended. During Carnival, for example, Brazilians dressed in indigenous costumes dance in African rhythms to the accompaniment of music played on European instruments.

Western Values

For many people today, the most important definition of the West involves adherence to "Western" values. The values typically identified as Western include democracy, individualism, universal human rights, toleration of religious diversity, ownership of private property, equality before the law, and freedom of inquiry and expression. These values, however, have not always been part of Western civilization. In fact, they describe ideals rather than actual realities; these values are by no means universally accepted throughout the West. Thus, there is nothing inevitable about these values; Western history at various stages exhibited quite different ones. Western societies seldom prized legal or political equality until quite recently. In ancient Rome and throughout most of medieval Europe, the wealthy and the powerful enjoyed more protection under the law than did slaves or the poor. Most medieval Christians were completely convinced of the virtue of making war against Muslims and heretics and curtailing the actions of Jews. Before the end of the eighteenth century, few Westerners questioned the practice of slavery and a social hierarchy of birth that remained powerful in the West through the nineteenth century; in addition, most women were excluded from equal economic and educational opportunities until well into the twentieth century. In many places women still do not have equal opportunities. In the twentieth century, millions of Westerners followed leaders who stifled free inquiry, denied basic human rights to many of their citizens, made terror an instrument of the state, and censored authors, artists, and journalists. The Holocaust, fascism, and communism were Western phenomena.

The values that define the West have not only changed over time, they also remain fiercely contested. One of the most divisive political issues today, for example, is that of "gay marriage." Both sides in this debate frame their arguments in terms of "Western values." Supporters of the legalization of same-sex marriages highlight equality and human rights: They demand that all citizens have equal access to the basic legal protections afforded by marriage. Opponents emphasize the centrality of the tradition of monogamous heterosexual marriage to Western legal, moral, and religious codes. What this current debate shows us is that no single understanding of "Western values," or of the West itself, exists. These values have always been contended, disputed, and fought over. In other words, they have a history. This text highlights and examines that history.

Asking the Right Questions

So how can we make sense of the West as a place and an identity, the shifting borders and definitions of the West, and Western civilization in general? In short, what has Western civilization been over the course of its long history—and what is it today?

Answering these questions is the challenge this book addresses. There are no simple answers to any of these questions, but there is a method for finding answers. The method is straightforward. Always ask the *what, when, where, who, how,* and *why* questions of the text.

The *What* Question

What is Western civilization? The answer to this question will vary according to time and place. In fact, for much of the early history covered in this book, "Western civilization" did not exist. Rather, a number of distinctive civilizations emerged in the Middle East, northern Africa, and Europe, each of which contributed to what later became Western civilization. As these cultures developed and intermingled, the idea of Western civilization slowly began to form. Thus, the understanding of Western civilization will change from chapter to chapter. The most extensive change in the place of the West was through the colonial expansion of the European nations between the fifteenth and twentieth centuries. Perhaps the most significant cultural change came with acceptance of the values of scientific inquiry for solving human and philosophical problems, an approach that did not exist before the seventeenth century but became one of the distinguishing characteristics of Western civilization. During the late eighteenth and nineteenth centuries, industrialization became the engine that drove economic development in the West. During the twentieth century, industrialization in both its capitalist and communist forms dramatically gave the West a level of economic prosperity unmatched in the non-industrialized parts of the world.

The *When* Question

When did the defining characteristics of Western civilization first emerge, and for how long did they prevail? Dates frame and organize the content of each chapter, and numerous short timelines are offered. These resources make it possible to keep track of what happened when. Dates have no meaning by themselves, but the connections *between* them can be very revealing. For example, dates show that the agricultural revolution that permitted the birth of the first civilizations unfolded over a long span of about 10,000 years—which is more time than was taken by all the other events and developments covered in this textbook. Wars of religion plagued Europe for nearly 200 years before Enlightenment thinkers articulated the ideals of religious toleration. The American Civil War—the war to preserve the union, as President Abraham Lincoln termed it—took place at exactly the same time as wars were being fought for national unity in Germany and Italy. In other words, by paying attention to other contemporaneous wars for national unity, the American experience seems less peculiarly an American event.

By learning *when* things happened, one can identify the major causes and consequences of events and thus see the transformations of Western civilization. For instance, the production of a surplus of food through agriculture and the domestication

MAP 1 CORE LANDS OF THE WEST These are the principal geographical features that will appear recurrently throughout this book.

of animals were prerequisites for the emergence of civilizations. The violent collapse of religious unity after the Protestant Reformation in the sixteenth century led some Europeans to propose the separation of church and state two centuries later. And during the nineteenth century many Western countries—in response to the enormous diversity among their own peoples—became preoccupied with maintaining or establishing national unity.

The *Where* Question

Where has Western civilization been located? Geography, of course, does not change very rapidly, but the idea of where the West is does change. By tracing the shifting relationships between the West and other, more distant civilizations with which it interacted, the chapters highlight the changing "where" of the West. The key to understanding the shifting borders of the West is to study how the peoples within the West thought of themselves and how they identified others as "not Western." During the Cold War, for example, many within the West viewed Russia as an enemy rather than as part of the West. In the previous centuries, Australia and North America came to be part of the West because the European conquerors of these regions identified themselves with European cultures and traditions and against non-European values.

The *Who* Question

Who were the people responsible for making Western civilization? Some were anonymous, such as the unknown geniuses who invented the mathematical systems of ancient Mesopotamia. Others are well-known—saints such as Joan of Arc, creative thinkers such as Galileo Galilei, or generals such as Napoleon. Most were ordinary. Humble people, such as the many millions who migrated from Europe to North America or the unfortunate millions who suffered and died in the trenches of World War I, also influenced the course of events.

Perhaps most often this book encounters people who were less the shapers of their own destinies than the subjects of forces that conditioned the kinds of choices they could make, often with unanticipated results. During the eleventh century when farmers throughout Europe began to employ a new kind of plow to till their fields, they were merely trying to do their work more efficiently. They certainly did not recognize that the increase in food they produced would stimulate the enormous population growth that made possible the medieval civilization of thriving cities and magnificent cathedrals. Answering the *who* question requires an evaluation of how much individuals and groups of people were in control of events and how much events controlled them.

The *How* Question

How did Western civilization develop? This is a question about processes—about how things change or stay the same over time. This book identifies and explores these processes in several ways.

First, woven throughout the story is *the theme of encounters and transformations.* What is meant by encounters? When the Spanish *conquistadores* arrived in the Americas some 500 years ago, they came into contact with the cultures of the Caribs, the Aztecs, the Incas, and other peoples who had lived in the Americas for thousands of years. As the Spanish fought, traded with, and intermarried with the natives, each culture changed. The Spanish, for their part, borrowed from the Americas new plants for cultivation and responded to what they considered serious threats to their worldview. Many native Americans, in turn, adopted European religious practices and learned to speak European languages. At the same time, Amerindians were decimated by European diseases, illnesses to which they had never been exposed. The native Americans also witnessed the destruction of their own civilizations and governments at the hands of the colonial powers. Through centuries of interaction and mutual influence, both sides became something other than what they had been.

The European encounter with the Americas is an obvious example of what was, in fact, a continuous process of encounters with other cultures. These encounters often occurred between peoples from different civilizations, such as the struggles between Greeks and Persians in the ancient world or between Europeans and Chinese in the nineteenth century. Other encounters took place among people living in the same civilization. These include interactions between lords and peasants, men and women, Christians and Jews, Catholics and Protestants, factory owners and workers, and capitalists and communists. Western civilization developed and changed, and still does, through a series of external and internal encounters.

Second, *features in the chapters* formulate answers to the question of how Western civilization developed. For example, each chapter contains an essay titled *Justice in History*. These essays discuss a trial or some other episode involving questions of justice. Some *Justice in History* essays illustrate how Western civilization was forged in struggles over conflicting values, such as the discussion of the trial of Galileo, which examines the conflict between religious and scientific concepts of truth. Other essays show how efforts to resolve internal cultural, political, and religious tensions helped shape Western ideas about justice, such as the essay on the *auto da fé*, which illustrates how authorities attempted to enforce religious conformity.

Some chapters include another feature as well. The *Encounters and Transformations* features show how encounters between different groups of people, technologies, and ideas were not abstract historical processes, but events that brought people together in a way that transformed history. For example, when the Arabs encountered the camel as an instrument of war, they adopted it for their own purposes. As a result, they were able to conquer their neighbors very quickly and spread Islam far beyond its original home in Arabia.

The *Different Voices* feature in each chapter includes documents from the period that represent contrasting views about a particular issue important at the time. These conflicting voices demonstrate how people debated what mattered to them and in the process formulated what have become Western values. During the Franco-Algerian War of the 1950s and early 1960s, for example, French military officers debated the appropriateness of torture when interrogating Algerian prisoners alleged to be insurgents. The debate about the use of torture against terrorist suspects continues today, revealing one of the unresolved conflicts over the appropriate values of the West.

The *Why* Question

Why did things happen in the way they did in history? This is the hardest question of all, one that engenders the most debate among historians. To take one persistent example, why did Hitler initiate a plan to exterminate the Jews of Europe? Can it be explained by something that happened to him in his childhood? Was he full of self-loathing that he projected onto the Jews? Was it a way of creating an enemy so that he could better unify Germany? Did he really believe that the Jews were the cause of all of Germany's problems? Did he merely act on the deeply seated anti-Semitic tendencies of the German people? Historians still debate the answers to these questions.

Such questions raise issues about human motivation and the role of human agency in historical events. Can historians ever really know what motivated a particular individual in the past, especially when it is so notoriously difficult to understand what motivates other people in the present? Can any individual determine the course of history? The *what, when, where, who,* and *how* questions are much easier to answer; but the *why* question, of course, is the most interesting one, the one that cries out for an answer.

This book does not—and cannot—always offer definitive answers to the *why* question, but it attempts to lay out the most likely possibilities. For example, historians do not really know what disease caused the Black Death in the fourteenth century that killed about one-third of the population in a matter of months. But they can answer many questions about the consequences of that great catastrophe. Why were there so many new universities in the fourteenth and fifteenth centuries? It was because so many priests had died in the Black Death, creating a huge demand for replacements. The answers to the *why* questions are not always obvious, but they are always intriguing; finding the answers is the joy of studying history.

20 The Age of the French Revolution, 1789–1815

On July 12, 1789, the French journalist Camille **Desmoulins** addressed an anxious crowd of Parisian citizens gathered outside the Palais-Royal, where public debate often took place. Playing upon fears that had been mounting during the past two months, Desmoulins claimed that the government of Louis XVI was preparing a massacre of Parisians. "To arms, to arms!" Desmoulins cried out, as he roused the citizens to their own defense. That night Parisians responded to his call by invading arsenals in the city in anticipation of the violence they thought was about to descend upon them. The next day they

THE STORMING OF THE BASTILLE, JULY 14, 1789 Parisian citizens attacked the Bastille not because it was a symbol of the Old Regime, but because it contained weapons that they needed to protect themselves from royalist troops.

LEARNING OBJECTIVES

20.1 ((•	20.2 ((•	20.3 ((•	20.4 ((•	20.5 ((•
Why did the Old Regime collapse in 1789, and what revolutionary changes took place during the next two years?	How did a second more radical revolution in 1792 create a regime that instituted the Reign of Terror?	In what ways did the political events of the revolution change French culture?	Did the rule of Napoleon from 1799 to 1814 confirm or betray the achievements of the French Revolution?	In what ways did the French Revolution change the course of European and Western history?

 Listen to Chapter 20 on MyHistoryLab

◉ Watch the Video Series on MyHistoryLab

Learn about some key topics related to this chapter with the *MyHistoryLab Video Series: Key Topics in Western Civilization*

continued to seize weapons and declared themselves members of the National Guard, a volunteer militia of propertied citizens.

On the morning of July 14, crowds of Parisians moved toward an ancient fortress known as the Bastille, where royal troops were stationed. The Parisians feared that the troops in the Bastille would take violent action against them, and they also wanted to capture the ammunition stored inside the building, which served as an arsenal and a prison. Negotiations with the governor of the Bastille were interrupted when some of the militia, moving into the courtyard of the fortress, demanded the surrender of the troops. Both sides fired shots, and the exchange led to a full-scale assault upon the Bastille by the National Guard.

After three hours of fighting and the death of 83 people, the governor surrendered. His captors, bearing the arms they had seized, then led him to face charges before the officers of the city government. The crowd, however, crying for vengeance against their oppressors, attacked the soldiers and crushed some of them underfoot. The governor was stabbed hundreds of times, hacked to pieces, and decapitated. The chief magistrate of the city suffered the same fate for his reluctance to issue arms to its citizens. The crowd then placed the heads of the two men on pikes and paraded through the city.

The storming of the Bastille was the first of many violent episodes that occurred during the sequence of events called the French Revolution. That revolution brought about some of the most fundamental changes in European political life since the end of Roman rule. It heralded the destruction of the Old Regime, the eighteenth-century political order that had been dominated by an absolute monarch and a privileged nobility and clergy. It led to the submission of the Catholic Church to state control. A more radical phase of the revolution, beginning in 1792, resulted in the destruction of the French monarchy and the declaration of a republic. It also led to a period of state-sponsored terrorism in 1793 and 1794, during which one group of revolutionaries engaged in a brutal campaign to eliminate their real and imagined enemies.

The excesses of the revolution led to a conservative reaction, and after a long period of rule by Napoleon Bonaparte between 1799 and 1815, the French monarchy was restored, marking the end of the revolutionary period. The ideas of the revolution, however, especially its commitment to democratic republicanism and its concept of the nation, continued to dominate politics in the West for the next two hundred years. This chapter will address this question:

How did the French Revolution permanently change the political culture of the West?

The First French Revolution, 1789–1791

20.1 Why did the Old Regime collapse in 1789, and what revolutionary changes took place during the next two years?

The French Revolution consisted of two distinct revolutions. The first, which began in 1789, resulted in a destruction of royal absolutism and the drafting of a constitution. The second and more radical revolution began in 1792 with the abolition of the monarchy and the formation of the French Republic.

The Beginning of the Revolution

The immediate cause of the revolution was a financial crisis that bankrupted the monarchy and deprived it of its authority. The government of Louis XVI (r. 1774–1792) had inherited considerable debts as a result of protracted periods of warfare with Great Britain. The opening of a new phase of this warfare in 1778, when France intervened in the American War of Independence on the side of the United States, pushed the government further into debt and strained the entire French economy. As the crisis deepened the king proposed a direct tax on all landowners. The nobility, however, objected to this plan, which would have perpetuated the absolutist policies of the royal government.

The deterioration of the government's financial condition finally forced the king to yield. When tax returns dried up as the result of an agricultural crisis in the summer months of 1788, the government could no longer pay its creditors. In a desperate effort to save his regime, Louis announced that he would convene the Estates General, a national representative assembly that had not met since 1614.

The meeting of the Estates General was set for May 1789. During the months leading up to its opening, public debates arose over how the delegates should vote. The Estates General consisted of representatives of the three orders or social groups, known as estates, which made up French society: the clergy, the nobility, and the **Third Estate**. The Third Estate technically contained all the commoners in the kingdom (about 96 percent of the population), ranging from the wealthiest merchant to the poorest peasant. The elected representatives of the Third Estate were propertied nonnoble elements of lay society, including many lawyers and military officers.

Before the meeting a dispute arose among the representatives over whether the three groups would vote by estate, in which case the first two estates would dominate the assembly, or by head, in which case the Third Estate would have about the same number of representatives as the other two estates. Each side claimed that it was the best representative of the "nation," a term meaning the entire body of French people.

After the king indicated that he would side with the clergy and the nobility, the Third Estate took the dramatic step of declaring itself a National Assembly and asked members of the other estates to vote with them. When the king locked the Third Estate

Third Estate The component of the Estates General in Old Regime France that technically represented all the commoners in the kingdom.

  Read the Document

Emmanuel Joseph Sieyès, *What Is the Third Estate?*

JACQUES-LOUIS DAVID, THE OATH OF THE TENNIS COURT The oath taken by the members of the Third Estate not to disband until France had a constitution led to the creation of the National Assembly and the legislation that destroyed royal absolutism and feudalism.

CHRONOLOGY: THE FIRST FRENCH REVOLUTION, 1789–1791

1788

August 8
Announcement of the meeting of the Estates General.

`1788`

1789

May 5
The Estates General opens at Versailles.
June 17
The Third Estate adopts the title of the National Assembly.
June 20
Oath of the Tennis Court.
July 14
The storming of the Bastille.
Late July
The Great Fear in rural areas.
August 4
Abolition of feudalism and privileges.
August 26
Declaration of the Rights of Man and Citizen.
October 5
March to Versailles; Louis XVI and National Assembly move to Paris.
November 2
Church property is nationalized.

`1789`

1790

July 12
Civil Constitution of the Clergy.
November 27
Decree requiring oath of loyalty from the clergy.

`1790`

1791

June 20
Royal family flees to Varennes, is apprehended by the National Guard.
October 1
Newly elected Legislative Assembly opens.

`1791`

out of their meeting place without explanation, the outraged members went to a nearby indoor tennis court and took a solemn oath (known as the Oath of the Tennis Court) that they would not disband until the country had been given a constitution. One week later the king ordered the nobility and the clergy to join the National Assembly.

As this political crisis was reaching a climax, a major social crisis, fueled by the high price of bread, caused a breakdown of public order. For many years French agriculture had experienced difficulty meeting the demands of an expanding population. A widespread harvest failure in 1788 reduced the supply even further. As the price of bread soared, demand for manufactured goods shrank, thus causing widespread unemployment among artisans. An increasing number of bread riots, peasant revolts,

((· 📖 Read the Document

"Petition of Women of the Third Estate"

and urban strikes contributed to a sense of panic at the very time that the government's financial crisis deepened. In Paris the situation reached a critical point in June 1789.

At that point the king, a man with little political sense, made the ill-advised decision to send 17,000 royal troops to Paris to restore order. The arrival of the troops gave the impression that the government was planning to attack the people of the city. In this atmosphere of public paranoia Parisians formed the National Guard and stormed the Bastille.

The fall of the Bastille unnerved the king. When he asked one of his aides, "Is it a revolt?" the aide replied, "No, sire, it is a revolution." The revolution had just begun. It moved into high gear two weeks later when the National Assembly responded to the outbreak of social unrest in the provinces. The scarcity of grain in the countryside gave rise to false rumors that the nobles were engaged in a plot to destroy crops and starve the people into submission. Peasants armed themselves and prepared to fight off the hired agents of the nobility. A widespread panic, known as the "Great Fear," gripped many parts of the country. Townspeople and peasants amassed in large numbers to defend themselves and save the harvest. In response to this panic, which reached its peak in the last two weeks of July, the National Assembly began to pass legislation that destroyed the Old Regime and created a new political order.

The Creation of a New Political Society

Between August 1789 and September 1790 the National Assembly took three revolutionary steps. First, it eliminated noble and clerical privileges. In August the assembly abolished the feudal dues that peasants paid their lords, the private legal jurisdictions of noblemen, the collection of tithes by the clergy, and the exclusive right of noblemen to hunt game on their lands. Ten months later the nobility lost their titles. Instead of a society divided into various corporate groups, each with its own privileges, France would now have only citizens, all of them equal at law. Social distinctions would be based on merit rather than birth.

The second step, taken on August 26, was the promulgation of the *Declaration of the Rights of Man and Citizen*. This document revealed the main influence of the Enlightenment on the revolution. It declared that all men, not just Frenchmen, had a natural right to liberty, property, equality before the law, freedom from oppression, and religious toleration. The statement that the "law is the expression of the general will" reflected the influence of Rousseau's *The Social Contract* (1762), while the statement that every citizen has the right to participate in the formation of that law either personally or through a representative embodied the basic principle of democracy. (See *Different Voices* in this chapter.)

The third step in this revolutionary program was a complete reorganization of the Church. To solve the problem of the national debt, the National Assembly placed land owned by the Church (about 10 percent of all French territory) at the service of the nation. The Civil Constitution of the Clergy of July 1790 in effect made the Church a department of the state, with the government paying the clergy directly. To retain their positions, the clergy were required to take an oath of loyalty to the nation.

In 1791 a newly elected Legislative Assembly—replacing the National Assembly— confirmed and extended many of these changes. A constitution, put into effect in October, formalized the end of royal absolutism. The king became a constitutional monarch, retaining only the power to suspend legislation, direct foreign policy, and command the armed forces.

The new constitution formally abolished hereditary legal privileges, thus providing equality of all citizens before the law. Subsequent legislation granted Jews and Protestants full civil rights and toleration. A law eliminating primogeniture (inheritance of the entire estate by the eldest son) gave all heirs equal rights to inherited property. The establishment of marriage as a civil contract and the right to end a marriage in divorce supported the idea of the husband and wife as freely contracting individuals.

This body of legislation destroyed the Old Regime and promoted a revolutionary view of French society as a nation composed of equal citizens possessing natural rights. Contemporaries recognized the significance of these changes. The Portuguese ambassador to France, who witnessed the events of 1789 firsthand, reported back to his government, "In all the world's annals there is no mention of a revolution like this."

The French Republic, 1792–1799

20.2 How did a second more radical revolution in 1792 create a regime that instituted the Reign of Terror?

Beginning in 1792 France experienced a second revolution that was much more radical than the first. During this revolution France was transformed from a constitutional monarchy into a republic. The state claimed far greater power than it had acquired in 1789, and it used that power to bring about a radical reform of French society.

The Establishment of the Republic, 1792

During the first two years of the revolution it appeared that the building of a new French nation would take place within the framework of a constitutional monarchy. There was little sentiment among the members of the Legislative Assembly, much less among the general population, in favor of abolishing the institution of monarchy. The only committed republicans—those supporting the establishment of a republic—in the Legislative Assembly belonged to a party known as the **Jacobins**, who found support in political clubs in Paris and in other parts of the country. By the late summer of 1792 this group of radicals, drawing upon the support of militant Parisian citizens known as ***sans-culottes*** (literally, those without breeches, the pants worn by noblemen), succeeded in bringing about the second, more radical revolution.

King Louis himself was in part responsible for this destruction of the monarchy. The success of constitutional monarchy depended on the king's willingness to play the new role assigned to him. In October 1789 Louis had agreed, under considerable pressure, to move his residence from Versailles to Paris, where the National Assembly had also relocated. The pressure came mainly from women, who formed the large majority of 10,000 demonstrators who marched from Paris to Versailles demanding a reduction in the price of bread. The king yielded to their demands and came to Paris. As he entered the city, accompanied by soldiers, monks, and women carrying guns and pikes, he reluctantly agreed to wear the tricolor cockade (a badge) to symbolize his acceptance of the revolution. Louis, however, could not disguise his opposition to the revolution, especially the ecclesiastical legislation of 1789. His

Jacobins A French political party supporting a democratic republic that found support in political clubs throughout the country and dominated the National Convention from 1792 until 1794.

sans-culottes The militant citizens of Paris who refused to wear the pants worn by noblemen and provided support for the Jacobins during the French Revolution; literally, those without breeches.

TRICOLOR COCKADE Louis XVI wearing the red liberty bonnet with the tricolor cockade on October 20, 1792. Refusing to be intimidated by a crowd of 20,000 people outside the royal palace, he donned the cap and proclaimed his loyalty to the constitution.

Different Voices
The Rights of Man and Woman

T he French Revolution gave rise to formal demands for the recognition and enforcement of the rights of man, but it also led to some of the earliest appeals for the equal rights of women. These two documents present the proclamation of the rights of man by the National Assembly and a parallel statement by a female writer who called for fundamental changes in the relations between men and women.

The passage of the Declaration of the Rights of Man and Citizen by the National Assembly on August 26, 1789, was one of the earliest and most enduring acts of the French Revolution. A document of great simplicity and power, it was hammered out during many weeks of debate. Its concern with natural rights and equality before the law reflected the ideas of the Enlightenment.

For Olympe de Gouges, the Declaration of the Rights of Man and Citizen did not guarantee women the same rights as men nor address existing inequalities between the sexes. In a pamphlet titled Declaration of the Rights of Women and the Female Citizen (1791), which is a founding document of modern feminism, de Gouges offered a set of principles that paralleled the rights claimed in the National Assembly's demand for universal human rights.

Declaration of the Rights of Man and Citizen (1789)

1. Men are born free and remain free and equal in rights. Social distinctions may be founded only on the common good.

2. The aim of all political association is the preservation of the natural and imprescriptible rights of man. These rights are liberty, property, security and resistance to oppression.

3. The principle of all authority rests essentially in the nation. No body nor individual may exercise any authority which does not emanate expressly from the nation.

4. Liberty consists in the freedom to do whatever does not harm another; hence the exercise of the natural rights of each man has no limits except those which assure to the other members of society the enjoyment of the same rights. These limits can only be determined by law. . . .

6. Law is the expression of the general will. Every citizen has the right to participate personally or through his representative in its formation. It must be the same for all, whether it protects or punishes. All citizens, being equal in the eyes of the law, are equally eligible to all dignities and to all public positions and occupations, according to their abilities, and without distinction except that of their virtues and talents.

7. No man may be indicted, arrested, or imprisoned except in cases determined by the law and according to the forms prescribed by law. . . .

10. No one should be disturbed for his opinions, even in religion, provided that their manifestation does not trouble public order as established by law.

11. The free communication of thoughts and opinions is one of the most precious of the rights of man. Every citizen may therefore speak, write, and print freely, but shall be responsible for any abuse of this freedom in the cases set by the law. . . .

17. Property being an inviolable and sacred right, no one may be deprived of it except when public necessity, determined by law, obviously requires it, and then on the condition that the owner shall have been previously and equitably compensated.

SOURCE: From P.-J.-B. Buchez and P.-C. Roux, Histoire parlementaire de la Révolution française (Paris, 1834).

Olympe de Gouges, Declaration of the Rights of Women and the Female Citizen (1791)

1. Woman is born free and lives equal to man in her rights. Social distinctions can be based only on common utility.

2. The purpose of any political association is the conservation of the natural and imprescriptible rights of woman and man; these rights are liberty, property, security, and especially resistance to oppression.

3. The principle of all sovereignty rests essentially with the nation, which is nothing but the union of woman and man; no body and no individual can exercise any authority which does not come expressly from it [the nation].

4. Liberty and justice consist of restoring all that belongs to others; thus, the only limits on the exercise of the natural rights of woman are perpetual male tyranny; these limits are to be reformed by the laws of nature and reason. . . .

6. The laws must be the expression of the general will; all female and male citizens must contribute either personally or through their representatives to its formation; it must be the same for all: male and female citizens, being equal in the eyes of the law, must be equally admitted to all honors, positions, and public employment according to their capacity and without other distinctions besides those of their virtues and talents.

7. No woman is an exception: she is accused, arrested, and detained in cases determined by law. Women, like men, obey this rigorous law. . . .

10. No one is to be disquieted for his very basic opinions; woman has the right to mount the scaffold; she must equally have the right to mount the rostrum, provided that her demonstrations do not disturb the legally established public order.

11. The free communication of thoughts and opinions is one of the most precious rights of woman, since this liberty assures the recognition of children by their fathers. Any female citizen thus may say freely, I am the mother of your child, without being forced by a barbarous prejudice to hide the truth; as long as she accepts responsibility for any abuse of this liberty [by lying about the paternity of the child] in cases determined by law. . . .

(continued on next page)

17. Property belongs to both sexes whether united or separated; for each it is an inviolable and sacred right; no one can be deprived of it, since it is a true patrimony of nature, unless public necessity, determined by law, requires it, and then only with a just compensation, settled in advance.

SOURCE: Olympe de Gouges, *Les Droits de la femme* (Paris, 1791).

For Discussion

1. What is the basis of Olympe de Gouges's demand for equal rights for women?
2. Did the two declarations differ in their views of the nation? Did they differ in their view of the proper function of law?

opposition led many people to suspect that he was encouraging the powers of Europe to invade France to restore the Old Regime.

Louis XVI had few personal resources upon which he might draw to win the confidence of his subjects. He was not as intelligent as his grandfather, Louis XV, nor did he have the skills necessary to dispel his subjects' growing distrust of him. Neither Louis nor his Austrian wife, Marie Antoinette, commanded much respect among the people. For many years the royal couple had been the object of relentless, sometimes pornographic satire. Critics lampooned the king for his rumored sexual inadequacies and the queen for a series of alleged infidelities with the king's brother and a succession of female partners. Whatever confidence Parisian citizens might have retained in the royal couple evaporated in June 1791, when the king and queen attempted to flee the country. The National Guard apprehended them at Varennes, close to the eastern French border, and forced them to return to Paris, where they were kept under guard at the palace of the Tuileries.

The development that actually precipitated the downfall of the monarchy and led to the establishment of a republic was the decision by the Legislative Assembly to go to war. After the flight to Varennes and the capture of the royal family, Frederick William II of Prussia and Emperor Leopold II of Austria, the brother of Marie Antoinette, signed an alliance and called upon the other European monarchs "to restore to the king of France complete liberty and to consolidate the bases of monarchical government." In response to this threat a small group of republicans, headed by the eloquent orator Jacques-Pierre Brissot (1754–1793), convinced the assembly that an international conspiracy against the revolution would end in an invasion of their country. Brissot and his supporters also believed that France could be lured into a foreign war, the king and queen would be revealed as traitors, and the monarchy would be destroyed. Exploiting xenophobic and revolutionary sentiment, and claiming that the strength of a citizen army would win a quick and decisive victory, Brissot and his allies won the support of the entire assembly. They also appealed to the international goals of the revolution, claiming that the French army would inspire revolution against "the tyrants of Europe" everywhere they went.

The Legislative Assembly declared war on Austria in April 1792. Instead of a glorious victory, however, the war resulted in a series of disastrous defeats at the hands of the Austrians and their Prussian allies. This military failure contributed to a mood of paranoia in France, especially in Paris. Fears arose that invading armies, in alliance with nobles, would undermine the revolution and destroy the assembly itself. In July the assembly officially proclaimed the nation to be in danger, calling for all citizens to rally against the enemies of liberty at home and abroad. Women petitioned for the right to bear arms. When the Austrians and Prussians threatened to torch the entire city of Paris and slaughter its population if anyone laid a hand on the royal family, Parisian citizens immediately demanded that the king be deposed.

On August 10 a radical republican committee overthrew the Paris commune, the city government that had been installed in 1789, and set up a new, revolutionary commune. A force of about 20,000 men, including volunteer troops from various parts of the kingdom, invaded the Tuileries, which was defended by about 900 Swiss guards. When the members of the royal bodyguard fled, members of the Paris crowds pursued them,

Le Sans Culotte intrépide

THE INTREPID *SANS-CULOTTE* In this satirical image of a *sans-culotte*, killing a nobleman conveys both the militancy of the *sans-culottes*, who were armed Parisian radicals who supported the Republic, and their distinctive dress. Male *sans-culottes* wore trousers rather than the breeches (*culottes*) that were in style among the members of the French nobility.

stripped them of their red uniforms, and hacked 600 of them to death with knives, pikes, and hatchets. The attack on the Tuileries forced the king to take refuge in the nearby Legislative Assembly. The assembly promptly suspended the monarchy and turned the royal family over to the commune, which imprisoned them in the Temple, a medieval fortress in the northeastern part of the city. The Assembly then ordered its own dissolution and called for the election of a new legislative body that would draft a new constitution.

The fall of the monarchy did nothing to allay the siege mentality of the city, especially after further Prussian victories in early September escalated fears of a Prussian invasion. The foreign invasion never materialized. On September 20, 1792 a surprisingly well-disciplined and well-trained army of French citizens, inspired by dedication to France and the revolution, repulsed the Prussian army at Valmy. This victory saved the revolution. Delegates to a new National Convention, elected by **universal male suffrage**, had already arrived in Paris to write a new constitution. On September 22 the Convention

universal male suffrage The granting of the right to vote to all adult males.

624

declared that the monarchy was formally abolished and that France was a republic. France had now experienced a second revolution, more radical than the first, but dedicated to the principles of liberty, equality, and fraternity, which soon became the motto of the revolution.

The Jacobins and the Revolution

By the time the Republic had been declared, the Jacobins had become the major political party in the Legislative Assembly. Soon, however, factional divisions began to develop within Jacobin ranks. The main split occurred between the followers of Brissot, known as **Girondins**, and the radicals known as Montagnards, or "**the Mountain.**" The latter acquired their name because they occupied the benches on the side of the convention hall, where the floor sloped upward. The Girondins occupied the lower side of the hall, while the uncommitted deputies, known as "the Plain," occupied the middle.

Both the Mountain and the Girondins claimed to be advancing the goals of the revolution, but they differed widely on which tactics to pursue. The Mountain took the position that as long as internal and external enemies threatened the state, the government needed to centralize authority in the capital. The Mountain thought of themselves as the representatives of the common people, especially the *sans-culottes* in Paris. Many of their leaders, including Georges-Jacques Danton (1759–1794), Jean-Paul Marat (1743–1793), and Maximilien Robespierre (1758–1794), were in fact Parisians. Their mission was to make the revolution even more egalitarian and to establish a republic characterized by civic pride and patriotism, which Robespierre referred to as the **Republic of Virtue**.

The Girondins, known as such because many of their leaders came from the southwestern department of Gironde, took a more conservative position than the Mountain on these issues. Favoring the economic freedom and local control desired by merchants and manufacturers, they were reluctant to support further centralization of state power. They believed that the revolution had advanced far enough and should not become more radical. They were also afraid that the egalitarianism of the revolution, if unchecked, would lead to a leveling of French society and result in social anarchy.

The conflict between the Girondins and the Mountain became apparent in the debate over what to do with the deposed king. Louis had been suspected of conspiring with the enemies of the revolution, and the discovery of his correspondence with the Austrian government led to his trial for treason against the nation. The Girondins had originally expressed reluctance to bring him to trial, preferring to keep him in prison. Once the trial began, they joined the entire National Convention in voting to convict him, but they opposed his execution. This stance led the Mountain to accuse the Girondins of being secret collaborators with the monarchy. By a narrow vote the Convention decided to put the king to death, and on January 21, 1793, Louis was executed at the Place de la Révolution, formerly known as the Place de Louis XV. (See *Justice in History* in this chapter.)

The instrument of death was the guillotine, an efficient and merciful but nonetheless terrifying decapitation machine first pressed into service in April 1792. It took its name from Dr. Joseph-Ignace Guillotin, who had the original idea for such a device, although he did not invent it. The guillotine was inspired by the conviction that all criminals, not just those of noble blood, should be executed in a swift, painless manner. The new device was to be put to extensive use during the next 18 months, and many Girondins fell victim to it.

The split between the Mountain and the Girondins became more pronounced as the republican regime encountered increasing opposition from foreign and domestic enemies. Early in 1793 Great Britain and the Dutch Republic allied with Prussia and Austria to form the First Coalition against France; within a month Spain and the Italian kingdoms of Sardinia and Naples joined them. The armies of these allied powers defeated French forces in the Austrian Netherlands in March of that year, and once again an invasion seemed imminent. At the same time internal rebellions against the revolutionary regime took place in various outlying provinces, especially in the

Girondins The more conservative members of the Jacobin party who favored greater economic freedom and opposed further centralization of state power during the French Revolution.

The Mountain Members of the radical faction within the Jacobin party during the French Revolution who advocated the centralization of state power and instituted the Reign of Terror.

Republic of Virtue The ideal form of government proposed by Maximilien Robespierre and other Jacobins during the French Revolution. Its proponents wished to make the republic established in 1792 more egalitarian and secular and inspire civic pride and patriotism in the people.

📖 Read the Document

Maximilien Robespierre, "Speech to National Convention"

district of the Vendée in western France. Noblemen and clerics led these uprisings, but they also had popular support, especially from tenant farmers who resented the increased taxation imposed by the new revolutionary government.

In the minds of Robespierre and his colleagues, the Girondins were linked to these provincial rebels, whom they labeled as *federalists* because they opposed the centralization of the French state and thus threatened the unity of the nation. In June 1793, 29 Girondins were expelled from the Convention for supporting local officials accused of hoarding grain. This purge made it apparent that any political opponent of the Mountain, even those with solid republican credentials, could now be identified as an enemy of the revolution.

The Reign of Terror, 1793–1794

To deal with its domestic enemies, the French republican government claimed powers that far exceeded those exercised by the monarchy in the age of absolutism. The Convention passed laws that set up special courts to prosecute enemies of the regime and authorized procedures that deprived those accused of their legal rights. These laws laid the legal

CHRONOLOGY: THE FRENCH REPUBLIC AND THE TERROR, 1792–1794

1792

April 20
Declaration of war against Austria.
August 10
Attack on the Tuileries; monarchy is suspended.
September 20
French victory at the Battle of Valmy.
September 21
National Convention meets.
September 22
Abolition of the monarchy and establishment of the Republic.

1793

January 21
Execution of Louis XVI.
February 1
Declaration of war against Great Britain and the Dutch Republic.
March 11
Beginning of rebellion in the Vendée.
June 2
Purge of Girondins from the Convention.
June 24
Ratification of a republican constitution.
October 16
Execution of Marie Antoinette.

1794

July 28
Tenth of *Thermidor*; execution of Robespierre.
November 12
Jacobin clubs closed.

foundation for the **Reign of Terror**, a campaign to rid the state of its internal enemies. A Committee of Public Safety, consisting of 12 members entrusted with the executive power of the state, superintended this process. Although technically subordinate to the Convention, the Committee of Public Safety became, in effect, a revolutionary dictatorship.

The man who emerged as the main figure on the Committee of Public Safety was Maximilien Robespierre. A brilliant student as a youth, Robespierre had taken offense when the royal carriage splashed him with mud as he was waiting to read an address to the king. A man with little sense of humor, he was passionate in his quest for justice. As a lawyer who defended indigent clients, Robespierre was elected to the Third Estate in 1789 and became a favorite of the *sans-culottes,* who called him "The Incorruptible." That he may have been, but he was also susceptible to the temptation to abuse power for partisan political purposes. Like Rousseau, whose work he admired, he was also willing to sacrifice individual liberty in the name of the General Will. He reasoned that because the General Will was indivisible, it could not accommodate dissent. Robespierre was primarily responsible for pushing the revolution to new extremes by establishing the program of state repression that began in the autumn of 1793.

The most intense prosecutions of the Terror took place between October 1793 and June 1794, but they continued until August 1794. By that time the revolutionary courts had executed 17,000 people, while 500,000 had suffered imprisonment. Another 20,000 either died in prison or were killed without any form of trial. Among the victims of the Terror were substantial numbers of clergy and nobility, but the overwhelming majority were artisans and peasants. One Parisian stableboy was guillotined for having said "f . . the Republic," while a baker from Alsace lost his head for predicting that "the Republic will go to hell with all its partisans."[1] Many of the victims came from the outlying regions of the country, especially the northeast, where foreign armies threatened the Republic, and the west, where a brutal civil war between the French army and Catholics and royalists was raging. Special surveillance committees identified these provincial enemies of the regime, and revolutionary tribunals tried them. The guillotine was by no means the only method of execution. In November and December 1793, about 1,800 rebels captured during the uprising in the Vendée were tied to other prisoners, placed in sinking boats, and drowned in the chilly waters of the Loire River.

Some of the most prominent figures of the Enlightenment fell victim to this paranoia. Among them was the Marquis de Condorcet, who believed passionately that all citizens, including women, had equal rights. Having campaigned against capital punishment, he committed suicide in a Parisian prison, just before he was to be executed. Another figure of the Enlightenment, the famous chemist Antoine Lavoisier (1743–1794), who had devoted himself to improving social and economic conditions in France, was executed at the same time. So too was the feminist Olympe de Gouges, who had petitioned for the equal rights of women. Many French revolutionaries, including Robespierre, used the political ideas of the Enlightenment to justify their actions, but the Terror struck down some of the most distinguished figures of that movement. In that sense the Terror marked the end of the Enlightenment in France.

The Committee of Public Safety then went after Danton and other so-called Indulgents who had decided that the Terror had gone too far. Danton's execution made everyone, especially moderate Jacobins, wonder who would be the next victim of a process that had spun completely out of control. In June 1794 the Terror reached a climax as 1,300 people went to their deaths. To stop the process, a group of Jacobins in the Convention organized a plot against Robespierre. Calling him a tyrant, they arrested him and more than 100 of his followers and guillotined them in late July 1794. In the provinces members of the White Terror, so named for the white Bourbon flag they displayed, executed leaders of local revolutionary tribunals. With these reprisals the most violent and radical phase of the French revolution came to an end.

The Reign of Terror had ended, but its memory would never be extinguished. Its horrors served as a constant warning against the dangers inherent in revolutionary

Reign of Terror A purging of alleged enemies of the French state between 1793 and 1794, superintended by the Committee of Public Safety, that resulted in the execution of 17,000 people.

 Read the Document

The National Convention, "Law on Suspects (1793)" and "Law of 22 Prairial Year II (1794)"

20.1

20.2

20.3

20.4

20.5

Justice in History
The Trial of Louis XVI

After the abolition of the monarchy and the proclamation of the French Republic in September 1792, the National Convention considered the fate of the deposed king. There was a broad consensus that Louis was guilty of treason against the nation and that he should answer for his crimes, but how he should do so became a subject of heated debate. The Convention was divided between the Girondins and the Mountain. Of the two, the Girondins were more inclined to follow due process, whereas the Mountain considered themselves to be acting as a revolutionary tribunal that had no obligation to adhere to existing French law. The Convention thus became a forum where Louis's accusers expressed competing notions of revolutionary justice.

The most divisive and revealing issue was whether there should be a trial at all. The Mountain originally took the position that because the people had already judged the king on August 10, when the monarchy had fallen and the king was taken prisoner, there was no need for a second judgment. They believed the death sentence should have been carried out immediately. Robespierre argued that a trial would have been counterrevolutionary, for it would have allowed the revolution itself to be brought before the court to be judged. A centrist majority, however, decided that the king had to be charged with specific offenses in a court of law and found guilty by due process before being sentenced.

A second issue, closely related to the first, was the technical legal question of whether Louis could be subject to legal action. Even in a constitutional monarchy, such as had been established in 1789, the legislative branch of the government did not possess authority over the king. The Convention based its decision to try Louis, however, on the revolutionary principle that he had committed crimes against the nation, which the revolutionaries claimed was a higher authority than the king. Louis, moreover, was no longer king but was now a citizen and, therefore, subject to the law in the same way as anyone else.

The third issue was Louis's culpability for the specific charges in the indictment. These crimes included refusing to call the Estates General, sending an army to march against the citizens of Paris, and conducting secret negotiations with France's enemies. The journalist and deputy Jean-Paul Marat added that "he robbed the citizens of their gold as a subsidy for their foes" and "caused his hirelings to hoard, to create famine, to dry up the sources of abundance that the people might die from misery and hunger." The king, who appeared personally to hear the

(continued on next page)

🔍 **View the Closer Look**   Execution of Louis XVI

EXECUTION OF LOUIS XVI, JANUARY 21, 1793 Although the king was convicted of treason by a unanimous vote, the vote to execute him carried by a slender majority of only 27 votes.

(continued from previous page)

20.1

20.2

20.3

20.4

20.5

indictment and then respond to the charges, based his defense on the laws in force at the times he was supposed to have committed his crimes. Thus, he defended his sending of troops to Paris on the grounds that in June and July 1789 he could order troops wherever he wanted. In the same vein, he argued that he had used force solely in response to illegal intimidation. These legalisms, however, only made the members of the Convention more contemptuous of the king. His defense failed to persuade a single Convention deputy. He was convicted of treason by a vote of 693–0.

The unanimous conviction of the king did not end the factional debates over the king's fate. Knowing that there was extensive support for the king in various parts of the country, the Girondins asked that the verdict be appealed to the people. They argued that the Convention, dominated by the Mountain and supported by militants in Paris, had usurped the sovereignty of the people. A motion to submit the verdict to the people for ratification lost by a vote of 424–283.

The last vote, the closest of all, determined the king's sentence. Originally, it appeared that a majority might vote for non-capital punishment. The Marquis de Condorcet, for example, argued that although the king deserved death on the basis of the law of treason, he could not bring himself to vote for capital punishment on principle. The radical response to this argument came from Robespierre, who appealed to the "principles of nature" that justified the death penalty in such cases, "where it is vital to the safety of private citizens or of the public." Robespierre's impassioned oratory carried the day. By a vote of 361–334 the king was sentenced to "death within 24 hours" rather than the alternatives of imprisonment followed by banishment after the war or imprisonment in chains for life. The following day Louis was led to the guillotine.

All public trials, especially those for political crimes, are theatrical events, in that the various parties play specific roles and seek to convey certain messages to their audiences. The men who voted to put Louis XVI on trial wanted to create an educational spectacle in which the already deposed monarch would be stripped of any respect he might still have commanded among the people. Louis was to be tried like any other traitor, and he was to suffer the same fate, execution by the guillotine. The attempt to strip him of all privilege and status continued after his death. His corpse, with his head placed between his knees, was taken to a cemetery, placed in a wooden box, and buried in the common pit. The revolutionaries were determined to guarantee that even in death the king would have the same position as the humblest of his former subjects.

For Discussion

1. How would you describe the standard of justice that the members of the National Convention upheld in voting to execute the king? How did this standard of justice differ from the standard to which King Louis XVI appealed?

2. Evaluate the argument of Robespierre that the death penalty can be justified only in cases of public safety. Compare his argument to that of Enlightenment thinkers such as Cesare Beccaria that capital punishment was an unjust, unnecessary, and uncivilized punishment.

Taking It Further

Jordan, David P. *The King's Trial: The French Revolution vs. Louis XVI.* 1979. The most thorough account of the trial.

Walzer, Michael (ed.). *Regicide and Revolution: Speeches at the Trial of Louis XVI.* 1974. A valuable collection of speeches with an extended commentary.

movements. The guillotine, the agent of a dysfunctional and indiscriminate state terrorism, became just as closely identified with the French Revolution as its famous slogan of "Liberty, Equality, Fraternity." The contrast between those two symbols, each of them emblematic of a different stage of the revolution, helps to explain how both conservatives and liberals in the nineteenth century would be able to appeal to the experience of the revolution to support their contradictory ideologies.

The Directory, 1795–1799

A desire to end the violence of the Terror allowed moderates in the National Convention to regain control of the state apparatus that Robespierre and his allies had used to such devastating effect. They dismantled the Paris Commune and stripped the Committee of Public Safety of most of its powers. In November 1794 they closed Jacobin clubs throughout the country, which had provided support for the Terror. The moderates who now controlled the government still hoped to preserve the gains of the revolution, while returning the country to more familiar forms of authority. A new constitution of 1795 bestowed executive power on a five-man Directorate, while an assembly consisting of two houses, the Council of Elders and the Council of Five Hundred, proposed and voted on all legislation. The franchise (the right to vote) was limited to property holders, allowing only two million men out of an adult male population of seven million to vote. A system of indirect election, in which a person voted for electors who then selected representatives, guaranteed that only the wealthiest members of the country would sit in the legislative councils.

Some of the wealthier and more entrepreneurial citizens of Paris welcomed the new regime, but opposition soon arose, mainly from Jacobins and *sans-culottes*. When the government relaxed the strict price controls that had been in effect under the Jacobins, the soaring price of bread and other commodities caused widespread social discontent among the populace. The continuation of the interminable war against foreign powers only aggravated the situation. Wherever French troops went, their constant need of food and other goods resulted in serious shortages of these commodities.

By the end of 1798 conditions had grown even worse. Inflation was running out of control. The collection of taxes was intermittent at best. The paper money known as *assignats*, first issued by the government in 1791 and backed by the value of confiscated Church lands, had become almost worthless. Late in 1797 the Directory, as the new regime was called, had to cancel more than half the national debt, a step that further alienated wealthy citizens who had lent money to the government. Military setbacks in 1798 and 1799 brought the situation to a critical point. The formation of a

CHRONOLOGY: THE DIRECTORY, 1795–1799

1795

August 22
The National Convention approves a new constitution.
October 5
Napoleon suppresses a royalist insurrection in Paris.
October 26
End of the Convention; beginning of the Directory.

1796

February 19
The issuing of *assignats* halted.
April 12
Beginning of a series of victories by Napoleon in Italy.

1798

May 13
Napoleon's expedition departs for Egypt.
May
Second Coalition (Britain, Austria, Russia, Naples, and Turkey) is formed against Napoleon.
July 21
Napoleon wins the Battle of the Pyramids.
August 1
Nelson destroys the French fleet at the Battle of the Nile.

1799

November 9–10
Napoleon's coup; Consulate established.

Second Coalition of European powers in 1799, which included Britain, Austria, Russia, Naples, and Turkey, presented a formidable challenge to French power and ensured that the war would not end soon. These military events produced a swing to the political left and raised the specter of another Jacobin coup.

In the face of this instability, Emmanuel-Joseph Sieyès, who had been elected as one of the directors two years earlier, decided to overthrow the government. Sieyès provided a link between the early years of the revolution, when he had defended the Third Estate, and the government of the Directory. Unlike many other prominent political figures, he had managed to avoid prosecution as the revolution had become more radical. When asked what he had done during the Reign of Terror, Sieyès replied, "I survived." Now he sought to provide the country with strong government, its greatest need in a period of political, economic, and social instability. The person Sieyès selected as his partner in this enterprise, who immediately assumed leadership of the coup, was Napoleon Bonaparte (1769–1821), a 30-year-old general who in 1795 had put down a royalist rebellion in Paris with a "whiff of grapeshot."

Napoleon had already established impressive credentials as a military leader. In 1796 and 1797 he had won major victories in Italy, leading to the Treaty of Campo Formio with Austria in 1797. Those victories and his short-lived success at the Battle of the Pyramids in Egypt had made him enormously popular in Paris, where he was received as a hero when he assumed command of the armed forces in the city in 1799. (See *Encounters and Transformations* in this chapter.) His popularity, his demonstrated military leadership, and his control of a large armed force made this "man on horseback" appear to have the best chance to replace the enfeebled civilian regime of the Directory.

On November 9, 1799, Napoleon addressed the two legislative councils. He reported the discovery of another Jacobin conspiracy and called for a new constitution to give the executive branch of the government more authority. Napoleon encountered resistance from some members of the Council of Five Hundred, who demanded that he be declared an outlaw. At this stage the president of the council, Napoleon's brother Lucien, intervened and called in troops to evict the members who opposed him. The following day France had a new government, known as the Consulate.

Executive power in the new government was to be vested in three consuls. It soon became clear, however, that Napoleon would dominate this trio. In the new constitution of December 1799, which the electorate ratified by **plebiscite** (a vote to accept or reject a proposal), Napoleon was named First Consul. This appointment made him the most powerful man in France and, for all practical purposes, a military dictator. The dictatorship became more apparent in 1802, when Napoleon was named Consul for Life.

plebiscite A popular vote for or against a form of government or rule by a particular person.

Cultural Change in France During the Revolution

20.3 In what ways did the political events of the revolution change French culture?

The French Revolution was primarily a political revolution, but it also brought about profound changes in French culture. It destroyed the cultural institutions of the Old Regime and created a new revolutionary culture.

The Transformation of Cultural Institutions

Between 1791 and 1794 many of the cultural institutions of the Old Regime were either destroyed or radically transformed, and new institutions under the control of the state took their place.

ACADEMIES The Parisian scientific and artistic academies established by Louis XIV (see Chapter 16) had a monopoly over the promotion and transmission of knowledge in the sciences and the visual arts. The academies were the epitome of privilege. They controlled their own membership, determined the recipients of their prizes, and monopolized their particular branches of knowledge. They were also heavily aristocratic institutions. As many as three-quarters of their members were nobles or clergy.

During the revolution the academies were abolished as part of a general attack on corporate bodies, and various government committees replaced them. For example, the Commission on Weights and Measures, which had been part of the Academy of Science, became an independent commission. Its task was to provide uniform weights and measures for the entire kingdom. In 1795 it established the meter, calculated as one ten-millionth of the distance from the North Pole to the equator, as the standard measure of distance. Like the decimal system, which was introduced at the same time, the metric system was subsequently adopted as a universal standard in all European countries.

The Popular and Republican Society of the Arts replaced the Royal Academy of Arts. The inspiration for this new republican society, which was open to artists of all social ranks, was Jacques-Louis David (1748–1825), the greatest painter of his generation. Employed at the court of Louis XVI, David became a vocal critic of the academy at the time of the revolution. He painted some of the most memorable scenes of the revolution, including the oath taken at the tennis court by the members of the National Assembly in 1789. During the Republic David depicted heroes of the revolution, such as Jean-Paul Marat (see the illustration on page 635), and he was later appointed First Painter to Napoleon. David presided over a revival of classicism in French painting, employing Greek and Roman motifs and exhibiting a rationalism and lack of sentiment in his work.

LIBRARIES Shortly after the revolution had begun, thousands of books and manuscripts from the libraries of monasteries, royal castles, residences of the nobility, and academies came into the possession of the state. Many of these became part of the Royal Library, which was appropriately renamed the National Library. The government also intended to catalog all the books held in libraries throughout the country. This effort to create the General Bibliography of France was never completed, and while the books were being cataloged, the government decided to get rid of those that dealt with "theology, mysticism, feudalism, and royalism" by sending them to foreign countries. This decision initiated a frenzy of book sales, mainly to private individuals. Altogether about five million books were lost or sold during these years.

MUSEUMS AND MONUMENTS The day after the abolition of the monarchy the Legislative Assembly created a Commission of the Museum, whose charge was "to collect paintings, statues and other precious objects" from royal residences, churches, and houses of émigrés. The museum was to be located in the Louvre, a royal palace that also served as an art gallery. When it opened in August 1793 the Louvre included a majority of paintings with religious themes. These religious works of art remained in the collection even though they appeared to be incompatible with the republican rejection of Christianity. The revolutionaries justified this decision on the grounds that this museum was intended to be entirely historical and have no relevance to contemporary culture.

The revolutionaries did not have the same respect for the bodies of their former kings. On August 10, 1793, the first anniversary of the deposition of Louis XVI, the National Convention ordered the destruction of all the tombs of past French kings. One by one the tombs were opened and the corpses, embalmed in lead, were removed. Metals and valuables were melted down for use in the war effort. The corpses were either left to disintegrate in the atmosphere or dragged unceremoniously to the cemetery, where they were thrown into the common pit. The corpse of Louis XIV landed on top of that of Henry IV. This disrespectful treatment of the remains of France's former kings was intended to erase the memory of monarchy.

The Creation of a New Political Culture

As the state was taking over and adapting the cultural institutions of the Old Regime, revolutionaries engaged in a much bolder and original undertaking: the production of a new, revolutionary political culture. Its sole purpose was to legitimize and glorify the new regime. This culture was almost entirely political; all forms of cultural expression were subordinated to the realization of a pressing political agenda.

The main political doctrine of the revolution was popular sovereignty: the claim that the people were the highest political power in the state. The new political culture was also popular in the sense that the entire populace, not simply the literate elite, adopted it. The people who embraced the new culture most enthusiastically were the *sans-culottes*—the radical shopkeepers, artisans, and laborers of Paris. The dress of these people influenced a change in fashion among the wealthier segments of society. A simple jacket replaced the ruffled coat worn by members of the upper classes, their powdered wigs gave way to natural hair, and long trousers replaced the shorter breeches. They also donned the red liberty cap, to which a tricolor cockade was affixed. The tricolor, which combined the red and blue colors of Paris with the white symbol of the Bourbon monarchy, identified the adherents of the revolution.

Symbols of revolution could be found everywhere. The commercialization of the revolution guaranteed that the tricolor flag, portraits of revolutionary figures, and images of the Bastille appeared on household objects as constant reminders of the public's support for the revolution. An order of the government in 1792 required all men to wear the tricolor cockade. Liberty trees, first planted by peasants as protests against local landlords, became a symbol of the revolution. By May 1792 more than 60,000 trees had been planted throughout the country.

The press, no longer tightly controlled by the government and the printers' guild, became a crucial agent of revolutionary propaganda and a producer of the new culture. Pamphlets, newspapers, brochures, and posters all promoted a distinctive revolutionary language, which became one of the permanent legacies of the revolution. Political leaders used the same rhetoric in their political speeches. *Sans-culottes* sang satirical songs and ballads, many of them to tunes well known in the Old Regime. The most popular of the songs of the revolutionary period was the *Marseillaise*, first sung by soldiers preparing for battle against the Austrians, but soon adopted by the civilian population and sung at political gatherings.

Much of this new political culture stemmed from the conviction that the doctrine of popular sovereignty should be practiced in everyday life. *Sans-culottes* did this by joining the political clubs organized by different factions within the National Assembly, by addressing others as citizens, and by using the more familiar form of the pronoun *you* (*tu* rather than *vous*) in all conversations. They also participated in the revolution by taking public oaths. On the first anniversary of the fall of the Bastille, as many as 350,000 people, many of them members of the "federations" of National Guards throughout the country, gathered on the royal parade ground outside Paris to take an oath "to the Nation, to the Law, to the King." Direct democracy was not possible in a society of 27 million people, but these cultural practices allowed people to believe that they were participating actively in the political process.

The new revolutionary culture was emphatically secular. In its most extreme form, it was blatantly anti-Christian. In September 1793 the radical Jacobin and former priest Joseph Fouché inaugurated a program of **de-Christianization**. Under his leadership, radical Jacobins closed churches and removed religious symbols such as crosses from cemeteries and public venues. In an effort to establish a purely civic religion, they forbade the public practice of religion and renamed churches "temples of reason." In their public pronouncements the architects of de-Christianization avoided reference to the Christian period of French history, which covered the entire national past.

de-Christianization A program inaugurated in France in 1793 by the radical Jacobin and former priest Joseph Fouché that closed churches, eliminated religious symbols, and attempted to establish a purely civic religion.

 Read the Document

Saint-Just on Democracy, Education, and Religion (1790s)

OATH TAKING On July 14, 1790, the first anniversary of the fall of the Bastille, as many as 350,000 people gathered on a field outside Paris to take an oath of loyalty to the new French nation. The event was referred to as the Feast of the Federation, because most of the oath takers were members of the regional federations of National Guards. The oath taking, which had many characteristics of a religious gathering, was led by the king himself, and it marked the most optimistic period of the revolution.

This de-Christianization campaign became the official policy of the Paris Commune and the National Convention. The program, however, did not win widespread support, and even some Jacobins claimed that in rejecting Christianity it had undermined a belief in God and the afterlife. In 1794 Robespierre attempted to modify the excesses of de-Christianization by launching the Cult of the Supreme Being. He promoted a series of festivals acknowledging the existence of a deity and the immortality of the soul. This new cult paid lip service to traditional religious beliefs, but it still served secular purposes. The cult was designed to direct the spiritual yearnings of the French people into patriotic undertakings and promote republican virtue.

In an effort to destroy all vestiges of the Old Regime, the government also instituted a new calendar in October 1793. The dates on the calendar began with September 22, 1792, the day the Republic was established. That became the first day of the year I, while the weeks now had ten days instead of seven. The new months were given names to evoke the different seasons, such as *Brumaire* for the first month of wintry weather, *Germinal* for the season of planting, and *Thermidor* for the warmest month of the summer. Hostile British contemporaries gave their own humorous renditions of these names, translating them as Freezy, Flowery, Heaty, and so on. The new calendar was intended to make the revolution a part of people's everyday consciousness. It remained in effect until the last day of 1805. The new revolutionary culture was disseminated widely, but it was always contested. Royalists trampled on the tricolor cockade, refused to adopt the new style of dress, and pulled up the liberty trees. During the Directory many wealthy members of society donned

JACQUES-LOUIS DAVID, *THE DEATH OF MARAT* (1793) The Jacobin journalist Jean-Paul Marat was stabbed to death in his bathtub by a noblewoman, Charlotte Corday, in July 1793. Marat holds the letter from his murderer that gave her entrance to his residence. The painting depicts the slain victim in the manner of the dead Christ in Michelangelo's *Pietà*. The painting thus shows how new secular culture of the revolution incorporated many elements of the Christian culture that had prevailed before the revolution began.

fancy and opulent clothes and revived the high social life of the capital. This resistance from counterrevolutionary forces guaranteed that, when the revolution was reversed, much of the new political culture would disappear. Napoleon did little to perpetuate it in the first decade of the nineteenth century, and the restored monarchy was openly hostile to it. Like the political revolution, however, some elements of revolutionary culture, such as the tricolor and the rhetoric of the revolutionary press, could never be suppressed. Not only did these cultural innovations inspire revolutionaries for the next 100 years, but they also became part of the mainstream of Western civilization.

The Napoleonic Era, 1799–1815

20.4 Did the rule of Napoleon from 1799 to 1814 confirm or betray the achievements of the French Revolution?

The coup d'état on November 9, 1799, or the eighteenth of *Brumaire* on the revolutionary calendar, marked a turning point in the political history of France. The Consulate ushered in a period of authoritarian rule. Liberty was restricted in the interest of order; republicanism gave way to dictatorship. The French Revolution had apparently run its course. But the period between 1799 and 1815 was also a time of considerable innovation, especially in the realm of politics and diplomacy. Those innovations were primarily the work of one man, Napoleon Bonaparte, who controlled the French government for the next 15 years.

Napoleon's Rise to Power

Napoleon Bonaparte was born on the Mediterranean island of Corsica. His father, Charles-Marie de Buonaparte, was an attorney who had supported the cause of winning Corsica's independence from the Italian state of Genoa. His mother, Letizia, came from an old noble family in the northern Italian region of Lombardy. In 1770 the new French government, which had gained control of the island the previous year, accepted the Buonaparte family as nobility. In 1779 the young Napoleon, whose native language was Corsican, received an appointment to a French military school. He survived both the rigors of the course of study and the taunting of his classmates, who mocked him for his accent and his poverty. Displaying a natural gift for military science, he won a position in the artillery section of the national military academy in Paris.

The events of the French Revolution made possible Napoleon's rapid ascent to military prominence and political power. When the revolution broke out, Napoleon returned to Corsica, where he organized the National Guard and petitioned the government to grant full rights of citizenship to his people. After becoming a Jacobin, he was commissioned to attack federalist and royalist positions in the south of France. Unlike many of his fellow Jacobins, he found favor with the Directory. In 1796 Napoleon was given command of the Army of Italy, at which time he abandoned the Italian spelling of his name for Bonaparte. His decisive victories against the Austrians and his popularity in Paris attracted the attention of Sieyès and others who wished to give the country strong, charismatic leadership.

Napoleon's personality was ideally suited to the acquisition and maintenance of political power. A man of unparalleled ambition, he was driven by an extraordinarily high assessment of his abilities. After one of his military victories he wrote, "I realized I was a superior being and conceived the ambition of performing great things." To the pursuit of his destiny he harnessed a determined and stubborn will and enormous energy. Temporary setbacks never seemed to thwart his single-minded pursuit of glory. He brought enormous energy to his military and political pursuits. He wrote more than 80,000 letters during his life, many of them transmitting orders to his officers and ministers. Authoritarian by nature, he used both intimidation and paternalism to cultivate the loyalty of his subordinates. Like many authoritarian leaders, he had difficulty delegating authority, a trait that weakened his regime. Finally, in an age dominated by high-minded causes, he exhibited an instinctive distrust of ideology and the doctrinaire pronouncements of philosophes such as Rousseau. Napoleon's military training led him to take a pragmatic, disciplined approach to politics, in which he always sought the most effective means to the desired end.

Napoleon's acquisition of power was systematic and shrewd. Playing on the need for a strong leader, and using the army as his main political tool, he maneuvered himself into the position of first consul in 1799. In 1802 he became consul for life, and two years later he crowned himself emperor of the French and his wife, Josephine, empress. The title of emperor traditionally denoted the height of monarchical power.

It is ironic that Napoleon, while continuing to hunt down and execute royalists, accepted a title of royalty himself and made his position, just like the French kingship, hereditary. By becoming emperor he not only betrayed his republican principles but also gave the French monarchy more power than it had in the Old Regime. As one royalist declared in 1804, "We have done more than we hoped. We meant to give France a king, and we have given her an emperor." Napoleon's coronation also made a negative impression outside France. The great German composer Ludwig van Beethoven, having dedicated his *Third Symphony* (1803) to Napoleon for overthrowing tyranny in France, scratched the emperor's name from the dedication after he assumed his new title the following year.

  Read the Document

Madame de Rémusat on the Rise of Napoleon

EMPEROR NAPOLEON CROWNING HIS WIFE, JOSEPHINE, EMPRESS OF THE FRENCH IN THE CATHEDRAL OF NOTRE DAME, 1804 This painting by Jacques-Louis David depicts secular and religious figures gathered around Napoleon not as members of privileged orders, but as representatives of the nation. Pope Pius VII remains seated as Napoleon places the crown on Josephine's head. Napoleon had already crowned himself emperor of the French.

SOURCE: Jacques-Louis David (1748–1825), "Consecration of the Emperor Napoleon I and Coronation of Empress Josephine," 1806–07. Louvre, Paris. Bridgeman-Giraudon/Art Resource, NY.

Napoleon and the Revolution

What was the relationship between Napoleon's rule and the French Revolution? Did Napoleon consolidate the gains of the revolution or destroy them? Did he simply redirect the revolutionary commitment to liberty, equality, and fraternity into more disciplined channels of expression after 1799? Or did he reverse the political trends that had prevailed from 1789 to 1799, crushing liberty in all its forms and establishing a ruthless, authoritarian dictatorship?

Napoleon always thought of himself as the heir of the revolution rather than its undertaker. He used the radical vocabulary of the revolution to characterize his domestic programs and his military campaigns. He presented himself as the ally of the common man against entrenched aristocratic privilege. He proclaimed a love for the French people and gave his support to the doctrine of popular sovereignty. He often referred to the rulers of other European countries as tyrants and presented himself as the liberator of their subjects.

Yet Napoleon's commitment to liberty was almost entirely rhetorical. Behind the appeals to the slogans of the revolution lurked a domineering will that was stronger than that of any eighteenth-century absolute monarch. Napoleon used the language of liberty and democracy to disguise a thoroughgoing authoritarianism, just as he used the rhetoric of republicanism to legitimize his own dictatorial regime. He orchestrated and controlled elections to make it appear that his rule reflected the will of the people. When

637

the empire was established he told his troops that they had the freedom to vote for or against the new form of government, but if they voted against it, they would be shot.

We can make a stronger case for Napoleon's egalitarianism. He demonstrated a commitment to providing equality of opportunity in the service of the state, and he supported the equality of all Frenchmen (but not Frenchwomen) before the law. This egalitarianism laid the foundation for the support he received from peasants, soldiers, and workers. He brought equality and political stability to France in exchange for political liberty. He synthesized the egalitarianism of the revolution with the authoritarianism of the Old Regime.

Napoleon was the heir of the revolution in two other ways. First, he continued the centralization and growth of state power and the rational organization of the administration that had begun in 1789. Each of the successive regimes between 1789 and 1815, even the Directory, had contributed to this pattern of state-building, and Napoleon's contribution was monumental. Second, he continued and extended France's military mission to export the revolution to its European neighbors. The two achievements are related to each other because the war effort necessitated the further growth and centralization of state power.

Napoleon and the French State

Once Napoleon had gained effective control of the French state, he sought to make it more efficient, organized, and powerful. In addition to turning the government into a de facto dictatorship, Napoleon settled the long struggle between Church and state, laid down a new law code that imposed legal uniformity on the entire country, and made the civil bureaucracy more centralized and uniform. He did all this with the intention of making the state an effective instrument of social and political control.

CONCORDAT WITH THE PAPACY Napoleon's first contribution to the development of the French state, achieved during the Consulate, was to resolve the bitter struggle between Church and state. A committed secularist, Napoleon was determined to bring the Church under the direct control of the state. This had been the main purpose of the Civil Constitution of the Clergy of 1790. Napoleon also realized, however, that the Civil Constitution had divided the clergy between those who had taken an oath to the nation and those who had refused. Clerical independence had also become a major rallying cry of royalists against the new regime, thereby threatening the stability of the country.

The death of Pope Pius VI (r. 1775–1799), an implacable foe of the revolution, gave Napoleon the opportunity to address this problem. The new pope, Pius VII (r. 1800–1823), who was more sympathetic to liberal causes, was eager to come to terms with the French government. The Concordat, which Napoleon and Pope Pius agreed to in 1801, gave something to both sides, although Napoleon gained more than he conceded. The pope agreed that all the clergy who refused to swear their loyalty to the nation would resign their posts, thus ending the bitter divisions of the past 12 years. The pope would appoint new bishops, but only with Napoleon's prior approval. The state would pay all clerical salaries, and the Church would abandon its claims to the ecclesiastical lands seized by the state at the beginning of the revolution.

These provisions represented formidable concessions to state power, and many French bishops found the terms of the Concordat too unfavorable to the Church. But the pope did manage to secure a statement that Roman Catholicism was the religion of the majority of citizens, and Napoleon agreed to scrap the secular calendar introduced in 1793, thereby restoring Sundays and holy days. Church attendance, having reached historic lows during the period of the Republic, began to rise. The Church regained respect and the freedom to function in French society, and more young recruits joined the clergy. Napoleon did not make many concessions to the Church, but they were significant enough to alienate a group of liberal philosophers and writers known as the Ideologues, who objected to what they saw as the return of "monkish superstition."

With the pope somewhat appeased, Napoleon took unilateral steps to regulate the administration of the French church. In a set of regulations known as the Organic Articles, which were added to the Concordat in 1802, the French church became a department of state, controlled by a ministry, just like any other bureaucratic department. Pronouncements from the pope required prior government approval, and the clergy were obliged to read government decrees from the pulpit. The state also gained control of Protestant congregations, which were given freedom of worship, and their ministers were also paid by the state. Jews received the protection of the state, but the government did not pay the salaries of rabbis.

THE CIVIL CODE Napoleon's most enduring achievement in the realm of state building was the promulgation of a new legal code, the Civil Code of 1804. A legal code is an authoritative and comprehensive statement of the law of a particular country. The model for modern legal codes in Europe was the *Corpus Juris Civilis* of the Roman Empire, which Justinian decreed at Constantinople between 529 and 534 C.E. That code had replaced the thousands of constitutions, customs, and judicial decisions that had been in effect during the Roman Republic and Empire. In compiling the new French code Napoleon, who had just proclaimed himself emperor of the French, imitated Justinian's legal achievement.

The Civil Code also met a long-standing set of demands to reform the confusing and irregular body of French law. Ever since the Middle Ages, France had been governed by a multiplicity of laws. In the southern provinces of the country, those closest to Italy, the law had been influenced by Roman law. In the north, the law was based on local or provincial customs. France needed a common law for all its people. Efforts to produce an authoritative written law code for all parts of the country had begun during the revolution, but Napoleon completed the project and published the code.

The Civil Code, which consisted of more than 2,000 articles, reflected the values of Napoleonic France. Articles guaranteeing the rights of private property, equality before the law, and freedom of religion enshrined key revolutionary ideas. The values promoted by the Civil Code, however, did not include the equality of the sexes. It granted men control of all family property. Women could not buy or sell property without the consent of their husbands. All male heirs were entitled to inherit equal shares of a family estate, but daughters were excluded from the settlement.

The Civil Code, which dealt only with the rights and relationships of private individuals, was the first and most important of six law codes promulgated by Napoleon. Others dealt with civil procedure (1806), commerce (1807), and criminal law (1811). Renamed the **Napoleonic Code** in 1806, the Civil Code had an impact on the law of several countries outside France. It became the basis for the codification of the laws of Switzerland, northern Italy, Poland, and the Netherlands, and it served as a model for the codes of many German territories controlled by France during the Napoleonic period. The Napoleonic Code also influenced the law of French-speaking North America, including the civil law of the state of Louisiana, which bears signs of its influence even today.

Napoleonic Code The name eventually given to the Civil Code of 1804, promulgated by Napoleon, which gave France a uniform and authoritative body of law.

ADMINISTRATIVE CENTRALIZATION Napoleon laid the foundation of modern French civil administration, which acquired the characteristics of rational organization, uniformity, and centralization. All power emanated from Paris, where Napoleon presided over a Council of State. This body consisted of his main ministers, who handled all matters of finance, domestic affairs, and war and oversaw a vast bureaucracy of salaried, trained officials. The central government also exercised direct control over the provinces. In each of the departments, the administrative divisions of France organized in 1790, an official known as a *prefect*, appointed by the central government, enforced orders coming from Paris (see **Map 20.1**). Paid the handsome annual salary of 20,000 francs, the prefects were responsible for the maintenance of public order. They enforced conscription, collected taxes, and supervised local public works, such as the construction and improvement of roads.

MAP **20.1** FRENCH DEPARTMENTS DURING THE REVOLUTION In 1790 France was divided into the 83 departments, each roughly equal in population. A preoccupation with uniformity, a product of the Enlightenment, became a major feature of French revolutionary culture. Note the departments of Vendée, a major center of counterrevolution in 1793, and Gironde, from which the Girondins, the moderate Jacobin party, took their name. In what other ways did the Enlightenment influence the French Revolution?

The men who served in the government of the French Empire belonged to one of two institutions: the civil bureaucracy and the army officer corps. The two were closely related, because the main purpose of the administrative bureaucracy was to prepare for and sustain the war effort. Both institutions were organized hierarchically, and those who held positions in them were trained and salaried. Appointment and promotion were based primarily on talent rather than birth.

The idea of "a career open to all talents," as Napoleon described it, ran counter to the tradition of noble privilege. This was one of the achievements of the revolution that Napoleon perpetuated during the empire. The new system did not amount to a **meritocracy**, in which advancement depends solely on ability and performance, because Napoleon himself made or influenced many appointments on the basis of friendship or kinship. The system did, however, allow people from the ranks of the bourgeoisie to achieve upward social mobility. To recognize their new status, Napoleon created a new order of nonhereditary noblemen, known as *notables*. Instead of inheriting status, these men acquired their titles by governmental service. Napoleon created more than 3,500 notables during his rule, thereby encouraging service to the state and strengthening loyalty to it.

meritocracy The practice of appointing people to office solely on the basis of ability and performance rather than social or economic status.

Napoleon, the Empire, and Europe

Closely related to Napoleon's efforts to build the French state was his creation of a sprawling European empire. This empire was the product of a series of military victories against the armies of Austria, Prussia, Russia, and Spain between 1797 and 1809. The instrument of these victories was the massive army that Napoleon assembled. With more than one million men under arms, it was the largest military force controlled by one man up to this time in European history.

Napoleon's victories against Austria in 1797 and 1800 resulted in territorial gains in Italy and control over the southern Netherlands, now called Belgium. A temporary peace with Britain in 1802 gave Napoleon free rein to reorganize the countries that bordered on France's eastern and southeastern boundaries. In Italy he named himself the president of the newly established Cisalpine Republic, and he transformed the cantons of Switzerland into the Helvetic Republic. Victories over Prussian forces at Jena and Auerstädt in 1806 gave him the opportunity to carve a new German kingdom of Westphalia out of Prussian territory in the Rhineland and to install his brother Jerome as its ruler. In the east Napoleon created the duchy of Warsaw out of Polish lands he seized from Prussia and Austria. In 1806 he formally dissolved the ancient Holy Roman Empire and replaced it with a loose association of 16 German states known as the Confederation of the Rhine (see **Map 20.2**).

Napoleon's final step in his effort to achieve mastery of Europe was the invasion and occupation of Spain. This campaign began as an effort to crush Portugal, an ally of Britain. In May 1808, as French armies marched through Spain en route to Lisbon, the Portuguese capital, a popular insurrection against Spanish rule occurred in Madrid. This spontaneous revolt, which led to the abdication of King Charles IV and the

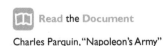

Read the Document

Charles Parquin, "Napoleon's Army"

MAP **20.2** THE EMPIRE OF NAPOLEON IN 1812 At its peak the official French Empire had 44 million inhabitants. The population of dependent states in Spain, Italy, Germany, and Poland brought the population of the "Grand Empire" to 80 million people. Why was Napoleon unable to include Russia in his Grand Empire?

CHRONOLOGY: THE CONSULATE AND THE EARLY YEARS OF THE EMPIRE, 1799–1806

1799
December 15
Proclamation of the Constitution of the Consulate.

1801
July 15
Concordat with the Papacy.

1804
March 21
The Civil Code promulgated.
December 2
Napoleon crowned emperor of the French.

1805
August
Third Coalition (Britain, Austria, and Russia) formed against France.

1806
August 6
Formal dissolution of the Holy Roman Empire.
October 14
French victories at the battles of Jena and Auerstädt.

succession of his son Ferdinand VII, was the first of many developments that caused the collapse of the Spanish Empire in America. In Europe it led to the absorption of Spain into the French Empire. Sensing that he could easily add one more territory to his list of conquests, Napoleon forced Ferdinand to abdicate and summoned his own brother, Joseph Bonaparte, to become king of Spain.

Joseph instituted some reforms in Spain, but the abolition of the Spanish Inquisition and the closing of two-thirds of the Spanish convents triggered a visceral reaction from the Spanish clergy and the general populace. Fighting for Church and king, small bands of local guerillas subjected French forces to intermittent and effective sabotage. An invasion by British forces under the command of Arthur Wellesley, later the Duke of Wellington (1769–1852), in what has become known as the Peninsular War (1808–1813), strengthened Spanish and Portuguese resistance.

Read the Document

Sir Harry Smith on Napoleon's Army in Spain

The Downfall of Napoleon

The turning point in Napoleon's personal fortunes and those of his empire came in 1810. After securing a divorce from Josephine in late 1809 because she had not borne him an heir, he married Marie-Louise, the daughter of the Habsburg emperor. This diplomatic marriage, which produced a son and heir to the throne the following year, should have made the French Empire more secure, but it had the opposite effect. For the first time during his rule, Napoleon faced dissent from both the right and the left, provoked in part by his negotiations with the Austrian Habsburgs. Despite the most stringent efforts at censorship, royalist and Jacobin literature poured off the presses. The number of military deserters and those evading conscription increased. Relations with the papacy reached a breaking point when Napoleon annexed the Papal States, at which point Pope Pius VII, who had negotiated the Concordat of 1801, excommunicated him.

Dissent at home had the effect of driving the megalomaniacal emperor to seek more glory and further conquests. In this frame of mind Napoleon made the ill-advised decision to invade Russia. The motives for engaging in this overly ambitious military campaign were not completely irrational. Victory over Russia promised to give France control of the Black Sea, and that in turn could ultimately have led to the control of Constantinople and the entire Middle East. More immediately, defeating Russia would have been necessary to enforce the French blockade of British goods, which Russia had refused to support.

The problem with a Russian invasion was that it stretched Napoleon's lines of communication too far and his resources too thin. Even before the invasion it was becoming increasingly difficult to feed, equip, and train the huge army he had assembled. The Grand Army that crossed from Poland into Russia in 1812 was not the efficient military force that Napoleon had commanded in the early years of the empire. Many of his best soldiers were fighting in the guerilla war in Spain. Casualties and desertions had forced Napoleon to call up new recruits who were not properly trained. Half the army, moreover, had been recruited from the population of conquered countries, making their loyalty to Napoleon uncertain.

The tactics of the Russians contributed to the failure of the invasion. Instead of engaging the Grand Army in combat, the Russian army kept retreating, pulling Napoleon further east toward Moscow. On September 7 the two armies clashed at Borodino, suffering a staggering 77,000 casualties in all. The Russian army then continued its retreat eastward. When Napoleon reached Moscow he found it deserted, and fires deliberately set by Muscovites had destroyed more than two-thirds of the city. Napoleon, facing the onset of a dreaded Russian winter and rapidly diminishing supplies, began the long retreat back to France. Skirmishes with the Russians along the way, which cost him 25,000 lives just crossing the Beresina River, conspired with the cold and hunger to destroy his army. During the entire Russian campaign his army lost a total of 380,000 men to death, imprisonment, or desertion. In the midst of this horror Napoleon, oblivious to the suffering of his troops, reported back to Paris, "The health of the emperor has never been better."

Not to be discouraged, Napoleon soon began preparing for further conquests. Once again his enemies formed a coalition against him, pledging to restore the independence of the countries that had become his satellites or dependents. Napoleon scored a few victories in the late summer of 1813, but in October allied forces inflicted a crushing defeat on him in the Battle of the Nations at Leipzig. Austrian troops administered another blow to the French in northern Italy, and the British finally drove them out of Spain. Napoleon's army was pushed back into France. A massive allied force advanced into Paris and occupied the city. After extensive political maneuvering, including a vote by the Senate to depose him, Napoleon abdicated on April 6, 1814. The allies promptly exiled him to the Mediterranean island of Elba. As he made the journey to the coast, crowds surrounding his coach shouted "Down with the tyrant!" while some villagers hanged him in effigy.

This course of events led to the restoration of the Bourbon monarchy. By the terms of the first Treaty of Paris in May 1814, the allies restored the brother of Louis XVI, the Count of Provence, to the French throne as Louis XVIII (r. 1814–1824). An implacable foe of the revolution, Louis strove to undermine its achievements. The white Bourbon flag replaced the revolutionary tricolor. Catholicism was once again recognized as the state religion. Exiled royalists returned to their high-ranking positions in the army. Nonetheless, Louis accepted a Constitutional Charter that incorporated many of the changes made between 1789 and 1791. Representative government, with a relatively limited franchise, replaced the absolutism of the Old Regime. The Constitutional Charter reaffirmed equality before the law, freedom of religion, and freedom of expression. Even more important, the powers of the state that the National Assembly and the Directory had extended and Napoleon had enhanced were maintained. The

Encounters and Transformations

The French Encounter the Egyptians, 1798–1801

Napoleon's expedition to Egypt in 1798 marked one of the few times during the revolutionary period that the French came in direct contact with non-Western peoples. The expedition resulted in the military occupation of the country for three years and set the stage for the first extensive encounters between Egyptians and Europeans since the Ottoman conquest of Egypt in the sixteenth century. At that time Egypt had become a semiautonomous province of the Ottoman Empire and had very little contact with the West. Egypt's isolation from the West meant that it had little exposure to the scientific and technological discoveries that had taken place in western Europe during the previous 300 years.

In addition to 38,000 soldiers, Napoleon brought with him 165 scholars who were organized in a Commission of Science and Arts. These men came from virtually every branch of learning: surveyors, cartographers, civil engineers, architects, botanists, physicians, chemists, and mineralogists. The commission also included artists, archaeologists, writers, and musicians. Their purpose was to give Napoleon information on the people and the resources of the country so that he could more easily subject it to French domination. A small group of these scholars set up an Institute of Egypt, whose mission was to propagate the Enlightenment and to undertake research on the history, people, and economy of the country. This involved the scholarly study of Egyptian antiquities, including the pyramids.

This work of the institute ushered in a long period in which many artifacts of Egyptian antiquity were taken from the country and transported to European museums and palaces. Members of the institute encouraged this cultural plundering, arguing that these Egyptian additions to the collections of the Louvre would embellish the glory of France. This ransacking of native Egyptian antiquities represented a form of cultural imperialism that continued unabated during the nineteenth century.

A description of Egypt, *Travels in Upper and Lower Egypt* (1802), written by a member of the institute, Dominique-Vivant Denon, reflected a different sort of French cultural imperialism. In this two-volume work, Vivant Denon described the different "races" of Egyptians whom he had encountered in the port town of Rosetta. He described the Copts, the most ancient Egyptians, as "swarthy Nubians" with flat foreheads, high cheekbones, and short broad noses and tendencies toward "ignorance, drunkenness, cunning, and finesse." He described the physical and personal characteristics of the Arabs and the Turks in more appealing terms, but they too were often reduced to the "degraded state of animals."

Expressions of French cultural superiority permeated other contemporary accounts of Napoleon's expedition. A multivolume work, *The Description of Egypt*, claimed that Napoleon wanted to procure for Egyptians "all the advantages of a perfected civilization." It praised him for bringing modern knowledge to a country that had been "plunged into darkness." These attitudes provided a justification for the subsequent economic exploitation of Egypt, first by the French and later by the British, during the nineteenth century.

JEAN-CHARLES TARDIEU, *THE FRENCH ARMY HALTS AT SYENE, UPPER EGYPT, ON FEBRUARY 2, 1799* This painting depicts a cultural encounter between French soldiers and Egyptians in the city of Syene (now Aswan) during the Egyptian campaign of 1798–1799. The soldiers are scribbling on the ruins of ancient Egypt, indicating a lack of respect for Egyptian culture.

SOURCE: Jean-Charles Tardieu (1765–1830), "Troops Halted on the Banks of the Nile, 2nd February 1812," oil on canvas. Chateau de Versailles, France/Lauros/Giraudon/The Bridgeman Art Library.

For Discussion

In what ways did Vivant Denon's work reflect the values that were cultivated during the Enlightenment?

administrative division of France into departments continued, and the Napoleonic Code remained in force. France had experienced a counterrevolution in 1814, but it did not simply turn the political clock back to 1788. Some of the political achievements of the previous 25 years were preserved.

Despite his disgrace and exile, Napoleon still commanded loyalty from his troops and large segments of the population. While in power he had constructed a legend that

JOAQUIN SOROLLA Y BASTIDA, *THE 2ND OF MAY IN MADRID* This painting depicts the unsuccessful Spanish revolt against Napoleon's military forces in Madrid on May 2, 1808. A French unit executed hundreds of the rebels the following day.

SOURCE: Art Resource XJL 186995.

CHRONOLOGY: THE DOWNFALL OF NAPOLEON, 1810–1815

1810

April 2
Marriage of Napoleon to Marie-Louise.

1810

1812

September 7
Battle of Borodino.
September 14
Napoleon enters Moscow.
October
Retreat from Moscow begins.

1812

1813

October 16–19
Battle of the Nations at Leipzig.

1813

1814

April 6
Abdication of Napoleon.
May 30
First Treaty of Paris.
September
Congress of Vienna assembles.

1814

1815

March
Napoleon escapes from Elba.
June 18
Battle of Waterloo.
November 20
Second Treaty of Paris.

1815

drew on strong patriotic sentiment. Supporters throughout France continued to promote his cause in the same way that royalists had maintained that of the Bourbon monarchy since 1792. The strength of the Napoleonic legend became apparent in March 1815, when Napoleon escaped from Elba and landed in southern France. Promising to rid the country of the exiled royalists who had returned and thereby save the revolutionary cause, he won over peasants, workers, and soldiers. Regiment after regiment joined him as he marched toward Paris. By the time he arrived, Louis XVIII had gone into exile once again, and Napoleon found himself back in power.

But not for long. The allied European powers quickly began to assemble yet another coalition. Fearing that the allies would launch a massive invasion of France, Napoleon decided to strike first. He marched an army of 200,000 men into the Austrian Netherlands, where the allies responded by amassing 700,000 troops. Near the small village of Waterloo, south of Brussels, Napoleon met the British forces of the Duke of Wellington, who had turned the tide against him during the Peninsula War. Reinforced by Prussian troops, Wellington inflicted a devastating defeat on the French army, which lost 28,000 men and went into a full-scale retreat. Napoleon abdicated once again and was exiled to the remote South Atlantic island of St. Helena, from which escape was impossible. He died there in 1821.

📖 Read the Document

Napoleon's Exile to St. Helena (1815)

MAP **20.3** EUROPE AFTER THE CONGRESS OF VIENNA, 1815 The Congress scaled back the boundaries of France to their status in 1790, ceded territory to Austria in western and northeastern Italy, and created the Kingdom of the Netherlands, a new German Confederation, and a new Kingdom of Poland ruled by Russia. The western part of Poland was ceded to Prussia. Which states benefited the most from this redrawing of the map of Europe?

Even before the Battle of Waterloo, the major powers of Europe had gathered in Vienna to redraw the boundaries of the European states that had been created, dismembered, or transformed during the preceding 52 years (see **Map 20.3**). Under the leadership of the Austrian foreign minister, Prince Klemens von Metternich (1773–1859), this conference, known as the **Congress of Vienna**, worked out a settlement that was intended to preserve the balance of power in Europe and at the same time uphold the principle of dynastic legitimacy. By the terms of a separate Treaty of Paris (the second in two years) the boundaries of France were scaled back to what they had been in 1790, before it had begun its wars of expansion. To create a buffer state on the northern boundary of France, the Congress annexed the Austrian Netherlands to the Dutch Republic, which now became the Kingdom of the Netherlands with William I, a prince of the House of Orange, as its king. The treaty ceded territory along the Rhineland to Prussia, while Austria, now named the Austrian Empire, gained territory in Italy. In place of the defunct Holy Roman Empire, the Congress established a new German Confederation, a loose coalition of 39 separate territories with a weak legislative assembly. The duchy of Warsaw, established in 1807 and renamed the Kingdom of Poland in 1812, was partitioned between Prussia and Russia. The five major powers that had drawn this new map of Europe—Britain, Austria, Prussia, Russia, and France—agreed to meet annually to prevent any one country, especially France but also Russia, from achieving military dominance of the European Continent.

Congress of Vienna A conference of the major powers of Europe in 1814–1815 to establish a new balance of power at the end of the Napoleonic Wars.

 Read the Document

The German Act of Confederation 1814

The Legacy of the French Revolution

20.5 In what ways did the French Revolution change the course of European and Western history?

With the conclusion of the Congress of Vienna a tumultuous period of European and Western history finally came to an end. Not only had France experienced a revolution, but every country in Europe and America had felt its effects. Governments were toppled in countries as far apart as Poland and Peru. Added to this turbulence was the experience of incessant warfare. France was at war for more than 20 years during the Republic and the Empire, and it had involved almost all European powers in the struggle. With armies constantly in need of provisions and supplies, high taxation, galloping inflation, and food shortages inflicted economic hardship on a large portion of the European population.

The cost of all this instability and warfare in terms of human life was staggering. Within the space of one generation almost two million European soldiers were killed in action, wasted by disease, or starved or frozen to death. In France alone just under 500,000 soldiers died during the revolutionary wars of 1792–1802 and another 916,000 during the wars of the Empire. Internal political disturbances took the lives of hundreds of thousands of civilians from all ranks of society, not only in France, but throughout Europe. Unprecedented fears of internal and external subversion fed the violence at all levels. Government officials, collaborators, counterrevolutionaries, and imagined enemies of the state were all executed. This spate of violence and death—much of it in the name of liberty—occurred almost entirely at the hands of the state or its enemies.

What was achieved at this extraordinary price? How did the France of 1815 differ from the France of 1788? What on balance had changed? Historians once argued that as a result of the revolution the bourgeoisie, composed of merchants, manufacturers, and other commoners of substantial wealth, had replaced the nobility as the dominant social and political class in France. This argument can no longer be sustained. The nobility certainly lost many of their privileges in 1789, and many of them went into exile during the revolutionary period, but the position they had in French society in 1815 did not differ greatly from what it had been under the Old Regime. In both periods there was considerable blurring of the distinctions between nobility and bourgeoisie. The revolutionary period did not witness the emergence of a new class of industrial entrepreneurs either. The only group that definitely profited from the revolution in the long run was men of property, regardless of their membership in any social category or "class." Wealthy men emerged triumphant in the Directory, found favor during the Napoleonic period, and became the most important members of political society after the monarchy was restored.

It would be difficult to argue that *women* of any social rank benefited from the revolution. During the early years of the revolution, women participated actively in public life. They were involved in many demonstrations in Paris, including the storming of the Bastille and the march to Versailles. But women never achieved the position of equality with men for which the Marquis de Condorcet and Olympe de Gouges had hoped. The radical Jacobins dealt that goal a major setback when they banned all women's clubs and societies on the grounds that female participation in public life would harm the institution of the family. This action ended the extensive participation of women in political life, which had begun during the eighteenth century, especially in the salons. During the nineteenth century French women exercised influence in the private sphere of the home, but not in the public sphere of politics.

It is even more difficult to identify permanent economic changes as a result of the revolution. The elimination of the remnants of feudalism may have made France marginally more capitalist than it had been before the revolution, but agricultural and mercantile capitalism had long been entrenched in French society. Nor did the Continental System, the blockade of British goods from all European ports initiated in 1806, allow French industry to catch up with that of Great Britain. Whatever economic gains were made under the protective shield of the state were offset by the adverse economic effects of 22 years of nearly continuous warfare. In the long run the revolutionary period delayed the process of industrialization that had entered its preliminary stages in France during the 1780s and retarded the growth of the French economy for the remainder of the nineteenth century.

The permanent legacy of the French Revolution lies in the realm of politics. First, the period from 1789 to 1815 triggered an enormous growth in the competence and power of the state. This trend had begun before the revolution, but the desire of the revolutionaries to transform every aspect of human life in the service of the revolution, coupled with the necessity of utilizing all the country's resources in the war effort, gave the state more control over the everyday life of its citizens than ever before. Fifteen years of Napoleonic rule only accentuated this trend, and after 1815 many of those powers remained with the government.

A second permanent political achievement of the French Revolution was the promotion of the doctrine of popular sovereignty. The belief that the people constituted the highest political authority in the state became so entrenched during the revolution that it could never be completely suppressed, either in France or in the other countries of Europe. Napoleon recognized its power when he asked the people to approve political changes he had already made by his own authority. After the restoration of the monarchy the doctrine of popular sovereignty was promoted mainly by the press, which continued to employ the new revolutionary rhetoric to keep alive the high ideals and aspirations of the revolution. The doctrine also contributed to the formation of two nineteenth-century ideologies, liberalism and nationalism, which will be discussed in Chapter 22.

CONCLUSION

The French Revolution and Western Civilization

The French Revolution was a central event in the history of the West. It began as an internal French affair, reflecting the social and political tensions of the Old Regime, but it soon became a turning point in European and Western history. Proclamations of the natural rights of humanity gave the ideals of the revolution widespread appeal, and a period of protracted warfare succeeded in disseminating those ideals outside the boundaries of France.

Underlying the export of French revolutionary ideology was the belief that France had become the standard-bearer of Western civilization. French people believed they were *la grande nation,* the country that had reached the highest level of political and social organization. They did not believe they had acquired this exalted status by inheritance. Unlike the English revolutionaries of the seventeenth century, the French did not claim that they were the heirs of a medieval constitution. French republicans of the 1790s attributed none of their national preeminence to the monarchy, whose memory they took drastic steps to erase. They considered the secular political culture that emerged during the French Revolution to be entirely new.

The export of French revolutionary political culture during the Republic and the Empire led to widespread changes in the established order. Regimes were toppled, French puppets acquired political power, boundaries of states were redrawn, and traditional authorities were challenged. Liberal reforms were enacted, new constitutions were written, and new law codes were promulgated. The Europe of 1815 could not be mistaken for the Europe of 1789.

The ideas of the French Revolution, like those of the Enlightenment that had helped to inspire them, did not go unchallenged. From the very early years of the revolution they encountered determined opposition, both in France and abroad. As the revolution lost its appeal in France, the forces of conservatism and reaction gathered strength. At the end of the Napoleonic period, the Congress of Vienna took steps to restore the legitimate rulers of European states and to prevent revolution from recurring. It appeared that the revolution would be completely reversed, but that was not the case. The ideas born of the revolution continued to inspire demands for political reform in Europe during the nineteenth century, and those demands, just like those in the 1790s, met with fierce resistance.

MAKING CONNECTIONS

1. Did the events of 1789 constitute a revolution in the sense that they brought about a fundamental change in the system of government? In what sense did the establishment of the Republic in 1792 represent a more radical change in French politics?
2. To what extent did the ideas of the Enlightenment inspire the events of the French Revolution?
3. How did the Jacobin commitment to equality lead to the Reign of Terror?
4. Did the French Revolution end in 1799 or did Napoleon perpetuate it in any significant ways?
5. Why did Napoleon fail to realize his diplomatic and military objectives?

TAKING IT FURTHER

For suggested readings see page R-1.

Chapter Review

The First French Revolution, 1789–1791

20.1 Why did the Old Regime collapse in 1789, and what revolutionary changes took place during the next two years?

A financial and political crisis due to the king's efforts to pay off debts from protracted periods of warfare, combined with a social crisis fueled by the high price of bread, caused a breakdown of social order. The revolution eliminated noble and clerical privileges, reorganized the Church, and instituted the idea that all men had a natural right to liberty, property, and equality before the law, freedom from oppression, and religious toleration. The king became a constitutional monarch, retaining only the power to suspend legislation, direct foreign policy, and command the armed forces.

The French Republic, 1792–1799

20.2 How did a second more radical revolution in 1792 create a regime that instituted the Reign of Terror?

Military failures abroad fueled paranoia at home, where fears that invading armies would undermine or destroy the revolution grew. The formal abolishment of the monarchy and the declaration of France as a republic dedicated to the principles of liberty, equality, and fraternity soon followed. Internal dissent within the government festered as the republican regime encountered increasing opposition from foreign and domestic enemies. The revolutionary courts executed 17,000 people, including substantial numbers of clergy and nobility, but a majority of the Terror's victims were artisans and peasants.

Cultural Change in France During the Revolution

20.3 In what ways did the political events of the revolution change French culture?

A new, revolutionary political culture was established, its sole purpose to legitimize and glorify the new government. All other forms of culture were subordinated to this new culture, with millions of books deemed to have royalist or religious themes sold off or lost, and museums like the Louvre created to house works of art that seemed incompatible with the republican rejection of Christianity.

The Napoleonic Era, 1799–1815

20.4 Did the rule of Napoleon from 1799 to 1814 confirm or betray the achievements of the French Revolution?

Napoleon combined the egalitarian values of the revolution with the authoritarianism of the Old Regime. He supported the equality of all Frenchmen, especially equality of opportunity in service of the state,

but his use of the language of liberty disguised what was essentially a dictatorship. He continued the centralization and growth of state power and administration begun during the revolution, and he extended France's military mission to spread the revolution throughout Europe.

The Legacy of the French Revolution

20.5 In what ways did the French Revolution change the course of European and Western history?

The French Revolution's legacy was mostly political. First, the revolutionaries' goal to transform every aspect of life in service of the revolution and the need to use all of the country's resources in the war effort supported the growth and power of the state. Second, the belief that the highest political authority in the state was its people is an idea that became so entrenched during the revolution that it could never be completely suppressed, either in France or in the other countries of Europe.

Chapter Time Line

1789 The storming of the Bastille. — 1789

1791 — **1791** Newly elected Legislative Assembly opens.

1792 Abolition of the monarchy and establishment of the Republic. — 1792

1793 — **1793** Execution of Louis XVI.

1795 End of the Convention; beginning of the Directory. — 1795

1799 — **1799** Napoleon's coup; Consulate established.

1804 Napoleon crowned emperor of the French. — 1804

1814 — **1814** Congress of Vienna assembles.

1815 Battle of Waterloo. — 1815

21 The Industrial Revolution

CHILD LABOR IN THE MINES A child hurrying coal through a tunnel in a mine.

n 1842 a 17-year-old girl, Patience Kershaw, testified before a British parliamentary committee regarding the practice of employing children and women in the nation's mines. When the girl made her appearance, the members of the committee observed that she was "an ignorant, filthy, ragged, and deplorable-looking object, such as one of uncivilized natives of the prairies would be shocked to look upon." Patience, who had never been to school and could not read or write, told the committee that she was one of ten children, all of whom had at one time worked in the coal mines, although three of her sisters now worked in a textile mill. She went to the pit at five in the morning and came out at five at night. Her job in the mines was to hurry coal, that is, to pull carts of coal through the narrow tunnels of the mine. Each cart weighed 300 pounds, and

LEARNING OBJECTIVES

21.1	21.2	21.3	21.4	21.5
What was the Industrial Revolution of the late eighteenth and nineteenth centuries?	What social and economic changes made industrial development possible?	How did industrialization spread from Great Britain to the European continent and America?	What were the economic, social, and cultural effects of the Industrial Revolution?	What was the relationship between Britain's industrial strength and the growth of its empire?

Listen to Chapter 21 on MyHistoryLab

👁 **Watch the Video Series on MyHistoryLab**

Learn about some key topics related to this chapter with the *MyHistoryLab Video Series: Key Topics in Western Civilization*

every day she hauled 11 of them one mile. The carts were attached to her head and shoulders by a chain and belt, and the pressure of the cart had worn a bald spot on her head. Patience hurried coal for 12 hours straight, not taking any time for her midday meal, which she ate as she worked. While she was working, the men and boys who dug the coal and put it in the carts would often beat her and take sexual liberties with her. Patience told the committee, "I am the only girl in the pit; there are about 20 boys and 15 men. All the men are naked. I would rather work in a mill than a coal pit."[1]

Patience Kershaw was one of the human casualties of a development that historians refer to as the Industrial Revolution. This process, which fundamentally transformed human life, involved the extensive use of machinery in the production of goods. Much of that machinery was driven by steam engines, which required coal to produce the steam. Coal mining itself became a major industry, and the men who owned and operated the mines tried to hire workers, many of them children, at the lowest possible wage. This desire to maximize profits led to the employment, physical hardship, and abuse of girls like Patience Kershaw.

The Industrial Revolution did more than create harrowing labor conditions. It resulted in a staggering increase in the volume and range of products made available to consumers, from machine-produced clothing to household utensils. It made possible unprecedented and sustained economic growth. The Industrial Revolution facilitated the rapid transportation of passengers as well as goods across large expanses of territory, mainly on the railroads that were constructed in all industrialized countries. It brought about a new awareness of the position of workers in the economic system, and it unleashed powerful political forces intended to improve the lot of these workers.

The Industrial Revolution thus played a crucial role in redefining and reshaping the West. Until the late nineteenth century industrialization took place only in Western nations. During that century "the West" gradually became identified with countries that had industrial economies. When some non-Western countries introduced mechanized industry in the twentieth century, largely by imitating Western example, the geographical boundaries of the West shifted.

This chapter will address the following question:

How did the Industrial Revolution transform Western civilization?

The Nature of the Industrial Revolution

21.1 What was the Industrial Revolution of the late eighteenth and nineteenth centuries?

The Industrial Revolution, which took place in Great Britain during the late eighteenth and early nineteenth centuries and in other European countries and America after 1815, consisted of four closely related developments: the introduction of new industrial technology, the utilization of mineral sources of energy, the concentration of labor in factories, and the development of new methods of transportation.

New Industrial Technology

The Industrial Revolution ushered in the machine age, and to this day machines are the most striking feature of modern industrial economies. In the late eighteenth century industrial machines were novelties, but their numbers increased dramatically in the early nineteenth century. For example, the power loom, a machine used for weaving cloth, was invented in Britain in 1787 but not put into widespread use until the 1820s. By 1836 there were more than 60,000 power looms in just one English county.

Machines became so common in Britain that machine-making itself became a major industry, supplying its products to other manufacturers rather than to individual consumers. Machines were introduced in the textile, iron, printing, papermaking, and engineering industries and were used in every stage of manufacture. Machines extracted minerals for use as either raw materials or sources of energy, transported those materials to the factories, saved time and labor in the actual manufacturing of commodities, and carried the finished products to market. Eventually machines were used in agriculture, facilitating both the plowing of fields and the harvesting of crops.

The most significant of the new machines were devices for producing textiles and the steam engine, which were first used in mining and the iron industry. These pieces of machinery became almost synonymous with the Industrial Revolution, and their invention in the 1760s appropriately marked its beginning.

TEXTILE MACHINERY Until the late eighteenth century, Europeans produced textiles entirely by hand. They spun yarn on spinning wheels and wove cloth on hand looms. Wool remained the main textile produced in Europe until the early eighteenth century, when a new material, cotton, became immensely popular, mainly because of its greater comfort. The demand for cotton yarn was greater than the quantities spinners could supply. To meet this demand a British inventor, James Hargreaves, in 1767 constructed a new machine, the spinning jenny, which greatly increased the amount of cotton yarn that could be spun and thus made available for weaving. The original jenny, a hand machine used in the homes of spinners, consisted of only eight spindles, but it later accommodated as many as 120.

📖 Read the Document

Richard Guest, *The Creation of the Steam Loom*

🔍 **View the Closer Look**   The Great Exhibition in London

EXHIBIT OF MACHINERY AT THE CRYSTAL PALACE EXHIBITION IN LONDON IN 1851 During the Industrial Revolution the manufacture of heavy machinery itself became an industry.

21.1

21.2

21.3

21.4

21.5

The spinning of yarn on the jenny required a stronger warp, the yarn that ran lengthwise on a loom. A power-driven machine, the water frame, introduced by the barber and wigmaker Richard Arkwright in 1769, made the production of this stronger warp possible. In 1779 Samuel Crompton, using tools he had purchased with his earnings as a fiddle player at a local theater, combined the jenny and the frame in one machine, called the mule. Crompton worked on his machine only at night to keep it secret, and the strange noises coming out of his workshop made his neighbors think his house was haunted. The mule, which could spin as much as 300 times the amount of yarn produced by one spinning wheel, became the main spinning machine of the early Industrial Revolution. Both the water frame and the mule required power, and that requirement led to the centralization of the textile industry in large rural mills located near rivers so that their water wheels could drive the machinery.

The tremendous success of the mule eventually produced more yarn than the weavers could handle on their hand looms. Edmund Cartwright, an Oxford-educated clergyman, supported by monies from his heiress wife, addressed that need with the invention of the power loom in 1787. In that same year he put his new invention to use in a weaving mill he built near the town of Doncaster. The power loom, like the spinning jenny, the water frame, and the mule, met a specific need within the industry. It also gave the producer a competitive advantage by saving time, reducing the cost of labor, and increasing production. Two power looms run by a 15-year-old boy, for example, could produce more than three times what a skilled hand loom weaver could turn out in the same time using only the old hand device, the flying shuttle. The net effect of all these machines was the production of more than 200 times as much cotton cloth in 1850 as in 1780. By 1800 cotton became Britain's largest industry, producing more than 20 percent of the world's cloth; by 1850 that percentage had risen to more than 50 percent. Indeed, by midcentury, cotton accounted for 70 percent of the value of all British exports.

Read the Document

Leeds Woolen Workers, "Petition"

THE STEAM ENGINE The steam engine was even more important than the new textile machinery because it was used in almost every stage of the productive process, including the operation of textile machinery itself. James Watt, a Scottish engineer, invented the steam engine in 1763. Watt's steam engine improved the engine invented by Thomas Newcomen in 1709, which had been used mainly to drain water from deep mines. The problem with Newcomen's engine was that the steam, which was produced in a cylinder heated by coal, had to be cooled to make the piston return, and the process of heating and cooling had to be repeated for each stroke of the piston. The engine was therefore inefficient and expensive to operate. Watt created a separate chamber where the steam could be condensed without affecting the heat of the cylinder. The result was a more efficient and cost-effective machine that could provide more power than any other source. Watt's pride in his invention was matched only by his pride in his Scottish nationality. Upon receiving a patent for the new device, he boasted, "This was made by a Scot."

After designing the steam engine, Watt teamed up with a Birmingham metal manufacturer, Matthew Boulton, to produce it on a large scale. Boulton provided the capital necessary to begin this process and hire the skilled laborers to assemble the machines. He also had ambitious plans for marketing the new invention throughout the world. "It would not be worth my while to make for three countries only," Boulton said, "but I find it well worth my while to make for the whole world."

The steam engine soon became the workhorse of the Industrial Revolution. Not only did it pump water from mines, but it also helped raise minerals such as iron ore from those mines. It provided the intense blast of heat that was necessary to re-smelt pig iron into cast iron, which in turn was used to make industrial machinery, buildings, bridges, locomotives, and ships. Once the engine was equipped with a rotating device, it drove factory machinery in the textile mills, and it eventually powered the railroad locomotives that carried industrial goods to market.

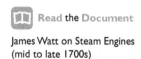

Read the Document

James Watt on Steam Engines
(mid to late 1700s)

Read the Document

Matthew Boulton and Manufacturing
(mid-1700s)

CHRONOLOGY: TECHNOLOGICAL INNOVATIONS OF THE INDUSTRIAL REVOLUTION

1763
James Watts's rotative steam engine.

1767
James Hargreaves's spinning jenny.

1769
Richard Arkwright's water frame.

1779
Samuel Crompton's mule.

1787
Edmund Cartwright's power loom.

1815
George Stephenson's steam locomotive.

1846
Elias Howe's sewing machine.

Mineral Sources of Energy

Until the late eighteenth century, either humans or beasts provided the power for most economic activity. Either people tilled the soil themselves, using a spade, or they yoked oxen to pull a plow. Either they carried materials and goods on their backs or they used horses to transport them. In either case the energy for these tasks came ultimately from organic sources, the food that was needed to feed farmers or their animals. If workers needed heat, they had to burn an organic material, wood or charcoal, to produce it. The amount of energy that these sources generated was therefore limited by the capacity of a geographical region to produce sufficient wood, charcoal, or food.

Organic sources of energy were of course renewable, in that new crops could be grown and forests replanted, but the long periods of time that these processes took, coupled with the limited volume of organic material that could be extracted from an acre of land, made it difficult to sustain economic growth. The only viable alternatives to organic sources of energy before the eighteenth century were those that tapped the forces of nature: windmills, which drained fields mainly in the Netherlands, and water wheels, which were driven by water pressure from river currents, waterfalls, or human-made channels that regulated the flow of water. The energy produced by wind and water was difficult to harness, however, and was available only in certain places. Moreover, these natural sources of energy could not produce heat.

The decisive change in harnessing energy for industrial purposes was the successful use of minerals, originally coal but in the twentieth century also oil and uranium, as the main sources of energy in the production and transportation of goods. These minerals were not inexhaustible, but the supplies could last for centuries,

PHILIPPE JACQUES DE LOUTHERBOURG, *COALBROOKDALE BY NIGHT* (1801) This painting depicts the intense heat produced by the coal bellows used to smelt iron in Coalbrookdale, an English town in the Severn Valley that was one of the key centers of industrial activity at the beginning of the nineteenth century.

and they were much more efficient than any form of energy produced from organic materials, including charcoal and peat. Coal produced the high combustion temperatures necessary to smelt iron, and unlike charcoal it was not limited by the size of a region's forests. Coal therefore became the key to the expansion of the British iron industry in the nineteenth century. It also became the sole source of heat for the new steam engine.

As the Industrial Revolution progressed, it relied increasingly on coal as its main fuel. Largely because of the demands of the mining, textile, and metal industries, coal mining became a major industry itself with an enormous labor force. By 1850 British mines employed about 5 percent of the entire national workforce. These miners were just as instrumental as textile workers in making Britain an industrial nation.

The Growth of Factories

During the Industrial Revolution, mechanized factories gradually replaced two types of workplaces in which most industrial production took place. These two predecessors of the factory were the rural industrial cottage and the large urban handicraft workshop.

Beginning in the late sixteenth century, capitalist entrepreneurs began employing families in the countryside to spin and weave cloth and make nails and cutlery. In this **domestic system** the entrepreneur provided the workers with raw materials and later paid them a fixed rate for each finished product. The workers performed their labor in their cottages, which were situated in agricultural areas. One feature of the domestic system was that all the members of the family, including children, participated in this industrial work, mainly when they were not engaged in planting or harvesting their crops.

In the early nineteenth century rural cottage industry gradually gave way to production in large factories. The great advantage of factory production over that of the rural cottage was mechanization, which became cost-efficient in a central industrial workplace. In factories, moreover, the entrepreneur could reduce the cost of labor and transportation, exercise tighter control over the quality of goods, and increase

domestic system An economic arrangement developed in the sixteenth century in which capitalist entrepreneurs employed families in rural areas to spin and weave cloth and make nails and cutlery.

productivity by concentrating workers in one location. Temporary labor shortages sometimes made the transition from rural industry to factory production imperative.

The second type of industrial workplace that the factory replaced was the large handicraft workshop. Usually located in towns and cities, rather than in the countryside, these workshops employed relatively small numbers of people with different skills who worked collectively on the manufacture of a variety of items, such as pottery and munitions. The owner of the workshop supplied the raw materials, paid the workers' wages, and gained a profit from selling the finished products.

The large handicraft workshop made possible a **division of labor**—the assignment of one stage of production to each worker or group of workers. The effect of the division of labor on productivity was evident even in the manufacture of simple items such as buttons and pins. In *The Wealth of Nations* (1776), the economist Adam Smith (1723–1790) used a pin factory in London to illustrate how the division of labor could increase per capita productivity from no more than 20 pins a day to the astonishing total of 4,800 pins in the same period of time.

Like the cottages engaged in rural industry, the large handicraft workshop eventually gave way to the mechanized factory. The main difference between the workshop and the factory was that the factory did not require a body of skilled workers. The factory worker's job was simply to tend to the machinery. The only skill factory workers needed was manual dexterity to operate the machinery. Only those workers who made industrial machinery remained craftsmen or skilled workers in the traditional sense of the word.

With the advent of mechanization, factory owners gained much tighter control over the entire production process. Indeed, they began to enforce an unprecedented discipline among their workers, who had to accommodate themselves to the boredom of repetitive work and a timetable set by the machines. Craftsmen who had been accustomed to working at their own pace now had to adjust to an entirely new and more demanding schedule. "While the engine runs," wrote one critical contemporary, "the people must work—men, women, and children yoked together with iron and steam. The animal machine—breakable in the best case, subject to a thousand sources of suffering—is chained fast to the iron machine which knows no suffering and no weariness."[2]

division of labor The assignment of one stage of production to a single worker or group of workers to increase efficiency and productive output.

  Read the **Document**

Adam Smith, *The Wealth of Nations*

MULE SPINNING A large mechanized spinning mill in northern England, about 1835. The workers did not require any great skill to run the machinery.

New Methods of Transportation

As industry became more extensive and increased its output, transport facilities, such as roads, bridges, canals, and eventually railroads, grew in number and quality. High industrial productivity required the efficient movement of raw materials to production sites and the transportation of finished products to markets. During the early phase of the Industrial Revolution in Britain, water transportation supplied most of these needs. A vast network of navigable rivers and human-made canals, eventually more than 4,000 miles in length, transported goods to and from areas that did not have access to the coast. For routes that had no access to water, the most common method of transportation was by horse-drawn carriages on newly built turnpikes or toll roads, many of them made of stone so that they were passable even in wet weather.

The most significant innovation in transport during the nineteenth century was the railroad. Introduced as the Industrial Revolution was gaining momentum, the railroad provided quick, cheap transportation of heavy materials such as coal and iron over long distances. Its introduction in Britain during the 1820s and throughout Europe and America during the following decades illustrated the transition from an economy based on organic sources of energy to one that relied on mineral sources of energy. Driven by coal-burning, steam-powered locomotives, the railroads freed transport from its dependence on animal power, especially the horses that were used

THE STOCKTON AND DARLINGTON RAILWAY The inaugural run of George Stephenson's locomotive on the Stockton and Darlington railway, the first in Britain, took place in 1825. The main function of the railway was to carry materials and goods to and from towns producing iron in the northern counties of England.

to pull coaches along turnpikes, barges along canals, and carts along parallel tracks in mines. Railroads rapidly became the main economic thoroughfares of the industrial economy. They linked towns and regions that earlier had not been easily accessible to each other. They also changed the travel habits of Europeans by making it possible to cover distances in one-fifth the time it took by coach.

The construction and operation of railroads became a major new industry, employing thousands of skilled and unskilled workers and providing opportunities for investment and profit. The industry created an unprecedented demand for iron and other materials used to build and equip locomotives, tracks, freight cars, passenger cars, and signals, thus giving a tremendous boost to the iron industry and the metal-working and engineering trades. By the 1840s the railroads had become the main stimulus to economic growth throughout western Europe and the United States. Transport in industrialized economies continued to experience frequent innovation. During the twentieth century, for example, new methods of transportation, including automobiles, airplanes, and high-speed rails, sustained economic growth in all industrialized countries; like the railroads, they have become major industries themselves.

View the Map

Great Britain: Railroads, ca. 1850

Conditions Favoring Industrial Growth

21.2   What social and economic changes made industrial development possible?

The Industrial Revolution occurred first in Britain because a set of social and economic developments encouraged the mechanization of industry. These conditions were the steady increase in the British population, improved agricultural productivity, the accumulation of large amounts of capital, and sufficient demand for manufactured goods.

Population Growth

Industrialization required a sufficiently large pool of labor to staff the factories and workshops of the new industries. One of the main reasons why the Industrial Revolution occurred first in Britain was that its population during the eighteenth century increased more rapidly than that of any country in continental Europe. Between 1680 and 1820 the population of England more than doubled, while that of France grew at less than one-third that rate, and the population of the Dutch Republic hardly grew at all.

One of the reasons this growth in the British population took place was that famines, which had occurred periodically throughout the early modern period, became less frequent during the eighteenth century. The last great famine in Britain took place in 1740, only a generation before industrialization began. Mortality from epidemic diseases, especially typhus, influenza, and smallpox, also decreased. Plague, which had decimated the European population periodically since the fourteenth century, struck England for the last time in the Great Plague of London in 1665. It made its last European appearance at Marseilles in 1720 but did not spread beyond the southern parts of France.

A second and even more important factor in British population growth was an increase in fertility. More people were marrying, and at a younger age, which increased the birthrate. The spread of rural industry encouraged this early-marriage pattern. Wage-earning textile workers tended to marry a little earlier than agricultural workers, probably because wage earners did not have to postpone marriage to inherit land or to become self-employed, as was the case with farm workers.

Increase in European Population, 1680–1820

	Population Totals (millions)	
	1680	*1820*
France	21.9	30.5
Italy	12.0	18.4
Germany	12.0	18.1
Spain	8.5	14.0
England	4.9	11.5
Netherlands	1.9	2.0
Western Europe	71.9	116.5
Percentage Growth Rates, 1680–1820		
England	133%	
Spain	64	
Italy	53	
Germany	51	
France	39	
Netherlands	8	
Western Europe	73	

SOURCE: E. A. Wrigley, "The Growth of Population in Eighteenth-Century England: A Conundrum Resolved," *Past and Present* 98 (1983): 122, by permission of Oxford University Press.

This increase in population facilitated industrialization by swelling domestic demand for manufactured goods and by increasing the number of people available to work in the factories and mines. The increase in the British population, however, was not so large that it retarded industrialization. If population growth was too rapid, it could lead to declining incomes, put pressure on agriculture to feed more people than possible, and prevent the accumulation of wealth. Most important, overpopulation could discourage factory owners from introducing costly machinery. If labor was plentiful and cheap, it could cost less for workers to produce the same volume of goods by hand. Industrialization therefore required a significant but not too rapid increase in population—the exact scenario that occurred in Britain during the eighteenth century.

Agricultural Productivity

Like population growth, expanding agricultural output fostered the Industrial Revolution in Britain. Between 1700 and 1800 British agriculture experienced a revolution, resulting in a substantial increase in productivity. A major reason for this increase was the consolidation of all the land farmed by one tenant into compact fields. During the Middle Ages and most of the early modern period, each tenant on a manorial estate leased and farmed strips of land scattered throughout the estate. Decisions regarding the planting and harvesting of crops in these "open fields" were made collectively in the manorial court. Beginning in the sixteenth century, some of the wealthier tenants on these estates agreed to exchange their strips of land with their neighbors to consolidate their holdings into large compact fields, with hedges, bushes, or walls defining their boundaries. This process of **enclosure** allowed individual farmers to exercise complete control over the use of their land. In the eighteenth and nineteenth centuries the number of enclosures increased dramatically when the British Parliament, most of whose members were landowners, passed legislation authorizing them.

With control of their lands, farmers could make them more productive. The most profitable change was to introduce new crop rotations, often involving the alternation of grains such as rye or barley with root crops such as turnips or grasses

enclosure The consolidation of scattered agricultural holdings into large, compact fields which were then closed off by hedges, bushes, or walls, giving farmers complete control over the uses of their land.

such as clover. These new crops and grasses restored nutrients to the soil and therefore made it unnecessary to let fields lie fallow once every three years. Farmers also introduced a variety of new fertilizers and soil additives that made harvests more bountiful. Farmers who raised sheep took advantage of discoveries regarding scientific breeding that improved the quality of their flocks.

More productive farming meant that fewer agricultural workers were required to feed the population. This made it possible for more people to leave the farms to work in the factories and mines. The expanded labor pool of industrial workers, moreover, was large enough that factory owners did not have to pay workers high wages; otherwise, the prospect of industrializing would have lost much of its appeal. The hiring of children and women to work in the factories and mines also kept the labor pool large and the costs of labor low.

Capital Formation and Accumulation

A third development that encouraged British industrialization was the accumulation of capital. The term **capital** refers to all the assets used in production. These include both the factories and machines that produce other goods (fixed capital) and the raw materials and finished products that go to market (circulating capital). Other forms of capital are the railroads and barges that transport raw materials to the places of production and finished products to market. Mechanized industry involves the extensive and intensive use of capital to do the work formerly assigned to human beings. An industrial economy therefore requires large amounts of capital, especially fixed capital.

Capital more generally refers to the money that is necessary to purchase these physical assets. This capital can come from individuals, such as wealthy landlords, merchants, or industrialists who invest the profits they have accumulated in industrial machinery or equipment. In many cases the profits derived from industrial production are reinvested in the firm itself. Alternatively, capital can come from financial institutions in the form of loans. Very often a number of individuals make their wealth available to an industrial firm by buying shares of stock in that company's operations. This, of course, is the main way in which most capital is accumulated today. In countries that have only recently begun to industrialize in Latin America and Southeast Asia, capital often comes from public sources, such as governments, or from international institutions, such as the International Monetary Fund.

In Britain the capital needed to achieve industrialization came almost entirely from private sources. Some of it was raised by selling shares of stock to people from the middle and upper levels of society, but an even larger amount came from merchants who engaged in domestic and international trade, landowners who profited from the production of agricultural goods (including those who owned plantations in America), and the industrial entrepreneurs who owned mines, ironworks, and factories. In Britain, where all three groups were more successful than in other parts of Europe, the volume of capital made available from these sources was substantial. These people could invest directly in industrial machinery and mines or, more commonly, make their wealth available to others indirectly in the form of loans from banks where they kept their financial assets.

Banks supplied a considerable amount of the funds necessary for industrialization. In Britain the possibilities for such capital were maximized in the late eighteenth century when financial institutions offered loans at low interest rates and when the development of a national banking system made these funds readily available throughout the country, especially in the new industrial cities, such as Leeds, Sheffield, and Manchester. The number of English banks rose from a mere dozen in 1750 to more than 300 in 1800. Many bankers had close ties with industrialists, thereby facilitating the flow of capital from the financial to the industrial sector of the economy.

capital All the physical assets used in production, including fixed capital, such as machinery, and circulating capital, such as raw materials; more generally the cost of these physical assets.

supply The amounts of capital, labor, and food that are needed to produce goods for the market as well as the quantities of those goods themselves.

demand The desire of consumers to acquire goods and the need of producers to acquire raw materials and machinery.

Demand from Consumers and Producers

The conditions for industrialization discussed so far all deal with **supply**, that is, the amounts of capital, labor, food, and skill necessary to support the industrial process. The other side of the economic equation is **demand**, which is the desire of consumers to purchase industrial goods and of producers to acquire raw materials and machinery. Much of the extraordinary productivity of the Industrial Revolution arose from the demand for industrial products. Many of the technological innovations that occurred at the beginning of the revolution also originated as responses to the demand for more goods. For example, the demand for more cotton goods spurred the introduction of the spinning jenny, the water frame, and the mule. Likewise, the demand for coal for industrial and domestic use led to the development of an efficient steam engine to drain mines so that those supplies of coal could be extracted.

During the early years of British industrialization the domestic market was the main source of demand for industrial products. Demand was especially strong among the bourgeoisie. A "consumer revolution" had taken place during the eighteenth century, as bourgeois individuals and families strove to acquire goods of all sorts, especially clothing and household products, such as pottery, cutlery, furniture, and curtains. The desire of the bourgeoisie to imitate the spending habits of the aristocracy helped to fuel this consumer revolution, while commercial manipulation, including newspaper advertising, warehouse displays, product demonstrations, and the distribution of samples, helped to facilitate it. An entirely new consumer culture arose, one in which women played a leading role. Advertisements promoting the latest female fashions, housewares, and children's toys became more common than those directed at adult male consumers. One ad in a local British paper in 1777, capitalizing on reports that mice were getting into ladies' hair at night, promoted "night caps made of silver wire so strong that no mouse or even a rat can gnaw through them." Advertisements therefore created a demand for new products and increased the demand for those already on the market.

If this consumer revolution had been restricted to the middle ranks of society, it would have had only a limited effect on the Industrial Revolution. The bourgeoisie constituted at most only 20 percent of the entire population of eighteenth-century Britain, and most of the goods they craved, with the exception of the pottery produced in Josiah Wedgwood's factories (which is still made today), were luxury items rather than the types of products that could be easily mass-produced. A strong demand for manufactured products could develop only if workers were to buy consumer goods such as knitted stockings and caps, cotton shirts, earthenware, coffeepots, nails, candlesticks, watches, lace, and ribbon. The demand for these products came from small cottagers and laborers as well as the middle class. The demand for stockings for both men and women was particularly strong. In 1831 the author of a study of the impact of machinery on British society declared, "Two centuries ago, not one person in a thousand wore stockings; one century ago, not one person in five hundred wore them; now not one person in a thousand is without them."[3]

Demand for manufactured products from the lower classes was obviously limited by the amount of money that wage earners had available for nonessential goods, and real wages did not increase very much, if at all, during the eighteenth century. Nevertheless, the income of families in which the wife and children as well as the father worked for wages did increase significantly both during the heyday of rural industry and during the early years of industrialization. In many cases family members worked longer and harder just so they could afford to buy new products coming on the market. As the population increased, so too did this lower-class demand, which helped sustain an economy built around industrial production.

The Spread of Industrialization

21.3 How did industrialization spread from Great Britain to the European continent and America?

The Industrial Revolution did not occur in all European countries at the same time. As we have seen, it began in Britain in the 1760s and for more than four decades was confined exclusively to that country (see **Map 21.1**). It eventually spread to other European and North American countries, where many industrial innovations were modeled on those in Britain. Belgium, France, Germany, Switzerland, Austria, Sweden, and the United States all experienced their own Industrial Revolutions by the middle of the nineteenth century. Only in the late nineteenth century did countries outside the traditional boundaries of the West, mainly Russia and Japan, begin to industrialize. By the middle of the twentieth century, industrialization had become a truly global process, transforming the economies of a number of Asian and Latin American countries.

Great Britain and the Continent

Industrialization occurred on the European continent much later than it did in Great Britain. Only after 1815 did Belgium and France begin to industrialize on a large scale, and it was not until 1840 that Germany, Switzerland, and Austria showed significant signs of industrial growth. Other European countries, such as Italy, Spain, and Russia, did not begin serious efforts in this direction until the late nineteenth century. It took continental European states even longer to rival the economic strength of Britain. Germany, which emerged as Britain's main competitor in the late nineteenth century, did not match British industrial output until the twentieth century.

Four factors explain the slower development of industrialization on the European continent. The first relates to the political situations in those countries. Well into the nineteenth century, most continental European states had numerous internal political barriers that impeded the transportation of raw materials and goods from one part of the country to another. In Germany, for example, which was not politically united until 1871, scores of small sovereign territorial units charged tariffs whenever goods crossed their boundaries. Only in 1834 did a customs union, the *Zollverein*, eliminate some of these barriers. In Poland the removal of customs barriers did not take place until 1851. The relatively poor state of continental roads and the inaccessibility of many seaports from production sites aggravated this political situation.

In contrast, Britain achieved economic unity early in the eighteenth century. After 1707, when Scotland was united to England and freedom of internal trade was established between the two countries, the United Kingdom of Great Britain constituted the largest free-trade zone in Europe. Raw materials and finished products could therefore move from one place to another in Britain, up to a distance of more than 800 miles, without payment of any internal customs or duties. The system of inland waterways was complete by 1780, and seaports were accessible from all parts of the country.

MAP **21.1** THE CONCENTRATIONS OF INDUSTRY IN GREAT BRITAIN, 1750–1820 The most heavily industrialized regions were in northern England, where the population of cities such as Manchester, Liverpool, and Sheffield grew rapidly. Why did northern England become more industrialized than the southern part of the country?

663

A second factor that weakened the industrial potential of many continental European countries was the imposition of protective tariffs on goods imported from other countries. The purpose of this mercantilist policy was to develop national self-sufficiency and maintain a favorable balance of trade, but it also had the negative effect of limiting economic growth. For example, in the Dutch Republic (the Kingdom of the Netherlands after 1815) a long tradition of protecting established industries prevented that country from importing the raw materials and machines needed to develop new industries. Because protectionism invited retaliation from trading partners, it also tended to shrink the size of potential overseas markets. Britain adopted a policy of free trade during the 1840s, and it pressured other European countries to adopt the same policy.

A third obstacle to European industrialization was aristocratic hostility, or at least indifference, to industrial development. British aristocrats were themselves often involved in capitalist enterprise and did not have the same suspicion of industry and trade that their counterparts in France and Spain often harbored. Many members of the British aristocracy, such as the entrepreneur "Turnip Townshend" (see Chapter 19), were agricultural capitalists who improved the productivity of their estates. Others were involved in mining. The Duke of Devonshire encouraged the exploitation of the copper mines on his estate, while the Duke of Bridgewater employed the engineer James Brindley to build a canal from the duke's coal mines in Worsley to the industrial city of Manchester in 1759. One reason for the British aristocracy's support for economic growth was that many of its members, especially the gentry, rose into its ranks from other social and economic groups. These individuals tended to be sympathetic to the values of a commercial and an industrial society. The same attitude toward commerce and industry did not exist among the nobility in France before the revolution, much less among German *Junkers*. These groups had little connection with industrial or commercial society, whose values they held in very low regard. Consequently, they rarely invested in industry.

A final reason for the slow industrialization of continental European countries was that they lacked the abundant raw materials that formed the basis of an industrial economy. Britain's large deposits of coal and iron ore, both of which were indispensable to industrialization, gave it an advantage over other European countries. France and Germany had some coal deposits, but they were more difficult to mine and they were not located near ocean ports. Continental countries also lacked access to other raw materials, especially cotton, which Britain could import from its overseas colonies. With a large empire on four continents and the world's largest merchant marine, Britain could import these raw materials less expensively and in larger quantities than its continental competitors.

View the Map

Interactive Map: European
Industrialization

Features of Continental Industrialization

During the first half of the nineteenth century, especially after 1830, Belgium, France, Switzerland, Germany, and Austria introduced machinery into the industrial process, used steam power in production, concentrated labor in large factories, and built railroads. This continental European version of the Industrial Revolution was often—but incorrectly—described as an imitative process, one in which entrepreneurs or government officials simply tried to duplicate Britain's economic success by following the British example. Although continental European nations did indeed rely to some extent on British industrial technology, each European nation, responding to its own unique combination of political, economic, and social conditions, followed its own course of industrialization. Three features, however, characterized these diverse industrial paths.

First, once countries such as Belgium and Germany began to industrialize, their governments played a much more active role in encouraging and assisting in the process. In contrast to Britain, whose government allowed private industry to function with few economic controls, continental governments became active partners in the industrial process. They supplied capital for many economic ventures, especially building railroads and roads. In Prussia the state owned a number of manufacturing and mining enterprises. Many continental governments also imposed protective tariffs to prevent an influx of cheap British goods from underselling the products of their own fledgling industries. In a few cases, continental European governments even provided financial support for investors in an effort to encourage capital formation (see **Map 21.2**).

A second major feature of continental European industrialization was that banks, particularly in Germany and Belgium, played an active role in industrial development. Drawing on the resources of both small and large investors, these corporate banks became in effect industrial banks, building railroads and factories themselves in addition to making capital available for a variety of industrial ventures.

A third distinct feature of continental European industrialization was that the railroads actually contributed to the beginning of industrial development. In Britain the railroads were introduced some 60 years after industrialization had begun and thus helped sustain an ongoing process of economic development. By contrast, the railroads on the European continent provided the basic infrastructure of its new economy and became a major stimulus to the development of other industries. Railroads also gave continental European governments the ability to transport military troops quickly in time of war, which helps to explain why governments supported railroad construction with such enthusiasm. In Belgium, which was the first continental European nation to industrialize, the new government built a national railroad system during the 1830s and 1840s not only to stimulate industry, but also to unify the newly independent nation.

MAP 21.2 CUSTOMS UNIONS IN CONTINENTAL EUROPE
One of the reasons for the relatively slow progress of industrialization on the European continent was the existence of internal tariff barriers. This map shows the dates when customs unions, such as the *Zollverein* of 1834 in the German Confederation, were established or the customs barriers were eliminated. By contrast, all internal customs duties within Great Britain had been eliminated more than a century earlier when England and Scotland were united in 1707. Why did continental European states find it more difficult than Britain to eliminate internal tariff barriers?

KRUPP STEELWORKS IN ESSEN, GERMANY, IN 1875 Smoke rises from the stacks of a steel mill in the Ruhr region, the center of German industry.

665

View the Image

Excelsior Iron Works

Industrialization in the United States

Industrialization in the United States began during the 1820s, not long after Belgium and France had begun to have their own industrial revolutions. It occurred first in the textile industry in New England, where factories using water power produced goods for largely rural markets. New England also began producing two domestic hardware products—clocks and guns—for the same market. In the 1840s New York began to produce products made from iron. Between 1850 and 1870 a second region between Pittsburgh and Cleveland became industrialized. This area specialized in heavy industry, especially steelmaking and the manufacture of large machinery, and it relied on coal for fuel. Railroads linked this industrialized region with that of the Northeast.

American industrialization included features of both the British and continental European patterns. As in Britain and France, the development of cottage industry in the United States preceded industrialization. As in most continental European countries, American railroads played a crucial role in the early years of industrialization. Most of the industrial machinery in the United States during the nineteenth century was modeled on imports from Britain. The most significant American technological innovation before 1900 was the sewing machine, which Elias Howe patented in 1846 and Isaac Singer improved in the 1850s. This new machine was then introduced in Europe, where it was used in the production of ready-to-wear garments.

The United States became known for its use of machinery in all industries and its efficient organization of factory labor. Toward the beginning of the twentieth century, American manufacturers streamlined the production process by introducing the assembly line, a division of labor in which the product passed from one operation to the next until it was fully assembled. The assembly line required the production of interchangeable parts, another American innovation, first used in the manufacture of rifles for the U.S. government.

Like Britain, the United States possessed vast natural resources, including coal. It also resembled Britain in the absence of governmental involvement in the process of industrialization. The main difference between the industrializations of the two countries was that during the nineteenth century labor in America was in relatively short supply. This placed workers in a more advantageous situation in dealing with their employers and prevented some of the horrors of early British industrialization from recurring on the other side of the Atlantic. Only with the influx of European immigrants in the late nineteenth century did the condition of American workers deteriorate and begin to resemble the early-nineteenth-century British pattern.

Industrial Regionalism

Although we have discussed the industrialization of entire states, the process usually took place within smaller geographical regions. There had always been regional specialization in agriculture, with some areas raising crops and others livestock. During the Industrial Revolution, however, entire economies acquired a distinctly regional character. Regional economies began to take shape during the days of the domestic system, when merchants employed families in certain geographical areas, such as Lancashire in England, to produce textiles. Related industries, such as those for finishing or dyeing cloth, also sprang up close to areas where spinning and weaving took place.

As industrialization spread outside Britain, this regional pattern became even more pronounced. In France the centers of the textile industry were situated near the northeastern border near Belgium and in the area surrounding Lyons in the east-central part of the country. Both of these areas had attracted rural household industry before the introduction of textile machinery. In Germany the iron industry was centered in the Ruhr region, where most of the country's coal was mined. In the city of Essen on the Ruhr River, the industrialist Alfred Krupp (1812–1887) established an enormous steelmaking complex that produced industrial machinery, railroad equipment, and guns for the Prussian army. Within the Habsburg Empire, most industry was located in parts of Bohemia (now the Czech Republic).

The development of regional economies did not mean that markets were regional. The goods produced in one region almost always served the needs of people outside that particular area. Markets for most industrial goods were national and international, and even people in small agricultural villages created a demand for manufactured goods. The French iron industry, for example, was centered in the eastern part of the country, but it catered to the needs of the wealthier segments of its own and other European populations, as did the iron industry in the Ruhr region in Germany and the textile industry in the north of England.

Regional industrial development helps to explain the striking contrast that persisted well into the twentieth century between the parts of countries that had become heavily industrialized and those that retained at least many of the appearances of a pre-industrial life. Some areas in all industrialized countries remained exclusively agricultural, while others continued a tradition of rural industry. This pattern was particularly evident in France, where mechanized industry was concentrated in a limited number of centers in the northeastern half of the country. In 1870 more than two-thirds of the French population still lived in rural areas. As economic growth and industrial development continued, however, agricultural regions eventually began to lose their traditional character. Even if industry itself did not arrive, the larger industrial economy made its mark. Agriculture itself became mechanized, while railroads and other forms of mechanized transport integrated these areas in a national economy.

The Effects of Industrialization

21.4 What were the economic, social, and cultural effects of the Industrial Revolution?

The Industrial Revolution had a profound impact on virtually every aspect of human life. The changes that it brought about were initially most evident in Britain, but over time they have occurred in every country that has industrialized, including the United States. Industrialization encouraged the growth of the population and the economy, affected the conditions in which people lived, changed family life, created new divisions within society, and transformed the traditional rural landscape.

Population and Economic Growth

The most significant of these changes was the sustained expansion of both the population and the economy. As we have seen, a significant population increase in the eighteenth century helped to make the Industrial Revolution in Britain possible. That growth had created a plentiful supply of relatively cheap labor, which in turn increased industrial output. As industry grew, population kept pace, and each provided a stimulus to the growth of the other.

Most contemporary observers in the late eighteenth century did not believe that this expansion of both the population and the economy could be sustained. The most pessimistic of these commentators was Thomas Malthus (1766–1834), an English clergyman who wrote *An Essay on the Principle of Population* in 1798. Malthus argued that population had a natural tendency to grow faster than the food supply. Thus, unless couples exercised restraint by marrying late and producing fewer children, the population would eventually outstrip the resources necessary to sustain it, resulting in poor nutrition, famine, and disease. These "positive checks" on population growth, sometimes aggravated by war, would drive population back to sustainable levels. These checks on population

21.1

21.2

21.3

21.4

21.5

Malthusian population trap The theory of Thomas Malthus (1766–1834) that the natural tendency of population to grow faster than the food supply would eventually drive the size of populations back to sustainable levels and end periods of economic expansion that usually accompany the growth of population.

growth also ended periods of economic expansion, which generally accompany increases in population. If this demographic and economic pattern had recurred, the significant expansion of the population and the economy that took place in eighteenth-century Britain would have reached its limits, just around the time that Malthus was writing.

This predicted cyclical contraction of both the population and the economy did not take place. Europe for the first time in its history managed to escape the **Malthusian population trap**. Instead of being sharply reduced after 1800, the population continued to expand at an ever-faster rate, doubling in Britain between 1800 and 1850. At the same time the economy, instead of contracting or collapsing, continued to grow and diversify.

Developments in industry explain why Europe was able to escape the Malthusian population trap. The accumulation of capital over a long period of time was so great that industry could employ large numbers of workers, even during the 1790s and 1800s, when Europe was at war. Because they had income from wages, workers were willing to marry earlier and have larger families. With lower food prices because of higher agricultural productivity, they could also afford to maintain a healthier diet and purchase more manufactured goods. Thus, the Industrial Revolution itself, coupled with the changes in agriculture that accompanied it, proved Malthus wrong.

While the increase of population in all industrialized societies is incontestable, the record of continued economic growth is not so clear. Economic growth in industrialized countries has not always been rapid or continuous. During the first six decades of industrialization in Britain, for example, economic growth was actually fairly slow, mainly because so much capital went into subsidizing the long war against France (1792–1802; 1804–1815). To claim that the Industrial Revolution resulted in sustained economic growth, we have to take a broad view, looking at an overall pattern of economic development and ignoring cyclical recessions and depressions. More important, industrialized nations have not yet experienced the type of economic contraction or collapse that Malthus predicted. For that reason, we can say that the Industrial Revolution has resulted in sustained economic growth in the West.

Standards of Living

Ever since the early years of the Industrial Revolution, a debate has raged over the effect of industrialization on the standard of living and the quality of life of the laboring population. The two main schools of thought on this issue are often referred to as the *optimists* and the *pessimists*. The optimists emphasize the positive effects of both the process of mechanization and the system of industrial capitalism that arose during the revolution. They focus on the success that industrialized nations have achieved in escaping the Malthusian population trap and in experiencing sustained economic growth. The Industrial Revolution, so they argue, has resulted in an unprecedented rise in individual income, which has made it possible for the mass of a country's population to avoid poverty for the first time in human history.

The main yardstick that the optimists use to measure the improvement in living standards is *per capita real income*, that is, income measured in terms of its actual purchasing power. Real income in Britain rose about 50 percent between 1770 and 1850 and more than doubled during the entire nineteenth century. This increase in income allowed workers to improve their diets as well as to purchase more clothing and other basic commodities. These increases, however, were only averages, concealing disparities among workers with different levels of skill. Only in the late nineteenth and twentieth centuries did industrialization raise the real income of all workers to a level that made the benefits of industrialization apparent.

The long-term increase in real income has never been substantial enough to persuade the pessimists that industrialization was on balance a positive good, at least for the working class. Pessimists have always stressed the negative effects of industrial development on the people on the lower levels of society. In their way of thinking, industrialization

Read the Document

Andrew Ure, from *The Philosophy of Manufactures*

was an unmitigated disaster. The cause of this disaster in their eyes was not mechanization itself, but the system of **industrial capitalism**. This form of capitalism, which is characterized by the private ownership of factories and the employment of wage labor, involved a systematic effort to reduce costs and maximize profits. In the pursuit of this goal, employers tried to keep wages as low as possible and increase production by introducing labor-saving technology, thus preventing workers from improving their lot.

Pessimists usually claim a moral basis for their position. In this respect they follow in a tradition begun by the poet William Blake (1757–1827), who referred to the new factories as "satanic mills," and the socialist Friedrich Engels (1820–1895), who in *The Condition of the Working Class in England in 1844* (1845) accused the factory owners in England of mass murder and robbery.

Most of the evidence that social critics use to support the pessimist position comes from the early period of industrialization in Britain, when workers' real wages either stagnated or declined and when conditions in factories and towns were most appalling. Working-class housing was makeshift and crowded, and there were few sanitary facilities. A new word, *slum,* was coined to refer to these poverty-stricken working-class neighborhoods. Poor drainage and raw sewage gave rise to a host of new hygienic problems, especially outbreaks of typhus and cholera. Between 1831 and 1866 four epidemics of cholera killed at least 140,000 people in Britain, most of whom lived in poorer districts.

The impact of industrialization and urbanization on the environment was no less harrowing. The burning of coal and the use of industrial chemicals polluted the urban atmosphere. The famous London fogs, which were actually smogs caused by industrial pollutants, presented a serious public health problem throughout the nineteenth century and did not begin to disappear until the introduction of strict regulations on the burning of coal in the 1950s.

While life in the city was bleak and unhealthy, working conditions in the factory were monotonous and demeaning. Forced to submit to a regimen governed by the operation of the machine, workers lost their independence as well as any control whatsoever over the products of their labor. They were required to work long hours, often 14 hours a day, six days a week, with few breaks. Factory masters locked the doors during working hours and assessed fines for infractions such as opening a window when the temperature was unbearable, whistling while working, and having dirty hands while spinning yarn. Work in the mines was a little less monotonous, but it was physically more demanding and far more dangerous. (See *Different Voices* in this chapter.)

Women, Children, and Industry

During the early Industrial Revolution in Britain, the industrial workforce, especially in the textile and mining industries, included large numbers of children and women. In the woolen industry in the western part of England, for example, female and child labor together accounted for 75 percent of the workforce. Children under age 13 made up 13 percent of the cotton factory workforce, and those under age 18 made up 51 percent. This pattern of employment reflected the demands of industrialists, who valued the hand skills and dexterity that children possessed as well as the greater amenability of both children and women to the discipline of factory labor. Some of the machines that were introduced into the textile industry in the late eighteenth century were specifically designed for women and children.

Female and child labor was both plentiful and cheap. Children received only one-sixth to one-third the wages of a grown man, while women generally took home only one-third to one-half of that adult male income. Yet women and children sought these low-paying jobs. In a family dependent on wages, everyone needed to work, even when a large labor pool kept wages depressed.

The participation of women and children in the workforce was *not* new. In an agricultural economy all members of the family contributed to the work, with parents

industrial capitalism A form of capitalism characterized by the ownership of factories by private individuals and the employment of wage labor.

21.1

21.2

21.3

21.4

21.5

and children, young and old, all being assigned specific roles. Rural industry also involved the labor of all members of the family. When people began working in the factories, however, they were physically separated from the home, making it impossible for workers to combine domestic and occupational labor.

As the workplace became distinct from the household, family life underwent a fundamental change, although it did not occur immediately. During the early years of the Industrial Revolution, members of many families found employment together in the factories and mines. Factory owners also tried to perpetuate many aspects of family life in the new industrial setting, defining the entire factory community as an extended family, in which the factory owner played the paternalistic role. Gradually, however, mothers found it impossible to care for their youngest children on the job, and most of them dropped out of the full-time workforce. The restriction of child labor by the British Factory Act of 1833 reinforced this trend and led to the establishment of a fairly common situation in which the male wage earner worked outside the home while his wife stayed home with the children. As one young girl who worked in the mines testified before a parliamentary commission investigation of child labor in 1842, "Mother takes care of the children." (See *Justice in History* in this chapter.)

The Industrial Revolution did nothing to improve the status of women. Neither the pay these women received nor the jobs they performed gave them financial autonomy or social prestige. Becoming an independent wage earner meant little when women's wages were on average one-third to one-half those of men. The jobs assigned to women within industry, such as operating textile machinery, generally required the least skill. When men and women worked in the same factory, the women were invariably subordinated to the authority of male workers or foremen, thereby perpetuating the patriarchal patterns that prevailed in preindustrial society. Even their exclusion from certain occupations, such as mining by an act of Parliament in 1842, only made the sexual division of labor more rigid than in preindustrial society.

Class and Class Consciousness

As Europe became more industrialized and urbanized, and as the system of industrial capitalism became more entrenched, writers began to use a new terminology to describe the structure of society. Instead of claiming that society consisted of a finely graded hierarchy of ranks to which individuals belonged by virtue of their occupations or their legal status, they divided society into three classes on the basis of the type of property people owned and the manner in which they acquired it. At the top of this new social hierarchy was the aristocracy, consisting of those who owned land and received their income in the form of rent. The middle class or bourgeoisie, which included the new factory owners, possessed capital and derived their income from profits, whereas the working class owned nothing but their own labor and received their income from wages.

Historians and social scientists disagree over the extent to which men and women in the nineteenth century were actually conscious of their membership in these classes. Some historians claim that the growth of wage labor, the exploitation of the working class, and conflicts between capital and labor encouraged workers to think of themselves not so much as individuals who occupied a position in a social hierarchy, but as members of a large class of workers who shared the same relationship to the means of production. These historians have pointed to the growth of trade unions, political campaigns for universal male suffrage, and other forms of working-class organization and communication as evidence of this awakening of **class consciousness**.

Other historians argue that people were less conscious of their class. True, at certain times in the early nineteenth century some workers thought of themselves as members of a class whose interests conflicted with those of factory owners and financiers. It was much more common, however, for them to think of themselves primarily as practitioners of a particular craft, as members of a local community, or as part

class consciousness The awareness of people from different occupations that they belonged to a class.

Different Voices

The Social and Cultural Effects of Industrialization

C ontemporaries and historians have debated whether the condition of the working class improved or deteriorated as a result of the Industrial Revolution. These two descriptions of the working class in England in the first half of the nineteenth century present evidence to support the two sides of the debate. In his history of the cotton industry, which he greatly admired, the English journalist Richard Guest focused on the improved educational opportunities offered to workers, mainly in the Sunday schools. The German social philosopher Friedrich Engels, who collaborated with Karl Marx (1818–1883) in writing The Communist Manifesto (1848), emphasized the exploitation and brutalization of the lower classes as they were turned into a wage-earning proletariat. In his first book, The Condition of the Working Class in England in 1844, which was inspired by his service as a manager in a factory in Manchester, Engels focused on the deplorable living conditions of industrial workers.

A Journalist Celebrates the Improvement in the Life of Industrial Workers

The progress of the cotton manufacture introduced great change in the manners and habits of the people. The operative workmen being thrown together in great numbers, had their faculties sharpened and improved by constant communication. Conversation wandered over a variety of topics not before essayed; the questions of peace and war, which interested them importantly, inasmuch as they might produce a rise or fall of wages, became highly interesting, and this brought them into the vast field of politics and discussions on the character of their government and the men who composed it. They took a greater interest in the defeats and victories of their country's arms, and from being only a few degrees above their cattle in the scale of intellect, they became political citizens.

To these changes the establishment of Sunday Schools has very much contributed; they have been a great means of forwarding this wonderful alteration. Before their institution the lower orders were extremely illiterate; very few of them could read, and still fewer of them could write, and when one of them learned to read, write and cast accounts, those requirements elevated him to a superior rank. His clerkly skill exempted him from manual labour, and as shopman, book-keeper or town's officer—perchance in the higher dignity of parish clerk or schoolmaster—he rose a step above his original station in life....

The facility with which the weavers changed their masters, the constant effort to find out and obtain the largest remuneration for their labor, the excitement to ingenuity which the higher wages for fine manufacturers and skilful workmanship produced, and a conviction that they depended mainly on their own exertions produced in them that invaluable feeling, a spirit of freedom and independence, and that guarantee for good conduct and improvement of manners, a consciousness of the value of character and of their own weight and importance.

SOURCE: Richard Guest, A Compendious History of the Cotton Manufacture (1823).

Friedrich Engels Deplores the Living Conditions of Industrial Workers

Since capital, the direct or indirect control of the means of subsistence and production, is the weapon with which this social warfare is carried on, it is clear that all the disadvantages of such a state must fall upon the poor man. For him no one has the slightest concern. Cast into the whirlpool, he must struggle through as well as he can. If he is so happy as to find work, i.e., if the bourgeoisie does him the favour to enrich itself by means of him, wages await him which scarcely suffice to keep body and soul together; if he can get no work he may steal, if he is not afraid of the police, or starve, in which case the police will take care that he does so in a quiet and inoffensive manner....

Every great city has one or more slums, where the working class is crowded together . . . these slums are pretty equally arranged in all the great towns of England, the worst houses in the worst quarters of the towns; usually one or two-storied cottage in long rows, perhaps with cellars used as dwellings, almost always irregularly built.... The streets are generally unpaved, rough, dirty, filled with vegetable and animal refuse, without sewer or gutters, but supplied with foul, stagnant pools instead. Moreover, ventilation is impeded by the bad, confused method of building of the whole quarter, and since many human beings here live crowded into a small space, the atmosphere that prevails in these working men's quarters may readily be imagined....

Liverpool, with all its commerce, wealth and grandeur yet treats its workers with the same barbarity. A full fifth of the population, more than 45,000 human beings, live in narrow, dark, damp, badly-ventilated cellar dwellings, of which there are 7,862 in the city. Besides these cellar dwellings there are 2,270 courts, small spaces built up on all four sides and having but one entrance, a narrow, covered passageway, the whole ordinarily very dirty and inhabited exclusively by proletarians.... In Nottingham there are in all 11,000 houses, of which between 7,000 and 8,000 are built back to back with a rear party-wall so that no through ventilation is possible, while a single privy usually serves for several houses.

SOURCE: Friedrich Engels, The Condition of the Working Class in England (1845).

For Discussion

1. Is it possible that these two accounts of working-class life in the industrial age could both be accurate? Which account do you find more persuasive and why?

2. How do the political agendas of the two authors influence their assessments of the effects of industrialization?

3. In what ways do these descriptions of industrial working class reflect the optimistic and pessimistic interpretations of industrialization discussed in this chapter?

CAPITAL AND LABOR This cartoon, drawn by the illustrator Gustave Doré, depicts wealthy industrialists gambling with workers tied together as chips.

of a distinct ethnic minority, such as the Irish in Britain. When they demanded the right to vote, workers based their claim on their historic constitutional rights, not the interests of all wage earners. When they demonstrated in favor of the 10-hour working day, they did so to improve the conditions in which they worked, not to advance the struggle of all workers against the middle class. The work experiences of laborers were too varied to sustain a widespread awareness that they belonged to one homogeneous group. Consequently, appeals for working-class solidarity to a large extent fell on deaf ears.

It is true that on certain occasions workers took violent action against their employers. In 1812 groups of hand loom weavers in the highly industrialized Midland region of England engaged in a determined campaign to destroy the new power looms that they blamed for rising unemployment and low wages. Often disguised and operating at night, these "Luddites," who took their name from their mythical leader Ned Ludd, smashed the new textile machinery that factory owners had introduced. (Even today people who object to the introduction of new technology are referred to as Luddites.) These men, however, did not identify with other British workers, especially those tending textile machinery in the factories.

Nevertheless, occasional encounters between workers and bourgeoisie did heighten an awareness of class divisions in British society. In August 1819, 60,000 workers gathered in St. Peter's Field in Manchester to demand the right to vote and better working conditions. Frightened by the size of the demonstration and opposed to the workers' demands, the volunteer cavalrymen of the city, who belonged to the middle class, attacked the crowd, killing 11 people and injuring another 400. This violent confrontation, known as the Peterloo Massacre, did not lead to revolution or sustained class warfare, but it did contribute to the perception, shared by an increasingly large number of people, that British society was divided into large groups of people based on their economic position in society.

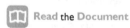 **Read the Document**

A Luddite Pamphlet

Justice in History

The Sadler Committee on Child Labor

Read the Document

British Parliament, "Inquiry into Child Labor"

The widespread use of child labor in British factories and mines during the early decades of the Industrial Revolution led to efforts by social reformers and Members of Parliament to regulate the conditions under which children worked. Parliament passed legislation restricting the number of hours that all children could work in textile mills in 1819 and 1829, but neither of these laws was enforced effectively, and they did not apply to all industries. Complaints of inhumane treatment, moral degradation, and exploitation of child workers continued to surface. In 1831 Michael Sadler (1780–1835), a Tory member of the British Parliament, introduced a bill in Parliament to limit the number of hours that all children could work to 10 hours per day. Like many social reformers, Sadler was inspired by what he considered his Christian duty to protect dependent members of the community.

Sadler chaired the committee to which his bill was referred. To muster support for the bill, Sadler held hearings in which child workers themselves came before the committee to report on the conditions under which they lived and worked. The success of his bill was by no means guaranteed. Many Members of Parliament were deeply committed to the policy of *laissez-faire*, according to which the government should not intervene in the operation of the economy, treating it instead as a self-regulating machine. Sadler had to convince his colleagues that they should modify that policy in the case of children, on the grounds that the state was obliged to provide for the welfare of children when their parents were unable to do so. He also needed to make the Members of Parliament and the broader public aware of the brutality of the conditions under which the children worked.

The hearings that took place were not a trial in the strict sense of the word, but they possessed many of the features of a judicial investigation, not unlike those conducted by American grand juries in criminal cases. Sadler intended the committee's proceedings to expose, condemn, and ultimately remedy misconduct by the factory owners. Procedurally the committee members had more latitude than courts of law. Because such parliamentary committees were designed to extract

CHILD LABOR IN THE TEXTILE INDUSTRY Children walking to work in a textile mill in northern England in the nineteenth century.

information rather than to bring offenders to trial, they did not need to adhere to any established judicial guidelines. There was no cross-examination of witnesses, nor could factory owners present a defense. The witnesses in this investigation were chosen because Sadler knew they would reveal the evils of the factory system.

The testimony presented to the Sadler Committee produced abundant evidence of the exploitation and physical abuse of child workers. Some of the most harrowing testimony came from the examination of a 17-year-old boy, Joseph Hebergam, on July 1, 1832. Hebergam revealed that he had begun the work of worsted spinning at age 7, that he worked at the factory from 5 A.M. until 8 P.M., and that he had only 30 minutes for lunch at noon, leaving him to eat his other meals while standing on the job. In the factory there were three overlookers (supervisors), one of whom was responsible for greasing the machinery and another for disciplining the workers. The latter overlooker walked continually up and down the factory with whip in hand.

When asked where his brother John was working, Joseph replied that he had died three years before at age 16. Sadler then inquired into the cause of his brother's death. The boy responded, "It was attributed to this, that he died from working such long hours and that it had been brought on by the factory. They have to stop the flies [part of the textile machinery] with their knees, because they go so swift they cannot stop them with their hands; he got a bruise on the shin by a spindle-board, and it went on to that degree that it burst; the surgeon cured that, then he was better; then he went to work again; but when he had worked about two months more his spine became affected, and he died." The witness went on to explain that his own severe labor had damaged his knees and ankles so much so that he found it painful to walk. His brother and sister would help carry him to the factory, but when they arrived late, even by as little as five minutes, the overlooker beat all three of them "till we were black and blue."[4] At the request of

(continued on next page)

673

(continued from previous page)

the committee, Joseph then stood up to show the condition of his limbs. He reported the death of another boy who had sustained massive injuries when he was caught in the shaft of the machinery he was running. Joseph concluded his testimony by recounting how the factory owners had threatened him and his younger brothers with losing their jobs if they testified before the committee.

Although widely publicized, the hearings of the Sadler Committee fell short of realizing their original objective. The bill, which eventually was approved by Parliament as the Factory Regulations Act of 1833, prohibited the employment of children under age nine in all factories. Boys and girls were allowed to work up to nine hours a day from age nine until their thirteenth birthday, and up to 12 hours a day from age 13 until their eighteenth birthday. Nevertheless, the long-term effect of this legislation was to establish in Western industrialized countries the principle that early childhood was a period of life set aside for education rather than work.

For Discussion

1. This investigation was concerned with the achievement of social justice rather than the determination of criminal culpability. What were the advantages of using legislative committees in such an undertaking?
2. Child labor was not a new phenomenon in the early eighteenth century. Why did the Industrial Revolution draw attention to this age-old practice?

Taking It Further

Horn, Pamela. *Children's Work and Welfare, 1780–1890.* 1996. An examination of the scale and nature of child employment in Britain and changing attitudes toward the practice.

The Industrial Landscape

As industry spread throughout Europe, urban and rural areas underwent dramatic changes. The most striking of these transformations took place in the new industrial towns and cities, some of which had been little more than country towns before the factories were built. Manchester, for example, grew from a modest population of 23,000 people in 1773 to a bustling metropolis of 105,000 by 1820. Large factories with their smokestacks and warehouses, ringed by long rows of houses built to accommodate the

THE PETERLOO MASSACRE, 1819 This drawing of the Peterloo Massacre shows the mounted yeomen of Manchester, with swords drawn, attacking the demonstrators, who had gathered to hear the speeches by the reformers on the platform above.

armies of new industrial workers, gave these cities an entirely new and for the most part grim appearance.

Cities experienced the most noticeable changes in physical appearance, but the countryside also began to take on a new look, mainly as a result of the transport revolution. The tunnels, bridges, and viaducts that were constructed to accommodate the railroad and the canals that were built to improve inland water transportation made an indelible imprint on the countryside. In many ways this alteration of the landscape demonstrated the mastery over nature that human beings had achieved at the time of the Scientific Revolution. The Industrial Revolution finally fulfilled the technological promise of that earlier revolution, and one of its effects was the actual transformation of the physical world.

The advent of modern industry also brought about a change in attitudes toward the landscape. The destruction of natural beauty in the interest of economic progress stimulated an appreciation of nature that had not been widespread during the medieval and early modern periods. Before the Industrial Revolution many features of the countryside, especially mountains, were viewed as obstacles to either travel or human habitation, not as objects of aesthetic appreciation. Urbanization and industrialization changed those perceptions, triggering a nostalgic reaction that became one of the sources of the romantic movement, which we shall consider in greater detail in the next chapter.

Industry did not always blight the landscape or offend artistic sensibilities. Some of the new industrial architecture, especially the viaducts and aqueducts that traversed valleys in the mountainous regions of the country, were masterpieces of modern engineering and architecture. Sir Walter Scott (1771–1832), the Scottish romantic novelist, claimed that the cast-iron Pontcysyllte aqueduct in Wales, which carried the waters of the Caledonian Canal 127 feet above the River Dee, was the most beautiful work of art he had ever seen. The railroad also had the ability to inspire the artistic imagination, as it did in Joseph Turner's (1775–1851) romantic painting *Rain, Steam and Speed*, which captured the railroad's speed and beauty.

JOSEPH M. W. TURNER, RAIN, STEAM AND SPEED: THE GREAT WESTERN RAILWAY (1844) This was one of the first oil paintings that had the railroad locomotive as its theme.

Industry, Trade, and Empire

21.5 What was the relationship between Britain's industrial strength and the growth of its empire?

n the middle of the nineteenth century, Britain towered above all other nations in the volume of its industrial output, the extent of its international trade, and the size of its empire. In industrial production it easily outpaced all its competitors, producing two-thirds of the world's coal, about half of its cotton cloth, half of its iron, and 40 percent of its hardware. Little wonder that Britain became known as "the workshop of the world." Britain controlled about one-third of the world's trade, and London emerged as the undisputed financial center of the global economy. Britain's overseas empire, which included colonies in Canada, the Caribbean, South America, India, Southeast Asia, and Australia, eclipsed those of all other European powers and continued to grow during the second half of the century.

These three great British strengths—industry, trade, and empire—were closely linked. Britain's colonies in both Asia and the Americas served as trading depots, while the promotion of trade led directly to the acquisition of new imperial possessions. Even when Britain did not formally acquire territory, it often established exclusive trading relationships with those countries, thereby creating an informal "empire of trade." Trade and empire in turn served the purposes of industry. Many of the raw materials used in industrial production, especially cotton, came from Britain's imperial possessions. Those possessions also provided markets for Britain's mass-produced manufactured goods. Such imperial markets proved immensely valuable when France blockaded its ports during the Napoleonic wars and thereby cut into British trade with the entire European continent.

The great challenge for British industrialists during the nineteenth century was to find new markets for their industrial products. Domestic demand had been strong at the beginning of the Industrial Revolution, but by the 1840s British workers did not possess sufficient wealth to purchase the increasingly large volume of hardwares and textiles manufactured in the mills and factories. Britain had to look overseas to find markets in which to sell the bulk of its industrial products. One possibility was to market them in other European countries, such as France and Germany, where demand for manufactured goods was high. These countries, however, were in the midst of their own industrial revolutions, and their governments had often legislated high protective tariffs against British goods to encourage the growth of their own industries. British industrialists, therefore, marketed their goods in less economically developed parts of the world, including British colonies. In all these areas, moreover, British military power and diplomatic influence advanced the interests of industry, trade, and empire.

East Asia: The Opium War, 1839–1842

British conflict with China provides the best illustration of the way in which the British desire to promote trade led to the acquisition of new colonies. For three centuries the Chinese had tightly controlled their trade with European powers. By 1842, however, British merchants, supported by the British government, managed to break down these barriers and give Britain a foothold in China, allowing it to exploit the East Asian market.

The conflict arose over the importation of opium, a narcotic made from poppy seeds and produced in great quantities in India. This drug, which numbed pain but also had hallucinogenic effects and could cause profound lethargy, was in widespread use in Europe and had an even larger market in Asia. In China opium had become a national addiction by the middle of the eighteenth century. The situation became much worse when British merchants increased the volume of illegal imports from India to China in the early nineteenth century. The Chinese government prohibited the use of opium, but because it had difficulty enforcing its own edicts, it decided to put an end to the opium trade.

Chinese efforts to stop British merchants from importing opium led to an increase in tensions between China and Britain. The situation reached a climax in 1839, when the Chinese seized 20,000 chests of opium in the holds of British ships and spilled them into the China Sea. It is unknown what effect the opium had on the fish, but the incident led to a British attack on Chinese ports. In this conflict, the first Opium War (1839–1842), the British had the advantage of superior naval technology, itself a product of the Industrial Revolution. The first iron-clad, steam-driven gunboat used in combat, the *Nemesis,* destroyed Chinese batteries along the coast, and an assault by 75 British ships on Chinkiang forced the Chinese to come to terms. In a treaty signed in 1842 China ceded the island of Hong Kong to the British, reimbursed British merchants for the opium it had destroyed, and opened five Chinese ports to international trade. As part of this settlement, each of these ports was to be governed by a British consul who was not subject to Chinese law. In this way Britain expanded its empire, increased its already large share of world trade, and found new markets for British manufactured goods in East Asia.

India: Annexation and Trade

The interrelationship of industry, trade, and empire became even clearer in India, which became known as the jewel in Britain's imperial crown. As we saw in Chapter 18, Britain gained control of the Indian province of Bengal in the eighteenth century and subsequently acquired other Indian states. After the Sepoy Mutiny of 1857 the British government brought all of India under its direct control.

Political control of India during the nineteenth century served the interests of British trade in two ways. First, it gave British merchants control of the trade between India and other Asian countries. Second, Britain developed a favorable balance of trade with India, exporting more goods to that country than it imported. Taxes paid to the British government by Indians and interest payments on British loans to India increased the flow of capital from Calcutta to London. The influx of capital from India was largely responsible for the favorable balance of payments that Britain enjoyed with the rest of the world until World War I. The capital that Britain received from these sources as well as from trade with China was funneled into the British economy or invested in British economic ventures throughout the world.

Control of India also served British interests by supplying British industries with raw materials while giving them access to the foreign markets they needed to make a profit. This promotion of British industry came at the expense of the local Indian economy. The transportation of cotton grown in India to British textile mills only to be returned to India in the form of finished cloth certainly retarded, if it did not destroy, the existing Indian textile industry. Resentment of this economic exploitation of India became one of the main sources of Indian nationalism in the late nineteenth century.

Latin America: An Empire of Trade

British policy in Latin America developed differently from the way it had in China and India, but it had the same effect of opening up new markets for British goods. Great Britain was a consistent supporter of the movements for independence that erupted in South America between 1810 and 1824 (see Chapter 18). Britain supported these movements not simply because it wished to undermine Spanish and Portuguese imperialism, but also because it needed to acquire new markets for its industrial products. Britain did not need to use military force to open these areas to British trade, as it did in China. Once the countries became independent, they attracted large volumes of British exports. In 1840 the British cotton industry shipped 35 percent of its exports to Latin American countries, especially to Argentina, Brazil, Uruguay, Mexico, and Chile. British financiers also exported large amounts of capital to these Latin American countries by investing vast sums of money in their economies. Britain thus established an informal "empire of trade" in Latin America. Britain did not govern these countries, but they developed the same economic relationship with Britain as other parts of the British Empire.

British investment and trade brought the newly independent states of Latin America into the industrial world economy. These countries, however, assumed a dependent position in that economy, not unlike the position India acquired about the same time. One effect of this dependence was to transform the small, self-sufficient village economies that had developed alongside the large plantations in Central and South America. Instead of producing goods themselves and selling them within their own markets, these villages now became suppliers of raw materials for British industry. This transformation made the Latin American population more dependent upon British manufactured goods, retarded or destroyed native Latin American industry, and created huge trade deficits for Latin American countries by the middle of the nineteenth century.

Ireland: The Internal Colony

Of all the imperial possessions with which Britain engaged in trade, the position of Ireland was the most anomalous. Despite its proximity to England, Ireland had always been treated as a colony. In 1801, after the unsuccessful Irish rebellion of 1798 discussed in Chapter 18, the British government incorporated Ireland into the United Kingdom and abolished the Irish Parliament. Although a small minority of Irishmen elected their representatives to sit in the British Parliament, and although Ireland thus became a part of the British state, Britain nonetheless continued to treat the country as an imperial possession.

Throughout the nineteenth century Ireland remained almost entirely agricultural. Industrialization occurred only in the northern province of Ulster, which produced ready-to-wear undergarments for women and shirts for men. Ireland's vast agricultural estates, many of them owned by absentee British landlords, provided Britain with large imports of grain. Unable to afford the high cost of grain, which British protectionist legislation priced artificially high, and without the opportunity to find employment in industry, Irish tenants eked out an existence on the land, relying on a diet consisting almost entirely of potatoes. When a blight destroyed the potato crop in 1845, the country experienced a devastating famine that killed more than one million people and forced another million to emigrate—many of them to the United States and Canada—between 1845 and 1848. The famine occurred despite the fact that Irish lands produced enough grain to feed the entire population. As the Lord Mayor of Dublin complained in 1845, British commercial policy inflicted on the Irish "the abject misery of having their own provisions carried away to feed others, while they themselves are left contemptuously to starve."[5] Thus, even in this internal colony, the British government's policy of promoting industry at home while importing resources from its imperial possessions served British economic interests at the expense of the countries under its control.

CONCLUSION

Industrialization and the West

By 1850 the Industrial Revolution had initiated some of the most dramatic changes in human life recorded in historical documents. Not since the Neolithic Age, when people began to live in settled villages, cultivate grains, and domesticate animals, did the organization of society, the patterns of work, and the landscape undergo such profound changes. In many ways the Industrial Revolution marked the watershed between the old way of life and the new. It gave human beings unprecedented technological control over nature, made employment in the home the exception rather than the rule, and submitted industrial workers to a regimen unknown in the past. It changed family life, gave cities an entirely new appearance, and unleashed new and highly potent political forces, including the ideologies of liberalism and socialism, which we discuss in the next chapter.

Industrialization changed the very definition of the West. In the Middle Ages Christianity shaped the predominant cultural values of Western countries, while in the eighteenth century the rational, scientific culture of the Enlightenment became central to the idea of the West. Now, in the nineteenth century, industrialization—and the system of industrial capitalism it spawned—increasingly defined the West. In discussing the prospects of industrialization in the Ottoman Empire in 1856, a British diplomat wrote that "Europe is at hand, with its science, its labor, and its capital," but that the Qur'an and other elements of traditional Turkish culture "are so many obstacles to advancement in a Western sense."[6] The Industrial Revolution thus created new divisions between the West and the non-Western world.

Until the late nineteenth century, industrialization took place only in nations that had traditionally been a part of the West. Beginning in the 1890s, however, countries that lay outside the West or on its margins began to introduce industrial technology and methods. Between 1890 and 1910 Russia and Japan underwent a period of rapid industrialization, and in the second half of the twentieth century many countries in Asia, the Middle East, and Latin America followed suit. This process of industrialization and economic development is often described as one of Westernization, and it has usually led to conflicts within those countries between Western and non-Western values. Whether those countries that have industrialized should be considered Western is not clear. Industrialization outside Europe and the United States reveals once again that the composition of the West changes from time to time and that its boundaries are often difficult to define.

MAKING CONNECTIONS

1. Why did the Industrial Revolution begin in Great Britain?
2. What are the strengths and weaknesses of the optimistic view of the Industrial Revolution?
3. What was the relationship between the growth of the population and the Industrial Revolution?
4. How did the Industrial Revolution change the definition of the West?

TAKING IT FURTHER

For suggested readings see page R–1.

Chapter Review

The Nature of the Industrial Revolution

21.1 What was the Industrial Revolution of the late eighteenth and nineteenth centuries?

Four key developments comprised the Industrial Revolution: the introduction and implementation of new industrial technology like textile machinery and the steam engine, the use of minerals like coal as sources of energy for the production and transportation of goods, the replacement of the rural cottage system to production in large factories, and the development of new methods of transportation, like the railroad, to transport goods.

Conditions Favoring Industrial Growth

21.2 What social and economic changes made industrial development possible?

An increase in the birthrate and a decrease in the occurrence of famines allowed population growth that encouraged industrial growth. The increase in farming productivity allowed more people to leave the farms to work in the factories and mines, and the substantial growth of capital and of a consumer culture also favored industrial development.

The Spread of Industrialization

21.3 How did industrialization spread from Great Britain to the European continent and America?

Scarce resources and political and social barriers meant that industrialization occurred at a slower rate on the European continent. Once countries started to industrialize, government involvement, banks, and the already existing railroad system became key factors in the process. In America, where natural resources were abundant, the process of industrialization more closely resembled Britain's, including the absence of governmental involvement.

The Effects of Industrialization

21.4 What were the economic, social, and cultural effects of the Industrial Revolution?

The accumulation of capital meant that industry could employ workers, who in turn used their income to marry earlier and successfully maintain larger families. But unhealthy working conditions and environmental pollution were also an effect of industrialization. Unable to combine domestic and occupational labor, women left the workforce. Cities, some built up around factories, and the countryside, where canals and bridges were built to transport goods, were transformed.

Industry, Trade, and Empire

21.5 What was the relationship between Britain's industrial strength and the growth of its empire?

British military power and diplomatic influence advanced the interests of industry, trade, and empire. Colonies in both Asia and the Americas served as trading depots, while the promotion of trade led directly to the acquisition of new imperial possessions. Many of the raw materials used in industrial production came from Britain's colonies, and those same colonies were also markets for Britain's mass-produced manufactured goods.

Chapter Time Line

1763 James Watts's rotative steam engine.

1767 James Hargreaves's spinning jenny.

1769 Richard Arkwright's water frame.

1779 Samuel Crompton's mule.

1787 Edmund Cartwright's power loom.

1815 George Stephenson's steam locomotive.

1846 Elias Howe's sewing machine.

22 Ideological Conflict and National Unification, 1815–1871

On March 18, 1871, the president of the French government, Adolphe Thiers, sent a small unit of troops to Paris to seize cannons that had been used against Prussian forces during their siege of the city a few months before. The cannons were in the possession of the National Guard, the citizen militia of Paris. The members of the National Guard felt that Thiers's government had abandoned them by recently concluding an armistice with the Prussians, who were still camped outside the city. They also believed that Thiers was determined to gain control of the city, which had refused to comply with the orders of the national government. When the troops reached the city, they encountered a hostile

EUGÈNE DELACROIX, *LIBERTY LEADING THE PEOPLE* (1830) The romantic representation of Liberty carrying the French tricolor during the Paris revolution of 1830 conveys the ideological inspiration and the violence of that armed uprising.

SOURCE: Eugène Delacroix (1798–1860), "July 28th, 1830; Liberty Guides the People," oil on canvas, 260 × 325 cm. Louvre, Dept. des Peintures, Paris, France. © Photograph by Erich Lessing/Art Resource, NY.

LEARNING OBJECTIVES

22.1 What were the main features of the four new ideologies of the early nineteenth century?

22.2 How did those ideologies shape the political history of Europe between 1815 and 1848?

22.3 How did liberal and conservative leaders use the ideology of nationalism to form nation-states?

22.4 How did warfare lead to political change in Russia and France between 1850 and 1871?

((∙ Listen to Chapter 22 on MyHistoryLab

👁 **Watch the Video Series on MyHistoryLab**

Learn about some key topics related to this chapter with the *MyHistoryLab Video Series: Key Topics in Western Civilization*

crowd of Parisians, many of whom were armed. The crowd surrounded the two generals who led the detachment, placed them up against a wall, and executed them.

This action led to a full-scale siege of Paris by government troops. In the city a committed group of radicals formed a new municipal government, the Paris Commune, a revival of the commune established during the French Revolution in 1792. The Commune took steps to defend the city against the government troops, and it implemented several social reforms. The Communards, as the members were known, set up a central employment bureau, established nurseries for working mothers, and recognized women's labor unions. For many decades the Commune served as a model of working-class government.

Yet the Paris Commune itself lasted only a few weeks. On May 21 the troops of the provisional government poured through the gates of the city, and during the "bloody week" that followed they took the city street by street, demolishing the barricades and executing the Communards. The Communards retaliated by executing a number of hostages, including the archbishop of Paris. They also burned down the Tuileries Palace, the hall of justice, and the city hall. During this one week at least 25,000 Communards were killed.

The short life of the Paris Commune marked the climax of a tumultuous period of European history. Between 1815 and 1871 Europe witnessed numerous movements for reform, periodic uprisings, and several revolutions. The people who participated in these momentous developments were inspired in large part by **ideologies**, theories of society and government that lay at the basis of political programs. The ideologies that developed during this period—liberalism, conservatism, socialism, and nationalism—endowed the West with a distinctive political culture. This chapter will address the following question:

ideologies Theories of society and government that form the basis of political programs.

How did these four ideologies affect the political and social history of the West from 1815 until 1871?

New Ideologies in the Early Nineteenth Century

22.1 What were the main features of the four new ideologies of the early nineteenth century?

The transformations of the West discussed in the last two chapters, the French Revolution and the Industrial Revolution, influenced the formation of the four new ideologies of the early nineteenth century.

Liberalism: The Protection of Individual Freedom

liberalism An ideology based on the conviction that individual freedom is of supreme importance and the main responsibility of government is to protect that freedom.

Liberalism is anchored in the belief that the main function of government is to promote political, social, and economic freedom. The primary objective of nineteenth-century liberals was to establish and protect individual rights, such as the freedom of the press, freedom of religion, and freedom from arbitrary arrest and imprisonment.

Liberals sought to guarantee these rights in written constitutions. Opposed to aristocratic privilege, they supported the principle of equality before the law. They also tended to be anticlerical, a position that led to frequent tension between them and the Roman Catholic Church. As defenders of individual freedom, they often campaigned to end slavery and serfdom.

The second objective of liberals was the extension of the franchise (the right to vote) to all property owners, especially the middle class. Liberals were usually opposed to giving the vote to the working class on the grounds that poor people, with little property of their own, could not be trusted to elect representatives who would protect property rights. Liberals also were opposed to giving the vote or any other form of political power to women. They believed that the proper arena for female activity was the home, where women occupied their natural domain. Liberals thus subscribed to the theory of separate spheres, which held that women were different in nature from men and that only male property holders should be allowed to participate in public affairs.

The third objective of liberals was to promote free trade with other nations and to resist government regulation of the domestic economy. This economic dimension of liberal ideology is usually referred to as **_laissez-faire_**, which means "let (people) do (as they choose)." Advocates of _laissez-faire_ held that the government should intervene in the economy only to maintain public order and protect property rights. As merchants and manufacturers, liberals favored a policy of _laissez-faire_ because it offered them the freedom to pursue their own self-interest without governmental interference and thereby realize greater profits.

One of the most influential proponents of liberal economic theory was David Ricardo (1772–1823), a British economist and stockbroker who argued that government efforts to regulate wages and prices would slow economic growth. In _Principles of Political Economy and Taxation_ (1819), Ricardo argued that if wages were left to the law of supply and demand, they would fall to near subsistence levels, leading workers to limit the size of their families. Lower wages and fewer consumers would in turn keep prices low. Industrialists found Ricardo's _laissez-faire_ theory appealing, but it was harder to convince workers that this "iron law of wages" would benefit them.

Liberalism found its greatest strength among the urban middle class. These people formed the group that felt most aggrieved by their exclusion from political life during the eighteenth and early nineteenth centuries and most eager to have government protect their property.

Conservatism: Preserving the Established Order

In the early nineteenth century the ideals of the Enlightenment and the radical changes ushered in by the French Revolution led to the formulation of a new ideology of **conservatism**, a set of ideas intended to prevent a recurrence of the revolutionary changes of the 1790s. The main goal of conservatives after 1815 was to preserve the monarchies and aristocracies of Europe against liberal movements.

The founder of modern conservative ideology was the Irish-born parliamentary orator Edmund Burke (1729–1797). In _Reflections on the Revolution in France_ (1790), Burke insisted that rights did not derive from human nature, as Enlightenment thinkers insisted, but were privileges that had been passed down through the ages and could be preserved only by a hereditary monarchy. Burke also contended that equality, so loudly proclaimed at the time of the French Revolution, was a dangerous myth that would undermine the social order. For Burke the social order was a partnership between the living, the dead, and those who had yet to be born. By introducing revolutionary change, the French Revolution had broken that partnership.

Early nineteenth-century conservatives justified the institution of monarchy on the basis of religion as well as history. The French writer Louis de Bonald (1754–1840) argued that Christian monarchies were the final creation in the development of both religious and political society. Only monarchies of this sort could preserve public order

 Read the Document

John Stuart Mill, Excerpts from _On Liberty_

laissez-faire The principle that governments should not regulate or otherwise intervene in the economy unless it is necessary to protect property rights and public order.

Read the Document

David Ricardo, _On Wages, "The Iron Law of Wages"_

conservatism A nineteenth-century ideology intended to prevent a recurrence of the revolutionary changes of the 1790s and the implementation of liberal policies.

and prevent society from degenerating into the savagery witnessed during the French Revolution. Like his fellow French writer, Joseph de Maistre (1754–1821), de Bonald rejected the entire concept of natural rights and reiterated the traditional doctrine of divine right, according to which kings received their power from God.

Socialism: The Demand for Equality

Socialism, the third new ideology of the early nineteenth century, arose in reaction against the development of industrial capitalism and the liberal ideas that justified it. Socialism calls for the ownership of the means of production (such as factories, machines, and railroads) by the community, with the purpose of reducing inequalities of income, wealth, opportunity, and economic power. In small communities, such ownership can be genuinely collective. In a large country, however, the only practical way to introduce socialism is to give the ownership of property to the state, which represents the people.

The main appeal of socialism was the prospect of remedying the deplorable social and economic effects of the Industrial Revolution. As we saw in Chapter 21, the short-term effects of industrialization included wretched working conditions, low wages, a regimentation of the labor force, and a declining standard of living. Socialists did not object to the mechanization of industry as such. Like liberals, they wanted society to be as productive as possible. They did, however, object to the system of industrial capitalism that accompanied industrialization and the liberal economic theory that justified it. (See *Different Voices* in this chapter.)

The earliest socialists, known as Utopian socialists, envisioned the creation of ideal communities in which perfect social harmony and cooperation would prevail. One of these Utopian socialists, the British industrialist and philanthropist Robert Owen (1771–1858), turned his mill in New Lanark, Scotland, into a model socialist community where he housed his workers and educated their children. In 1825 he established a similar community in New Harmony, Indiana. Utopian socialism was not particularly concerned with the granting of political rights to workers, nor did it encourage class consciousness or class tensions.

socialism An ideology calling for the ownership of the means of production by the community with the purpose of reducing inequalities of income, wealth, opportunity, and economic power.

View the Closer Look   Socialist Utopia in New Harmony, Indiana

ROBERT OWEN'S DESIGN FOR A SOCIALIST UTOPIA IN NEW HARMONY, INDIANA The symmetry of the city's design recalls the classical notions of an ordered life.

Different Voices
Liberals and Socialists View the Middle Class

N ineteenth-century liberals, who stressed individual rights and free trade, extolled the virtues of the middle class, whom they regarded as the most progressive and productive members of society. Socialists, however, viewed the middle class or bourgeoisie as exploitative capitalists who oppressed the working class. In the first document, the liberal British economist and political philosopher James Mill (1773–1836), who supported the effort to give the middle class greater representation in the British Parliament, argues that the working class should follow the advice and example of the middle class. Karl Marx and Friedrich Engels were the leading philosophers of communism, the form of socialism that emphasized class warfare and called for a dictatorship of the proletariat. In the second document Marx and Engels condemn the middle class for their oppression and exploitation of the proletariat.

James Mill Praises the Wisdom and Leadership of the Middle Class

It is to be observed, that the class which is universally described, as both the most wise, and the most virtuous part of every community, the middle rank, are wholly included in that part of the community which is not the aristocratical. It is also not disputed, that in Great Britain the middle rank are numerous, and form a large proportion of the whole body of the people. Another proposition may be stated, with a perfect confidence of the concurrence of all those men who have attentively considered the formation of opinions in the great body of society, or, indeed, the principles of human nature in general. It is, that the opinions of that class of the people, who are below the middle rank, are formed, and their minds are directed by that intelligent and virtuous rank, who come the most immediately in contact with them, who are in the constant habit of intimate communication with them, to whom they fly for advice and assistance in all their numerous difficulties, upon whom they feel an immediate and daily dependence, in health and in sickness, in infancy and in old age; to whom their children look up as models for their imitation, whose opinions they have daily repeated, and account it their honour to adopt. There can be no doubt whatever that the middle rank, which gives their most distinguished ornaments to science, to art, and to legislation itself, to every thing which exalts and refines human nature, is that part of the community of which, if the basis of representation were now so far extended, the opinion would ultimately decide. Of the people beneath them, a vast majority would be sure to be guided by their advice and example.

SOURCE: From James Mill, *Essay on Government* (1820).

Karl Marx and Friedrich Engels Assail the Middle Class for Their Exploitation of Workers

The modern bourgeois society that has sprouted from the ruins of feudal society has not done away with class antagonisms. It has but established new classes, new conditions of oppression, new forms of struggle in place of the old ones. Our epoch, the epoch of the bourgeoisie, possesses, however, this distinct feature: it has simplified class antagonisms. Society as a whole is more and more splitting up into two great hostile camps, into two great classes directly facing each other—bourgeoisie and proletariat....

The bourgeoisie, wherever it has got the upper hand, has put an end to all feudal, patriarchal, idyllic relations. It has pitilessly torn asunder the motley feudal ties that bound man to his "natural superiors," and has left remaining no other nexus between man and man than naked self-interest, than callous "cash payment." It has drowned the most heavenly ecstasies of religious fervor, of chivalrous enthusiasm, of philistine sentimentalism, in the icy water of egotistical calculation. It has resolved personal worth into exchange value, and in place of the numberless indefeasible chartered freedoms, has set up that single, unconscionable freedom—Free Trade. In one word, for exploitation, veiled by religious and political illusions, it has substituted naked, shameless, direct, brutal exploitation....

The bourgeoisie has through its exploitation of the world market given a cosmopolitan character to production and consumption in every country. To the great chagrin of Reactionists, it has drawn from under the feet of industry the national ground on which it stood. All old-established national industries have been destroyed or are daily being destroyed. They are dislodged by new industries, whose introduction becomes a life and death question for all civilized nations, by industries that no longer work up indigenous raw material, but raw material drawn from the remotest zones; industries whose products are consumed, not only at home, but in every quarter of the globe. In place of the old wants, satisfied by the production of the country, we find new wants, requiring for their satisfaction the products of distant lands and climes. In place of the old local and national seclusion and self-sufficiency, we have intercourse in every direction, universal interdependence of nations. The bourgeoisie, by the rapid improvement of all instruments of production, by the immensely facilitated means of communication, draws all, even the most barbarian, nations into civilization. The cheap prices of commodities are the heavy artillery with

(continued on next page)

(continued from previous page)

which it batters down all Chinese walls, with which it forces the barbarians' intensely obstinate hatred of foreigners to capitulate. It compels all nations, on pain of extinction, to adopt the bourgeois mode of production; it compels them to introduce what it calls civilization into their midst, i.e., to become bourgeois themselves. In one word, it creates a world after its own image.

SOURCE: From Karl Marx and Friedrich Engels, *The Communist Manifesto* (1848).

For Discussion

1. How do the authors of these two documents differ in their descriptions of the relationships between the middle class and the working class?
2. What is the basis of Mill's praise for the middle class and Marx and Engels' condemnation of it?
3. How might a liberal like Mill have responded to the publication of the *Communist Manifesto*? How might a conservative have responded?

A second generation of socialists became more concerned with using the power of the state to improve their lot. The most influential of these socialists was the French democrat Louis Blanc (1811–1882), who proposed that the state guarantee workers' wages and employment in times of economic depression. He also wanted the state to support the creation of workshops where workers would sell the product of their labor directly without middlemen. The principle underlying Blanc's concept of the social order was "From each according to his abilities; to each according to his needs." Blanc's brand of socialism began a long tradition in which workers tried to improve their circumstances by influencing government. This initiative was closely related to the radical democratic goal of universal male suffrage, which became one of the main objectives of many socialists after 1840.

The German social philosopher Karl Marx (1818–1883) formulated the most radical form of nineteenth-century socialism. Marx was much more preoccupied than other socialists with the collective identity and political activities of the working class. Reading about working conditions in France during the early 1840s, he became convinced that workers in industrial society were the ultimate example of human alienation and degradation. Marx and his co-author Friedrich Engels began to think of workers as part of a capitalist system, in which they owned nothing but their labor, which they sold to capitalist producers for wages.

dialectic The theory that history advanced in stages as the result of the conflict between different ideas or social groups.

dialectical materialism The socialist philosophy of Karl Marx according to which history advanced as the result of material or economic forces and would lead to the creation of a classless society.

proletariat The word used by Karl Marx and Friedrich Engels to identify the class of workers who received their income from wages.

communism The revolutionary form of socialism developed by Karl Marx and Friedrich Engels that promoted the overthrow of bourgeois or capitalist institutions and the establishment of a dictatorship of the proletariat.

Marx and Engels worked these ideas into a broad account of historical change in which society moved inevitably and progressively from one stage to another. They referred to the process by which history advanced as the **dialectic**. Marx acquired the idea of the dialectic from the German philosopher Georg Wilhelm Friedrich Hegel (1770–1831), who believed that history advanced in stages as the result of the conflict between one idea and another. Marx disagreed with Hegel on the source of historical change, arguing that material or economic factors rather than ideas determined the course of history. Hence, Marx's socialist philosophy became known as **dialectical materialism**.

According to Marx and Engels, the first stage of the dialectic had taken place when the bourgeoisie, who received their income from capital, seized political power from the aristocracy, who received their income from land, during the English and French revolutions. Marx and Engels predicted that the next stage of the dialectic would be a conflict between the bourgeoisie and the working class or **proletariat**, which received its income from wages. This conflict, according to Marx and Engels, would result in the triumph of the working class. Led by a committed band of revolutionaries, the proletariat would take control of the state, establish a dictatorship so that they could implement their program without opposition, and usher in a classless society.

Marx and Engels issued this call to action in *The Communist Manifesto* (1848), which ended with the famous words, "Working men of all countries unite!" Marx's brand of socialism, **communism**, takes its name from this book. Communism is a revolutionary ideology that advocates the overthrow of "bourgeois" or capitalist institutions and the transfer of political power to the proletariat. Communism differs from other forms of socialism in its call for revolution, its emphasis on class conflict, and its

 Read the Document

Karl Marx and Friedrich Engels, from the *Communist Manifesto*

686

insistence on complete economic equality. Communism belongs to a tradition that originated among members of the extreme wing of the democratic movement at the height of the French Revolution. One of those radicals, François-Noël Babeuf (1760–1797), demanded economic and political equality, called for the common ownership of land, and spoke in terms of class warfare. Marx's achievement was to place Babeuf's radical ideas in the framework of dialectical materialism in his monumental three-volume work, *Capital* (1867–1894).

Nationalism: The Unity of the People

Nationalism, the fourth new ideology of the early nineteenth century, also took shape during and after the French Revolution. A **nation** in the nineteenth-century sense of the word refers to a large community of people who believe that they have a common homeland and share a similar culture. The ideology of **nationalism** is the belief that the people who form this nation should have their own political institutions and that the interests of the nation should be defended and promoted at all costs.

The geographical boundaries of nations, however, do not often correspond to the geographical boundaries of states, which are administrative and legal units of political organization. For example, in the early nineteenth century Germans often referred to their nation as comprising all people who spoke German. At that time there were more than a dozen German states, including Prussia, Bavaria, and Baden, and there were also many German speakers

KARL MARX Karl Marx, the German social philosopher who developed the revolutionary socialist doctrine of communism.

living in non-German lands, such as Bohemia. A primary goal of nationalists is to create a **nation-state**, a single political entity that governs all the members of a particular nation. The doctrine that justifies this goal is **national self-determination**, the claim that any group that considers itself a nation has the right to be ruled only by members of its own nation and to have all the members of the nation included in this state.

The ideology of nationalism had roots in the French Revolution. Most of the revolutionary steps taken in France during the 1790s were undertaken in the name of a united French people—the French *nation*. Article 3 of the *Declaration of the Rights of Man and Citizen* (1789) declared that "the principle of all authority rests essentially in the nation." The French Republic was constructed as the embodiment of the French nation. It gave an administrative unity to the French people and encouraged them to think of themselves as sharing a common cultural bond. Instead of a collection of regions, France had become *la patrie,* or the people's native land.

Nationalists emphasized the antiquity of nations, arguing that there had always been a distinct German, French, English, Swiss, or Italian people living in their respective homelands. This claim involved a certain amount of fiction, because in the past the people living in those lands possessed little cultural or linguistic unity. There was little uniformity, for example, in the languages spoken by people whom nineteenth-century nationalists identified as German, French, or Italian. Until the eighteenth century most educated Germans wrote in French, not German. Only a small percentage of Italians

nation A large community of people who possess a sense of unity based on a belief that they have a common homeland and share a similar culture.

nationalism The belief that the people who form a nation should have their own political institutions and that the interests of the nation should be defended and promoted at all costs.

nation-state A political structure sought by nationalists in which the boundaries of the state and the nation are identical, so that all the members of a nation are governed by the same political authorities.

national self-determination The doctrine advanced by nationalists that any group that considers itself a nation has the right to be ruled only by the members of their own nation and to have all members of the nation included in that state.

spoke Italian (the language spoken in Tuscany), and the main language of many Italian nationalists of the nineteenth century was French. Even after nation-states were formed, a large measure of linguistic, religious, and ethnic diversity persisted within those states, making true cultural unity impossible. The nation is, therefore, something of a myth—an imagined community rather than an objective reality.

The ideal of the nation-state has proved almost impossible to realize. The boundaries of nations and states have never fully coincided. Patterns of human settlement are too fluid to prevent some members of a particular cultural group from living as a minority in a neighboring state. Some Poles, for example, have always lived in Germany, Spaniards in Portugal, and Italians in Switzerland. France at the time of the French Revolution probably came closest to realizing the ideal of a nation-state, claiming jurisdiction over most French people. Nevertheless, different cultural identities, such as those of the Basques in southwest France and the Flemish in the far northeast, both of whom spoke their own language, prevented the emergence of a powerful sense of national identity in all parts of France until the late nineteenth or early twentieth century.

In Britain the creation of a nation-state was a complicated process. **National consciousness**, which is a people's belief that they belong to a nation, developed earlier in England than in any other country in Europe. In the sixteenth century almost all English people spoke the same language, and they were also subject to the same common law. In 1536, however, the principality of Wales was united to the kingdom of England, thereby including two nations, the English and the Welsh, in the same state. In 1707 England and Scotland were united in a new state, the **United Kingdom** of Great Britain, and in 1801 Ireland was brought into the United Kingdom as well. Thus, the United Kingdom in the nineteenth century included four nations: the English, the Welsh, the Scots, and the Irish. In this multinational state, the task of building a British nation, as opposed to an English or a Scottish nation, has taken time. To this day, Britons are more accustomed to think of themselves as English, Welsh, or Scottish than as British.

Other peoples faced even more daunting obstacles in constructing nation-states. Many nations were subsumed within large empires, such as Hungarians and Croatians in the Austrian Empire and Greeks and Serbs in the Ottoman Empire. In those empires, nationalist movements often took the form of separatist revolts or wars of independence, in which a nationalist group attempted to break off and form a nation-state of its own. A very different situation prevailed in Germany and Italy, where people who shared some linguistic and cultural traditions lived under the control of many different states. In these cases, nationalist movements sought to unite the smaller states into a larger nation-state.

One of the great paradoxes of nationalism is that the acquisition of colonies overseas often strengthened nationalist sentiment at home. The military conquest of these lands became a source of pride for the people in the metropolis, and also gave them a sense of cultural superiority. The main source of British national pride was the rapid spread of British control over one-quarter of the world's surface during the eighteenth and nineteenth centuries. Nationalism could also promote the supremacy of one's own nation over others. The French revolutionaries who conquered a large part of the European continent in the early nineteenth century justified their expansion on the grounds that they were superior to the rest of the human race. In 1848 a fervent German nationalist declared his support for "the preponderance of the German race over most Slav races." The Italian national leader Giuseppe Mazzini (1805–1872) preferred to be called a patriot rather than a nationalist on the grounds that nationalists were imperialists who sought to encroach on the rights of other peoples.

Nationalism was often linked to liberalism during the early nineteenth century, when both movements supported revolutionary programs to realize the goal of national self-determination. Liberals believed that representative government and a limited expansion of the franchise would provide a firm foundation for the establishment

national consciousness The awareness or belief of people that they belong to a nation.

United Kingdom The name of the British state formed by the union of England and Scotland in 1707. In 1801 Ireland became part of the United Kingdom; however, after the establishment of the Irish Free State in 1922, only the six Irish counties in the northern province of Ulster remained united to Britain.

of the nation-state. The two ideologies, however, differed in emphasis. Liberalism stressed individual freedom, whereas nationalism was more concerned with political unity. At times those different ideals came into conflict with each other. The liberal doctrine of free trade, for example, ran into conflict with the doctrine of economic nationalism, which encouraged the protection of national industries.

Nationalism was just as capable of supporting conservatism as liberalism in the early nineteenth century. Because nationalists viewed the nation as having deep roots in the distant past, some of them glorified the monarchical and hierarchical political arrangements that prevailed in the Middle Ages. In 1848 conservative Prussian landlords rallied around the cause of "God, King, and Fatherland." Later in the nineteenth century, nationalism became identified almost exclusively with conservatism when the lower middle classes began to prefer the achievement of national glory, either in warfare or in imperialistic pursuits, to the establishment of individual freedom.

Culture and Ideology

The four new ideologies of the early nineteenth century were influenced by two powerful cultural traditions: scientific rationalism and romanticism. These two traditions represented sharply divergent sides of modern Western culture.

SCIENTIFIC RATIONALISM Scientific rationalism originated in the Scientific Revolution and reached its full flowering in the Enlightenment. This tradition has provided a major source of Western identity ever since the late eighteenth century. It stresses the powers of human reason and considers science superior to all other forms of knowledge. Scientific rationalism is essentially a secular tradition, in that it does not rely on theology or Christian revelation for its legitimacy. The effort to construct a science of human nature, which was central to Enlightenment thought, belongs to this tradition, while the Industrial Revolution, which involved the application of scientific knowledge to production, was one of its products.

During the nineteenth century, scientific rationalism continued to influence Western thought and action. As scientific knowledge expanded, and as more people received a scientific education, the values of science and reason were proclaimed more boldly. Scientific knowledge and an emphasis on the importance of empirical data (that which can be tested) became essential components of much social thought. The clearest statement that science was the highest form of knowledge and would lead inevitably to human progress was the secular philosophy of **positivism**.

The French philosopher Auguste Comte (1798–1857) set forth the main elements of positivism. Like many thinkers in the Enlightenment tradition, Comte argued that human society passed through a succession of historical stages, each leading to a higher level. It had already passed through two stages, the theological and the metaphysical, and it was now in the third, the positive or scientific stage. The word *positive* in this context means that which has substance or concrete reality, as opposed to that which is abstract or speculative. Comte predicted that in the final positive stage of history the accumulation of factual or scientific knowledge would enable thinkers, whom we now call sociologists, to discover the laws of human behavior and thus make possible the improvement of society. This prediction of human progress, and Comte's celebration of the liberation of knowledge from its theological shackles, had particular appeal to liberals, especially those who harbored hostility to the Roman Catholic Church.

The values of science and the belief in its inevitable advance also influenced the social thought of Karl Marx. Friedrich Engels called Marx's ideology of communism scientific socialism, in that it too offers a vision of history determined solely by positive, in this case material or economic, developments. Marxism rejects the metaphysical, idealistic world of Hegel and the theology of all Christian religion and thus fits into the same scientific tradition to which positivism and earlier Enlightenment thought belongs.

positivism The philosophy developed by Auguste Comte in the nineteenth century according to which human society passed through a series of stages, leading to the final positive stage in which the accumulation of scientific data would enable thinkers to discover the laws of human behavior and bring about the improvement of society.

 Read the Document

Auguste Comte, "Course of Positive Philosophy"

22.1

22.2

22.3

22.4

romanticism An artistic and literary movement of the late eighteenth and nineteenth centuries that involved a protest against classicism, appealed to the passions rather than the intellect, and emphasized the beauty and power of nature.

ROMANTICISM The cultural tradition that posed the greatest challenge to scientific rationalism was **romanticism**. This tradition originated as an artistic and literary movement in the late eighteenth century, but it soon developed into a more general worldview. The artists and writers who identified themselves as romantics recognized the limits of human reason in comprehending reality. Unlike scientific rationalists, they used intuition and imagination to penetrate deeper levels of being and to comprehend the entire cosmos. Romantic art, music, and literature therefore appealed to the passions rather than the intellect.

Romantics did not think of reality as being simply material, as did the positivists. For them it was also spiritual and emotional, and their purpose as writers and artists was to communicate that nonempirical dimension of reality to their audiences. Romantics also had a different view of the relationship between human beings and nature. Instead of standing outside nature and viewing it objectively, in the manner of a scientist analyzing data derived from experiments, they considered themselves part of nature and emphasized its beauty and power.

As an art form, romanticism was a protest against classicism and, in particular, the classicism that prevailed in the late eighteenth century. As we discussed in Chapter 19, classicism reflects a worldview in which the principles of orderliness and rationality prevail. Classicism is a disciplined style that demands adherence to formal rules that govern the structure and the content of literature, art, architecture, and music. By contrast, romanticism allows the artist much greater freedom. In literature the romantic protest against classicism led to the introduction of a new poetic style involving the use of imagery, symbols, and myth. One example of this style is "Rime of the Ancient Mariner" (1798) by the English poet Samuel Taylor Coleridge (1772–1834). The poem uses the sun and moon as powerful symbols in describing a nightmarish sea voyage.

Many romantic works of literature, such as the novels of the Scottish author Sir Walter Scott (1771–1832), were set in the Middle Ages, which they saw not as a dark age of superstition but as an era that fostered spiritual and artistic pursuits. To emphasize the limits of scientific rationalism, other romantics explored the exotic, the weird, the mysterious, and even the satanic elements in human nature. Mary Shelley's introspective novel, *Frankenstein* (1818), an early example of science fiction, incorporated many of these themes. The novel, which tells the story of the creation of a large, ugly monster by the idealistic Swiss scientist Victor Frankenstein, reveals the preoccupation of romantic literature with the exotic and the mysterious. Frankenstein's rejection of the monster leads this freak of nature to kill the scientist's brother, his friend, his wife, and, ultimately, Frankenstein himself. Filled with self-loathing, this creature of modern science sets off to throw himself on his own funeral pyre.

Within the visual arts, romanticism also marked a rebellion against the classicism that had dominated eighteenth-century culture. Classicism emphasized formality and symmetry in art, and it celebrated the culture of an ideal Greek and Roman past. By contrast, romantic painters depicted landscapes that evoked a mood and an emotion rather than an objective pictorial account of the surroundings. Romantic paintings sought to evoke feeling rather than to help the viewer achieve intellectual comprehension. Some of their works conveyed the power of nature while others depicted its majesty and grandeur.

Romantic music, which also appealed to the emotions, marked a similar but more gradual departure from formal classicism. The inspirational music of Ludwig van Beethoven (1770–1827), the son of a German court musician from Bonn, marked the transition from classical to romantic forms. Beethoven's early work conformed to the conventions of classical music, but some of his later compositions, which defied traditional classical harmonies, were intended to evoke an emotional response. His famous "Ode to Joy" in his ninth and final symphony remains unequaled in its ability to rouse the passions. Another early romantic composer, Franz Schubert (1797–1828), who was born in Vienna, blended classical forms with romantic themes by incorporating

View the Closer Look

Cult of the Unattainable

CASPAR DAVID FRIEDRICH, *THE WANDERER ABOVE THE SEA OF FOG* (1818) This early nineteenth-century painting of a man observing a landscape covered by fog conveys the mystery and majesty of nature, which was a main theme of romantic art. It is unclear, however, whether the man, whose back is turned to the viewer, was awestruck by what he observed or was contemplating the difficult task of achieving human mastery over nature.

Hungarian and gypsy folk music into his compositions. The emotionally powerful operas of the German composer Richard Wagner (1813–1883), many of which were set in the mythical German past, marked the height of the romantic movement in music. That style attained its greatest popularity during the second half of the nineteenth century with the lyrical symphonies and concertos of Johannes Brahms (1833–1897) in Germany and the symphonies, ballets, and operas of Peter Tchaikovsky (1840–1893) in Russia.

Romanticism, like the rational and scientific culture it rejected, had powerful political implications, leaving its mark on the ideologies of the modern world. In the early nineteenth century, romanticism appealed to many liberals because it involved a protest against the established order and emphasized the freedom of the individual. The French romantic author Victor Hugo (1802–1885), whose epic novels *The Hunchback of Notre Dame* (1831) and *Les Misérables* (1862) depicted human suffering with great compassion, identified romanticism as "liberalism in literature." For Hugo a relationship existed between liberty in art and liberty in society. Romanticism could, however, support conservatism by idealizing the traditional social and political order of the Middle Ages and the central importance of religion in society.

Romanticism has a closer association with nationalism than with any other ideology. In the most general sense romanticism invested the idea of "the nation" with mystical qualities, thus inspiring devotion to it. Romantics also had an obsessive interest in the cultural, literary, and historical roots of national identity. The German philosopher and literary critic Johann Gottfried von Herder (1744–1803), for example, promoted the study of German language, literature, and history with the explicit purpose of giving the German people a sense of national unity.

In other parts of Europe, especially in Poland and the Balkans, romantic writers and artists gave nationalists the tools necessary to construct a common culture and history of their nations. The Polish romantic composer Frédéric Chopin (1810–1849), who emigrated to Paris in 1831, inspired Polish nationalists by drawing on native Polish dances in his works for the piano. At the same time the romantic poet Adam Mickiewicz (1798–1855), another Polish exile in Paris, wrote *The Books of the Polish Nation* (1832), exalting his country as the embodiment of freedom and predicting that by its long suffering it would eventually liberate the human race.

Ideological Encounters in Europe, 1815–1848

22.2 How did those ideologies shape the political history of Europe between 1815 and 1848?

The four new ideologies of the nineteenth century—liberalism, conservatism, socialism, and nationalism—interacted in a variety of ways, sometimes reinforcing each other and at other times leading to direct and violent political conflict. During the years between 1815 and 1831 the main ideological encounters occurred between liberalism, sometimes infused with nationalism, and conservatism. In 1815, at the time of the Congress of Vienna, it appeared that conservatism would carry the day. The determination of the major European powers to suppress any signs of revolutionary activity made the future of liberalism and nationalism appear bleak. The power of the new ideologies, however, could not be contained. Liberal and nationalist revolts took place in three distinct periods: the early 1820s, 1830, and 1848. During the latter two periods the demands of workers, sometimes expressed in socialist terms, added to the ideological mixture. In all these encounters conservatives had their say, and in most cases they emerged victorious.

Liberal and Nationalist Revolts, 1820–1825

Between 1820 and 1825 a sequence of revolts in Europe revealed the explosive potential of liberalism and nationalism and the determination of conservatives to crush those ideologies. These revolts also reflected the strength of movements for national self-determination. The three most significant revolts took place in Spain, Greece, and Russia.

THE LIBERAL REVOLTS OF 1820 IN SPAIN AND PORTUGAL The earliest clash between liberalism and conservatism occurred in Spain, where liberals ran into determined opposition from their king, Ferdinand VII (r. 1808–1833). Ferdinand had been restored to power in 1814 after his forced abdication in 1808. In 1812, during the rule of Joseph Bonaparte, the Spanish *Cortes*—the representative assembly in that kingdom—had approved a liberal constitution. This constitution provided a foundation for a limited monarchy and the protection of Spanish civil liberties. In keeping with the ideas of the French Revolution, it also declared that the Spanish nation, not the king, possessed sovereignty. The tension began when King Ferdinand declared that he would not recognize this constitution. Even worse for disheartened liberals, Ferdinand decided to reestablish the Spanish Inquisition, invited exiled Jesuits to return, and refused to summon the *Cortes*. In 1820, when the Spanish Empire in the New World had already begun to collapse (see Chapter 18), liberals in Madrid, in alliance with some military officers, seized power.

This liberal revolt proved to be a test for the **Concert of Europe**, the mechanism established at the Congress of Vienna to preserve the balance of power in Europe and prevent further revolution wherever it might arise. Klemens von Metternich, the Austrian foreign minister who had been responsible for proposing this cooperation of the major powers, urged intervention in Spain. Although the British refused because they wanted to protect their trading interests with the Spanish colonies, Austria, Prussia, and Russia agreed. These conservative powers restored Ferdinand to the throne, and again he renounced the liberal constitution of 1812. The liberals not only lost this struggle, but they also suffered bitter reprisals from the government, which tortured and executed their leaders. The situation became only marginally better in 1833, when Ferdinand died and the liberal ministers of his young daughter, Queen Isabella II (r. 1833–1868), drew up another constitution. Her reign was marked by civil war, instability, and factional strife in which liberals made few substantial gains.

Shortly after the Spanish revolt of 1820, a similar rebellion based on liberal ideas took place in Portugal. The royal family had fled to Brazil during the Napoleonic wars, leaving Portugal to be governed by a regent. A group of army officers removed the regent and installed a liberal government, which proceeded to suppress the Portuguese Inquisition, confiscate church lands, and invite King John (r. 1816–1826) to return to his native land as a constitutional monarch. After the king returned in 1822, his enthusiasm for liberal government waned. His granddaughter, Maria II (r. 1826–1853), kept the liberal cause alive, relying on support from Portugal's traditional ally, Britain, but she struggled against the forces of conservatism and had only limited success.

22.1

22.2

22.3

22.4

Concert of Europe The joint efforts made by Austria, Prussia, Russia, Britain, and France during the years following the Congress of Vienna to suppress liberal and nationalist movements throughout Europe.

THE NATIONALIST REVOLT OF 1821 IN GREECE A revolt in Greece in 1821, inspired more by nationalism than liberalism, achieved greater success than did the rebellions of 1820 in Spain and Portugal. It succeeded because other members of the Concert of Europe, not just Britain, lent their support to the revolt. Greece had long been a province in the sprawling Ottoman Empire, but a nationalist movement, organized by Prince Alexander Ypsilantis (1792–1828), created a distinct Greek national identity and inspired the demand for a separate Greek state. In 1821 a series of revolts against Ottoman rule took place on the mainland of Greece and on some of the surrounding islands. These rebellions received widespread support in Europe from scholars who considered Greece the cradle of Western civilization and from religiously inspired individuals who saw this as a struggle of Christianity against Islam. Hundreds of European volunteers joined the Greek rebel forces. Thus, the insurrection became not only a liberal and national revolt, but also a broad cultural encounter between East and West. The English romantic poets George Lord Byron (1788–1824) and Percy Shelley (1792–1822) became active and passionate advocates for Greek independence, while the romantic painter Eugène Delacroix (1798–1863) depicted the horror of the Turkish massacre of the entire population of the Greek island of Chios in 1822. The link between nationalism and romanticism could not have been more explicit.

The Greek revolt placed the powers allied in the Concert of Europe in a quandary. On the one hand,

EUGÈNE DELACROIX, *THE MASSACRE AT CHIOS* (1824) In 1821 the Greeks on the Aegean Islands rebelled against their Turkish rulers, and in April 1822 Turkish reprisals reached their peak in the massacre of the inhabitants of Chios. Romantic paintings were intended to evoke feelings, in this case horror, at the genocide perpetrated by the Turks against the Greek rebels. The painting reveals the close association of romantic art with the causes of liberalism and nationalism.

they were committed to intervene on behalf of the established order to crush any nationalist or liberal revolts, and they condemned the insurrection on those grounds when it first erupted. On the other hand, they were Western rulers who identified the Ottoman Turks with everything that was alien to Christian civilization. Moreover, Russia wanted to use this opportunity to dismember its ancient enemy, the Ottoman Empire. The European powers eventually took the side of the Greek rebels. In 1827 Britain, France, and Russia threatened the Turks with military intervention if they did not agree to an armistice and grant the Greeks their independence. When the Turks refused, the combined naval forces of those three countries destroyed the fleet of the Turks' main ally, Egypt, at Navarino off the Greek coast. This naval action turned the tide in favor of the Greeks, who in 1833 finally won their independence and placed a Bavarian prince, Otto I (r. 1833–1862), on the throne. Thus, the Greek war of independence effectively ended the Concert of Europe. Originally intended to crush nationalist and liberal revolts, the Concert in this case helped one succeed.

THE DECEMBRIST REVOLT OF 1825 IN RUSSIA The least successful of the early liberal revolts took place in Russia, where a number of army officers, influenced by liberal ideas while serving in western Europe during the Napoleonic wars, staged a rebellion against the government of Tsar Nicholas I (r. 1825–1855) on the first day of his reign. The officers, together with other members of the nobility, had been meeting for almost a decade in political clubs, such as the Society of True and Faithful Sons of the Fatherland in St. Petersburg. In these societies they articulated their goals of establishing a constitutional monarchy and emancipating the serfs.

The rebels, known as **Decembrists** for the month in which their rebellion took place, could not agree on the precise form of government they wished to institute. That disagreement, coupled with a reluctance to take action at the critical moment, led to their failure. When Tsar Alexander I died suddenly in 1825, the Decembrists hoped to persuade his brother Constantine to assume the throne and establish a representative form of government. Their hopes were dashed when Constantine refused to tamper with the succession and accepted the reign of his brother Nicholas. The reactionary Nicholas had no difficulty suppressing the revolt, executing its leaders, and leaving Russian liberals to struggle against police repression for the remainder of the nineteenth century.

Decembrists Russian liberals who staged a revolt against Tsar Nicholas I on the first day of his reign in December 1825.

Liberal and Nationalist Revolts, 1830

A second cluster of early-nineteenth-century liberal and national revolts in 1830 achieved a greater measure of success than the revolts of the early 1820s. These revolutions took place in France, the kingdom of the Netherlands, and the kingdom of Poland.

THE FRENCH REVOLUTION: THE SUCCESS OF LIBERALISM The most striking triumph of liberalism in Europe during the early nineteenth century occurred in France, where a revolution took place 15 years after the final defeat of Napoleon at Waterloo. This liberal success did not come easily. During the first few years of the restored monarchy, conservatives had their way, as they did elsewhere in Europe. Louis XVIII had approved a Charter of Liberties in 1814, but he was hardly receptive to any further liberal reforms. Between 1815 and 1828 ultraroyalists dominated French politics. These reactionaries sponsored a "white terror" (so called because they displayed the white flag of the Bourbon monarchy) against liberals and Protestants. Two men nicknamed Three Slices and Four Slices, indicating the number of pieces into which they butchered their Protestant enemies, were the main instigators of this terror.

In 1824, when the conservative Charles X (r. 1824–1830) ascended the throne and took steps to strengthen the Church and the nobility, there appeared to be little hope for liberalism. Nevertheless, liberal opposition to the monarchy gained support from

CHRONOLOGY: LIBERAL AND NATIONALIST REVOLTS, 1820–1833

1820
Liberal revolt in Spain; liberal army officers seize power in Portugal.

1820

1821

1821
Beginning of Greek revolt against the Ottoman Empire.

1825
Decembrist revolt in Russia against Nicholas I.

1825

1829

1829
Liberals gain majority in French Chamber of Deputies.

1830
Revolution in Paris, Louis-Philippe I becomes king of France; Belgium becomes independent and adopts a liberal constitution; beginning of the Polish rebellion against Nicholas I of Russia.

1830

1833

1833
Greece becomes independent; Otto I becomes king.

merchants and manufacturers, as well as from soldiers who still kept the memory of Napoleon alive. Fears that Charles would claim absolute power and a serious economic crisis in 1829 helped liberals gain a majority in the Chamber of Deputies, the French legislature.

Charles then embarked upon a perilous course. In what became known as the July Ordinances he effectively undermined the principles of the 1814 Charter of Liberties. These ordinances dissolved the new Chamber of Deputies, ordered new elections under a highly restrictive franchise, and censored the press. The public reaction to this maneuver caught the king by surprise. Thousands of students and workers, liberals and republicans alike, poured onto the streets of Paris to demonstrate. Unable to restore order, the king abdicated in favor of his grandson, but the liberals offered the crown instead to the Duke of Orléans, who was crowned as Louis-Philippe I (r. 1830–1848).

Louis-Philippe accepted a revised version of the Charter of 1814 and doubled the franchise, giving the vote to middle-class merchants and industrialists. The king catered to this bourgeois constituency by encouraging economic growth and restricting noble privilege. His reign, which is often referred to as the "bourgeois monarchy," also achieved a measure of secularization when the Chamber of Deputies declared that Roman Catholicism was no longer the state religion. In keeping with liberal ideals, however, he did nothing to encourage republicanism or radical democracy, much less socialism. Efforts to depict him as the heir to the French Revolution did not persuade the bulk of the population. When the government brought the ashes of Napoleon from St. Helena to Paris, thousands of French men and women turned out to pay homage to the former emperor. Much to his disappointment, Louis-Philippe gained little political benefit from the move. France had acquired a liberal monarchy, but it stood on a precarious foundation.

THE BELGIAN REVOLUTION: THE SUCCESS OF NATIONALISM The French Revolution of 1830 triggered the outbreak of a liberal and nationalist revolution in the neighboring country of Belgium. In 1815 the Congress of Vienna had united the Austrian Netherlands and the Dutch Republic in the new Kingdom of the Netherlands. This union of the Low Countries did not work out; soon after the formation of the new kingdom, the Belgians began pressing for their independence as a nation. With a Dutchman, William I, as king and with the seat of government in Holland, the Dutch were the dominant partner in this union, a situation that caused considerable resentment in Belgium. Moreover, most Belgians were Catholics, whereas the majority of Dutch people were Protestants. With their own history and culture, Belgians thought of themselves as a separate nation. They also were more liberal than their Dutch neighbors, advocating free trade and the promotion of industry, while resenting the high tariffs imposed by the Dutch government.

The two main political parties in Belgium, the Liberals and the Clericals, joined forces to achieve national independence. When the news of the revolution in Paris reached Brussels, fighting broke out between workers and government troops. A Belgian national congress gathered to write a new constitution; when the Dutch tried to thwart the rebellion by bombarding the Belgian city of Antwerp, Britain assembled a conference of European powers to devise a settlement. The powers agreed to recognize Belgium's independence, and they arranged for a German prince, Leopold of Saxe-Coburg, uncle of the future British Queen Victoria, to become king. The Dutch, however, refused to recognize the new government, and they renewed their military attacks on Belgium. Only in 1839 did all sides accept the new political arrangement.

THE POLISH REBELLION: THE FAILURE OF NATIONALISM The French Revolution of 1830 triggered a second uprising, this one unsuccessful, in the kingdom of Poland (see **Map 22.1**). Poland had suffered many partitions at the hands of European powers during the eighteenth century, and in 1815 the Congress of Vienna had redefined its borders once again. The congress established a separate Polish kingdom, known as Congress Poland, with Warsaw as its capital and the Russian tsar, Alexander I (r. 1815–1825), as its king. The western part of Poland, the Duchy of Poznan, went to the kingdom of Prussia, while Cracow became a free city.

With a Russian king the independence of Poland was mere fiction, but Alexander had approved a liberal Polish constitution in 1815. He grew to regret this decision, and his rule as king of Poland gradually alienated Polish liberals within the national legislature, the *Sejm*. The accession of Nicholas in 1825 aggravated those tensions. An uncompromising conservative, Nicholas accused the Polish opposition of complicity with the Russian Decembrist rebels. He brought them to the brink of rebellion when he made plans to send the Polish army, together with Russian troops, to suppress the French Revolution of 1830 and prevent the Belgians from receiving their independence.

The revolt began when army cadets in the officers' school in Warsaw attacked

MAP **22.1** EUROPEAN CENTERS OF REBELLION AND REVOLUTION, 1820–1848 All these political disturbances were inspired by ideology. Why did Britain not experience a rebellion or revolution during these years?

the residence of the Grand Duke Constantine, the governor-general of Poland, and it quickly gained the support of the entire army and the urban populace. The revolt appealed to both liberals and nationalists, and it drew inspiration from a group of romantic poets who celebrated the achievements of the Polish past. The rebels established a provisional Polish government at Warsaw, but the liberal members of the *Sejm* were unwilling to enlist the peasantry in the conflict, fearful that they would rise against Polish landlords rather than the Russians. When the powers of western Europe refused to intervene on behalf of this liberal cause, Nicholas was able to crush the rebellion, abolish the *Sejm,* and deprive the kingdom of Poland of its autonomous status. Nicholas visited a terrible revenge upon the leaders of the revolt, confiscated the lands of those who had emigrated, and shut down the University of Warsaw. His brutal repression set back the cause of liberalism and nationalism in Poland for another two generations.

22.1

22.2

22.3

22.4

View the Image

The Clemency of the Russian Monster-British Cartoon, 1832

Liberal Reform in Britain, 1815–1848

The challenges that liberals faced in Britain were somewhat different from those they confronted in most other European countries. Having maintained the status quo during the era of the French Revolution, the forces of British conservatism, which bore the ideological stamp of Edmund Burke, remained formidable. At the same time, however, Britons already enjoyed many of the rights that liberals on the European continent demanded, such as freedom of the press and protection from arbitrary imprisonment. The power of the British monarchy was more limited than in almost any other European country. The ideology of liberalism, which had deep roots in British political and social philosophy, defined the political creed of many Whigs, who formed the main opposition to the ruling Conservative or Tory party after 1815.

In this relatively favorable political climate, British liberals pursued three major goals that amounted to a program for reform rather than revolution. The first was the repeal of legislation that denied political power to Catholics and "nonconformist" Protestants who did not attend the services of the Anglican Church. Liberals were opposed on principle to religious discrimination, and many of them belonged to nonconformist congregations. The Tory prime minister, the Duke of Wellington, who had defeated Napoleon at Waterloo, eventually agreed to liberal demands. The Protestant nonconformists were emancipated in 1828 and the Catholics one year later.

The second liberal cause was the expansion of the franchise, which was realized when the Whigs, who came to power in 1830, passed the Great Reform Bill of 1832. The legislation expanded the franchise to include most of the urban middle class, created a number of new parliamentary boroughs (towns that elected representatives to sit in the House of Commons) in regions where industrial growth had led to an increase in population, and established a uniform standard for the right to vote throughout the country. In keeping with the principles of liberalism, however, the bill restricted the vote to property owners. It rejected the demands of radicals for universal male suffrage and denied all women the vote.

The third liberal cause was free trade. The target of this campaign was a series of protective tariffs on the import and export of hundreds of commodities, including raw materials used in production. The most hated protective tariff was on grain (known in Britain as corn), which kept the price of basic food commodities high to protect the interests of landlords and farmers. In 1837 a group of industrialists and radical reformers formed the Anti-Corn Law League with the purpose of bringing about the repeal of the Corn Law of 1815, which greatly restricted the importation of foreign grain into Britain. This campaign against protectionism did not succeed until 1845, when the Conservative prime minister, Sir Robert Peel, brought about repeal by securing the votes of some of his own party and combining them with those of the Whigs, all of whom favored free trade. Peel took this action only after the potato famine in Ireland, which was discussed in Chapter 21, had begun to cause widespread starvation.

 Read the Document

Karl Marx on the Question of Free Trade (1848)

Chartists A British group of workers and middle-class radicals who drafted a People's Charter in 1837 demanding universal male suffrage and other political reforms.

  Read the Document

Chartist Movement: The People's Petition of 1838

Unlike the liberals, socialists and radical democrats achieved little success in Britain during the first half of the nineteenth century. In 1837 workers and middle-class radicals drew up a People's Charter, demanding universal male suffrage, annual parliaments, voting by secret ballot, equal electoral districts, the elimination of property qualifications for Members of Parliament, and the payment of salaries to those same members. These **Chartists**, as they were known, gained widespread popular support when economic conditions deteriorated, but British workers showed little inclination to take to the streets. The government's reduction of indirect taxes during the 1840s, coupled with the effective use of the police force and the strict enforcement of the criminal law, also helped prevent Britain from experiencing revolution in 1848. The price of this failure was that further liberal reforms, such as the extension of the franchise to include workers, did not take place in Britain for another two decades.

The Revolutions of 1848

Unlike Britain, almost every country on the European continent experienced revolution in 1848. The revolutions took place during a period of widespread economic discontent. European countries had suffered bad harvests in 1845 and 1846 and an economic recession in 1847, leading to a decline in the standard of living for both industrial and agricultural workers. Discontent took the form of mass protests and demonstrations,

THE MEETING ON KENNINGTON-COMMON.—FROM A DAGUERREOTYPE.

THE LAST GREAT CHARTIST RALLY IN BRITAIN, APRIL 10, 1848 Government precautions, including the appointment of special constables to handle the crowd, and rain kept the number of demonstrators in London lower than anticipated. The government ordered the leader of the movement, Feargus O'Connor, to stop the planned march to Parliament.

which increased the likelihood of violent confrontation. The revolutions of 1848 were more widespread than the revolts of the 1820s and 1830, and more people participated. These revolutions also gave more attention to both nationalist and socialist issues.

THE FRENCH REVOLUTIONS OF 1848 The first of the revolutions of 1848 took place in France, where the liberal government of Louis-Philippe faced mounting criticism. Declining economic conditions led to a series of demonstrations in Paris for the right of workers to vote and receive state assistance for their trades. When troops from the Paris National Guard fired on the demonstrators and killed 40 people, the barricades once again appeared in the streets and the rebels seized government buildings. France experienced its third revolution in 60 years. To save his regime, Louis-Philippe abdicated in favor of his grandson, but the revolutionaries abolished the monarchy and declared the Second French Republic.

The Chamber of Deputies selected a provisional government that included republicans, liberals, and radical democrats. It also included two socialists, Louis Blanc and a worker who preferred to be called by the single name of Albert. The French Revolution

CHRONOLOGY: THE REVOLUTIONS OF 1848

1848
February
Revolution in Paris.
March
Insurrection in Berlin, peasant unrest in the countryside, formation of liberal governments in Prussia and other German states; revolutions in Milan and Venice; Ferdinand II issues a new constitution in Naples.
April
Elections for a new National Assembly in France.
May
Meeting of the Frankfurt Parliament; meeting of the Prussian Assembly.

1848

June
Suppression of working-class resistance in Paris; Pan-Slav Congress in Prague; suppression of the rebellion in Prague.
October
Suppression of revolution in Vienna.
December
Election of Louis-Napoleon as president of the Second French Republic; Frankfurt Parliament issues *Declaration of the Basic Rights of the German People;* Frederick William dissolves Prussian Assembly.

1849
March
King Frederick William rejects the German crown offered by the Frankfurt Parliament.
April
Frankfurt Parliament promulgates a new constitution; Hungarian Diet proclaims Magyar independence.

1849

May–June
Fall of the liberal ministries in German states.
August
Venetian Republic surrenders to Austrian forces; suppression of the Hungarian movement for independence.

of 1848 offered the socialists their first opportunity to realize the goal of a democratic and socialist republic. Many of the 200 clubs formed in Paris at this time, some of which were exclusively female, were either republican or socialist in their orientation. The socialist agenda included not only universal male suffrage, which the government granted immediately, but also active support for unemployed workers. Blanc secured the establishment of national workshops to give the unemployed jobs on public projects. Ordinances reduced the length of the workday to 10 hours in the city and 12 hours in rural areas.

These bold socialist initiatives did not last long. By the summer the euphoria of the revolution had dissipated and the aspirations of workers had been crushed. The elections held in April 1848 to constitute a new National Assembly and write a new constitution seated an overwhelming majority of conservative monarchists and only a small minority of republicans and socialists. Resentment of the provisional government's assistance to urban workers and anger at the levying of a surtax to pay for government programs revealed the lack of broad popular support for radical political programs. Tension between the new conservative assembly and the forces of the left mounted when the government closed the workshops and sent Parisian workers either into the army or into exile in the provinces.

These newly adopted policies led to further working-class violence in Paris in June 1848. When General Louis Cavaignac, known as "the butcher," was called in to restore order, regular army troops killed at least 1,500 insurgents and sent another 4,000 into exile in French colonies. These confrontations appeared to Karl Marx to constitute class warfare, a prelude to the proletarian revolution he predicted for the future. Louis Blanc, who was implicated in these uprisings, fled to England, where Marx himself would soon arrive and spend the rest of his life.

The revolution ended with the election of Napoleon's nephew, Louis-Napoleon Bonaparte (1808–1873), as the president of the Second French Republic in December 1848. As president, Louis-Napoleon drew support from conservatives, liberals, and moderate republicans. He also benefited from the legend that his uncle had created and the nationalist sentiment it inspired. Because the first Napoleon had become emperor, even those who preferred an empire to a republic could vote for his nephew. The younger Napoleon followed in his uncle's footsteps, dissolving the National Assembly in December 1851 and proclaiming himself emperor of the French one year later. This step brought the Second Republic to an end and established the Second Empire. The new emperor called himself Napoleon III, in deference to the uncrowned Napoleon II, the son of Napoleon I who had died in 1823.

THE REVOLUTIONS OF 1848 IN GERMANY, AUSTRIA, HUNGARY, AND BOHEMIA
Before 1848, liberalism and nationalism had achieved little success in Germany. German university students, inspired by the slogan "Honor, Freedom, Fatherland," had staged a number of large rallies during the early years of the nineteenth century, but the forces of conservatism had kept them in check. The Carlsbad Decrees of 1819, intended to suppress university radicalism, inaugurated a period of severe repression throughout Germany. The only success achieved by German liberals and nationalists prior to 1848 was the establishment of the *Zollverein,* a customs union of the various German states, in 1834. Even that project, which promoted free trade within German lands, did not attract support from all liberals.

A major opportunity for the liberal cause in Germany came in 1848 in the immediate wake of the February Revolution in France. As in France, however, radical demands from democrats and socialists for universal suffrage, including equal rights for women, competed with the more moderate liberal agenda. German radicals also demanded government assistance for artisans and workers who had suffered economic hardship as a result of industrialization. In Berlin, the capital of Prussia, these discontents led radicals to barricade the streets. The protests escalated after troops fired into the crowd, killing some 250 people. The violence spread to the countryside, where peasants demanded that landlords renounce their privileges and grant them free use of their lands. In response to these pressures, King Frederick William IV summoned an assembly, elected by universal male suffrage, to write a new Prussian constitution. Other German states also yielded to liberal pressure, establishing liberal governments known as the "March ministries."

As these events were unfolding, the contagion of revolution spread to Austria, the other major German kingdom, which formed the nucleus of the sprawling Austrian Empire. News of the revolution in Paris led to demonstrations by students and workers in Vienna. An assortment of Austrian liberal aristocrats, middle-class professionals, and discontented workers demanded an end to the long rule of the conservative minister, Klemens von Metternich. In response to the demands of these groups, Emperor Ferdinand I (r. 1835–1848) summoned a constitutional assembly and installed a moderate government. A conservative Prussian observer feared that these concessions had broken "the most secure dam against the revolutionary tide."

The main difference between the revolutions of 1848 in Austria and the other German lands was that events in Vienna awakened demands of Hungarians and Czechs for national autonomy within the empire. In Hungary the nationalist leader Lajos Kossuth (1802–1894) pushed for a program of liberal reform and national autonomy. This initiative created further tensions between the Magyars and the various national minorities within the kingdom of Hungary. Similar problems arose in Bohemia, where a revolution in Prague led to demands from the Czechs for autonomy within the Austrian Empire. In June 1848 the Czech rebels hosted a Pan-Slav Congress in Prague to advance a nationalist plan for achieving unity of all Slavic people. This idealistic proposal could not be realized, for there were many distinct Slavic nationalities, each of which had a desire to establish its autonomy. In addition, there was a large German-speaking population within Bohemia that identified with other German territories in the Confederation.

The most idealistic and ambitious undertaking of the revolution in central Europe was the meeting of the Frankfurt Parliament in May 1848. Some 800 middle-class liberals, most of whom were lawyers, officials, and university professors, came from all the German states to draft a constitution for a united Germany. The parliament produced powerful speeches in support of both liberal and nationalist ideals, and in December 1848 it promulgated a *Declaration of the Basic Rights of the German People*. This document recognized the equality of all German people before the law; freedom of speech, assembly, and religion; and the right to private property. (See *Justice in History* in this chapter.) Like so many liberal assemblies, however, the Frankfurt Parliament failed to address the needs of the workers and peasants. The delegates rejected universal male suffrage as a "dangerous experiment" and refused to provide protection for artisans who were being squeezed out of work by industrialization. For these reasons, the parliament failed to win broad popular support.

In April 1849 the Frankfurt Parliament drafted a new constitution for a united Germany, which would have a hereditary "emperor of the Germans" and two houses of parliament, one of which would be elected by universal male suffrage. Austria, however, voted against the new plan; without Austrian support, the new constitution had little hope of success. The final blow to German liberal hopes came when King Frederick William of Prussia refused the Frankfurt Parliament's offer of the German crown, which he referred to as coming from the gutter and "reeking of the stench of revolution." At that point the Frankfurt Parliament disbanded and the efforts of German liberals to unite their country and give it a new constitution came to an inglorious end.

By the middle of 1849, conservative forces had triumphed in the various German territories and the Austrian Empire. In Prussia the efforts of the newly elected assembly to restrict noble privilege triggered a reaction from the conservative nobles known as Junkers. Frederick William dismissed his liberal appointees, sent troops to Berlin, and disbanded the assembly. A similar fate befell the other German states, such as Saxony, Baden, and Hanover, all of which had installed liberal governments in the early months of the revolution. In Austria Prince Alfred Windischgrätz, who had crushed

Read the Document

Metternich on the Revolutions of 1848

Justice in History

Prostitution, Corporal Punishment, and Liberalism in Germany

In March 1822 municipal authorities in the northern German city of Bremen arrested Gesche Rudolph, a poor, uneducated 25-year-old woman, for engaging in prostitution without registering with the police. Ever since the days when troops from five different European states had occupied her neighborhood, Rudolph had been selling her sexual services as her only form of livelihood. After her arrest she was not given a formal trial, but was summarily expelled from the city and banned from ever returning. Unable to earn a living through prostitution in a village outside the city, where she resided with a brother who physically abused her, Rudolph returned to the city, where she was arrested once again for prostitution. This time she was sentenced to 50 strokes of the cane and six weeks in jail, after which she was once again expelled from the city. Returning again to Bremen, she was arrested in a drunken stupor in a whorehouse and subjected to a harsher sentence of three months' imprisonment and 150 strokes before another expulsion. This pattern of arrest, punishment, expulsion, and return occurred repeatedly during the next two decades, with the number of strokes rising to 275 and the period of imprisonment to six years. During a portion of her prison sentence she was given only bread and water for nourishment.

Rudolph's arrest in 1845 at the end of a six-year imprisonment and her subsequent expulsion and return to Bremen led to the appointment of a liberal lawyer, Georg Wilhelm Gröning, to represent her. After reviewing her case and calculating that she had been whipped a total of 893 times and imprisoned for a cumulative period of 18 years, Gröning appealed her sentence to the senate of Bremen on the grounds that her treatment was not only futile but immoral. His appeal addressed an issue that went far beyond this particular case or even the prosecution of the crime of prostitution. Gröning's action raised the controversial issue of the legitimacy and value of corporal punishment, an issue that divided liberals and conservatives, who had different notions of justice.

Until the eighteenth century the penal systems of Europe had prescribed corporal punishments, administered publicly, for most crimes. These punishments ranged from whippings and

CORPORAL PUNISHMENT IN THE NINETEENTH CENTURY A man receives the sixth of 30 lashes in 1872.

placement in the stocks for minor offenses to mutilation, hanging, and decapitation for felonies. They were justified mainly on the grounds that they provided retribution for the crime and deterred the criminal and those who witnessed the punishment from committing further crimes. These two main functions of retribution and deterrence are the same functions that capital punishment allegedly serves today. Corporal punishments were also intended to humiliate the criminal by violating the integrity of the body and subjecting the prisoner to the mockery and sometimes the maltreatment of the crowd. The torture of suspects to obtain evidence also served some of these functions, although judicial torture took place during the trial, not as part of the sentence.

The entire system of corporal punishment and torture came under attack during the eighteenth century. Prussia abolished torture in 1754, and the Prussian General Law Code of 1794 eliminated many forms of corporal punishment. This code reflected the concern of Enlightenment thinkers that all such assaults on the body were inhumane and denied the moral dignity of the individual. Because most of the people who incurred corporal punishment were poor, the system also violated the liberal principle of equality before the law.

Despite these efforts at reform, the illegal administration of corporal punishment by public and private authorities continued in Prussia and the other German states. Conservatives, who had a different notion of justice from that of liberals, defended these sentences. For them any reference to natural rights and human dignity were "axioms derived from abstract philanthropic speculation." The president of the Prussian police, Julius Baron von Minutoli, expressing the conservative position on the issue, claimed that corporal punishment was more effective than imprisonment in preventing crime, as it alone could instill terror in the criminal.

It was apparent that in the case of Gesche Rudolph, 893 strokes had not instilled terror in her or deterred her from her crime. The Senate made the young woman Gröning's ward and suspended her sentence. Gröning arranged for Rudolph to live

(continued on next page)

(continued from previous page)

in the countryside under the strict supervision of a competent countryman. This compromise solution at least broke the cycle of expulsion, return, and punishment that had failed to reform her. We do not know whether she gave up her life of prostitution.

Soon after Gesche Rudolph became Gröning's ward, the liberal critics of corporal punishment in Germany celebrated a victory. King Frederick William IV of Prussia formally abolished the practice in May 1848. Shortly thereafter the Frankfurt Parliament included freedom from physical punishment by the state in its *Declaration of the Basic Rights of the German People*. Most German states and municipalities, including Bremen, wrote this right into law in 1849. The failure of the Frankfurt Parliament, however, and the more general failure of liberalism in Germany after 1849 led to a strong conservative campaign to reinstate corporal punishment in the 1850s. They succeeded only in maintaining corporal punishment within the family, on manorial estates, and in the prisons. Liberalism had not succeeded in completely establishing its standard of justice, but it did end exposure to public shame as a punishment for crime.

For Discussion

1. Why did liberals object to corporal punishment?
2. In addition to inflicting physical pain, corporal punishment produces social shame. What is the difference between social shame and legal guilt? In what ways does shame still play a role in punishments today?

Taking It Further

Evans, Richard. *Tales from the German Underworld: Crime and Punishment in the Nineteenth Century*. 1998. Provides a full account of the prosecution of Gesche Rudolph.

the Czech rebels in June, dispersed the rebels in Vienna in October. When Hungary proclaimed its independence from the empire in April 1849, Austrian and Russian forces marched on the country and crushed the movement.

THE REVOLUTIONS OF 1848 IN ITALY The revolutions of 1848 also spread to Austrian possessions in the northern Italian territories of Lombardy and Venetia. In Milan, the main city in Lombardy, revolutionary developments followed the same pattern as those in Paris, Berlin, and Vienna. When the barricades went up, some of the Milanese insurgents used medieval pikes stolen from the opera house to fight off Austrian troops. Their success triggered rebellions in other towns in Lombardy, in Venice, and in the southern Kingdom of the Two Sicilies. In that kingdom the Spanish Bourbon king, Ferdinand II (r. 1830–1859), after suppressing a republican revolt in January, was forced to grant a liberal constitution. The spread of these revolts inspired the hope of unifying all Italian people in one nation-state.

This Italian nationalist dream had originated among some liberals and republicans during the first half of the nineteenth century. Its most articulate proponent was Giuseppe Mazzini, a revolutionary from Genoa who envisioned the establishment of a united Italian republic through direct popular action. In 1831 Mazzini founded Italy's first organized political party, Young Italy, which pledged to realize national unification, democracy, and greater social equality. Mazzini combined a passionate commitment to the ideals of liberalism, republicanism, and nationalism.

Yet in 1848 an Italian prince, not Mazzini or Young Italy, took the first steps toward Italian unification. King Charles Albert ruled Piedmont-Sardinia, the most economically advanced of the Italian states. In 1848 his army, which included volunteers from various parts of Italy, marched into Lombardy and defeated Austrian forces. Instead of moving forward against Austria, however, Charles Albert decided to consolidate his gains, hoping to annex Lombardy to his own kingdom. This decision alienated republicans in Lombardy and in other parts of Italy. The rulers of the other Italian states feared that Charles Albert's main goal was to expand the limits of his own kingdom at their expense. By August 1848 the military tide had turned. Fresh Austrian troops defeated the Italian nationalists outside Milan. The people of that city turned against Charles Albert, forcing him to return to his own capital of Turin. The Italian revolutions of 1848 had suffered a complete defeat.

THE FAILURE OF THE REVOLUTIONS OF 1848 The revolutions of 1848 in France, Germany, the Austrian Empire, and Italy resulted in victory for conservatives and defeat for liberals, nationalists, and socialists. All the liberal constitutions passed during the early phase of the revolutions were eventually repealed or withdrawn. The high hopes of national unity in Germany, Italy, and Hungary were dashed. Workers who built the barricades in the hope of achieving improvements in their working conditions gained little from their efforts.

The revolutions failed because of divisions among the different groups that began the revolutions, particularly the split between the liberals who formulated the original goals of the revolution and the lower-class participants who took to the streets. Liberals used the support of the masses to bring down the governments they opposed, but their ideological opposition to broad-based political movements and their fear of further disorder sapped their revolutionary fervor. Divisions also emerged between liberals and nationalists, whose goals of national self-determination required different strategies from those of the liberals who supported individual freedom.

National Unification in Europe and America, 1848–1871

| 22.3 | How did liberal and conservative leaders use the ideology of nationalism to form nation-states? |

Prior to 1848 the forces of nationalism, especially when combined with those of liberalism, had little to show for their efforts. Besides the Greek rebellion of 1821, which succeeded largely because of international opposition to the Turks, the only successful nationalist revolution in Europe took place in Belgium. Both of these nationalist movements were secessionist in that they involved the separation of smaller states from larger empires. Efforts in 1848 to form nations by combining smaller states and territories, as in Italy and Germany, or by uniting all Slavic people, as proposed at the Pan-Slav Congress, had failed. Between 1848 and 1871, however, movements for national unification succeeded in Italy, Germany, and the United States, each in a different way. In the vast Austrian Empire a different type of unity was achieved, but it did little to promote the cause of nationalism.

Italian Unification: Building a Fragile Nation-State

The great project of Italian nationalists, the unification of Italy, faced formidable obstacles. Austrian military control over the northern territories, which had thwarted the nationalist movement of 1848, meant that national unification would not be achieved peacefully. The dramatic economic disparities between the prosperous north and the much poorer south posed a challenge to any plan for economic integration. A long tradition of local autonomy within the kingdoms, states, and principalities made submission to a strong central government unappealing. The unique status of the papacy, which controlled its own territory and which influenced the decisions of many other states, served as another challenge. Despite these obstacles, however, the dream of a resurgence of Italian power, reviving the achievements of ancient Rome, had great emotive appeal. Hatred of foreigners who controlled Italian territory, which dated back to the fifteenth century, gave further impetus to the nationalist movement.

The main question for Italian nationalism after the failure of 1848 was who could provide effective leadership of the movement. It stood to reason that Piedmont-Sardinia, the strongest and most prosperous Italian kingdom, would be central to that undertaking. Unfortunately its king, Victor Emmanuel II (r. 1849–1861), was more known for his hunting, his carousing, and his affair with a teenage mistress than his statesmanship. Victor Emmanuel did, however, appoint a nobleman with liberal leanings, Count Camillo di Cavour (1810–1861), as his prime minister. Cavour displayed many of the characteristics of nineteenth-century liberalism. He favored a constitutional monarchy, the restriction of clerical privilege and influence, and the development of a capitalist and industrial economy. He was deeply committed to the unification of the Italian peninsula, but only under Piedmontese leadership, and preferably as a federation of states. In many ways, Cavour was the antithesis of the republican Mazzini, the central figure in Italian unification. Mazzini's idealism and romanticism led him to think of national unification as a moral force that would lead to the establishment of a democratic republic, which would then undertake an extensive program of social reform. Mazzini often wore black, claiming that he was in mourning for the unrealized cause of unification.

Mazzini's strategy for national unification involved a succession of uprisings and invasions. Cavour, however, adopted a diplomatic course of action intended to gain the military assistance of France against Austria. In 1859 French and Piedmontese forces defeated the Austrians at Magenta and Solferino and drove them out of Lombardy. One year later Napoleon III signed the Treaty of Turin with Cavour, allowing Piedmont-Sardinia to annex Tuscany, Parma, Modena, and the Romagna, while ceding to France the Italian territories of Savoy and Nice. This treaty resulted in the unification of all of northern and central Italy except Venetia in the northeast and the Papal States in the center of the peninsula (see **Map 22.2**).

MAP **22.2** THE UNIFICATION OF ITALY, 1859–1870 The main steps to unification took place in 1860, when Piedmont-Sardinia acquired Tuscany, Parma, Modena, and the Romagna and when Garibaldi seized control of the Kingdom of the Two Sicilies in the name of King Victor Emmanuel of Piedmont-Sardinia. Who was most responsible for achieving Italian unification?

Mafia Organizations of armed men who took control of local politics and the economy in late nineteenth-century Sicily.

The main focus of unification efforts now turned to the Kingdom of the Two Sicilies in the south. A rebellion against the Bourbon monarch Francis II, protesting new taxes and the high price of bread, had taken place there in 1860. At that point the third figure in the story of Italian unification, the militant republican adventurer Giuseppe Garibaldi (1807–1882), intervened with decisive force. Garibaldi, who was born in Nice and spoke French rather than Italian as his main language, was determined no less than Cavour and Mazzini to drive all foreigners out of Italy and achieve its unification. Originally a supporter of Mazzini's republican goals, Garibaldi gave his support in the 1860s for Italian unification within the framework of a monarchy. A charismatic military leader, Garibaldi put together an army of volunteers, known as the Red Shirts for their colorful makeshift uniforms. In 1860 he landed in Sicily with an army of 1,000 men, took the main Sicilian city of Palermo, and established a dictatorship on behalf of King Victor Emmanuel. Garibaldi then landed on the mainland and took Naples. Shortly thereafter the people of Naples, Sicily, and most of the Papal States voted their support for union with Piedmont-Sardinia. In March 1861 the king of Sardinia assumed the title of King Victor Emmanuel of Italy (r. 1861–1878). Complete unification was achieved when Austria ceded Venetia to Italy in 1866 and when French troops, which had been protecting a portion of the Papal States, withdrew from Rome in 1870.

The achievement of Italian unification did not fully realize the lofty nationalist goals of creating a culturally unified people or a powerful central state. Economic differences between northern and southern Italy became even greater after unification than before. The overwhelming majority of the people continued to speak their local dialects or even French rather than Italian. Traditions of local political autonomy and resentment against the concentration of wealth in the north retarded the development of loyalty to the new Italian state and inspired a series of bloody rebellions in the former Kingdom of the Two Sicilies during the 1870s and 1880s.

The widespread practice of banditry in the southern mainland aggravated this instability. Bandits were peasants who, in the hope of preserving a world that appeared to be vanishing, swept through towns, opened jails, stole from the wealthy, and sacked their houses. Closely related to banditry was the growth in Sicily of the **Mafia**, organizations of armed men who took control of local politics and the economy. The Mafia originated during the struggle for unification in the 1860s and strengthened their position in Sicily once the country had been unified. Their power, the prevalence of banditry, and the enduring strength of Italian loyalty to the local community all made it difficult for the new Italian state to flourish. The movement for national unification had driven the French and the Austrians out of the peninsula, but it had failed to create a model nation-state.

GIUSEPPE GARIBALDI The uniform Garibaldi is wearing was derived from his days as a guerilla fighting in the civil war in Uruguay (1842–1846). Garibaldi also spent two years in asylum in the United States.

German Unification: Conservative Nation-Building

Like Italy, Germany experienced a successful movement for national unification after the disappointments of 1848. The German movement, like the Italian, benefited from the actions of crafty statesmen and the decisions made by other states. Unlike Italy, however, Germany achieved unification under the direction of highly conservative rather than liberal forces.

The kingdom of Prussia, with its largely German-speaking population, its wealth, and its strong army, assumed leadership of the nationalist movement. The key figure in this process was Count Otto von Bismarck (1815–1898), a lawyer and bureaucrat from an old Junker family whom King William I of Prussia appointed as his prime minister in 1862. By birth, training, and instinct, Bismarck was an inflexible conservative, determined to preserve and strengthen the Prussian nobility and monarchy and make the Prussian state strong and powerful. To achieve his goals, Bismarck did not hesitate to make alliances with any political party, including the liberals. This subordination of political means to their ends, and Bismarck's willingness to use whatever tactics were necessary, regardless of any moral considerations, made him a proponent of *Realpolitik*, the adoption of political tactics solely on the basis of their realistic chances of success.

Bismarck pursued the goal of national unification through the exercise of raw military and political power. "The great questions of the day," he said in 1862, "will not be settled by speeches and majority decisions—that was the error of 1848 and 1849—but by iron and blood." Bismarck did not share the romantic devotion of other German nationalists to the Fatherland or their desire to have a state that embodied the spirit of the German people. His determination to achieve German national unification became synonymous with his goal of strengthening the Prussian state. This commitment to the supremacy of Prussia within a united Germany explained his steadfast exclusion of the other great German power, Austria, from his plans for national unification.

Bismarck achieved German unification mainly through Prussian success in three wars (see **Map 22.3**). The first, a war against Denmark in 1864, gave Prussia and Austria joint control of the Danish duchies of Schleswig and Holstein, which had large German-speaking populations. The second war, the Austro-Prussian War of 1866, resulted in the formation of a new union of 22 German states, the North German Confederation. This new political structure replaced the German Confederation, the loose association of 39 states, including Austria, established in 1815. The North German Confederation had a central legislature, the *Reichstag*. The king of Prussia became its president and Bismarck its chancellor. Most significantly, it did not include Austria.

The third war, which completed the unification of Germany, was the Franco-Prussian War of 1870–1871. This conflict began when Napoleon III, the French emperor, challenged Prussian efforts to place a member of the Prussian royal family on the vacant Spanish throne. Bismarck welcomed this opportunity to take on the French, who controlled German-speaking territories on their eastern frontier and who had cultivated alliances with the southern German states. Bismarck played his diplomatic cards brilliantly, guaranteeing that the Russians, Austrians, and British would not support France. He then used the army that he had modernized to invade France and seize the towns of Metz and Sedan. The capture of Napoleon III during this military offensive precipitated the end of France's Second Empire and the establishment of the Third French Republic in September 1870.

As a result of its victory over France, Prussia annexed the predominantly German-speaking territories of Alsace and Lorraine. Much more important, the war led to the proclamation of the German Empire, with William I of Prussia as emperor. The empire, which included many German states, was formally a federation, just like the North German Confederation that preceded it. In practice, however, Prussia

  Read the Document

A Letter from Otto von Bismarck (1866)

Realpolitik The adoption of political tactics based solely on their realistic chances of success.

MAP **22.3** THE UNIFICATION OF GERMANY, 1866–1871 Prussia assumed leadership in uniting all German territories except Austria. Prussia was responsible for the formation of the North German Confederation in 1866 and the German Empire in 1871. Why was Austria not included in a united Germany?

View the Map

The German Empire

dominated this political structure, and the new German imperial government, just like that of Prussia, was highly autocratic. The government won the support of the middle class by adopting policies supporting free trade, but the ideologies that the imperial government promoted were those of conservatism and nationalism, which encouraged devotion to "God, King, and Fatherland."

Unification in the United States: Creating a Nation of Nations

At the same time that Italy and Germany were achieving national unification by piecing together disparate kingdoms, provinces, and territories, the United States of America engaged in a process of territorial expansion that brought lands acquired by purchase or conquest into the union as states. This process of unification, which proceeded in a piecemeal fashion, took much longer than the unifications of Italy and Germany in the 1860s. It included the annexation of Florida in 1819 and the admission of Texas,

PROCLAMATION OF THE GERMAN EMPIRE IN THE HALL OF MIRRORS AT VERSAILLES, JANUARY 21, 1871 King William I of Prussia, standing on the dais, is being crowned emperor of Germany. At the center of the picture, dressed in a white uniform jacket, is Otto von Bismarck, the person most responsible for the unification of all German territory in one empire.

an independent republic for nine years, to the union in 1845. After establishing its independence from Mexico in 1846, California joined the union in 1850. This process of gradual unification did not end until 1912, when New Mexico and Arizona, the last territories in the contiguous 48 states, were admitted to the union.

The great test of American unity came during the 1860s, when 11 southern states, committed to the preservation of the economic system of slavery, and determined that it should be extended into new territories acquired by the federal government, seceded from the union and formed a confederation of their own. The issue of slavery had helped to polarize North and South, creating deep cultural and ideological divisions that made the goal of national unity appear remote. The constitutional issue underlying the Civil War was the preservation of the union. In a famous speech made in 1858, Abraham Lincoln, who became president in 1861, declared that "a house divided against itself cannot stand . . . this government cannot endure permanently half slave and half free." When the war ended and slavery was abolished, that union was not only preserved but strengthened. Amendments to the U.S. Constitution provided for equal protection of all citizens under the law. The South, which had its own regional economy, was integrated into the increasingly commercial and industrial North. Gradually, the people of the United States began to think of themselves as a united people, drawn from many different nations of the world. The United States became "a nation of nations."

Nationalism in Eastern Europe: Preserving Multinational Empires

The national unifications that took place in Germany and Italy formed part of a *western* European pattern in which the main units of political organization would become nation-states. Ethnic minorities would always live within the boundaries of these states, but the states would encourage the growth of national consciousness among all their citizens. In France, Britain, and Spain, all of which achieved national unification by the beginning of the nineteenth century, the state played a central role in this process. Minority populations within these large western European states have occasionally threatened to establish a separate political identity as nations. However, with the one notable exception of Ireland, the southern portion of which became independent of Britain in the twentieth century, the large states of western Europe have maintained their unity and promoted nationalist sentiment to sustain it.

In *eastern* Europe a very different pattern prevailed, especially in the Austrian and Russian Empires. Instead of becoming unified nation-states, these two empires remained large, multinational political formations, embracing many different nationalities. This pattern was most obvious in the large, sprawling Austrian Empire, which encompassed no fewer than 20 different ethnic groups, each of which thought of itself as a nation (see **Map 22.4**). The largest of these nationalities were the Germans in Austria and the Bohemians and the Magyars in Hungary, but the Czechs, Slovaks, Poles, Slovenes, Croats, Romanians, Ukrainians, and Italians (before 1866) all formed sizable minority populations. Map 22.4 illustrates this diversity. The various nationalities within the empire had little in common except loyalty to the Austrian emperor, who defended the Catholic faith and the privileges of the nobility. National unification of the empire presented a much more formidable task than those that confronted Cavour and Bismarck.

The ideology of nationalism threatened to tear apart this precariously unified empire. It awakened demands of Hungarians, Czechs, and others for national autonomy and also spawned a movement for the national unity of all Slavs. The emperor, Francis Joseph (r. 1848–1916), recognized the danger of nationalist ideology. He also feared that liberalism, which was often linked to nationalism, would at the same time

MAP **22.4** NATIONALITIES WITHIN THE AUSTRIAN EMPIRE The large number of different nationalities within the Austrian Empire made it impossible to accommodate the demands of all nationalities for their own state. In what way did the Austrian Emperor Francis Joseph differ from Bismarck in his attitude toward the ideology of nationalism?

undermine his authority, which he had reasserted with a vengeance after the failure of the revolutions of 1848. He therefore repressed these nationalist aspirations at every turn. This policy had disastrous consequences for the future history of Europe, as Slavic nationalism and separatism have remained a source of political instability in southeastern Europe until the present day.

During this volatile period Francis Joseph made only one major concession to nationalist sentiment within his sprawling empire. In 1867 he agreed to create the Dual Monarchy of Austria-Hungary, in which he would be both king of Hungary and emperor of Austria. Each monarchy would have its own parliament and bureaucracy, although matters of foreign policy and finance would be handled in Vienna. This *Ausgleich* (settlement) represented a concession to the Magyars, the dominant ethnic group in Hungary and the second largest nationality in the empire. It gave very little, however, to all the other nationalities within the two kingdoms of Austria and Hungary. The *Ausgleich* officially recognized the equality of all nationalities within the Dual Monarchy and allowed schooling to be conducted in the local language, but it permitted only Germans in Austria and Magyars in Hungary to acquire their own political identity. Instead of a unified nation-state, the emperor now presided over two multinational monarchies.

International Conflict and Domestic Politics, 1853–1871

22.4 How did warfare lead to political change in Russia and France between 1850 and 1871?

Between 1853 and 1871 two wars between European powers, one on the boundaries of the West and the other at its center, had a significant effect on domestic politics. The Crimean War of 1853–1856 led to a reluctant adoption of liberal reforms in Russia, while the Franco-Prussian War of 1870–1871 set back the cause of both liberalism and socialism in France for the remainder of the nineteenth century.

Russia and the Crimean War, 1853–1856

The Crimean War was the direct result of Russian imperial expansion. It began when Russia occupied the principalities of Moldavia and Wallachia (present-day Romania) in the Ottoman Empire to gain access to the Straits of Constantinople. Russians justified this incursion by claiming they were protecting Orthodox Christians in the Balkans from their Muslim Turkish oppressors. They also claimed that they were promoting the national unity of all Slavic people under Russian auspices. This Russian version of Pan-Slavism was, in effect, an extreme form of Russian imperialism that sought to curb the nationalist aspirations of individual Slavic minorities.

When Russia occupied Moldavia and Wallachia, the Turks responded by declaring war on Russia. Britain joined the conflict on the side of the Turks, ostensibly to preserve the balance of power in Europe, but also to prevent Russia from invading India, Britain's most important colony. The French joined the British, and both powers sent large armies to begin a siege of the port of Sebastopol on the Black Sea.

The poorly trained British forces, commanded by officers who had purchased their commissions and who had no sound knowledge of military tactics, suffered staggering losses, more of them from disease than from battle. The most senseless episode of the war occurred when a British cavalry unit, the Light Brigade, rode into a deep valley near Balaklava, only to be cut down by Russian artillery perched on the surrounding hills.

Read the Document

Emancipation Manifesto (1861)

Nevertheless, Britain, France, and Turkey, together with Piedmont-Sardinia, which entered the war in 1855, prevailed, and Russia suffered its most humiliating defeat of the nineteenth century. The defeat contributed to a crisis that led to a number of liberal reforms during the rule of Tsar Alexander II (1855–1881). Alexander, an indecisive man who had inherited the throne in the middle of the Crimean War, was hardly a liberal (he once referred to the French system of government as "vile"), but he did yield to mounting liberal pressure to emancipate 50 million serfs in 1861. Alexander also established elected local assemblies in which 40 percent of peasants had the vote, implemented a new judicial system, and instituted educational reforms.

France and the Franco-Prussian War, 1870–1871

The defeat of France in the Franco-Prussian War of 1870–1871 had a negative effect on the fortunes of both liberalism and socialism in France. When Napoleon III established the Second Empire in 1852, he tried to mask his usurpation of power by preserving the tradition of universal male suffrage and by submitting his rule to popular ratification. During the 1860s his government became known as "the Liberal Empire," a strange mixture of conservatism, liberalism, and nationalism. "The little Napoleon" gradually allowed a semblance of real parliamentary government, relaxed the censorship of the press, and encouraged industrial development. To this mixture he added a strong dose of nationalist sentiment by evoking the memory of his uncle, Napoleon I.

CHRONOLOGY: FRENCH POLITICS, 1848–1871

1848
February 25
Establishment of the Second Republic.
December
Election of Louis-Napoleon as president of the Second Republic.

1851
December 2
Louis Napoleon dissolves the National Assembly.

1852
November
Establishment of the Second Empire under Napoleon III.

1870
July 19
Beginning of the Franco-Prussian War.
September 2
Surrender of Napoleon III to Prussia at Sedan.
September 4
End of the Second Empire and proclamation of the Third Republic.

1871
February
National Assembly meets at Bordeaux.
March
Rising of the Paris Commune.
May 10
End of the Franco-Prussian War.
May 21–27
"Bloody Week"; suppression of the Paris Commune.

EXECUTION OF PARIS COMMUNARDS, MAY 1871 Troops of the provisional French government killed at least 25,000 Parisians during the uprising.

Military defeat, however, destroyed the regime of Napoleon III. The emperor himself was taken captive at the Battle of Sedan—a personal and national humiliation. The Second Empire collapsed. The establishment of the Third Republic in September 1870 led to a major ideological shift in French politics. The following January Adolphe Thiers (1797–1877), a veteran French statesman who hoped to establish a conservative republican regime or possibly a restoration of the monarchy, negotiated an armistice with Bismarck. This prospect gained strength when elections to a new National Assembly returned a majority of monarchists. The National Assembly then elected Thiers as president of a provisional government.

The provisional government was determined to assert its authority over the entire French nation. In particular, it wanted to curb the independence of the city of Paris. Parisians, however, were just as determined to carry on the struggle against Prussia and keep alive the French radical tradition that had flourished in the city in 1792 and again in 1848. The socialist and republican ideals of the new Paris Commune, coupled with its determination to preserve the independence of the city, culminated in the bloodshed described at the beginning of this chapter. The crushing of the Commune marked a bitter defeat for the forces of French socialism and radicalism. The Third French Republic endured, but its ideological foundation was conservative nationalism, not liberalism or socialism.

View the Map

The Paris Commune

CONCLUSION

The Ideological Transformation of the West

The ideological encounters that took place between 1815 and 1871 resulted in significant changes in the political cultures of the West. As the early nineteenth-century ideologies of liberalism, conservatism, socialism, and nationalism played out in political movements and revolutions, the people who subscribed to these ideologies often redefined their political objectives. Many British and French socialists, for example, recognizing the necessity of assistance from liberals, abandoned their call for creating a classless society and sought instead to increase wages and improve working conditions of the lower classes. The demands of socialists for greater economic equality pressured liberals to accept the need for more state intervention in the economy. The realities of conservative politics led liberal nationalists in Germany and Italy to accept newly formed nation-states that were more authoritarian than they had originally hoped to establish. Recognizing the strength of the ideologies to which they were opposed, conservative rulers such as Emperor Napoleon III and Tsar Alexander II agreed to adopt liberal reforms. Liberals, conservatives, socialists, and nationalists would continue to modify and adjust their political and ideological positions during the period of mass politics, which began in 1870 and which will be the subject of the next chapter.

The Western ideologies that underwent this process of adaptation and modification had a broad influence on world history. In the twentieth century, three of the four ideologies discussed in this chapter have inspired political change in parts of the world that lie outside the geographical and cultural boundaries of the West. Liberalism has provided the language for movements seeking to establish fundamental civil liberties in India, Japan, and several African countries. In its radical communist form, socialism inspired revolutions in Russia, a country that for many centuries had straddled the boundary between East and West, and in China. Nationalism has revealed its explosive potential in countries as diverse as Indonesia, Thailand, and the Republic of the Congo. Ever since the nineteenth century, Western ideologies have demonstrated a capacity both to shape and to adapt to a variety of political and social circumstances.

MAKING CONNECTIONS

1. Why did liberals and socialists, both of whom opposed conservatives, disagree with each other?
2. How did romanticism provide support for liberalism, nationalism, and conservatism?
3. Why did the revolutions of 1848 fail?
4. Why did the pattern of national unification succeed in western Europe and America but fail in eastern Europe?

TAKING IT FURTHER

For suggested readings see page R-1.

Chapter Review

New Ideologies in the Early Nineteenth Century

22.1 What were the main features of the four new ideologies of the early nineteenth century?

Establishing and protecting individual rights and freedoms, like that of the press and religion, was the primary focus of liberalism in the nineteenth century. Conservatism aimed to preserve the monarchies, aristocracies, and other hereditary rights against liberal movements, and socialism sought to reduce power and economic inequalities by allowing the community ownership of all means of production. Finally, nationalism is the belief that the unique political institutions and interests of a nation should be defended and promoted at all costs.

Ideological Encounters in Europe, 1815–1848

22.2 How did those ideologies shape the political history of Europe between 1815 and 1848?

Revolutions in European countries in the 1820s, 1830, and 1848 revealed both the potential of liberalism and nationalism and the determination of conservatives to overcome them. These revolutions achieved varying degrees of success, but in many states, especially Germany and Austria, liberal gains achieved early in the revolutions of 1848 were reversed. Ideological divisions between liberals and socialists contributed to the failure of these movements

National Unification in Europe and America, 1848–1871

22.3 How did liberal and conservative leaders use the ideology of nationalism to form nation-states?

Italian advocates of national unification appealed to a desire to revive the power of ancient Rome and to expel foreigners from their country. Bismarck achieved German unity mainly by political and military force, but the German Empire established in 1871 won conservative support from German nationalists by appealing to support for the German Fatherland. The United States cultivated a common American nationality among immigrants from other nations and by integrating the Southern states into the national economy after the Civil War. The Austrian Empire appeased Hungarian nationalist sentiment by creating the Dual Monarchy but prevented other ethnic minorities within the Austrian Empire from realizing their nationalist goals.

International Conflict and Domestic Politics, 1853–1871

22.4 How did warfare lead to political change in Russia and France between 1850 and 1871?

Russia's defeat in the Crimean War contributed to a political crisis that led Tsar Alexander II to adopt certain liberal reforms, including freeing the serfs and establishing elected assemblies in the localities. In France, conservative forces triumphed when Napoleon III was captured and defeated during the Franco-Prussian War. The collapse of his empire, which had made concessions to both nationalist and liberal groups, and the institution of a conservative republican regime defeated the forces of socialism and radicalism.

Chapter Time Line

1821 Greek revolt. — 1821

1825 — **1825** Decembrist revolt in Russia.

1830 Revolution in France. — 1830

1832 — **1832** Great Reform Bill in Britain.

1848 Revolutions in France, Germany, Italy, and Austria. — 1848

1852 — **1852** Establishment of the Second French Empire.

1866 Formation of the North German Confederation. — 1866

1870–1871 — **1870–1871** Franco-Prussian War.

1871 Rising of the Paris Commune. — 1871

23 The Coming of Mass Politics, 1870–1914

I n the spring of 1881, a harrowing scene took place in St. Petersburg, capital of the Russian Empire. A 28-year-old woman, Sofia Perovskaia, was scheduled to be executed for her part in the assassination of Tsar Alexander II. Although born into wealth and privilege, Perovskaia had joined the revolutionary socialist movement. She became a leader of the People's Will, a small revolutionary group that sought to topple the tsarist regime through sabotage and assassination. On March 1, 1881, six People's Will members stationed themselves along the streets of St. Petersburg. At Perovskaia's signal, they released their bombs and assassinated one of the most powerful men in Europe.

THE EXECUTION OF THE PEOPLE'S WILL Condemned to hang because of their role in the assassination of Tsar Alexander II, members of the revolutionary terrorist group the People's Will mount the scaffold on April 15, 1881.

LEARNING OBJECTIVES

23.1 ((•

What developments transformed Western economies and social life after 1870?

23.2 ((•

How did Western ruling classes respond to the new mass politics?

23.3 ((•

What forms did mass politics assume during this era?

23.4 ((•

How did the emergence of feminism in this period demonstrate the potential and the limits of political change?

((• Listen to Chapter 23 on MyHistoryLab

⊙ Watch the Video Series on MyHistoryLab

**Learn about some key topics related to this chapter with the *MyHistoryLab Video Series:
Key Topics in Western Civilization***

The assassins, however, were quickly arrested and sentenced to death. On the day of Perovskaia's execution, she mounted the scaffold calmly, but when the noose was placed around her neck, she grabbed hold of the platform below with her feet. It took the strength of two men to pry her feet loose so that she could hang.

The image of Sofia Perovskaia clinging to the platform with her bare feet while her executioners strained to push her to her death captures the ferocity of political struggle in Europe at the end of the nineteenth century. As we discussed in Chapter 22, ideological conflicts among liberals, conservatives, and socialists shaped the political culture of the West in the nineteenth century. These conflicts intensified and widened after 1870. The economic and social changes associated with the Industrial Revolution helped to create **mass politics**—new national political cultures characterized by the participation of men (but not yet women) outside the upper and middle classes. As industrialization spread across Europe, individuals and groups traditionally excluded from power fought for a voice in national political affairs. But, like Sofia Perovskaia's executioners, the governing classes often struggled to pry newcomers off the platform of political power—and they often succeeded. Examination of these encounters answers a key question:

mass politics A political culture characterized by the participation of non-elites.

How did the new mass politics reshape definitions of the West by the beginning of the century?

Economic Transformation

23.1 What developments transformed Western economies and social life after 1870?

Three economic developments helped shape Western actions and attitudes between 1870 and 1914: the economic depression that began in 1873, the expansion and transformation of the Industrial Revolution, and accelerated urbanization and immigration. The violent social encounters often produced by these developments helped transform the political structures and ideologies of the West.

Economic Depression and Industrial Expansion

In the 1870s, Europe's economy tilted downward—prices, interest rates, and profits all fell and remained low in many regions until the mid-1890s. Agriculture was hit hardest. By the 1890s, the price of wheat was only one-third of what it had been in the 1860s. Farmers across Europe found it difficult to make a living. Industry and commerce fared better than agriculture but declining prices for manufactured goods—often by as much as 50 percent—squeezed business profit margins.

What caused this depression? Ironically, the answer rests with the success of the Industrial Revolution. As we saw in Chapter 21, between 1760 and 1860 economic production changed dramatically, first in Britain, then in parts of western Europe. After 1860, the Industrial Revolution spread across the European continent. Railways increasingly linked Europe's diverse regions into a single economic

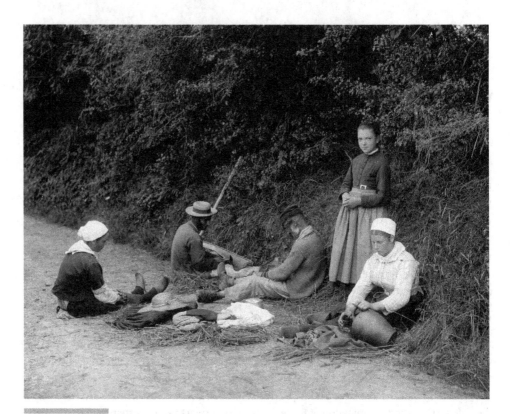

PRE-INDUSTRIAL CONTINUITIES This photograph of a French peasant family taking time off for a meal highlights the patchy nature of industrialization even in western Europe. Not until the 1880s and 1890s did many rural regions come within the embrace of the modern industrial economy.

network. This development opened European markets to cheap grain from the American Midwest and Ukraine—and so sent much of Europe's farming sector into economic crisis.

The spread of the Industrial Revolution is also linked to the economic depression more generally: As regions and nations industrialized, they produced more goods; yet, many industrial workers, agricultural laborers, and landowning peasants had little money to spend on industrial products. In other words, by the 1870s, a mass consumer society had not yet emerged to match the mass production created by industrialization. As production exceeded consumption, long-term agricultural and industrial depression resulted.

Industrial Change

The expansion of industrialization across Europe and the United States coincided with a new phase in the Industrial Revolution—what some historians even call the **Second Industrial Revolution**. Three factors made this industrial era different from what had come before: first, the emergence of important new industries as a result of major scientific and technical innovations; second, greater complexity in industrial organization; and third, important shifts in the marketing of industrial goods.

Second Industrial Revolution A new phase in the industrialization of the processes of production and consumption, which was underway in Europe in the 1870s.

While textiles and coal had dominated the first Industrial Revolution, the Second Industrial Revolution rested on chemicals, steel, and electricity. The development of synthetic dyes and new techniques for refining petroleum made the chemical and oil industries into important sectors of the West's economy in the decades after 1870. Similarly, a series of new technologies and techniques enabled manufacturers to produce steel cheaply and in huge quantities, which in turn expanded production in railroads and shipbuilding.

The new steel industry also transformed building construction. Combined with the inventions of the mechanical crane and stonecutter, the new steel technologies allowed builders to reach to the skies. Cityscapes changed as these new constructions thrust upward. For example, the engineering firm of Gustave Eiffel (1832–1923) built an iron and steel tower to celebrate the Paris World's Fair of 1889. Modeled on the structural supports of railway viaducts, the Eiffel Tower was ridiculed by critics as a "truly tragic street lamp" and a "half-built factory pipe," but it soon came to symbolize both Paris and the new age of industrial modernity.

The development of electric power also characterized the Second Industrial Revolution. In 1866 the English scientist Michael Faraday (1791–1867) designed the first electromagnetic generator. In 1879, the American Thomas Edison (1847–1931) invented the light bulb. These developments created a huge energy-producing industry. They also accelerated the production and distribution of other industrial goods as factories, shops, and the train and tram lines that serviced them were linked to city power grids.

Industrial organization changed as well. Businesses became larger and more complex. To control production costs in a time of declining profits, business owners developed new organizational forms, including *vertical integration*—buying the companies that supplied their raw materials and those that bought their finished products—and *horizontal integration,* linking up with companies in the same industry to fix prices, control competition, and ensure a steady profit (often called trusts or cartels). The Standard Oil Company exemplifies both trends. Formed in 1870 by John D. Rockefeller (1839–1937), Standard Oil monopolized 75 percent of the petroleum business in the United States by the 1890s, and controlled iron mines, timberland, and manufacturing and transportation businesses.

Within these new, huge, often multinational companies, organization grew more complex and impersonal. The small family firm run by the owner became rarer as layers of managers and clerical staff separated worker from owner. Even identifying "the owner" grew difficult. The need for capital to fuel these huge enterprises drove businesses to *incorporate*—to sell "shares" in the business to numerous stockholders, each of whom now shared ownership in the company.

The marketing of goods also changed. During these decades, a revolution in retailing occurred, one that culminated in a new type of business aimed at middle-class customers—the department store. In a traditional shop, the retailer (who was often also the producer) offered a small selection of products in limited quantities at fairly high prices. In contrast, in the new department stores—Bon Marché in Paris, Macy's in New York, Whiteley's in London—a vast array of products confronted the consumer. These new enterprises made their profits from a quick turnover of a large volume of low-priced products. To stimulate sales, they sought to make shopping a pleasant experience by providing well-lighted expanses filled with appealing goods sold by courteous, well-trained clerks. In-store reading rooms and restaurants pampered shoppers. Another innovation, mail-order catalogs, offered the store's delights to distant customers. Advertising became a crucial industry as business sought to persuade potential customers of new needs and desires.

On the Move: Emigration and Urbanization

Economic depression and the expansion and transformation of the Industrial Revolution accelerated patterns of urbanization and immigration. The depression hit agricultural regions particularly hard, just when population growth exerted greater pressure on land and jobs. In addition, industrial expansion undercut rural handicraft production. As a result, men and women from traditional villages sought new economic opportunities in the industrializing cities of Europe, the Americas, and Australia.

THE BICYCLE REVOLUTION The bicycle exemplifies the way mass industrial production revolutionized aspects of daily life. For the first time, ordinary individuals, too poor to afford a horse or automobile, could purchase their own private means of transportation that would get them where they wanted to go in one-quarter of the time that walking required. As this engraving shows, the bicycle also contributed to the expansion of the woman's sphere.

European cities grew dramatically after 1870. In 1800, only 23 European cities had more than 100,000 inhabitants. By 1900, there were 135 cities of such a size. The European population as a whole continued to expand in this period, but the cities increased at a much faster pace. For example, in 1800 the city of Odessa in Ukraine held 6,000 inhabitants. By 1914, Odessa contained 480,000 people.

Seeking opportunities, inhabitants of industrially underdeveloped regions migrated to more economically advanced areas. Italians headed to France and Switzerland, while the Irish poured across the Irish Sea into Liverpool and Glasgow. Some immigrants headed not for the nearest city, but for a different continent. Between 1860 and 1914, more than 52 million Europeans crossed the oceans in quest of a better life. Over 70 percent of these transoceanic immigrants traveled to North America, 21 percent to South America, and the rest to Australia, New Zealand, or colonies in Asia and Africa.[1] Emigrants from eastern Europe accounted for an ever-larger share of those bound for America. In the 1880s 100,000 Poles moved to the United States. By the 1900s, however, between 130,000 and 175,000 Poles were heading to the United States *each year*.

Growing Social Unrest

Rapid economic change, combined with accelerated urbanization and immigration, heightened social tensions and destabilized political structures. The freefall in prices that characterized the depression eroded capitalist profit margins. In response, businessmen sought to reduce the number of their employees and to increase labor productivity. Workers reacted angrily. Reduced prices did mean that the living standards of *employed* workers rose, but so, too, did unemployment and underemployment. Heightened class hostilities thus characterized these decades.

In rural regions such as Spain and Ireland, the collapse in agricultural prices fostered social and economic crises. Agricultural laborers and peasants turned to violence to enforce their calls for a fairer distribution of land. The spread of industrialization into southern and eastern Europe led to unrest as handicraft producers and independent artisans fought to maintain their traditional livelihoods.

The flow of immigrants into Europe's cities raised social tensions. Cities were often unable to cope with their dramatic increases in population. Newcomers battled with established residents for jobs and apartments. The mixture of nationalities and ethnic groups often proved particularly explosive.

((• 📖 Read the Document

Adelheid Popp, "Finding Work: Women Factory Workers"

Defining the Nation

23.2 How did Western ruling classes respond to the new mass politics?

The economic and social changes detailed in the last section helped create mass politics. Because industrial expansion broke down local and regional cultures, loyalties, and mindsets, it cleared the way for the development of new national political identities and interests. The railroads, telegraph, and telephone shattered the barriers of distance, while new printing technologies made newspapers cheap and available to ordinary people. With access to information, they could now form opinions and participate in national and international debate as never before. The dramatic expansion of cities also created the environments in which mass political movements could grow.

Faced with the challenge of this new political culture, political leaders sought to quell social discontent and ensure the loyalty of their populations. They did so in the context of the turbulent international climate created by the national unification of Italy and Germany and the continuing decline of the Ottoman Empire (see Chapter 22). As the European balance of power shifted, governments scrambled to strengthen their states at home as well as abroad.

Nation-Making

After 1870, all but the most authoritarian European leaders recognized the importance of "nation-making," of creating a sense of national identity to overcome the conflicting regional, social, and political loyalties that divided their citizens and subjects. But while European political elites sought to make ordinary men feel a part of political life, they also tried to retain their dominant social and political position. As socialism challenged both liberal and conservative regimes, those in power had to figure out how to stay there.

FRANCHISE EXPANSION One way to stay in power was to share it, as the British example proved. In the first half of the nineteenth century, Britain's landed elite had accommodated middle-class demands for greater influence without relinquishing its own dominance. Landed aristocrats and gentlemen played leading roles in both major political parties—the Liberals and the Conservatives (also called "Tories")—but both parties encouraged industrial growth and policies that benefited the middle classes. In the last third of the century, this system expanded to include working-class men. In 1867, many urban working men won the right to vote, and in 1884 this right was extended to rural male laborers. Although Britain did not achieve universal male suffrage until after World War I, this gradual expansion of the franchise convinced many British working-class men that there was no need for revolution.

Similar patterns emerged across Europe in this era as aristocratic and middle-class politicians extended the vote to lower-class men. These political leaders regarded franchise reform as a way to avoid socialist revolution by incorporating potential revolutionaries within the system.

SOCIAL REFORM New voters, however, had to be wooed and wowed. They had to be persuaded to vote the way their leaders wished. Political parties thus turned to social welfare legislation. Both liberal and conservative politicians used social welfare reform to convince working-class voters that they had a stake in the existing political system—and thus to reduce the appeal of revolutionary socialism.

In the 1880s, for example, German Chancellor Otto von Bismarck introduced some of the most thoroughgoing social welfare measures yet seen in Europe. Bismarck, a fiercely conservative aristocrat, sought to ensure German stability and national unity. Alarmed by the popularity of the socialist German Social Democratic Party (SPD), Bismarck outlawed it in 1878, and then enacted laws to attract working-class voters. He initiated sickness benefits in 1883, coverage for industrial accidents in 1884, and old-age pensions and disability insurance in 1889.

Like their conservative opponents, liberal politicians also saw social reform as a way to stay in power and create national unity. In 1906, British trade unionists and socialists formed the Labour Party. Alarmed by this socialist threat, Britain's Liberal government enacted welfare measures, including state-funded lunches for school-children, pensions for the elderly, and sickness and unemployment benefits for some workers. A similar process occurred in Italy. Frightened by the growing appeal of revolutionary socialist parties, the Liberal Party leader Giovanni Giolitti (1842–1928) tried to improve workers' lives and convince them that real change did not require revolution. Giolitti legalized trade unions, established public health and life insurance programs, cracked down on child labor, and established a six-day workweek.

SCHOOLING THE NATION Like social welfare programs, state elementary schools served as important tools in the effort to build internally united (and therefore externally competitive) nation-states. During the late nineteenth century, most of the nations of western and central Europe established free public elementary education systems. Such schools helped foster loyalty to the nation and its leaders. In the 1880s,

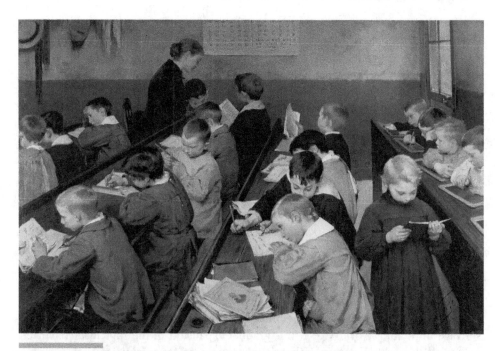

MASS SCHOOLING Jean Jules Henri Geoffroy, *The Junior Class,* 1889. Geoffroy presented this painting at the World's Fair of 1889 in celebration of the 100th anniversary of the French Revolution. In France, supporters of the Republic saw the state school system as one of the French Revolution's central achievements and regarded the state school teacher as an embodiment of republican (as opposed to religious or monarchical) ideals. In keeping with these revolutionary and republican ideals, Geoffroy's classroom contains both middle-class boys (wearing white collars) and their lower-class peers.

for example, French student teachers were instructed that "their first duty is to make [their pupils] love and understand the fatherland."[2]

Schools helped forge a national identity in three ways. First, they ensured the triumph of the national language. Required to abandon their regional dialect (and sometimes brutally punished if they did not), children learned to read and write in the national language. Second, history and geography lessons taught children versions of the past that strengthened their sense of belonging to a superior people and often served a specific political agenda. For example, wall maps of France in French classrooms included the provinces of Alsace and Lorraine, even though Germany had seized these regions after the Franco-Prussian War in 1871. Finally, the schools, with their essentially captive populations, participated fully in nationalistic rituals, including singing patriotic songs such as *Deutschland Über Alles* ("Germany Over All") or *Rule Britannia,* and observing special days to commemorate military victories or national heroes.

INVENTING TRADITIONS Nationalistic ritual was not confined to the schoolroom. Making nations often meant *inventing* traditions to capture the loyalty of the mass electorate. German policymakers, for example, invented "Sedan Day." This new national holiday celebrated the victory over France in the Franco-Prussian War that helped create the new German Empire. It featured parades, flag raisings, and special services to foster a sense of German nationalism among its citizens.

Inventing a set of traditions around the monarchy and making the royal family the center of the nation were also effective nation-making tools. When the German states united in 1871, the king of Prussia, William I, became the new German emperor. William I, however, tended to identify himself more as a Prussian than a German. It was his grandson, William II (r. 1888–1918), who used personal appearances and militaristic pageantry to make the monarchy a symbolic center of the new nation. In Britain, the anniversaries of Queen Victoria's accession to the throne (the Silver Jubilee of 1887 and the Diamond Jubilee of 1897) were elaborately staged and orchestrated to make ordinary Britons feel close to the queen and therefore part of a powerful, united nation. Mass printing and production helped support this new mass politics of nationality.

GERMAN EMPEROR WILLIAM II AND HIS ENTOURAGE William preferred to wear military regalia when he appeared in public. In this way, William himself symbolized the link between the German state and Germany's military might.

At the Jubilees, participants could purchase illustrated commemorative pamphlets, plates etched with the queen's silhouette, teapots in the shape of Victoria's head, or even an automated musical bustle that played *God Save the Queen* whenever the wearer sat down.

Nation-Making: The Examples of France, the Russian Empire, and Ireland

By the late nineteenth and early twentieth centuries, political leaders recognized that fostering a sense of national identity among their citizens or subjects would both lessen the appeal of socialism and strengthen the nation-state in war with competitors (see **Map 23.1**). The examples of France, the Russian Empire, and Ireland, however, demonstrate the complexities of nation-making.

FRANCE: A CRISIS OF LEGITIMACY At the end of the last chapter, we saw that defeat in the Franco-Prussian War of 1870–1871 led France to return to a republican form of government, based on universal manhood suffrage. This "Third Republic" faced a crisis of legitimacy. Many Frenchmen argued that the Republic was the product of

MAP 23.1 EUROPE AT THE END OF THE NINETEENTH CENTURY Compare this map with Map 20.3 ("Europe After the Congress of Vienna in 1815," page 646). How does this comparison show the impact of modern nationalism on European political geography? What changes in political borders have occurred and why?

military defeat and therefore not worth their loyalty or support. These opponents of the Third Republic included monarchists who wanted a king, Bonapartists longing for a Napoleonic empire, Catholics disturbed by republican efforts to curb the political power of the Church, and aristocrats opposed to democracy.

To understand the opposition to the Third Republic in France after 1871, it is essential to remember that "republicanism" in France meant more than "no king, no emperor." Rooted in the radical Jacobin Republic of 1792 (see Chapter 20), republicanism rested on a vision of an ideal France of male equals—small shopkeepers and independent artisans—governed by reason, not religion. Such a vision clashed with the interests and ideals of monarchists, Bonapartists, and Catholics. The clash of these rival ideologies generated chaos in French politics.

The **Dreyfus Affair** exemplified this ideological clash and revealed the lack of consensus about French political identity. (See *Justice in History* in this chapter.) In 1894, a French military court wrongly convicted Captain Alfred Dreyfus (1859–1935) of espionage. French intellectuals took up Dreyfus's case, and supporters and opponents of Dreyfus battled in the streets and the legislature. Support for Dreyfus, who was Jewish, became equated with support for the secular ideals of the Republic. The anti-Dreyfusards, in contrast, saw the affair as a symptom of everything wrong with the Republic. They believed that true French nationalism should center on the Catholic religion and respect for the military.

In some ways, the supporters of Dreyfus—and therefore of the Republic—won. Dreyfus was declared "not guilty" in 1906, and the government placed the army under civilian control and removed the Catholic Church from its privileged position. With these measures politicians aimed to separate citizenship from religious affiliation and unite the nation around the ideal of a secular Republic. In 1914, on the eve of World War I, the Third Republic was thus stronger than it had been two decades earlier.

It had not yet, however, gained the approval of all of French society. Royalist and Catholic opposition remained strong. At the same time, working-class disaffection was growing. The Radical Party, which represented the interests of small store-owners and independent craftsmen, not industrial workers, dominated political life and drew its support from rural and small-town constituencies. The Radicals opposed the high taxes necessary to establish social welfare programs and dragged their feet on social legislation such as the 10-hour workday (not passed until 1904) and old-age pensions (not established until 1910). As a result, French factory workers increasingly turned to violence.

RUSSIA: REVOLUTION AND REACTION In the sprawling and multiethnic Russian Empire, the task of nation-making was immense, but well underway by 1914. As we saw in Chapter 22, in the 1860s Tsar Alexander II instituted the "Great Reforms," which included the emancipation of 50 million serfs, the creation of a new judicial system, and the vesting of local governmental authority in elected assemblies (for which 40 percent of the peasantry was able to vote). The Reforms energized Russian provincial and press culture and enlivened local politics. As new opportunities arose for lawyers, clerks, shopkeepers, accountants, journalists, and the like, the middle classes expanded.

Many of these middle-class men and women embraced liberal political ideals and sought the reform of the tsar's autocratic regime and the expansion of political representation. Others concluded that only violent revolution would bring meaningful political change. Terrorist groups like the People's Will, as we saw at the beginning of this chapter, turned to assassination as a political weapon.

The new Russian working class also grew increasingly politicized. In the 1890s, the western regions of the Russian Empire underwent dramatic industrialization. By 1900, only Britain, Germany, and the United States produced more steel—and Russia supplied 50 percent of the industrialized world's oil. Coal mines and steel mills dotted Ukraine, and huge state-run factories dominated Moscow and St. Petersburg.

Dreyfus Affair The trials of Captain Alfred Dreyfus on treason charges dominated French political life in the decade after 1894 and revealed fundamental divisions in French society.

 Watch the Video

Russian Terrorism

Justice in History

The Dreyfus Affair: DEFINING NATIONAL IDENTITY

IN FRANCE

On September 27, 1894, French counterespionage officers examined a disturbing document—an unsigned, undated cover letter for documents containing information on French military equipment and training. The officers concluded that the letter was intended for the German military attaché in Paris. Someone in the French officer corps was selling military secrets to the Germans.

After a brief investigation, the French investigators concluded that the traitor was Captain Alfred Dreyfus, a candidate officer on the General Staff. An unlikely traitor, Dreyfus had compiled a strong record during his military career and, by all accounts, was a staunch French patriot. Moreover, because his wife was wealthy, he had no need to sell his country for money. He was, however, an aloof arrogant man, disliked by most of his fellow officers. He was also a Jew.

Convicted of treason, Dreyfus was exiled in 1895 to Devil's Island, a former leper colony 12 miles off the coast of French Guyana in the Caribbean. Many believed he had gotten off too lightly. Public and press clamored for his execution.

The case seemed closed. But some months later, the new chief of the Intelligence Bureau, Major Marie-Georges Picquart, discovered that someone was continuing to pass military secrets to the Germans. Picquart set out to trap the man he believed to be Dreyfus's accomplice. The evidence he uncovered, however, convinced him that Dreyfus was innocent.

Picquart's efforts created a national crisis. On January 13, 1898, one of France's most famous authors, Émile Zola, alleged in a Paris newspaper that the French military was engaged in a cover-up. In an article headlined *"J'accuse!"* ("I accuse!"), Zola charged that the General Staff had deliberately convicted an innocent man. Over the next six weeks, riots broke out in French cities.

In 1899, a second military court tried Dreyfus and again found him guilty. In the subsequent riots in Paris, 100 people were wounded and 200 jailed. Ten days later, the French president pardoned Dreyfus to heal the divisions opened by the trial.

The Dreyfus Affair drew international attention, polarized French politics, and tore apart Parisian society. It sparked violent protests, duels, and trials for assault, defamation, and libel. The question "Are you for or against Dreyfus?" divided families and destroyed friendships. During the height of the controversy, for example, the painter Edgar Degas ridiculed Camille Pisarro's paintings. When reminded that he had once admired these same works, Degas said, "Yes, but that was before the Dreyfus Affair." Degas was a passionate anti-Dreyfusard, Pisarro a Dreyfus supporter.[3]

Why did the Dreyfus Affair change one painter's perception of another's work? Why was this trial not simply a case, but an *affair,* a matter of public and private debate, as well as political upheaval?

To comprehend the Dreyfus Affair, we must understand that it was less about Captain Alfred Dreyfus than about the very existence of the Third Republic, founded in 1871 in the wake of military defeat in the Franco-Prussian War and the collapse of Napoleon III's empire. The intellectuals and politicians who supported Dreyfus were defending this Republic. They sought to limit the army's involvement in France's political life and upheld a secular definition of the nation that treated Catholics no differently from Protestants, Jews, or atheists.

Dreyfus's opponents, in contrast, regarded the Third Republic as a betrayal of the true France. They wanted a hierarchical, Catholic, imperial state, steeped in military traditions. By defending the military conviction of Dreyfus, they supported the army and the authoritarian traditions that the Republic had jettisoned. The Dreyfus Affair was thus an encounter between competing versions of French national identity.

The question "What is France?" however, could not be answered without considering a second question: "Who belongs

THE DREYFUS AFFAIR GAME This board game, with portraits of the key players in the Dreyfus Affair, illustrates the dominant role of the "Affair" in late nineteenth-century French culture.

(continued on next page)

(continued from previous page)

in France?"—or more specifically, "What about Jews?" France's small Jewish community (less than 1 percent of the population) had enjoyed the rights of full citizenship since 1791—much longer than in most of Europe. Yet the Dreyfus Affair showed that even in France, the position of Jews in the nation remained uncertain. Although anti-Semitism played little role in the initial charges against Dreyfus, it quickly became a dominating feature of the affair. For many anti-Dreyfusards, Dreyfus's Jewishness explained everything. The novelist and political theorist Maurice Barrès insisted, "I have no need to be told why Dreyfus committed treason. . . . That Dreyfus is capable of treason I conclude from his race."[4] Anti-Semites such as Barrès regarded Jewishness as a kind of hereditary disease that made Jews unfit for French citizenship. To the anti-Semitic nationalist, "the Jew" was a person without a country, unconnected by racial or religious ties to the French nation—the opposite of a patriot.

In 1906, a French high court exonerated Dreyfus. Not until 1995, however, did the French military acknowledge his innocence. Dreyfus survived to serve his country with distinction in the First World War.

Like Dreyfus, the Third Republic survived the Dreyfus Affair. Outrage over the army's cover-up led republican leaders to limit the powers of the army and so lessened the chances of a military coup. Anti-Semitism, however, remained pervasive in French politics and cultural life well into the twentieth century.

For Discussion

1. What does the Dreyfus Affair reveal about definitions of national identity in late-nineteenth-century Europe?
2. Many French men and women believed that for the sake of the national interest, Dreyfus's conviction had to be upheld—whether he was actually guilty or not. In what situations, if any, should "national interest" override an individual's right to a fair trial?

Taking It Further

Begley, Louis. *Why the Dreyfus Affair Matters*. 2009. Begley, a novelist and a lawyer, uses the history of the Dreyfus Affair to reflect on contemporary political and legal issues.

Burns, Michael. *France and the Dreyfus Affair: A Documentary History*. 1999. An accessible collection of primary documents.

Industrialization created a small but significant urban working class. With a literacy rate approaching 70 percent, these workers had access to both liberal and socialist political ideas.

Such ideas, however, clashed with the absolutist convictions of the tsarist regime. Convinced that God had appointed them to rule, Alexander III (r. 1881–1894) and Nicholas II (r. 1894–1917) clung to absolutism. To catch up with the West, the tsarist regime adopted Western industrialization but had no intention of accepting Western ideas of representative government. It could not, however, completely block the flow of these ideas into the Russian Empire.

Nor could it stamp out the social upheaval created by economic change. Rapid state-imposed industrialization produced cities simmering with discontent. Factory workers labored 11 hours a day in poor conditions, but both strikes and unions were illegal. In the countryside, heavy taxation and rapid population growth increased competition for land and intensified peasant discontent.

The tsarist regime's efforts at "nation-making" proved even more divisive. Under Alexander III and even more intensely under Nicholas II, **Russification** became official state policy throughout the empire. Originally designed to limit Polish influence in the western borderlands of the empire, Russification required that the Russian language be used in schools and government institutions and that traditional local legal and social customs conform to those imposed by the central, Russian state. Russification also meant an increasing emphasis on the Russian Orthodox religion as an element of "Russianness." Orthodox believers who did not conform to official Russian Orthodox practice, as well as Roman Catholics and Lutherans, faced increasing persecution. So, too, did non-Christians, including Buddhists, Muslims, and especially Jews.

While Russification did enhance the national identity of Orthodox, Russian-speaking subjects of the tsar, it aroused hostility among even formerly loyal peoples. The Finns, for example, who had come under Russian imperial rule in 1809, had generally regarded the tsarist state as far preferable to their former Swedish overlords. The tsarist efforts to Russify Finland, which began in the 1890s, rapidly destroyed the Finns' positive view of the tsarist regime. In areas such as Poland, Lithuania, and Ukraine, too, Russification intensified nationalist resentment against Russian imperial rule.

 Read the Document

"Working Conditions of Women in the Factories," M. I. Pokrovskaia

Russification Tsarist policy from the 1890s until the outbreak of World War I; Russification imposed the use of Russian language and emphasized Russian Orthodox religious and cultural practices.

⊗ **View the Closer Look** Bloody Sunday, St. Petersburg, 1905

THE REVOLUTION OF 1905 IN THE MOVIES On Bloody Sunday, January 22, 1905, Russian troops opened fire on more than 100,000 citizens who had gathered in St. Petersburg to present a petition to the tsar. Rather than subduing the revolt, the massacre sparked a revolution. This photograph, supposedly of the moment when the tsar's troops began to shoot the demonstrators, is one of the most familiar images of the twentieth century—yet it is *not* in fact a documentary record. Instead, it is a still taken from *The Ninth of January,* a Soviet film made in 1925.

In 1905, popular and nationalist discontent flared into revolution. That year Japan trounced the Russian Empire in a war sparked by competition for territory in Asia. This military disaster made the tsarist regime seem incompetent and provided an opening for political reformers and nationalist groups. On a day that became known as "Bloody Sunday" (January 22, 1905), 100,000 workers and their families attempted to present to the tsar a petition calling for higher wages, better working conditions, and political rights. Troops fired on the unarmed crowd. At least 70 people were killed and more than 240 wounded. The massacre strengthened the call for revolution. Across the empire, workers went on strike and demanded economic and political rights. In June, parts of the navy mutinied. Nationalist groups grabbed the opportunity to demand autonomous states.

With the empire in chaos, Tsar Nicholas II gave in to demands for the election of a national legislative assembly, the Duma. Yet the revolution continued. In December a military mutiny sparked an uprising in Moscow. As buildings burned and street battles raged, revolutionary socialists controlled parts of the city.

By the time the first Duma met in April of 1906, however, tsarist forces had regained the offensive and terrorized much of the opposition. Because most of the army remained loyal, the tsarist regime was able to quell the Moscow uprising and then move to suppress revolutionary forces across the empire. But just as importantly, the violence and radicalism displayed in Moscow horrified middle-class liberals, who now refused to cooperate with revolutionary or socialist groups. Nicholas succeeded in limiting the Duma's legislative role and, by 1907, regained many of his autocratic powers.

CHRONOLOGY: INSTABILITY WITHIN THE RUSSIAN EMPIRE

1881
Assassination of Tsar Alexander II; accession of Alexander III. — 1881

1882 — **1882**
May Laws reimpose restrictions on Russian Jews.

1890s
Industrialization accelerates under Witte. — 1890s

1894 — **1894**
Accession of Nicholas II.

1904
Outbreak of Russo-Japanese War. — 1904

1905 — **1905**
Revolution.

The Revolution of 1905, then, did not overthrow the tsarist regime or transform it into a limited or liberal monarchy. Yet it was not a complete failure. Trade unions, strikes, and political parties were now legal. The Duma did exist and helped connect the still-thriving provincial and urban political cultures with the central state. The revolution's most important success, however, was the loosening of censorship. The already influential local press expanded further, as did the numbers of all sorts of publications. Public opinion now became a crucial force in Russian imperial politics. Nicholas's unshaken commitment to autocracy and Russification, however, ensured that the Empire remained politically unstable.

THE IRISH IDENTITY CONFLICT Chapter 21 described Ireland as an "internal colony," officially part of the United Kingdom since 1801 but governed with British rather than Irish economic interests in mind. In this internal colony, the growth of Irish nationalism led to political instability and the threat of civil war.

The United Kingdom comprised two islands—Britain and Ireland—and four nations—the English, the Welsh, the Scottish, and the Irish. By the 1870s, a chasm yawned between the first three overwhelmingly Protestant and industrialized nations, and the largely Roman Catholic, largely peasant culture of Ireland. Economic grievances fused with a deeply rooted sense of political and religious repression among Irish Catholics and convinced many of the need for independence from Britain. Not all Irish nationalists, however, were Roman Catholic. Many Irish Protestants also embraced the ideal of an independent Ireland.

Irish nationalism took two forms. A minority of Irish nationalists was revolutionary and republican: These "Fenians" (from the Old Irish word for "warrior") sought an Irish republic with no ties to the British monarchy or the British Empire. Convinced that the only way to achieve this republic was through armed struggle, they carried out a number of terrorist attacks in Ireland and Britain from the 1860s on. The larger, more moderate group of Irish nationalists aimed not at an independent republic but rather at the more limited ideal of "Home Rule"—an Irish Parliament in Dublin to govern Irish domestic issues.

Faced with growing Irish nationalism, the British government resorted time and again to martial law, accompanied by attempts to resolve peasant grievances through land reform. Such reform measures were always too little, too late. Then, in the 1880s, Liberal Party leader William Gladstone embraced Irish Home Rule as the only path to peace. The issue of Home Rule for Ireland split the Liberal Party and convulsed British parliamentary politics for the rest of the nineteenth century.

Even more significantly, the prospect of Home Rule frightened many Irish Protestants who feared becoming a minority within a Catholic-governed state. "Home Rule," they said, equaled "Rome Rule." The descendants of English and Scottish settlers, Protestants constituted a minority of the Irish population as a whole, but made up the majority in the northernmost province of Ulster. These Ulstermen, or "Unionists," defined their national identity as "British" rather than "Irish" and made it clear that they would fight to defeat Home Rule and preserve the union of Ireland with Britain.

By 1914, such a fight looked inevitable. The Liberals, back in office, were determined to achieve Irish Home Rule. The Conservatives were just as determined to oppose it, even to the point of backing military rebellion. In Ireland, nationalists and Unionists formed paramilitary organizations as they prepared to fight. Only the outbreak of war in Europe postponed civil war in Ireland (see **Map 23.2**).

MAP **23.2** THE UNITED KINGDOM OF GREAT BRITAIN AND IRELAND IN 1910 What were the factors weakening the Union between Great Britain and Ireland by 1910? In what ways did the emergence of the Unionist movement (in favor of retaining the Union) further destabilize the political status quo?

The New Mass Politics

23.3 What forms did mass politics assume during this era?

We have seen that by expanding the franchise, passing social welfare legislation, and inventing nationalist traditions, liberal and conservative political leaders sought to win the loyalty of the lower classes. Mass support for socialist and racist-nationalist political parties, however, challenged the power of traditional political leaders and parties.

The Politics of the Working Class

The rise of working-class socialist political parties and the emergence of more radical trade unionism reflected an escalation of class hostilities. Workers often rejected the political authority of their bosses and landlords and sought power on their own terms.

THE WORKERS' CITY The impact of agricultural crisis and industrial expansion created large working-class communities in the rapidly growing industrial cities. At the same time, technological developments such as electrified tram lines and the expansion of the railway system enabled wealthy Europeans to retreat from overcrowded, dirty, disease-ridden city centers to the new suburbs. Increasingly isolated from the middle and upper classes, industrial workers developed what sociologists call "urban villages," closely knit neighborhoods in which each family had a clear and publicly acknowledged place.

Sharply defined gender roles played an important part in ordering this world. The home became the woman's domain (although many working-class women also worked outside the home). Wives often controlled the family income and made most decisions about family life. Men built their own cultural and leisure institutions—the corner pub, the music hall, the football club, the brass band. These institutions not only provided an escape from the confines of work and home, they also secured the bonds of male working-class identity. This identity rested on a sharp distinction between "Us"—ordinary men, workers, neighbors—and "Them," bosses, owners, landlords, those with privilege and power.

WORKING-CLASS SOCIALISM AND THE REVOLUTIONARY PROBLEM The emergence of working-class socialist political parties embodied this class identity. By 1914, 20 European countries had socialist parties.

Why socialism? As we saw in Chapter 22, by 1870 Karl Marx had published his economic and political theory of revolutionary socialism. Not many workers had the time, education, or energy to study Marx's complex ideas. But Marx's basic points, presented to workers by socialist activists and organizers, resonated with many workers. Quite simply, these laborers had already identified their boss as the enemy, and Marx assured them that they were right. His insistence that class conflict was inherent within the industrial system accorded with workers' own experience of social segregation and economic exploitation. The onset of economic depression in the 1870s also appeared to confirm Marx's prediction that capitalism would produce economic crises until it finally collapsed.

The most dramatic socialist success story was in Germany. In the elections of 1912, the socialist SPD won 35 percent of the national vote and became the largest party in the German Reichstag or parliament. German socialism was, however, more than just party politics. The SPD provided German workers with an alternative community. They could send their children to socialist day care centers and bury their parents in socialist cemeteries. They could spend their leisure time in socialist bicycling clubs and chess teams. They could read socialist newspapers, sing socialist songs, save their money in socialist banks, and shop at socialist cooperatives.

By the 1890s, the rapid growth of socialist parties throughout Europe persuaded many activists that working-class revolution was just around the corner. In 1885 the SPD leader August Bebel (1840–1913) declared, "Every night I go to sleep with the thought that the last hour of bourgeois society strikes soon."[5]

Yet Bebel was wrong. Ironically, the immediate success of socialist parties ensured their long-term failure to foment a working-class revolution. To continue to attract voters, socialist parties needed to pass legislation that would appeal to workers. But minimum wage laws, pension rights, and the like improved workers' lives within a *non-socialist* system—and so made socialist revolution more remote. Why resort to violent revolution when participation in parliamentary politics was paying off? Why overthrow capitalism when workers were benefiting from it?

In Germany, the quest for an answer to these questions led to **socialist revisionism**, a set of political ideas most closely associated with Eduard Bernstein (1850–1932). Bernstein rejected the Marxist faith in inevitable violent revolution and argued instead for the gradual and peaceful evolution of socialism through parliamentary politics. He called for German socialists to form alliances with middle-class liberals and carry out social and economic reforms.

In 1899, the SPD condemned Bernstein's revisionism and reaffirmed its faith in the inevitability of capitalism's collapse and violent, working-class revolution. Bernstein had lost the battle—but he won the war. For, in practice if not in theory, the SPD acted like any other parliamentary party. It focused on improving the lot of its constituency through legislative change. As a result, the German political system grew more responsive to workers' needs—and workers grew less revolutionary.

Read the Document

"Socialism: The Gotha Program"

socialist revisionism The belief that an equal society can be built through participation in parliamentary politics rather than through violent revolution.

Socialist parties across Europe tended to follow the pattern of the SPD: They voiced the rhetoric of revolution while working for gradual change through parliamentary politics. Despite the almost hysterical fears of many middle- and upper-class Europeans, the successes of socialist political parties strengthened parliamentary politics more than they stirred up revolution.

RADICAL TRADE UNIONISM AND THE ANARCHIST THREAT Much of the support for socialist parliamentary parties came from the trade union movement. As we have seen, the onset of economic depression in the 1870s shattered middle-class confidence and shrank capitalists' profit margins. Looking to cut costs, businessmen sought to reduce the number of laborers, increase production, and decrease wages. To protect workers from this onslaught, unions grew more radical. First, while the unions of the 1850s and 1860s had tended to be small, craft-based groupings of skilled workers, the new unions aimed to organize all the male workers in an entire industry—for example, all male textile workers, rather than just the skilled weavers. And second, these new unions were also more willing to resort to strikes and violence. Unionized workers in barbershops were even encouraged to "inflict nonfatal cuts on the clients of their capitalist masters."[6]

syndicalism Ideology of the late nineteenth and early twentieth century that sought to achieve a working-class revolution through economic action, particularly through mass labor strikes.

general strike Syndicalist tactic that called for every worker to go on strike and thus disrupt the capitalist economy and force a political revolution.

anarchism Ideology that views the state as unnecessary and repressive and rejects participation in parliamentary politics in favor of direct, usually violent action.

The ideology of **syndicalism** further radicalized the union movement. Syndicalists sought to use the economic clout of the working class to topple capitalism and create a worker-controlled, egalitarian society. In the syndicalist vision, if every worker in a nation went on strike—a **general strike**—the resulting disruption of the capitalist economy would lead to working-class revolution. The French syndicalist leader Georges Sorel (1847–1922) did not actually believe that a general strike was possible, but he argued that the *idea* of the general strike served as an essential myth, an inspirational idea that would give workers the motivation and self-confidence to make a revolution.

In their rejection of parliamentary politics and their willingness to use violence to achieve their revolutionary ends, syndicalists were influenced by **anarchism**. Anarchists shunned politics and opted for direct action such as street fighting and assassination. Whereas Marxists sought working-class control of the state, anarchists aimed to destroy the state entirely. The Russian anarchist Mikhail Bakunin (1814–1876) insisted that the great obstacle to a just and egalitarian society was the state itself, not capitalism or the industrial middle class.

The combined impact of both syndicalism and anarchism created a climate of social unrest and political turmoil in much of Europe before 1914. In the 1890s anarchists carried out a terrorist campaign in Paris that began with a series of bombings and culminated in the fatal stabbing of President Sadi Carnot. Other anarchist victims included Empress Elisabeth of Austria in 1898, King Umberto I of Italy in 1900, and U.S. President William McKinley in 1901.

 Read the Document

Mikhail Bakunin, "Principles and Organization of the International Brotherhood"

The Politics of Race and Nation

Just as "the masses" consisted of more than urban factory workers, so mass politics were not limited to socialism, syndicalism, and anarchism. Members of the lower middle class (or "petit-bourgeoisie"), for example, rarely joined socialist parties or trade unions: Fighting to protect their middle-class status, these clerks, shop assistants, and small store owners regarded the socialist vision of working-class rule as a nightmare. Socialism also possessed little appeal in areas just beginning to industrialize, such as much of eastern Europe, which still contained many independent artisans and peasants threatened by the modernization that socialism represented. Many within these social groups turned to political parties based on ethnic identity or racism rather than class.

nationalist-racist politics Anti-liberal politics that appeal to race-based identities and fears.

Part of the appeal of **nationalist-racist politics** lay in its radical style. Possessing only a basic education, most of the newly enfranchised had little time for reading or

ANARCHISM AND ASSASSINATION The anarchist Luigi Lucheni assassinated Empress Elisabeth of Austria-Hungary in 1898. Lucheni targeted the empress not for anything she had done, but simply for who she was. He wrote in his diary, "How I would like to kill someone, but it must be someone important so it gets in the papers."

sustained intellectual work. They worked long hours and needed to be entertained. They needed a new style of politics—one based more on visual imagery and symbolism than on the written word. Nationalist politics fit the bill perfectly. Unlike socialists, who placed faith in education and rational persuasion, nationalist-racist politicians relied on emotional appeals. By waving flags, parading in historical costumes or military uniforms, and singing folk songs, they tapped into powerful personal and community memories to persuade voters of their common identity, based not on shared economic interests but on ethnic, religious, or linguistic ties—and a mistrust of those who did not share those ties.

NATIONALISM IN THE OTTOMAN AND AUSTRO-HUNGARIAN EMPIRES: THE POLITICS OF DIVISION Nationalist mass politics proved powerful in the multiethnic, industrially underdeveloped Ottoman and Austro-Hungarian Empires. These regions possessed a diversity of ethnic, linguistic, and religious groups. Nationalist ideology taught these groups to identify themselves as nations and to demand independent statehood.

By the 1870s, as we saw in Chapter 22, nationalism had already weakened the Ottoman Empire's rule over its European territories. Determined to hold on to his empire, the Ottoman sultan in 1875 and 1876 suppressed nationalist uprisings in Bosnia-Herzegovina and Bulgaria with ferocity. But this repression gave Russia the excuse it needed to declare war on behalf of its Slavic "little brothers" in the Balkans. As a result of this Russo-Turkish War (1877–1878), the Ottomans lost most of their remaining European territories. **Map 23.3** shows that Montenegro, Serbia, and Romania became independent states, while Austria-Hungary took Bosnia-Herzegovina. Bulgaria received autonomy, which the Bulgarians widened into full independence in 1908. A series of Balkan Wars in the early twentieth century meant even more losses for the Ottoman Empire.

Ottoman weakness appeared to make Austria-Hungary stronger. The appearance of strength, however, was deceptive. Straining under the pressures of late industrialization, Austria-Hungary's numerous ethnic and linguistic groups competed for power and privileges (see Map 22.4, page 710). In the age of mass politics, these divisions shaped political life.

Language became a key battleground in this political competition. In a multilingual empire, which language would be taught in the schools or used in official communications or guarantee career advancement? Politicians agitated for the primacy of their own native language and pushed for the power needed to ensure it. In the Hungarian half of the empire, for example, the ruling Magyar-speaking Hungarian landlords redrew constituency boundaries to give maximum influence to Magyar speakers in parliament and undercut the power of other ethnic groups. "Magyarization"

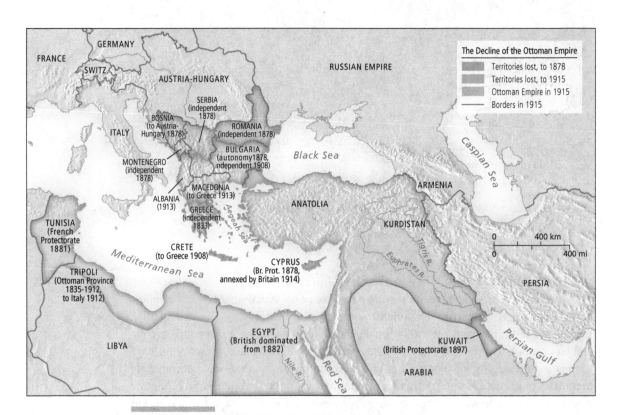

MAP **23.3** THE DISINTEGRATION OF THE OTTOMAN EMPIRE During the nineteenth century, the Ottoman regime lost territory and political control over much of its once-mighty empire to both nationalist independence movements and to rival European powers. From the 1870s on, mass nationalism accelerated Ottoman disintegration. What territories had the Ottoman regime lost by 1880? What territories were lost between 1880 and 1915? How did the disintegration of the Ottoman Empire change the balance of power in Europe?

in governmental offices and schools bred resentment among non-Hungarians. They formed their own political parties and began to dream of political independence. Similarly, in the Austrian half of the empire, the struggle between Germans and Czechs over language laws became so intense that no party could establish a majority in parliament, and in 1900 Emperor Francis Joseph (r. 1848–1916) resorted to ruling by decree.

ANTI-SEMITISM IN MASS POLITICS   Anti-Semitism played a central role in the new nationalist mass politics. Across Europe, anti-Semitic parties emerged, while established conservative parties adopted anti-Semitic rhetoric to attract voters. Three developments explain this heightened anti-Semitism.

Anti-Semitism grew stronger after 1870, first, because of an increasing tendency to racialize national identity. Concepts such as "the English race" or the "racial heritage" of the French had no scientific basis, but the perception of the racial roots of nationhood was powerful. Nationalism raised the question, "Who does *not* belong to the nation?" For many Europeans and Americans, race provided the answer. As the "nation" came to be defined in racial terms, so did "Jewishness." This shift from a religious to a more racial definition of Jewishness strengthened anti-Semitism. If national identity grew from racial roots, then for many, Jews were foreign plants, outsiders who threatened national unity.

Growing immigrant Jewish populations in much of Europe and the United States in the 1880s and 1890s heightened the perception of Jews as outsiders. Mass Jewish immigration is thus the second factor that helps explain the heightened anti-Semitism after 1870. Events in the Russian Empire help explain the upsurge in Jewish immigration. We saw at the beginning of this chapter that a group of terrorists assassinated Tsar Alexander II in 1881. Tsar Alexander III believed that a Jewish conspiracy was responsible for his father's assassination and responded with the May Laws of 1882. The May Laws reimposed restrictions on Jewish economic and social life within the Russian Empire, which now included most of Poland, the heartland of European Jewry. **Pogroms**—mass attacks on Jewish homes and businesses, sometimes organized by local officials—escalated. Fleeing this persecution, Jews migrated to Paris, London, Vienna, and other European cities.

The encounter between these immigrant Jewish communities and their hosts was often hostile. Extremely poor, the immigrants spoke Yiddish rather than the language of their new home, dressed in distinctive clothing, and sometimes practiced an ardently emotional style of Judaism that resisted assimilation. As the numbers of Jews rose in Europe's cities, these clearly identifiable immigrants were blamed for unemployment, disease, crime, and any other difficulty for which desperate people sought easy explanations.

A third factor in explaining later nineteenth-century anti-Semitism is what one historian has labeled the "rise of the Jews,"[7] a development linked to Jewish emancipation and assimilation. At the start of the nineteenth century, most European Jews had few political rights and were often confined to specific economic roles and required to live in restricted territories or city districts. In the second half of the century, however, most European Jews were *emancipated*: They gained civil and political rights. Many Jews assumed new economic roles and moved into new regions; not surprisingly, as economic newcomers, they often took up positions in the newest sectors of the industrial economy. They became department store owners or newspaper editors rather than farmers or small craftsmen.

During this period, many Jews also *assimilated* into European societies: They dropped distinctive dress styles, stopped speaking Yiddish, and discarded or modernized their practice of Judaism. Because many assimilated Jews secularized the traditional Jewish emphasis on studying the Torah into an emphasis on educational and artistic excellence, they also moved into professional and cultural fields.

pogroms An organized and often officially encouraged riot or attack to persecute a particular ethnic or religious group, especially associated with eastern European attacks against Jews.

THE RESULTS OF ANTI-SEMITISM In this 1905 painting by Samuel Hirszenberg, Hasidic Jews in Russian-governed Poland bury the victim of a pogrom. Hirszenberg called his painting *The Black Banner* in reference to both "The Black Hundreds," armed thugs who belonged to the anti-Semitic "Union of the Russian People," and *The Russian Banner*, the Union's newspaper that was partially funded by the tsar.

As a result of both emancipation and assimilation, then, Jewish communities became significant in European economic, artistic, and intellectual life. In Budapest in 1900, for example, Jews formed 25 percent of the population, yet they accounted for 45 percent of the city's lawyers, more than 40 percent of its journalists, and more than 60 percent of its doctors. In Germany, Jews owned almost all the large department stores; in the German cities of Frankfurt, Berlin, and Hamburg, Jews owned all the large daily newspapers.

While most Jews remained very poor, this visible Jewish success in emerging areas of the industrial economy meant that many Europeans linked Jewishness to industrialization and modernity. For many independent shopowners, traditional artisans, and small farmers with much to lose from industrialization, Jews became the symbol of the modernity that they feared.

ZIONISM: JEWISH MASS POLITICS The heightened anti-Semitism of the late nineteenth century convinced some Jews that the Jewish communities of Europe would be safe only when they gained their own state. The ideology of Jewish nationalism became known as **Zionism** because many Jewish nationalists called for the establishment of a Jewish state in "Zion," the biblical land of Palestine.

Zionism became a mass movement under the guidance of Theodor Herzl (1860–1904), an Austrian Jewish journalist. In his early adulthood, Herzl epitomized the assimilated Jew. He was a proud German who did not practice Judaism and refused to allow his son to be circumcised. In the 1890s, however, Herzl witnessed the rise to power of Vienna mayor Karl Lueger, whose Christian Social party attracted voters with an explicitly anti-Semitic platform. Herzl concluded that Jews would always be outsiders in Europe. In 1896, he published *The Jewish State,* a call for Jews to build a state of their own.

By 1914 some 90,000 Jews had settled in Palestine, where they hoped to build a Jewish state. Zionism, however, faced strong opposition. The idea of Palestine as the Jewish "homeland" aroused Arab nationalists, whose vision of an independent Arab state free from Ottoman control included Palestine and its population of 700,000 Arabs. Ultraorthodox Jews also condemned Zionism because they believed that only God could accomplish the Jewish return to Zion. In addition, many Jews in western European nations such as Britain feared that Zionism played into the hands of anti-Semites who argued that Jews could not be trusted to be good citizens or loyal subjects within European states.

Zionism Nationalist movement that emerged in the late nineteenth century and sought to establish a Jewish political state in Palestine (the Biblical Zion).

The Women's Revolt

23.4 How did the emergence of feminism in this period demonstrate the potential and the limits of political change?

As more men from the laboring classes received the vote, middle-class women demanded that they, too, receive this key political right. The campaign for women's suffrage, however, was only part of a multifaceted international middle-class **feminist movement**. For feminists, the vote was a way to transform cultural values and expectations. Nineteenth-century feminism rejected the liberal ideology of separate spheres—the insistence that both God and biology destined middle-class men for the public sphere of paid employment and political participation, and women for the private sphere of the home. In seeking political rights, feminists sought not just to enter the public, masculine sphere, but to obliterate many of the distinctions between the public and private spheres altogether.

feminist movement International movement that emerged in the second half of the nineteenth century and demanded broader political, legal, and economic rights for women.

 Watch the Video

British Women's Suffrage

Changes in Women's Experiences and Expectations

The nineteenth-century feminist movement was almost entirely a middle-class event. One important explanation for the lack of working-class involvement rests in a revolutionary change that occurred in middle-class, but not in working-class, families. In the last third of the nineteenth century, middle-class couples began to limit the size of their families by using already well-known methods of birth control such as abstinence, withdrawal, and abortion. For example, the average British middle-class family in the 1890s had fewer than three children, versus an average of six children in 1850. This basic change meant that married middle-class women no longer spent much of their adult life pregnant or nursing and were thus free to pursue other interests, including feminist activism.

Why did working-class families not follow the same pattern? The answer is largely economic. As economic depression cut into business profits, middle-class families looked to cut expenses. Family limitation made sense: Middle-class children remained in school through much of their teenaged years and so constituted a long-term drain on family resources. Working-class children, however, left school by age 11 or 12 and so began to contribute to the family income much earlier. Because children constituted an economic asset rather than a drain, working-class families remained large. To women struggling to rear large families in poverty, the vote must have seemed largely irrelevant.

Moreover, politically active working-class women tended to agree with Karl Marx that class, not gender, was the real dividing line in society. To better their lives, they turned to labor unions and socialism. The British activist Selina Cooper (1868–1946), for example, fought hard for women's rights, but within the British Labour movement. Cooper, who was sent to work in a textile mill at age 10, viewed the widening of women's opportunities and the achievement of working-class political power as two sides of the same coin.

Read the Document

Doris Viersbeck, "Life Downstairs: A Servant's Life"

Changing economic and social conditions for middle-class women also help explain the emergence of the feminist movement. In 1850, the unmarried middle-class woman who had to support herself had little choice but to become a governess or a paid companion to a widow. But by the 1870s, the expansion of the Industrial Revolution and the widening of state responsibilities created new opportunities. Middle-class single women became typists, telephone and telegraph operators, sales clerks, and bank tellers. During the 1860s in England, the number of women working as commercial clerks and accountants increased tenfold.

MIDDLE-CLASS WOMEN MOVING INTO THE PUBLIC SPHERE Julius LeBlanc Stewart, *The Goldsmith Girls in a Peugeot Voiturette in the Bois de Boulogne in 1897*, 1901. As this turn-of-the-century painting testifies, new leisure opportunities for women challenged the middle-class ideal of the "Angel in the House."

The same period saw governments assume greater responsibility for the welfare and education of the poor. Middle-class women, who had served as volunteers and charity workers, quickly claimed both paying and elected positions in the new local and state bureaucracies. Women served on school and welfare boards, staffed government inspectorates, and managed poorhouses. In some states, they voted in local (but not national) elections and were elected to local (but not national) office. Compulsory mass education also created a voracious demand for teachers and thus a new career path for unmarried women.

Expectations also began to change for married middle-class women as they moved into a new public role as consumers. It was the woman who was the principal target of the new advertising industry, the woman whom the new department stores sought to entice with their window displays and courteous clerks, the woman who rode the new tram lines and subways to take advantage of sales.

As middle-class women's opportunities widened, they confronted legal, political, and economic disabilities. An international feminist movement emerged and fought for four goals: removing the legal impediments faced by married women, widening opportunities for female employment and higher education, erasing the double standard of sexual conduct, and obtaining national women's suffrage.

Married Women and the Law

In the nineteenth century, European legal systems strongly reinforced the liberal ideology of separate spheres for men and women. Law codes often classified women with children, criminals, and the insane. Article 231 of the Napoleonic Code, the legal system of France and the basis of the legal codes of much of Europe, declared that "the husband owes protection to his wife; the wife owes obedience to her husband." In Russia a woman could not travel without her father's or husband's permission, and the husband was also the legal guardian of all children. He alone picked their schools, determined their punishments, and approved their marriage partners. In Prussia only the husband could decide when his baby should stop breastfeeding. According to English common law, "the husband and wife are one person in law," and that person was the husband. Most property brought into a marriage, given to a woman, or earned by her while married became the property of her husband.

From the mid-nineteenth century on, women's groups fought to improve the legal rights of married women. The results were uneven. By the end of the 1880s, English married women could own their own property, control their own income, and keep their children. Two decades later, French women could claim similar rights. In contrast, the German Civil Code of 1900 granted all parental authority to the husband—even over his stepchildren. While married women could keep money they earned, all property owned by the wife before marriage or given to her after marriage became the husband's.

Read the Document

Henrik Ibsen, *A Doll's House*, Act Two

Finding a Place: Employment and Education

Feminists also worked to widen women's educational and employment opportunities. Even girls from privileged families rarely received rigorous educations before 1850. The minority who did go to school spent their time learning ladylike occupations such as fancy embroidery, flower arranging, and piano playing. Posture was more important than literature or science. Widening the world of women's education, then, became a crucial feminist aim and an area in which they achieved considerable, but limited, success.

Feminists' educational campaigns had three main emphases: improving the quality of girls' secondary education, expanding the number of girls' secondary schools, and opening universities to women. The fight to upgrade the quality of girls' secondary education was difficult. Many parents opposed an academic curriculum for girls, a position reinforced by medical professionals who argued that girls' brains could not withstand the strain of an intellectual education. Dorothea Beale (1831–1906) established one of the first academic high schools for girls in London in the 1850s, but she faced an uphill battle persuading parents to allow her to teach their daughters mathematics. In France, feminists achieved their goal of a state system of secondary schools for girls in the 1880s. They lost the battle for a university-preparatory curriculum, however, which made it difficult for girls to pass the exams necessary to enter the French university system.

Opportunities for university education for women varied. While few women entered French universities in this period, in the United States, one-third of all students in higher education were women by 1880. In Germany, however, women were not admitted as full-time university students until 1901. In Russia, full-time university study became available to women in Moscow in 1872, and by 1880 women in Russia had some of the best opportunities for higher education in Europe. But then in 1881, as we saw at the start of this chapter, a group of young assassins killed Alexander II—a group that included Sofia Perovskaia, an educated woman. The tsarist government concluded that revolutionary politics and advanced female education went hand in hand and cut off women's access to the universities.

Despite such limitations and reverses, the range of jobs open to European women did broaden. In 1900, French women won the right to practice law, and in 1903 a French woman lawyer presented a case in a European court for the first time. In 1906, the Polish-born physicist and Nobel Prize winner Marie Curie became the first woman to hold a university faculty position in France. By the early twentieth century, women doctors, although still unusual, were not unheard of. In Russia, women accounted for 10 percent of all physicians by 1914.

No More Angels

The campaigns for women's legal rights and the expansion of employment and educational opportunities helped women move into the public sphere. But the third goal of feminist activity—eradicating the double standard of sexual conduct—posed a more radical challenge to separate-sphere ideology. By arguing that the same moral standards should apply to men and women, feminists questioned whether separate spheres should exist at all.

The ideology of separate spheres glorified women's moral purity and held that the more aggressive, more animal-like natures of men naturally resulted in such pastimes as heavy drinking and sexual adventurism. The laws and the wider culture reflected these assumptions. For example, in France, a woman with an illegitimate child could not institute a paternity suit against the father: Premarital sex was a crime for the woman, but not for the man. Similarly, the English divorce legislation of 1857 declared that a woman's adultery was sufficient for a husband to sue for divorce; however, for a wife to divorce her husband, she had to prove that he had committed not just adultery, but bigamy, incest, or bestiality.

To feminists, applying different moral standards to men and women degraded men and blocked women's efforts to improve their own lives and society as a whole. As the French feminist leader Maria Deraismes explained, "To say that woman is an angel is to impose on her, in a sentimental and admiring fashion, all duties, and to reserve for oneself all rights. . . . I decline the honor of being an angel."[8]

To erase the moral distinctions between men and women, feminists fought on several fronts. One key struggle was over the regulation of prostitution. By the 1870s, many European countries, as well as the United States, had established procedures that made it safer for men to hire prostitutes, while still treating the women involved as criminals. In England, the Contagious Diseases Act, passed in 1870 to address the problem of venereal disease, declared that the police could require any woman suspected of being a prostitute to undergo a genital exam. Feminists such as Josephine Butler (1857–1942) contended that such legislation made it easier for men to indulge their sexual appetites, while punishing the impoverished women who had to sell their bodies to feed themselves and their children. For almost 20 years Butler led a campaign both to repeal the legislation that regulated prostitution and to focus public attention on the lack of employment opportunities for women.

Abuse of alcohol was another battleground for the women's movement. Feminists argued that the socially accepted practice of heavy male drinking impoverished families and caused domestic violence. The temperance or prohibitionist cause thus became a women's rights issue. Temperance organizations spread across much of the western world and, between 1916 and 1919, succeeded in pushing through prohibitionist legislation in Iceland, Finland, Norway, the United States, and many Canadian provinces. Prohibition, however, did little to transform gender relations, proved difficult to enforce, and was fairly rapidly repealed.

Other feminist moral reform campaigns achieved only limited success. The regulation of prostitution did end in England in 1886 and in the United States, France, and the Scandinavian countries by 1914, but remained in effect in Germany. By 1884 in France, a husband's adultery, like a wife's, could end a marriage; in England, however, the grounds for divorce remained differentiated by gender until 1923. In all European countries and in the United States, the sexual double standard remains embedded in much of middle- and working-class culture.

The Fight for Women's Suffrage

The slow pace and uneven progress on both the legal and moral fronts convinced many feminists that they needed the political clout of the *national* suffrage to achieve their goals. In 1867 the National Society for Women's Suffrage was founded in Britain. Over the next three decades, suffrage societies emerged in the rest of Europe. The French feminist leader Hubertine Auclert (1848–1914) described the vote as "the keystone that will give [women] all other rights." She refused to pay taxes on the grounds of "no

Different Voices
The Debate over Women's Suffrage

T he debate over a woman's right to vote did not divide along gender lines. Many men supported women's suffrage, and many women, including Britain's Queen Victoria, regarded it as a violation of the natural order. The following excerpts present arguments in the women's suffrage debate. The best-selling British novelist Mary Ward—or, as she always presented herself, Mrs. Humphry Ward (1851–1920)—wrote the first document, a letter to the editor of an influential magazine, in 1889. Many well-known and influential women signed the letter. The second excerpt comes from a French suffragist pamphlet published in 1913.

An Anti-Suffrage Argument: Mrs. Humphry Ward

We, the undersigned, wish to appeal to the common sense and the educated thought of the men and women of England against the proposed extension of the Parliamentary suffrage to women.

While desiring the fullest possible development of the powers, energies and education of women, we believe that their work for the State, and their responsibilities towards it, must always differ essentially from those of men, and that therefore their share in the working of the State machinery should be different from that assigned to men. . . . To men belong the struggle of debate and legislation in Parliament; the working of the army and navy; all the heavy, laborious, fundamental industries of the State, such as those of mines, metals, and railways; the lead and supervision of English commerce, the service of that merchant fleet on which our food supply depends.

At the same time we are heartily in sympathy with all the recent efforts which have been made to give women a more important part in those affairs of the community where their interests and those of men are equally concerned; where it is possible for them not only to decide but to help in carrying out, and where, therefore, judgment is weighted by a true responsibility, and can be guided by experience and the practical information which comes from it. As voters for or members of School Boards, Boards of Guardians, and other important public bodies, women have now opportunities for public usefulness which must promote the growth of character, and at the same time strengthen among them the social sense and habit. But we believe that the emancipation process has now reached the limits fixed by the physical constitution of women, and by the fundamental difference which must always exist between their main occupations and those of men. The care of the sick and the insane; the treatment of the poor; the education of children: in all these matters, and others besides, they have made good their claim to larger and more extended powers. We rejoice in it. But when it comes to questions of foreign or colonial policy, or of grave constitutional change, then we maintain that the necessary and normal experience of women does not and can never provide them with such materials for sound judgment as are open to men.

In conclusion: nothing can be further from our minds than to seek to depreciate the position or the importance of women. It is because we are keenly alive to the enormous value of their special contribution to the community, that we oppose what seems to us likely to endanger that contribution. We are convinced that the pursuit of a mere outward equality with men is for women not only vain but demoralizing. It leads to a total misconception of women's true dignity and special mission. It tends to personal struggle and rivalry, where the only effort of both the great divisions of the human family should be to contribute the characteristic labour and the best gifts of each to the common stock.

SOURCE: Mrs. Humphry Ward. "An Appeal Against Female Suffrage," *Nineteenth Century* 147 (June 1889): 781–785.

A Pro-Suffrage Argument: The French Union for Womens' Suffrage

We are going to try to prove that the vote for women is a just, possible and desirable reform. . . .

A woman has responsibility in the family; she ought to be consulted about the laws establishing her rights and duties with respect to her husband, her children, her parents.

Women work—and in ever greater numbers; a statistic of 1896 established that . . . the number of women workers was 35 percent of the total number of workers, both male and female.

If she is in business, she, like any businessman, has interests to protect. . . .

If a woman is a worker or a domestic, she ought to participate as a man does in voting on unionization laws, laws covering workers' retirement, social security, the limitation and regulation of work hours, weekly days off, labor contracts, etc.

. . . .

Finally, her special characteristics of order, economy, patience and resourcefulness will be as useful to society as the characteristics of man and will favor the establishment of laws too often overlooked until now.

The woman's vote will assure the establishment of important social laws.

All women will want:

To fight against alcoholism, from which they suffer much more than men;

To establish laws of health and welfare;

To obtain the regulation of female and child labor;

To defend young women against prostitution;

Finally, to prevent wars and to submit conflicts among nations to courts of arbitration.

SOURCE: A report presented to Besançon Municipal Council by the Franc-Comtois Group of the Union Française pour le Suffrage des Femmes. Besançon, March 1913, 6–9.

For Discussion

1. How does the argument of Mrs. Humphrey Ward reflect the liberal ideology of separate spheres for men and women?
2. What is the basic argument presented by the French Union for Women's Suffrage? Why did the suffragists argue that the women's vote would create a better world?
3. How does this argument in the pro-suffrage pamphlet reflect rather than reject separate sphere ideology?

suffragists Feminists who sought to achieve the national vote for women through rational persuasion and parliamentary politics.

suffragettes Feminist movement that emerged in Britain in the early twentieth century. Unlike the suffragists, who sought to achieve the national vote for women through rational persuasion, the suffragettes adopted the tactics of violent protest.

  Read the Document

Emmeline Pankhurst, "Freedom or Death"

taxation without representation" and was the first woman to describe herself as a "feminist," a word that entered the English language from French around 1890.

Auclert and other **suffragists** had little success. Only in Finland (1906) and Norway (1913) did women gain the national franchise in this period. The social upheaval of World War I brought women the vote in Russia (1917), Britain (1918), Germany (1918), Austria (1918), the Netherlands (1919), and the United States (1920). But women in Italy had to wait until 1945, in France until 1944, and in Greece until 1949. Swiss women did not vote until 1971.

As these dates indicate, feminists faced significant obstacles in their battle for the national franchise. (See *Different Voices* in this chapter.) In Roman Catholic countries such as France and Italy, the women's suffrage movement met two key barriers. First, the Church opposed the women's vote. Second, Catholicism empowered women in different ways. In its veneration of the Virgin Mary and other female saints, in its exaltation of family life, in the opportunity it offered for religious vocation as a nun, Catholicism provided women with many non-political avenues for emotional expression and intellectual satisfaction.

In Britain, feminists' failure to win the national franchise persuaded some activists to abandon the suffragist emphasis on working through the political system and to adopt more radical tactics. Led by the imposing mother-and-daughters team of Emmeline (1858–1928), Christabel (1880–1958), and Sylvia Pankhurst (1882–1960), the **suffragettes** formed a breakaway women's suffrage group in 1903. The suffragettes argued that male politicians would never simply give the vote to women; instead, they had to grab it by force. Adopting as their motto the slogan "Deeds, Not Words," suffragettes disrupted political meetings, chained themselves to the steps of the Houses of Parliament, shattered shop windows, burned churches, destroyed mailboxes, and even, in a direct attack on a cherished citadel of male middle-class culture, vandalized golf courses.

In opting for violence, suffragettes assaulted a central fortification of middle-class culture—the ideal of the passive, homebound woman. Their opponents reacted with fury. Police broke up suffragette rallies with sexually focused brutality: They dragged suffragettes by their hair, stomped on their crotches, punched their breasts, and tore off their blouses. Once in jail, hunger-striking suffragettes endured the horror of forced feedings. Jailers pinned the woman to her bed while the doctor thrust a tube down her throat, lacerating her larynx, and pumped in food until she gagged.

CONCLUSION

The West in an Age of Mass Politics

The clash between the suffragettes and their jailers was only one of a multitude of encounters, many of them violent, among those seeking access to political power and those seeking to limit that access, between 1870 and the start of World War I in 1914. Changing patterns of industrialization and accelerated urbanization gave rise to other sorts of encounters—between the liberal and the socialist, or between the manager seeking to cut production costs and the employee aiming to protect his wages, or between newly arrived immigrants in the city and long-established residents who spoke different languages.

Out of such encounters emerged key questions about the definition of "the West." Did democracy define the West? Should it? Was the West synonymous with white, western European men or could people with olive-colored or black skin—or women of any color—participate fully in Western culture and politics? Was "the West" defined by its rationality? In the eighteenth century, Enlightenment thinkers had looked to reason as the path to social improvement. The rise of nationalist politics, based on emotional appeal and often racist hatred, challenged this faith in reason. But at the same time, developments in industrial organization and technology, which helped expand European national incomes, pointed to the benefits of rational processes.

As we will see in the next chapter, the expansion of Western control over vast areas of Asia and Africa in this period led many Europeans and Americans to highlight economic prosperity and technological superiority as the defining characteristics of the West. Confidence, however, was accompanied by anxiety as these years also witnessed a far-reaching cultural and intellectual crisis. Closely connected to the development of mass politics and changes in social and gender relations, this crisis eroded many of the pillars of middle- and upper-class society and raised questions about Western assumptions and values.

MAKING CONNECTIONS

1. How did the economic transformation of the West after 1870 contribute to changes in middle-class women's roles—and in at least some women's expectations?
2. How did both socialism and racist-nationalist politics challenge the liberal definition of "the West"?
3. Why did anti-Semitism emerge as a powerful political force after 1870?

TAKING IT FURTHER

For suggested readings, see page R-1.

Chapter Review

Economic Transformation

23.1 What developments transformed Western economies and social life after 1870?

An economic depression and industrial changes led to accelerated emigration and urbanization patterns that eventually contributed to social unrest. Social tensions were heightened and political structures weakened when businessmen reacted to the depression by reducing employees and attempting to increase productivity. The results were angry workers, a rise in unemployment, and violent social encounters.

Defining the Nation

23.2 How did Western ruling classes respond to the new mass politics?

Political and social elites tried to eliminate social discontent and win the loyalty of the populations in three ways: by expanding the franchise, by providing social welfare programs, and by creating a sense of national identity that could rise above conflicting loyalties. At the same time they were committed to retaining their domination of social and political positions.

The New Mass Politics

23.3 What forms did mass politics assume during this era?

On the left side of the political spectrum, the ideologies of socialism, syndicalism, and anarchism all promised radical change and a more equal society. While socialist parties used the rhetoric of revolution and proved popular among urban workers, they increasingly worked for gradual change through political and legislative routes. Nationalist-racist politics dominated rightwing mass politics and proved appealing in areas that industrialized late and that contained competing ethnic and linguistic groups.

The Women's Revolt

23.4 How did the emergence of feminism in this period demonstrate the potential and the limits of political change?

The international feminist movement fought to remove legal barriers faced by married women, increase opportunities for female employment and higher education, eliminate the double standard of sexual conduct, and obtain the right to vote for all women. In all instances, the pace was slow and success uneven, although opportunities for women did increase.

Chapter Time Line

1867
Formation of National Society for Women's Suffrage in Britain inaugurates women's suffrage movement; Failed Fenian rebellion against British rule of Ireland.

1867

1871

1871
Unification of Germany; formation of French Third Republic.

1873
Onset of Great Depression in Trade and Agriculture; Irish Home Rule League formed.

1873

1878

1878
Russo-Turkish war ends; Ottoman Empire loses most of its European territories.

1879
Edison invents the light bulb.

1879

1881

1881
Assassination of Tsar Alexander II of Russia.

1882
Passage of May Laws in Russia intensifies persecution of Russian Jews.

1882

1894

1894
Accession of Tsar Nicholas II in Russia intensifies Russification.

1895
Conviction of Captain Alfred Dreyfus for treason in France sparks the Dreyfus Affair.

1895

1896

1896
Zionist leader Theodor Herzl publishes *The Jewish State*.

1905
Revolution in Russia.

1905

1906

1906
Finland passes women's suffrage.

1912
Socialist SPD becomes largest party in Germany.

1912

24 The West and the World: Cultural Crisis and the New Imperialism, 1870–1914

I n the summer of 1898, British troops invaded the Sudan in northeast Africa. On September 2, 40,000 Sudanese soldiers retaliated against British defenses at Omdurman. The Sudanese soldiers possessed a reputation for military fierceness, but they attacked with swords, spears, and outdated firearms. Equipped with repeating rifles and Maxim guns (a type of early machine gun), British troops simply mowed them down. After only five hours of fighting, 11,000 Sudanese lay dead. The British lost just 40 men. According to one soldier—the future prime minister Winston Churchill—the biggest danger to the British troops was boredom: "The mere physical act [of loading, firing, and reloading] became tedious." In contrast, Churchill recalled, "all the time out on the plain on the other side bullets were shearing through flesh, smashing and splintering bone; blood spouted from terrible wounds; valiant men were struggling through a hell of whistling metal, exploding shells, and spurting dust— suffering, despairing, dying."[1]

The lopsided Battle of Omdurman was one episode in the story of new imperialism, the final phase in the Western conquest of the globe. This often violent encounter between the West and the rest of the world was closely connected to the

LEARNING OBJECTIVES

24.1 ((
How did scientific developments during this period lead to both optimism and anxiety?

24.2 ((
Why did many Europeans in this period believe they were living in a time of cultural crisis?

24.3 ((
What were the causes and consequences of the new imperialist ideology for the West and non-Western societies?

((Listen to Chapter 24 on MyHistoryLab

ADELBERT SELIGMANN, *GERMAN SURGEON THEODOR BILLROTH AT WORK IN VIENNA* (1890) Modern surgery in the making: The patient has been anesthetized, but the modern operating room does not yet exist, nor are the doctors wearing gloves or masks. Billroth, the director of the Second Surgical Clinic in Vienna, pioneered surgical techniques for gastrointestinal illnesses and cancer.

👁 Watch the Video Series on MyHistoryLab

Learn about some key topics related to this chapter with the *MyHistoryLab Video Series: Key Topics in Western Civilization*

📖 Read the Document

Winston Churchill, *The River War: Chapter 15 The Battle of Omdurman*

political and economic upheavals examined in Chapter 23. An understanding of new imperialism, however, also demands a close look at scientific, intellectual, and cultural developments between 1870 and 1914. As Western adventurers risked life and limb to chart Africa's rivers and exploit Asia's resources, artists and scientists explored new worlds of thought and perception that challenged the social order and even the meaning of reality itself. This chapter examines the scientific, artistic, and physical explorations that characterized these decades and asks:

In what ways did these explorations redefine the West and its relationship with the rest of the world?

Scientific Transformations

24.1 How did scientific developments during this period lead to both optimism and anxiety?

Scientific advances after 1870 improved the health and hygiene of the Western world. Yet these changes also deepened the cultural anxiety of Europeans and Americans in this period as they pushed men and women into new encounters with the human body and the wider physical universe. In the crowded cities, the threat of contagious disease forced policymakers, physicians, and scientists to rethink the way the human body interacted with other bodies, human and microscopic. The work of biologists highlighted the way bodies had evolved to meet the challenges of survival, while the experiments of chemists and physicists exposed key flaws in the accepted model of the physical world.

Medicine and Microbes

In the nineteenth century, a series of developments transformed the practice of Western medicine. Before this time, physicians assumed that bad blood caused illness and so relied on practices such as leeching (attaching leeches to the skin) and bloodletting (slicing open a vein). Ignorant of the existence of bacteria and viruses, doctors attended one patient after another without bothering to wash their hands or surgical instruments. The only anesthetic available was alcohol. Patients and doctors regarded pain as inevitable, something to be endured rather than eased.

Urbanization overwhelmed such traditional medical practices. Expanding urban populations served as seedbeds for contagious diseases. Cholera outbreaks first forced doctors and public officials to pay attention to the relationship between overcrowding, polluted water, and epidemic disease. In 1848, for example, a cholera epidemic persuaded British officials to build the sewer system that still serves London today.

Neither officials nor doctors, however, understood the causes of disease until the 1860s, when the chemist Louis Pasteur (1822–1895) discovered the source of contagion to be microscopic living organisms—bacteria. Building on this discovery, Pasteur developed vaccines against anthrax, rabies, and many other diseases. (His process of purifying milk and fermented products is still known as pasteurization.) Following Pasteur, Robert Koch (1843–1910), professor of public health in Berlin, isolated the tuberculosis bacillus in 1882 and the bacteria that cause cholera in 1883. The work of Pasteur, Koch, and other scientists in tracing the transmission of disease improved Western medical practice. Between 1872 and 1900, the number of European deaths from infectious diseases dropped by 60 percent.

The use of anesthetics marked another important medical advance. In 1847 a Scottish physician first delivered a baby using chloroform to dull the mother's pain. Although condemned by theologians (who regarded pain as a necessary part of sinful human existence), the use of anesthetics spread quickly. Britain's Queen Victoria, who gave birth to nine children, expressed the feelings of many patients when she greeted the use of anesthetics in the delivery room with delight: "Oh blessed chloroform!"

These medical advances gave Europeans genuine confidence that the scientific conquest of nature would create a healthier environment. But the widespread awareness of germs also heightened anxiety. After the 1870s, Europeans were aware that they lived in a world populated by potentially deadly but invisible organisms, carried on the bodies of their servants, their employees, their neighbors, and their family members. Isolation of the bacilli that caused an illness did not immediately translate into its cure, and viral infections such as measles continued to be killers. Those who could afford to isolate themselves from danger often did so. As wealthy Europeans fled from urban centers of contagion, suburbs and seaside resorts multiplied.

The Triumph of Evolutionary Science

Developments in geology and biology also led to both confidence and anxiety. Evolutionary science provided a scientific framework in which educated Europeans could justify their own superior social and economic positions. Yet it challenged basic religious assumptions and depicted the natural world in new and unsettling ways.

Christians had long relied on the opening chapters of the Bible to understand the origins of nature and humanity, but nineteenth-century geologists challenged the biblical account. Although a literal reading of the Bible dated the Earth at 6,000 years old, geologists such as Charles Lyell (1797–1875) argued that the Earth had formed over millions of years. In *Principles of Geology*—a best-seller that went through 11 editions—Lyell refuted the orthodox Christian position that the biblical account of Noah's flood and other divine interventions explained geological change and the extinction of species. He argued that the material world must be seen as the product of natural forces still at work, still observable today.

But how did natural processes explain the tremendous variety of plant and animal species in the world? The British scientist Charles Darwin (1809–1882) answered this question in a way that proved satisfying to large numbers of educated Europeans—and horrifying to others. In the 1830s Darwin participated in a global expedition. On this trip he observed that certain species of animal and plant life, isolated on islands, had developed differently from related species on the coast. After returning to Britain, Darwin read the population theory of Thomas Malthus (see Chapter 21). Malthus argued that all species produce more offspring than can actually survive. Putting together Malthus's theory with his own observations, Darwin concluded that life is a struggle for survival, and that small biological variations can help an individual member of a species win this struggle. From this understanding came the **Darwinian theory of evolution**.

Darwin's evolutionary hypothesis rested on two ideas: *variation* and *natural selection*. Variation refers to the biological advantages that assist in the struggle for survival. A bird with a slightly longer beak, for example, might gain easier access to scarce food supplies. Over generations, the individuals with the variation displace those without. Variation, then, provides the means of natural selection, the process by which new species evolve.

Darwinian theory of evolution
Scientific theory associated with the nineteenth-century scientist Charles Darwin that highlights the role of variation and natural selection in the evolution of species.

 Read the Document

Charles Darwin, *Autobiography*

DARWIN'S DISTURBING MIRROR Simplified and often ridiculous versions of Darwin's ideas almost immediately entered popular culture. Here a monkey version of Darwin holds up a mirror to his fellow creature, who seems surprised by his reflection.

Darwin provided an explanation for evolutionary change, but two factors remained problematic. First, the process of variation that he described required many, many generations. Could it account for the multitude of variations apparent in the biological world? Second, how did variations first emerge and how are they inherited?

The answers lay embedded in the research of an Austrian monk, Gregor Mendel (1822–1884). Experimenting in his vegetable garden, Mendel developed the laws of genetic heredity. Mendel's work, however, was ignored until the end of the nineteenth century, when the Dutch botanist Hugo DeVries (1848–1935) used Mendel's data to hypothesize that evolution occurred through radical mutations in the reproductive cells of an organism, which pass on to offspring at the moment of reproduction. Mutations that offer an advantage in the struggle for existence enable the mutated offspring to survive—and to produce more mutant offspring. Thus, evolution can proceed by leaps, rather than over a very long period of time.

Long before these genetic underpinnings of evolution were understood, however, Darwin's theories proved influential. Published in 1859, *On the Origin of Species* aroused immediate interest and debate. Controversy intensified when, in 1871, Darwin published *The Descent of Man*, in which he argued that human beings, like other species, evolved over time. This denial of humanity's special place within the universe horrified many Christians. They found the Darwinian view of nature even more troubling. According to orthodox Christian theology, the beauty of nature reveals God to the believer. In the Darwinian universe, however, nature does not display God's hand at work. Instead, it is a blood-filled arena in which organisms compete for survival—"nature red in tooth and claw," as the British poet Alfred Lord Tennyson put it. In such a universe, ideas of purpose and meaning seemed to disappear.

Nevertheless, many Europeans and Americans welcomed Darwin's evolutionary theory because it seemed to confirm their faith in the virtues of competition and in the inevitability of progress. As Darwin himself wrote, because "natural selection works solely by and for the good of each being, all [physical] and mental development will tend to progress toward perfection."

Social Darwinism and Racial Hierarchies

While Darwin used his theory of evolution to explain biological change, the British writer Herbert Spencer (1820–1902) insisted that evolutionary theory should be applied to social policy as well. A champion of *laissez-faire* economics (see Chapter 22), Spencer coined the phrase "the survival of the fittest." He argued that charity or government assistance for the poor slowed the evolution of a better society by enabling the weak—the less fit—to survive.

Social Darwinists applied Spencer's concept of the survival of the fittest to entire races. They argued that the nonwhite races in Africa and Asia stood below white

Social Darwinists Followers of the later-nineteenth-century application of the theory of evolution to entire human societies.

Europeans on the evolutionary ladder. Hence, G. A. Henty, a British novelist and Social Darwinist, insisted that the "intelligence of the average negro is about equal to that of a European [male] child of ten years old."[2] Social Darwinists used such pseudoscientific arguments to justify Western imperialism. Evolutionary backwardness, they argued, doomed the nonwhite races to conquest and even extinction. These lines from a bestselling British novel sum up the Social Darwinist worldview: "Those who are weak must perish; the earth is to the strong. . . . We run to place and power over the dead bodies of those who fail and fall; ay, we win the food we eat from out the mouths of starving babes. It is the scheme of things."[3]

Social Darwinists used evolution to justify not only racial but also gender hierarchies. Arguing that the bodies of women were less evolved than those of men, they identified women as mentally and physically inferior. Such ideas spread throughout Western culture in the late nineteenth century. Leading intellectuals such as the psychiatrist Sigmund Freud, for example, argued that "the female genitalia are more primitive than those of the male," while the French social theorist Gustave Le Bon compared the average female brain to that of a gorilla.

Wrenched out of its biological framework and misapplied to social and international affairs, evolutionary theory thus justified the central assumptions of nineteenth-century society: the benefits of competition, the rightness of white rule and male dominance, and the superiority of Western civilization. Yet evolutionary science also worked to undermine Western confidence because with the idea of evolution came the possibility of *regression*: Was the traffic on the evolutionary ladder all one-way, or could species descend to a lower evolutionary level? Could humanity regress to its animal origins?

The concept of the **inheritance of acquired characteristics**, associated with the work of the French scientist Jean-Baptiste Lamarck (1744–1829), strengthened these fears of regression. More than 50 years before Darwin published his *Origin of Species,* Lamarck theorized that "acquired characteristics"—traits that an individual developed in response to experience or the environment, such as the stooped back of a miner, the poor vision of a lace maker, or the promiscuity of a prostitute—could be "acquired" by the individual's children. Because the process of genetic reproduction was not yet understood, Lamarck's theories remained influential throughout the nineteenth century. Middle-class Europeans and Americans feared that the impoverished masses in the expanding city slums were acquiring undesirable characteristics, ranging from physical deformity to sexual immorality and violent criminality. Using Lamarck's theories, they concluded that if growing numbers of poor children inherited these traits, the evolutionary ascent of the West could slow or even reverse.

 Read the Document

Herbert Spencer, "Illustrations of Universal Progress"

inheritance of acquired characteristics Now discredited scientific theory of evolutionary change, powerful in the nineteenth century.

The Revolution in Physics

A revolution in physics also began in this era. Although its most dramatic consequences—atomic weapons and nuclear energy—would not be realized for another half century, this revolution contributed to both the exhilaration and the uncertainty that characterized Western intellectual and cultural history after 1870.

At the core of the revolution in physics lay the question, "What is matter?" The triumph of the theories of Isaac Newton had ensured that, for 200 years, educated Westerners had a clear, certain answer: Matter was what close observation and measurement showed it to be (see Chapter 17). Three-dimensional material bodies, made up of the building blocks called atoms, moved against a fixed backdrop of space and time. Like a machine, nature was predictable. Using reason, observation, and common sense, then, human beings could understand, control, and improve the material world.

A series of discoveries and experiments challenged this commonsense view of the universe and offered in its place a more mysterious and unsettling vista. The discovery of the X-ray in 1895 disrupted prevailing assumptions about the solidity of matter. These assumptions crumbled further when the Polish chemist Marie Sklodowska Curie (1867–1934) found a new element, radium, which did not behave the way matter was supposed to behave: Continually emitting subatomic particles, radium did not possess a

MARIE SKLODOWSKA CURIE AND PIERRE CURIE IN THEIR LABORATORY IN 1904 Both Curies won Nobel Prizes.

theory of relativity Albert Einstein's revolutionary model of the physical universe as four-dimensional.

constant atomic weight. Two years later, the German scientist Max Planck (1858–1947) theorized that a heated body radiates energy not in the continuous, predictable stream most scientists envisaged, but rather in irregular clumps, which he called *quanta*. Most scientists dismissed Planck's hypothesis as contrary to common sense, but soon his "quantum theory" helped shape a new model of a changeable universe.

These scientific discoveries provided the context for the work of Albert Einstein (1879–1955), the most famous scientist of the twentieth century. Bored by his job as a patent clerk, Einstein passed the time speculating on the nature of the cosmos. In 1905, he directly challenged the Newtonian model of the universe by publishing his **theory of relativity**. With this theory, Einstein offered a model of a four-dimensional rather than three-dimensional universe. To height, width, and depth, Einstein added *time*. He theorized that time and space are not fixed. They shift, relative to the position of the observer. Similarly, matter itself shifts because the mass of a material object changes with its motion. In the Einsteinian model, then, time, space, and matter intermingle in a universe of relative flux. Einstein used his own everyday experiences to explain his model. He noticed that as the streetcar in which he was traveling passed a fixed object, like a house, the object appeared to narrow. The faster the streetcar, the more the object narrowed. In other words, the dimension of width varies according to the speed and position of the viewer.

Despite such efforts at everyday explanation, the revolution in physics made much of science incomprehensible to ordinary men and women. Most importantly, the new science challenged the basic assumptions that governed nineteenth-century thought by offering a vision of the universe in which what you see is *not* what you get, in which objective reality might well be the product of subjective perception.

Social Thought: The Revolt Against Positivism

Just as the revolution in physics presented a new and unsettling picture of the physical universe, so also troubling theories about the nature of human society surfaced in "social thought" (the research and publications that lay the foundations for disciplines such as sociology, psychology, and anthropology). As Chapter 22 explained, the mainstream of nineteenth-century thought was **positivist**: It placed great faith in human reason. At the end of the century, however, social thinkers revolted against positivism by emphasizing the role of nonrational forces in determining human conduct.

Gustave Le Bon (1841–1931), for example, developed his theory of crowd or collective psychology by studying how appeals to emotion, particularly in the form of symbols and myths, influenced group actions. For Le Bon, the new mass politics (see Chapter 23) was a form of such crowd behavior: Uneducated voters made choices on the basis of emotion, not logical argument. Le Bon concluded that democracy relinquished political control to the irrational masses and so would lead only to disaster.

While Le Bon focused on the crowd, the German social theorist Max Weber (1864–1920) explored the "bureaucratization" of modern life—the tendency of political and economic institutions to become more and more bureaucratic, and therefore standardized and impersonal. Weber saw the triumph of bureaucracy as generally positive, the victory of reason and science over tradition and prejudice. But he also recognized that bureaucracies could crush ideals and individuals and so threaten personal freedom.

Troubled by the vision of individuals trapped within "the iron cage of modern life," Weber in 1898 suffered a nervous breakdown. According to his wife, "an evil something out of the subterranean unconscious . . . grasped him by its claws."[4] This view of the individual as a captive of the unconscious was central to the revolt against positivism and reached its fullest development in the influential work of the Viennese scientist and physician Sigmund Freud (1856–1939). Freud's effort to treat patients suffering from nervous disorders persuaded him that the conscious mind plays a limited role in shaping an individual's actions. In *The Interpretation of Dreams* (1900), Freud argued that beneath the rational surface of each human being surge all kinds of hidden desires, including such irrational drives as the longing for death and destruction. Freud believed that he could understand human behavior (and treat mental illness) by diving below the rational surface and exploring the submerged terrain of unconscious desire. The emergence of Freudian psychology, however, convinced many educated Western individuals not that the irrational could be uncovered and controlled, but rather that the irrational was *in* control.

positivist The emphasis on the use of the scientific method to reach truth; a stress on observable fact.

Cultural Crisis: The *Fin-de-Siècle* and the Birth of Modernism

24.2 Why did many Europeans in this period believe they were living in a time of cultural crisis?

The recognition of the power of the irrational contributed to a growing cultural crisis. The French phrase *fin-de-siècle*, literally translated as "end of the century," served as a shorthand term for the mood of uneasiness that characterized much of Western society in this era. Fast-moving economic, technological,

fin-de-siècle French term for the "turn of the century"; used to refer to the cultural crisis of the late nineteenth century.

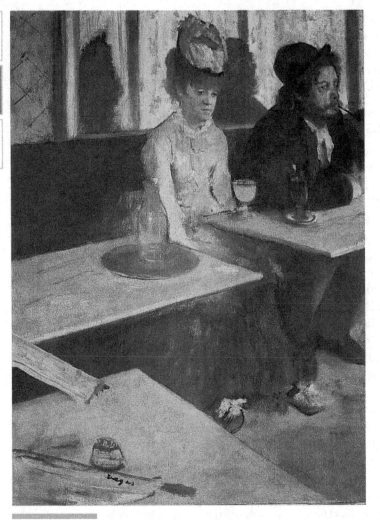

EDGAR DEGAS, *ABSINTHE* (1876–1877) Parisian café-goers often indulged in absinthe, a strong alcoholic drink flavored with anise. Degas's portrait of one such absinthe drinker is a picture of deterioration: This woman's lined face, weary posture, and isolation provide an evocative image of the *fin-de-siècle*.

SOURCE: Edgar Degas, "The Glass of Absinthe," 1876. Oil on canvas, 36 × 27 in. Musee d'Orsay, Paris. Scala/Art Resource, NY.

modernism Term applied to artistic and literary movements from the late nineteenth century through the 1950s. Modernists sought to create new aesthetic forms and values.

 Read the Document

Emile Zola, *Nana*

and social changes, coupled with new scientific theories, convinced many that old solutions no longer worked. The quest for new answers fostered the birth of **modernism**, a broad label for a series of unsettling and inspiring developments in thought, literature, and art. Many Europeans and Americans celebrated modernism as a release from restraining middle-class codes. Others, however, responded fearfully.

The *Fin-de-Siècle*

The sense that the West was in a state of decline fostered *fin-de-siècle* anxiety. A number of factors contributed to these fears of degeneration. As cities spread, so did perceptions of rising crime rates. Such perceptions went hand in hand with the reality of increasing drug and alcohol use. Diners in high society finished their sumptuous meals with strawberries soaked in ether, and respectable bourgeois men offered each other cocaine as a quick "pick-me-up" at the end of the working day. Middle-class mothers fed restless babies opium-laced syrups, while workers bought enough opium-derived laudanum on Saturday afternoon to render them unconscious until work on Monday morning. Using Lamarck's theory of the inheritance of acquired characteristics, scientists contended that criminality and drug addictions would be passed on from generation to generation, thus contributing to social decline.

Popular novels also contributed to the fear of degeneration by depicting Western culture as diseased or barbaric. In *Nana* (1880), the French novelist Émile Zola (1840–1902) used the title character, a prostitute, to embody his country. Watching as French soldiers march to defeat in the Franco-Prussian War, Nana is dying of smallpox, her face "a charnel-house, a heap of pus and blood, a shovelful of putrid flesh."[5] Works such as *Dr. Jekyll and Mr. Hyde* (1886) and *Dracula* (1897) showed that beneath the cultured exterior of a civilized man lurked a primitive, bloodthirsty beast.

The writings of the German philosopher and poet Friedrich Nietzsche (1844–1900) epitomized the mood of the *fin-de-siècle*. Nietzsche dismissed most members of modern society as little more than sheep, penned in by outdated rules and beliefs. Middle-class morality, rooted in Christianity, had sapped Western culture of its vitality. "Christianity has taken the side of everything weak," Nietzsche insisted.

Nietzsche traced the weakness of Western culture beyond Christianity, however, back to the ancient Greek emphasis on rationality. He argued that by overemphasizing rational thought, Western societies repressed powerful instinctive and emotional forces. Even the style of his publications reflected Nietzsche's impatience with reason. Rather than write carefully constructed essays that proceeded logically from one fact to another, he adopted an elusive, poetic style characterized by disconnected fragments, more accessible to intuitive understanding than to rational analysis.

Nietzsche's call to "become what you are" attracted young enthusiasts throughout Europe in the 1890s. These Nietzsche fans embraced his conviction that the confining codes of middle-class morality held back the individual from personal liberation. "God is dead," Nietzsche proclaimed, "and we have killed him." If God is dead, then "there is nobody who commands, nobody who obeys, nobody who trespasses." Such declarations alarmed other readers, who viewed Nietzsche's work as a cause rather than a critique of Western decay.

Tightening Gender Boundaries

Fear of degeneration also expressed itself in late-nineteenth-century efforts to strengthen the boundaries that separated "maleness" from "femaleness." The feminist and the homosexual joined the criminal, the drug addict, and the prostitute in the list of dangerous and degenerate beings. (See *Justice in History* in this chapter.)

📖 **Read the Document**

Richard Freiherr von Krafft-Ebing, *Psychopathia Sexualia*

In the decades after 1870, as middle-class women began to move into the public spheres of university education and paid employment, feminism emerged as a political force (see Chapter 23). Many Europeans and Americans viewed these developments with alarm. They argued that the female body and brain could not withstand the strains of public life. In the antifeminist view, a woman who pursued higher education or a career not only risked her own physical and mental breakdown, she also tended to produce physically and morally degenerate children and so threatened the evolutionary advance of Western societies.

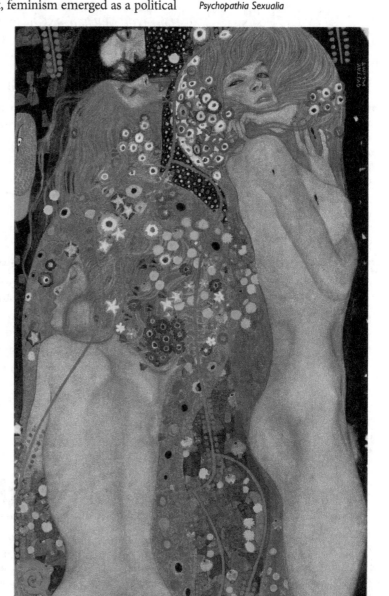

Like feminists, homosexuals were singled out as threats to the social order in this period. Before 1869, *homosexual* was not a word: Coined by a Hungarian scientist seeking a new label for a new concept, it entered the English language in 1890. Traditionally, Europeans and Americans had viewed same-sex sexual practice as a form of immoral behavior, indulged in by morally lax—but otherwise normal—men. (Few considered the possibility of female homosexual behavior.) In the later nineteenth century, however, the emphasis shifted from *actions* to *identity*, from condemning a type of behavior to denouncing a type of person: the homosexual.

Three developments heightened the fear of homosexuality. First, the anonymity and mobility of urban life offered homosexuals space in which they could express a more confident homosexual identity. Throughout Western cities, homosexual subcultures became more numerous and more visible—and, therefore, more threatening.

Second, the rise of corporate capitalism (see Chapter 23) undercut the liberal masculine ideal. Liberal ideology depicted middle-class men as aggressive, self-reliant initiators. Now these men found themselves bound to desks and taking orders. No longer masters of their own fates, they were now bit players in the drama of corporate capitalism. Condemnation of not only homosexuality but also feminism provided a way to redefine and strengthen masculine identity.

Finally, a new science of sexuality contributed to new fears. During the final decades of the nineteenth century, scientists made important breakthroughs in the understanding of human reproduction and sexual physiology. In 1879, for example, scientists first witnessed, with the aid of the microscope, a sperm

GUSTAV KLIMT, *WATER SERPENTS* (1904–1907) Klimt's paintings often featured women as alluring but engulfing elemental forces. Here he uses the mythological imagery of sea serpents to depict women as unabashedly sensual, even as creatures on the prowl—quite a contrast to the passive woman of separate-sphere ideology.

cell penetrating an egg. Greater understanding of sexual *physiology*, however, went hand in hand with the effort to define normal sexual *practice* and to the medical condemnation of homosexuality as pathology.

Heightened concern about gender boundaries pervaded not only the science, but also the art of the late-nineteenth-century West. In the visual arts, women often appeared as elemental forces, creatures of nature rather than civilization, who threatened to trap, emasculate, engulf, suffocate, or destroy the unwary man. The Austrian Gustav Klimt (1862–1918) frequently painted women as creatures of nature, often provocatively sexual. Such images recur even more graphically in the work of Klimt's student, Egon Schiele (1890–1918). In his short life Schiele created more than 3,000 works on paper and 300 paintings, many of these depictions of dangerous women. Works such as *Black-Haired Girl with Raised Skirt* (1911) used harsh colors and brazen postures to present an unsettling vision of female sexuality.

The Birth of Modernism

modernist movement Term applied to the artistic and literary movements from the late nineteenth century through the 1950s. Modernists sought to create new aesthetic forms and values.

Schiele's disturbing paintings exemplify the new **modernist movement**. In the final decades of the nineteenth century, modernist artists such as Schiele tossed aside the rules and embarked on a series of bold experiments. No single style characterized modernism, but modernist artists, musicians, and writers shared an impatience with the middle-class liberal worldview.

Modernists challenged liberalism, first, by rejecting the idea of art as an instrument of moral or emotional uplift. Liberals believed that the arts served a useful purpose in civilized society. Visiting art galleries was a popular activity, rather like going to the movies today. Respectable workers and middle-class men and women crowded into exhibitions where they viewed paintings that told an entertaining story and had a clear moral message. In contrast, modernists declared "art for art's sake." Modernist painters did not seek to tell a story or to preach a sermon, but rather to experiment with line, color, and composition.

Second, modernists rejected the middle-class faith in the power of human reason and observation, and instead emphasized the role of individual experience and intuition in shaping human understanding. In Paris, for example, a group of artists centered on

Justice in History
The Trial of Oscar Wilde

In March 1895 the Marquis of Queensberry left a message with the porter of a gentleman's club in London. The message, written on Queensberry's calling card, read "To Oscar Wilde, posing as a *somdomite*." What Queensberry meant to write was *sodomite,* a common term for a man who engaged in sexual relations with other men. By handing the card to the porter, Queensberry publicly accused Wilde, a famous novelist and playwright, of homosexual activity. Ten years earlier the British Parliament had declared illegal all homosexual activity, even consensual relations between adults in a private home. Queensberry's accusation, then, was serious. Oscar Wilde responded by suing Queensberry for libel—and set in motion a legal process that led to Wilde's imprisonment, and indirectly, to his early death.

Wilde made a reckless mistake when he chose to sue for libel, for in fact Queensberry had not libeled him. Wilde was a homosexual. He and Queensberry's son, Lord Alfred Douglas, were lovers. Why, then, did Wilde dare to challenge Queensberry? Perhaps he thought that the fact that he was married, with two children, shielded him against the charge. Or perhaps his professional successes gave Wilde a sense of invulnerability. With two of his plays then appearing on the London stage to favorable reviews, he stood at the pinnacle of his career in the spring of 1895.

Wilde had built that career by flouting middle-class codes of morality. He saw himself as an artist and insisted that art should be freed from social convention and moral restraint. His "High

(continued on next page)

Society" comedies about privileged elites living scandalous lives and exchanging witty epigrams were far from the morally uplifting drama expected by middle-class audiences.

Wilde also used his public persona to attack the conventional, the respectable, and the orthodox. Widely recognized for his outrageous clothing and conversation, he had consciously adopted the mannerisms of what nineteenth-century Britons called a "dandy"—a well-dressed, irreverent, artistic, leisured, and effeminate man. Before his trial, such effeminacy did not serve as a sign of, or a code for, homosexual inclinations, but it did signal to many observers a lavish—and loose—lifestyle. Oscar Wilde, then, was a man many British men and women loved to hate.

Even so, when his trial opened Wilde appeared to be in a strong position. Because Wilde had Queensberry's card with the "sodomite" charge written on it, Queensberry faced certain conviction un-

OSCAR WILDE AND LORD ALFRED DOUGLAS Although the British government pursued its case against Wilde, it made no effort to put together a case against Douglas.

How do we account for the intensity of Wills's language and the severity of Wilde's sentence? Why did the condemnation of homosexuality grow harsher in the closing decades of the nineteenth century? One answer is that in a time of rapid change, boundaries became more important, a way to create and enforce social order. Wilde crossed those boundaries and so seemed to threaten social stability.

Secondly, by the end of the nineteenth century, the state had assumed new responsibilities. Desperate to enhance national strength in a period of heightened international competition, Western governments intervened in areas previously considered to be the domain of the private citizen. To strengthen national productivity and military viability, governments now compelled parents to send their children to school, regulated the hours adults could work, supervised the sale of food and drugs, set new standards for housing construction—and policed sexual boundaries.

less he could show that Wilde had engaged in homosexual activity. Wilde knew that Queensberry would not risk shining the legal spotlight on his own son's homosexuality.

At first, Queensberry's attorney, Edward Carson, focused on Wilde's published works, trying to use Wilde's own words to showcase his immorality. It proved an ineffective strategy. On the witness stand, Wilde reveled in the attention and made Carson seem like a man of little culture and no humor.

On the second day of the libel trial, however, Carson interrogated Wilde about his associations with male prostitutes. Suddenly the issue was no longer the moral worth of Wilde's published writings, but rather his sexual life. At this point, Wilde withdrew his libel charge against Queensberry, and the court declared the marquis not guilty.

If Queensberry was innocent of libel in calling Wilde a sodomite, then by clear implication, Wilde was guilty of homosexual activity and therefore a criminal. On May 25, 1895—just three months after Queensberry had left his misspelled message with the club porter—Wilde was found guilty of seven counts of gross indecency with other men. The presiding judge, Sir Alfred Wills, characterized the trial as "the worst case I have ever tried," and described Wilde as "the centre of a circle of extensive corruption of the most hideous kind." Wills declared, "I shall under the circumstances be expected to pass the severest sentence the law allows. In my judgment it is totally inadequate for such a case." He sentenced Wilde to two years at hard labor. The physical punishment took its toll. Wilde died in 1900 at age 46.

The policing of sexual boundaries became easier after the well-publicized Wilde trial because it provided a homosexual personality profile, a "Wanted" poster to hang on the walls of Western culture. Wilde became the embodiment of The Homosexual, a particular and peculiar type of person, and a menace to cultural stability. The Wilde trial linked "dandyism" to this new image. Outward stylistic choices such as effeminacy, artistic sensibilities, and flamboyant clothing and conversation became, for many observers, the telltale signs of inner corruption. Thus, the Wilde case marked a turning point in the construction and the condemnation of a homosexual identity.

For Discussion

1. How does this trial illustrate the role of medical, legal, and cultural assumptions in shaping sexual identity in the late nineteenth century?
2. Did the trial of Oscar Wilde achieve justice? If so, what kind and for whom?

Taking It Further

An Ideal Husband. 1999. This film adaptation of Oscar Wilde's hilarious play exemplifies his lighthearted but devastating critique of conventional manners and morals.

The Real Trial of Oscar Wilde: The First Uncensored Transcript of The Trial of Oscar Wilde vs. John Douglas (Marquess of Queensberry), 1895. 2003. Includes an introduction by Wilde's grandson Merlin Holland.

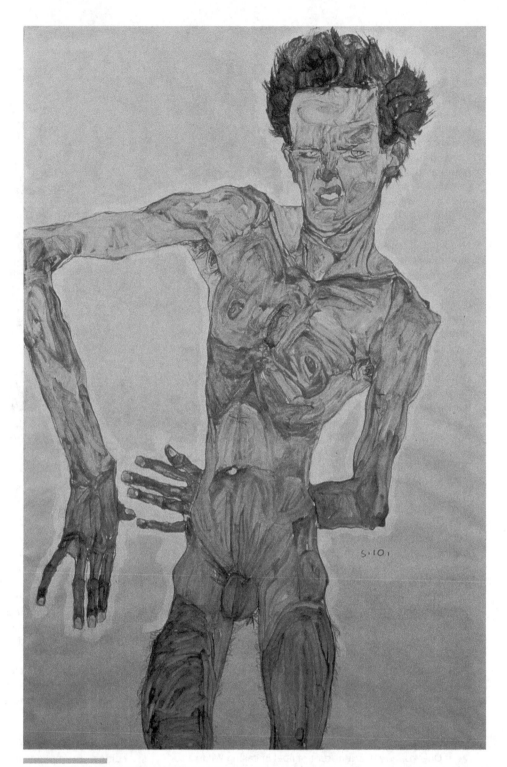

EGON SCHIELE, *NUDE SELF-PORTRAIT WITH OPEN MOUTH* (1910) Schiele's paintings exemplify the Expressionist movement with their bold use of color and their no-holds-barred exploration of human emotion and sexuality.

SOURCE: Egon Schiele (1890–1918), "Standing Nude, Facing Front (Self Portrait), 1910." Graphische Sammlung Albertina, Vienna, Austria/ The Bridgeman Art Library.

Cubists Followers of the early twentieth century modernist artistic movement that emphasized the fragmentation of human perception through visual experiments with geometric forms.

Expressionism Modernist artistic movement of the early twentieth century that used bold colors and experimental forms to express emotional realities.

the Spaniard Pablo Picasso (1881–1973) juxtaposed different perspectives and points of view on a single canvas. They called themselves **Cubists**. In one cultural historian's apt description, "Cubists cracked the mirror of art."[6] Their fragmented, jagged, energetic works no longer reflected the world "out there," but instead revealed the artist's fluid and contradictory vision. (See *Encounters and Transformations* in this chapter.)

This emphasis on art as a personal expression is also seen in the **Expressionist** movement, centered not in France as was Cubism, but in central and eastern Europe.

Expressionists such as Egon Schiele argued that art should express the artist's interior vision, not the exterior world. In nude self-portraits, Schiele depicted himself as ugly and emaciated, a graphic expression of his tormented internal universe.

Finally, modernists challenged the liberal worldview by insisting that history was irrelevant. Liberals viewed history as an important source of moral lessons and as a key to understanding the present and improving the future. Modernists, however, argued that fast-moving industrial and technological change shattered the lines connecting past, present, and future. Painters such as the Futurists in Italy (one of the many artistic movements that clustered under the modernist umbrella) reveled in the new machine age, a world cut off from anything that had gone before. In their paintings they depicted human beings as machines in motion, moving too fast to be tied down to history. The Futurists also challenged traditional ways of living, epitomized in their declaration of war on spaghetti.

New musical styles emerging in popular and high culture in these decades also demonstrated this modernist sense of discontinuity. Ragtime, for example, combined syncopation with unexpected rhythms and sudden stops, while jazz, which developed around the turn of the century in black urban neighborhoods in the United States, created a musical universe of constant spontaneous change. In Europe, symphonic musicians such as Russian composer Igor Stravinsky (1882–1971) and his Austrian counterpart Arnold Schoenberg (1874–1951) shocked their audiences with pieces that broke all the rules. In Stravinsky's ballet, *The Rite of Spring* (1913), the meter shifts 28 times in the final 34 bars of the central dance. Similarly, Schoenberg eliminated repetition from his works and used rapid tempo changes.

Audiences tended to greet modernist works with incomprehension and outrage. At the first performance of Schoenberg's *Five Orchestral Pieces* in London in 1912, one listener reported that "the audience laughed audibly all through . . . and hissed vigorously at the end." The next year in Vienna, the performance of a different Schoenberg piece had to be abandoned after the audience rioted. Similarly, reviewers routinely condemned modernist painting as sick, pornographic, or simply insane. One London critic

24.1

24.2

24.3

View the **Closer Look**

Futurism: Unique Form of Continuity in Space

GINO SEVERINI: *SUBURBAN TRAIN ARRIVING AT PARIS,* 1915 The interlapping geometric forms and images of tilting buildings, as well as the subject matter—a train arriving—illustrate the Futurist emphasis on change and movement, as well as their delight in the new machine age.

WILLIAM HOLMAN HUNT, *THE LIGHT OF THE WORLD* (1852) In this devotional painting, Jesus, the light of the world, stands knocking at the closed door of a lost soul. The overgrown weeds and fallen fruit symbolize sin and the lantern stands for Christ's illuminating power. The stars and crescents on the lantern represent Holman Hunt's hope for the conversion of Jews and Muslims to Christianity. The popularity of this work highlights the limited appeal of modernist art in the pre-1914 era.

SOURCE: William Holman Hunt (1827–1910), "The Light of the World," C. 1852, oil on canvas. © Manchester Art Gallery, UK/TheBridgeman Art Library.

dismissed the painter Paul Cézanne (1869–1954) as "an artist with diseased retinas."

This hostility to modernism shows that most audiences remained firmly within a cultural milieu in which paintings revealed pretty scenes, novels told a moral tale, and music offered harmonious charm. In the early twentieth century, one of the most popular pieces of art in the English-speaking world was *The Light of the World* by William Holman Hunt (1827–1910). This moralistic piece with its easy-to-understand and uplifting story, at odds with every modernist principle, triumphantly toured the British Empire from 1905 to 1907. Enthusiastic crowds jostled for tickets and hailed the painting as a religious and artistic masterpiece.

Popular Religion and Secularization

As the response to Holman Hunt's depiction of Jesus reveals, religious belief remained a powerful force in the decades after 1870. In Britain, Sunday worship continued to be a central aspect of middle-class culture, and the still-strong Sunday School movement and religious instruction in state schools ensured that working-class children were taught the fundamentals of the Christian faith. On the Continent, many Europeans connected unbelief with revolutionary anarchy after the Communards—the Parisian radicals who tried to set up a revolutionary government in 1871—executed the Archbishop of Paris. The excesses of the Paris Commune (discussed in Chapter 22) thus contributed to a religious revival. Popular Catholic religiosity often focused on the cult of the Virgin Mary: By the 1870s, the shrine at Lourdes, the site of Mary's miraculous appearance in 1858, was attracting hundreds of thousands of Catholic pilgrims.

Three additional factors contributed to the religiosity of late-nineteenth-century Europe. First, the high rate of immigration meant that many people found themselves searching for something familiar in foreign cities. They often turned to the religious cultures of the homeland. In English cities, for example, Irish immigrants looked to the local Roman Catholic Church for spiritual solace, material support, and social contacts. Second, in many regions nationalism strengthened religious belief and practice. Hence, for Polish nationalists dreaming of independence from Russian rule, Roman Catholicism was a key part of a separate national identity. Finally, as we shall see in the next section, the expansion of Western empires across the globe appeared to provide clear evidence of the ongoing triumph of Christianity.

Yet this triumphalism met growing anxiety as Christians faced new challenges. As we saw in our discussion of Darwin, developments in biology undermined the orthodox Christian view of nature as harmonious and divinely directed. Medical advances also narrowed the appeal of traditional religion. People had once accepted diseases

PILGRIMAGES IN FRANCE—DEPARTURE FROM A PROVINCIAL STATION OF "SACRED HEART" PILGRIMS FOR LOURDES.

PILGRIMAGE TO LOURDES This 1873 engraving from an American newspaper shows "Sacred Heart" pilgrims in France departing from a provincial station near Lourdes to continue their journey on foot.

such as cholera as "acts of God," but now they understood their natural causes. Scientists, in other words, seemed able to answer questions previously thought the province of theologians. Finally, the emergence of the social sciences directly challenged Christianity by dismissing the question of religious truth and asking instead, what is the function of religious belief in a society? Emile Durkheim (1858–1917), one of the founders of French sociology, dared to lump Christianity with "even the most barbarous and the most fantastic rites and the strangest myths." Durkheim insisted that no religion was more true than any other—each filled a social need.[7]

The Christian response to these challenges varied. Many Protestants embraced the scientific method as a gift from God. They argued that the study of the Bible as a historical and literary document—as a collection of divinely inspired texts produced by all-too-human writers—promised to free Christians *from* antiquated beliefs impossible to sustain in the new scientific age and *for* a more relevant, reform-oriented religious life. Protestant fundamentalists, however, insisted on retaining a belief in the literal, historical, and scientific accuracy of the Christian scriptures, a stance that led them to oppose science as the enemy of religion.

The Roman Catholic papacy also adopted a defiant pose in the face of modern challenges. In 1864, Pope Pius IX (r. 1846–1878) issued a *Syllabus of Errors,* which condemned the notion that the pope should "harmonize himself with progress, with liberalism, and with modern civilization." Six years later, a church council—the first called since the sixteenth-century Catholic Reformation—proclaimed the doctrine of **papal infallibility**. According to this doctrine, when the pope issues a decree that concerns matters of faith and morality, that decree is free from error and valid for all time and all places. The proclamation of papal infallibility rebuked those Catholic theologians who argued that Christianity had to adapt to the modern world.

The Roman Catholic Church also faced important political challenges in these decades. In countries with a large Catholic population, the Church's alliance with conservatism pushed **anticlericalism** to a dominant position on the liberal agenda. In France, for example, Catholics dominated the political parties that demanded a return

Read **the Document**

Matthew Arnold, *Dover Beach*

Read **the Document**

Pope Leo XIII, *Of New Things*

papal infallibility The doctrine of the Roman Catholic Church proclaimed at the First Vatican Council in 1870 that the pope could not err when making solemn declarations regarding faith or morals.

anticlericalism Opposition to the political influence of the Roman Catholic Church.

to monarchical or authoritarian rule; liberal Frenchmen who wanted the Third Republic to survive thus fought to reduce the Church's influence. More generally, the spread of socialism provided European workers with a belief system and source of communal life outside of, and opposed to, the Church.

The most significant challenge faced by religious institutions after 1870, however, emerged not from parliamentary assemblies, socialist rallies, or scientific laboratories, but rather from the department stores and sports fields. In the growing industrial cities, working- and middle-class individuals enjoyed new, secular sources of entertainment, inspiration, and desire. Energies once focused on religious devotion centered increasingly on the activities of consumption and recreation. Whereas shared religious worship had once cemented community life, the rituals of spectator sports now forged new bonds of loyalty and identity. The ever-changing array of colorful products displayed in shop windows promised fulfillment and satisfaction in the here and now, an earthly paradise rather than a heavenly reward.

The New Imperialism

24.3 What were the causes and consequences of the new imperialist ideology for the West and non-Western societies?

Many of those items on display behind the new plate-glass shop windows were the products of imperial conquest. **New imperialism** intertwined with many of the developments we have already examined in this chapter and in Chapter 23. Telegraphs ensured rapid communication from far-flung empires and mass printing technologies guaranteed that illustrated tales of imperial achievement made their way into homes and schools. Social Darwinism supplied a supposedly scientific justification for the conquest of peoples deemed biologically inferior, while swift military victories over other societies helped quell anxiety about European degeneration. For many Europeans—particularly the British, who presided over the largest empire in the world—imperialist domination served as reassuring evidence of the apparent superiority of Western civilization.

new imperialism The third phase of modern European imperialism that occurred in the late nineteenth and early twentieth centuries and extended Western control over almost all of Africa and much of Asia.

Understanding the New Imperialism

Imperialism itself was not new. In the fifteenth century, Europeans had embarked on the first phase of imperialism, with the extension of European control across coastal ports of Africa and India, and into the New World of the Americas (see Chapter 13). In the second phase, which began in the late seventeenth century, European colonial empires in Asia and the Western Hemisphere expanded as governments sought to increase their profits from international trade (see Chapter 18).

As in these earlier phases of imperialism, trade motivated much of the imperial activity after 1870 as well. The need to protect existing imperial interests also impelled further conquests. For example, the desire to protect India—the "Jewel in the Crown" of the British Empire—explains much of British imperial acquisition throughout the nineteenth century. Britain's annexation of Burma and Kashmir, its establishment of spheres of influence in the Middle East, and its interests along the coast of Africa were all linked to its empire in India.

Defense of existing empires and commercial considerations, however, do not fully explain new imperialism. After 1870 and particularly after 1880, the West's expansion became much more aggressive. In just 30 years, European control of the globe's land surface swelled from 65 to 85 percent. In addition, new players joined the expansionist game. Recently formed nation-states such as Germany and Italy jostled for colonial territory in Africa, the United States began to extend its control over the Western Hemisphere, and Japan initiated its imperialist march into China and Korea. What factors lay behind this new imperialism?

◉ **Watch the Video**

The Origins of Modern Imperialism and Colonialism

24.1

24.2

24.3

TECHNOLOGY, ECONOMICS, AND POLITICS Part of the answer lies in the economic developments examined in Chapter 23. Because of the Second Industrial Revolution, European and American economies increasingly depended on raw materials available only in regions such as Asia, Africa, and South America. Rubber insulated the electrical and telegraph wires now encircling the globe—but rubber trees did not grow in Europe or the United States. Palm oil from Africa provided the lubricant needed for industrial machinery. The slaughter of Africa's once-plentiful elephant herds provided the ivory for many of the new consumer goods now decorating middle-class parlors, such as piano keys and billiard balls. Relying on these primary resources, Western states were quick to respond to perceived threats to their economic interests. The Germans even coined a word to describe this fear of losing access to essential raw materials: *Torschlusspanik,* or "fear of the closing door."

Competition for markets also accelerated imperial acquisition. With the onset of economic depression in the 1870s (discussed in Chapter 23), industrialists faced declining demand for their products in Europe. Imperial expansion seemed to provide a solution, with annexed territories seen as captive markets. As a French newspaper editorial explained in 1891, "every gunshot opens another outlet for French industry."[8]

By the mid-1890s, however, the depression had ended in most regions—yet the pace of imperialist expansion did not slow. Instead, a global investment boom ensured continuing imperialist expansion. European capital financed railway lines, mines, and public utilities across the world. With each railroad or coal mine or dam, European interests in non-European regions expanded, and so did the pressure on European governments to assume formal political control should outside competitors or local political instability threaten those interests.

In addition to these economic factors, domestic political pressures encouraged imperialist acquisition. In the age of mass politics, political leaders needed to find issues that would appeal to new voters. Tales of dangerous explorations and decisive military victories proved popular. Imperialist conquest assured ordinary men that they were part of a superior, conquering people.

As the *Different Voices* feature in this chapter illustrates (see page 763), international competition also fostered imperialism. Newly formed nations such as Italy and Germany sought empires outside Europe as a way to gain power and prestige within Europe. The nineteenth-century German historian Heinrich von Treitschke explained, "All great nations in the fullness of their strength have desired to set their mark on barbarian lands and those who fail to participate in this great rivalry will play a pitiable role in time to come."[9] Similar concerns about status and strategic advantages motivated nations such as Britain and France to defend and expand their empires.

THE IMPERIAL IDEA New imperialism functioned as a belief system that permeated middle-class and mass culture in the decades after 1870. To educate viewers in the "imperial idea," exhibitions and fairs displayed goods and peoples from conquered regions. Images of empire appeared in boys' adventure stories, glossy ads for soap and chocolates, picture postcards, cookie tins, and cheap commemorative china plates and mugs. In the music halls and theaters, imperialist songs and dramas received popular applause.

At the center of the imperial idea stood the assumption that Western dominance over the world was a good thing. Europeans would not have sought to remake the world in the European image had they not been convinced of the superiority of that image. What led them to believe they had the right and the responsibility to take charge of other cultures and continents?

W w   *W w*

W is the Word
    Of an Englishman true:
When given, it means
    What he says, he will do.

A LESSON IN THE IMPERIAL IDEA As this alphabet reader makes clear, education in imperial ideology began early.

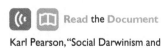

Read the Document

Karl Pearson, "Social Darwinism and Imperialism"

One key factor was the perceived link between Western Christianity and "civilization." Christian missionaries served as a vanguard of Western culture throughout the nineteenth century. The celebrated Scottish explorer David Livingstone (1813–1873), who mapped out much of central and southern Africa, was a Protestant missionary (although not a very successful one—his only convert eventually renounced the Christian faith). Missionary society publications introduced their readers to exotic territories, while the societies themselves lobbied for Western territorial expansion to promote the spread of Christian missions.

Technology also seemed to justify Western imperialism. Before the eighteenth century, the technological gap between the West and other societies had not loomed large. In some cases, such as China, non-Western societies had held the technological advantage. Industrialization, however, gave the West the technological edge. Thus, the British adventurer Mary Kingsley (1862–1900) wrote, ". . . . [W]hen I come back from a spell in Africa, the thing that makes me proud of being one of the English is . . . a great railway engine. . . . [I]t is the manifestation of the superiority of my race."[10]

Finally, Social Darwinism seemed to provide scientific authority for the imperial idea. The British Lord Milner (1854–1925) explained in a speech in South Africa in 1903: "The white man must rule, because he is elevated by many, many steps above the black man; steps which it will take the latter centuries to climb, and which it is quite possible that the vast bulk of the black population may never be able to climb at all."[11]

Imperialists believed that empire—whether ordained by God or by biology—was a moral duty: Men and women in the West were obliged to bring the benefits of their civilization to the rest of the world. The British poet Rudyard Kipling (1865–1936) famously articulated this idea in 1899, in a poem urging American policymakers to conquer the Philippines:

> *Take up the White Man's burden—*
> *Send forth the best ye breed—*
> *Go bind your sons to exile,*
> *To serve your captives' need;*
> *To wait in heavy harness*
> *On fluttered folk and wild—*
> *Your new-caught sullen peoples,*
> *Half devil and half child.*[12]

Different Voices
Advocates of New Imperialism

N ew imperialism resulted from a variety of fears and ambitions, as these two documents illustrate. While some advocates of imperial expansion sought to convert the world's populace to Christianity, others insisted that overseas possessions strengthened a nation's ability to compete with its rivals, not only in the economic but also in the military, diplomatic, and even cultural arenas.

Jules Ferry, Speech Before French National Assembly, July 1883

Jules Ferry (1832–1893), who served two terms as premier (prime minister) of France, supported French imperial expansion. As the interruptions and objections to his speech reveal, Ferry faced opposition, particularly from socialist politicians.

M.[*] JULES FERRY: Gentlemen. . . . I believe that there is some benefit in summarizing . . . the principles, the motives, and the various interests by which a policy of colonial expansion may be justified.

In the area of economics, I will allow myself to place before you . . . the considerations which justify a policy of colonial expansion from the point of view of that need, felt more and more strongly by the industrial populations . . . of our own rich and hard working country: the need for export markets. . . . Why? Because next door to us Germany is surrounded by barriers, because beyond the ocean, the United States of America has become protectionist . . . because not only have these great markets . . . become more difficult of access for our industrial products, but also these great states are beginning to pour products not seen heretofore onto our own markets. . . .

Gentlemen, there is a second point . . . the humanitarian and civilizing side of the question. On this point the honorable M. Camille Pellatan [an anti-imperialist opponent of Ferry's] has jeered in his own refined and clever manner; he jeers, he condemns, and he says "What is this civilization which you impose with cannonballs? What is it but another form of barbarism? Don't these populations, these inferior races, have the same rights as you? Aren't they masters of their own houses? Have they called upon you? You come to them against their will, you offer them violence, but not civilization." . . .

Gentlemen, I must speak from a higher and more truthful plane. It must be stated openly that, in effect, superior races have rights over inferior races. *[Movement on many benches on the far left.]*

M. JULES MAIGNE [a socialist opponent]: Oh! You dare to say this in the country which has proclaimed the rights of man! . . . .

FERRY: I repeat that superior races have a right, because they have a duty. They have the duty to civilize inferior races. . . . *[Approbation from the left. New interruptions from the extreme left and from the right.]* . . .

Gentlemen, there are certain considerations which merit the attention of all patriots. The conditions of naval warfare have been profoundly altered. ["Very true! Very true!"][†] At this time, as you know, a warship cannot carry more than 14 days' worth of coal . . . and a ship which is out of coal is a derelict on the surface of the sea, abandoned to the first person who comes along. Thence the necessity of having on the oceans provision stations, shelters, ports for defense and revictualling. *[Applause at the center and left. Various interruptions.]* And it is for this that we needed Tunisia, for this that we needed Saigon and the Mekong Delta, for this that we need Madagascar . . . and will never leave them! *[Applause from a great number of benches.]* Gentlemen, in Europe as it is today, in this competition of so many rivals which we see growing around us, . . . in a Europe, or rather in a universe of this sort, a policy of peaceful seclusion or abstention is simply the highway to decadence! . . .

France . . . cannot be merely a free country . . . she must also be a great country, exercising all of her rightful influence over the destiny of Europe . . . she ought to propagate this influence throughout the world and carry everywhere that she can her language, her customs, her flag, her arms, and her genius. *[Applause at center and left.]*

Friedrich Fabri, *Does Germany Need Colonies?* (1879)

A pastor and theology professor, Friedrich Fabri (1824–1891) directed an interdenominational German missionary society that worked in southern Africa and the East Indies. In 1879, Fabri published Does Germany Need Colonies? His answer was unequivocal.

In looking for colonial possessions Germany is not prompted by the desire for expanding its power; it wants only to fulfill a national, we may even say a moral duty. . . .

The German nation has long experience on the oceans, is skilled in industry and commerce, more capable than others in agricultural colonization, and furnished with ample manpower like no other modern highly cultured nation. Should it not also enter successfully upon this new venture? . . . There is much bitterness, much poisonous partisanship in our newly united Germany; to open a promising new course of national development might have a liberating effect, and move the national spirit in a new direction.

Even more important is the consideration that a people at the height of their political power can successfully maintain their historic position only as long as they recognize and prove themselves as the bearers of a cultural mission. That is the only way which guarantees the stability and growth of national prosperity, which is the necessary basis for an enduring source of power. In past years Germany has contributed only its intellectual and literary work to this century; now we have turned to politics and become powerful. But if the goal of political power becomes an end in itself, it leads to hardness, even to barbarism, unless that

*[*]"M."= abbreviation for "Monsieur" ("Mister").

[†] These words were shouted out in the assembly by other legislators.

(continued on next page)

(continued from previous page)

nation is willing to undertake the inspirational, moral, and economic leadership of the times. . . . [L]ook around the globe and assess the ever-increasing colonial possessions of Great Britain, the strength which it draws from them, the skills of its administration, and the dominant position which the Anglo-Saxon stock occupies in all overseas countries. . . . It would be well if we Germans began to learn from the colonial destiny of our Anglo-Saxon cousins and emulate them in peaceful competition. When, centuries ago, the German empire stood at the head of the European states, it was the foremost commercial and maritime power. If the new Germany wants to restore and preserve its traditional powerful position in future, it will conceive of it as a cultural mission and no longer hesitate to practice its colonizing vocation.

SOURCES: Jules Ferry, Speech Before French National Assembly, 1883, in Ralph A. Austin (ed.), *Modern Imperialism: Western Overseas Expansion and Its*

Aftermath, 1776–1965 (Lexington, Mass.: D.C. Heath, 1969), 70–73. Friedrich Fabri, *Does Germany Need Colonies?* (Gotha, Germany: Perthes, 1879). Translated by Theodore von Laue. In Perry et al., *Sources of the Western Tradition*, 4th ed., Vol. 2. (New York: Houghton Mifflin, 1999), 235–237. Copyright © 1999 Wadsworth, a part of Cengage Learning, Inc. Reproduced by permission. www.cengage.com/permissions.

For Discussion

1. What are the four reasons Ferry gives for imperial expansion? Do they differ from Fabri's?
2. Which sections of these documents might any nineteenth-century imperialist of any nationality have articulated? Which sections make sense only within the specific French and German contexts?
3. The "imperial idea" played an important role in shaping Western identities at the end of the nineteenth century. How would Ferry and Fabri have defined the West? How would Ferry's parliamentary opponents?

Not all Europeans and Americans embraced the idea of the "White Man's burden," and many rejected the imperialist assumption of Western superiority. As the example of Picasso makes clear (see *Encounters and Transformations* in this chapter), some modernist artists looked to non-Western cultures for artistic inspiration. The Fauves ("wild beasts"), a Paris-based circle of artists that included Henri Matisse (1869–1954) and Paul Gauguin (1848–1903), condemned most Western art as artificial, and sought in their own brilliantly colored works to rediscover the vitality that they found in non-Western cultures.

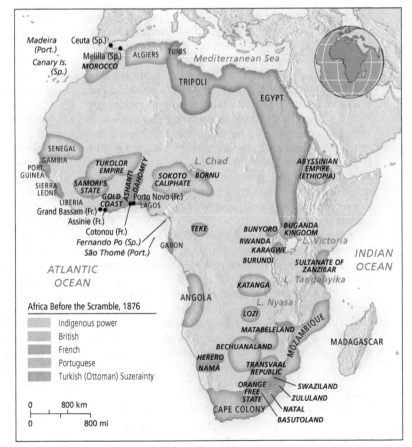

MAP **24.1** (A) AFRICA BEFORE THE SCRAMBLE, 1876 AND (B) AFRICA AFTER THE SCRAMBLE, 1914 A comparison of these two maps reveals the dramatic impact of the new imperialism on African societies. Indigenous empires such as the Sokoto Caliphate came under Western rule, as did tribal societies such as the Herero. Even states ruled by whites of European descent came under European rule, as the examples of the Transvaal and the Orange Free State in South Africa illustrate. Which African states remained independent of European control? What was the impact of Western imperialism on Ottoman power in north Africa?

Critics of empire often focused on its domestic political and economic implications. The British economist J. A. Hobson (1858–1940) charged that overseas empires benefited only wealthy capitalists while distracting public attention from the need for political and economic reform at home. Hobson argued that unregulated capitalism led almost inevitably to imperialist expansion because it generated huge surpluses in capital for a small elite, who must then find somewhere to invest these surpluses. Hobson's ideas influenced European socialists, who condemned imperialism along with capitalism.

The Scramble for Africa

New imperialism reached its zenith in Africa. As **Maps 24.1A** and **24.1B** show, in just 30 years, between 1875 and 1905, Europeans established 30 new colonies and protectorates encompassing 10 million square miles of territory and controlling 110 million Africans. By 1905, 90 percent of Africa was under European control. The conquest of the African continent was so rapid and dramatic that as early as 1884 mystified Europeans began to talk about the **Scramble for Africa**.

OVERCOMING THE OBSTACLES European efforts to establish settlements in the African interior faced three key obstacles: the climate, disease, and African resistance. The inhospitable climate meant that Africa was known as "the white man's grave." Over 75 percent of the white soldiers sent to West Africa in the early nineteenth century died there, and another 20 percent became invalids. Temperatures of more than 100 degrees Fahrenheit in some regions and constant rainfall in others made travel extremely difficult. The mosquito and the tsetse fly made it deadly. Mosquito bites brought malaria, while the tsetse fly carried trypanosomiasis, or sleeping sickness, an infectious illness that ended in a deadly paralysis. Sleeping sickness killed livestock as well as people.

Scramble for Africa The frenzied imposition of European control over most of Africa that occurred between 1870 and 1914.

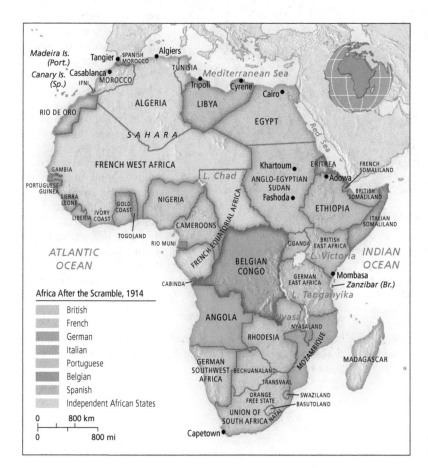

Africa After the Scramble, 1914

- British
- French
- German
- Italian
- Portuguese
- Belgian
- Spanish
- Independent African States

0   800 km

0   800 mi

MAP **24.1** (B)

Encounters and Transformations
Picasso Goes to the Museum

A fter months of work and more than 800 preparatory sketches, Pablo Picasso judged the painting finished at last. But when he showed *Les Demoiselles d'Avignon* to his friend and rival Matisse, the Frenchman thought the work a joke. Another friend and fellow painter, Georges Braques, found it appalling. Picasso did not exhibit the painting for several years and it remained largely unknown until 1939 when it went on display at the Museum of Modern Art in New York City. Today, *Demoiselles* is one of the most well-known modernist works of art in the Western world, "the amazing act on which all the art of our century is built."[13] It helped transform the history of Western art and even, perhaps, the history of perception itself.

With its in-your-face sexuality, *Demoiselles* retains its ability to shock. Five naked whores (*demoiselles* means "prostitutes") advertise for trade, twisting their bodies into erotic, even pornographic poses. The painting's eroticism alone, however, does not explain its impact.

The painting as we now know it resulted from a specific encounter that occurred when Picasso went to a museum in Paris. Sometime in 1906 or 1907, when he was already deeply involved in this painting, Picasso viewed African tribal masks on exhibit at the Ethnographic Museum in the Trocadero. This museum visit profoundly excited and upset the Spanish painter. His girlfriend Fernande Olivier reported, "Picasso is going crazy over Negro works and statues."[14] In Picasso's view, these "Negro works and statues" possessed the vitality and authenticity missing from Western art. Picasso and many modernists believed that Western civilization, with its urbanization and industrialism, its organizations and academies, its codes and regulations, had stifled artistic expression. They saw most modern art as weak and lifeless—the tired-out product of a worn-out society. In contrast, they argued, African art resembled the pictures drawn by children: energetic, playful, creative, colored outside the lines.

PABLO PICASSO, *LES DEMOISELLES D'AVIGNON* (1907)

This notion of African culture as childlike, of course, reflected the imperialist idea of "backward peoples." Picasso and other modernists rejected the imperialist notion of Western superiority and criticized Western empires, yet they could not escape imperialist stereotypes. Within the limits of these stereotypes, however, some modernists turned the cultural relationship of the West and Africa upside down. Picasso went to African art to learn, not to conquer.

Picasso's encounter with the African masks transformed this specific painting and modern art itself. After his Trocadero visit, Picasso reconfigured the faces of the two women on the right so that their mask-like appearances now clash awkwardly with those of the three other prostitutes. This step destroyed any unity of narrative or composition in the painting: The five figures are no longer part of a single story or share a single point of view. Picasso also fragmented each of the bodies, flattening them and reducing them to jutting geometric forms. Thus, *Demoiselles* pushed Picasso toward Cubism, one of the most influential artistic styles of the twentieth century (see page 756). As the art historian John Golding has written, "In the *Demoiselles* Picasso began to shatter the human figure. . . . He spent the rest of his artistic life dissecting, reassembling, and reinventing it."[15] After Picasso, Western artists spent the rest of the twentieth century dissecting, reassembling, and reinventing the way we see and depict our world.

For Discussion

How did Picasso use the art of a different culture to explain and challenge his own? Did *Demoiselles* challenge or did it affirm Western imperialist ideas?

In regions with endemic trypanosomiasis, such as equatorial, southern, and eastern Africa, the use of horses and oxen was impossible. Despite these difficulties, Europeans did endeavor to establish inland settlements in Africa, but were usually defeated by African resistance. In the seventeenth century, for example, the Portuguese set up forts and trading centers in modern Zimbabwe but were driven out by local African populations.

Beginning around 1830, however, a series of developments altered the relationship between Europe and Africa and made European conquest possible. First, European explorers changed the Western understanding of Africa. Between 1830 and 1870, adventurers mapped out the chief geographical features of Africa's interior and so illuminated the "Dark Continent" for Europeans. They discovered that central Africa was not the empty desert that Europeans had assumed, but rather a territory with abundant agricultural and mineral resources—and lots of people, all of them potential consumers of European goods.

The shift in the European vision of Africa—from desert to treasure house—coincided with important political changes within Africa itself. Many of these political shifts were the unintended consequences of Western efforts to abolish the slave trade. In the 1830s, Britain and other European powers, pressured by humanitarian and missionary groups, sought to wipe out the West African slave trade. They succeeded—and the slave trade shifted to central and eastern Africa. This shift caused great political instability. African slaving nations relied on frequent military raids to obtain their human merchandise. These raids—carried out by Africans against Africans—disrupted agricultural production, shattered trade networks, and undermined the authority of existing political rulers. With political systems in disarray, many African regions were vulnerable to European encroachment.

Finally, three specific inventions shifted the balance of power in the West's favor. First, steam power proved crucial in enabling Western imperialists to overcome the obstacles to traveling through Africa by allowing them to use the continent's extensive but shallow river system. While steam enabled Westerners to penetrate the African interior, the quinine prophylaxis helped them survive once they got there. Doctors had long prescribed quinine for malaria. Death and disability rates from the disease remained high, however, until some chance discoveries revealed the importance of taking quinine prophylactically—of saturating the system with quinine *before* any infection. By the 1860s, Westerners routinely ingested quinine in preparation for postings in Africa—and their death rates dropped dramatically.

African death rates, however, soared because of the third crucial invention of imperialism—the repeating, breech-loading rifles Europeans carried from the 1870s on. Before the development of these rifles, Europeans used muskets or muzzle-loading rifles. These weapons fouled easily, particularly in damp weather, and could be loaded only one ball at a time—usually while the rifleman was standing up. The musket-armed European did not gain a significant military advantage, even over spears. With the repeating rifle, however, "any European infantryman could now fire lying down, undetected, in any weather, 15 rounds of ammunition in as many seconds at targets up to half a mile away." As we saw at the beginning of this chapter, the repeating breech-loader and its descendant, the machine gun, made the European conquest of regions such as the Sudan "more like hunting than war."[16]

SLICING THE CAKE: THE CONQUEST OF AFRICA   In the decades after 1870, convinced that the conquest of African territories would guarantee commercial prosperity and strengthen national power, European states moved quickly to beat out their rivals and grab a piece of the continent. As King Leopold II of Belgium (1865–1909) explained in a letter to his ambassador in London in 1876, "I do not want to miss a good chance of getting us a slice of this magnificent African cake."[17]

Leopold's slice proved enormous. He wanted the Congo, a huge region of central Africa comprising territory more than twice as large as central Europe. After a decade of quarreling, representatives of the European powers met in Berlin in 1884 and agreed to Leopold's demands. They also used this Berlin Conference to regulate the Scramble for Africa. According to the terms established in Berlin, any state claiming a territory in Africa had to establish "effective occupation" and to plan for the economic development of that region.

But as the history of the Congo Free State demonstrated, such economic development served European, not African, interests. Leopold's personal mercenary army turned the Congo into a hellhole of slavery and death. By claiming all so-called vacant land, Leopold deprived villagers of the grazing, foraging, and hunting grounds they needed to survive. He levied rubber quotas for each village, forcing villagers to harvest wild rubber for up to 25 days each month while their families starved. Brutal punishments ensured compliance: Soldiers chopped off the hands of villagers who failed to meet their quota. The Belgians also forced Africans to serve as human mules, a practice that spread sleeping sickness from the western coast into the interior. As an estimated three million people died from the combined effects of forced labor, brutal punishments, starvation, and disease, Leopold II's enormous profits from the Congo enabled him to indulge his hobby of building elaborate tourist resorts on the Riviera.

King Leopold's brand of imperialism proved so scandalous that in 1908 the Belgian government replaced Leopold's personal rule with state control over the Congo. Yet the king's exploitation of the Congo differed only in degree, not in kind, from the nature of European conquest elsewhere in Africa. Forced labor was common throughout European-controlled areas, as were brutal punishments for any Africans who dared resist. Faced with tribal revolt in Southwest Africa, the German colonial army commander in 1904 ordered the extermination of the entire Herero tribe. His soldiers drove 20,000 men, women, and children from their villages into the desert to die of thirst.

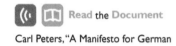 Read the Document

Carl Peters, "A Manifesto for German Colonization"

AFRICAN RESISTANCE As the Herero rebellion demonstrated, Africans frequently resisted imperial regimes, but to no avail. The only successful episode of African resistance to European conquest occurred in northern Africa, in the kingdom of Ethiopia (also called Abyssinia). By the time of the European Scramble for Africa, Ethiopia had developed not only a modern standing army, but also an advanced infrastructure and communications system. In 1896 these factors enabled the Ethiopian nation to defeat the Italian army at the Battle of Adowa.

Adowa, however, was the exception. The technological gap between the indigenous peoples and their European conquerors doomed most African resistance. Africans did have guns, the result of a booming arms trade between European rifle manufacturers and African states. Frequently, however, the arms shipped to Africa were inferior models—muskets or single-firing muzzle-loaders rather than the up-to-date and deadly efficient repeating rifles and early machine guns possessed by the European invaders. African military leaders who did obtain advanced weaponry often failed to make the strategic leap necessary to adapt their military tactics to new technologies. (As we will see in Chapter 25, European military leaders made similar mistakes in World War I.)

Asian Encounters

Unlike most of Africa, many of the diverse states of Asia had already been woven into the web of the Western economy well before 1870 as a part of the eighteenth-century mercantilist empires established by Dutch, British, Portuguese, and French trading companies (see Chapter 18). Throughout the nineteenth century, European governments strengthened their control over many of these regions, primarily to protect trade routes or to ensure access to profitable commodities such as rubber, tin, tobacco, and sugar. The Dutch, for example, expanded their East Indies empire, moving from control of the island of Java in 1815 to domination over almost the entire archipelago several decades later (see **Map 24.2**).

Four factors accelerated the pace of imperialist acquisition in Asia after 1870. First, in the age of steam, Western powers needed Pacific islands to serve as coaling stations for their commercial and naval fleets. Second, new industrial processes heightened the economic value of many of these regions. The development of a process for producing dried coconut, for example, made Samoa so valuable that Germany, Britain, and the United States competed for control over the tiny islands. Third, as in Africa, international competition accelerated imperialism. Territorial gains by one power led to anxiety and a quicker pace of expansion by its rivals.

Finally, the steady erosion of Chinese political stability—itself a result of encounters with the West—intensified this "Scramble for Asia." As Western powers competed for access to Chinese markets, Western empires expanded throughout Asia. The quest for a protected trade route to China, for example, impelled the French to extend their control over neighboring Indochina. By 1893, the Union of French Indochina included the formerly independent states of Laos, Cambodia, Annam, and Tonkin—the latter two better known by their contemporary name of Vietnam.

Read the Document

"Letter of Phan Chu Trinh to the French Governor-General"

MAP **24.2** IMPERIALISM IN ASIA, 1914 The impact of the new imperialism on Asia was not as dramatic as in Africa, but the spread of Western rule is significant nonetheless. This map shows a key development: the entry of non-European powers—Japan and the United States—into the imperialist game. What it does not show is the extent of Western and Japanese influence in China. Profoundly destabilized by foreign intervention, China in 1914 was in the midst of revolution. Which states emerged as the most powerful in Asia by 1914?

EXPANDING THE WEST: THE UNITED STATES AND AUSTRALIA In the latter half of the nineteenth century, the United States and Australia established themselves as extensions of the West. As these states expanded and consolidated their territories and subdued indigenous populations, race-based versions of national identity that had justified European imperialist adventures came to be applied to all peoples of color.

For the United States, the acquisition of an empire in Asia followed consolidation of control over most of North America. After emerging victorious from a war with Mexico in 1846, the United States gained the territories of California, Nevada, Utah, Arizona, New Mexico, and southern Colorado. The completion of the transcontinental Union Pacific railroad in 1869 accelerated the pace of westward settlement. The conquest of the continent, however, depended on the defeat, and often decimation, of its indigenous peoples. A series of "Indian wars" punctuated the decades from 1860 through 1890 as the United States expanded westward.

Once its borders reached the Pacific Ocean, the United States quickly emerged as an imperialist power in Asia. In 1853, Commodore Matthew Perry used his squadron of four warships to open Japan to American commerce; during the 1860s and 1870s the United States participated with the European powers in chipping away at China's national sovereignty to ensure favorable terms of trade there. By the end of the century, the United States had annexed Hawaii and part of Samoa, and as a result of the Spanish-American War had acquired Guam, the Philippines, Cuba, and Puerto Rico.

American acquisition of empire in Asia heightened anti-Asian sentiment within the United States. The Chinese Exclusion Act of 1882 (renewed in 1902) prohibited Chinese immigration. In 1913, the Alien Land Law, which outlawed land ownership by noncitizens, sought to restrict the property rights of Japanese immigrants.

These efforts paralleled attempts in the American South to construct a version of national identity confined to whites. Southern legislators used literacy tests, poll taxes, and violent intimidation to deprive blacks of their right to vote, while **Jim Crow** or segregation laws defined blacks as second-class citizens.

Australia's territorial expansion and its emergence as a Western state resembled the United States' development in many respects. After Captain James Cook discovered and claimed Australia for the British Crown in 1770, the British government used it as a dumping ground for convicts. But with the expansion of the wool industry in the decades after 1830, the six British colonies established in Australia became a center of British immigration. In 1901, these colonies joined together in the Commonwealth of Australia, part of the British Empire but a self-governing political entity—and a self-defined "Western" nation, despite its geographical location in the Eastern Hemisphere. Many Australians, including the first prime minister, Edmund Barton, identified the "West" as "white." Barton campaigned on a platform calling for a "White Australia."

As in the United States, the process of extending Western civilization demanded the defeat of the indigenous population. At the start of Britain's occupation of Australia, King George III had forbidden anyone to "wantonly destroy [the Aboriginal peoples] or give them any unnecessary interruption in the exercise of their several occupations."[18] But the settlement of whites intent on building cities, planting farms, and fencing in land for pastures interrupted the nomadic way of life for the estimated 500,000 inhabitants of Australia, living in scattered tribal groupings.

The British divided over how to treat the Aborigines. Many British settlers and, as the decades passed, many in the growing group of Australia-born whites regarded the Aborigines as a threat to white settlements. Massacres of Aborigines resulted. Christian and humanitarian groups, and the British government in London, denounced this violence and insisted that the Aborigines should be westernized and Christianized, rather than exterminated. From the 1820s on, mission stations housed and educated Aboriginal children. Forcibly removed from their homes, these children were schooled in British ways and then at age 15 placed in employment as apprentices and domestic

Jim Crow Series of laws mandating racial segregation throughout the American South.

servants. Despite these missions, few Aborigines assimilated to the Western way of life. In the final decades of the nineteenth century, official policy shifted from assimilation to "protection." The Australian government declared Aborigines and mixed-race individuals to be legal wards of the state and required them to live on reserves. Aborigines did not receive Australian citizenship until 1967.

Many white Australians perceived not only Aborigines but also Asian immigrants as threats to their Western identity. By the 1850s, tens of thousands of Chinese had migrated to Australia. Arriving as indentured servants, they worked under brutal conditions. Many labored in the gold mines, where they received one-twelfth of the wages paid to a European. As the numbers of Chinese immigrants grew, so, too, did anti-Chinese sentiment. One newspaper editor noted, "The Chinese question never fails. At every meeting . . . visions of millions of the barbarians swooping upon the colony . . . rise in the mental horizons of every man present."[19] In 1888, the Australian government turned back ships containing Chinese immigrants. Legislation to restrict Chinese immigration soon followed.

THE CONTINUED EXPANSION OF THE RUSSIAN EMPIRE As in the United States and Australia, imperial expansion in nineteenth-century Russia took the form of territorial consolidation across a continent. **Map 24.3** shows that by 1914, the Russian Empire stretched from Warsaw in central Europe to Vladivostok on the Sea of Japan—one-seventh of the global land surface. Ethnic Russians accounted for only 45 percent of the population of this empire.

The colonization of Siberia began in the sixteenth century when Russian serfs fled eastward in search of land and freedom. The end of serfdom actually accelerated the flow to Siberia, because peasants now needed to escape the debts imposed on them by the emancipation legislation of 1861 (see Chapter 22). The tsarist policy of exiling political dissenters to Siberia added to the outflow, while the completion of the trans-Siberian railway in the 1890s made the journey easier. Between 1800 and 1914, seven million Russians settled in or were deported to Siberia.

Just as American expansion westward and the British conquest of Australia dramatically depleted Indian and Aboriginal numbers, so Russian migration into Siberia displaced that region's original population. Until 1826 Russians could trade Siberians as slaves and many died because of brutal treatment. In addition, the immigrants

MAP **24.3** THE EXPANSION OF THE RUSSIAN EMPIRE Throughout the nineteenth century, the Russian Empire expanded to the west and south. After Russia's acquisition of territories in the Caucasus and Black Sea region, more Muslims lived under tsarist rule than in the Ottoman Empire. Which states were threatened by Russian expansion?

Read the Document

Prince Aleksandr Gorchakov,
"The Gorchakov Circular"

brought with them new epidemic diseases and the booming fur trade depleted the animal herds that served as the Siberians' main food source. Disease and famine decimated the Siberian population.

Russia also expanded southward into central Asia, primarily as a preemptive response to the growth of British power in India. Fearing that the British might push northward, the Russians pushed south. By 1885, the Black Sea region, the Caucasus, and Turkestan had all fallen to Russian imperial control, and Muslims constituted a significant minority of the tsar's subjects. Over the next three decades the oil fields of the Caucasus became a crucial part of the Russian industrial economy.

The expansion of the Russian Empire eastward encroached upon Chinese territory and thus helped destabilize China. It also led to growing hostilities between Russia and Japan, as both regimes coveted Chinese Manchuria. We saw in Chapter 23 that the growing antagonism between Russia and Japan led to the Russo-Japanese War in 1904 and that defeat in this war helped provoke the Russian Revolution of 1905. Imperialism could be a risky business.

JAPANESE INDUSTRIAL AND IMPERIAL EXPANSION Japan's victory over Russia in 1905 signaled its rise to global power and its emergence as an imperialist player. In the 1630s the Japanese emperor sealed Japan from the West by closing Japanese ports to all foreigners except a small contingent of Dutch and Chinese traders confined to the city of Nagasaki. The Japanese government rebuffed all Western overtures until 1853, when, as we have seen, Commodore Perry forced Japan to open two of its ports to American ships. Over the next 15 years, Western powers pushed to expand their economic influence in Japan, and Japanese elites fought over how to respond. Anti-Western terrorism became endemic, civil war broke out, and a political revolution ensued.

Japan emerged from this turbulent time with a new government. For more than 200 years effective political control had rested in the hands not of the Japanese emperor, but rather of the "Shogun," the military governor of Japan. In 1868, however, Japan's warrior nobility tossed the Shogun from power and restored the young Emperor Mutsuhito (1867–1912) to effective rule—the Meiji Restoration.

Japan's new government determined that the only way to resist Western conquest was to adopt Western industrial and military technologies and techniques. Over the next four decades, a revolution from the top occurred, as a modern centralized state, modeled on France, replaced Japan's feudal political system and as a system of state schools, modeled on U.S. public schools, was constructed. Funds poured into building a modern navy, modeled on Britain's, and a powerful conscript-based army, modeled on Germany's. An imperial decree of 1871 even ordered that government officials abandon kimonos for western suits.

Beginning in the 1890s, Japan also adopted western-style imperialism. Wars with China in 1894 and Russia in 1904 led to the Japanese seizure of Taiwan and Korea, and expanded Japanese economic influence in Manchuria. One writer, Tokutomi Soho (1863–1957), proclaimed that Japan's imperial conquests showed that "civilization is not a monopoly of the white man."[20] Certainly imperialist violence was not a white man's monopoly: The Japanese brutally punished Koreans and Taiwanese who dared to protest against their new rulers.

SCRAMBLING IN CHINA While Japan used its encounter with the West to modernize and militarize its society, China proved less successful in withstanding Western hegemony. Throughout the nineteenth century, Chinese national sovereignty slowly eroded as European powers, the United States, and Japan jostled for access to China's markets and resources. In 1899, European states with interests in China did agree to back the American "open door" policy, which opposed the formal partitioning of China (as had just occurred in Africa). This policy, however, actually increased rather than blocked Western interference in Chinese economic and political affairs.

THE BOXER REBELLION QUELLED Although never formally controlled by Western powers, China was, by the end of the nineteenth century, a Western "sphere of influence," as the aftermath of the Boxer Rebellion of 1900 made clear. At the insistence of the Western powers, the Chinese government publicly executed the Boxer ringleaders in front of the foreign troops who had defeated the rebels.

Many Chinese resented Western encroachment, and in 1900, a secret society devoted to purging China of Western influence began attacking foreigners. Because members of the society practiced the martial arts, this event was called the Boxer Rebellion. With the covert support of the Chinese government, the rebels attacked European diplomatic headquarters in Beijing and killed more than 200 missionaries and several thousand Chinese Christians. The West responded in fury. A combined military force, drawing 16,000 soldiers from Russia, Germany, Austria-Hungary, France, Britain, Japan, and the United States, crushed the rebellion and sacked Beijing. Required to grant further trade and territorial concessions to its invaders, the Chinese central government was fatally weakened. In 1911, revolution engulfed China and propelled it into four decades of political and social tumult.

A Glimpse of Things to Come: The Boer War

In the 1840s, a British journalist in China urged the Chinese to accept what he regarded as the crucial lesson of history: "Ever since the dispersion of man, the richest stream of human blessings has, in the will of Providence, followed a western course." To many Europeans, Australians, and Americans, the rapid expansion of Western imperial control across the globe after 1870 confirmed this lesson. At the end of the nineteenth

CHRONOLOGY: ASIA ENCOUNTERS THE WEST

1853 — 1853
Commodore Matthew Perry forces Japan to open its markets to the United States.

1868 — **1868**
The Meiji Restoration in Japan; Japan begins rapid modernization.

1885 — 1885
Russia establishes control over Central Asia.

1893 — **1893**
Union of French Indochina includes Laos, Cambodia, Tonkin, and Annam.

1894–1895 — 1894–1895
The Sino-Japanese War: China defeated.

1898 — **1898**
Spanish-American War; United States annexes Puerto Rico, Philippines, Hawaii, and Guam; establishes protectorate over Cuba.

1899 — 1899
"Open door" policy in China proclaimed by United States.

1900–1903 — **1900–1903**
Boxer Rebellion in China.

1901 — 1901
Commonwealth of Australia formed.

1904–1905 — **1904–1905**
Russo-Japanese War: Russia defeated.

1911 — 1911
Revolution in China: Overthrow of Manchu Dynasty.

century, however, the British found themselves embroiled in a conflict that challenged this complacency. The Boer War of 1899–1902 shook British self-confidence and foreshadowed the total warfare and the crumbling of empires that marked the experience of the West in the twentieth century.

The Boer War was the culmination of a century of hostility among British imperialists, Dutch settlers (called Boers, the Dutch word for "farmer"), and indigenous Africans in the southern triangle of Africa. Germany's move into Southwest Africa in 1884 worsened this conflict: The British in the Cape Colony (see **Map 24.4**) feared that the Boers would work with Germany against British interests. The discovery in 1886 of diamonds and gold in the Transvaal, an independent Boer republic, intensified the conflict. British investors in the profitable diamond and gold mines resented Boer taxation and labor policies, and pressed the British government to invade the Boer republics and place them under British rule.

In 1899, these imperialists got the war they had demanded, but it turned out to be different from what they expected. The Boers proved formidable enemies, skilled riflemen who knew the land and were fighting for their homes. Mired in a guerilla war, the British command decided to smoke out the Boer fighters through a scorched-earth policy. British troops burned more than 30,000 farms to the ground and confined Boer women and children, and their black African servants, in poorly provisioned concentration camps. Diseases such as diphtheria and typhus soon took their toll. Almost 20,000 Boer women and children, and at least 14,000 blacks, died in these camps.

The British finally defeated the Boers in April 1902, but two factors limited this victory. First, the Boer states came under British control, but the Boers (or Afrikaners) outnumbered other whites in the newly created Union of South Africa. After South Africa received self-government in 1910, the Afrikaners dominated the political system and created a nation founded on racial segregation. Second, Britain emerged from the Boer War with its military and its humanitarian reputation severely tarnished. The war aroused strong opposition inside Britain and showed that popular support for imperialism would rapidly disappear if the costs proved too high.

The sort of conflict between imperialism's opponents and supporters would be repeated many times over the next several decades as nationalist challenges against

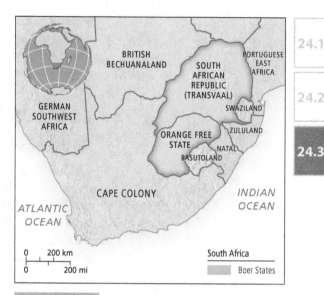

MAP **24.4** SOUTH AFRICA After the defeat of the Boer states—the Transvaal and the Orange Free State—in the Boer War in 1902, the Union of South Africa comprised the Cape Colony and the two Boer republics. Why did the British government regard South Africa as a crucial part of the British Empire?

👁 **Watch the Video**

John Cox, *The Origins of the Holocaust*

CHRONOLOGY: THE STRUGGLE FOR CONTROL IN SOUTH AFRICA

1806
Britain takes control of the Cape Colony from the Dutch.

1837
Boers establish independent republics of Transvaal and Orange Free State.

1884
German annexation of Southwest Africa.

1886
Gold discovered in the Transvaal.

1899
Anglo-Boer War begins.

1910
Self-government granted to South Africa.

imperial rule multiplied and the imperial idea grew less and less persuasive. More ominously, the sight of noncombatants confined—and dying—in concentration camps would soon become all too familiar. The Boer War thus served as a prophetic opening to the twentieth century.

CONCLUSION

Reshaping the West: Expansion and Fragmentation

Africans and Asians who saw their political and social structures topple under the imperialist onslaught would probably have agreed with the Austrian poet Hugo von Hoffmansthal (1874–1929) when he wrote in 1905 that "what other generations believed to be firm is in fact sliding." Hoffmansthal, however, was not commenting on Africa or Asia. He was describing the Western cultural and intellectual landscape that, like colonial political boundaries, underwent enormous and disturbing change in the decades after 1870. In this era, matter itself began to slide, as the Newtonian conception of the world gave way to a new, more unsettling picture of the physical universe. Changes in medical practice, the triumph of Darwin's evolutionary theory, and the revolt against positivism helped undermine established assumptions and contributed to the sense that the foundations of Western culture were shifting. So, too, did the birth of modernism and broader changes, such as middle-class women's move into the public sphere and the redefinition of sexual boundaries, push Western culture in a new direction.

In the later nineteenth century, then, a series of encounters reshaped the West. Its geographic boundaries expanded as non-European regions such as the United States emerged as significant economic and imperial powers. With Australians claiming Western identity, "the West" even spilled over into the Eastern Hemisphere. Yet fragmentation as well as expansion characterized the Western experience after 1870. At the same time that social thinkers proclaimed white cultural superiority, European artists such as Gauguin and Picasso embraced the artistic styles of non-European, nonwhite societies in an effort to push open the boundaries of Western culture. While scientific and technological achievements convinced many Europeans and Americans that the West would conquer the globe, others regarded these developments with profound uneasiness.

The next chapter will show that the sense that old certainties were slipping led some Europeans to welcome war in 1914 as a way to restore heroism and moral purpose to Western society. The trenches of World War I, however, provided little solidity. Many nineteenth-century political, economic, and cultural structures slid into ruin under the impact of total war.

MAKING CONNECTIONS

1. How did Social Darwinism contribute to the mood of cultural uneasiness that characterized the *fin-de-siècle*? How did Social Darwinism and the sense of crisis inherent in the *fin-de-siècle* help shape the new imperialism?
2. What factors strengthened religious beliefs and allegiances in late-nineteenth-century Europe? Given these factors, why did many Western Christians feel that Christianity was under attack in this era?
3. Compare the patterns of territorial and political expansion in the United States, Australia, and Russia. How did these developments change the definition and power of the West?

TAKING IT FURTHER

For additional readings, see page R-1.

On MyHistoryLab

Take the Study Plan for Chapter 24,
The West and the World: Cultural Crisis
and the New Imperialism, 1870–1914,
on MyHistoryLab

Chapter Review

Scientific Transformations

24.1 How did scientific developments during this period lead to both optimism and anxiety?

Medical advances in disease prevention inspired confidence in the power of scientific discoveries to benefit humankind, but an increased awareness and fear of germs increased anxiety. Developments in evolutionary science were used to justify existing social and economic hierarchies, but also contributed to unease since they challenged basic religious assumptions and heightened fears of racial and national degeneration. New research in the social sciences highlighted the power of irrational forces in determining human conduct. Finally, the revolution in physics unseated traditional depictions of the natural world and made much of science incomprehensible to ordinary men and women.

Cultural Crisis: The *Fin-de-Siècle* and the Birth of Modernism

24.2 Why did many Europeans in this period believe they were living in a time of cultural crisis?

Perceptions of rising rates of crime and disease in the rapidly growing cities, combined with the unsettling impact of changing gender roles, contributed to the sense that the West was in a state of decline. So, too, did modernist art and literature, which challenged central middle-class ideas about the role of art in society. A growing sense of religious crisis also heightened anxieties, although popular religiosity remained vibrant.

The New Imperialism

24.3 What were the causes and consequences of the new imperialist ideology for the West and non-Western societies?

Competition for captive markets, pressure to secure global investments in these markets by formally controlling them, and the fact that Western dominance over the world appealed to voters eager to think of themselves as a superior people were factors in the rapid imperial acquisition of the time. Speedy and dramatic conquests of entire continents, like Africa and Australia, reassured many Westerners of their own racial and cultural superiority, while decimating indigenous cultures.

Chapter Time Line

1859
Publication of Darwin's *Origin of Species.*
1859

1870
1870
Proclamation of papal infallibility.

1875–1905
Scramble for Africa.
1875–1905

1895
1895
Oscar Wilde trial.

1899
Boer War.
1899

1905
1905
Einstein publishes his theory of relativity.

1907
Picasso completes *Desmoiselles d'Avignon.*
1907

1911
1911
Revolution in China.

25 The First World War

On the morning of July 1, 1916, in the fields of northern France near the Somme River, tens of thousands of British soldiers crawled out of ditches and began to walk across a muddy expanse filled with shards of metal and decomposing human bodies. Weighed down with 60-pound backpacks, they trudged forward. The soldiers expected little opposition. For a week British heavy artillery had pummeled the Germans who lay on the other side of the mud. But the German troops had waited out the bombardment in the safety of "dugouts"—fortified bunkers scooped from the earth beneath the trenches. When the attack began, they raced to their gunnery positions and raked the evenly spaced lines of British soldiers with machine-gun fire. More than 20,000 British soldiers died that day, thousands within the first minutes of the attack. Another 40,000 were wounded. Yet the attack went on. Between July 1 and November 18, 1916, when the Battle of the Somme finally ended, almost 420,000 soldiers from Britain and the British Empire were killed or

THE BATTLE OF THE SOMME, 1916
British (left) and German troops recover casualties during a lull in the fighting.

LEARNING OBJECTIVES

25.1)))
What factors led Europe into war in 1914?

25.2)))
When, where, and how did the Allies defeat the Central Powers?

25.3)))
How did total war structure the home fronts?

25.4)))
What were the consequences of this war for the European and the global political order?

))) Listen to Chapter 25 on MyHistoryLab

⊙ Watch the Video Series on MyHistoryLab

Learn about some key topics related to this chapter with the *MyHistoryLab Video Series:
Key Topics in Western Civilization*

wounded. Their French allies lost 200,000 men to death or injury. German casualties are estimated at 450,000.

Such carnage became commonplace during the First World War. Between 1914 and 1918, European commanders sent more than eight million men to their deaths in a series of often futile attacks. The total number of casualties—killed, wounded, and missing—reached more than 37 million. These casualty figures were in part the products of the Industrial Revolution, as the nations of the West used their factories to churn out ever more efficient tools of killing. The need for machine guns, artillery shells, poison gas canisters, and other implements of modern warfare meant that World War I was the first **total war**, a war that demanded that combatant nations mobilize their industrial economies and their armies, and thus a war that erased the distinction between civilian and soldier. In total war, victory depended on the woman in the munitions factory as well as the man on the front lines.

This first total war redefined the West. By shattering the authoritarian empires of eastern and central Europe and integrating the United States more fully in European affairs, the war ensured that commitment to democratic values became central to one dominant twentieth-century definition of "the West." But the war also strengthened anti-democratic forces: It catapulted into power a communist regime in Russia, intensified eastern Europe's ethnic and nationalist conflicts, and undermined many of the economic structures on which Western stability and prosperity rested. This chapter explores a key question:

How did the encounter with total war transform Western cultures?

The Origins of the First World War

25.1 What factors led Europe into war in 1914?

On June 28, 1914, ethnic Serbian terrorists assassinated Archduke Franz Ferdinand (1863–1914), the heir to the throne of the Austro-Hungarian Empire. One month after the archduke's death, Austria declared war on Serbia. One week later, Europe was at war. Germany entered the war on Austria's side. These two **Central Powers** squared off against not only small Serbia, but also the colossal weight of the **Allies**, the combined forces of Russia, France, and Britain. By the time the war ended in late 1918, it had embraced states from around the globe.

Why did the murder of one man on the streets of a Balkan city lead to the deaths of millions? To understand the origins of World War I, we need to examine four interlocking factors: the destabilizing impact of eastern European nationalism, the creation of rival alliance systems, the requirements of an industrialized military, and the "will to war"—the conviction among both policymakers and ordinary people that war provided a resolution to social and cultural crisis.

((∘)) 🕮 **Read the Document**
"British Soldiers on the Battle of the Somme"

total war A war that demands extensive state regulation of economic production, distribution, and consumption; and that blurs (or erases entirely) the distinction between civilian and soldier.

Central Powers Germany and Austria-Hungary in World War I.

Allies During World War I, the states allied against the Central Powers of Germany and Austria-Hungary. During World War II, the states allied against the regimes of Nazi Germany, fascist Italy, and imperial Japan.

Nationalism in Eastern Europe: Austria-Hungary and the Problem of Serbia

In eastern Europe, where ethnic, religious, or linguistic identities rather than political citizenship defined the "nation," nationalism served as an explosive force. For the Czechs, Slovenians, Serbs, Poles, Ukrainians, and many other groups, translating national identity into political identity—creating a "nation-state"—demanded the breakup of empires and a redrawing of political boundaries.

The divisive impact of nationalism in eastern Europe explains why officials within the Austro-Hungarian Empire regarded the small state of Serbia as a major threat. A multiethnic, multilinguistic empire, Austria-Hungary's survival depended on damping down the fires of nationalism wherever they flamed up. Yet Serbian politics centered on fanning the nationalist flame. In 1903, a group of Serbian army officers had shot Serbia's despised king and queen, chopped their bodies into bits, and threw the pieces out the window. To remain in power and avoid such a grisly fate, the new king catered to the demands of radical nationalists who sought the unification of all Serbs into a Greater Serbian state. Because more than seven million Serbs lived not in Serbia, but in Austria-Hungary, the Austrian monarchy regarded this call for Serbian unification as a serious threat to the Austro-Hungarian Empire.

The hostile relations between Serbia and Austria-Hungary led directly to the outbreak of the war. In 1908 Austria annexed Bosnia, a region with a large Serbian population. The Serbian government responded by encouraging Bosnian Serb separatist and terrorist groups. One such group, the Black Hand, assassinated Archduke Franz Ferdinand in the summer of 1914. That assassination convinced Austrian officials to declare war on Serbia.

Read the Document

Borijove Jevtic, "The Murder of Archduke Franz Ferdinand at Sarajevo, 1914"

ARREST OF GAVRILO PRINCIP Princip was only 18 years old when he assassinated Archduke Franz Ferdinand and set into motion the sequence of events that led to the First World War. Because of his age, he did not receive the death penalty but instead was sentenced to 20 years in prison. He died at age 22 of tuberculosis.

International Competition and Rival Alliance Systems

To understand what transformed this Austro-Serbian conflict into a European war, we need to look at the rival alliance systems that helped escalate a regional conflict into a European and then a global war. These alliances emerged in response to heightened international competition.

The unification of Germany in 1871 upset the balance of power by creating a military and economic powerhouse in the middle of Europe. Until 1890, however, the diplomatic maneuvers of Otto von Bismarck, the new Germany's chancellor, ensured stability. Bismarck recognized that the Franco-Prussian War of 1870 (which brought about German unification) had made antagonism toward Germany central to French foreign policy. He also recognized that Germany's position in the center of Europe made it vulnerable to encirclement, should France succeed in forming an anti-German alliance with another European state. To avoid such encirclement, Bismarck maintained alliances with Russia, Austria, and Italy. The Dual Alliance between Germany and the Austro-Hungarian Empire in 1879 became the **Triple Alliance** of 1882, which joined Germany, Austria, and Italy in a defensive treaty. With the Reinsurance Treaty of 1887, Russia and Germany agreed to remain neutral if either was attacked.

Triple Alliance Defensive alliance of Germany, Austria-Hungary, and Italy, signed in 1882.

But in 1888, a new emperor, Kaiser William II (r. 1888–1918), ascended the German throne. William, an ambitious and impatient young man, dismissed Bismarck in 1890 and launched Germany down a more dangerous path. The new kaiser broke with Bismarck's policies in two areas. First, William let the Reinsurance Treaty with Russia lapse, thus allowing anti-German France to join with Russia in the Franco-Russian Alliance of 1894. Germany now faced exactly the sort of encirclement by hostile powers, and the resulting threat of a two-front war, that Bismarck had sought to avoid.

Second, William favored a new "world policy" (*Weltpolitik*) for Germany that alienated Britain. Whereas Bismarck had confined Germany's interests to Europe, William and many prominent Germans wanted to see Germany claim its "place in the sun" as a global power: Germany needed a mighty overseas empire and a navy to defend it. Such policies were guaranteed to aggravate the British. As an island state dependent on its overseas empire, Britain based its defense on its naval supremacy. From the British point of view, a strong German navy challenged British national security and an expanding German empire conflicted with British imperial interests.

Hostility toward German ambitions overcame Britain's long tradition of "splendid isolation" from continental entanglements. In the first decade of the twentieth century, a series of military and economic arrangements formed ever-tighter links between Britain, Russia, and France, clearing the way for the formation of the **Triple Entente** among these three powers. An informal association rather than a formal alliance, the Triple Entente did not *require* Britain to join in a war against Germany. Many British officials, however, viewed Germany as the major threat to British interests.

Triple Entente Informal defensive agreement linking France, Great Britain, and Russia before World War I.

In this situation, German policymakers placed heavy emphasis on the alliance with Austria-Hungary. Strengthening this crucial ally became paramount. In July 1914, then, when Austrian officials debated their response to the assassination of Franz Ferdinand, the German government urged a quick and decisive blow against Serbia. Kaiser William assured the Austrian ambassador that Germany would stand by Austria no matter what the cost.

Both German and Austrian policymakers recognized that the cost might well be war with Russia. Eager to expand its influence in the Balkan region (and so gain access to the Mediterranean Sea), the Russian imperial regime had for decades positioned itself as the champion of Slavic peoples in the Balkans and as the protector of independent Slavic states such as Serbia. Thus, if Austria attacked Serbia, Russia might well mobilize in Serbia's defense.

German officials gambled, however, that Russia was not yet strong enough to wage war on Serbia's behalf. A decade earlier, Russia's defeat in the Russo-Japanese

War (see Chapter 23) had exposed its military weakness. Yet if Russia did choose war, then, the German chancellor Theobald von Bethmann-Hollweg explained, Germany's chances of victory were "better now than in one or two years' time."[1] Bethmann-Hollweg and his advisers knew that the tsarist government, in response to its loss to Japan, had implemented a military reform and rearmament program. Russia would only grow stronger.

Mobilization Plans and the Industrialized Military

The alliance system helps explain the beginnings of World War I: Germany's alliance with Austria emboldened Austrian policymakers to attack Serbia, while the links between Serbia and Russia made it likely that this attack would pull in the Russian Empire—and Russia was allied with France. Alliances alone, however, did not transform the Austro-Serbian conflict into a European war. No alliance *required* either Russia or Britain to enter the fray. Moreover, Italy, a member of the Triple Alliance with Germany and Austria, did not join these two powers in declaring war in August 1914. In fact, when Italy entered the war in 1915, it fought *against* Germany and Austria (see **Map 25.1**).

MAP **25.1** EUROPE, AUGUST 1914 In August 1914 each of the Central Powers faced the challenge of war on two fronts, but the entry of the Ottoman Empire into the war on the side of the Central Powers in November 1914 blocked Allied supply lines to Russia through the Mediterranean. What advantages did the alliance with the Ottoman Empire confer on Germany and Austria-Hungary?

To understand the origins of World War I, then, we need to look not only at the impact of rival alliance systems, but also at the widening gap between the expectations of traditional diplomacy and the requirements of an industrialized military. This growing gap ensured that when preparations for war began in the summer of 1914, control of the situation slipped out of the hands of the diplomats and their political superiors and into the grasp of the generals. The generals had planned for a European war. Once set in motion, their plans dictated events.

An important factor in these plans was the railroad, which enabled military planners to move large numbers of men quickly to precise locations. The speed with which governments could now throw armies into battle muddled the distinction between mobilization and actual war. *Mobilization* refers to the transformation of a standing army into a fighting force—calling up reserves, requisitioning supplies, enlisting volunteers or draftees, moving troops to battle stations. Traditionally, mobilization meant preparation for a possible fight, a process that took months and could be halted if the diplomats succeeded in avoiding war. But the railroads accelerated the mobilization process and thereby altered military planning. Aware that the enemy could also mobilize quickly, planners stressed the importance of preventive attacks, of striking before being struck. Once a state mobilized, the momentum toward war seemed almost irresistible.

These developments help explain the **Schlieffen Plan**, the military blueprint that structured German actions—and Allied reactions—in the summer of 1914. After the creation of the Franco-Russian Alliance in 1894, German military planners had to prepare for a two-front war. They devised the Schlieffen Plan for just that eventuality. The plan assumed that Russia's mobilization would take time: The vastness of its territory and the underdevelopment of its industrial infrastructure (including railroads) would slow its military mobilization and so guarantee that Russian troops would not pose an immediate threat to German borders. According to the Schlieffen Plan, then, the smaller Austrian army would hold off the slowly mobilizing Russians while the German army moved with lightning speed against France (see **Map 25.2**). After a quick knock-out blow against France, the Germans would concentrate on defeating Russia.

The Schlieffen Plan's need for speed thus pressured German politicians to treat a Russian declaration of mobilization as a declaration of war itself. As soon as Russia began to mobilize, German military leaders pushed their political counterparts to break off diplomatic negotiations so that the troop-laden trains could set off. Only two days elapsed between Russia's order of mobilization and the German declaration of war.

The need for speed also dictated that the attack against France would proceed via Belgium. Because German planners knew that the French expected any German attack to come through Alsace and Lorraine (the provinces that the Germans had taken from France after the Franco-Prussian War), the Schlieffen Plan called for the bulk of the German army to avoid France's fortified northeastern border (see Map 25.2) and instead swing to the west. Moving in a wide arc, the German army would flood into France through Belgium, encircle Paris, and scoop up the French forces before their generals knew what had hit them. With France out of the fight, the German troops would then board trains and speed back to the Eastern Front to join their Austrian allies.

By invading Belgium, German policymakers knew they risked bringing Britain into the war, as a longstanding international agreement appointed Britain Belgium's protector. Yet German policymakers gambled that Britain would stay out of the conflict. Again their gamble failed. Convinced that Germany threatened British economic and imperial interests, Britain's policymakers regarded the German invasion of Belgium as the pretext they needed to enter the war with mass support. Thus, just six weeks after a Serbian terrorist shot an Austrian archduke in Bosnia, British and German soldiers were killing each other in the mud of northern France.

Schlieffen Plan German military plan devised in 1905 that called for a sweeping attack on France through Belgium and the Netherlands.

MAP **25.2** (A) THE SCHLIEFFEN PLAN, 1905 AND (B) THE ACTUAL GERMAN ADVANCE, 1914 Count Alfred von Schlieffen's original plan of 1905 called for the sleeves of the German soldiers on the right flank to brush the English Channel: The German army would sweep in a huge arching movement west. In the fall of 1914 Helmuth von Moltke modified Schlieffen's plan: Compare these two maps. Why do some military historians argue that Schlieffen's plan would have succeeded if carried out in its original form?

The Will to War

The needs of an industrialized military outweighed traditional diplomacy and pushed those soldiers into that mud. Similarly, new pressures from public opinion constrained diplomats in the summer of 1914. This public pressure, or the "will to war," constituted the fourth factor in the outbreak of World War I.

Still drawn largely from the aristocracy, diplomats sought to maintain the balance of power in a Europe unbalanced by the forces of not only nationalism and industrial change, but also mass politics. The widening of the franchise meant that public opinion now played a role in international relations. Most new voters relied on the popular press—cheap newspapers marketed to a semiliterate public—for their understanding of foreign affairs. The banner headlines, large photographs, and short, simplified stories in these newspapers transformed the dense complexities of foreign relations into a compelling drama of Good Guys versus Bad Guys. Well-schooled in national identity, ordinary Europeans by 1914 tended to view foreign affairs as a giant nationalistic competition. They wanted evidence that "we" were ahead of "them."

In the last weeks of July 1914, pro-war crowds gathered in large cities, but not all Europeans welcomed the prospect of war. In Berlin, for example, 30,000 middle-class men and women paraded through the streets on the evening of July 25, singing patriotic songs and massing around statues of German heroes, while in working-class neighborhoods antiwar demonstrations received solid support. The declaration of war, however, silenced these demonstrations. Opposition to the war muted after August 1914, even among working-class socialists. National loyalty proved stronger than class solidarity.

What made the idea of war so appealing to so many in 1914? Some Europeans saw war as a powerful cleanser that would scour society of corruption. As Chapter 24

June 28
Assassination of Archduke Franz Ferdinand.

July 28
Austro-Hungarian declaration of war against Serbia.

July 30
Russian mobilization.

July 31
French, Austrian, and German mobilization.

August 1
German declaration of war on Russia.

August 3
German declaration of war on France.

August 4
German invasion of Belgium; British declaration of war against Germany.

explained, fears of racial degeneration and gender confusion marked the years before 1914. War seemed to provide an opportunity for men to reassert their virility and their superiority. It also offered them the chance to be part of something bigger than themselves—to move beyond the boundaries of their often-restricted lives and join in what was presented as a great national crusade. Carl Zuckmayer, a German playwright and novelist who volunteered to fight, later explained that men like him welcomed the war as bringing "liberation . . . from . . . the saturation, the stuffy air, the petrifaction of our world."[2]

For political leaders, war provided the opportunity to mask social conflicts and to displace domestic hostilities onto the battlefield. Violent trade unionism, socialist demands for revolutionary changes, anarchist-inspired assassinations, ethnic terrorism, and feminist protests had shaken the West in the decades before 1914. To many European elites, their society seemed on the verge of disintegration. But, as the future British prime minister Winston Churchill explained, war united societies with "a higher principle of hatred."

The war for which university students cheered, politicians schemed, and generals planned was not anything like the war that happened, however. Most people anticipated a short war. Theorists argued that the cost of waging an industrial war was so high that no state could sustain a conflict for long. The men who marched off to war in August 1914 expected that they would be home by Christmas. Instead, if they survived, which few of them did, they would spend not only that Christmas, but the next three, in the midst of unprecedented horror.

The Experience of Total War

25.2   When, where, and how did the Allies defeat the Central Powers?

Counting on *élan*, the French military spirit, to see them to victory, French troops swung into battle sporting bright red pants and flashy blue tunics. At their head rode the cream of the French military education system, the graduates of the Saint-Cyr military academy, who charged wearing their parade dress of white gloves and plumed hats. All that color and dash made easy targets for the German machine guns. As one military historian wrote, "Never have machine-gunners had such a heyday. The French stubble-fields became transformed into gay carpets of red and blue."[3] Those "gay carpets," colored with the blood and broken bodies of young French men, signaled that this would be a war of unexpected slaughter.

The Western Front: Stalemate in the Trenches

Implementing a modified version of the Schlieffen Plan (see Map 25.2), German troops swept through Belgium into France. By the first week of September they seemed poised to take Paris. This rapid advance, however, overstretched German supply lines, allowing French and British forces to turn back the Germans at the Marne River. In an episode that signaled the importance of the internal combustion engine—and the oil that fueled it—in modern warfare, an ingenious French commander exploited a gap in the German lines by moving troops rapidly from Paris to the front in the only vehicles available: taxicabs. (The army paid the drivers full fare for the trip.)

Taxicabs saved Paris, but the Allied forces failed to push the Germans out of France. By the middle of October, German, British, and French soldiers huddled in trenches that eventually extended more than 300 miles from the Belgian coast to the borders of Switzerland. There they stayed for the next four years.

HOLES AND DITCHES Siegfried Sassoon, a British poet and a World War I veteran, insisted that "when all is said and done, this war was a matter of holes and ditches."[4] From the strategic point of view, these holes and ditches—the trenches—were defensive fortifications, and the long stalemate on the Western Front shows that they worked well. Attacking infantry units walked forward against an enemy armed with machine guns and sheltered behind wide barbed-wire fences and a thick wall of dirt and sandbags. Despite numerous attempts between the fall of 1914 and the spring of 1918, neither side was able to break through the enemy line.

A discussion of trench strategy, however, conveys nothing of the appalling misery summed up by the term *trench warfare*. Imagine standing in a ditch about seven or eight feet deep and about three or four feet wide. The walls of the ditches are packed mud, propped up with sandbags. Wooden boards cover the floor, but the mud squelches between them. Piles of sandbags and barbed-wire barricades on the enemy's side of the ditch deepen your sense of being underground. Moreover, the trenches do not run in tidy straight lines. Instead, they zigzag at sharp angles, restricting the range of fire for enemy snipers and limiting the impact of explosives, but also ensuring that everywhere you look you see a wall of mud. Because you are in northern France, it is probably raining. Thus, you are standing not on but *in* mud—if you are lucky. In some parts of the line, soldiers stand in muddy water up to a foot deep. On the other side of your sandbag defenses stretches **no-man's-land**, the territory dividing the British and French trench systems from the German. Pocked with deep craters from heavy shelling, often a sea of mud churned up by the artillery, no-man's-land is littered with stinking corpses in various states of decomposition—all that is left of the soldiers who

no-man's-land The area between the combatants' trenches on the Western Front during World War I.

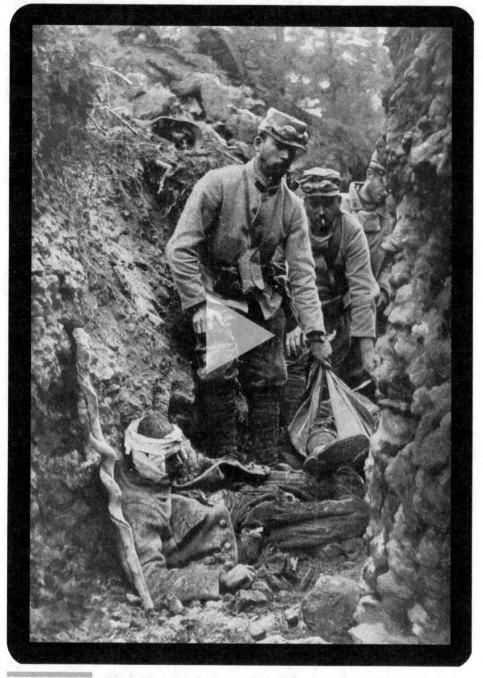

LIFE AND DEATH IN THE TRENCHES The dead, the dying, and the surviving jostle one another in a French trench.

died during previous attacks. Your constant companions are lice (the term *lousy* was coined on the Western Front) and rats. For the rats, the war is an endless feast as they grow enormously fat, nibbling their way through the piles of dead.

From 1915 on, the horror of the Western Front escalated with the introduction of a new killing tool—poison gas, first deployed by the Germans in the spring of 1915. The Allies condemned the use of poison gas as inhumane, but within months the British and French, too, were firing poison gas canisters across the lines. The consequences were appalling: blinded eyes, blistered skin, seared lungs, death by asphyxiation. By

A BATTERY SHELLED BY PERCY WYNDHAM LEWIS (1919) The mechanical nature of the war on the Western Front dominated many soldiers' accounts. Seeking the chance to be heroes, men volunteered to fight and found themselves reduced to interchangeable parts in a colossal war machine. In works such as *A Battery Shelled*, British artist Percy Wyndham Lewis (1882–1957) used modernist techniques to represent the reality of mechanized war. Lewis served in a British artillery unit and, in 1917, became an "Official War Artist," charged with recording and memorializing the war through painting. In this work, a burial party digs a grave for a gunner killed by enemy shells. The three soldiers in the foreground, however, seem utterly detached, as distanced from the death as the men who fired the shells.

SOURCE: Bridgeman IWM 28827.

1916, with the gas mask a standard part of every soldier's uniform, military companies resembled hordes of insects.

And, like insects, they were easily squashed. In the summer of 1915 an average of 300 British men became casualties on the Western Front every day, not because they were wounded in an attack, but because they were picked off by snipers, felled by an exploding shell, or wasted by disease brought on by living in the mud amid putrefying corpses.

THE OFFENSIVES The offensives, the attacks launched by both sides on the Western Front, sent the numbers of dead and wounded soaring. None of the elderly commanders—the Germans Helmuth von Moltke and Erich von Falkenhayn, the French Joseph Joffre and Ferdinand Foch, and the British Douglas Haig and John French—knew what to make of trench warfare. Schooled to believe that war was about attacking, they sought vainly to move this conflict out of the ditches by throwing masses of both artillery and men against the enemy lines. But time and time again the machine gun foiled these mass attacks.

The Battle of the Somme, described in the opening of this chapter, illustrates a typical offensive on the Western Front. By the end of 1917, the death tolls on the Western Front rose to astonishing levels, yet neither side had gained much ground. Many soldiers, who enlisted not for a specific term or tour of duty but "for the duration"—until the war ended—became convinced that only the dead escaped from the trenches. (See *Different Voices* in this chapter.)

The War in Eastern Europe

The Western Front was only one of several theaters of war. The Italian and Austrian armies, for example, fought along a stationary front for two brutal years after Italy joined the war on the Allies' side. Characterized by futile offensives and essential immobility, the war in Italy mirrored the conflict on the Western Front. In eastern Europe, however, a different plot unfolded.

Read the Document

Erich Maria Remarque, *All Quiet on the Western Front*

Different Voices

The Cultural Impact of the Western Front

M any of the upper- and middle-class officers fighting on the Western Front volunteered out of love for their country, an idealistic view of war as a heroic mission, and a longing for adventure. British recruiting posters described the war as the "Greatest Game of All." Trench warfare defied these expectations. The following poems, written by two young upper-middle-class British officers, illustrate the shift from the initial enthusiasm for the war to later disillusionment and despair. Neither man survived the war: Rupert Brooke died of blood-poisoning on his way to Gallipoli in 1915. Wilfred Owen was killed in battle in 1918, just days before the war ended.

In the sonnet series "1914," written just as the war began, Rupert Brooke not only welcomed the war but, as his first subtitle indicates, linked the outbreak of war, and the chance of heroic death, to the coming of internal or personal peace.

1914. I. Peace

Now, God be thanked Who has matched us with His hour,
And caught our youth, and wakened us from sleeping,
With hand made sure, clear eye, and sharpened power,
To turn, as swimmers into cleanness leaping,
Glad from a world grown old and cold and weary
Leave the sick hearts that honor could not move,
And half-men, and their dirty songs and dreary,
And all the little emptiness of love.

Oh! we, who have known shame, we have found release there,
Where there's no ill, no grief, but sleep is mending,
Naught broken save the body, lost but breath;
Nothing to shake the laughing heart's song peace there
But only agony, and that has ending;
And the worst friend and enemy is but Death.

1914. III. The Dead

Blow out, you bugles, over the rich Dead!
There's none of these so lonely and poor of old,
But, dying, has made us rarer gifts than gold.
These laid the world away; poured out the red
Sweet wine of youth; gave up the years to be
Of work and joy, and that unhoped serene,
That men call age; and those who would have been,
Their sons, they gave, their immortality.
Blow, bugles, blow! They brought us, for our dearth,
Holiness, lacked so long, and Love, and Pain.
Honour has come back, as a king, to earth,
And paid his subjects with a royal wage;
And Nobleness walks in our ways again;
And we have come into our heritage.

SOURCE: From "Peace" from "1914" Five Sonnets by Rupert Brooke. London: Sidgwick & Jackson, 1915.

Owen composed this piece, one of the most famous poems written during World War I, in several drafts between October 1917 and March 1918. The poem flatly describes a soldier being asphyxiated by poison gas while Owen and the rest of the company watch.

Dulce et Decorum Est by Wilfred Owen

Bent double, like old beggars under sacks,
Knock-kneed, coughing like hags,
we cursed through sludge,
Till on the haunting flares we turned our backs
And towards our distant rest began to trudge.
Men marched asleep. Many had lost their boots
But limped on, blood-shod. All went lame; all blind;
Drunk with fatigue; deaf even to the hoots
Of tired, outstripped Five-Nines that dropped behind.
Gas! Gas! Quick, boys!—An ecstasy of fumbling,
Fitting the clumsy helmets just in time;
But someone still was yelling out and stumbling
And flound'ring like a man in fire or lime . . .
Dim, through the misty panes and thick green light,
As under a green sea, I saw him drowning.
In all my dreams, before my helpless sight,
He plunges at me, guttering, choking, drowning.

If in some smothering dreams you too could pace
Behind the wagon that we flung him in,
And watch the white eyes writhing in his face,
His hanging face, like a devil's sick of sin;
If you could hear, at every jolt, the blood
Come gargling from the froth-corrupted lungs,
Obscene as cancer, bitter as the cud
Of vile, incurable sores on innocent tongues,—
My friend, you would not tell with such high zest
To children ardent for some desperate glory,
The old Lie: "Dulce et decorum est
Pro patria mori."*

SOURCE: "Dulce et Decorum Est" from Poems by Wilfred Owen, with an Introduction by Siegfried Sassoon. London: Chatto and Windus, 1920.

For Discussion

1. Why did Brooke see the war as a path to some sort of personal peace? How might his enthusiasm for war reflect the power of what Owen labeled "The old Lie"?
2. Compare the language and imagery in the two poems. How do the words themselves demonstrate a shift in the view of war?
3. Did disillusionment of soldiers on the Western Front differ from the disillusionment experienced by most soldiers, regardless of time or place? Is not the experience of combat always a rude awakening from innocence into brutal knowledge?

*"It is sweet and right to die for one's country."

A WAR OF MOVEMENT If the war on the Western Front was a war of mud and ditches, the conflict on the Eastern Front was a war of movement. For three years, massive armies surged back and forth, as the plains and mountains of eastern Europe echoed with the tumult of spectacular advances, headlong retreats, escalating ethnic conflict, and, finally, political revolution.

When the war began in August 1914, Russian troops headed in a two-pronged onslaught against Germany and against Austria (see **Map 25.3**). Although surprised by the speed of the Russian advance, German troops in East Prussia turned the Russian tide at the Battle of Tannenberg and then advanced steadily into the Russian Empire. The next year, a combined German and Austrian assault forced the Russian army to retreat more than 300 miles into its own territory. Russian military losses by the end of 1915 were astounding, with well over one million soldiers killed, another million wounded, and 900,000 taken prisoner. Russian soldiers pushed back into Austria-Hungary in June 1916, but could not sustain the attack. They advanced again in the summer of 1917, but this offensive also soon disintegrated into a retreat.

These retreats revealed that the Russian Empire's economic and political structures could not withstand the pressures of total war. Russian supply lines were so overextended that the poorly fed and inadequately clothed Russian troops found themselves without ammunition and unable to press ahead. Demoralized, they began to desert in large numbers.

Civilians within the Russian Empire also suffered enormously. As its army retreated, the tsarist regime ordered a "scorched earth" policy: Russian soldiers bombed their own cities, dismantled factories, burned farm buildings and crops, and killed livestock. Many groups who lived in the borderlands and were judged potentially disloyal—including Poles, German-speaking Lutherans, and Jews—were deported to the east. These deportations, combined with the scorched earth policy that left millions without a means of subsistence, created a massive wave of refugees, what one historian has termed "a whole empire walking."[5]

By 1917 the Russian Empire hovered on the brink of collapse. Soldiers, workers, and peasants grew impatient with wartime deprivations and demands. Linguistic and religious minorities, particularly those who endured forcible deportation, turned increasingly to anti-Russian nationalist politics.

This disaffection and disintegration led to the Russian Revolution. As we will explore in detail later in this chapter, revolution forced the tsar to abdicate in February 1917. In October, a small group of socialist revolutionaries called the Bolsheviks seized control and moved quickly to pull Russia out of the war.

View the Map

Russian Armies on the Eastern Front in World War I

MAP **25.3** THE EASTERN AND MIDDLE EASTERN FRONTS, 1914–1918 Unlike the Western Front, the Eastern Front was far from stationary. How does this map help explain why many Germans found their country's defeat in November 1918 to be incomprehensible?

GERMANY AND THE EAST The German army thus *defeated* its enemy on the Eastern Front. From 1915 on, the German army

"A WHOLE EMPIRE WALKING" This hand-colored slide features a group of refugees in wartime Russia. By 1917, approximately seven million refugees wandered the Russian Empire, subject to months or years of hunger, cold, disease, rape, looting, and beatings.

occupied huge swathes of what had been the Russian Empire. The **Treaty of Brest-Litovsk**, signed in 1918, confirmed this occupation by ceding to Germany all of imperial Russia's western territories and one-third of its population.

Many of the regions that German soldiers occupied between 1915 and 1919 were less industrially developed and urbanized than Germany; moreover, these lands had been systematically "scorched" by the retreating Russian troops. Confronted with societies in the midst of chaos, the Germans concluded that "the East" was primitive and barbaric, in need of German civilization and order.

German rule, however, only intensified the suffering of the borderland populations. High taxation rates, forced labor, and the confiscation of scarce food and supplies resulted in famine in many occupied areas by 1917. Rather than Germanizing these peoples, German rule helped strengthen national identities. As Lithuanians, Poles, Ukrainians, and others fought for survival, they increasingly began to think of themselves in national terms.

THE FORGOTTEN FRONT: THE BALKANS In southeastern Europe, World War I was in many ways the "Third Balkan War," yet another installment in an ongoing competition for territory and power. In 1912 and again in 1913, Greece, Bulgaria, Romania, and Serbia had fought each other in the First and Second Balkan Wars. Hence, in 1915 Bulgaria allied with the Central Powers to gain back the territory it had lost in the Second Balkan War while Romania joined the Allies in 1916 to protect its hold on that territory.

For most of the war, the Central Powers controlled the Balkans. A joint Bulgarian, German, and Austro-Hungarian invasion crushed Romania. The Serbian experience was even bleaker. By November of 1915, the Serbian army had been pushed to the Albanian border. Some 200,000 Serbian soldiers fled over the snow-swept mountains of Albania to the Adriatic Sea in the disastrous "Winter March." Austrian troops occupied Serbia and placed the country under military rule. By the war's end, approximately 25 percent of Serbian citizens lay dead.

Treaty of Brest-Litovsk Treaty between Germany and Bolshevik-controlled Russia, signed in March 1918, that ceded to Germany all of Russia's western territories.

The World at War

The imperialist expansion of the later nineteenth century ensured that as soon as the war began, it jumped outside European borders. The British and French Empires supplied the Allies with invaluable military and manpower resources. Australia, New Zealand, Canada, India, South Africa, and Ireland supplied no less than 40 percent of Britain's military manpower during the war. More than 650,000 men from Indochina, Algeria, and French West Africa assisted the French war effort.

Fighting fronts multiplied around the globe as combatants struggled for imperial and European supremacy (see **Map 25.4**). Portugal joined the Allies largely because it hoped to expand its colonial possessions in Africa. Japan seized the opportunity to snatch German territories in China while using its navy to protect Allied troop and supply ships. By the end of 1914, Japanese, Australian, and New Zealander troops occupied most of Germany's island colonies in the Pacific as well.

The Middle East also became a key theater of war. Once the Ottoman Empire joined the Central Powers, Britain's Middle Eastern economic and military interests lay vulnerable. Britain was desperate to protect Allied access to the Suez Canal—a vital link to the soldiers and supplies of India, Australia, and New Zealand—and to Persian oil fields, an important source of fuel for the British navy.

MAP **25.4** THE WORLD AT WAR Imperialist relationships and global economics ensured that a European conflict became a world war. In Africa, for example, Portuguese and South African troops fought a bush war against German and native soldiers. How does this map illustrate the emergence of Japan and the United States as global powers? Why do you think that several Latin American countries declared war on Germany in April 1917?

To defeat the Ottoman Empire in the Middle East, the British joined forces with Arab nationalists. Led by a British soldier named T. E. Lawrence (1888–1935)—better known as "Lawrence of Arabia"—and inspired by promises of postwar national independence, Arab nationalists used guerilla warfare to destroy what remained of Ottoman rule in the Middle East. By 1917 the Ottomans had lost control of almost the entire coastal region of the Arabian Peninsula bordering the Red Sea, and Lawrence and his Arab allies had captured Jerusalem.

THE WAR AT SEA AND THE ENTRY OF THE UNITED STATES While infantrymen rotted in trenches and froze in mountain passes, the German and British navies fought a critical war at sea. German submarines sought to cut Britain's imperial lifeline and starve out its civilian population by sinking ships before they could reach British ports. Almost 14,000 British sailors and civilians died in these submarine attacks. In turn, British destroyers stretched a blockade across all ocean and sea passageways to Germany and its allies.

The Allied blockade prevented food and other essential raw materials from reaching Germany, Austria-Hungary, and their associates. Food shortages sparked riots in more than 30 German cities in 1916. When the potato crop that year failed and eliminated one of the only remaining sources of nutrition, children's rations fell to *one-tenth* of their actual needs.

Desperate to win the war quickly, German policymakers in 1917 decided to escalate their submarine war against Britain. Suspecting (correctly) that supposedly neutral American passenger ships were delivering essential war materiel to Britain, the German government ordered its submarines to sink without warning any ship heading for British shores. The Germans recognized that this unrestricted submarine warfare would probably pull the United States into the war. But Germany stood on the brink of economic collapse, and German policymakers decided they had no choice. They gambled that they would defeat the Allies in a last-ditch effort before the United States' entry into the war could make much of a difference.

The United States declared war on Germany in April 1917. Outrage over American deaths at sea served as the most immediate cause of American entry into the war. Four other factors also played a role. First, Franco-British news stories about German atrocities during the invasion of Belgium persuaded many Americans that right rested on the Allied side. Second, the Russian Revolution removed an important obstacle to American cooperation with the Allies—the tsarist regime. Americans had balked at the idea of allying with the repressive government of Tsar Nicholas II, but the February Revolution, which overthrew Nicholas, offered American policymakers a more acceptable wartime partner. Third, by the time President Woodrow Wilson asked the U.S. Congress for a declaration of war, the American economy was intertwined with that of the Allies. Trade between the United States and the Allied states had grown from $825 million in 1914 to more than $3 billion in 1916, and American bankers

A WORLD AT WAR: ALGERIAN SOLDIERS Crammed into a freight car, Algerian soldiers receive drinks before heading to the Western Front. Forces from Europe's overseas empires fought on both the Western and Eastern Fronts.

had loaned more than $2 billion to the Allied governments. Finally, the German government committed a serious blunder in the spring of 1917 when it offered to assist Mexico in recovering New Mexico, Arizona, and Texas in exchange for Mexican support should war break out between Germany and the United States. The interception of a telegram sent by the German foreign minister Arthur Zimmermann exposed this offer and inflamed anti-German sentiment in the United States. The German policy of unrestricted submarine warfare, then, put flame to kindling that was already in place.

The U.S. declaration of war (followed by those of Brazil, Costa Rica, Cuba, Guatemala, Haiti, Honduras, Nicaragua, and Panama) provided an immediate psychological boost for the Allies, but several months passed before American troops arrived on the battlefield in significant numbers. By July 1918, however, the United States was sending 300,000 fresh soldiers to Europe each month. The Allies now had access to an almost unlimited supply of military materials and men. Eventually nearly two million American soldiers were sent to Europe and almost 49,000 American soldiers died in battle.

BACK IN MOTION: THE WESTERN FRONT IN 1918 Faced with the prospect of having to fight fresh American forces, German policymakers decided to gamble one more time. On March 2, 1918—before the bulk of the U.S. army had been deployed—the German army launched an overwhelming ground assault against British and French lines. The gamble almost succeeded. In just 30 minutes the German troops broke through the British front line. By April the German army stood just 50 miles from Paris.

What explains this sudden shift on the Western Front from a conflict characterized by stalemate to a war of decisive movement? As we have seen, in the first years of the war commanders remained committed to offensive techniques suited to an age of preindustrial warfare—the mass charge, the cavalry attack—even though industrial technologies such as the machine gun had transformed the power of defensive war. Certainly, Western commanders were well-acquainted with the killing potential of the machine gun. In the imperial conflicts discussed in Chapter 24, the machine gun enabled small European forces to defeat larger indigenous armies. But on the Western Front, both sides possessed the machine gun. In other words, both sides were good on defense but poor on offense.

In 1918, however, the Germans came up with new offensive strategies. Instead of a frontal assault dictated by commanders sitting well behind the lines, Germany's offensive of 1918 consisted of a series of small group attacks aiming to cut behind British and French positions rather than straight on against them. In addition, the Germans in 1918 scrapped the preliminary artillery barrage that signaled when and where an attack was about to begin. In place of the barrage they employed sudden gas and artillery bursts throughout the offensive. The rapid German advance in the spring of 1918 showed that technique had caught up with technology.

In July, however, the Allies stopped the German advance. In August they broke through the German lines and began to push the German army backward. Throughout the summer the push continued. By September the Western Front, which had stood so stationary for so long, was rolling eastward at a rapid clip.

The final German gamble failed for three reasons: First, the rapidity of the advance overstrained German manpower and supply lines. Second, the Allies learned from their enemies and adopted the same new offensive strategies. And third, the Allies figured out how to make effective use of a new offensive technology—the tank. Developed in Britain, the tank obliterated the defensive advantages of machine-gun-fortified trenches. A twentieth-century offense met a twentieth-century defense, and the war turned mobile.

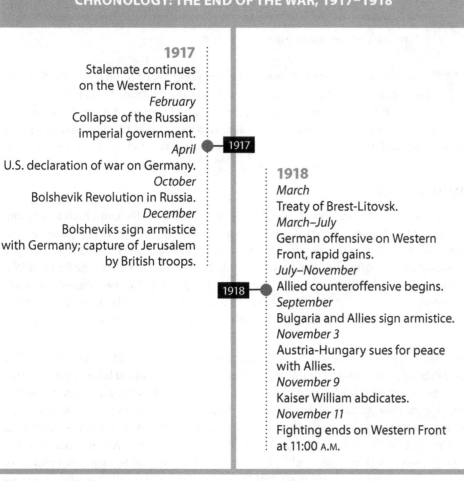

CHRONOLOGY: THE END OF THE WAR, 1917–1918

1917
Stalemate continues
on the Western Front.
February
Collapse of the Russian
imperial government.
April
U.S. declaration of war on Germany.
October
Bolshevik Revolution in Russia.
December
Bolsheviks sign armistice
with Germany; capture of Jerusalem
by British troops.

1917

1918
March
Treaty of Brest-Litovsk.
March–July
German offensive on Western
Front, rapid gains.
July–November
Allied counteroffensive begins.
September
Bulgaria and Allies sign armistice.
November 3
Austria-Hungary sues for peace
with Allies.
November 9
Kaiser William abdicates.
November 11
Fighting ends on Western Front
at 11:00 A.M.

1918

Reinforced with fresh American troops and the promise of more to come, the Allied forces surged forward against the hungry and demoralized Germans. When the Bulgarian, Ottoman, and Austrian armies collapsed in September and October, Germany stood alone. On November 11, 1918, German leaders signed an armistice and the war ended. The Treaty of Brest-Litovsk was declared void, and in 1919 German troops withdrew from the eastern lands they had occupied.

A VERY DIFFERENT BATTLE As the war drew to a close in 1918, a very different battle began. In the spring, American soldiers training at Camp Funston, Kansas, began to sicken with a severe form of influenza—the flu. When American units from the camp arrived on the Western Front, the flu virus traveled along with them and soon spread throughout the armies and then, via demobilized soldiers, nurses, and administrators, back to their home countries. By August, a flu pandemic was underway.

The influenza pandemic of 1918–1919 claimed the lives of approximately 50 million victims—far more than died in battle during the war. (Some estimates range as high as 100 million.) No other recorded epidemic killed so many people so quickly. Few people at the time, however, realized the extent of the outbreak. Horrified by what the pandemic might do to civilian morale in a time of total war, governments on both sides censored press reports. Ironically, the pandemic came to be known as the Spanish Flu, because in neutral Spain the government did not restrict press coverage.

 Read the Document

Anna Eisenmenger, "A German Soldier Returns Home"

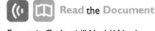

Read the Document

Francois Carlotti, "World War I:
A Frenchman's Recollections"

The Home Fronts

25.3 How did total war structure the home fronts?

he term *home front* was coined during World War I to highlight the fact that this conflict was fought not only by soldiers on the front lines, but also by civilians at home. Total war demanded the mobilization of a combatant state's productive capacity. Total war recast and in some cases revolutionized not only the economies, but also the political, social, and gender relations of the states involved.

Industrial War

World War I was the first industrial war. Poison gas and machine guns, barbed wire and shovels, canned foods and mass-produced uniforms—all poured out of factories and helped shape this war. Industrialization made it possible for governments to deploy the masses of men mobilized in this conflict. While 170,000 men fought in the Battle of Waterloo in 1815 and 300,000 soldiers in the Battle of Sedan in 1870, *one million* combatants were swept up in the Battle of the Marne in 1914. Only industrialized production could keep these huge armies supplied with weapons, ammunition, and other necessities.

THE EXPANSION OF THE STATE At first, no government realized the crucial role that industrial labor would play in this war. Both military and political leaders believed that the war would end quickly and that success depended on throwing as many men as possible into the front lines. In France, even munitions factories were shut down and their workers sent to the front. Governments practiced "business as usual"—letting the free market decide wages, prices, and supply—with disastrous results. Soaring inflation, growing black markets, public resentment over war profiteering (the practice of private businessmen making huge profits off the war), and, most crucially, shortages of essential military supplies, including ammunition, proved that a total war economy needed total regulation.

Beginning in 1915, both the Allied and Central Powers' governments gradually assumed the power to requisition supplies, dictate wages, limit profits, and forbid workers to change jobs. In Germany, the increasing regulation of the economy was called *war socialism*, a misleading term because it was big business that benefited. The German army worked in partnership with large industrial firms to ensure the supply of war materiel to the front lines, while the Auxiliary Service Law of 1916 drafted all men age 17 to 60 for war work. Measures such as these greatly expanded the size and power of the central governments in the combatant states. For example, in 1914 the British office in charge of military purchases employed 20 clerks. By 1918, it had become the Department of Munitions, a bureaucratic empire with 65,000 employees overseeing more than three million workers in government-owned and -operated munitions plants.

This expansion of governmental power corresponded with restricted individual freedom, even in traditionally liberal states such as Britain. Flying in the face of tradition, in 1916 Britain's government imposed the draft—a clear example of the requirements of the state overriding the desires of the individual. By the war's end, the British government had also restricted the hours that pubs could be open (as a way of encouraging workers to show up for work sober) and tampered with time itself by inventing Daylight Saving Time as a means of maximizing war production.

THE POLITICS OF TOTAL WAR The war's reliance on industrial production greatly empowered industrial producers—the workers. In 1915 both France and Britain abandoned political party competition and formed coalition governments that included socialist and working-class representatives. In return, French and British union leaders agreed to a ban on labor strikes and accepted the temporary "deskilling" of certain jobs—a measure that allowed unskilled laborers, particularly women, to take the place of skilled workers at lower rates of pay.

Nevertheless, the number of labor strikes rose in Britain and France in 1916 and in 1917. Faced with the potential of disintegration on the home front, British and French political leaders reacted similarly. They formed war governments committed to total victory. In Britain, David Lloyd George (1863–1945) became prime minister at the end of 1916. A Welsh artisan's son who had fought hard to reach the top of Britain's class-bound, English-dominated political system, Lloyd George was not a man to settle for a compromise peace. One year later, Georges Clemenceau (1841–1929) became prime minister of France. Nicknamed "the Tiger," Clemenceau demanded victory. When asked to detail his government's program, he replied simply, *"Je fais la guerre!"* ("I make war!").

But making war, French and British officials realized, demanded public support. They cultivated this support in two ways. First, they sought to depict the war as a struggle between democracy and authoritarianism—a crusade not for national power or economic gain, but for a better world. Second, they recognized that if they failed to meet the basic needs of ordinary citizens, civilian morale would plummet. Both governments intervened regularly in the economy to ensure that workers received higher wages, better working conditions, and a fair distribution of food stocks. In state-owned munitions factories, workers for the first time received benefits such as communal kitchens and day care. Food rationing actually improved the diets of many poor families. Living standards among employed workers in France and in Britain rose during the war.

The situation in Germany differed significantly. Until the last weeks of the war German political leadership remained in the hands of the conservative elite and the military. Increasingly, Generals Hindenburg and Ludendorff—the heroes of the Battle of Tannenberg—dictated political affairs. The army and big industrial firms seized control of German economic life. Given the power to set prices and profit

BERLIN, 1917. As German civilians line up for scarce food supplies in Berlin in the winter of 1917, an elderly woman collapses, most likely from hunger.

margins, industrialists—not surprisingly—made a killing. Their incomes soared, while escalating inflation and chronic food shortages ground down ordinary workers. In 1917, industrial unrest slowed German war production, civilian discontent reached dangerous levels, and the success of the Allied blockade meant Germans were starving.

The World Turned Upside Down

By the war's end, changes in the relations among classes and between men and women caused many Europeans to feel as if their world had turned upside down. European workers grew more radical as they realized the possibilities of their own collective power and the potential of the state as an instrument of social change. The fact that by 1917 many of these workers were women also had revolutionary implications. In the work world and in society at large, gender roles, like class relations, underwent a marked shift.

THE WAR'S IMPACT ON SOCIAL RELATIONS In the trenches and on the battlefields, World War I had a leveling effect. For many young, middle-, and upper-class soldiers, the war provided their first sustained contact with both manual labor and manual laborers. In letters home, they testified to a newfound respect for both, as the horrors of the war experience broke down rigid class barriers.

On the home front, however, social relations grew more rather than less hostile. During the war years, inflation eroded the savings of middle-class men and women and left them scrambling to maintain their social and economic status. In Germany and throughout eastern Europe, food shortages and falling wages produced a revolutionary situation. By contrast, in Britain and France, a rising standard of living demonstrated to workers the benefits of an interventionist state. Yet class hostilities rose in western Europe, too. Working-class activists demanded that the state continue to regulate the economy in peacetime to improve the standard of living of ordinary workers. Having finally tasted the economic pie, workers fought for a bigger piece, while the middle class struggled to defend its shrinking slice.

THE WAR'S IMPACT ON GENDER RELATIONS By 1916, labor shortages in key military industries, combined with the need to free up as many men as possible for fighting, meant that governments on both sides actively recruited women for the paid workforce. Women were suddenly visible in the public sphere as bus drivers, elevator operators, and train conductors. In eastern Europe, the agricultural labor force came to consist almost entirely of women. In western Europe, women took on dangerous positions in munitions factories, worked just behind the front lines as ambulance drivers and nurses, and in 1917 and 1918 often led the way in walking off the job to demand better conditions.

The impact of the war on women's roles should not be exaggerated, however. Throughout the war, more women continued to work in domestic service—as cooks, maids, nannies—than in any other sector of the economy. The great majority of the women who did move into skilled industrial employment were not new to the paid workforce. Before 1914 they had worked in different, lower-paying jobs. And they certainly were not treated as men's equals. In government-run factories in Britain, women received as little as 50 percent of men's wages for the same job.

Nevertheless, for many women, the war was a liberating experience. With their husbands away, many wives made decisions on their own for the first time. Female munitions workers in Britain received wages three times higher than their prewar earnings. But middle- and upper-class women experienced the sharpest change. In the prewar years, immobility and passivity continued to mark the lives of many middle-class girls—sheltered within the family home, subject to paternal authority, waiting for a marriage proposal. The war threw women into the public space. The middle-class girl who before 1914 was forbidden to travel without a chaperone might be driving an ambulance, splashing through the mud and blood, or washing the bodies of naked working-class soldiers.

At the same time that the war smashed many of the boundaries that had restricted women, it narrowed the world of the middle-class male soldier. While women were on the move—driving buses, flying transport planes, ferrying the wounded—men were stuck in the mud, confined to narrow ditches, waiting for orders. Expecting to be heroic men of action, they found themselves instead living the sort of immobile, passive lives that had characterized the prewar middle-class woman's experience. In total war, even gender roles turned upside down.

Yet when the war ended, many of these radical changes proved to be only temporary. The wartime movement of women into skilled factory jobs and public positions such as bus drivers and train conductors was rapidly reversed. For example, by the terms of the British Restoration of Pre-War Practices Act (1919), women who had taken up skilled factory jobs received two weeks' pay and a train ticket home.

Other changes appeared more permanent. France in 1919 possessed 10 times as many female law students and three times as many female medical students as it had in 1914. British women over age 30 received the vote on a limited basis; in the United States, Germany, and most of the new states in eastern Europe, meanwhile, the achievement of female suffrage was more complete. Cultural changes also seemed to signal a gender revolution. Women smoked in public, raised their hemlines, cut their hair, and threw away their corsets.

ROLE REVERSAL The imagery in this British Red Cross poster infantilized the soldier while making the nurse into a figure of saintly power. Many men found the forced confinement and passivity of trench warfare profoundly unsettling, while many women experienced the war as a time of liberation.

Identifying the Enemy: From Propaganda to Genocide

Many of the changes in gender and class relations resulted from government efforts to regulate the economy for total war. To ensure that their citizens remained committed to the war effort, governments also sought to regulate the production and distribution of ideas. Pacifists and war objectors faced prison sentences and even execution. In France, journalists and rival politicians—even the former prime minister—who dared suggest negotiations with Germany were thrown in prison.

Wartime governments worked to create ideas that would encourage a total war mentality. Propaganda emerged as a crucial political tool. By censoring newspapers and doctoring photographs, politicians ensured that the public viewed the war positively. Poster campaigns using new techniques developed in the advertising industry aroused patriotic fervor.

Fostering a total war mentality also required stirring up hatred for those labeled as the Enemy. In words that were soon set to music and became a popular wartime song, poet and army private Ernst Lissauer (1882–1937) urged Germans to "hate [England] with a lasting hate. . . . Hate of seventy millions, choking down."[6] Meanwhile in Britain, anti-German feelings ran so high that the royal family changed its name from Hanover

THE HARVEST OF WAR The Turkish massacre of more than one million Armenians illustrates the destructive consequences of combining nationalist hatred with total war. This criminal horror is often seen as foreshadowing the Jewish Holocaust during World War II.

to Windsor in an effort to erase its German lineage. In the ethnic cauldron of eastern Europe, hatred of the enemy often fed hostility toward ethnic minorities, perceived as the enemy within. In Austria-Hungary, for example, more than 500 Bosnian Serbs and hundreds of Ukrainians were shot without trial because they were seen as Russian sympathizers.

The most horrific result of the tendency to look for the enemy at home occurred in the Ottoman Empire, where suspicion of the Armenian minority resulted in mass murder. The brutal "solution" to the so-called "Armenian question" began in April 1915. After arresting Armenian elites (and thus removing potential resistance leaders from Armenian communities), Turkish troops rounded up and killed Armenian men. In some cases, soldiers marched the men outside their town or village and then shot them. In other instances, they were pushed into caves and asphyxiated by fires blocking the entrances. The Ottoman government then ordered the women, children, and the elderly deported to Syria. Driven from their homes on short notice, they marched through mountain and desert terrain without food or water. Rapes and executions were commonplace. Between 1915 and 1918, more than one million Armenian men, women, and children died in this attempt at **genocide**, the murder of an entire people.

genocide The murder of an entire people.

  Read the Document

"A Turkish Officer Describes the Armenian Massacres"

War and Revolution

25.4 What were the consequences of this war for the European and the global political order?

Total war tore at the social and political fabric of European societies. As seams began to fray and gaping holes appeared, many welcomed the opportunity to tear apart the old cloth and weave something new. Some of these revolutionaries were Marxists, aiming to build a socialist Europe. Others were nationalists, determined to assert the rights of their ethnic or linguistic group, or to overthrow their colonial rulers. Yet not all revolutionaries belonged to underground or terrorist groups. The president of the United States, Woodrow Wilson, also demanded a new world order. The peace settlement, however, failed to realize these revolutionary expectations.

The Russian Revolutions

Tsarist Russia began the war already divided. In regions such as Latvia, Lithuania, Poland, and Ukraine, anti-Russian sentiment flared high, and nationalists saw the war as opening the door to independent statehood. Throughout the empire, the clash between Tsar Nicholas II's vision of Russia as a divine autocracy and the political demands of the growing middle and working classes created an explosive situation.

The war brought political chaos to the Russian Empire. Nicholas, a man with a remarkable capacity for self-delusion, insisted on going to the front and commanding his army. He left political affairs in the hands of his wife Alexandra (1872–1918) and her spiritual mentor Grigori Rasputin (1869–1916). Rasputin is one of the more intriguing characters in twentieth-century history. An illiterate, unwashed faith healer from a peasant background, he possessed a well-documented and still-unexplained ability to stop the bleeding of Alexei, the young hemophiliac heir to the throne. Many high-ranking Russians, however, argued that Rasputin was not a miracle worker but a traitor. Because Rasputin opposed the war against Germany, they perceived him as a voice of treason whispering in the German-born tsarina's ear. In 1916 Russian noblemen murdered Rasputin, in hopes of restoring authority and stability to the tsarist government.

THE FEBRUARY REVOLUTION Rasputin's removal achieved little. The French ambassador in Russia wrote in January 1917, "I am obliged to report that, at the present moment, the Russian Empire is run by lunatics."[7] Almost two million Russian soldiers had died and many more had been wounded or taken prisoner. Economic and communications networks had broken down, bread prices were rising, and people were hungry. Even members of the tsarist government began to ask not *if* revolution would occur, but *when*.

The answer came on February 24, 1917 (March 8 on the western calendar). A group of women workers in Petrograd (formerly St. Petersburg) demonstrated to protest inadequate food supplies. Over the course of the next few days, similar demonstrations flickered across the city. On February 27, they coalesced into revolutionary fire when the troops who were ordered to put down the protest joined it instead. Governmental orders lost all authority, and on March 2 Tsar Nicholas was forced to abdicate. The Russian Revolution had begun.

Who now controlled Russia? Two competing centers of power emerged: the Provisional Government and the Petrograd Soviet. On March 12, the Duma, or Russian parliament, created a Provisional Government from among its members. Like the Duma, the new Provisional Government was dominated by members of the gentry and middle classes: professionals, businessmen, intellectuals, bureaucrats. These men tended to be liberals who believed that Russia was now moving along the path toward a parliamentary democracy. They quickly enacted important reforms such as universal suffrage, the eight-hour workday, and civic equality for all citizens. The Provisional Government, however, was exactly what its name indicated: provisional. Its members believed they should not take any drastic measures. Their task was to serve as a caretaker government until an elected Constituent Assembly wrote a constitution for the new Russia.

But at the same time that the Provisional Government was struggling to bring order to the chaos of revolutionary Russia, across the empire socialists, industrial workers, and soldiers formed **soviets**, or councils, to articulate their grievances and hopes.

soviets Workers' and soldiers' councils formed in Russia during the Revolution of 1917.

THE REVOLUTIONARY SPARK On March 8, 1917, thousands of women took to the streets of Petrograd to protest the imposition of bread rationing. Their cries for "Peace and Bread" sparked the Russian Revolution.

The Petrograd Soviet, led by revolutionary socialists, soon became a powerful political rival to the less radical Provisional Government.

But neither the liberals in the Provisional Government nor the socialists in the Petrograd Soviet could control the revolution. A *popular* revolution—a revolution *of the people*—had overthrown Nicholas II, and at the core of this popular revolution stood a simple demand: "Peace, Land, Bread." Soldiers—and most Russians—wanted an immediate end to a war that had long ceased to make any sense to them. Peasants, as always, wanted land, their guarantee of survival in a chaotic world. And city dwellers wanted bread—food in sufficient quantities and at affordable prices.

The Provisional Government could not satisfy these demands. It did promise the gradual redistribution of royal and Church lands, but peasants, unconstrained by the liberal regard for law and the rights of private property, wanted land immediately. More important, by the summer of 1917 no Russian government could have provided bread without providing peace. Russia no longer had the resources both to continue its war effort and to reconstruct its economy. The urban population dwindled as food disappeared from the shops, factories ceased operation because of shortages of raw materials, and the currency lost all value. Peace appeared impossible, however. Not only did Russia have commitments to its allies, but German armies stood deep within Russian territory. A separate peace with Germany would mean huge territorial losses. Only a constitutionally elected government would have the legitimacy to take such a drastic step, most Provisional Government members believed. And so the war continued.

And so, too, did the revolution. Peasants made their own land reform by seizing the land they wanted. Soldiers declared their own peace by deserting. (Of every 1,000-man Russian troop sent to the front, fewer than 250 men made it into combat. The rest deserted.) The Provisional Government grew more unpopular. Not even the appointment of the well-liked socialist and Petrograd Soviet member Alexander Kerensky (1881–1970) as prime minister stabilized the government's position.

THE OCTOBER REVOLUTION This tumultuous situation created the opportunity for the **Bolsheviks**, one of the socialist factions in the Petrograd Soviet, to seize control. In April 1917, the Bolshevik leader, Vladimir Lenin (1870–1924), returned from almost 20 years in exile. While still in his teens, Lenin had committed himself to revolution after his older brother was executed for trying to assassinate Tsar Alexander III. Iron-willed and ruthlessly pragmatic, Lenin argued that a committed group of professional revolutionaries could force a socialist revolution on Russia. In a largely peasant society, the agent of revolutionary change could not be the urban industrial working class (as Karl Marx had theorized). The masses could not make the revolution, and so the Bolshevik or Communist Party, the revolutionary "vanguard," must make it for them.

By the fall of 1917, Bolshevik membership had grown from 10,000 to 250,000, and the party held a majority in the Petrograd Soviet. Lenin now demanded the immediate overthrow of the Provisional Government. On October 25 (November 7 on the Western calendar), Bolshevik fighters captured the Winter Palace in Petrograd, where the Provisional Government was meeting.

The *second* Russian Revolution was underway. The Bolsheviks declared a policy of land and peace—land partition with no compensation to estate owners and an immediate peace with Germany, regardless of the cost. (As we have seen, the cost was high: According to the terms of the Treaty of Brest-Litovsk, signed with Germany in 1918, Russia lost its western territories.)

Promises of peace and land did not win over everyone in Russia, however. Civil war erupted as rival socialists, liberals, and tsarist supporters resisted Bolshevik rule. These "Whites" (distinguished from "Red" Bolsheviks) received assistance from foreign troops. Fearing the spread of communist revolution, 14 countries (including the United States, Britain, France, and Japan) sent 100,000 soldiers to Russia. Non-Russian nationalists fighting for independent statehood joined in the conflict. (See *Justice in History* in this chapter.)

As the war raged, transportation systems shut down, the water supply ceased to run, and furniture became the only source of fuel. When the furniture ran out, entire families froze to death inside apartment blocks. Urban areas emptied as their inhabitants fled to the countryside. By 1921, Moscow had lost half its residents and Petrograd (formerly St. Petersburg) lost two-thirds. Yet rural conditions were also brutal, a consequence of the Bolshevik policy of "War Communism": the nationalization of all land and industry, the suppression of private trade, and a food levy that deprived peasants of almost all they produced. The peasants resisted—actively, with violence, and passively, by refusing to plant crops. Famine resulted.

The civil war killed off more combatants than had World War I, but by 1922 the Bolsheviks emerged victorious over the Whites and many of the nationalist uprisings. Poland, Finland, and the Baltic states (Estonia, Latvia, and Lithuania) retained their

25.1

25.2

25.3

25.4

Bolsheviks Minority group of Russian socialists, headed by Vladimir Lenin, who espoused an immediate transition to a socialist state. It became the Communist Party in the Soviet Union.

Q View the **Closer Look**

Bolshevik Revolution Propaganda Poster

  Read **the Document**

"Bolshevik Seizure of Power, 1917"

Justice in History
Revolutionary Justice: THE NONTRIAL
OF NICHOLAS AND ALEXANDRA

O n July 16, 1918, Bolshevik revolutionaries shot and killed Nicholas II, tsar of Russia; his wife, the tsarina Alexandra; his heir, 14-year-old Alexei; their four daughters—Olga (age 23), Tatiana (age 21), Maria (age 19), and Anastasia (age 17); their three servants; and their physician.

When leaders in other states heard the news of the deaths, they condemned the killings as murders. The Bolsheviks, however, termed them acts of revolutionary justice.

(continued on next page)

(continued from previous page)

After the October Revolution, the Bolsheviks imprisoned the tsar and his family in a house in Ekaterinburg, 900 miles east of Moscow in a region controlled by the Bolshevik Ural Regional Soviet. Throughout the spring of 1918, the Bolshevik government prepared to try Nicholas publicly for crimes against the Russian people.

But the trial never happened. By July, an anti-Bolshevik army was

TSAR NICHOLAS II AND FAMILY Tsar Nicholas II, the Tsarina Alexandra, and their family.

pattern of escalating violence that characterized World War I and its revolutionary aftermath.

In the blood of these killings, however, we can also see reflected two ideas that shaped Bolshevik politics: the subordination of law to the revolutionary state and the concept of collective guilt. The Bolsheviks dismissed the liberal ideal of impartial justice as a myth. They

approaching Ekaterinburg. If these troops freed the imperial family, they would score a crucial victory. The Ural Soviet decided—probably with Lenin's approval—to execute the tsar and his family immediately.

Pavel Medvedev, one of the tsar's guards, recounted the events of the evening of July 16. As he watched, the royal family entered a downstairs room: "The Tsar was carrying the heir [Alexei] in his arms. . . . In my presence there were no tears, no sobs and no questions." Medvedev's commander ordered him to leave. When he returned a few minutes later, he said,

. . . . [I] saw all the members of the Tsar's family lying on the floor with numerous wounds to their bodies. The blood was gushing. The heir was still alive—and moaning. [The commander] walked over to him and shot him two or three times at point blank range. The heir fell still.[8]

Medvedev did not relate the more gruesome details of the execution. Trying to preserve part of the family fortune, the tsar's daughters wore corsets into which they had sewn diamonds. When they were shot, the bullets, in the words of one eyewitness, "ricocheted, jumping around the room like hail."[9] Even after several pistols were emptied, one of the girls remained alive. The guards resorted to bayonets.

The Ural Regional Soviet announced the tsar's execution, but said nothing about his family. The official statement from Moscow reported that "the wife and son of Nicholas Romanov were sent to a safe place."[10]

These lies reveal the Bolsheviks' own uneasiness with the killings. Why, then, did they shoot the family? Determination to win the civil war provides part of the answer. According to Trotsky, Lenin "believed we shouldn't leave the Whites [the anti-Bolshevik forces] a live banner to rally around."[11] Any member of the royal family could have become such a banner. In addition, Trotsky argued, the killings were essential "not only to frighten, horrify, and to dishearten the enemy, but also in order to shake up our own ranks, to show them that there was no turning back, that ahead lay either complete victory or complete ruin."[12] The killing of Tsar Nicholas and his family thus formed part of the

argued that justice is never blind, that it always serves the interests of those in power. In a discussion of the tsar's killing, a Bolshevik pamphlet admitted, "Many formal aspects of bourgeois justice may have been violated." But, the pamphlet argued, such a violation of "bourgeois" standards of justice did not matter because "worker-peasant power was manifested in the process."[13] "Worker peasant power," embodied in the revolutionary state, trumped such "formal aspects of bourgeois justice" as legal rights.

While this concept of the law as subordinate to the state helps us understand the tsar's execution without trial, the concept of collective guilt provides a context for the killing of his children. The Bolshevik model of socialism assumed that *class* constituted objective reality. Aristocratic and middle-class origins served as an indelible ink, marking a person permanently as an enemy of the revolutionary state—regardless of that person's own actions or inclinations. From the Bolshevik perspective, royal origins tainted the tsar's children. When their continuing existence threatened the revolution, they were shot. Over the next four decades, the concept of collective guilt contributed to millions of deaths in the former Russian Empire.

For Discussion

1. How was the murder of the Russian royal family the by-product of total war rather than the result of any revolutionary ideals?
2. Were the Bolsheviks correct in arguing that "justice" is never blind, that legal systems reflect the interests of a society's dominant groups? Is there such a thing as impartial justice?

Taking It Further

Kozlov, Vladimir, and Vladimir Khrustalëv. *The Last Diary of Tsaritsa Alexandra.* 1997. A translation of Alexandra's diary from 1918.

Steinberg, Mark, and Vladimir Khrustalëv. *The Fall of the Romanovs.* 1999. A detailed account of the last two years of the tsar and his family, based on archives opened only after the collapse of the Soviet Union.

CHRONOLOGY: REVOLUTION IN RUSSIA, 1917–1922

1917

1917

February 24
St. Petersburg/Petrograd women's protest; revolution begins.
March 2
Establishment of Provisional Government and abdication of tsar.
October 25
Bolshevik overthrow of the Provisional Government.

1918–1922

1918–1922
Civil war.

hard-won independence. The "Union of Soviet Socialist Republics" (USSR, or Soviet Union) replaced the Russian Empire.

THE SPREADING REVOLUTION The victory of the Russian Bolsheviks inspired socialists across Europe and around the world. In January 1919, communists in Buenos Aires, Argentina, led by Russian immigrants, controlled the city for three days until they were crushed by the Argentine army. British dockworkers struck in support of the Bolshevik Revolution, and in French cities general strikes caused chaos. In Austria, revolutionaries attempted to take control of government buildings in Vienna but were quickly defeated by the Austrian army. In Hungary, Bela Kun, a journalist who had come to admire the Bolsheviks while a prisoner of war in Russia, established a short-lived soviet regime in the spring of 1919.

Revolution also swept through defeated Germany. In October 1918, its military commanders recommended that the German government enter into peace negotiations, but the Allies refused to negotiate until the Germans democratized their political system. As a result, representatives of left-wing and centrist parties—including the SPD, the largest socialist party in Europe—joined the German government.

This "revolution from above" coincided and competed with a "revolution from below." Inspired by the Bolshevik Revolution, many German socialists condemned the SPD as too moderate; instead, they supported the more radical Spartacists (named after Spartacus, the gladiator who led a slave revolt against Rome in the first century B.C.E.). Directed by Karl Liebknecht (1871–1919) and Rosa Luxemburg (1870–1919), the Spartacists demanded an immediate communist revolution. By November 8, German communists declared the establishment of a Soviet republic in the province of Bavaria and the Red Flag—symbol of communism—flew over 11 German cities.

On November 9, the kaiser abdicated and the head of the SPD, Friedrich Ebert (1871–1925), became chancellor of Germany. From the window of the Reichstag building in Berlin, one of Ebert's colleagues in the SPD proclaimed that Germany was now a parliamentary democracy. Almost at that very moment, Karl Liebknecht stood at another window in Berlin (in the occupied royal palace) and announced that Germany was now a revolutionary communist state. With two opposing versions of revolution on offer, civil war raged until the spring of 1919, when the SPD defeated the communists.

THE REVOLUTION HALTED Even after the failure of communist revolution in Germany, however, Lenin hoped that the communist revolution would spread throughout western Europe. The Polish-Soviet War of 1919–1921 inspired and then crushed this hope of a European communist revolution.

Partitioned among Prussia, Austria, and Russia in the eighteenth century, Poland was reconstructed after World War I. Its eastern borders, however, remained unclear because of the ongoing civil war and nationalist conflicts in Bolshevik Russia. Poland's leader, Josef Pilsudski (1867–1935), aimed to create a federation consisting of Poland and independent Ukraine, Belarus, and the Baltic states, a kind of twentieth-century version of the early modern Polish-Lithuanian Commonwealth. Nationalists within these states, however, refused to cooperate. Although Pilsudski's army controlled much of this territory by May 1920, a Soviet counterattack in June forced the Poles to retreat.

This successful Soviet push into Poland led Lenin to believe that the revolution was unstoppable. Once the Soviets conquered Poland, Lenin argued, they could use it as "a base against all the contemporary states."[14] Thus, Lenin termed the Battle of Warsaw of August 1920 a "turning point for the world."[15] Instead, Pilsudski and his forces held Warsaw and drove the Red Army back. The Peace of Riga of 1921 ended the war between Bolshevik Russia and Poland and set the limits of the Bolshevik Revolution.

The Failure of Wilson's Revolution

At the beginning of 1919, representatives of the victorious Allies gathered in Paris to draw up the peace treaties. These officials aimed for more than ending the war. They wished to construct a new Europe. At the center of this high endeavor was the American college professor-turned-president Woodrow Wilson. Wilson based his version of revolutionary change on the ideal of national self-determination—a world in which "every people should be left free to determine its own polity, its own way of development, unhindered, unthreatened, unafraid, the little along with the great and powerful." Wilson foresaw a new map of Europe, with independent, ethnically homogenous, democratic nation-states replacing the old authoritarian empires.

Wilson envisioned that these new nation-states would interact differently from the empires of the past. In what he called his **Fourteen Points**, Wilson demanded a revolution in international relations. He argued that "Points" such as freedom of the seas, freedom of trade, and open diplomacy (an end to secret treaties) would break down barriers and guarantee peace and prosperity for all peoples. The cornerstone of this new world order would be an international organization, the **League of Nations**. By overseeing the implementation of the Fourteen Points and resolving disputes between states through negotiation, the League would guarantee that World War I was "the war to end all wars." Because all states—big and small, European and non-European—would have an equal voice in the League, the systems of secret diplomacy and Great Power alliances that had led to total war would disappear.

Wilson's vision, however, went unrealized. In Paris in 1919 and 1920, the Allies and their defeated enemies signed a series of treaties, the most important of which was the Treaty of Versailles with Germany. The treaty writers sought to create a new international order based on three features: a democratic Germany, national self-determination in eastern Europe, and a viable system of international arbitration headed by the League of Nations. They failed in all three.

THE TREATY OF VERSAILLES AND GERMAN DEMOCRACY At the center of the new Europe envisioned by Woodrow Wilson was to be a new democratic Germany, but the French leader, Georges Clemenceau, did not share this vision. After surviving two German invasions of his homeland, he wished to ensure that Germany could never again threaten France. Clemenceau proposed the creation of a Rhineland state in Germany's industrialized western region as a buffer zone between France and Germany and as a way to reduce Germany's economic power. The British leader David Lloyd George promised his people that he would squeeze Germany "until the pips squeak"

Fourteen Points The principles outlined by U.S. President Woodrow Wilson as the basis for a new world order after World War I.

League of Nations Association of states set up after World War I to resolve international conflicts through open and peaceful negotiation.

and publicly supported Clemenceau's hard-line approach. In private, Lloyd George feared that this approach would feed the flames of German resentment and undermine the structures of German democracy.

Lloyd George's fears proved well-grounded. The German people bitterly resented the **Versailles Treaty**, which they perceived as unjustly punitive. By the terms of the treaty, Germany lost all of its overseas colonies, 13 percent of its European territory, 10 percent of its population, and its ability to wage war. The treaty limited the German army to a defensive force of 100,000 men, with no aircraft or tanks. Clemenceau failed to create a separate Rhineland state, but the Rhineland was demilitarized, emptied of German soldiers and fortifications. In addition, the Versailles Treaty ceded the coal-fields of the Saar region to France for 15 years (see **Map 25.5**).

Most significantly, the treaty declared that German aggression had caused the war and therefore that Germany must recompense the Allies for their costs. In 1921, the Allies presented Germany with a bill for **reparations** of 132 billion marks ($31.5 billion). As Chapter 26 details, this reparations clause helped set up an economic cycle that proved devastating for both global prosperity and German democratic politics.

THE FAILURE OF NATIONAL SELF-DETERMINATION The peace settlement sought to redraw eastern Europe on national lines. Map 25.5 shows that the old multinational empires of eastern and central Europe disappeared, replaced with independent nation-states. Poland again became a state, with pieces carved out of the German, Austro-Hungarian, and Russian Empires. One entirely new state—Czechoslovakia—was formed out of the rubble of the Austro-Hungarian Empire. Romania, Greece, and Italy all expanded as a result of serving on the winners' side, while Serbia became the heart of the new Yugoslavia. The defeated states shrank, some dramatically. Austria, for example, became a mere rump of what had been the mighty Habsburg Empire, and Hungary was reduced to one-third of its prewar size. All that remained of the Ottoman Empire was Turkey.

President Wilson heralded these changes as the victory of "national self-determination." But as Wilson's own secretary of state complained, "This phrase is simply loaded with dynamite. It will raise hopes which can never be realized." Wilson had called for "every people" to be left free to determine its political destiny—but who constituted "a people"?

Even after the peace settlements redrew the map, 30 million eastern Europeans remained members of minority groups. Fewer than 70 percent of Hungarians, for example, lived in Hungary—more than three million were scattered in other states. Over nine million Germans resided outside the borders of Germany. In the newly created

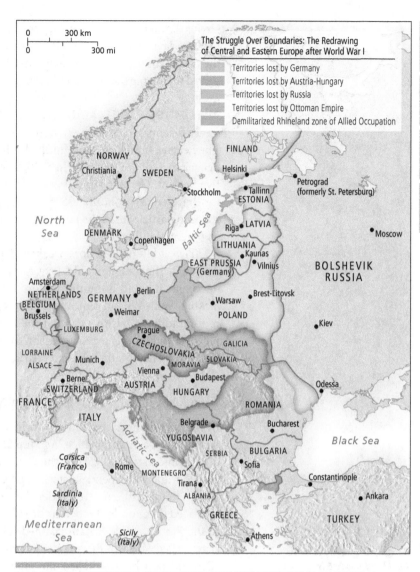

MAP **25.5** THE STRUGGLE OVER BOUNDARIES: THE REDRAWING OF CENTRAL AND EASTERN EUROPE AFTER WORLD WAR I Compare this map with Map 25.1 on page 782. How did the war redraw the political map of central and eastern Europe? Which states gained and which states lost territory? Which states were new creations?

Versailles Treaty Treaty between Germany and the victorious Allies after World War I.

reparations Payments imposed upon Germany after World War I by the Versailles Treaty to cover the costs of the war.

 View the Image

LA Times Cartoon: France Demands War Reparations from Germany

View the Map

"Shifting Borders: Eastern Europe after World War II"

Czechoslovakia, one-third of the population was neither Czech nor Slovak. The new state of Yugoslavia contained an uneasy mixture of several ethnic groups, most resentful of the dominant Serbs. Rather than satisfying nationalist ambitions, the peace settlements served to inflame them, thus creating a volatile situation for the post-World War I world.

THE LIMITS OF THE LEAGUE True to Wilson's vision of a new international order, the treaty makers included the Covenant of the League of Nations in each of the treaties. The League, however, never fulfilled Wilson's hopes of making war obsolete. When the League met for the first time in 1920, three significant world powers had no representative present: Germany and the Soviet Union were excluded, and, in a stunning defeat for President Wilson, the U.S. Senate rejected membership. The failure of these three states to participate in the League at its beginning stripped the organization of much of its potential influence.

Two additional factors weakened the League. First, it had no military power. Although the League could levy economic sanctions against states that flouted its decisions, it could do nothing more. Second, the will to make the League work was lacking. With Wilson removed from the picture, European leaders pursued their own more traditional visions of what the League should be. French politicians, for example, believed that its primary reason for existence was to enforce the provisions of the Versailles Treaty rather than to restructure international relations.

The Making of the Modern Middle East

In the Middle East, the end of World War I meant an entirely new map, but not the end of European dominance. As **Map 25.6** shows, under terms set by the new League of Nations, the Allies carved the Ottoman territory in the Middle East into separate and nominally independent states. The League, however, judged these states as "not yet able to stand by themselves under the strenuous conditions of the modern world" and so placed them under French or British control (or "Mandate"). Syria and Lebanon fell to the French, while Britain claimed Iraq (Mesopotamia), Palestine, and Transjordan (later called Jordan). Britain also continued to exercise its influence over Egypt, Iran (Persia), and what would become Saudi Arabia.

Three factors explain why this remaking of the Middle East failed to effect a lasting settlement in the region. First, the new boundaries violated wartime promises and so created a long-lasting legacy of mistrust and resentment against the West. Second, the new states imposed on the region were artificial, the creation of the Allied victors rather than a product of historical evolution or of the wishes of the inhabitants themselves. And finally, Western mandatory supervision (which in actual practice differed little from old-fashioned imperial rule) brought with it Western practices and concepts that destabilized regional social and economic structures.

The early history of Iraq exemplifies these three factors. In 1915, Sharif Husayn (Hussein) ibn Ali, head of the Hashemite dynasty that guarded the Islamic holy sites, agreed to fight the Central Powers in exchange for British support of an independent Arab state. The British argued they fulfilled this promise when they placed Husayn's son Faisal on the throne of the newly created Iraq. Husayn and his supporters, however, felt betrayed. They believed that the British had reneged on the promise of an independent Arab kingdom centering on what became Syria and including Palestine.

The artificiality of Iraq also created a revolutionary situation. In creating Iraq, the Allies glued together three provinces—Basra, Baghdad, and Mosul—that the Ottomans had never treated as a single political or economic unit. The population of this new state

View the Video

The Continuing Legacy of World War I in the Middle East

MAP **25.6** THE MIDDLE EAST AFTER WORLD WAR I In the wake of the war, the newly created League of Nations redrew the political boundaries of the Middle East under a new system of "mandates." Whose interests did this new system serve?

FAISAL AT THE HEAD OF HIS TROOPS, 1917 Sharif Husayn ibn Ali's son Faisal led Arab troops in an alliance with the British against Ottoman forces. After the war, Faisal became king of Iraq.

consisted of a volatile mixture of ethnicities (including Arab, Kurd, and Assyrian) and religions (including Shi'ite and Sunni Muslims, Christians, Jews, and Zoroastrians). These groups did not identify as "Iraqi" nor did they feel any sense of allegiance to their new ruler. They regarded Faisal as an imperialist puppet, jumping as British "advisers" pulled the strings.

Finally, the British inadvertently destabilized Iraq's social structures by introducing British legal and economic concepts that destroyed indigenous traditions. For example, by applying the concept of private land ownership to Iraqi customary relations, the British transformed the traditional tie between tribal sheikh and tribesmen into an economic arrangement between landowner and tenants—one that tended to enrich the landowner while impoverishing the tenants.

The settlement of Palestine destabilized the Middle East even further. Husayn and his supporters believed that the British government had promised them an independent Arab kingdom that would include Palestine. Yet during the war British officials also pledged support for a Jewish state in Palestine. Influenced by the anti-Semitic myth of a powerful Jewish elite wielding influence over world affairs, British policymakers believed (wrongly) that Jewish influence could determine whether the United States entered and Russia remained in the war. Desperate to ensure both, the British government in 1917 issued the **Balfour Declaration**, which announced that Britain favored the Zionist goal of a Jewish national homeland in Palestine.

After the war, Palestine passed into British hands as a League of Nations mandate. The British remained formally committed to the Balfour Declaration. Some 90 percent of the inhabitants of Palestine in 1920, however, were Arabs (both Christians and Muslims). They viewed the Balfour Declaration as an effort to take away their land and give it to Europeans. Arab protests and riots in Palestine erupted, and by 1922 the British government decided to slow the pace of Jewish immigration into the region to alleviate Arab fears. Over the next two decades the British faced continuous pressure from both Arab and Jewish nationalist forces. Like the remaking of eastern Europe, the remaking of the Middle East ushered in decades of political turmoil and violence.

 Read the Document

"The Balfour Declaration"

Balfour Declaration Declaration of 1917 that affirmed British support of a Jewish state in Palestine.

CONCLUSION

The War and the West

The idea of "the West" changed as a result of World War I. The entry of American forces in the final year of the war signaled that, in the twentieth century, the United States would feature in any definition of "Western culture" or "Western civilization." At the same time, the spread of the war to the Middle East and Africa and the significant role played by soldiers from imperial territories such as Tunisia, India, and Australia demonstrated the global framework that complicated and constrained Western affairs.

The war's revolutionary aftermath also had consequences for formulations of "Western identity." With the triumph of the Bolshevik Revolution, two versions of modernity now presented themselves—one associated with the United States and capitalism, and the other represented by Russia and its communism. The Bolshevik Party's intellectual roots lay in Marxism, a Western ideology shaped by Western ideals of evolutionary progress and the triumph of human reason. But after the Russian Revolution, many in the West viewed communism as the "Other" against which the West identified itself.

The carnage of World War I challenged the faith of many Europeans that industrial development ensured the West's continual moral and material progress. In the final decades of the nineteenth century, European and American soldiers had used repeating rifles and machine guns to conquer huge sections of the globe in the name of Western civilization. In 1914, European and American soldiers turned their machine guns on each other. The world the war created was one of unprecedented destruction. Millions lay dead, with millions more maimed for life. Vast sections of northern France and eastern Europe became giant cemeteries filled with rotting men and rusting metal. Across central and eastern Europe, starvation continued to claim thousands of victims. In the new world shaped by relentless conflicts such as the Battle of the Somme, the pessimism and sense of despair that had invaded the arts in the decade before the war became more characteristic of the wider culture. For many Europeans, the optimism and confidence of nineteenth-century liberalism died in the trenches.

Yet, paradoxically, the war also fostered high hopes. Wilson declared that this had been the war to end all wars. The fires of revolution burned brightly and many in the West believed that, on top of the ashes of dismantled empires, they would now build a better world. The task of reconstruction, however, proved immense. Seeking stability, many Europeans and Americans did their best to return to prewar patterns. The failure of the peace settlement ensured that the "war to end all wars" set the stage for the next, more destructive total war.

MAKING CONNECTIONS

1. Compare and contrast the Eastern, Western, and Middle Eastern Fronts in World War I: How and why did the experiences of ordinary soldiers in these war zones differ? Which front was more important for shaping the postwar West?
2. What do the phrases "total war politics" and a "total war mentality" mean? How did total war politics and mentalities affect European women? The working class? National minorities?
3. How did the Wilsonian and Leninist visions of postwar Europe differ? Which was more "Western" and why? Which was more successful and why?

TAKING IT FURTHER

For suggested readings, see page R-1.

Chapter Review

The Origins of the First World War

25.1 What factors led Europe into war in 1914?

The volatile force of nationalism in Eastern Europe increased over-all tensions, while a complicated system of international alliances heavily influenced who declared war and when. Once in motion, the machine of war was difficult to stop given the widening gap between traditional diplomatic policy and the needs of an increasingly indus-trialized military. Public sentiment was heavily swayed toward the idea of war as a way to prove national superiority.

The Experience of Total War

25.2 When, where, and how did the Allies defeat the Central Powers?

The war was fought in the muddy trenches on the Western Front, in a series of advances and retreats in Eastern Europe, around the globe in places like the Middle East, and at sea in the form of blockades and submarine attacks. Germany proved victorious on the Eastern Front by the beginning of 1918 but the struggling Allies received needed reinforcements when the United States entered the war. A final surge against the starving and demoralized Germans led to the fall of the Central Powers and eventually Germany's withdrawal from the east-ern lands its troops had occupied.

The Home Fronts

25.3 How did total war structure the home fronts?

The crucial role of industrial production in total war empowered industrial workers. Class relations shifted when workers, many of whom were women, realized the importance of their collective power. Gender relations also shifted as women moved into more public roles. To maintain morale and shape public perception of the war, states turned to censorship and propaganda. Demonization of the enemy and the need for a total war mentality fostered a climate of violence and even genocide.

War and Revolution

25.4 What were the consequences of this war for the Euro-pean and the global political order?

The strain of total war led to revolution in Russia and the establishment of the world's first communist state. The punitive peace imposed on Germany weakened the new democratic German state while the re-drawing of state boundaries in central and eastern Europe heightened rather than resolved nationalist tensions. Similarly, the remapping of the Middle East betrayed wartime promises to competing national groups and failed to foster political stability or economic prosperity in the region.

Chapter Time Line

1914
June
Assassination of Archduke Francis Ferdinand of Austria-Hungary.
August
Outbreak of World War I.
October
Stalemate on the Western Front begins.

1914

1916

1916
Food shortages in German cities.

1917
February
Popular revolution in Russia.
April
U.S. joins the Allies.
October
Bolshevik Revolution in Russia.

1917

1918
March
Treaty of Brest-Litovsk: Germany victorious in East.
August
Global flu pandemic underway.
November
Germany surrenders.

1918

26 Reconstruction, Reaction, and Continuing Revolution: The 1920s and 1930s

O n September 14, 1927, a convertible accelerated down a street in Nice in southern France. In its passenger seat sat Isadora Duncan, who let her long silk shawl whip in the wind. One of the most famous dancers in the Western world, Duncan had pioneered a revolutionary style of dance that replaced toe shoes and tutus with bare feet and simple tunics. Attacking classical ballet as an artificial form that deformed the female body, the American-born Duncan created dances that did not impose movement on the body, but instead flowed from the body itself. Speeding down the streets in a convertible, Duncan provides a fitting image for Western culture after World War I. She was an American, and in these decades American culture came to represent for many Europeans the limitless future. Like Duncan in her car, Americans and Europeans in the postwar era wanted to move in new directions, break traditional barriers, and push toward greater liberation. Even

OTTO DIX, *FLANDERS* (1934–1935) In this painting, the bodies of soldiers shape the Flanders landscape. Like these soldiers—and much of postwar European culture—Dix, a veteran, could not escape the war. His paintings reveal a man permanently wounded.

LEARNING OBJECTIVES

26.1 ((	26.2 ((	26.3 ((	26.4 ((	26.5 ((	26.6 ((
What was the impact of World War I on European cultural life?	What circumstances explain the collapse of democracy throughout much of interwar Europe?	How did the Nazis succeed in establishing a dictatorship in Germany?	Why did the Soviet Union seem a success and how did the democracies respond?	What changed, and what did not, in women's experiences after World War I?	How did the interaction between the West and the world outside change after World War I?

((Listen to Chapter 26 on MyHistoryLab

26.1

26.2

26.3

26.4

26.5

26.6

👁 Watch the Video Series on MyHistoryLab

Learn about some key topics related to this chapter with the *MyHistoryLab Video Series: Key Topics in Western Civilization*

Duncan's clothing—loose tunics, free-flowing scarves, fluid shawls—symbolized a love of freedom and mobility.

Yet freedom is sometimes dangerous and movement can be violent. On that autumn day in 1927 Duncan's scarf became entangled in the wheel of the car and strangled the dancer. Gruesome as it is, this image, too, symbolizes the West in the turbulent interlude between World War I and World War II. The American president, Woodrow Wilson, hailed World War I as the "final war for human liberty." Many Europeans agreed. They thought that the war would propel their society down a new road. In much of Europe, however, the drive toward freedom ended with the triumph of ideologies that viewed human liberty as an illusion and mass murder as a tool of the state.

The strangulation of democracy in eastern and southern Europe during these decades highlights a central theme of this book: the contested definition of "the West." In the Wilsonian vision, the West promoted individual freedom through democratic politics and capitalist economics. But in the 1920s and 1930s, anti-democratic and anti-capitalist ideologies defined the West differently. Examination of the aftermath of World War I answers the question:

Why was the link between "Western" and "democratic" so fragile in this era?

Cultural Despair and Desire

26.1 What was the impact of World War I on European cultural life?

After World War I, many in the West turned from the future in despair. Others, however, dreamed of building a new world.

The Waste Land

Within a few years of the war's end, war memorials dotted cities and villages throughout France and Britain. These memorials rarely celebrated the Allies' victory. They focused instead on dead soldiers—on slaughter, not success. At Verdun, for example, the memorial was an ossuary, a gigantic receptacle for the skulls and bones of 130,000 men. In some ways, European culture after the war took the form of an ossuary, as intellectuals and artists looked at the death tolls from the war and concluded that the end product of human reason and scientific endeavor was mass destruction.

In the English-speaking world, "The Waste Land" (1922), a poem by the American expatriate T. S. Eliot (1888–1965), supplied an evocative portrait of postwar disillusion. Like a Cubist painting, this lengthy poem contains no straightforward narrative. Instead, it comprises fragments of conversation, literary allusions, disjointed quotations, and mythological references, all clashing in a modernist cry of despair:

> White bodies naked on the low damp ground
> And bones cast in a little low dry garret,
> Rattled by the rat's foot only, year to year.

26.1

26.2

26.3

26.4

26.5

26.6

existentialism Twentieth-century philosophy that emerged in the interwar era and influenced many thinkers and artists after World War II. Existentialism emphasizes individual freedom in a world devoid of meaning or coherence.

Pessimism also marked theology and philosophy. In the nineteenth century, theologians and philosophers emphasized humanity's progressive evolution, but World War I raised doubts about the moral progress of human society. In his writings, the Swiss theologian Karl Barth (1886–1968) emphasized human sinfulness and argued that an immense gulf separated humanity from God. Human intellectual effort could not bridge the gap. Reaching God demanded a radical leap of faith.

Barth's German colleague Rudolf Bultmann (1884–1976) made the leap of faith even more radical. Bultmann argued that the Jesus Christ depicted in the New Testament—the foundation of Christianity—was largely fictional. In Bultmann's view, the New Testament resembled Eliot's "Waste Land" in its layered fragments originating from myth and folk tale, capable of multiple interpretations. Bultmann, a Lutheran pastor, argued that in this Christian mythology persons can find spiritual—although not scientific or historical—truth.

Bultmann's form of Christianity is often called Christian **existentialism** because Bultmann put a Christian twist on the existentialist philosophy that emerged in the interwar era. Existentialists such as Jean-Paul Sartre (1905–1980) taught that existence has no built-in meaning—no religious purpose or moral value. It just *is*. To overcome the fear, alienation, even *Nausea* (the title of one of Sartre's novels, published in 1938) of mere existence, a person must consciously choose actions that create meaning and a sense of self. As Sartre put it, each person is "condemned to be free."

Building Something Better

In *Flanders,* painted in 1934, the war veteran Otto Dix (1891–1969) depicted a nightmare of trench soldiers, rotting like blasted trees. Stuck in the mud, Dix's soldiers provide a haunting image of interwar culture. A different vision, however, takes shape when we examine the work of Dix's contemporaries in the *Bauhaus.* Established in Berlin in 1919 as a school for architects, craftsmen, and designers, the Bauhaus epitomized postwar Western idealism rather than despair. Its members sought to eliminate the barriers between "art" (what we put on our walls or see in museums) and "craft" (what we actually use in daily life: furniture, textiles, dishes, and the like). By making daily living more effective, efficient, and beautiful, the Bauhaus's founder Walter Gropius (1883–1969) and his students hoped to become "the architects of a new civilization."[1] Like Gropius, many artists abandoned the prewar modernist ideal of "art for art's sake" and produced work steeped in political passion and the hope of radical social change.

Faith in technology characterized this optimistic side of interwar culture. Having demonstrated the destructive power of machines during World War I, human beings would now use their mechanical powers to reconfigure modern society. Architecture illustrated this mechanical faith. A house, explained the Swiss architect Le Corbusier (1887–1965), was "a machine for living in." Le Corbusier and his fellow modernist architects stripped their buildings of ornamentation and exposed the machinery—the supporting beams, the heating ducts, the elevator

ARCHITECTS OF A NEW CIVILIZATION This Bauhaus design for a "public transport interconnecting stop, electric transformer and urinal" first appeared in a French architecture journal in 1925. Many architects and city planners saw public transport systems as the means of making modern urban life not only more efficient but also more connected and cohesive.

26.1

26.2

26.3

26.4

26.5

26.6

shafts. Concrete, steel, and glass became the building materials of choice as modernist skyscrapers—glittering rectangles—transformed urban skylines and testified to the triumph of the human-made.

This enthusiasm for the mechanical also influenced interwar popular culture. The chorus line embodied the interwar obsession with mechanization, with each dancer reduced to working as a standardized component in a mass formation. Similarly, in the Charleston, a dance craze of the 1920s, the dancers' arms and legs fired like pistons, the entire body a fast-moving machine.

Along with the movies, the car and the airplane symbolized this new era of technological possibilities. The export of the assembly line from the United States to Europe cut the cost of automobile manufacturing: The rich man's toy became a middle-class necessity. The airline industry also took off in this era, with air passenger service between London and Paris beginning in 1919. In 1927, when the American Charles Lindbergh (1902–1974) completed the first solo flight across the Atlantic, he became an international hero, a symbol of human resourcefulness and technological mastery.

Scientific Possibilities

The ongoing scientific revolution also offered new possibilities. As Chapter 24 explained, from the 1890s on, a new model of the universe began to take shape. By the 1920s, Albert Einstein's concept of matter as "frozen energy" engaged scientists from all over the world. In theory, if the energy could be "thawed out," then this energy could be released. But could this theory become reality? In 1936, the British scientist Ernest Rutherford (1871–1937), head of one of the most important research laboratories in the West, dismissed the idea of unlocking the atom to release energy as "moonshine."

Four years earlier, however, a scientist working in Rutherford's laboratory had in fact found the key to unlocking the atom, although no one realized it at the time. In 1932, James Chadwick (1891–1974) discovered that atoms contain not only positively charged protons and negatively charged electrons, but also neutrons. Because neutrons possess no electrical charge, neither the protons nor electrons repel them. Thus, a bombardment of heavy neutrons could, in theory, split an atom's nucleus—a process called *nuclear fission*. The split nucleus itself would then emit neutrons, which would burst open other atoms, which in turn would emit further neutrons . . . and on and on in a nuclear chain reaction. The result: a colossal burst of energy that could be harnessed for industrial production—or for military destruction.

Such possibilities remained theoretical until 1938 when German scientists Otto Hahn (1879–1968) and Fritz Strassmann (1902–1980) broke open the uranium atom. Within a year, more than 100 articles on the implications of this discovery appeared in scientific journals. As one historian noted, "Physicists viewed the discovery of nuclear fission like the finding of a lost treasure map."[2]

Read the Document

Werner Heisenberg, "Uncertainty"

The Appeal of Authoritarianism and the Rise of Fascism

26.2 What circumstances explain the collapse of democracy throughout much of interwar Europe?

The extremes of pessimism and utopianism that characterized cultural developments in the post-World War I era were mirrored in the increasing polarization of political life. Facing the mass destruction wrought by total war, many in the West concluded that the age of liberalism, with its faith in individual reason

26.1

26.2

26.3

26.4

26.5

26.6

and the give-and-take of parliamentary democracy, had ended and that the new era demanded authoritarian, single-party politics. As we will see in the next section, many turned leftward, to the communism of the Soviet Union. But others turned in the other direction, to conservative authoritarianism, or even further, to the new politics of fascism.

The Collapse of Democracy in Eastern and Central Europe

We saw in Chapter 25 that the politicians and diplomats who drew up the peace settlements after World War I envisioned a new Europe of independent, democratic nation-states. As **Map 26.1** shows, postwar eastern Europe certainly *looked* markedly different from its prewar counterpart. Lines on the map, however, did not change key political realities. Few of these new states had any democratic traditions or history, and few of their new political leaders had mastered the consensus-building essential to stable parliamentary government.

MAP **26.1** EUROPE IN THE 1920S AND 1930S This map shows the political boundaries of European states in the interwar period. How did these boundaries clash with national identities and ambitions?

26.1

26.2

26.3

26.4

26.5

26.6

More importantly, the lines drawn on the new map actually worked to destabilize these new states. Rather than quelling nationalist hostilities, the peace settlement inflamed them. Ethnic nationalism formed the ideological basis of these new states: Poland for the Poles, Czechoslovakia for Czechs and Slovaks, Latvia for Latvians, and so forth. Yet all of these nation-states contained sizeable ethnic minorities—groups who did not regard themselves (or were not regarded by the majority) as part of the "nation" that now controlled the state. Some resorted to violence: In Poland, for example, Ukrainian nationalist groups waged a terrorist campaign throughout the 1920s and 1930s to subvert the new Polish state. Other groups turned to parliamentary politics. They formed ethnically based political parties that sought to destroy the postwar political settlement. In many of the new states, then, forming an effective government became impossible as political allegiances fractured and parties found no common ground. In Poland, where Jewish, Ukrainian, and German minorities made up one-third of the population, 18 different parties contended for control.

Economic problems exacerbated these nationalist conflicts. Much of eastern, southern, and central Europe remained a world of impoverished peasants and aristocratic landlords. In Romania, Poland, and Hungary, at least 60 percent of the population worked the land. In Bulgaria and Yugoslavia, the figure was 80 percent (versus 20 percent in industrialized Britain). With little industrial growth in these regions and few cities to absorb labor, unemployment rates rose and land hunger grew more intense. Parliaments torn apart by nationalist hostilities failed to devise effective economic development policies.

In contrast, authoritarianism offered at least the illusion of strong leadership. In every eastern European state except Czechoslovakia, democracy gave way to authoritarian government during the 1920s or 1930s.

View the Map

Authoritarian Regimes in Europe in the Mid-1930s

CHRONOLOGY: THE RETURN OF AUTHORITARIAN RULE TO EASTERN EUROPE

1923
1923
Boris III establishes a royalist dictatorship in Bulgaria.

1926
1926
May
Marshal Josef Pilsudski establishes a military dictatorship in Poland.
December
Smetona establishes dictatorship in Lithuania.

1928
1928
A new constitution gives King Zog in Albania almost unlimited powers.

1929
1929
Alexander I establishes a royal dictatorship in Yugoslavia.

1932
1932
Fascist leader Gyula Gömbös appointed prime minister in Hungary.

1934
1934
Dictatorships established in Latvia and Estonia.

1938
1938
King Carol establishes a royal dictatorship in Romania.

26.1

26.2

26.3

26.4

26.5

26.6

fascism Twentieth-century political ideology that rejected the existing alternatives of conservatism, communism, socialism, and liberalism. Fascists stressed the authoritarian power of the state, the efficacy of violent action, the need to build a national community, and the use of new technologies of influence and control.

The Fascist Alternative

At the same time, developments in Italy highlighted a new type of authoritarian politics—**fascism**. Conceived in the coupling of wartime exhilaration and postwar despair, fascism offered an alternative to existing political ideologies. Fascism was more than a set of political ideas, however. As presented by its creator, Benito Mussolini (1883–1945), fascism was an ongoing performance, a spectacular sound-and-lights show with a cast of millions.

MUSSOLINI'S RISE TO POWER Fascism originated in Italy as a product of World War I. When Italy entered the war on the side of the Allies in 1915, many Italians welcomed the war as a cleansing force, a powerful disinfectant that would purify Italian society. Mussolini, a socialist journalist, shared these views. Because the Socialist Party opposed Italy's entry into the war, Mussolini broke with the socialists, joined the army, and fought until he was wounded in 1917. When the war ended, he sought to create a new politics that would build on the camaraderie and exhilaration of combat.

In March 1919, Mussolini and about 100 men and some women gathered in Milan and declared themselves the fascist movement. Like Mussolini, many of these "fascists of the first hour" were war veterans. A number had served in the *arditi*, elite commando units that fought behind enemy lines. The arditi uniform, a black shirt, became the fascist badge of identity. The arditi slogan, *me ne frego* ("I don't give a damn"), became the blackshirts' creed, a fitting expression of their willingness to throw aside conventional standards and politics.

Just three and a half years after the first fascist meeting in Milan, Mussolini became prime minister of Italy. His rise to power occurred against a backdrop of social turmoil. In 1919 and 1920, more than one million workers were on strike and a wave of socialist-inspired land seizures spread across the countryside. Fearing that communist revolution would engulf Italy just as it had destroyed tsarist Russia, landowners and industrialists looked to Mussolini's fascists for help. Fascist squads disrupted Socialist Party meetings, broke up strikes, beat up trade unionists, and protected aristocratic estates from attack. By 1922, the fascists were a powerful political force with 35 parliamentary seats. In October, King Victor Emmanuel III (r. 1900–1946) asked Mussolini to become prime minister. Fascists from all over Italy converged in the "March on Rome," a piece of street theater designed to demonstrate the disciplined might of Mussolini's followers.

Over the next four years Mussolini used legal and illegal methods, including murder, to eliminate his political rivals and remake Italy as a one-party state. By 1926, he had succeeded. Party politics, an independent press, and the trade union movement disappeared. Victor Emmanuel remained on the throne, the official head of state, but power lay in Mussolini's hands. The restored death penalty and a strong police apparatus stood ready to crush dissent and fortify the fascist state.

THE FASCIST REVOLUTION IN ITALY But what was fascism? As a political ideology, fascism was, first, intensely *nationalistic*. The interests of the nation took precedence over any tradition, class, or individual. Fascism was also *statist* and *anti-democratic*. A centralized state, governed by a single party and led by an authoritarian leader, protected the nation's interests. Finally, fascism was *militaristic*. It exalted violence and military action. Influenced by Social Darwinism (see p. 748), Mussolini believed that nations, like species, competed for survival in a hostile world. Only the strong would—and should—survive.

Mussolini presented fascism as the politics of change. With a strong leader at the wheel, with violent action as its fuel, the fascist state would crash through social and economic barriers and transport the nation into the modern age. Yet Mussolini's supposedly radical revolution in fact reinforced traditional upper-class interests. Early

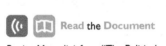

Read the Document

Benito Mussolini, from "The Political and Social Doctrine of Fascism" fascist promises of land redistribution were never realized. In theory, fascism promised to replace capitalist competition and the profit motive with **corporatism**: Committees (or "corporations") made up of representatives of workers, employers, and the state would direct the economy for the good of the nation. In actuality, workers' rights disappeared while industrialists' profits remained untouched.

Although Mussolini had no intention of giving *genuine* political power to ordinary people, he did recognize the importance of giving them the *illusion* of power. Fascism made individuals feel a part of a mighty nation. "After-work" recreational groups connected ordinary people to the fascist state by serving as a channel for fascist propaganda and occupying their leisure hours.

The "Cult of the Duce" also fostered a sense of national community. Mussolini insisted, "I am Fascism." Choreographed public appearances gave ordinary Italians the chance to see, hear, and adore their Duce ("Leader"), and, through contact with his person, to feel a part of the new Italy. Mussolini paid careful attention to his public image. He ordered the press to ignore his birthdays and the births of his grandchildren: The Duce could not be seen to age. Instead, Mussolini appeared as a man of action. Depicted in planes, trains, and racing cars, he was always on the move, always pressing forward. (See *Different Voices* in this chapter.)

Mussolini combined up-to-date advertising and mass media technologies with age-old rituals inspired largely by the Catholic Church. Huge public rallies set in massive arenas, carefully staged with lighting and music, inspired his followers. A popular fascist slogan summed up the leadership cult: "Believe, Obey, Fight." Italians were not to think or question. They were to *believe*. What were they to believe? Another slogan provided the answer: "Mussolini is always right."

THE GREAT DEPRESSION AND THE SPREAD OF FASCISM AFTER 1929 In the 1920s, fascism possessed little appeal outside Italy. The key factor in the spread of fascism was the **Great Depression**. On October 24, 1929, the U.S. stock market collapsed. Over the next two years, the American economic crisis evolved into a global depression as banks closed, businesses collapsed, and unemployment rates rose to devastating levels.

corporatism The practice by which committees (or "corporations") made up of representatives of workers, employers, and the state direct the economy.

26.1
26.2
26.3
26.4
26.5
26.6

View the **Closer Look**

The Face of Fascism: Benito Mussolini

Great Depression Calamitous drop in prices, reduction in trade, and rise in unemployment that devastated the global economy in 1929.

CHRONOLOGY: MUSSOLINI'S RISE TO POWER

1915–1917
Serves in the Italian army.

1919
Participates in the creation of the fascist movement.

1921
Fascist Party wins 35 seats in parliament.

1922
Becomes prime minister.

1925–1926
Abolishes party politics and establishes himself as dictator.

26.1

26.2

26.3

26.4

26.5

26.6

The Depression spread so quickly because World War I had shifted the world's economic center from Europe to the United States. To pay for the war, European states had sold off their assets and borrowed heavily. By the end of 1918 Allied states owed the United States more than $9 billion. New York's stock market rivaled London's, and the United States moved from the position of debtor to creditor. The problem of wartime indebtedness soon became entangled with the issue of German reparations. Britain, France, and Italy could pay off their debts to the United States only if Germany paid reparations to them. American credit became the fuel that kept the European economy burning. American investors loaned money to Germany, which used the money to pay reparations to the Allies, which in turn used the money to pay back the United States. With the collapse of the U.S. stock market, however, American creditors liquidated European investments, and European economies tumbled.

The political and social disarray that accompanied the Great Depression enhanced the appeal of fascist promises of stability, order, and national strength. Over the next decade fascist movements emerged across Europe and existing authoritarian regimes adopted fascist trappings to stay in power.

Nazism and the Defeat of Democracy in Germany

| 26.3 | How did the Nazis succeed in establishing a dictatorship in Germany? |

On the political spectrum, fascism comes under the heading of the **Radical Right**. Unlike nineteenth-century conservatism, Radical Right ideologies rejected existing social and political hierarchies, and fought not to defend but to uproot the status quo. In Germany, the Nazi Party offered a different version of Radical Right ideology. Just as the emergence of fascism was inextricably linked to Benito Mussolini, so **Nazism** cannot be separated from Adolf Hitler (1889–1945). To understand the Nazi revolution in Germany, we need first to explore the weakness of German democracy, and then Hitler's rise to power and the impact of Nazi rule on ordinary people.

The Weakness of the Weimar Republic

The peace settlement after World War I dismantled the imperial structures of Germany and replaced them with a democratic parliamentary system: the **Weimar Republic**. This political structure, however, sat precariously atop anti-democratic foundations. The kaiser was gone, but powerful anti-democratic forces remained to weaken the new Germany.

The survival of authoritarian attitudes and institutions resulted in part from the civil war that raged throughout Germany in the fall of 1918 and the first months of 1919. In this struggle, German communists, inspired by the Bolshevik Revolution in Russia, fought the more moderate socialist party (the SPD) that now governed Germany. Anxious to impose order, the SPD leaders chose to work with rather than replace the existing civil service, even though this meant allying with pro-authoritarian aristocrats who had served the kaiser. To win the civil war, the SPD also abandoned its longstanding loathing of the German military and deployed regular army units and the "Free Corps" (volunteer paramilitary units, often comprising demobilized soldiers addicted to violence) against communist rebels.

Radical Right Refers to extremist ideologies on the far right of the political spectrum, such as fascism and Nazism.

Nazism Twentieth-century political ideology associated with Adolf Hitler that adopted many fascist ideas but with a central focus on racism and particularly anti-Semitism.

Weimar Republic The democratic German state constructed after defeat in World War I and destroyed by the Nazis in 1933.

26.1

26.2

26.3

26.4

26.5

26.6

By the spring of 1919, this strange alliance of moderate socialists, traditional aristocrats, and thugs had crushed the communist uprising. The SPD had won—and yet it lost. By allying with the civil service, the army, and the Free Corps, the SPD crushed not only the communist revolution, but also its own chances of achieving significant social change. Many of the officers in the army and aristocrats in the civil service opposed democracy. Continuing in positions of power and influence, they constituted an authoritarian force at the heart of the new Germany. The approximately 400,000 men who made up the Free Corps also regarded democracy with contempt—"an attempt of the slime to govern."[3] Its slogan summed up the Free Corps attitude: "Everything would still have been all right if we had shot more people."[4] (See *Justice in History* in this chapter.)

Resentment of the Versailles Treaty strengthened these anti-democratic forces. Many Germans could not separate the birth of the Weimar Republic from the national humiliation imposed by Versailles. They blamed the moderate socialist government that signed the treaty for this humiliation. Army officers encouraged the idea that Germany could have kept on fighting had the SPD not "stabbed it in the back." This "stab-in-the-back" legend helped undermine support not only for the SPD's moderate socialism, but for democracy itself.

Hyperinflation further weakened Weimar democracy. In 1923, the German mark collapsed completely and paper money ceased to have any value. The mark, which in 1914 could be traded for the American dollar at a rate of 4:1, plummeted by October 1923 to an exchange rate of 440,000,000:1. Families who had scrimped for years found they had only enough savings to buy a loaf of bread.

This hyperinflation resulted from the Weimar government's effort to force the Allies to reconsider the reparations payments demanded by the Versailles Treaty. In 1922, the government halted payments and requested a new economic agreement. When the French retaliated by sending troops into Germany's Ruhr Valley to seize coal as a form of reparations, German miners went on strike. To pay the striking workers, the German government began printing money with abandon. The inflation rate surged upward—and then out of control.

Faced with the potentially disastrous collapse of the German economy, Allied and German representatives drew up the Dawes Plan in 1924, which renegotiated reparations. By the end of 1924, the German economy had stabilized. But hyperinflation seriously eroded support for the Weimar Republic. For many Germans, democracy meant disorder and degradation.

GEORGE GROSZ, *THE PILLARS OF SOCIETY* (1926) A World War I veteran like Otto Dix (see page 814), the Expressionist artist and communist George Grosz used his art to criticize the Weimar Republic. In this painting, a drunken military chaplain preaches while soldiers rampage behind his back. In the foreground sits a lawyer, supposedly a modern professional, but out of his head bursts a cavalry officer bent on destruction. To the lawyer's right, a publisher with a chamber pot on his head clutches the newspapers that guarantee his fortune and delude the masses. To the lawyer's left totters an SPD politician. His pudgy, drink-reddened cheeks, the steaming pile of excrement on his head, and the pamphlet he presses to his chest (headlined "Socialism Is Work") indicate Grosz's contempt for reformist socialism.

hyperinflation Catastrophic price increases and currency devaluation, such as that which occurred in Germany in 1923.

26.1

26.2

26.3

26.4

26.5

26.6

Hitler's Rise to Power

These events provide the backdrop for the emergence of Adolf Hitler and his Nazi movement as a force in German politics. Hitler, a German nationalist, was not a citizen of Germany for most of his life. Born in the Austrian half of the Austro-Hungarian Empire, Hitler came of age in Vienna, where he made a meager living as a painter while absorbing the anti-Semitic German nationalism that permeated this capital city. By the time World War I broke out, however, Hitler had settled in Germany. Delighted by the chance to fight the war in a German rather than an Austrian uniform, Hitler regarded army life as "the greatest of all experiences." He served as a German soldier until he was temporarily blinded by poison gas in 1918. Hitler then returned to Munich, home to large bands of unemployed war veterans and a breeding ground for nationalist and racist groups.

The Nazi Party began as one of these groups, with Hitler quickly emerging as its leader. *Nazi* is shorthand for National Socialist German Workers' Party, but this title, like all of Nazi ideology, was an empty promise. Nazism opposed socialism, communism, and trade unionism. Like fascism, Nazism was a nationalist, statist, anti-democratic, and militarist ideology.

In Nazism, however, racism, particularly anti-Semitism, played the central role. To Hitler, all history was the history of racial struggle; in that racial struggle, the Jews were always the principal enemy. Hitler regarded Jewishness as a biological rather than a religious identity, a toxic infection that threatened "Aryans," a linguistic term that Hitler misused to identify the "racially pure"—white northern Europeans. In Hitler's distorted vision, Jewishness and communism formed two parts of the same evil whole. He saw the Bolshevik victory in Russia as part of a wider struggle for Jewish world domination, and he promised his followers that the Aryan race would defeat the forces of "Judeo-Bolshevism" and establish a mighty empire encompassing all of eastern Europe, including the Soviet Union.

The early Nazi movement appealed to men like Hitler, individuals without power or, apparently, much chance of getting it—unemployed ex-soldiers, small shopkeepers wiped out by postwar inflation, lower middle-class clerks anxious to preserve their shaky social status, and workers who had lost their jobs. Nazism offered a simple explanation of history, a promise of future glory, and someone to blame for personal and national woes. By November 1923, party membership stood at about 55,000—a small, insignificant fringe party.

That month, however, Hitler and his supporters achieved national renown by attempting to overthrow the Weimar government. Although this "Beer Hall Putsch," as it came to be called (because it originated in a beer hall), failed miserably, it won Hitler a wide audience. His speeches during the ensuing trial for treason and *Mein Kampf* ("My Struggle"), the book he wrote while in prison, publicized his racialized view of German political history.

After Hitler emerged from prison, he concentrated on transforming the Nazis into a persuasive political force. To infiltrate German society at all levels, Nazis formed university and professional groups, labor unions, and agrarian organizations, while the Nazi paramilitary organization, the SA (*Sturmabteilung*), terrorized opponents. The party held meetings and rallies incessantly, not just during election periods, and so ensured that Germany was saturated with its message. Even so, in the elections of 1928, Nazi candidates won only 2.6 percent of the vote.

The Great Depression shifted the political playing field in Hitler's favor. As German industrial output fell by 46 percent and its number of jobless grew to more than six million, the Weimar political system began to collapse. No German political leader could put together a viable governing coalition. In all of 1932 the federal parliament met for only 13 days. With the mechanisms of parliamentary democracy faltering, political polarization accelerated. By July 1932, the Nazis were the largest party

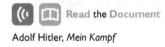

Read the Document

Adolf Hitler, *Mein Kampf*

26.1

26.2

26.3

26.4

26.5

26.6

Justice in History
The Trial of Adolf Hitler

On February 24, 1924, Adolf Hitler appeared in court in Munich on a charge of high treason. The trial marked a turning point in Hitler's career. It gave him a national platform and convinced him of the futility of an armed offensive against the state. From 1925 on, Hitler would work through the parliamentary system to destroy it. But the trial of Adolf Hitler was also significant in what it revealed about the power of anti-democratic forces in the new Germany. The trial made clear that many in positions of authority and responsibility in the Weimar Republic shared Hitler's contempt for the democratic state. By treating Hitler not as a traitorous thug, but rather as an honorable patriot, his prosecutors helped weaken the already fragile structures of German democracy.

Hitler's attempt to overthrow the Weimar Republic by force occurred at the height of hyperinflation. By November 8, 1923, when Hitler took up arms, the German mark was worth only one-trillionth of its prewar value. As the currency eroded, the Weimar government saw its political legitimacy seeping away as well. Hitler believed he could channel this political discontent into a national revolution. His supporters included one of the most important men in Germany, the World War I hero, General Erich von Ludendorff. Seeking to avoid the blame for Germany's defeat in 1918, Ludendorff insisted that his army could have won the war had it not been stabbed in the back by the Social Democratic politicians who now ran the government. Like many German conservatives—and like Hitler—Ludendorff viewed the Weimar Republic as illegitimate.

On November 8 Hitler made his move. Standing in a Munich beer hall, he declared that the German federal government had been overthrown and that he was now the head of Germany, with Ludendorff as his commander-in-chief. Around noon the next day, Hitler, Ludendorff, and several thousands of their followers marched toward one of Munich's main squares. Armed police blocked their passage and the ensuing firefight killed 17 men. Despite the bullets whizzing through the air, Ludendorff marched through the police cordon and stood in the square awaiting arrest. Hitler ran away. Police found him two days later, cowering in a supporter's house.

HITLER IN LANDSBERG PRISON, 1924 This photo of Hitler during his short imprisonment was made into a postcard, to be purchased by his supporters.

The Beer Hall Putsch had failed. In jail awaiting trial, Hitler contemplated suicide. Yet later he described his defeat as "perhaps the greatest stroke of luck in my life." The defeat meant a trial and a trial meant a national audience.

During the trial Hitler admitted that he had conspired to overthrow the democratically elected Weimar government. He insisted, however, that he was not guilty of treason, that the real treason occurred in November 1918, when the Social Democratic government surrendered to the Allies: "I confess to the deed, but I do not confess to the crime of high treason. There can be no question of treason in an action which aims to undo the betrayal of this country in 1918. . . . I consider myself not a traitor but a German."

In his testimony, Hitler depicted himself as a patriot, a nationalist motivated by love of Germany and hatred of communists and socialists. "The eternal court of history" would judge him and his fellow defendants "as Germans who wanted the best for their people and their Fatherland, who were willing to fight and to die."[5]

Despite Hitler's admission of conspiring against the government, the presiding judge could persuade the three lay judges (who took the place of a jury) to render a guilty verdict only by arguing that Hitler would soon be pardoned. The reluctance of the judges to convict Hitler highlights the extraordinary sympathy shown to him and to his political ideas throughout the trial and during his imprisonment. The chief prosecutor offered a rather surprising description of an accused traitor: "Hitler is a highly gifted man, who has risen from humble beginnings to achieve a respected position in public life, the result of much hard work and dedication." In delivering the verdict, the judge emphasized Hitler's "pure patriotic motives and honorable intentions." Rather than being deported as a foreign national convicted of a serious crime (Hitler was still an Austrian citizen), he was given a slight sentence of five years, which made him eligible for parole in just six months. Prison officials treated Hitler like a visiting dignitary—they exempted him from work

(continued on next page)

(continued from previous page)

26.1

26.2

26.3

26.4

26.5

26.6

and exercise requirements, cleaned his rooms, and provided a special table decorated with a swastika banner in the dining hall. When Hitler was released in September, his parole report described him favorably as "a man of order."[6]

Hitler's gentle treatment revealed the precarious state of democratic institutions in Germany after World War I. Many high-ranking Germans in positions of power and influence (such as judges and prosecutors) loathed parliamentary democracy. The trial also revealed the willingness of conservative aristocrats to ally with Radical Right groups such as the Nazis. Not yet strong, the Nazis in 1923 were easily reined in. A decade later, however, the conservatives who thought they could ride Hitler to power found that they were no longer in control.

For Discussion

1. Imagine you are a German war veteran reading about this case in the newspaper in 1924. Why might you be attracted to the party of Adolf Hitler?
2. Hitler appealed to the "eternal court of history." What do you think he meant? How would Hitler have defined "justice"?

Taking It Further

The Hitler Trial Before the People's Court in Munich, trans. H. Francis Freniece, Lucie Karcic, and Philip Fandek (3 vols.). 1976. An English translation of the court transcripts.

Kershaw, Ian. *Hitler 1889–1936: Hubris.* 1999. A compelling (and massive) account of Hitler's early life and rise to power.

CHRONOLOGY: HITLER'S RISE TO POWER

1914–1918
Serves in the German army.

1919–1923
Establishes himself as a right-wing activist in Munich.

1923
Fails to overthrow the government with the Beer Hall Putsch.

1929
Collapse of the U.S. stock market; onset of Great Depression.

1930
Nazis win 107 seats in German parliament.

1932
Nazis win 230 seats; become largest party in German parliament.

1933
January
Hitler becomes chancellor.
February
Hitler uses Reichstag fire as pretext to gain emergency powers.
March
Hitler uses the Enabling Act to destroy democracy in Germany.

Read the Document

Heinrich Hauser, "With Germany's Unemployed"

in the parliament, winning 37 percent of German votes. Support for their communist rivals also continued to grow.

In this unstable climate, Chancellor Heinrich Bruning turned to an emergency measure in the German constitution—rule by presidential decree. This practice meant that power shifted from parliament to the president, the World War I hero General

26.1

26.2

26.3

26.4

26.5

26.6

Paul von Hindenburg. Already in his 80s, Hindenburg was a weak man who was easily manipulated by a small circle of aristocratic advisers. These men, terrified of communism and convinced that the Nazis could be easily controlled, persuaded Hindenburg to offer Hitler the position of chancellor in January 1933. One of the group, Baron Franz von Papen, reassured a friend that Hitler posed "no danger at all. We have hired him for our act. In two months' time we'll have pushed Hitler so far into the corner, he'll be squeaking."[7]

It was a poor prediction. Almost as soon as Hitler took office he persuaded Hindenburg to pass an emergency decree ordering the seizure of all Communist Party presses and buildings. Then in February a fire destroyed the German parliament building. Declaring (wrongly) that the fire was part of a communist plot against the state, Hitler demanded the power to imprison without warrant or trial. Arrests of more than 25,000 of his political opponents followed—communists, socialists, and anyone who openly opposed him. At the end of March, German politicians, cowed by Nazi threats of imprisonment, passed the Enabling Act, giving Hitler the power to suspend the constitution and pass legislation without a parliamentary majority. By the summer of 1933, Hitler had destroyed German democracy and established a dictatorship.

Life (and Death) in the Nazi Dictatorship

Often presented as a model of authoritarian efficiency, the Nazi dictatorship was actually a confusing mass of overlapping bureaucracies, in which ambitious officials competed with each other for power and influence. This planned chaos ensured that none of Hitler's deputies acquired too much authority. It also enhanced the mystery of the state. The individual citizen attempting to make a complaint or resolve a problem would soon feel as if he were engaged in a battle with a multi-limbed monster.

This monster, however, had only one head: Adolf Hitler. Like Mussolini, Hitler realized the importance of personalizing his rule. In his early years of power, he was constantly on the move, using cars and planes to visit city after city, to deliver speech after speech, to touch person after person. Leaders of the Hitler Youth swore this oath: "Adolf Hitler is Germany and Germany is Adolf Hitler. He who pledges himself to Hitler pledges himself to Germany."[8]

NATIONAL RECOVERY When the Nazis seized control in 1933, depression gripped the German economy. The rules of economic orthodoxy dictated that in times of depression, a government should cut spending and maintain a balanced budget. Hoping to jump-start the stalled economy, Hitler's immediate predecessors in office had set aside these rules and begun to plan programs based on deficit spending. Hitler took these plans and ran with them. He invested heavily in public works and after 1936 poured money into rearmament. These programs created thousands of jobs. Unemployment dropped from 44 percent in 1932 to 14.1 percent in 1934 to less than 1 percent in 1938—while unemployment rates in the double digits persisted in democratic states such as Britain and France.

Germans and non-Germans alike hailed Nazi Germany as an economic success, yet under Nazi rule, real wages fell and workers' rights disappeared. Emphasis on rearmament led to shortages in food supplies and in consumer goods. Still, many Germans *believed* themselves to be much better off. The expansion of social welfare assistance (for those considered "Aryan") helps explain this perception, as does the establishment of the "Strength through Joy" program that provided workers with cheap vacations, theater and concert tickets, and weekend outings. But most important, under the Nazis, Germans were working. The abundance of jobs—despite the low wages, despite the disappearance of workers' rights, despite the food shortages—made Hitler an economic savior to many.

26.1

26.2

26.3

26.4

26.5

26.6

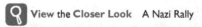
View the **Closer Look**   A Nazi Rally

HEIL (HAIL) *HITLER!* An enthusiastic crowd salutes Hitler at a Nazi Party rally. The women in the traditional costumes illustrate a key aspect of the Nazis' appeal: their promise to restore women to their traditional domestic roles. The men in military uniform indicate a second source of Nazi popularity: the restoration of military strength and national pride.

Many Germans also viewed him as a national savior who restored Germany's pride and power. German payments of war reparations halted in 1930 because of the global economic crisis. Hitler never resumed payment. He also ignored the treaty's military restrictions and rebuilt Germany's armed forces. By 1938, parades featuring row after row of uniformed troops signaled the revitalization of German military might. For many ordinary Germans, traumatized and shamed by the sequence of national disasters—military defeat, loss of territory, hyperinflation, political and fiscal crises, unemployment—the sight of troops goose-stepping under the German flag meant personal and national renaissance. As one Nazi song proclaimed, "And now the me is part of the great We."[9] (See *Different Voices* in this chapter.)

CAMPAIGNS OF REPRESSION AND TERROR The creation of the "great We" depended on the demonization and repression of the "not Us," those defined as outside or opposed to the nation. Hitler used the existing German police force and his own paramilitary troops—the brownshirted SA and the blackshirted SS (*Schutzstaffel*)—to terrorize those he defined as enemies of the nation. By 1934 half of the 300,000 German Communist Party members were in prison or dead and most of the rest had fled the country. The Nazis also persecuted specific religious groups on the basis of their actual or presumed opposition to the Nazi state. Roman Catholics faced constant harassment and about half of Germany's 20,000 Jehovah's Witnesses were sent to concentration camps. Homosexuals, too, faced harsh persecution. Between 1933 and 1939, 10,000 Germans were killed by the Nazi regime.

The groups that the Nazis deemed biologically inferior suffered most severely. Beginning in 1933, the Nazi regime forced the sterilization of the mentally and physically handicapped and mixed-race children (in most cases, the offspring of German women and black African soldiers serving in the French occupation force in the Rhineland). The campaign was soon extended to the Roma (Gypsies). By 1939, 370,000 men and women had been sterilized.

The brunt of Nazi racial attacks, however, fell on Germany's Jewish community—less than 1 percent of the population. To Nazi anti-Semites, Hitler's accession to the German chancellorship was like the opening of hunting season. They beat up Jews in the streets, vandalized Jewish shops and homes, threatened German Christians who associated with Jews, and violently enforced boycotts of Jewish businesses. Anti-Jewish legislation piled up. In 1933, the Nazi government dismissed "non-Aryans" (Jews) from the civil service and the legal profession, and restricted the number of Jewish students in high schools and universities. Every organization in Germany—youth clubs, sports teams, labor unions, charitable societies—underwent "Nazification," which meant the dismissal of all Jewish members and the appointment of Nazis to leadership roles. In 1935, the "Nuremberg Laws" deprived German Jews of their citizenship and declared marriage or sexual relations between German Jews and non-Jews a serious crime. By 1938, 25 percent of Germany's Jewish population had fled the country.

26.1

26.2

26.3

26.4

26.5

26.6

The Soviet Alternative and the Democracies' Response

26.4 Why did the Soviet Union seem a success and how did the democracies respond?

The apparent successes of fascist Italy and Nazi Germany appealed to many Europeans and Americans disenchanted with democracy. During this period, the Soviet Union also seemed a success story. While the capitalist states struggled with high unemployment rates and falling industrial output, the Soviet Union appeared to be performing economic miracles. Politics in the West thus became increasingly polarized into the Radical Left and the Radical Right. Politicians and policymakers in the United States and in western Europe struggled to maintain the middle ground, to retain democratic values in the face of extremist challenges.

The Soviet Union: Revolution Reconstructed, Terror Extended

Created out of the rubble of revolution and civil war, the new Soviet Union embarked on a different path from the rest of the West in the post–World War I period. Under the dictatorial rule of the Bolshevik—now called the Communist—Party, peoples of over 100 different national groups, speakers of over 200 languages and dialects, struggled to create a new political order.

NEP AND NATIONALITIES We saw in Chapter 25 that after four years of bitter fighting, the Bolsheviks won the civil war. Once in power, Lenin imposed single-party rule, silenced debate, and used intimidation and murder to crush dissent. The rule of the tsar gave way not to democracy, but to the rule of the commissar, the Communist Party functionary. Party bureaucrats became a privileged upper class, with access to the best jobs, food, clothing, and apartments.

Even the harshest authoritarian control could not, however, make up for the immense economic damage wrought by the years of civil war. With famine in the countryside and the economy in disarray, Lenin in 1921 declared a strategic retreat from "War Communism" and the effort to abolish capitalist enterprise. Under the **New Economic Policy (NEP)**, peasants were allowed to sell their produce for profit. Although the state continued to control heavy industry, transport, and banking, NEP actually encouraged small private businesses and farms. Under this policy the Soviet

 Read the Document

Nadezhda Krupskaya, "What a Communist Ought to Be Like"

New Economic Policy (NEP) Vladimir Lenin's economic turnaround in 1921 that allowed and even encouraged small private businesses and farms in the Soviet Union.

 Read the Document

A. Dubova, "Living Someone Else's Life"

26.1

26.2

26.3

26.4

26.5

26.6

economy stabilized, small businessmen (called "Nepmen") increased in number, and many peasants prospered.

The New Economic Policy accompanied a new nationalities program. The Soviet Union included enormous numbers of non-Russians. Recognizing that many of these peoples resented the tsar's Russification policies (see p. 727), Lenin abandoned Russification. Rather than crushing non-Russian national identities, the new program sought to foster local language and cultures—and thus, Lenin hoped, win the allegiance of non-Russians to the new communist order. The Soviet Union itself was a federation of the semi-autonomous republics of Russia, Ukraine, Byelorussia (Belarus), and Transcaucasia. Ethnic Russians living in non-Russian republics were required to learn local languages, and local elites were encouraged to join the Communist Party and take on leadership positions.

FROM LENIN TO STALIN The deputy who helped Lenin create the nationalities program was himself a non-Russian from Georgia, as his last name—Dzhugashvili—indicated. But most Soviets knew him by his revolutionary name: Stalin, man of steel. Like Lenin, Joseph Stalin (1879–1953) was a professional revolutionary, an "old Bolshevik" who had labored in the underground opposition to the tsarist regime. Although an important man in the party, he was not widely expected to succeed Lenin as leader when Lenin died in 1924. As party secretary, however, Stalin controlled who belonged to this all-powerful group. By the mid-1920s, large numbers of ordinary communists owed their party privileges and their livelihoods to him. After a protracted leadership struggle, Stalin emerged in 1927 as Lenin's successor and the head of the Soviet Union.

To solidify and expand his authority, Stalin constructed a gargantuan personality cult. Innumerable posters and statues ensured that Stalin's figure remained constantly in front of Soviet citizens. Textbooks rewrote the history of the Bolshevik Revolution and linked every scientific, technological, or economic advance in the Soviet Union to him. The scores of letters personally addressed to "Comrade Stalin" testify that millions of Soviet citizens saw Stalin as their protector. (See *Different Voices* in this chapter.)

In many of the omnipresent images of Stalin, he appeared alongside Lenin, as Stalin always carefully (and deceptively) painted himself as Lenin's chosen heir. The key characteristics of Leninism—authoritarian rule and the use of terror as a tool of state—not only remained central but grew more pronounced under Stalin. We will see, however, that in important ways Stalin shifted the direction of Soviet policies.

THE "REVOLUTION FROM ABOVE": COLLECTIVIZATION Once Stalin established his control over the Soviet Union, he dismantled Lenin's New Economic Policy and launched the Soviet economy into full-scale industrialization. This economic transformation, however, rested on dead bodies, millions of dead bodies, as mass murder became even more an integral part of the Soviet regime.

To catapult the Soviet Union into the ranks of the industrialized states, Stalin called for "the revolution from above"—the abandonment of NEP and the acceleration of state control over the economy. The first stage of this revolution was **collectivization**, the replacement of private and village farms with large cooperative agricultural enterprises run by communist managers according to directives received from the central government. Regarded as more modern and efficient, collective farms were expected to produce an agricultural surplus and thereby raise the capital needed for industrialization. In addition, collectivization would realize communist ideals by eradicating the profit motive, abolishing private property, and transforming peasants into modern state employees.

To initiate collectivization, Stalin announced at the end of 1929 that the **kulaks** would be "liquidated as a class." A "kulak" was a wealthier peasant, depicted in

collectivization The replacement of private and village farms with large cooperative agricultural enterprises run by state-employed managers. Collectivization was a key part of Joseph Stalin's plans for modernizing the Soviet economy and destroying peasant opposition to communist rule.

kulak Russian term for a peasant who is relatively prosperous.

26.1

26.2

26.3

26.4

26.5

26.6

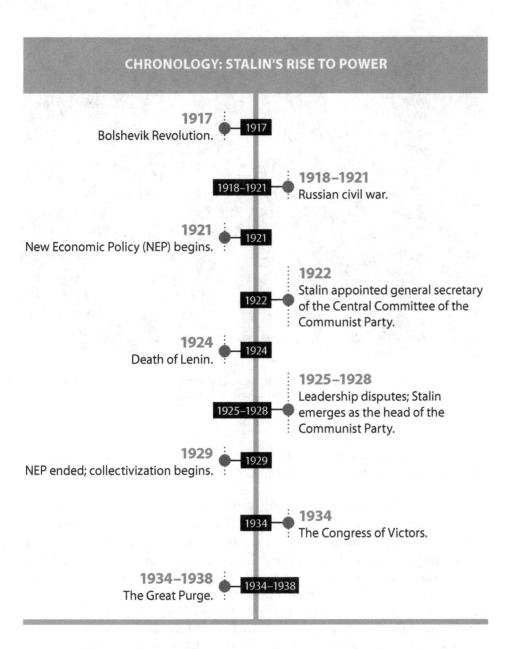

CHRONOLOGY: STALIN'S RISE TO POWER

1917
Bolshevik Revolution.
1917

1918–1921
1918–1921
Russian civil war.

1921
New Economic Policy (NEP) begins.
1921

1922
1922
Stalin appointed general secretary of the Central Committee of the Communist Party.

1924
Death of Lenin.
1924

1925–1928
1925–1928
Leadership disputes; Stalin emerges as the head of the Communist Party.

1929
NEP ended; collectivization begins.
1929

1934
1934
The Congress of Victors.

1934–1938
The Great Purge.
1934–1938

Soviet propaganda as an oppressor who grew fat off the labor of others, an enemy of the ongoing revolution. Kulaks tended to be the leaders in their localities, those who had prospered under NEP and those with the most to lose from collectivization. Over the next few years, almost two million kulaks were stripped of all their possessions, forced onto freezing freight cars, and deported to **the Gulag**, the network of forced labor camps and special settlements that stretched across Siberia and Kazakhstan.

The "liquidation" of the kulaks served as the opening onslaught in what became an undeclared war against Soviet peasants, who resisted collectivization by burning their crops, slaughtering their livestock, and fighting with shovels and hoes. They proved no match for the armed might of the Stalinist state.

Peasant resistance did, however, disrupt agricultural production. Faced with low harvest yields in 1932, Stalin responded by deploying starvation as a weapon. Brigades of communist activists moved into rural regions and confiscated all food supplies. The numbers of deaths resulting from collectivization and famine remain controversial, but the available evidence points to death figures between five and seven million.

the Gulag Term for the network of forced labor and prison camps in the Soviet Union.

 Read the Document

Irina Ivanovna Kniazeva, "A Life in a Peasant Village"

829

26.1

26.2

26.3

26.4

26.5

26.6

"THE PEOPLE'S VERMIN" This photograph from 1930 shows a public display used as publicity for the collectivization campaign. The gigantic masks depict the kulaks as vermin to be eradicated.

Ukraine and Kazakhstan were hardest hit. Over three million Ukrainians died, as did almost 40 percent of the Kazakh population.

THE "REVOLUTION FROM ABOVE": INDUSTRIALIZATION While class war raged in the countryside, city dwellers embarked on the second stage of the "revolution from above"—industrialization. In 1931 Stalin articulated the task facing the Soviet Union: "We are fifty or a hundred years behind the advanced countries. We must catch up this distance in ten years. Either we do it or we go under."[10] "Doing it" demanded, first, fierce labor discipline. If fired, a worker was automatically evicted from his or her apartment and deprived of a ration card. "Doing it" also demanded reducing personal consumption. Eighty percent of all investment went into heavy industry, while domestic construction and light industry—clothing, furniture, dishes, appliances, and the like—were ignored. Scarcity became the norm, long lines and constant shortages part of every city-dweller's existence. Soviet citizens endured an estimated 40 percent fall in their already low standard of living between 1929 and 1932.

While millions starved in the countryside and urban living standards plummeted, young communists acclaimed these years of hardship and horror as an era of heroism. They volunteered to organize collective farms, to work in brutal conditions at construction sites, to labor long hours in factories and mines. Propaganda campaigns aimed at persuading laborers to work harder kept this enthusiasm at a fever pitch. The most productive workers earned medals and material gifts. Publicity focused on gargantuan engineering achievements—the cities built atop swampland, the hydroelectric projects with their enormous dams and power plants, the Moscow subway system. Such publicity made party members feel part of a mighty endeavor. A popular song announced, "We were born to make fairy tales come true."[11]

No propaganda campaign and no amount of effort from enthusiastic communists, however, could provide the Soviet Union with the labor it needed to catch up with the West in 10 years. Forced labor was crucial. Throughout the 1930s, Gulag prison camps housed up to two million men, women, and children at any one time. Many of the huge engineering triumphs of the decade rested on the backs of these prisoners.

By the end of the 1930s, Stalin's "revolution from above" had achieved its aim. The pouring of resources into heavy industry and the wringing of every ounce of labor out of an exhausted, cold, and hungry populace succeeded in building the foundations of an industrial society, one that would pass the test of total war in the 1940s. Press censorship ensured that the mass killing and forced labor that fueled this economic transformation remained hidden.

STALIN'S CONSOLIDATION OF POWER: THE GREAT PURGE AND SOVIET SOCIETY The 17th Communist Party Congress in 1934 called itself the "Congress of Victors," as the party celebrated its industrial successes and the achievement of collectivization. But within five years, half of the 2,000 delegates had been arrested. Of the 149 elected members of the Congress's Central Committee, 98 were shot dead. These Congress delegates fell victim to the "**Great Purge**." So, too, did an estimated 700,000 of their fellow Soviet citizens, with millions more imprisoned and deported.

The most well-known victims of the Great Purge were top-ranking Communist Party officials, "old Bolsheviks" like Stalin who had fought in the revolution. By charging these powerful men with conspiring against the communist state, Stalin reduced the chances that any competitor might oust him. The purge, however, moved beyond the top ranks of the party and swallowed up low-level party members, managers in state agencies, factory directors, and engineers—and their families and friends. Many were killed without trial, others executed after a legal show, and still others deported to labor camps to be worked to death on Stalin's construction projects.

In 1937 the Purge broadened even further. Even prisoners already in the Gulag were not safe: In the Siberian city of Omsk, for example, the Gulag chief and his men shot 1,300 people in one single night. This phase of the Purge targeted members of national minorities, particularly ethnic Poles. Party officials who had faithfully implemented Lenin's nationalities program and worked to develop non-Russian languages and cultures found themselves condemned for the crime of fostering "bourgeois nationalism." An estimated 250,000 Soviet citizens were executed in 1937 and 1938 on the grounds of their nationality.

Through deportation, mass killing, and general terror, the Great Purge consolidated Stalin's hold on the Soviet Union. It eliminated all potential competitors and, strangely, it gave many people a reason to believe in their leader. Individuals who moved into the positions left vacant by the purge's victims had a material and psychological stake in believing that these victims were guilty and that the purge was justified.

The Response of the Democracies

In the 1930s, democratic states faced powerful challenges, as many in the West concluded that democracy simply did not work. Yet in western Europe and the United States, governments took important steps to ensure that democracy survived.

A THIRD WAY? THE SOCIAL DEMOCRATIC ALTERNATIVE The effort to meet the challenge of the Great Depression accelerated the development of the political model that would dominate western Europe after World War II: **social democracy**. In a social democracy, a democratically elected government accepts the responsibility of ensuring a decent standard of living for its citizens. To achieve this goal, the government assumes two functions—first, regulating an economy containing both private enterprise and

26.1

26.2

26.3

26.4

26.5

26.6

Read the Document

John Scott, Excerpt from *Behind the Urals: An American Worker in Russia's City of Steel*

Great Purge Period of mass arrests and executions particularly aimed at Communist Party members in the Soviet Union.

social democracy Political system in which a democratically elected parliamentary government endeavors to ensure a decent standard of living for its citizens through both economic regulation and the maintenance of a welfare state.

26.1

26.2

26.3

26.4

26.5

26.6

Different Voices

The Cult of the Leader

S talinism stood on the extreme left of the political spectrum; Nazism and fascism, on the extreme right. Mussolini's fascists came to national prominence by beating up socialists, and Hitler ranked communists alongside Jews as enemies of the German nation. Yet Radical Right and Radical Left states resembled each other in many ways. Fascist Italy, Nazi Germany, and the Stalinist Soviet Union shared contempt for individual rights and a willingness to use violence as an instrument of the state. These states also all relied on the cult of personality (or the leadership cult). Searching for a way to mobilize the masses without granting them actual political power, Mussolini, Hitler, and Stalin used their own images to personify and personalize the state and to make their authoritarian rule more extensive and more acceptable. The following excerpts illustrate the cults of personality that helped shape the West in the 1930s.

I. Description of an Early Nazi Rally by Louise Solmitz, Schoolteacher

The April sun shone hot like summer and turned everything into a picture of gay expectation. There was immaculate order and discipline . . . the hours passed. . . . Expectations rose. There stood Hitler in a simple black coat and looked over the crowd. Waiting. A forest of swastika pennants swished up, the jubilation of this moment was given vent in a roaring salute. . . . How many look up to him with a touching faith! As their helper, their savior, their deliverer from unbearable distress—to him who rescues the Prussian prince, the scholar, the clergyman, the farmer, the worker, the unemployed, who leads them from the parties back into the nation.

SOURCE: "Description of an Early Nazi Rally by Louise Solmitz, Schoolteacher," copyright © 1988 by Claudia Koonz. From *Mothers in the Fatherland: Women, the Family, and Nazi Politics* by Claudia Koonz. New York: St. Martin's Press, 1987.

II. Letter from a Nazi Party member, a "Party Comrade," to Hitler, 1936

My Führer! . . . I feel compelled by unceasing love to thank our creator daily for, through his grace, giving us and the entire German people such a wonderful Führer, and in a time . . . where our beautiful dear Fatherland was threatened with the most horrible destruction through Jewish bolshevism. It does not bear thinking about what floods of tears, what blood after the scarcely healed wounds of the World War, would have flowed, if you, my beloved Führer, in all your anguish for such a great people had not found the courage, with at that time a small band of seven men, to win through as the saviour of 66 million Germans, in that through your great love of every individual, from the smallest child to the most aged, you captured all, all, women, men, and the whole of German youth. . . . It is a pleasure for me, not a compliment, not hypocrisy, to pray for you, my Führer, that the Lord God who has created you as a tool for Germany should keep you healthy, that the love of the people towards you should grow, firm and hard like the many oak trees which have been planted in love and honour to you, my Führer, even in the smallest community in Germany. . . . A Heil to the Führer for victory with all the former front-line fighters who still remain today devoted to the Führer to death. For Germany must live even if we must die.

SOURCE: Quoted in Ian Kersaw, *The Hitler Myth,* Oxford: Oxford University Press, 1987, p. 81. By permission of Oxford University Press. Copyright © 1987 by Ian Kershaw.

III. Account by Maria Demchenko, collective farm laborer, of her meeting with Stalin at an award ceremony

Comrade Stalin was standing among his assistants smiling, waving his hand to us (like this!) and looking at the *kolkhozniks* very, very closely and with a special kind of warmth. When the cheers had quieted down, he looked at me and said, 'Well, comrade Demchenko, tell us your story. . . . "

I told him everything.

I was looking at comrade Stalin—at how he was listening, and I could tell by his face that he hadn't missed a single word: now he would smile, then look thoughtful, or nod like this his head, as if to say that's right!

After the *kolkhoz* women he started talking himself. His whole speech, his every word as so engraved on my memory that I'll never forget them. . . .

SOURCE: "Account by Maria Demchenko, collective farm laborer, of her meeting with Stalin at an award ceremony," from *Stalin's Peasants: Resistance and Survival in the Russian Village After Collectivization* by Sheila Fitzpatrick. Copyright © 1994 by Oxford University Press, Inc. Published by permission of Oxford University Press.

IV. Speech by a Woman Delegate at a Workers' Conference in the Soviet Union

Thank you comrade Stalin, our leader, our father, for a happy, merry kolkhoz* life!

He, our Stalin, put the steering-wheel of the tractor in our hand. . . . He, the great Stalin, carefully listens to all of us in this meeting, loves us with a great Stalinist love (*tumultuous applause*), day and night thinks of our prosperity, of our culture, of our work. . . .

Long live our friend, our teacher, the beloved leader of the world proletariat, comrade Stalin! (*Tumultuous applause, rising to an ovation. Shouts of "Hurrah!"*)

SOURCE: "Speech by a Woman Delegate at a Worker's Conference in the Soviet Union," from *Stalin's Peasants: Resistance and Survival in the Russian Village After Collectivization* by Sheila Fitzpatrick. Copyright © 1996 by Oxford University Press, Inc. Published by permission of Oxford University Press.

For Discussion

1. Why did Radical Right and Radical Left movements include cults of personality? Do these excerpts reveal any differences between the leadership cults of these states?

2. How and why did the cult of personality take on religious dimensions? Should we view modern nationalism as a secular religion?

3. Can we take these documents at face value? In a dictatorial state, where any dissent risks punishment and even death, people often hide their true feelings and beliefs. How do we know that the individuals speaking here were not putting on an act to survive or to get ahead?

*kolkhoz = collective farm

26.1

26.2

26.3

26.4

26.5

26.6

nationalized, or state-controlled, businesses, and second, overseeing a welfare state, which guarantees citizens access to unemployment and sickness benefits, pensions, family allowances, and health services. Although social democracy did not triumph in the West until after a second total war, interwar Western societies took important steps on this third path, an alternative to the extremes of the Radical Right and the Radical Left.

One of the most striking experiments in changing the relationship between democratic governments and the economy occurred in the United States. Franklin Delano Roosevelt (1882–1945) was elected president in 1932 at the height of the Great Depression, when unemployment stood at 24 percent and federal troops in Washington, D.C. fought rioting unemployed veterans. Promising a "New Deal" of "Relief, Recovery, Reform," Roosevelt tackled the depression with an activist governmental policy that included agricultural subsidies, public works programs, and the Social Security Act of 1935, which set the foundations of the U.S. welfare program.

Yet even with this sharp upswing in government activity, unemployment in the United States remained high—10 million workers were without jobs in 1939—and the gross national product (GNP) did not recover to 1929 levels until 1941. In the view of some economists, Roosevelt failed to solve the problem of unemployment because he remained committed to the ideal of a balanced budget. In contrast, the British economist John Maynard Keynes (1883–1946) insisted that in times of depression the state should not reduce spending and endeavor to live within its budget, but instead should adopt a program of deficit spending to stimulate economic growth. Only when prosperity returned, Keynes advised, should governments increase taxes and cut expenditures to recover the deficits.

The experience of Sweden appeared to confirm **Keynesian economics**. The Swedish Social Democratic Party took office in 1932 with the intention of using the powers of the state to revive the economy. The government allowed its budget deficit to climb while it financed public works and increased welfare benefits, ranging from unemployment insurance to maternity allowances to subsidized housing. By 1937 unemployment was shrinking rapidly as the manufacturing sector boomed.

Throughout most of western Europe, however, governments proved reluctant to embrace new policies. For example, Britain's limited economic recovery in the later 1930s stemmed largely from the emergence of new private industries aimed at domestic consumption (such as radios and other small electronics). In the areas hardest hit by depression—northern British cities, home to export industries such as coal, shipbuilding, textiles, and steel—the lack of government intervention meant continuing unemployment and widespread poverty throughout the 1930s.

POPULAR FRONTS IN FRANCE AND SPAIN The limited success of democratic governments in addressing the problems of the Great Depression meant that many experienced the 1930s as a hard, hungry decade. The examples of France and Spain illustrate the political polarization occurring in Europe in the 1930s, as well as the sharp limits on governments seeking both to maintain democratic politics and to improve living conditions.

The Great Depression hit France later than most other European states, but in 1931 the French economy plummeted. Social unrest grew, and so, too, did the appeal of fascism. The fascist threat, combined with the deepening national emergency, led to the formation of the **Popular Front**, a coalition comprising radicals, socialists, and communists. In 1936, the Popular Front won the national elections and Socialist Party leader Léon Blum (1872–1950) took office as prime minister. Over the next year, Blum nationalized key industries and gave workers pay increases, paid vacations, and a 40-hour workweek.

Many conservative French voters saw Blum's policies of social reform as the first step on the road to Stalinism. They cried, "Better Hitler than Blum!"—in other words,

Keynesian economics Economic theories associated with the British economist John Maynard Keynes that advocate using the power of the democratic state to ensure economic prosperity.

Popular Front A political coalition of liberals, socialists, and communists to defeat fascist and racist-nationalist political rivals.

26.1

26.2

26.3

26.4

26.5

26.6

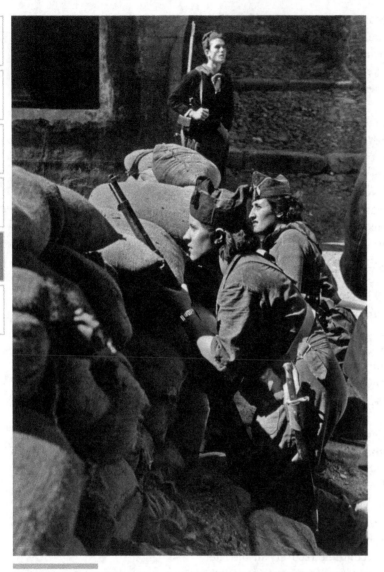

THE SPANISH CIVIL WAR The Spanish Civil War mobilized women as well as men. These soldiers, fighting in the uniform of the anarchist militia, are defending the barricades of Barcelona against rebel attack.

better the Radical Right than the Stalinist Left. The global business community pulled capital out of France, which brought on a major financial crisis and the devaluation of the French franc. Dependent on foreign loans, Blum's government tried to retreat from its social and economic reforms. Its working-class constituency responded with riots, and the Popular Front in France disintegrated.

In Spain, the Popular Front was defeated not by economic pressures, but by civil war. In 1931, a democratically elected republican government replaced the Spanish monarchy; in 1936, a Popular Front government, comprising socialists and communists, took office. Army officers, led by General Francisco Franco (1892–1975), rebelled and civil war began.

The struggle between the left-wing Republican government and the right-wing rebels quickly became an international issue. Fascist Italy and Nazi Germany supported the rebellion. The Republic of Spain appealed to the democracies for aid, but the only state that came to its assistance was the Soviet Union. Unnerved by Soviet involvement, the French, British, and American governments remained neutral, although 15,000 of their citizens joined the International Brigades to fight for Spanish democracy. All total, over 59,000 volunteers from 55 countries fought in these brigades.

The Spanish Civil War raged until March 1939, when the last remnants of the Republican forces surrendered to Franco. At least 400,000 men and women died in the war, and Franco executed another 200,000 after he took power and established an authoritarian state.

The Reconstruction of Gender

26.5 What changed, and what did not, in women's experiences after World War I?

We saw in Chapter 25 that the demands of total war meant that women moved into economic areas previously designated as "men only." World War I seemed an important turning point in the history of Western women. But here, as in the democratization of eastern and central Europe, World War I was in many ways the turning point that failed to turn.

The New Woman

At first sight, the postwar period seemed to be an era of profound change for women. In the films, magazines, novels, and popular music of the 1920s, the "New Woman" took center stage. Living, working, and traveling on her own, sexually active, she stepped out of the confines of home and family. Women's dress and hairstyles reinforced the sense of change. Whereas nineteenth-century women's clothing had accentuated the

26.1

26.2

26.3

26.4

26.5

26.6

womanly body while restricting movement, the clothing of the 1920s ignored a woman's curves and became less confining. Sporty new "bobs" replaced the long hair that had long been a sign of proper femininity.

This perception of the New Woman rested on changing political and economic expectations. By 1920 women in the United States and many European countries had received the right to vote in national elections and to hold national office. In all the industrialized countries, expansion of the health care and service sectors meant new jobs for women as nurses, social workers, secretaries, telephone operators, and clerks. Women's higher education opportunities also widened in this period.

The biggest change affecting the lives of ordinary women, however, was more intimate: the spreading practice of family limitation. We saw in Chapter 23 that by the 1870s middle-class women in Western countries were practicing birth control. In the 1920s and 1930s, an increasing number of working-class women began to do so as well. Fewer pregnancies and fewer mouths to feed improved women's health and living standards.

The Reconstruction of Traditional Roles

Despite these important changes, however, women's *roles* altered little in the two decades after World War I. Governments and ordinary citizens recoiled from wartime gender upheaval and worked to reconstruct nineteenth-century masculine and feminine ideals.

THE "NEW WOMAN" Almost every aspect of the "New Woman" (captured in this 1927 French magazine illustration) offended traditionalists: The bobbed hair, manly fashions, and aggressive strutting crossed the border into masculine terrain.

The war's lengthy casualty lists and the drop in the average family size provoked widespread fear about declining populations—and thus declining national strength. Governments, religious leaders, and commercial entrepreneurs joined together to convince women that their destiny lay in motherhood. Sales and purchases of birth control devices became illegal during the 1920s in France, Belgium, Italy, and Spain. France outlawed abortions in 1920. In Britain after 1929, a woman who had an abortion could be sentenced to life imprisonment. To encourage population growth, governments expanded welfare services. By providing family allowances, subsidized housing, school lunches, health insurance, and prenatal and well-baby care, politicians and policymakers hoped to ensure that married women stayed at home and produced large families.

Eugenics (the effort to improve the physical and intellectual capacities of the population by encouraging individuals with "desirable" traits to reproduce) played an important role in this legislation. National leaders wanted to increase not only the quantity, but the quality of the population. On the positive side, this meant improving the health of babies and mothers. More ominously, welfare policy rhetoric often focused on separating the "fit" from the "unfit," with class and race used to designate who was "fit" to produce children for the nation.

Despite the calls for women to remain at home, many women had to work in paid employment. In the work world, just as in the family, traditional roles strengthened

eugenics The effort to improve the physical and intellectual capacities of the population by encouraging individuals with "desirable" traits to reproduce and/or by discouraging those individuals designated as "undesirable" from reproducing.

26.1

26.2

26.3

26.4

26.5

26.6

after World War I. Most working women returned to jobs in domestic service or to factory positions labeled unskilled and therefore low-paying. Because employers still tended to bar women from management positions, assign them to the most repetitive tasks, and pay them by piecework, the wage gap between male and female laborers remained wide. The numbers of women employed in the clerical and service sectors did rise in this era, but the movement of women into these positions meant such jobs were reclassified as "women's work," a guarantee of low pay and little power.

WOMEN AND THE RADICAL RIGHT Fascism and Nazism promised to restore order to societies perceived to be on the verge of disintegration. Restoration of order meant the return of women to their proper place. According to Nazi propaganda, "the soil provides the food, the woman supplies the population, and the men make the action."[12] Hitler proclaimed, "The Nazi Revolution will be an entirely male event." Mussolini agreed: "Woman must obey. . . . In our State, she must not count."[13]

The Nazi government offered financial and cultural incentives to encourage women to stay at home and produce babies. These measures ranged from marriage loans (available only if the wife quit her job) and income tax deductions for families to the establishment of discussion, welfare, and leisure groups for housewives. The Nazis also used disincentives. One of the first actions of Hitler's government was to restrict women's employment in the civil service and to rule that female physicians could work only in their husbands' practices. By 1937, female physicians and women with PhDs had lost the right to be addressed as "Doctor" or "Professor." Women could no longer work as school principals. Coeducational schools were abolished. Birth control became illegal and penalties for abortion increased while prosecutions doubled.

In fascist Italy, Mussolini's government focused its legislation on both men and women. Unmarried men over age 30 had to pay double income tax (priests were exempt) and fatherhood became a prerequisite for men in high-ranking public office. Quotas limited the number of women employed in the civil service and in private business, while women found themselves excluded entirely from jobs defined as "virile," a list that included boat captains, diplomats, high school principals, and history teachers. A wide-ranging social welfare program that included family allowances, maternity leaves, and marriage loans sought to strengthen the traditional family. Despite these provisions, birth rates in Italy actually declined because low wages meant families could not afford more children.

WOMEN IN THE SOVIET UNION In contrast to these efforts to reinforce traditional family structures, in Russia the Bolsheviks promised to revolutionize gender roles. Lenin believed that the family was a middle-class institution doomed to "wither away." He declared that in the ideal communist society, marriage would be a mutually beneficial—and in many cases temporary—arrangement between two equally educated and equally waged partners, and housework and child care would move from the private domestic household into the public sphere of paid employment. Nevertheless, in revolutionary Soviet society, too, continuities linked the pre- and postwar experience of women.

One month after seizing power, the Bolsheviks legalized divorce and civil marriages. In 1918, a new family legal code declared women and men equal under the law and abolished the distinction between legitimate and illegitimate children. To free women from housework—described by Lenin as "barbarously unproductive, petty, nervewracking, and stultifying drudgery"[14]—the Bolsheviks promised communal child care centers, laundries, and dining rooms. In 1920, just as other states were outlawing

Read the Document

Gertrud Scholtz-Klink, "Speech to the Nazi Women's Organization" abortion, the practice became legal in Bolshevik Russia. A Women's Bureau instructed women in their new rights, challenged the traditional patriarchy of peasant households, and encouraged Muslim women to remove their veils.

But in 1922, as we have seen, Lenin retreated from communist ideology by instituting the New Economic Policy. NEP also meant reversals in the gender revolution. By 1923, the dining halls had closed and more than half of the day care centers shut down. Throughout the 1920s, Soviet women's wages averaged 65 percent of men's. Moreover, in rural and Islamic regions, the Bolshevik attempt at gender revolution aroused strong and sometimes violent resistance. The majority of Soviet women remained in subordinate roles.

This retreat from gender revolution accelerated once Stalin took control of the Soviet Union. In 1936, the Soviet government outlawed abortion and made divorce more difficult. Like Western leaders, Stalin also tried to increase birth rates by granting pregnant women maternity stipends and improving prenatal care.

Stalin made no effort to pull women out of the workforce, however. Of the more than four million new workers entering the labor force between 1932 and 1937, 82 percent were women. Soviet women continued to have access to higher education and professional jobs—working as doctors, engineers, scientists, and high-ranking government officials—and, like men, they were deported and executed in huge numbers.

"WORKING WOMEN IN THE STRUGGLE FOR SOCIALISM AND THE STRUGGLE AGAINST RELIGION" This Soviet propaganda poster proclaims a new age of liberation for Soviet women. The light of socialism, reached through Lenin's writings (top left) and visible in clean, modernist design (top right), penetrates the darkness of superstition and patriarchal abuse (bottom left and right). The woman who dominates the poster, an architect designing the socialist future, represents the ideal Soviet woman.

The West and the World: Imperialism in the Interwar Era

((• 📖 Read the Document

Soviet Union "Law Code on Marriage" and "Law Code on Motherhood"

26.6 How did the interaction between the West and the world outside change after World War I?

During World War I the Allies championed national self-determination in Europe, but they had no intention of allowing the nations under their imperial rule to determine their own government. Britain and France emerged from the war with their empires greatly expanded: They divided up Germany's overseas colonies in Africa and Asia, and became the dominant powers in the Middle East. Belgium and Portugal retained their African colonies, while in Asia, some of the spoils went to Japan, Australia, and New Zealand. Popular imperialism reached its zenith after the war as well, as filmmakers and novelists found that imperial settings formed the perfect backdrop for stirring tales of individual heroism and limitless adventure.

26.1
26.2
26.3
26.4
26.5
26.6

26.1

26.2

26.3

26.4

26.5

26.6

The Irish Revolution

In this period, however, important challenges to the imperial idea emerged. The most successful occurred in Ireland. World War I radicalized the Irish nationalist movement. We saw in Chapter 23 that before 1914, the mainstream of Irish nationalism supported "Home Rule"—Irish political autonomy within the framework of the British Empire. By 1919, Home Rule was too little, too late, and popular opinion had swung behind the radical demand for an Irish Republic independent of Britain.

The British response to the Easter Rising of 1916 helped push popular Irish nationalism in a radical direction. A small group of revolutionary nationalists mounted an armed rebellion on Easter Monday in Dublin. Few Irish men or women participated and many condemned the Rising—but then the British government made the fatal error of executing the leaders of the rebellion and treating the population of Dublin with brutality. Public opinion shifted rapidly. The executed leaders became martyrs for the sacred cause of nationhood.

The British decision in 1918 to impose military conscription in Ireland aroused further anger and completed the radicalization process. The result was the Anglo-Irish War of 1919–1921, in which the Irish rebels utilized the tactics of guerilla warfare to battle against their much stronger foe.

With much of its public weary of war, the British government in 1921 offered a peace settlement based on limited independence for Ireland: The new "Irish Free State" was to retain its membership within the British Empire, and the six northern counties within the province of Ulster, dominated by Protestants of English and Scottish descent who opposed Irish independence, were to remain part of the United Kingdom.

Appalled that Irish leaders would have to continue to swear an oath of allegiance to the British monarchy and that the island would be partitioned, a minority of the Irish rejected the peace settlement—and declared war against the new Irish Free State. The Irish Civil War of 1922–1923 created lasting divisions in Irish political and cultural life. The Irish Free State finally severed its ties with the British Empire and became the Republic of Eire in 1949. Northern Ireland today retains its constitutional links to Britain (see **Map 26.2**).

Changing Power Equations: Ideology and Economics

Ireland's revolt against British imperial rule was unusual in this era because it succeeded. In other regions, European powers were able to retain imperial control. Nevertheless, during the 1920s and 1930s, mass nationalist movements grew stronger in many regions, the result of both the spread of communist ideology and the impact of the Great Depression.

Communist ideology played an important role in undermining European empires. Lenin argued that capitalist competition for markets led inevitably to imperialism and thus that anti-capitalism and anti-imperialism went hand in hand. Declaring itself the defender of oppressed nationalities everywhere, the Soviet Union provided ideological and material assistance to nationalist independence movements in Indonesia, Indochina, Burma, and, most significantly, China, where Soviet advisers helped form the Communist Party in 1921.

MAP **26.2** IRELAND AND BRITAIN The treaty of 1921 that ended the Anglo-Irish War partitioned the Irish island. Six northern counties (or "Ulster") remain part of the British state (officially the United Kingdom of Great Britain and Northern Ireland). The rest of Ireland became the Irish Free State, an independent state within the British Empire. In 1937, a new constitution changed the name of the Free State to Eire. Eire declared itself a republic in 1949. What was the significance of this 1949 declaration?

Economic developments proved as important as ideological arguments, however. The Great Depression brought a sharp fall in the prices of primary products across the globe. The price decline spelled disaster for many colonial regions that relied on the production of cash crops for export. More directly, the response of imperial regimes to the economic challenges of the Depression diminished their own effectiveness. Looking for ways to reduce expenditures, European governments cut funds to colonial schools, public services, and health care. Direct taxation rates rose while unemployment rates soared. In response, nationalist movements exploded.

Postwar Nationalism, Westernization, and the Islamic Challenge

Anti-Western sentiment in imperial territories also took religious form. In Africa, for example, a revival of animist religion expressed an explicit rejection of the Christian teachings brought by European and American missionaries and an implicit refusal of Western cultural and political styles.

Throughout many African regions and in much of Asia, however, Islam possessed the most potent appeal. In the growing cities, immigrants cut off from their villages and traditional religious practices found that Islam provided an alternative cultural identity to the one offered by their European rulers.

The end of World War I marked the beginning of a new era in Islamic history. The Ottoman Empire had symbolized a unified Islam: As caliph, the Ottoman sultan claimed religious authority over all Muslims, even those not under Ottoman political rule. The collapse of the Ottoman Empire and the abolition of the Ottoman caliphate in the wake of World War I created a new religious and political environment for Muslims. Many followed Western secular models. Others, however, found spiritual solace and political identity in Islamic revival movements.

NATIONALIST MODELS For many Muslims in the Middle East, **pan-Arabism** emerged as a powerful form of ethnic nationalism. Just as pan-Slavism promoted the ideal of a single Slavic state (see p. 701), so pan-Arabism insisted that all Arabs—including the minority who were not Muslim—should unite in an Arab state.

Not all Arab nationalists, however, embraced pan-Arabism. In states such as Egypt, where the national boundaries had not been imposed by Western armies or institutions, nationalism tended to coalesce around the state itself. Hence, in Egypt, the nationalist political party, *Wafd,* called for Egyptian national freedom, not for pan-Arabic unity.

For nationalists such as those in Wafd, the successful nationalist revolution in Turkey provided a source of inspiration. In the tumultuous period immediately following the end of World War I, Turkish nationalists led by Mustafa Kemal Pasha overthrew the Ottoman sultan and forced the Allies to back away from imposing a treaty that would have limited the new state of Turkey's national sovereignty.

But while Kemal had no intention of letting Western powers control Turkey, he was not anti-Western. Kemal viewed the West as modern—and he wanted to modernize Turkey. Thus, he declared Turkey a secular republic, outlawed polygamy, granted women civil and legal rights, and required all Turks to take surnames. He became known as Kemal "Ataturk" ("Father of the Turks"). A mass literacy program aimed to teach Turks how to read and write using the Latin alphabet. Schoolmasters who dared use Arabic lettering were arrested. Ataturk even condemned the traditional form of Turkish headwear, the fez, as "an emblem of ignorance, negligence, fanaticism, hatred of progress and civilization."[15] To represent Turkey's new Western orientation, Turkish men were ordered to wear Western suits and English bowler hats.

Read the Document

Ho Chi Minh, "Equality!"

Read the Document

Jomo Kenyatta, from Facing Mt. Kenya: The Tribal Life of the Gokuyu

26.1

26.2

26.3

26.4

26.5

26.6

pan-Arabism Nationalist ideology that called for the political unification of all Arabs, regardless of religious affiliation.

26.1

26.2

26.3

26.4

26.5

26.6

Ataturk was less enthusiastic about English political freedom. Despite setting up a parliament elected by universal suffrage, he used executive power to govern with an iron grip over a one-party state. He also continued the Ottoman policies of repression toward Turkey's Armenian minority.

Kemal Ataturk's secularist, Westernized model of nationalism proved alluring. During the 1920s and 1930s nationalists in the Middle East, Africa, and Asia tended to embrace Western models, even as they rejected Western (or Western-imposed) rulers. They formed parliamentary political parties, advocated Western political ideologies such as liberalism and communism, regarded the state as secular, and saw political independence as a crucial step toward industrial modernization and economic prosperity.

THE ISLAMIC CHALLENGE Beneath the surface of political life, however, different movements with different aims were coalescing. Throughout the new states of the Middle East, soaring sales of popular biographies of the Prophet Muhammad and the proliferation of Islamic leagues and clubs hinted that many ordinary people found secular nationalism as alien as the faces of their Western-imposed rulers and as meaningless as the boundaries on the new map. These sentiments did not harden into political movements until the 1940s; during the interwar decades, however, the Wahhabi religious revival in central Arabia and the Muslim Brotherhood in Egypt set a new direction for Islam's relationship to the West.

Founded by Muhammad Abd al-Wahhab (1703–1787) in the eighteenth century, **Wahhabism** sought to purify Islam by returning to a strict interpretation of the *Sharia*, or Islamic law. Wahhabism revived in the tumultuous period after World War I because its reassertion of fundamental truths and practices proved reassuring in a time of unsettling political change. Moreover, the postwar Wahhabi revival had a powerful patron: Abd al-Aziz Ibn Saud (ca. 1888–1953), the head of the Saudi dynasty whose conquests on the Arabian peninsula became the basis for the kingdom of Saudi Arabia. Wahhabism's call for Islamic purification soon embraced sharp opposition to Western culture.

A different sort of movement that had similar goals emerged in Egypt in 1928. Like the Wahhabis, the Islamic Brotherhood (or *Ikhwan*) rejected modernizing interpretations of Islam, reasserted the universal jurisdiction of Islamic law, and viewed Western societies as corrupt. For the Brotherhood, Islam governed not just religious belief, but all areas of life. Working through youth groups, educational institutes, and business enterprises, the Brotherhood spread from its Egyptian base throughout the Middle East during the 1930s.

Wahhabism A religious reform and revival movement founded by Muhammad Abd al-Wahhab (1703–1787) in the eighteenth century to purify Islam by returning to a strict interpretation of the *Sharia*, or Islamic law. Revived during the 1920s in Saudi Arabia.

Moral Revolution in India

During this era, an anti-Western protest movement also took shape in India under the leadership of Mohandas Gandhi (1869–1948). Gandhi had spent 20 years in South Africa fighting to improve the lot of indentured Indian laborers under British imperial rule and developing his commitment to social and political change through nonviolent protest and civil disobedience.

After he returned to India in 1916, Gandhi transformed Indian nationalism into a mass movement by appealing to traditional Indian customs and religious identities. He did not oppose modernization, but he argued that modernization did not mean Westernization. India could—and should—follow its own path. Gandhi rejected Western dress and presented himself in the role of the religious ascetic, a familiar and honored figure in Indian culture. In his insistence that the nationalist struggle be one of "moral force" rather than a physical fight, Gandhi drew on the Hindu tradition of nonviolence. He was careful, however, not to equate "Indian" with "Hindu." Gandhi strove to incorporate the minority Muslim community into the nationalist movement, and he broke with the traditional Hindu caste system by campaigning for the rights of those deemed "untouchable." (*See Encounters and Transformations* in this chapter.)

26.1

26.2

26.3

26.4

26.5

26.6

Encounters and Transformations

From Mohandas to Mahatma:
GANDHI'S TRANSFORMATION

I n April 1893, a young, well-dressed Indian lawyer purchased a first-class train ticket from Durban to Pretoria (South Africa). The first part of the journey proceeded uneventfully, but then another traveler, a white man, entered the first-class compartment. He turned around and returned with two guards, who demanded that the Indian man sit in third class, with the other "colored" passengers. The young lawyer refused and so was thrown off the train at the next stop.

Mohandas Gandhi's experience on the train to Pretoria was not unusual. The Indian immigrant community in South Africa had long endured legal discrimination, economic exploitation, and frequent violence, while the black African community suffered far worse. But the 24-year-old Gandhi knew little about such things. Growing up as the spoiled youngest son in an upper-caste family in India, he had known privilege rather than prejudice. Even the three years he spent in London studying law did not expose him to racial discrimination. Gandhi, in fact, felt that when he left Britain he was leaving "home." He returned to India in 1891 convinced of the superiority of British law and culture. He banned Indian-style clothing from his household, insisted that his illiterate young wife learn English, and decreed that his children eat porridge and cocoa for breakfast. He saw himself as a successful British lawyer.

But others did not see him that way. When Gandhi asked a British official for a favor for his brother, he was humiliated and actually pushed out the door by a servant. "This shock changed the course of my life," Gandhi later noted.[16] Offered a job in South Africa, he went—and on that train to Pretoria encountered further humiliation. By the time Gandhi finally reached Pretoria, he had decided to fight. He became the leader of the Indian civil rights movement in South Africa.

Gandhi lived in South Africa for 21 years. During these decades, the westernized, Britain-loving lawyer became a Hindu

THE MAHATMA Gandhi drew on Hindu and Western traditions in formulating his moral protest.

holy man. Mohandas became Mahatma, the "great-souled one." This transformation occurred in part because of Gandhi's sense of betrayal as he encountered the racial discrimination embedded in British imperialism. His time in London had taught Gandhi that Britain epitomized the Western ideals of impartial justice and individual rights. But the British colonial regime he encountered in South Africa violated those ideals. Disillusioned, Gandhi turned back to his Hindu roots.

Western culture also, however, played a positive role in Gandhi's transformation. During his time in South Africa, Gandhi read widely in Christian and Western texts, including the New Testament, and books by nineteenth-century European social and cultural critics that exposed the spiritual and material failures of industrial society. Gandhi's intellectual encounter with these texts helped him formulate the idea of Satyagraha ("Truth-Force"). In its most specific sense, Satyagraha is a political tool. Through nonviolent mass civil disobedience, the powerless persuade the powerful to effect political change. But Satyagraha is also a spiritual act, the victory of goodness over violence and evil.

Gandhi's specific encounters with the injustice of imperial rule, first in the home of a British official in India and then on his South African train ride, forced him to embark on a different sort of spiritual and political journey, an exploration of both Western and Hindu thought. This journey transformed Gandhi from Mohandas into Mahatma and led him to Satyagraha—and the transformation of Indian nationalism into a mass movement. By 1948, this movement made it impossible for the British to govern India.

For Discussion

Encounters with Western ideas and Western people helped transform Gandhi "from Mohandas to Mahatma." How have Gandhi's ideas transformed Western culture and politics?

26.1

26.2

26.3

26.4

26.5

26.6

Unable to decide whether to arrest Gandhi as a dangerous revolutionary or to negotiate with him as a representative of the Indian people, the British did both. In 1931, Gandhi and the viceroy of India (literally the "vice-king," the highest British official in India) met on equal terms for a series of eight meetings. A few months later Gandhi was in prison, along with 66,000 of his nationalist colleagues.

Successive British governments passed a series of measures granting Indians increasing degrees of self-government, but Gandhi and the Indian National Congress demanded full and immediate national independence. The resulting impasse led to escalating unrest and terrorist activity, despite Gandhi's personal commitment to nonviolence. India remained the jewel in Britain's imperial crown, but the glue holding it in place was deteriorating rapidly by the end of the 1930s.

📖 Read the Document

Jawaharlal Nehru, from *The Autobiography of Jawaharlal Nehru*

THE POWER OF THE PRIMITIVE When the American dancer Josephine Baker first hit the stage in Paris in 1925, her audience embraced her as the image of African savagery, even though Baker was a city kid from St. Louis. A Parisian sensation from the moment she arrived, Baker's frenetic and passionate style of dancing—and her willingness to appear on stage wearing nothing but a belt of bananas—epitomized for many Europeans the freedom they believed their urbanized culture had lost, and that the United States and Africa retained. Baker's belt of bananas, designed by her white French employer, shows that racist stereotypes shaped this idealization of the primitive. Yet Baker's blackness and her Americanness represented a positive image of liberation to many Parisians.

The Power of the Primitive

When asked what he thought of "Western civilization," Gandhi replied, "I think it would be a very good idea." Just as nationalists outside of the West such as Gandhi began to challenge the equation of the West with civilization, so too did Westerners themselves. In the nineteenth century, imperialists insisted that "civilization" gave the West the right to rule the "barbarians" in the rest of the world. But by 1918, in the wake of the war, at least some Europeans asked, "Who is the barbarian now?"

Developments in psychology further eroded the boundaries between barbarian or "primitive" and modern cultures. In his postwar writings, Sigmund Freud emphasized that human nature was fundamentally aggressive, even bestial. Freud's three-part theory of personality, developed in the 1920s, argued that within each individual the *id*, the unconscious force of primitive instinct, battles against the controls of the *ego*, or conscious rationality, and the *superego*, the moral values imposed by society. Although Freud taught that the continuity of civilization depended on the repression of the id, many Freudian popularizers insisted that the individual should allow his or her primitive self to run free.

The work of Freud's onetime disciple Carl Jung (1875–1961) also stressed the links between the primitive and the modern. Jung contended that careful study of an individual's dreams will show that they share common images and forms—"archetypes"—with ancient mythologies and world religions. These archetypes point to the existence of the "collective unconscious," shared by all human beings, regardless of when or where they lived. Thus, in Jung's analysis the boundary between "civilized" and "primitive," "West" and "not West," disappeared.

In the work of other thinkers and artists, that boundary remained intact, but Western notions of cultural superiority turned upside down. The German novelist Hermann Hesse (1877–1962) condemned modern industrial society as spiritually

26.1

26.2

26.3

26.4

26.5

26.6

barren and celebrated Eastern mysticism as a source of power and wisdom. Many writers agreed that the West needed to look to outside its borders for vibrancy and vitality. The belief that Western culture was anemic, washed out, and washed up also led to a new openness to alternative intellectual and artistic traditions. As the energetic rhythms of African American jazz worked their way into white musical traditions, they transformed popular music.

Similarly, the *Négritude* movement stressed the history and intrinsic value of black African culture. Founded in Paris in 1935 by French colonial students from Africa and the West Indies, Négritude condemned European culture as weak and corrupted and called for blacks to recreate a separate cultural and political identity. The movement's leading figures, such as Leopold Senghor (1906–2001), who later became the first president of independent Senegal, opposed Western imperialism and demanded African self-rule. Drawing together Africans, Afro-Caribbeans, and black Americans, Négritude assumed the existence of a common black culture that transcended national and colonial boundaries. The movement stole the white racists' stereotype of the "happy dancing savage" and refigured it as positive: Black culture fostered the emotion, creativity, and human connections that white Western industrial society destroyed.

CONCLUSION

The Kingdom of Corpses

In 1921, the Goncourt Prize, the most prestigious award in French literature, was awarded not to a native French writer, but to a colonial: René Maran, born in the French colony of Martinique. Even more striking than Maran's receiving the prize was the content of the novel for which he was honored. In *Batouala*, Maran condemned Western culture: "Civilization, civilization, pride of the Europeans and charnel house of innocents. . . . You build your kingdom on corpses."[17]

For many in the West, Maran's description of Europe as a kingdom of corpses appeared apt in the aftermath of total war. During the 1920s and 1930s Soviet communism on the left and Nazism and fascism on the right rejected such key Western ideals as individual rights and the rule of law. These extremist ideologies seemed persuasive in the climate of despair produced not only by the war, but also by the postwar failure of democracy in eastern Europe and the collapse of the global economy after 1929. As a result, the kingdom of corpses grew: in Nazi Germany, in Spain, and most dramatically in the Soviet Union. The kingdom of corpses was, however, a particularly expansionist domain. As the 1930s ended, the West and the world stood on the brink of another total war, one in which the numbers of dead spiraled to nearly incomprehensible levels.

MAKING CONNECTIONS

1. The Soviet Union stood on the far left of the political spectrum; fascist Italy and Nazi Germany stood on the far right. Yet these ideological opponents shared many common features: What were they? How do you explain these commonalities?
2. What were the key developments in governmental policies toward women, welfare, and the family in the interwar era? How can we explain the similarities in Radical Right, democratic, and Radical Left policies?

TAKING IT FURTHER

For suggested readings, websites, and films, see page R-1.

On MyHistoryLab

✓ Take the Study Plan for Chapter 26,
Reconstruction, Reaction, and Continuing
Revolution: The 1920s and 1930s,
on MyHistoryLab

Chapter Review

Cultural Despair and Desire

26.1 What was the impact of World War I on European cultural life?

The massive destruction of total war led many Europeans to embrace pessimistic assessments of human nature and human society. Others, however, argued that the war had created the possibility of radical social improvement, particularly through technological and scientific research and development.

The Appeal of Authoritarianism and the Rise of Fascism

26.2 What circumstances explain the collapse of democracy throughout much of interwar Europe?

Nationalist conflicts and economic underdevelopment weakened the new democracies of eastern Europe. As the Great Depression stalled the global economy, many voters and politicians embraced aspects of fascism, a new form of Radical Right politics that emerged in Italy after World War I. An intensely nationalistic ideology, fascism exalted the power of the state, dismissed democracy as weak, and glorified military action. It also used mass spectacles to generate enthusiasm and a sense of belonging to a mighty movement.

Nazism and the Defeat of Democracy in Germany

26.3 How did the Nazis succeed in establishing a dictatorship in Germany?

The Nazis remained a fringe party until the Great Depression weakened German democracy and polarized voters and political leaders. Once in political power, the Nazis used terror and intimidation to destroy all that remained of German democracy. The Nazi economic program lowered the standard of living for many Germans but also lowered unemployment rates. Nazi racial and political ideology demonized many groups, most particularly Germany's Jewish community.

The Soviet Alternative and the Democracies' Response

26.4 Why did the Soviet Union seem a success and how did the democracies respond?

Through violence and dictatorial rule, Stalin imposed mass modernization on the Soviet economy but the vast cost of his collectivization of Soviet agriculture and his industrial program remained largely hidden. In western Europe and the United States, governments moved toward social democratic programs and policies. In France and Spain, Popular Front governments sought to unite non-fascist parties together in democratic governments but faced defeat or overthrow.

The Reconstruction of Gender

26.5 What changed, and what did not, in women's experiences after World War I?

In many, although not all, western states, women received the national franchise after World War I and had wider employment and educational opportunities. Gender ideology, however, did not change very much. Both World War I's high cost in human life and falling birth rates after the war impelled political leaders to find ways to encourage women to remain in the home and to produce more children.

The West and the World: Imperialism in the Interwar Era

26.6 How did the interaction between the West and the world outside change after World War I?

The French and British empires grew as a result of the war, but so, too, did anti-colonialist nationalist movements. The Great Depression strained the economies of overseas territories and increased indigenous resentment against European imperial rule. The growth of anti-Western Islamic movements in the 1920s and 1930s also weakened the hold of European powers on their empires and dependencies. At the same time, many Western thinkers and artists began to see non-Western cultures as a source of the vitality and creativity that they believed to be disappearing from industrial societies.

On MyHistoryLab

✓ Take the Study Plan for Chapter 26, Reconstruction, Reaction, and Continuing Revolution: The 1920s and 1930s, on MyHistoryLab

Chapter Time Line

1921
Communists victorious in Russian civil war; Lenin institutes NEP.

1921

1922

1922
Irish Free State established.

1925
Mussolini establishes fascist dictatorship in Italy.

1925

1928

1928
Stalin emerges as head of the Soviet Union.

1929
Onset of the Great Depression; Stalin orders the collectivization of Soviet farms; Onset of Great Depression.

1929

1931

1931
Gandhi imprisoned by British authorities in India.

1933
Hitler establishes Nazi dictatorship in Germany.

1933

1936

1936
Spanish Civil War begins.

27 World War II

In the final weeks of World War II in Europe, many allied soldiers faced their most difficult assignment yet. Combat veterans, accustomed to scenes of slaughter, broke down and cried as they encountered a landscape of horror beyond their wildest nightmares: the Nazi concentration and death camps. As one American war correspondent put it, "We had penetrated at last to the center of the black heart, to the very crawling inside of the vicious heart."[1] The American soldiers who opened the camp in Mauthausen, Austria, never forgot their first sight of the prisoners there: "By the thousands they came streaming. . . . Hollow, pallid ghosts from graves and tombs, terrifying, rot-colored figures of misery marked by disease, deeply ingrained filth, inner decay. . . . squat skeletons in rags and crazy grins."[2]

Similarly, the sights they saw at Bergen-Belsen in Germany left an indelible mark on the British troops who liberated that camp. Bergen-Belsen had become the dumping ground for camp inmates from eastern Europe as the German army retreated in front of the advancing Soviet army. Sick and starving, these prisoners were packed, 1,200 at a time, into barracks built to accommodate a few hundred. By March 1945, drinking water and food had disappeared, excrement dripped from bunk beds and coated the floors, and dead bodies piled up everywhere. In these conditions, the only living beings to flourish were the

THE MASS GRAVES AT BERGEN-BELSEN
British soldiers liberated the Nazi concentration camp of Bergen-Belsen on April 15, 1945. For many prisoners, however, death provided their only "liberation."

LEARNING OBJECTIVES

27.1 (((
How did military and political expectations lead to World War II?

27.2 (((
How did Nazi Germany conquer the continent of Europe by 1941?

27.3 (((
Why did the Allies win in 1945?

27.4 (((
What were the context, causes, and consequences of genocide during World War II?

27.5 (((
What did total war mean for civilians in the occupied regions and on the home front?

(((Listen to Chapter 27 on MyHistoryLab

⊙ Watch the Video Series on MyHistoryLab

Learn about some key topics related to this chapter with the *MyHistoryLab Video Series: Key Topics in Western Civilization*

27.1

27.2

27.3

27.4

27.5

microorganisms that caused typhus. Floundering in this sea of want, British soldiers, doctors, and nurses did what they could. Even so, 28,000 of Bergen-Belsen's 60,000 inmates died in the weeks following liberation.

In Mauthausen and Bergen-Belsen, in the piles of putrefying bodies and among the crowds of skeletal survivors, American and British soldiers encountered the results of Adolf Hitler's effort to redefine the West. In Hitler's vision, Western civilization comprised ranks of white, northern Europeans, led by Germans, marching in step to a cadence dictated by the all-powerful state. To realize this vision, Hitler turned to total war and mass murder.

This quest to reconfigure the West as a race-based German empire led Hitler to join hands with an ally outside the West: Japan. The German-Japanese alliance transformed a European war into a global conflict. Understanding World War II thus demands that we look not only at the results of Nazi racial ideology, but also at global power relations and patterns of economic dependency. The Pacific war constituted the most brutal in a long series of encounters between Japanese elites and the West. Like Hitler, Japan's governing elites longed for an empire—in their case, an Asian empire to ensure access to the resources and domination over the peoples of the Pacific region. With such access and such domination, they hoped to insulate Japan's economic and political structures from Western influence or control.

As we examine both the European and the Pacific theaters of war, we will need, then, to ask how competing definitions of "the West" helped shape this conflict. We will also confront the question of results:

How did the cataclysm known as World War II redefine the West?

The Coming of War

27.1 How did military and political expectations lead to World War II?

World War I was supposed to be the "war to end all wars." Instead, a little more than 20 years later, total war again engulfed Europe and then the world. Hitler's ambitions for a German empire in eastern Europe accounted for the immediate outbreak of war in September 1939. But a complete explanation of the origins of World War II extends beyond Hitler's aims and actions.

An Uneasy Peace

The Second World War originated in the settlement of the First. Three factors accounted for the fragility of the peace settlement. First, the Versailles Treaty created great resentment among Germans, helped weaken postwar Western economies, and enhanced Hitler's appeal. Second, the League of Nations, created to replace the alliance

THE PRELUDE TO WORLD WAR II The Japanese resumption of their war in China in 1937 added to the horrors of the 1930s. Here a photographer captured the agony of a baby separated from its parents in the railway station in Shanghai.

systems that many blamed for starting World War I, could not realize the high hopes of its planners. Lacking military power, boycotted by the United States, and at various times excluding the key states of Germany and the Soviet Union, the League proved too weak to serve as the basis of a new international order. Finally, the redrawing of the map of eastern and central Europe, intended to create cohesive nation-states, instead worsened national conflict throughout eastern and southern Europe.

The onset of the Great Depression in 1929 further destabilized the peace. Economic nationalism intensified as governments erected tariff walls to protect their own industries. Some sought to escape economic difficulties through territorial expansion. Japan, threatened by the collapse of export markets for raw silk and cotton cloth, invaded Manchuria (in eastern China) in 1931 and Italy invaded Ethiopia in 1935. The Ethiopians endured many of the horrors soon to come to the European continent, including the saturation bombing of civilians, the use of poison gas, and the establishment of concentration camps. At the end of June 1936, Ethiopia's now-exiled Emperor Haile Selassie (1892–1975) addressed the Assembly of the League of Nations and warned, "It is us today. It will be you tomorrow."[3]

One year after Italian troops invaded Ethiopia, civil war broke out in Spain. As Chapter 26 explained, the victory of General Francisco Franco's rebels seemed to signal that aggressors could act with impunity. While the Spanish Civil War raged, the Japanese resumed their advance in China. In what became known as the Rape of Nanking (Nanjing), soldiers used babies for bayonet practice, gang-raped as many as 20,000 young girls and women, and left the bodies of the dead to rot in the street.

The Expansion of Nazi Germany

Against this backdrop of military aggression and the democracies' inaction, Hitler made his first moves to establish a German empire in Europe (see **Map 27.1**). In 1933, he withdrew Germany from the League of Nations and two years later announced the creation of a German air force and the return of mass conscription—in deliberate violation of the terms of the Versailles Treaty. In 1936, Hitler allied with Mussolini in the **Rome-Berlin Axis** and again violated his treaty obligations when he sent German troops into

Rome-Berlin Axis Alliance between Benito Mussolini's Italy and Adolf Hitler's Germany formed in 1936.

the Rhineland, the industrially rich region on Germany's western border. Yet France and Britain did not respond. Two years later, in March 1938, Germany broke the Versailles Treaty once more by annexing Austria.

After the successful *Anschluss* ("joining") of Germany and Austria, Hitler demanded that the Sudetenland, the western portion of Czechoslovakia inhabited by a German-speaking majority, be joined to Germany as well. He seemed finally to have gone too far. With France and the Soviet Union pledged to protect the territorial integrity of Czechoslovakia, Europe stood on the brink of war. The urgency of the situation impelled Britain's prime minister Neville Chamberlain (1869–1940) to board an airplane for the first time in his life and fly to Munich to talk with Hitler. After negotiations that excluded the Czech government, Chamberlain and French prime minister Edouard Daladier agreed to grant Hitler the right to occupy the Sudetenland immediately. Assured by Hitler that this **Munich Agreement** satisfied all his territorial demands, Chamberlain flew home to an enthusiastic welcome. Crowds cheered when he declared "peace in our time." (See *Different Voices* in this chapter.)

"Peace in our time" lasted for six months. In March 1939, Hitler's promises were proven worthless as German troops occupied the rest of Czechoslovakia. Hitler then took out an insurance policy against fighting a two-front war by persuading Stalin to sign the **German-Soviet Non-Aggression Pact**. The pact publicly pledged the two powers not to attack each other. It also secretly divided Poland between them and promised Stalin substantial territorial gains in eastern Poland and the Baltic regions.

On September 1, 1939, German troops invaded Poland and within weeks were implementing racial policies that murdered millions of Poles. The British and French declared war against Germany on September 3. Two weeks after German troops crossed Poland's borders in the west, the Soviets pushed in from the east and imposed a regime characterized by mass deportations and death. World War II had begun.

Evaluating Appeasement

Could Hitler have been stopped before he catapulted Europe into World War II? The debate over this question has centered on British policy during the 1930s. With France weakened by economic and political crises, the United States remaining aloof from European affairs, and the communist Soviet Union regarded as a pariah state, Britain assumed the initiative in responding to Hitler's rise to power and his demands.

British policymakers—particularly Neville Chamberlain, who was prime minister in the late 1930s—pursued a policy of conciliation and negotiation in their dealings with Hitler. After World War II broke out, that policy was called **appeasement**, a word now equated with passivity and cowardice. Chamberlain, however, was not a coward and was far from passive. Convinced he had a mission to save Europe from war, he actively sought to accommodate Hitler.

MAP 27.1 THE EXPANSION OF GERMANY IN THE 1930s Beginning with the remilitarization of the Rhineland in 1936, Hitler embarked on a program of German territorial expansion. This map also indicates the expansion of the Soviet Union into Poland as a result of the secret terms of the German-Soviet Non-Aggression Pact. Which of Germany's expansionist moves could Hitler argue were based on "national self-determination"?

The Expansion of Germany in the 1930s
- Germany in 1933
- Remilitarized in 1936
- Annexed in 1938 – April 1939
- Satellite state, March 1939
- Conquered by Germany, September 1939
- Annexed by Soviet Union, September 1939
- International boundaries, 1936
- Prewar boundaries of Poland

Munich Agreement The agreement in 1939 between the governments of Nazi Germany, Britain, and France that granted Germany sovereignty over the Sudetenland; part of the effort to appease the Nazi government and avoid a second total war in Europe.

German-Soviet Non-Aggression Pact Signed by Joseph Stalin and Adolf Hitler in 1939, the agreement publicly pledged Germany and the Soviet Union not to attack each other and secretly divided up Poland and the Baltic states between the two powers.

View the Map
German Expansion Under the Third Reich

Read the Document
Adolf Hitler, The Obersalzberg Speech, 1939

appeasement British diplomatic and financial efforts to stabilize Germany in the 1920s and 1930s and so avoid a second world war.

27.2

27.3

27.4

27.5

For Chamberlain, and many other Europeans, the alternative to appeasement was a total war that would destroy Western civilization. They remembered the last war with horror and agreed that the next war would be even worse, for it would be an air war. The years after 1918 saw the aviation industry take off in Europe and the United States, and both military experts and ordinary people recognized the disastrous potential of airborne bombs. Stanley Baldwin (1867–1947), Chamberlain's predecessor as prime minister, told the British public, "The bomber will always get through." The civilian casualties inflicted by the Italian air force in Ethiopia and by the bombing of Spanish cities in the Spanish Civil War convinced many that Baldwin was right, and that war was, therefore, unacceptable.

Motivated by the desire to avoid another horrible war, appeasement rested on two additional pillars—the assumption that many of Germany's grievances were legitimate and the belief that only a strong Germany could neutralize the threat posed

CHRONOLOGY: ON THE ROAD TO WORLD WAR II

1919
Versailles Treaty.
1919

1929
1929
Onset of the Great Depression.

1931
Japan invades Manchuria.
1931

1933
1933
Hitler becomes chancellor of Germany.

1935
Hitler announces a German air force and military conscription; Italy invades Ethiopia.
1935

1936
German troops occupy the Rhineland; civil war breaks out in Spain; Hitler and Mussolini form the Rome-Berlin Axis.
1936

1937
Japan advances against China; Rape of Nanking.
1937

1938
March
Germany annexes Austria (the *Anschluss*).
September
Munich Conference: Germany occupies the Sudetenland.
1938

1939
March 15
Germany invades Czechoslovakia.
August 23
German-Soviet Non-Aggression Pact.
September 1
Germany invades Poland.
September 3
Great Britain and France declare war on Germany.
1939

by Soviet communism. During the 1920s, many scholars and policymakers studied the diplomatic records concerning the outbreak of World War I. They concluded that the treaty makers at Versailles were wrong in blaming Germany for starting the war. Convinced that the Versailles Treaty had treated Germany unjustly, British leaders sought to renegotiate reparations, to press the French into softening their anti-German policies, and to draw Germany back into the network of international diplomatic relations. Hitler's rise to power gave added impetus to a policy already in place. British leaders argued that they could rob Hitler of much of his appeal by rectifying legitimate German grievances. Fear of communism reinforced this desire to stabilize Germany. Many politicians applauded Hitler's suppression of German communists and welcomed a remilitarized Germany as a strong barricade against the threat posed by Soviet Russia. The startling announcement of the German-Soviet Non-Aggression Pact in the summer of 1939, however, revealed this barricade to be hollow.

Europe at War, 1939–1941

27.2 How did Nazi Germany conquer the continent of Europe by 1941?

Within just two years, Hitler appeared to have achieved his goal of establishing a Nazi empire in Europe. By the autumn of 1941, almost all of continental Europe was either allied to or occupied by Nazi Germany.

A New Kind of Warfare

The four-year stalemate on the Western Front in World War I demonstrated that an entrenched defense, armed with machine guns, could easily withstand an infantry assault. Postwar German military strategists, seeking to avoid the stalemate of trench warfare, theorized that the airplane and the tank could together act as an "armored fist" strong and swift enough to break through even the most well-fortified enemy defenses. The bomber plane would provide a mobile bombardment to shatter fortifications, break communication links, and clog transport routes. Simultaneously, motorized infantry and tank formations would punch through enemy lines.

Germany's successes in the first years of World War II illustrated the effectiveness of a mobile, mechanized offensive force. Germany's only defeat during these years came in the Battle of Britain, when Germany confronted a mobile, mechanized defense. Like Germany's victories, this defeat highlights a crucial theme of this chapter: the central role of industrial production in modern war.

BLITZKRIEG During the invasion of Poland, most of the German army moved on foot or horseback, as soldiers had done for centuries. Motorized divisions, however, bludgeoned through the Polish defenses, penetrated deep into enemy territory, and secured key positions. While these units wreaked havoc on the ground, the Luftwaffe—the German air force—rained ruin from the air. Over 1,300 planes shrieked across the Polish skies and destroyed the Polish air force.

Western newspaper reporters christened Nazi Germany's offensive techniques **blitzkrieg**—lightning war. Western Europeans experienced blitzkrieg firsthand in the spring of 1940 when the German army invaded Denmark and Norway in early April and moved into western Europe in May. The Netherlands fell in four days. Belgium, supported by French and British units as in World War I, held out for two weeks.

By the end of May, the Germans had trapped the British army and several divisions of the French force in a small pocket on the northern French coast called Dunkirk. While the British Royal Air Force (RAF) held off the Luftwaffe, the British navy and a

blitzkrieg "Lightning war"; an offensive military tactic making use of airplanes, tanks, and motorized infantry to punch through enemy defenses and secure key territory. First demonstrated by the German army in World War II.

 Read the Document

Marc Bloch, *Strange Defeat*

Vichy regime Authoritarian state established in France after defeat by the German army in 1940.

🔍 **View the Map**

The Division of France

flotilla of fishing and recreational boats piloted by British civilians evacuated the troops. By June 4, 110,000 French and almost 240,000 British soldiers had been brought safely back to Britain. But, as the newly appointed British prime minister, Winston Churchill (1874–1965), reminded his cheering people, "Wars are not won by evacuation."

On June 14, German soldiers marched into Paris. The French Assembly voted to disband and to hand over power to the World War I war hero Marshal Philippe Pétain (1856–1951), who established an authoritarian government. On June 22 this new **Vichy regime** (named after the city Pétain chose for his capital) signed an armistice with Germany and pledged collaboration with the Nazi regime. Theoretically, Pétain's authority extended over all of France, but as **Map 27.2** illustrates, in actuality the Vichy regime was confined to the south (and to the French colonial regions). As of June 1940, Germany not only occupied western and northern France, but—with its allies and satellites—held most of the continent.

THE BATTLE OF BRITAIN After the fall of France, Hitler hoped that Britain would accept Germany's domination of the continent and agree to a negotiated peace, but his hopes went unrealized. The failure of appeasement and the subsequent military disasters had thoroughly discredited Prime Minister Neville Chamberlain. A member of Chamberlain's own party spoke for the nation, "In the name of God, go!" Chamberlain went. The British parliament suspended party politics for the duration of the war, and power passed to an all-party coalition headed by Winston Churchill, a critic of Britain's

MAP **27.2** THE NAZI EMPIRE, 1939–1942 By 1942, Nazi Germany controlled most of Europe and much of North Africa and the Middle East. Which states were conquered by Germany? Which allied with Germany? Which states remained neutral?

Different Voices

Appeasement and the Munich Agreement

A fter World War I the victorious Allies redrew the map of central Europe and assigned the Sudetenland, a crescent-shaped region on the edge of what had been the Austro-Hungarian province of Bohemia, to Czechoslovakia. During the 1920s and 1930s, ethnic German Sudetenlanders experienced discrimination in education, employment, and political life, while German nationalist politicians fanned the flames of discontent and, in some cases, worked secretly with Hitler to prepare the ground for a Nazi takeover. In 1938, following his successful annexation of Austria, Hitler demanded the Sudetenland. After a series of meetings, Hitler, the British prime minister Neville Chamberlain, and the French premier Eduard Daladier announced the "Munich Agreement," which gave the Sudetenland to Germany. On his return to Britain, Chamberlain made his infamous proclamation of "peace in our time." The majority of British citizens cheered the Munich Agreement. One who did not was Winston Churchill, a member of Chamberlain's Conservative Party, but a critic of Chamberlain's appeasement policy.

In the first excerpt, Chamberlain defends appeasement in a speech before the House of Commons. In the second excerpt, Churchill attacks the Munich Agreement.

I. Neville Chamberlain in the House of Commons, 1938

War today . . . is a different thing . . . from what it used to be. . . . When war starts today, in the very first hour, before any professional soldier, sailor or airman has been touched, it will strike the workman, the clerk, the man-in-the-street or in the 'bus, and his wife and children in their homes. . . . [Y]ou cannot ask people to accept a prospect of that kind . . . unless you feel yourself, and can make them feel, that the cause for which they are going to fight is a vital cause—a cause that transcends all the human values. . . .

Since I first went to Berchtesgaden* more than 20,000 letters and telegrams have come to No. 10, Downing Street.† . . . the people who wrote did not feel that they had such a cause for which to fight. . . . That is my answer to those who say that we should have told Germany weeks ago that, if her army crossed the border of Czechoslovakia, we should be at war with her. . . .

What is the alternative to this bleak and barren policy of the inevitability of war? . . . we should seek by all means in our power to avoid war, by analysing possible causes, by trying to remove them, by discussion in a spirit of collaboration and good will. . . . even if it does mean the establishment of personal contact with dictators. . . .

I am asked how I can reconcile an appeal to the country to support the continuance of [the rearmament program]‡

*"Berchtesgarden": Hitler's mountain retreat where the political leaders met.
†"No. 10, Downing Street"—the address of the British prime minister's residence.
‡British governments adopted a policy of increased expenditure on armaments from 1934 on.

with . . . my belief that we might have peace for our time . . . I never meant to suggest that we should [secure peace] by disarmament, until we can induce others to disarm too. Our past experience has shown us only too clearly that weakness in armed strength means weakness in diplomacy. . . .

SOURCE: *Parliamentary Debates.* Fifth Series. Volume 339. House of Commons Official Report (London, 1938), 544–552.

II. Winston Churchill in the House of Commons, October 5, 1938

[W]e have sustained a total and unmitigated defeat. . . . The utmost my right hon. Friend the Prime Minister has been able to secure . . . has been that the German dictator, instead of snatching the victuals from the table, has been content to have them served to him course by course. . . .

After [Germany's] seizure of Austria in March . . . I ventured to appeal to the Government . . . to give a pledge that in conjunction with France and other Powers they would guarantee the security of Czechoslovakia while the Sudeten-Deutsch [Sudeten-German] question was being examined either by a League of Nations Commission or some other impartial body. . . . Between submission and immediate war there was this third alternative, which gave a hope not only of peace but of justice. It is quite true that such a policy in order to succeed demanded that Britain should declare straight out and a long time beforehand that she would, with others, join to defend Czechoslovakia against an unprovoked aggression. . . .

All is over. Silent, mournful, abandoned, broken, Czechoslovakia recedes into the darkness. . . . I think you will find that in a period of time which may be measured by years, but may be measured only by months, Czechoslovakia will be engulfed in the Nazi regime. . . .

It must now be accepted that all the countries of Central and Eastern Europe will make the best terms they can with the triumphant Nazi power. . . . Many of those countries . . . have already got politicians, Ministers, Governments, who were pro-German, but there was always an enormous popular movement in Poland, Rumania, Bulgaria, and Yugoslavia which looked to the Western democracies and loathed the idea of having this arbitrary rule of the totalitarian system thrust upon them, and hoped that a stand would be made. All that has gone by the board. . . .

The Prime Minister desires to see cordial relations between this country and Germany. There is no difficulty at all in having cordial relations between the peoples. . . . But never will you have friendship with the present German Government. You must have diplomatic and correct relations, but there can never be friendship between the British democracy and the Nazi power. . . .

(continued on next page)

(continued from previous page)

I do not grudge our loyal, brave people . . . the natural, spontaneous outburst of joy and relief when they learned that the hard ordeal would no longer be required of them at the moment; but they should know the truth. They should know that there has been gross neglect and deficiency in our defences; they should know that we have sustained a defeat without a war . . .

And do not suppose that this is the end. This is only the beginning of the reckoning. This is only the first sip, the first foretaste of a bitter cup which will be proffered to us year by year unless by a supreme recovery of moral health and martial vigour, we arise again and take our stand for freedom as in the olden time.

SOURCE: http://www.winstonchurchill.org/i4a/pages/index.cfm?pageid=1189. Accessed 12-12-07.

For Discussion

1. How did Chamberlain defend the Munich Agreement? What was he trying to achieve?
2. What alternatives did Churchill offer to the Munich Agreement? How realistic were these alternatives?
3. At the end of 1918, ethnic German delegates from Bohemia and Moravia rejected inclusion in Czechoslovakia and instead declared the union of German-majority regions (such as the Sudetenland) with Austria. In response, the new Czech government mobilized its army to enforce its boundaries—even though these boundaries contained over three million ethnic Germans. Does awareness of this history change your assessment of the Munich Agreement? If so, how and why?

appeasement policy since 1933. Never a humble man, Churchill wrote that when he accepted the position of prime minister, "I felt as if I were walking with Destiny, and that all my past life had been but a preparation for this hour and this trial . . . I was sure I should not fail." In his first speech as prime minister, Churchill promised, "Victory—victory at all costs."

Faced with the British refusal to negotiate, Hitler ordered his General Staff to prepare for a land invasion of Britain. But placing German troops in the English Channel while the RAF still controlled the skies would be a certain military disaster. The destruction of Britain's air power had to come first. On July 10, German bomber raids on English southern coastal cities opened the Battle of Britain, a battle waged in the air and in the factories, and Germany's first significant defeat.

The British had three important advantages in the Battle of Britain. First, RAF pilots were flying in the skies above Britain—which meant that pilots who survived crashes could be rescued to fight again, whereas German survivors sat out the rest of the war as prisoners. Second, the rearmament program begun in 1934 had constructed a chain of anti-aircraft gun installations and radar stations that protected the British Isles and increased German losses. And finally, and most significantly for the future course of the war, Britain's industrial productivity outweighed Germany's. In the summer of 1940, British factories each month produced twice the number of fighter aircraft coming out of German plants. On September 17, 1940, Hitler announced that the invasion of Britain was "postponed."

The Invasion of the Soviet Union

Third Reich Term for Adolf Hitler's Germany; articulates the Nazi aim of extending German rule across Europe.

War against Britain had never been one of Hitler's central goals, however. His dreams of the **Third Reich**, a German empire that was to last a thousand years, centered on capture of the agricultural and industrial resources of the Soviet Union. But Hitler sought far more than resources. He envisioned war with the Soviet Union as an apocalyptic clash of Good versus Evil: the superior German race against the twin evils of "Judeo-Bolshevism." The Soviet Union was, of course, the center of global "Bolshevism," or communism, while the majority of European Jews lived in Soviet-controlled eastern Polish lands or in the Soviet Union itself.

A CRUCIAL POSTPONEMENT In July 1940, as the Battle of Britain began, Hitler ordered his military to plan a Soviet invasion. By December the plan was set: German troops were to invade the Soviet Union in April 1941. But they did not. Hitler postponed the invasion for two crucial months because the ambitions of an incompetent ally—Mussolini—threatened to undermine the economic base of the Nazi war machine.

Hoping to expand his Mediterranean empire, Mussolini ordered Italian troops into British imperial territories in North Africa in July 1940, followed by an invasion of Greece in October. But with a military budget one-tenth the size of Germany's, outdated tanks and aircraft, no aircraft carriers or anti-aircraft defenses, and a limited industrial base, Italy was ill-equipped to fight a total war. By the spring of 1941, the British army had pushed the Italians back into Libya while the Greeks mounted a strong resistance.

Hitler feared the consolidation of British power in Africa and was even more terrified of a British advance into eastern Europe. If Britain were able to build air bases in Greece, the Balkans would lie open to British bombing runs that could cripple the German war effort. Germany received 50 percent of its cereal and livestock from the Balkan region, 45 percent of its aluminum ore from Greece, 90 percent of its tin from Yugoslavia—and most of its oil from Romania. Without oil, there would be no *blitz* in *blitzkrieg*.

These considerations led Hitler to delay the invasion of the Soviet Union while the German army mopped up Mussolini's mess in the Balkans and North Africa. In April 1941, German armored units punched through Yugoslavian defenses and encircled the Yugoslav army. Greece came next. Meanwhile, in North Africa German troops recaptured all the territory taken by the British the previous year. As Map 27.2 shows, by the summer of 1941, Germany stood triumphant, with dramatic victories in North Africa and the Balkans. But these victories came at a high price: the postponement of the German invasion of the Soviet Union from April to June.

EARLY SUCCESS At first, that postponement seemed to matter little. On June 22, 1941, the largest invading force the world had yet seen began to cross the Soviet borders. Three million German soldiers, equipped with 2,770 modern aircraft and 3,350 tanks, went into battle. In a matter of days, most of the Soviet air force was destroyed. By October, the Germans had taken Kiev, besieged Leningrad, and stood 80 miles from Moscow. Almost 45 percent of the Soviet population was under German occupation, and the Germans controlled access to much of the Soviet Union's natural and industrial

GERMAN MASSACRE AT KERCH In one of the most famous Soviet photographs taken during the war, relatives try to identify their dead after German troops massacred all the men in the village of Kerch. Such atrocities as this strengthened the will of the Polish, Baltic, and Soviet peoples to resist their German occupiers.

resources, including more than 45 percent of its grain and 65 percent of its coal, iron, and steel. On October 10, Hitler's spokesman announced to the foreign press corps that the destruction of the Soviet Union was assured. German newspapers proclaimed, "CAMPAIGN IN THE EAST DECIDED!"[4]

Why was Germany so successful at the start of the invasion? Blitzkrieg provides part of the answer. Germany's spearhead force of tank and motorized infantry divisions shattered the Soviet defensive line and seized key targets. Stalin's stubborn refusal to believe that Hitler would violate the Non-Aggression Pact also weakened Russian defenses. Soviet intelligence sources sent in more than 80 warnings of an imminent German attack. Stalin classified these messages as "doubtful" and ordered the messengers themselves punished. Moreover, the initial German advance occurred in territories where Soviet rule had brought enormous suffering and where, therefore, the population had little reason to defend the Soviet state. Ukraine, for example, was still recovering from the Stalinist-inflicted famine of the 1930s, while eastern Poland and the Baltic states, which Stalin had gained through the German-Soviet Non-Aggression Pact, were still bleeding from the Soviet takeover in 1939.

THE FATAL WINTER Yet in the winter of 1940–1941, the German advance stalled. Leningrad resisted its besiegers, and Moscow remained beyond the Germans' reach. Three obstacles halted the German invasion. First, German atrocities strengthened local resistance against the occupiers. The troops in occupied Soviet territory treated the local populations with utter cruelty. SS and army units moved through eastern Poland, the Baltics, and Soviet lands, seizing key resources and murdering at will. The Nazi governor of Ukraine insisted, "I will pump every last thing out of this country."[5] By 1941, human-made famine devastated Ukraine and Galicia.

As partisan units worked behind the German lines, sabotaging their transportation routes, hijacking their supplies, and murdering their patrols, they found the Germans vulnerable to guerilla attack because of the second factor in halting the

REBUILDING THE INDUSTRIAL MIGHT OF THE SOVIET UNION The stalling of the German offensive in the winter of 1941–1942 gave the Soviet Union the essential advantage of time: time to rebuild their industrial strength. Thousands of factories were dismantled and shipped to safety east of the Urals. In this photo, workers begin the massive job of putting their factory back together. Before the war, they made railway cars. Now they would build tanks.

invasion: Germany's overstretched lines. Since June the German army had advanced so far so fast that it overstrained its supply and communication lines.

The weather, the third and most crucial obstacle for the Germans, worsened these logistical problems. Had the Germans invaded in April, as originally planned, they might have captured Moscow and pushed even further east well before winter set in. Instead, the crucial postponement meant that German troops were first mired in mud and then stuck in snow. An early October snowfall, which then melted, turned Russia's dirt roads to impassable mud. By the time the ground froze several weeks later, the German forces, like Napoleon's army 130 years earlier, were fighting the Russian winter. Subzero temperatures wreaked havoc with transportation lines. Horses froze to death, and machinery refused to start. Men fared just as badly. Dressed in lightweight spring uniforms, German soldiers fell victim to frostbite. By the end of the winter, the casualty list numbered more than 30 percent of the German East Army.

At the start of 1942, this army still occupied much of the Soviet Union and controlled the majority of its agricultural and industrial resources. More than three million Soviet soldiers had been killed and another three million captured. But the failure to deal the Soviets a quick death blow in 1941 gave Stalin and his high command a crucial advantage—*time*. During the German advance, Soviet laborers dismantled entire factories to transport them east, to areas out of German bombing range. Between August and October 1941, 80 percent of the Soviet war industry was in pieces. The *time* gained in the winter of 1941–1942 allowed the Soviets to put these pieces back together: They rebuilt their factories and focused the colossal productive power of the Soviet Union on the war effort. By 1943, Russia was outproducing Germany: 24,000 tanks versus 17,000; 130,000 artillery pieces versus 27,000; 35,000 combat aircraft versus 25,000. In a total war, in which victory occurs on the assembly line as well as on the front line, these statistics threatened Hitler's dreams of a German empire.

CHRONOLOGY: EUROPE AT WAR

1939
September
German-Soviet conquest of Poland.

1940
April 9
German blitzkrieg against Denmark and Norway begins.
May 10
Germans attack western Europe.
June 22
Fall of France.
July 10
Battle of Britain begins.
September 7
London Blitz begins.
September 17
Hitler cancels plans for invasion of Britain.

1941
March
U.S. Congress passes Lend-Lease Act.
April
German invasion of the Soviet Union postponed; German offensives in Yugoslavia, Greece, and North Africa.
June 22
German invasion of the Soviet Union begins.
December
German advance halted outside Moscow.

The World at War, 1941–1945

I n December 1941, as the German advance slowed in the Soviet Union, Japanese expansionism in the Pacific fused with the war in Europe and drew the United States into the conflict. Over the next four years, millions of soldiers, sailors, and civilians lost their lives in a gargantuan and complicated conflict waged around the world.

The Globalization of the War

Even before 1941, Europe's imperialist legacy ensured that World War II was not confined to Europe. Mussolini's desire to expand his Mediterranean empire pushed the fighting into North Africa, while Britain would never have been able to stand alone in 1940 against the German-occupied continent without access to the manpower and materials of its empire. German efforts to block British access to these resources spread the war into the Atlantic, where British merchant marines battled against German submarines to keep open the sea lanes to Britain.

Those sea lanes provided a crucial connection between Britain and the still-neutral United States, on whose resources Britain drew heavily. In March 1941, the U.S. Congress passed the **Lend-Lease Act**, which guaranteed that the United States would supply Britain with necessary military supplies, with payment postponed until after the war ended. The passage of Lend-Lease was one of the most important decisions in all of World War II. It gave first Britain and then the Soviets access to American industrial might.

As the United States drew closer to Britain, its relations with Japan grew more hostile. In 1941 the Japanese occupied Indochina, and the United States responded by placing an embargo on trade in oil with Japan. Japanese policymakers viewed the embargo as tantamount to an act of war. Japan's imperial ambitions demanded that it move decisively before its oil ran out. The South Pacific, a treasure house of mineral and other resources, beckoned.

Between December 7 and 10, 1941, Japanese forces attacked American, British, and Dutch territories in the Pacific—Hong Kong, Wake and Guam Islands, the Philippines, Malaya, and the American naval base at Pearl Harbor, Hawaii. After an attack that lasted only a few hours, the U.S. Pacific fleet lay gutted. Guam fell immediately, while Wake Island held out until December 23 and Hong Kong surrendered on Christmas Day. February saw both Malaya and Singapore in Japanese hands. By May, Japanese forces had conquered Indonesia, Burma, and the Philippines. As **Map 27.3** illustrates, in just a few months, the Japanese established themselves as imperial overlords of the South Pacific, with its wealth of raw materials.

The audacity of the Japanese attack impressed Hitler. Although he had long feared American industrial power, he joined Japan by declaring war on the United States on December 11, 1941. In Europe Germany now faced an alliance of Britain, the Soviet Union, and the United States. Yet even against this alliance, Germany appeared to occupy a strong position. By January a spectacular offensive in North Africa brought German forces within 200 miles of the strategically vital Suez Canal. In June the German army resumed its advance in the Soviet Union and soon threatened Russia's oil fields in the southern Caucasus. With Germany on the offensive in the Middle East and the Soviet Union, and Japan controlling the Pacific, the Allies looked poised to lose the war.

The Turning Point: Midway, El Alamein, and Stalingrad

Twelve months later the situation had changed, and the Allies were on the road to eventual victory. The second half of 1942 proved the turning point as three very different

---

Lend-Lease Act Passed in March 1941, the act gave Britain access to U.S. industrial products during World War II, with payment postponed for the duration of the war.

Read the Document

Japanese Total War Research Institute, Plan for the Greater East Asia Co-Prosperity Sphere, 1942

MAP **27.3** JAPAN'S TERRITORIAL AMBITIONS Lacking its own supply of natural resources, Japan embarked on imperial conquest. What mineral and agricultural resources were crucial? Which European powers lost territory to Japan?

battles transformed the course of the war. In the Pacific, victory at the Battle of Midway gave the U.S. forces a decisive advantage. In North Africa, British forces experienced their first battlefield victory at El Alamein. And in Europe, the Battle of Stalingrad dealt Germany a blow from which it never recovered.

THE BATTLE OF MIDWAY The Battle of Midway resulted from the Japanese effort to ensure its air supremacy by destroying U.S. aircraft carriers. To do so, the Japanese attacked Midway Island, a U.S. outpost, on June 4, 1942. By mid-morning the Japanese had shot down two-thirds of the American planes. But then an American dive-bomber group, which had gotten lost, suddenly found itself above the main Japanese carriers. Their decks cluttered with gas lines and bombs, these ships were caught in the act of refueling and rearming the strike force. In five minutes, the bombers destroyed three of Japan's four carriers. The fourth sank later in the day. The destruction of the Japanese carriers dealt Japan a blow from which it could not recover. The United States possessed the industrial resources to rebuild its lost ships and airplanes. Japan did not. In five explosive minutes at Midway the course of the Pacific war changed.

THE BATTLE OF EL ALAMEIN In contrast, the Battle of El Alamein marked the culmination of over two years of fighting in North Africa. As we have already seen, in the spring of 1941 German troops came to the aid of retreating Italian forces in Libya; by June 1941, they had muscled the British back into Egypt. For more than a year the two armies pushed each other back and forth across the desert. But finally the British caught the Germans by surprise at El Alamein in October 1942.

One month later combined British and American forces landed in Morocco and Algeria. Over the next six months they pushed Germany out of North Africa and secured a jumping-off point for their invasion of southern Italy in July 1943. El Alamein thus marked a turning point in the war. Churchill said of it, "It is not the beginning of the end, but it may be the end of the beginning."[6]

THE BATTLE OF STALINGRAD Churchill's apt description also fits the third turning point of 1942, the Battle of Stalingrad. In July the German army was sweeping south toward the oil-rich Caucasus. Hitler ordered the southern offensive split into two, with one arm reaching up to conquer Stalingrad on the Volga River. The conquest of Stalingrad would give the Germans control over the main waterway for the transport of oil and food from the Caucasus to the rest of the Soviet Union. But by dividing his offensive, Hitler widened his front from 500 to 2,500 miles. When the Germans reached Stalingrad on August 23, their resources were overstretched.

Stalin's generals assured him they could destroy the exposed German army—but only if Stalingrad could hold on for almost two months while they assembled the necessary men and machinery. An epic urban battle ensued, fought street by street, house by house, room by room. By November, Soviet troops had surrounded the Germans. When the German commander, General Friedrich von Paulus (d. 1953), requested permission to surrender, Hitler replied, "The army will hold its position to the last soldier and the last cartridge."[7] Paulus disobeyed orders and surrendered on January 30, 1943, but by then his army had almost ceased to exist. The Germans never made up the losses in manpower, material, or morale they suffered at Stalingrad.

The Allied Victory in Europe

Map 27.4 illustrates that the Allies moved to the offensive in 1943. The destructive fury of total war increased exponentially, as German military death statistics reveal: By July of 1944, 2.8 million German soldiers had died; in the remaining nine months of the war, another 4.8 million were killed.

THE INVASION OF ITALY Stalin had long been pleading with his Allies to relieve the pressure on Soviet troops by opening a "Second Front" in Europe. On July 10, 1943, British and American forces landed in Sicily, prepared to push up the Italian peninsula, described by Churchill as the "soft underbelly" of German-controlled Europe. The Italian offensive at first appeared a success. Within just 15 days, Mussolini had been overthrown and his successor opened peace negotiations with the Allies.

Yet the Italian invasion did not prove decisive. The German army occupied Italy, rescued Mussolini, and pushed back against the Allied offensive. Ridged with mountains and laced with rivers, the Italian peninsula formed a natural defensive fortress. In an eight-month period, Allied forces advanced only 70 miles.

THE DECISIVE FRONT The European war was thus decided not in the mountains of Italy, but in the East. Beginning in the summer of 1943, the Soviets steadily pushed back the Germans on a front that ran from Leningrad in the far north to the Crimea in the south. The battles between the Soviet Union and Nazi Germany were some of the largest military confrontations in history. An estimated 75 percent of German military losses in World War II came on the Eastern Front.

MAP **27.4** ALLIED VICTORY IN EUROPE, 1942–1945 In 1943, Allied forces moved onto the offensive. Where and when were the crucial battles? How does this map illustrate the pivotal role of the Eastern Front in deciding the outcome of the war?

The Soviet advance from 1943 on demonstrated that the Red Army had mastered and improved upon German blitzkrieg tactics. The Soviets concentrated their tanks into forces that combined motorized infantry regiments, tanks, antitank battalions, and mobile anti-aircraft artillery. They also multiplied their number of radios and field telephones to avoid the organizational chaos that had greeted the invasion of 1941.

Such mobile armored forces depended on factories churning out steel, rubber, oil, and all the various machine parts needed by a modern army. Achievements in industrial production thus constituted a key factor in the Soviet victory. While Lend-Lease supplied the Soviet Union with the basics needed to keep its army moving—aircraft and tanks, rails and locomotives, trucks and gasoline, and 15 million pairs of boots—the Soviets did not rely on imports alone. In 1943, Russia manufactured four times as many tanks as it imported, and Soviet production of tanks and antitank guns doubled Germany's.

THE FALL OF GERMANY As the Red Army closed in on Germany from the east, the British, Canadians, and Americans pushed in from the west. On June 6, 1944, the Allies carried out the largest amphibious operation in history. Five seaborne divisions (two American, two British, and one Canadian) and three airborne divisions (two American and one British) crossed the English Channel and landed on the coast of northern France. The **D-Day** landings illustrated the Allied advantage in manpower and material. Against the Allies' eight divisions, the Germans had four and against the Allies' 5,000 fighter planes, the Germans could send up 169.

Yet the strength of the German resistance—particularly on Omaha Beach, where U.S. troops sustained more than 4,000 casualties—signaled that the road to Berlin

D-Day Common term for June 6, 1944, when 150,000 Allied troops landed on the shores of northern France to open an effective second front against German-occupied Europe.

CHRONOLOGY: 1942: THE TURNING POINT

1941

December 7
Japan bombs Pearl Harbor.
December 11
Germany declares war
on United States.

[1941]

1942

January 21
German offensive begins in North
Africa.
February 15
Surrender of British forces to Japan
at Singapore.
April 22
British retreat from Burma.
May 6
Japan completes conquest
of the Philippines.
June 4
Battle of Midway.
August 7
First U.S. Marine landing
on Guadalcanal.
August 23
German Sixth Army reaches
Stalingrad.
October 23
Battle of El Alamein begins.
November 8
Anglo-American landing in North
Africa begins.
November 23
German Sixth Army cut off
at Stalingrad.

[1942]

would not be easy. The Allies faced the task of uprooting the Germans from territory where they had planted themselves five years earlier. For 10 months, American, British, and other Allied troops fought a series of hard-won battles.

As these troops pushed in on Germany from the west, the Soviets accelerated their onslaught in the east. Just over two weeks after D-Day—and three years to the day since Germany had invaded the Soviet Union—the Soviet army mounted Operation Bagration, described by one historian as "the most overwhelming single military assault in history."[8] Two and a half million Soviet troops attacked along a 450-mile front that ran from the Baltics through Byelorussia (Belarus). Outmanned and outgunned, the Germans broke. One Polish civilian, who saw the Germans retreating, wrote, "They were no longer soldiers, but moving human tatters."[9] By early August, Soviet tank units were within reach of Warsaw, and Hitler's dream of a 1,000-year Reich was crumbling (see Map 27.4).

In March 1945, the Soviet army approached Berlin from the east and the British and American armies reached Germany's Rhine border. The Allies agreed to leave the conquest of Berlin to the Soviet Army. In this climactic battle of the European war, 320,000 Germans, many of them young boys, fought three million Soviet troops. Even so, it took 11 days before the city's commander surrendered on May 2. Two days earlier, Hitler took a cyanide capsule and then shot himself. On May 7, 1945, General Alfred Jodl (1890–1946) signed the unconditional surrender of German forces.

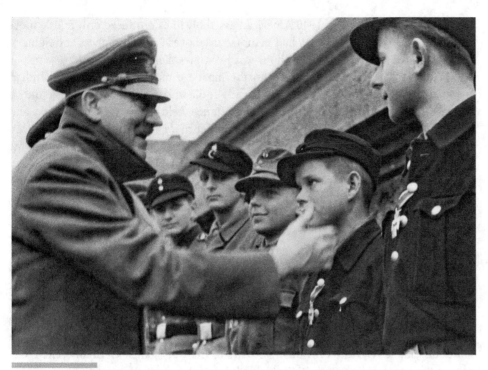

THE BATTLE FOR BERLIN On April 20, 1945, Hitler celebrated his fifty-sixth birthday and made a rare visit out of his Berlin bunker to visit with the troops defending his city. As this photograph shows, these "soldiers" were just children. Ten days later, Hitler committed suicide.

The Air War, the Atom Bomb, and the Fall of Japan

When Germany surrendered in the spring of 1945, the war in the Pacific still raged. After the Midway battle of 1942, the United States steadily, but slowly, agonizingly, pushed the Japanese back island by island. Japanese industry could not make up for the weapons and ammunition expended in these battles. In contrast, American factories were

CHRONOLOGY: THE LONG MARCH TOWARD ALLIED VICTORY

1943

February
German surrender at Stalingrad;
Red Army goes on the offensive;
Allied round-the-clock bombing
of Germany begins. — **1943**
May
German surrender in North Africa.
July 10
Allied invasion of Italy begins.

1944

January
Lifting of the siege of Leningrad.
June 4
Allies liberate Rome.
June 6 — **1944**
D-Day landings; Allied offensive
in France begins.
June 22
Operation Bagration begins.
August 24–26
Allied liberation of Paris.
September
Allies liberate the Netherlands,
Belgium, and Luxembourg.
October
U.S. invasion of the Philippines.

just gearing up. Whereas in 1940 American assembly lines produced only a little more than 2,000 aircraft, by 1944 they had manufactured over 96,000 bombers and fighters. American productivity per worker hour was five times that of Japan.

While U.S. troops moved closer to the Japanese mainland, British and Indian troops rebuffed a Japanese attempt to invade India and pushed the Japanese out of Burma. Australian forces, with American assistance, held the line at New Guinea and forestalled a Japanese invasion of Australia. By February 1945, then, when American marines landed on the small island of Iwo Jima, just 380 miles from Japan's home islands, the Japanese war effort was in tatters and an Allied victory ensured.

Obtaining this final victory, however, was not easy. In the month of fighting on Iwo Jima, one-third of the American landing force died or suffered injury. The April conquest of Okinawa was even more hard-won. Outnumbered two to one, the Japanese endured staggering losses—110,000 of the 120,000 soldiers on the island died. Yet they still inflicted serious damage on the attacking force, killing or wounding 50,000 Americans before the fight was over. Nobody counted how many Okinawans died in a battle they had done nothing to provoke, although estimates ranged as high as 160,000.

THE AIR WAR After the capture of Iwo Jima and Okinawa, American forces had the bases needed to bomb Japanese cities. This air war utilized tactics and technologies the Allies developed over the previous five years in the war against Germany. Their victory in the Battle of Britain in 1940 shielded the British from an invasion but not from bombing. By May 1941, German planes had bombed almost every major industrial city in Britain, killing 43,000 noncombatants. But from January 1941 on, British bombers retaliated in kind, and as the war wore on, developed new techniques of airborne destruction. In May 1942, for example, British planes destroyed Cologne with the world's first 1,000-bomber raid. One year later, the British bombing of Hamburg created the world's first **firestorm**. In this human-made catastrophe, fires (caused by incendiary bombs) combine with winds to suck the oxygen out of the air and raise temperatures to combustible levels. As one survivor of the Hamburg bombing recalled, "The smallest children lay like fried eels on the pavement."[10] More than 500,000 German civilians died in Allied bombing attacks. Twenty percent of those were children.

To defeat Japan, the U.S. air command adopted the tactics that the British had perfected in the skies over Germany. On a single March evening, American bombs and the ensuing firestorm killed 85,000 residents of Tokyo. Over the next five months, American bombers hit 66 Japanese cities, burned 180 square miles, and killed approximately 330,000 Japanese. At the same time, a U.S. naval blockade cut Japan off from its supply lines.

THE MANHATTAN PROJECT While American bombers pulverized Japanese cities during the spring and summer of 1945, a multinational group of scientists fought a different battle in a secret military installation in New Mexico. The **Manhattan Project**, the code name for the joint British-American-Canadian effort to construct an atom bomb, was an extraordinary endeavor, the biggest and most expensive weapons development project up to that point in history. Yet even American vice president Harry Truman did not know about the project until after President Roosevelt died.

The Manhattan Project originated as part of the war against Nazi Germany. When the European war began, a number of scientists—many of them eastern and central European émigrés who had fled the Nazis, and many of them Jewish—feared that Germany might develop an atom bomb. They pressured the British and American governments to build the Bomb before Hitler did. Britain took the initial lead by creating a committee to oversee atomic research in the spring of 1940. British research persuaded the Americans that an atom bomb could be constructed and in October 1941—two months *before* Japan bombed Pearl Harbor—Roosevelt and Churchill created an atomic partnership. For three years the Manhattan Project scientists labored to unlock the atom's

firestorm Catastrophe in which fires combine with winds to suck the oxygen out of the air and raise temperatures to combustible levels. First experienced during the British bombing of the German city of Hamburg in World War II.

Manhattan Project Code name given to the secret Anglo-American project that resulted in the construction of the atom bomb during World War II.

power. They succeeded on July 16, 1945, when the world's first atomic explosion—the Trinity test—detonated over the desert of New Mexico. But by the time of the Trinity test, Nazi Germany had already fallen. The threat of a Nazi atom bomb disappeared.

The Pacific War, however, raged on. The decision to use atom bombs against Japan generated immediate controversy. Many of the scientists on the Manhattan Project opposed the decision as a step across a crucial moral dividing line, as did important American military officials such as General Dwight Eisenhower (1890–1969), supreme commander of the Allied forces in Europe, and General Douglas MacArthur (1880–1964), supreme Allied commander in the Pacific. Those in favor of the decision argued that if atom bombs were not used, the Allies would have to invade Japan. U.S. Army planners warned that if casualty rates were as high as those on Okinawa, the numbers of Americans killed in the first phase of the invasion could reach 50,000. Admiral William Leahy (Truman's Chief of Staff) and others, however, argued that an invasion was not necessary, that if the Allies maintained the naval blockade and continued to attack Japanese cities with conventional bombs, Japan would surrender by the end of the year. From President Truman's perspective, however, continuing the war—with or without an invasion of Japan—meant continuing to put Allied soldiers in harm's way. The Bomb promised to end the war quickly and bring Allied servicemen home.

A LIGHT BRIGHTER THAN A THOUSAND SUNS At 8:15 A.M. on August 6, 1945, an American plane named the *Enola Gay* (after the pilot's mother) dropped an atom bomb above the city of Hiroshima (see Map 27.3). A light "brighter than a thousand suns" flashed in the sky. Temperatures at the site of the atomic explosion reached 5,400 degrees Fahrenheit. All those exposed within two miles of the center suffered primary thermal burns—their blood literally boiled and their skin peeled off in strips. Of Hiroshima's wartime population of 400,000, 140,000 died by the end of 1945, with another 60,000 dying in the next five years.

The Japanese reacted to the atomic bombing of Hiroshima with incomprehension and confusion. They did not know what had hit them. Within the high levels of the Japanese government, gradual realization of the atomic bomb's power strengthened the position of those officials who recognized that Japan must now give up. A hard-line faction of the military, however, wished to fight on.

Then, on August 8, the Soviet Union declared war on Japan. The next day American forces dropped an atom bomb on the city of Nagasaki and killed 70,000 outright (with another 70,000 dying over the next five years). On August 10, Emperor Hirohito (1901–1989) told his military leaders to surrender. Viewed in the West as an implacable warlord, Hirohito actually possessed fairly limited political power and had been pressing for peace since June. Negotiations between the Allies and the Japanese continued until August 15, when the war ended.

Read the Document

The Franck Report

Read the Document

John Siemes, An Eyewitness to Hiroshima

MUSHROOM CLOUD The detonation of the atomic bomb over Hiroshima on August 6, 1945, produced what would become one of the most familiar images of the post–World War II age.

CHRONOLOGY: THE END OF WORLD WAR II, 1945

March 16
American victory on Iwo Jima. — **March**

April
April
Red Army encircles Berlin.
April 11
American troops reach Elbe River
in Germany.
April 30
Hitler commits suicide.

May 7
VE Day: Official German surrender. — **May**

June — *June 22*
American victory at Okinawa.

August 6
United States drops atomic
bomb on Hiroshima.
August 8
Soviet Union enters war — **August**
against Japan.
August 9
United States drops atomic
bomb on Nagasaki.

September — *September 2*
V-J Day: Formal Japanese
surrender.

In Hiroshima and Nagasaki, however, another fight was underway, this time against an unseen and at first unrecognized enemy: radiation. The lingering horror of radiation sickness, which many Americans and British first dismissed as Japanese propaganda, signaled that the atom bomb was not just a bigger weapon. In the months after the war's end, both policymakers and ordinary people came to recognize that the revolutionary new force of atomic power had introduced the world to new possibilities—and new horrors.

The Wars Within the War

27.4 What were the context, causes, and consequences of genocide during World War II?

Armies and advanced weaponry tell only part of the story of World War II. Inside and alongside the military war, other wars raged.

THE EASTERN KILLING ZONE Most of the killing occurred in what the historian Timothy Snyder has termed the "bloodlands," the multilinguistic, multiethnic regions from central Poland in the west to western Russia in the east and embracing Ukraine, Belarus, and the Baltics.[11] The "bloodlands" first endured the expansion of Stalinist rule and then became a laboratory for genocide. Civilian death counts in this killing zone are staggering. By the war's end, 20 percent of Poland's prewar population was dead. So, too, were over three million Ukrainian civilians. Half of the prewar population of Belarus had either died or been displaced.

As specified in the secret clauses of the German-Soviet Non-Aggression Pact, the Soviet Union occupied eastern Poland and the Baltic states in 1939. Immediately the inhabitants of these regions endured the full ferocity of Stalinist terror. In Poland, for example, over 400,000 individuals, primarily ethnic Poles and Jews, were deported to the Gulag—pulled out of their homes, deprived of their possessions, crowded onto freezing freight cars, and trundled hundreds of miles eastward. Another 30,000 were executed as Stalinist forces moved to establish control over Polish society, including 22,000 army officers who were gunned down and buried in ditches in the Katyn forest and surrounding region.

Meanwhile, German-occupied Poland became the staging ground for the Nazi racial reordering of Europe. As **Map 27.5** shows, Germany annexed much of western Poland, which Hitler envisaged as prime territory for German "re-colonization." Between September 1939 and June 1941, a brutal deportation program forced Poles and Jews out of their homes. The remainder of German-held Poland, or the "General Government," became the dumping ground for deported Poles and Jews and a vast labor reservoir for the German war effort. Hitler intended the Slavic populations, defined in his racist hierarchy as biologically inferior, to serve as a labor pool for their German superiors. To reduce the Polish people to slaves, the Nazis attempted to destroy Polish society and culture. They seized businesses and bank accounts, replaced Polish place names with German names, closed universities and high schools, and murdered Polish intellectuals and professionals.

The German invasion of the Soviet Union (including Soviet-occupied Poland and the Baltics) intensified this race-based violence and extended the killing zone. As we saw earlier in this chapter, the advancing German army treated the local populations with horrifying brutality and deployed mass starvation as a weapon of war. Dreaming of transforming Ukraine into a vast German agricultural colony, the Nazis viewed the local populations as completely expendable.

MAP **27.5** POLAND DURING WORLD WAR II In September 1939, the Germans and Soviets invaded and divided Poland between them. The Germans split their territory in two. Western Poland became part of Greater Germany, with the Polish and Jewish residents displaced to make room for new German settlers. The rest of German-occupied Poland became the General Government, a vast forced labor and killing zone. Where were the death camps located? What factors explain this location?

The War Against the Jews

The war against the Jews, usually called the **Holocaust** or the Shoah, took place within this political context of racial reordering and within the physical context of the "bloodlands." According to Nazi racial ideology, two "races" posed an inherent threat to the Reich: the Roma (Gypsies) and Jews. War gave the Nazis the opportunity to attempt what had seemed impossible: the complete destruction of these peoples. Somewhere between 220,000 and 600,000 Romani died in the *Porajmos*—the Devouring—including almost all those living in the Baltic states and Czechoslovakia. The much larger Jewish population of Europe was, however, the special target of Hitler's hatred. The Holocaust claimed the lives of approximately six million Jews. Children were especially vulnerable. Of the Jewish children living in 1939 in the regions already or soon to be under German control, only 11 percent survived.

Holocaust Adolf Hitler's effort to murder all the Jews in Europe during World War II.

View the Map

The Holocaust

867

THE EVOLUTION OF THE "FINAL SOLUTION" In 1939, the Nazi government had no defined "Jewish policy," even as the conquest of western Poland brought almost two million Jews under German control. Amidst vague plans of exporting the Jewish population eastward or even to the African island of Madagascar, German officials in Poland focused on identifying Jews and moving them into isolated and easily controlled areas. Under this policy of "ghettoization," the German occupiers expelled Jews from their homes and confined them in ghettos sealed off from their non-Jewish neighbors. Packed into overcrowded apartments, with inadequate food and sanitation, the ghetto populations lived in a nightmare of disease, starvation, and death. In the almost two-year period between the invasion of Poland and the invasion of the Soviet Union, an estimated 30,000 Jews died, killed outright by German soldiers or dead from starvation and disease as a result of deportation and ghettoization. Yet the suffering had only begun.

The invasion of the Soviet Union provided the context in which Nazi policy shifted to outright mass murder. Alongside the regular German army marched special units of the SS called *Einsatzgruppen* ("strike forces"). With the army providing logistical support, these small motorized units (about 3,000 men in all) took on the task of murdering Jews. Most of these murders followed the same general pattern: SS soldiers—often aided by local populations—rounded up all of the Jewish men, women, and children in a town or village and marched them in batches to a field or woods. They ordered the first batch to dig a large ditch. They stripped their victims of their clothing, lined them up on the edge of the ditch, and shot them at point-blank range. They then lined up subsequent batches and shot them as well, so that by the end of a day's worth of killing, dead and dying bodies filled the ditch. A thin layer of soil thrown on top transformed the ditch into a mass grave. Estimates of the final death count of the Einsatzgruppen actions range from 1.5 to 2 million, including almost the entirety of the historic Jewish communities in the Baltics and Ukraine.

In December of 1941, with the German military offensive in the Soviet Union stalled, Hitler called for the total annihilation of European Jews, whom he blamed for Germany's military disasters. On January 20, 1942, senior German officials met in a villa in Wannsee, outside Berlin, to draw up plans for genocide, which they termed the **Final Solution**. Even the Jewish populations in neutral countries such as Sweden and Ireland showed up on the target list. The Wannsee Conference marked the beginning of a more systematic approach to murdering European Jews.

This systematic approach built on the experience in mass murder gained by the Einsatzgruppen. By trial and error, these squads discovered the most efficient ways of identifying and rounding up Jews, shooting them, and burying the bodies. But the Einsatzgruppen actions also revealed the limits of conventional methods of killing. Shooting took time, used up valuable ammunition, and required many men. Moreover, even well-trained and indoctrinated soldiers cracked under the strain of shooting unarmed women and children at close range. The Nazis needed a technological approach, one that would provide a comfortable distance between the killers and the killed. The death camp filled this need.

Final Solution Nazi term for the effort to murder every Jew in Europe during World War II.

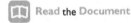 Read the Document

The Wannsee Protocol

 Watch the Video

The Origins of the Holocaust

GENOCIDE BY ASSEMBLY LINE *Death camps* were not the same as *concentration camps*. From 1933 on, Hitler's government sentenced communists, homosexuals, Jehovah's Witnesses, Romani, and anyone else defined as an enemy of the regime to forced labor in concentration camps. After the war began, the camp system expanded dramatically throughout German-controlled Europe. Concentration camps became an essential part of the Nazi war economy. Important German businesses set up factories inside or right next to camps, to have ready access to their supplies of slave labor. Concentration camp inmates died in huge numbers from brutal physical labor, torture, and diseases linked to malnutrition, inadequate shelter, and poor sanitation. Yet death in these camps was a by-product rather than central aim. In contrast, the death camps of

EINSATZGRUPPEN ACTION   A soldier shoots the last remaining Jew in a Ukrainian village.

Belzec, Majdanek, Sobibor, and Treblinka had only one purpose: murder, primarily the murder of Jews.

Beginning in early 1942, Jewish ghettos throughout Poland emptied. Selected in batches, groups received orders to gather at the railway station for deportation to "work camps" farther east. Soldiers packed them into cattle cars, more than 100 people per car, all standing up for the entire journey. Deprived of food and water, with hardly any air, often for several days, many died en route. (See *Justice in History* in this chapter.)

The survivors stumbled off the trains into a vast machine of death. Forced to undress, they were then herded into a fake communal shower—actually a gas chamber. After the poison had done its work, Jewish slaves emptied the chamber and buried the bodies in mass graves or burned the bodies in crematoria, modeled after industrial bake ovens. The death camps thus used the techniques and technologies of industrial production for human destruction. Along a murderous assembly line, the human raw material moved from arrival through selection to undressing rooms to the gas chamber to the crematoria.

THE DEATH FACTORY OF AUSCHWITZ-BIRKENAU Auschwitz-Birkenau combined the labor camp with the death camp. Auschwitz originated in 1940 as a concentration camp for Poles and, after 1941, for Soviet POWs. It grew into an industrial complex covering several square miles, with barracks for 70,000 prisoners who slaved in its coal mines, synthetic rubber and oil factories, and several smaller military industries. Its inmate population eventually included not only Poles and Russians, but also peoples from across Europe. Given just enough food for survival (the official diet permitted a prisoner to remain alive for an average of three months), Auschwitz's inmates endured daily hard labor and the constant, indiscriminate brutality of their captors.

Once the "Final Solution" was underway, Auschwitz's cruel empire expanded to encompass a death camp: Birkenau. Jews deemed strong enough (never more than 20 percent of a typical transport) were selected for hard labor in the main camp. The rest perished in Birkenau's gas chambers, their bodies burned in one of five crematoria. The writer Elie Wiesel, deported to Auschwitz with his family when he was 15, recalled the selection process:

> 'Men to the left! Women to the right!' Eight words spoken quietly, indifferently, without emotion. Eight short, simple words. Yet that was the moment when I parted from my mother.[12]

Wiesel's mother and younger sister, and almost one million others, died in the gas chambers of Auschwitz-Birkenau.

Read the Document

The Holocaust—Memoirs from the Commandant of Auschwitz

THE ALLIES' RESPONSE Allied leaders had access to information about the Holocaust from very early on. In July 1939, before the war had begun, Polish Intelligence provided the British government with a copy of "Enigma," the German coding machine. Throughout the war, then, British code breakers translated German military radio transmissions such as this one from an Einsatzgruppen unit in the Soviet Union on August 27, 1941: "Regiment South shot 914 Jews; the special action staff with police battalion 320 shot 4,200 Jews." By June 1942, Allied leaders knew that death camps existed and in December of that year the British and American governments issued an inter-Allied declaration that described and condemned Hitler's efforts to murder European Jews.

Despite this public acknowledgment, the Allies did not act directly to stop the killings. Should the Allies then be considered bystanders in the crime of the Holocaust? Some historians contend that anti-Semitism in both British and American societies prevented their leaders from exploring ways to stop the Holocaust (such as sending in commando units, bombing the rail lines into the death camps, or even bombing the camps themselves). Other historians argue that these alternatives were not militarily feasible and that the Allies did the only thing they could do for Europe's Jews: Win the war as quickly as possible.

In the months after the war ended, Allied leaders struggled to bring Nazi leaders to trial to account for their crimes. What one participant called "the greatest trial in history" opened in November 1945. For 11 months, a four-man tribunal—American, British, French, and Soviet—sat in a courtroom in the German city of Nuremberg to judge 19 prominent German military, political, and industrial leaders. The **Nuremberg trials** introduced the category of "crimes against humanity" into international law. The participation of the Soviets, however, undercut the trials' effectiveness. The judges carefully avoided any mention of the Soviets' own war crimes of forcible deportation and mass murder.

Nuremberg trials Post-World War II trials of members of the Nazi Party and German military; conducted by an international tribunal.

Watch the Video

Conformity and Opposition in Nazi Germany

Resistance Label given to the many different underground political and partisan movements directed against Nazi rule in German-occupied Europe during World War II.

The Resistance and Its Limits

Throughout German-occupied Europe, Jewish and non-Jewish Europeans joined the **Resistance**, the underground struggle against Nazi rule. Resistance movements hid

Justice in History
The Trial of Adolf Eichmann

O n May 23, 1960, David Ben-Gurion (1886–1973), the prime minister of Israel, made a spectacular announcement: Israeli secret service agents had kidnapped Adolf Eichmann, a wanted Nazi war criminal, and smuggled him into Israel to await trial. As the head of the Gestapo's Jewish Affairs unit, Eichmann had sorted through the complicated bureaucratic procedures to ensure that European Jews moved expeditiously along the murderous assembly line, from identification to ghettoization to deportation to death. After the war Eichmann fled to Argentina, where, as "Ricardo Klement," he lived a quiet, respectable life with his wife and children—until 1960.

From the moment of Ben-Gurion's sensational announcement, the Eichmann case occupied the attention of the world. Six hundred foreign correspondents attended the trial, one of the first to be filmed by television cameras. More than 120 witnesses, many of them Holocaust survivors, testified.

The Eichmann trial told the story of Jewish suffering during World War II to the widest possible audience. Both Ben-Gurion and the chief prosecutor, Gideon Hausner, saw the trial as "a living record of a gigantic human and national disaster" that would educate the world in the causes and consequences of the Holocaust.[13] In his emotional opening statement, Hausner described himself as the spokesman for "six million accusers . . . [whose] ashes were piled up in the hills of Auschwitz and in the fields of Treblinka, or washed away by the rivers of Poland."[14]

By the time the prosecution rested its case, it was clear that Eichmann had played an essential role in the murder of millions. Yet the Eichmann trial attracted an enormous amount of criticism and continues to arouse great controversy. Critics charged that to achieve *moral justice* for Holocaust victims and survivors, the Israeli court committed a *legal injustice* against Eichmann. Not only did Eichmann's kidnapping violate international law, but the trial itself was filled with irregularities, including the introduction of testimony that did not pertain to the specific crimes charged. Critics also disputed Israel's legal right to try Eichmann: The crimes had not occurred in Israeli territory, nor were Eichmann's victims Israeli citizens. (The state of Israel did not exist until 1948.)

EICHMANN ON TRIAL Adolf Eichmann sits behind bulletproof glass and is guarded by Israeli soldiers.

In reply to these critics, Hausner and other supporters of the prosecution insisted that justice demanded that Eichmann be brought to trial and that the Israeli government had pursued the only course of action open to it. In the Eichmann trial, then, we confront a case in which what was legal on the one hand and what was just on the other appeared very much at odds. There is no doubt that Eichmann was guilty of horrendous crimes. There is also no doubt that the Israeli government stepped beyond established legal boundaries in trying and condemning Eichmann.

The Eichmann trial also raised important questions about the nature of the Holocaust. Was it a crime perpetrated by a few evil men, or did the evil penetrate deep into German, and European, society? The prosecution's case sought to depict Eichmann as a monster, a demonic mastermind responsible for the deaths of millions of Jews. As Hausner contended, "it was [Eichmann's] word that put gas chambers into action; he lifted the telephone, and railway trains left for the extermination centers; his signature it was that sealed the doom of tens of thousands."[15] Such a depiction provided a comforting explanation for the Holocaust—monstrous devils rather than ordinary human beings perpetrated this colossal crime.

Yet many trial observers and subsequent historians argued that such a depiction was wrong. This argument structured the most well-known critique of the prosecution— Hannah Arendt's *Eichmann in Jerusalem: A Report on the Banality of Evil,* published in 1963. Arendt (1906–1975), a Jewish philosopher who had fled Nazi Europe in 1941, argued that the trial showed Eichmann to be a plodding bureaucrat obsessed with trivial details—an ordinary man, capable of extraordinary evil.

Should ordinary men be held responsible for following evil orders? Defense attorney Robert Servatius insisted that the Holocaust was an "act of state," a crime carried out by a political regime, for which no civil servant could bear the blame. Eichmann only did as he was told. Servatius concluded his arguments by

(continued on next page)

(continued from previous page)

asking Eichmann how he viewed "this question of guilt." Eichmann replied,

> Where there is no responsibility, there can be no guilt. . . . I condemn and regret the act of extermination of the Jews which the leadership of the German state ordered. But I myself could not jump over my own shadow. I was a tool in the hands of superior powers and authorities.[16]

Eichmann's judges disagreed. In declaring Eichmann guilty of genocide, they argued,

> We reject absolutely the accused's version that he was nothing more than a "small cog" in the extermination machine. . . . He was not a puppet in the hands of others. His place was among those who pulled the strings.[17]

Eichmann died by hanging on May 31, 1962, the first execution in Israel, which had abolished capital punishment for all crimes except genocide.

For Discussion

1. What if Eichmann really was only "a tool in the hands of superior powers and authorities"? Would he still have been responsible for his actions?
2. In the Eichmann case, the letter of the law and justice appeared at odds. In what situations—if any—must we break the law to ensure that justice prevails? Who has the authority to make such a judgment?

Taking It Further

Cesarini, David. *Becoming Eichmann: Rethinking the Life, Crimes, and Trial of a "Desk Murderer."* 2004. A fascinating exploration of Eichmann's life and significance.

The Trial of Adolf Eichmann: Record of Proceedings in the District Court of Jerusalem. Vols. 1–9. 1993–1995. The basic primary source.

Jews and others on the run, disrupted transportation systems, assassinated Nazi officials, and relayed secret information to the Allies. In Poland, the Resistance developed into a secret "state within a state" that included an underground parliament, school system, printing press, and a "Home Army" of 350,000 men and women. In areas where the terrain offered shelter for guerillas (such as parts of the Soviet Union and the mountainous regions of Yugoslavia, Italy, and southern France), the Resistance formed partisan groups that attacked German army units.

The story of the Resistance is one of great heroism, yet only a minority of Europeans joined. The Germans' military strength and ruthlessness made resistance seem futile. In one of the best-known cases, Jews in the Warsaw ghetto rose up in the spring of 1943 and—armed with only one or two submachine guns and a scattering of pistols, rifles, hand grenades, and gasoline bombs—held off the Germans for more than a month. But in the end, the Germans leveled the ghetto and deported its survivors to death camps.

The German policy of exacting collective retribution also undercut mass support for anti-German efforts. In 1942, for example, British intelligence forces parachuted Czech agents into German-held Czechoslovakia. The agents assassinated the chief SS official in the region, Reinhard Heydrich (1904–1942), but they were immediately betrayed. In retaliation, the Germans massacred the entire population of the village of Lidice.

In countries allied to (rather than conquered by) the Germans, potential resisters had to convince themselves that patriotism demanded working against their own government. Thus, in France until 1943, joining the Resistance meant opposing the lawfully instituted collaborationist Vichy government. As a result, many French men and women viewed Resistance fighters as traitors, not heroes. By 1943, however, an alternative focus of national loyalty had emerged: the Free French headed by General Charles De Gaulle (1890–1970). De Gaulle had gone into exile rather than accept the armistice with Nazi Germany. After the Anglo-American landings in North Africa in November 1942, De Gaulle claimed Algeria as a power base, declared himself the head of a Free French provisional government, and called on all loyal French men and women to resist Nazi rule and Vichy collaboration.

Civil War and Nationalist Savagery

Divisions within the Resistance both limited its impact and increased the human costs of the war. In Greece, for example, the communist-dominated National Liberation Front battled a rival Resistance group that fought for the return of the Greek monarchy.

View the **Closer Look**   Liberating the Concentration Camps

27.1

27.2

27.3

27.4

27.5

THE LIBERATION OF BUCHENWALD CONCENTRATION CAMP IN GERMANY, APRIL 25, 1945 A German woman cries as she is led, with other German citizens, past a pile of murdered prisoners at Buchenwald. The crowd in this picture is a group of people from a nearby town, brought to view the camps so they could not deny what had taken place.

There was, then, no single "Resistance," and fighting among Resistance groups often shaded into civil war.

The bloodletting in Yugoslavia exemplifies this link between the Resistance and civil war. The Nazi puppet state of Croatia, established after the German invasion of 1941, enthusiastically adopted policies of mass murder aimed at Jews, Muslims, and Serbs. The Resistance movement that emerged in Croatia and the rest of Yugoslavia split along both nationalist and political lines. The "Chetniks," Serbian guerillas who supported the return of the exiled Serb monarchy and the restoration of Serbian supremacy in Yugoslavia, not only fought Croats and Germans (and slaughtered Jews and Muslims), but also battled the communist "Partisans." Led by Josip Broz (1892–1980), alias "Tito," these Partisans won the civil war, drove the Germans out of Yugoslavia, and established a postwar communist state. Beneath the uniform surface created by communist ideology, however, the jagged edges of nationalist division in Yugoslavia remained sharp.

In the killing zones of the East—the Baltic states, Belarus, Ukraine, and eastern Poland—the retreat of German forces from 1943 on ushered in a period of vicious conflict between nationalist groups who sought to position themselves for postwar supremacy. Ukrainian guerilla groups, for example, attacked German and Polish settlements in territory that they had staked out for an independent Ukraine. At least 50,000 Poles died, with tens of thousands of others forced to flee westward. "Liquidate all Polish traces," a Ukrainian partisan ordered, "pay attention to the fact that when something remains that is Polish, then the Poles will have pretensions to our land."[18] In response, Polish units in Galicia and eastern Poland turned on their Ukrainian neighbors.

Under Occupation and on the Home Front

27.5 What did total war mean for civilians in the occupied regions and on the home front?

For the men, women, and children in the occupied zones of Europe, there was no "home front"; the war's reach extended everywhere. But even in states not under enemy occupation, the home front was not a place of safety, but a place where a different kind of war was underway. World War II obliterated the distinction between combatant and noncombatant, blurred gender roles, and provoked calls for radical social change.

Occupation Policies and Forced Labor

We have already seen in this chapter that in German-occupied Europe, Nazi racial ideals determined ordinary people's reality. The Nazis drew a sharp line between western Europeans—the Dutch, Norwegian, Danes, and Flemish, all considered of racially superior "Germanic stock"—and the Slavs of eastern Europe. The Nazis believed that "Germanic" peoples could be taught to become good Nazis and therefore spared them the extreme violence that characterized German occupation in the east.

Yet German occupation in the west, although less brutal than in the east, remained harsh. Anyone who spoke out against the Nazis faced imprisonment or death. The Nazis forced occupied countries to pay exorbitant sums to cover the costs of their own occupation and to sell manufactured products and raw materials to Germany at artificially low prices. The occupation grew even more fierce after 1943 as German military losses piled up, stocks of food and other supplies dwindled, and German demands for civilian labor increased.

For millions of men and women in both eastern and western Europe, the war meant forced labor in Germany. With the need to free up men for the front lines, the Nazis faced labor shortages in almost every economic sector. Placing the economy on an all-out war footing would have meant imposing unpopular measures such as conscripting women for industrial labor, lengthening working hours, and prohibiting holidays. The Nazis chose instead to "recruit" labor from conquered territories. By August 1944, German farmers and factory owners employed over 5.7 million foreign civilian laborers (one-third of whom were women) and almost two million POWs. These foreign workers accounted for more than half the labor in German agriculture and munitions plants and one-third of the labor force in key war industries such as mining, chemicals, and metals.

Foreign labor not only fueled the German war machine, it also maintained German civilian morale. Foreign labor cushioned Germans on the home front from the impact of total war and reassured them that they belonged to a superior race. Nazi regulations stipulated that German workers regard themselves as the masters of the foreigners working alongside them. Many German factory owners were relieved to find they now employed laborers with few political rights. The director of one aircraft manufacturing firm explained, "The great advantage of employing foreigners . . . is that we only have to give orders. There is no refusal, no need to negotiate."[19]

ΟΙ ΗΡΩΙΔΕΣ ΤΟΥ 1940

"THE HEROINES OF 1940" Designed in 1946, this Greek poster commemorated the contributions of women in the Greek Resistance movement.

The Women's War

World War II was in every way a women's war. The bombs falling on urban neighborhoods did not distinguish between sexes; forced labor, mass deportation, and genocide all swept up women as well as men. In occupied countries, women fought and died in the Resistance. In countries not occupied by enemy forces, women tended to bear the brunt of home front deprivation, as they were usually the ones who had to get a meal on the table and clothe their children in the face of severe rationing. Basic household goods such as frying pans, toothbrushes, bicycle tires, baby bottles, and batteries almost disappeared. Food was in short supply and clothing had to be recycled. Women became experts at "make do and mend," as British government pamphlets advised.

In total war, military victory depended on the women in the assembly lines as well as the men in the front lines, and so women were mobilized for war work. British women did not serve in combat, but they were drafted for service in civilian defense, war-related industry, or the armed forces. Women accounted for 25 percent of the civilians who worked in Britain's Air Raid Protection services as wardens, rescuers, and telephone operators. The numbers of women employed in male-dominated industries such as metals and chemicals rose dramatically.

Only the Soviet Union mobilized women more fully than Britain. Soviet women constituted 80 percent of the agricultural and 50 percent of the industrial labor force. All Soviet adult men and women under age 45 who were not engaged in essential war work were required to work 11 hours a day constructing defenses. Soviet women also served in combat. By 1944, 246,000 women were in front-line units. For all Soviet citizens, male and female, life on the home front meant endless labor, inadequate food supplies, and constant surveillance under martial law.

Until 1943, the German home front contrasted sharply with that of Britain and the Soviet Union. The Nazi policy toward female employment rested on Hitler's conviction that Germany had lost World War I in part because of the collapse of morale on the home front. In the first years of the war, then, the Nazi government did not dramatically cut consumption levels. Moreover, Hitler believed that the future of the "German race" depended on middle-class women being protected from the strains of paid labor so that they could bear healthy Aryan babies. The use of foreign labor took the place of the full-scale mobilization of women, until military necessity undercut Nazi gender ideology.

The fall of Stalingrad marked the turning point for German women. With losses on the Eastern Front averaging 150,000 men per month, the German army needed more men. Hitler's deputy Joseph Goebbels (1897–1945) ordered a total mobilization of the home front. The final, desperate year of the war saw a concentrated use of female labor in Nazi Germany.

Of all the combatant states, the United States stood out as unique with regard to the home front. More than 70 percent of American women remained outside the paid workforce. Rationing was comparatively minimal and consumption levels high. In fact, for many families, the war years brought prosperity after years of economic depression. American cities were never bombed, and thus the United States was able to maintain a clear distinction between soldier and civilian, man and woman—a distinction that was blurred in other combatant nations.

What Are We Fighting For?

To mobilize their populations for total war, governments had to convince their citizens to support the war effort. Maintaining morale and motivating civilians and soldiers to endure deprivation and danger demanded that leaders supply a persuasive answer to the question: What are we fighting for?

MYTH AND MORALE All states—democratic or authoritarian—rely on *myths,* on stories of origins and identity, to unify disparate individuals, classes, and groups. In times of total war, such myths become crucial. Combatant governments enlisted artists, entertainers, and the technologies of the mass media for mythmaking and morale-building. In Britain, for example, Henry Moore's (1898–1986) drawings of ordinary people in air raid shelters (completed under an official commission) evoked the survival of civilized values in the midst of unspeakable degradation. In Germany, strict censorship before the war had already subordinated the arts and entertainment industries to the demands of the Nazi state. The war heightened this control as censorship tightened even further, paper shortages limited the production of books and periodicals, and the threat of being drafted for the Eastern Front kept artists in line.

During the war, film came into its own as an artistic form capable of creating important myths of national unity. Laurence Olivier's version of Shakespeare's *Henry V* (1944) comforted British moviegoers with its classic story of a stirring English military victory against huge odds. In Italy, a group of filmmakers known as the Neo-Realists created a set of films that dramatized the Resistance spirit of national unity. Shot on location, with amateur actors and realistic sets, movies such as Roberto Rossellini's *Open City* (1945) depicted lower-class life with honesty and respect and called for the creation of a better society from the rubble of the old.

PLANNING FOR RECONSTRUCTION Rossellini's call for the creation of a new society was echoed throughout Europe during the war. A consensus emerged on the need for social democracy, a society in which the state intervenes in economic life to ensure both public welfare and social justice (see p. 831). As early as December 1942, a British government committee set out a radical plan for postwar society. In rather unusual language for an official document, the committee's report identified "five giants on the road to reconstruction": Want, Disease, Ignorance, Squalor, and Idleness. To slay these giants, the committee recommended that the state assume responsibility for ensuring full employment and a minimum standard of living for all through the provision of family allowances, social welfare programs, and a national health service. The Beveridge Report (named after the committee's chairman) became a best-seller in Britain and the basis for a number of postwar European social welfare plans.

Three factors explain this radical reorientation of European politics. First, and most important, as the war dragged on and the death tolls mounted, European men and women demanded that their suffering be worthwhile. They wanted to know that they were fighting not to rebuild the depressed and divided societies of the 1930s, but to construct a new Europe. In France, for example, the Resistance Charter of 1944 demanded the construction of a "more just social order" through the nationalization of key industries, the establishment of a comprehensive social security system, and the recognition of the rights of workers to participate in management.

Second, the war (and the ongoing revelations of Nazi atrocities) discredited the politics of the far right. This sort of politics, whether fascist, Nazi, or conservative-authoritarian, disappeared from legitimate political discussion. But in Europe (although less so in the United States) the liberal ideal of the free and self-interested individual competing in an unregulated economy also lay in ruins, the victim of the prewar Great Depression. The new Europe, then, had to be built along different lines.

Finally, both the Resistance and the experience of wartime mobilization taught that the power of the state could be used to improve the well-being of its citizens without trampling on the rights of the individual. In the 1930s, Hitler and Mussolini on the Radical Right, and Stalin on the Radical Left, had persuaded many that the individual was not important, that only the state mattered. But the Resistance reasserted the essential significance of the individual and the choices he or she makes. At the same time, the combatant nations' success in mobilizing their economies for total war indicated the positive possibilities of state action. If governments could regulate economies to fight wars, why could they not regulate economies for peacetime prosperity and greater social justice? In the postwar era, then, democracy reclaimed the activist state from fascism and Nazism on the one hand and Stalinism on the other.

CONCLUSION

The New West: After Auschwitz and the Atom Bomb

The wartime encounter with the Nazi vision of the West as a race-based authoritarian order was crucial. From it emerged a sharpened commitment within the West to the processes and values of democracy. But to present the Second World War as a conflict between democracy and Nazism is to oversimplify. To defeat Nazi Germany, the democracies of Britain and the United States allied with Stalin's Soviet Union, a dictatorial regime that matched Hitler's Germany in its contempt for democratic values and human rights and that surpassed it in state-sanctioned mass murder.

The Soviet Union emerged from the war as the dominant power in eastern Europe. As we will see in the next chapter, the presence of the Soviet Army obliterated any chance to establish democratic governments in this region. The tensions inherent in the Anglo-American alliance with the Soviets led directly to the Cold War, the ideological and political conflict that dominated the post-World War II world and that again forced a redefinition of the West. From 1949 until 1989, drawing the West on any map was easy: One shaded in the United States and the countries allied to it—and against the Soviet Union. At the same time, however, a new division emerged. World War II marked the beginning of the end of European imperial control over the non-European world. The postwar era would thus see growing tensions between "North" and "South"—between the industrially developed nations and the underdeveloped regions seeking to shrug off their colonial past.

Much of the impetus for imperial control over non-European regions had come from the conviction of Western supremacy. During World War II, however, Japanese victories had exposed the illusion of Western military invincibility. And after the war, the gradual realization of the full horror of the Holocaust demolished any lingering claim to Western cultural superiority. What sort of superior position could be claimed by a culture in which educated, supposedly civilized men sent children into gas chambers disguised as showers? The atomic bombings of Hiroshima and Nagasaki added more questions to the ongoing debate about the meaning of the West. With the best of intentions, some of the greatest minds in the Western world had produced weapons designed to kill and maim tens of thousands of civilians within seconds. Had Western technology outdistanced Western ethics? And what about the implications of such technologies in a democratic society? For example, would the need to control such weapons lead to measures that eroded individual freedom?

Thus, the assembly-line techniques of mass murder developed by the Nazis and, in very different ways, the sheer efficiency of the atom bomb in obliterating urban populations forced both individuals and their political leaders to confront the destructive potential of Western industrialism. For centuries, the use of the methods of scientific inquiry to uncover truth and achieve both material and moral progress had supported Westerners' self-identification and their sense of cultural superiority. But World War II demonstrated that the best of science could produce the worst of weapons, that technology and technique could combine in the death factory. The task of accepting this knowledge, and facing up to its implications, helped shape Western culture after 1945.

MAKING CONNECTIONS

1. Why do historians assert that World War II in Europe was won on the Eastern Front?
2. How did the home fronts of World War I differ from those in World War II? What explains the similarities? The differences?

TAKING IT FURTHER

For suggested readings, films, and websites, see page R-1.

Chapter Review

The Coming of War

27.1 How did military and political expectations lead to World War II?

Supposed to be the "war to end all wars," World War I set up World War II. The peace settlements exacerbated nationalist tensions in eastern Europe and aroused German and Japanese resentment at the same time that the destruction of total war convinced many Europeans of the necessity of avoiding war at all costs. Throughout the 1930s, both Germany and Japan expanded their territorial base and military might.

Europe at War, 1939–1941

27.2 How did Nazi Germany conquer the continent of Europe by 1941?

With the techniques and technologies of blitzkrieg, German military strategists overcame the defensive stalemate that had characterized the Western Front during World War I. Although frustrated in the Battle of Britain, the Germans experienced initial success in the invasion of the Soviet Union.

The World at War, 1941–1945

27.3 Why did the Allies win in 1945?

In the defeat of Nazi Germany, the fighting on the Eastern Front proved crucial. In addition, Great Britain, the Soviet Union, and the United States outpaced Nazi Germany and its allies, including Japan, in the industrial production and scientific developments that fueled total war. Nazi atrocities also strengthened resistance throughout occupied Europe.

The Wars Within the War

27.4 What were the context, causes, and consequences of genocide during World War II?

The conquest of western Poland marked the beginnings of the Nazi regime to reorder the racial/ethnic composition of eastern Europe. With the invasion of the Soviet Union, the so-called Final Solution, which included the industrialization of mass murder in the death camps, took shape. At the same time, World War II heightened nationalist and ethnic tensions that in many areas erupted into civil war. It also provided further incentives for the Stalinist government of the Soviet Union to tighten its murderous hold on the peoples under its control.

Under Occupation and on the Home Front

27.5 What did total war mean for civilians in the occupied regions and on the home front?

Many Europeans were forced to labor for the Nazi war effort, while others opted to join the Resistance, the underground fight against the Nazi regime. Total war also meant the experience of massive bombing campaigns as well as the unprecedented economic and military mobilization of women. In western Europe, government efforts to ensure civilian morale, as well as the more general experience of wartime suffering, produced a widespread commitment to the idea and ideals of social democracy.

Chapter Time Line

1933
Hitler becomes chancellor of Germany.

1933

1939

1939
Germany invades Poland; German-Soviet conquest of Poland.

1940
Battle of Britain begins.

1940

1941

1941
U.S. Congress passes Lend-Lease Act; German invasion of the Soviet Union begins; Japan bombs Pearl Harbor.

1942
Battle of Midway; Battle of El Alamein begins; German Sixth Army cut off at Stalingrad.

1942

1943

1943
Allied invasion of Italy begins.

1944
D-Day landings; Allied offensive in France begins; Operation Bagration begins.

1944

1945

1945
VE Day: Official German surrender; United States drops atomic bomb on Hiroshima; V-J Day: Formal Japanese surrender.

28 Redefining the West After World War II

O n an apparently ordinary day in August 1961, western European television viewers witnessed an extraordinary sight. While the news cameras rolled, policemen from East Berlin—the section of Berlin controlled by East Germany's communist government—played tug-of-war with firemen from West Berlin, the half of the city that belonged to the democratic state of West Germany. Between them, however, was not the usual length of rope, but rather a middle-aged woman. As East Berlin policemen tried to pull this woman back into an apartment building, West Berlin firemen struggled to pull her out.

The construction of the Berlin Wall set this bizarre contest in motion. During the 1950s a growing number of East Germans sought to flee communist rule by crossing into (free) West Berlin. Finally in 1961, the East German and Soviet authorities took action. In the early morning hours of Sunday, August 13, they erected a barbed-wire fence along Berlin's east-west dividing line and blocked anyone from crossing this fence into West Berlin. In some cases, however, the dividing line ran right through apartment buildings and so, for the next few weeks, these apartments provided literal "windows to the west." West Berlin firemen waited with blankets ready to catch anyone

LEARNING OBJECTIVES

28.1	28.2	28.3	28.4
Why and how did the world step from World War II to the Cold War?	What was the impact of decolonization and the Cold War on the global balance of power?	What patterns characterized the history of the Soviet Union and eastern Europe after the death of Stalin?	What patterns characterized the history of western Europe in the 1950s and 1960s?

Listen to Chapter 28 on MyHistoryLab

TUG-OF-WAR AT THE BERLIN WALL Caught by the television cameras, this woman sought to escape through her window into West Berlin. She succeeded.

⊙ Watch the Video Series on MyHistoryLab

Learn about some key topics related to this chapter with the *MyHistoryLab Video Series:*
Key Topics in Western Civilization

28.1

28.2

28.3

28.4

willing to jump out of a window—and out of communist eastern Europe. These windows closed quickly. The communist authorities first bricked up windows facing West Berlin. Later they leveled entire apartment buildings. The barbed-wire fence became a concrete wall buttressed by gun towers, lit by searchlights, and patrolled by armed guards with "shoot to kill" orders.

The unidentified woman dangling out of the window, literally caught between West and East, symbolizes Europe during the 1950s and 1960s. In these decades, the Cold War between the United States and the Soviet Union helped shape European politics, culture, and society. As the woman's desperation to reach the West indicates, American influence in western Europe did not parallel Soviet domination of eastern Europe. Nevertheless, many Europeans in the West as well as the East felt that they no longer fully controlled their own societies.

The Cold War was in part an encounter of two clashing ideologies, as much a battle of ideas and values as weapons and warriors. Both sides laid claim to universal cultures—to have achieved a way of life that would benefit *all* human societies. This ideological encounter forced a redefinition of "the West." Previous chapters have described the way in which this cultural construct shifted over time. By the late nineteenth century, Christianity, although still important, played a less central role in defining "the West" than did such factors as industrial technology, the illusion of white racial superiority, and faith in capitalist economics and liberal political values. The Cold War added fears of the Soviet Union and communist ideology to the mix. These fears at times eroded the Western commitment to democracy, particularly within the developing world.

Significantly, the Cold War turned "hot" not in Europe, but in places such as Korea, Cuba, and Vietnam. This era witnessed a widening economic gap between "North" and "South"—between the industrialized nations, largely located in the Northern Hemisphere, and economically underdeveloped regions, many south of the equator, many now shrugging off colonial rule. As the Cold War moved beyond Europe's borders to the developing regions two different contests—North versus South and West versus East—intertwined.

How, then, did these contests shape the ever-evolving idea of the West?

A Dubious Peace, 1945–1949

28.1 Why and how did the world step from World War II to the Cold War?

World War II ended in the spring and summer of 1945, but the killing did not. Postwar purges, deportations, and civil wars ensured that the death totals continued to mount. As the "hot" war waned, the Cold War began between the Soviet Union and the countries it controlled on the one hand and the United States and its Western allies on the other.

Devastation, Death, and DPs

Germany's surrender in May 1945 did not bring immediate peace to Europe. Many regions in southern and eastern Europe experienced civil war, while in other areas victors turned with vengeful fury against the vanquished. In the Baltic states and Ukraine, guerilla groups opposed to Soviet annexation fought until the early 1950s. Those left alive in post-World War II Europe faced the overwhelming task of reconstruction. Intensive bombing rendered most highways, rail tracks, and waterways unusable. With laborers, seed, fertilizer, and basic equipment all in short supply, agricultural production in 1945 stood below 50 percent of prewar levels. Less visible, but just as devastating, was the destruction of the financial system. Few European currencies were worth much. In defeated Germany, cigarettes replaced marks as the unit of exchange.

Map 28.1 indicates one of the most serious problems facing postwar Europe: that of the refugees or displaced persons (DPs). The DP problem stemmed, first, from

MAP **28.1** AFTER WORLD WAR II: SHIFTING BOUNDARIES, SHIFTING POPULATIONS World War II and its aftermath resulted in the movements of millions. Political ambitions and military concerns fused with racial and ethnic hatreds and the emerging Cold War to create new state boundaries that resulted in the exchange of entire populations. One boundary line, shifted one-quarter inch on a map, meant hundreds of thousands of men, women, and children were forced out of their homes and into strange new cities or villages, in the midst of postwar economic breakdown and social upheaval. What were the significant changes in state borders after the war? Which populations were most affected by these changes?

the war itself, with millions made homeless by invasions and mass bombing. Second, Hitler's attempts at racial reordering also caused DP numbers to skyrocket, as concentration and death camp survivors now stumbled through the wreckage of war-torn Europe.

A third factor in the worsening DP problem was the peace settlement itself, which redrew the boundaries of Germany and reaffirmed the Soviet annexation of eastern Poland and the Baltic states. In a brutal resolution to what was perceived as the problem of national minorities, the Allies and eastern European governments agreed on a policy of population transfers. More than 18 million Europeans were forced out of their homes and homelands, as ancient multi-linguistic and multi-ethnic communities were destroyed, replaced by ethnically homogenous nation-states. Germans suffered particularly severely as the Soviet, Polish, Czech, Romanian, Yugoslav, and Hungarian governments all forcibly deported their German populations. Often forced on the road with no food or supplies, approximately two million Germans died in this postscript to World War II.

From Hot to Cold War

The conflict that posed the greatest threat to the dubious peace after 1945 was the **Cold War**, the struggle for global supremacy between the United States and the Soviet Union. Within just a few years of the defeat of Germany and Japan, the allies became enemies, and what Winston Churchill called the **"Iron Curtain"** dropped between eastern and western Europe.

THE DELICATE FABRIC OF THE WARTIME ALLIANCE A common wartime enemy rather than shared postwar aims wove together the alliance of Britain, the Soviet Union, and the United States. To ensure Soviet (and his own) security and power, Joseph Stalin demanded that Soviet boundaries extend westward and that the Soviet "sphere of influence" include the states along the Soviet Union's western borders. He noted bluntly, "The more you've got, the safer you are."[1]

Stalin's demands for "friendly" and therefore communist-dominated governments in eastern Europe conflicted with American and British aims. The American president, Franklin D. Roosevelt, saw the establishment of democracies throughout Europe—including along the Soviet borders—as essential to international security and American prosperity. One American official explained to Congress, "If you create good governments in foreign countries, you will have better markets for ourselves."[2] The third Allied leader, Winston Churchill, the British prime minister, regarded the extension of Soviet influence westward as a threat to the European balance of power. He saw Stalin's plans for Poland as a particular problem: Britain had gone to war in September 1939 because of the Nazi invasion of Poland and over 200,000 Polish soldiers were fighting for the Allies.

Poland was very much on the agenda in November 1943 when the **Big Three**— Stalin, Churchill, and Roosevelt—met together for the first time in the Tehran Conference. Stalin insisted on the restoration of the *1940* Polish-Soviet border—the boundary line drawn by the secret clauses of the German–Soviet Non-Aggression Pact. Churchill and Roosevelt recognized that if they agreed, they would be affirming the brutal Soviet invasion of eastern Poland in 1939. Yet they also knew that Soviet soldiers were dying by the millions on the Eastern Front and they were eager to retain Stalin's full commitment to the alliance. At Tehran, then, they agreed—secretly—that Poland's postwar borders would shift hundreds of miles westward.[3]

By February 1945, when the Big Three met in the Crimean seaside town of Yalta, Stalin stood in an even stronger negotiating position. As he said, "Everyone imposes his own system as far as his armies can reach"—and in 1945, the Soviet army had a long reach, with its soldiers occupying Poland, Romania, Bulgaria, Hungary, and much of

Cold War Struggle for global supremacy between the United States and the Soviet Union, waged from the end of World War II until 1990.

Iron Curtain Metaphor for the Cold War division of Europe after World War II.

 Read the Document

Winston Churchill, "Iron Curtain Speech"

Big Three Term applied to the British, Soviet, and U.S. leaders during World War II: until 1945, Winston Churchill, Joseph Stalin, and Franklin Roosevelt; by the summer of 1945, Clement Attlee, Joseph Stalin, and Harry Truman.

THE BIG THREE I (YALTA, FEBRUARY 1945) From 1941 until April 1945, the Big Three meant Churchill, Roosevelt, and Stalin. At the very end of the war, however, the composition of the Big Three suddenly changed, as Harry Truman replaced Roosevelt and Clement Attlee replaced Churchill.

Yalta Conference Meeting in 1945 of the leaders of the Allied states of Britain, the Soviet Union, and the United States to devise plans for postwar Europe.

Czechoslovakia. Roosevelt's desire to obtain Stalin's commitment to enter the war against Japan also strengthened Stalin's hand. The **Yalta Conference** thus produced a contradictory compromise. Stalin promised free and democratic elections in eastern Europe while Roosevelt and Churchill agreed that such freely elected democratic governments should be pro-Soviet. They did not, however, define "free" or "democratic," and made no arrangements to oversee or regulate the elections. Stalin noted privately, "A freely elected government in any of these countries would be anti-Soviet, and that we cannot allow."[4]

The Big Three also differed on the fate of Germany. Stalin hoped to wring every available resource out of Germany to pay for Soviet reconstruction. Roosevelt, however, became convinced that the economic revival of Europe depended on a prosperous Germany. Moreover, he and Churchill feared that a weak or partitioned German state would invite Soviet expansion into central Europe. At Yalta, the Big Three did not resolve the issue of Germany's future, but they agreed to divide Germany and the symbolically and strategically vital city of Berlin into occupation zones controlled by the United States, the Soviet Union, France, and Britain (see Map 28.1).

Reluctant to place too much pressure on the alliance's fraying seams, Roosevelt opted for postponing the hard decisions at Yalta. He hoped that a new international body, the United Nations (UN), would settle the controversial questions after the war. If the Soviet Union refused to participate, however, the UN, like the interwar League of Nations, would be a failure. Therefore, Roosevelt sought to avoid confrontations that might give Stalin a reason to block Soviet membership.

Roosevelt also hoped that new international economic structures would stabilize the postwar order. In 1944 leading American and European economists had gathered in New Hampshire to construct a system for postwar economic revival. Aware of the economic chaos that had followed World War I and desperate to avoid a repeat of the Great Depression of the 1930s, they drew up the **Bretton Woods Agreement**, the framework for the Western postwar economic order. To keep the global economy

Bretton Woods Agreement Agreement signed in 1944 that established the post-World War II economic framework in which the U.S. dollar served as the world's reserve currency.

running smoothly, Bretton Woods recognized the American dollar as the world's reserve currency and fixed currency exchange rates. It also established two new international economic institutions—the International Monetary Fund (IMF), to maintain the stability of member currencies, and the World Bank, to encourage global economic development.

FRAYING SEAMS, 1945–1946 The final Big Three conference in the German city of Potsdam in July 1945 did not bridge the gap between the Soviet Union and its allies. Stalin faced two unfamiliar negotiating partners. The new American president Harry Truman (1884–1972) replaced Roosevelt, who had died in April, and midway through the summit, the new British prime minister, the Labour Party leader Clement Attlee, arrived to take Churchill's place. The changes made little difference. Stalin demanded control over the territories occupied by his armies, while the British and Americans increasingly saw this demand as a threat to democratic ideals and the European balance of power.

Two additional factors heightened the hostility between the Allied leaders during the **Potsdam Conference**. First, the British foreign secretary, Ernest Bevin (1881–1951), the man who largely determined foreign policy in Attlee's government, had a history of fighting communist efforts to control British unions. A fierce anti-Stalinist as well as an ardent British nationalist, Bevin believed that a stronger Soviet Union threatened Britain's status as a Great Power. He urged the United States to stand tough against Soviet demands.

The second factor was more dramatic. During the summit Truman received a telegraph informing him of the successful Trinity test of the atomic bomb in New Mexico (see Chapter 27). This news meant that the war against Japan would soon be over—and that the Americans and British no longer needed or wanted Stalin to join the war in the Pacific. An important Western incentive for placating Stalin disappeared.

Yet the wartime alliance remained intact after Potsdam. Truman resisted the idea of a permanent American military presence in Europe and so for the next few months sought to resolve the conflicts that divided the Allied leaders. Stalin, too, was unwilling to push too far. He feared American military might and hoped to reduce military expenditures to revive the Soviet economy. Thus, in regions that he viewed as part of the Western sphere of influence, Stalin adopted a policy of passivity. He refused to assist communists seeking to overthrow the British-backed monarchy in Greece, and he ordered communist parties in western Europe to participate with noncommunists in coalition governments.

TORN IN TWO, 1946–1948 Stalin, however, adopted no such policy of passivity in eastern Europe. Throughout 1945 and 1946 communists in these states used legal and illegal methods—including intimidation, torture, and kidnapping—to expand their power base and to co-opt, silence, or expel noncommunist leaders. In Poland, for example, Stalin ordered top-ranking members of the wartime underground government secretly arrested, flown to Moscow, and thrown into prison. Those Poles who had fought in the Home Army against German rule were shipped to Soviet labor camps.

Disagreements over the fate of Germany also helped tear apart the alliance. At Yalta the Allies had agreed to share the postwar occupation, and at Potsdam, Truman and Attlee gave in to Stalin's demand for German reparations: The British, American, and French occupying governments shipped manufactured goods and machines from the more industrialized western regions of Germany to the largely agricultural Soviet zone in the east. In exchange, the Soviets agreed to provide food and raw materials from their zone to the western territories. The Soviets, however, proved more interested in plundering their zone than in establishing a workable joint economic policy. By 1946, British and American authorities recognized that Germans faced starvation. Convinced that economic recovery must be made an immediate priority, they

Potsdam Conference The meeting in July 1945 of the Allied leaders of Britain, the Soviet Union, and the United States in the German city of Potsdam.

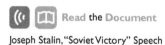

Read the Document

Joseph Stalin, "Soviet Victory" Speech

28.2

Truman Doctrine Named after U.S. president Harry Truman, the doctrine that in 1947 inaugurated the Cold War policy of resisting the expansion of communist control.

28.3

28.4

Marshall Plan The use of U.S. economic aid to restore stability to Europe after World War II and so undercut the appeal of communist ideology.

combined their zones into a single economic unit and stopped reparations deliveries to the Soviets. With all pretense of a united Allied policy in Germany now dropped, Truman reversed his initial plan to withdraw American troops from Germany as soon as possible. "We are staying here," declared Secretary of State James Byrnes in September 1946. And stay they did: As of 2013, American forces remain in Germany.

The announcement of the **Truman Doctrine** in 1947 exposed the widening rift between Stalin and the West. An American policy, the Truman Doctrine evolved in response to British actions. In February 1947 the British government informed Truman's administration that it could not afford to continue to assist the Greek government in its fight against communist rebels. The United States immediately assumed Britain's role in Greece. More important, Truman used this development to issue the Truman Doctrine, which committed the United States to the policy of containment: resisting communist expansion wherever in the world it occurred.

The **Marshall Plan**—and more particularly, Stalin's rejection of it—reinforced the division of Europe into two hostile camps. In 1947, U.S. Secretary of State George Marshall (1880–1959) toured Europe and grew alarmed at the devastation and despair that he observed. Fearing that hungry Europeans might turn to communism, Marshall proposed that the United States underwrite Europe's economic recovery. Marshall's proposal at first received little attention, but in Britain Foreign Secretary Ernest Bevin heard a report of it on the radio. Convinced that an ongoing American presence in Europe would serve British interests, Bevin hailed the Marshall Plan as "a lifeline to sinking men."

Bevin's French counterpart, Foreign Minister Georges Bidault (1899–1983), shared his enthusiasm, and together they helped make the Marshall Plan a reality. With representatives from 12 other European states, Bevin and Bidault devised a four-year plan for European economic reconstruction that accelerated western Europe's leap into postwar prosperity. Eventually the United States sent $13 billion to Europe, and a new international body, the Organization for European Economic Cooperation (OEEC), worked to eliminate trade barriers and stabilize currencies.

By some estimates, the wealth that the Soviet Union siphoned from eastern Europe roughly equaled the amount of Marshall aid that the United States injected into western Europe. The United States offered aid to every European state; if a state did accept aid, however, it also had to join the OEEC. Because Stalin viewed the OEEC as an instrument of American domination, he banned eastern European governments from receiving Marshall funds. When the Czechs tried to do so, Stalin engineered a communist coup in February 1948 that destroyed what remained of democracy in Czechoslovakia—and the last remnant of parliamentary democracy in eastern Europe.

THE COLD WAR BEGINS Over the next few years, eastern Europeans endured what Soviet citizens had suffered in the 1920s and 1930s: the extension of Communist Party control over the armed forces and the state bureaucracy, forced collectivization, the sacrifice of the standard of living to fuel heavy industrialization—and Stalinist terror.

Stalin's tightening grip over eastern Europe solidified American and western European suspicions of Soviet aims. Yet the spread of Stalinism in eastern Europe originated in part from Stalin's *loss* of control over a key eastern European state. In 1948, the Yugoslav communist leader, Tito, broke with Stalin. Alarmed by Tito's independence, Stalin cracked down across the rest of eastern Europe. He first purged eastern European Communist Parties of any potential "titoists"—leaders who might threaten his dominance. Between 1948 and 1953 more communists were killed by their own party members than had died at the hands of the Nazis during World War II. (See *Justice in History* in this chapter.) The terror then spread beyond communist ranks. Labor and prison camps dotted the eastern European landscape. Only Stalin's death in 1953 caused the wave of persecution to recede.

Stalin's break with Tito and the resulting spread of terror throughout eastern Europe coincided with the first "battle" of the Cold War. In June 1948, Stalin ordered

Justice in History
Show Time: THE TRIAL OF RUDOLF SLÁNSKÝ

O n the night of July 31, 1951, Rudolf Slánský, general secretary of the Communist Party of Czechoslovakia (CPC), left his fiftieth birthday party and headed home, a frightened man. Outwardly, nothing was wrong. The CPC had celebrated the day in style. The communist president, Klement Gottwald, presented Slánský with the medal of the Order of Socialism, the highest honor awarded in Czechoslovakia. Congratulations poured in from all over the country. But Slánský knew he was in trouble: Stalin had not acknowledged his birthday. In the upper ranks of Czechoslovakia's Communist Party in 1951, signs of Stalin's approval or disapproval were literally matters of life or death. The Stalinist purge of eastern Europe was raging, with thousands arrested, tortured, imprisoned, or killed.

Slánský knew he was vulnerable on three counts. First, he held a rank high enough to ensure a spectacular show trial. As the Soviet Great Purge of the 1930s had demonstrated, trials and executions of leading communists cemented mass loyalty to the regime by rousing ordinary citizens to perpetual vigilance—but for a trial to be a genuine show, the defendant had to be worth showing. Any trial with Slánský, the CPC general secretary, as defendant would be the perfect show.

Second, Slánský was a Czech, and Stalin viewed his Czech colleagues with particular suspicion. Czechoslovakia was the only state in eastern Europe with a history of successful democracy. Moreover, the CPC had participated with noncommunists in a coalition government longer than any other eastern European communist party. Such differences linked the CPC to the ideology of "national communism," which taught that each state should follow its own route to communism, that the Soviet path was not the only way. After the Yugoslav communist leader Tito had dared to defy Stalin's leadership in 1948, Stalin became obsessed with rooting out "national communism" and punishing any potential "titoists."

Finally, Slánský knew that he occupied a vulnerable position because he was a Jew. Aiming to establish a Soviet presence in the Middle East after the war, Stalin had tried to persuade the new state of Israel to align with the Soviet Union by offering diplomatic recognition and arms deals. But Stalin's efforts failed. By 1950, Israel had become an ally of the United States. In response, Stalin regarded all Jews as potential "Zionists" (that is, as pro-Israel and therefore pro-Western and anti-Soviet in their allegiances).

Slánský's birthday fears turned out to be correct. Shortly before midnight on November 24, 1951, security agents arrested him at his home. A lifelong atheist, Slánský could say nothing except "Jesus Maria." He knew what was coming. Instrumental in initiating the Stalinist terror in Czechoslovakia, Slánský had approved the arrests and torture of many of his colleagues. Ironically, he had drafted the telegram asking Stalin to send Soviet advisers to assist in the Czech purge—the very same advisers who decided to target Slánský.

For the next year, Slánský endured mental and physical torture, directed by these advisers. Common torture tactics included beatings and kickings; prolonged periods in a standing position and/or without sleep, food, or water; and all-night interrogation sessions. One interrogator recalled, "Instead of getting evidence, we were told that they were villains and that we had to break them."[5]

Before the show trial began on November 20, 1952, party officials had already determined the verdict and sentences. Prosecutors, defense attorneys, judges, and the accused spoke the lines of a script written by security agents. Slánský pleaded guilty to the crimes of high treason, espionage, and sabotage. This founding member of the CPC said he had conspired to overthrow the communist government. This Resistance fighter confessed to collaborating with the Nazis. This zealous Stalinist announced that he was a titoist-Zionist working for the United States.

RUDOLF SLÁNSKÝ ON TRIAL Slánský, already a broken man, bows his head as he hears his death sentence on November 27, 1952.

(continued on next page)

Why did Slánský make such a ludicrous confession? Fear of further torture was clearly one motive, but other factors also came into play. Communists such as Slánský believed that the interests of the party always came first, ahead of individual rights, ahead of abstractions such as "truth." Slánský may have believed that his confession, false though it was, served the party. As one experienced interrogator noted about a different defendant, "He'll confess; he's got a good attitude toward the party."[6] In addition, Slánský may have been promised, as were other show trial defendants, that his life would be spared and his family protected if he confessed.

Slánský hanged on December 3, 1952. His family was deported with only the barest essentials to a designated district and assigned to manual labor.

For Discussion

1. How did Cold War concerns shape Slánský's trial?
2. Slánský supervised the start of the Terror in Czechoslovakia. Did he, then, "get what he deserved"? What sort of justice was served in the trial of Rudolf Slánský?

Taking It Further

Lukes, Igor. "The Rudolf Slánský Affair: New Evidence." *Slavic Review* 58, 1 (Spring 1999): 160–187. Illuminating study of the role of Cold War intrigue in determining Slánský's fate.

Kaplan, Karel. *Report on the Murder of the General Secretary*. 1990. Kaplan emigrated from Czechoslovakia to West Germany in the late 1970s and wrote this report.

the western sectors of the city of Berlin—those areas controlled by the United States, France, and Britain—blockaded. Stalin hoped to force the Western powers to resume the delivery of reparations payments from western Germany or, at the very least, to give up control of West Berlin. Instead, the British and Americans responded with the Berlin Airlift. For almost a year, planes landed in West Berlin every three minutes, day and night, delivering 12,000 tons of daily supplies. In May 1949 Stalin recognized

CHRONOLOGY: THE OUTBREAK OF THE COLD WAR

1944 *August* Soviet Army advances into Balkans.

1945 *January* Soviet Army advances into Poland. *February* Yalta Conference. *July* Potsdam Conference. *August* United States drops atomic bombs on Hiroshima and Nagasaki.

1946 *March* Churchill gives his "Iron Curtain" speech in Missouri.

1947 *February* Truman Doctrine announced. *June* Marshall Plan announced.

1948 *February* Communist coup in Czechoslovakia destroys last democracy in eastern Europe. *June* Split between Yugoslavia's communist leader Tito and Stalin, Stalinist terror throughout eastern Europe widened; Soviet blockade of West Berlin, Berlin Airlift.

1949 *April* Formation of North Atlantic Treaty Organization (NATO). *May* Official formation of West Germany (Federal Republic of Germany). *August* Soviet atomic bomb test.

defeat and called off the blockade. The city of Berlin, like Germany itself, remained divided for the next 40 years.

In 1949, three additional developments wove the final threads into the basic Cold War pattern. First, the British and American zones of occupied Germany, joined with the French zone, became the Western-allied state of West Germany, while the Soviet zone became communist East Germany. Second, in April 1949 nine western European nations allied with the United States and Canada in the **North Atlantic Treaty Organization (NATO)**, a military alliance specifically aimed at repelling a Soviet invasion of western Europe. And third, on August 29, 1949, the Soviet Union tested its own atomic bomb. Over the next few years, Stalin forced his eastern European satellites into an anti-Western military alliance (finalized as the **Warsaw Pact** in 1955), and the United States and the Soviet Union developed hydrogen or thermonuclear bombs, weapons with far more destructive might than their atomic predecessors. Europe stood divided into two hostile military blocs, each dominated by a superpower in possession of a nuclear arsenal.

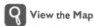 **View the Map**

Shifting Borders—Eastern Europe After World War II

28.1

28.2

North Atlantic Treaty Organization (NATO) Defensive anti-Soviet alliance of the United States, Canada, and the nations of western Europe established in 1949.

28.3

Warsaw Pact Military alliance of the Soviet Union and its eastern European satellite states in the Cold War era.

28.4

The West and the World: Decolonization and the Cold War

28.2 What was the impact of decolonization and the Cold War on the global balance of power?

The conflict between East and West soon blended with a very different struggle, one between the peoples of the developing nations and European imperialism. The Soviet Union and the United States used economic and military aid, as well as covert action, to cajole and coerce newly independent nations into choosing sides in what became the global Cold War conflict.

The End to the Age of European Empires

In the economic hard times following World War II, European governments regarded their empires as more crucial than ever. States such as Britain and France looked to their imperial possessions to give them international power and prestige. Britain's Foreign Minister Ernest Bevin, for example, saw the British Empire as the means "to develop our own power and influence to equal that of the U.S. of A. and the U.S.S.R."[7] The war, however, strengthened colonial independence movements, with nationalists highlighting the inherent contradiction between the Allies' fight for democracy in Europe and the denial of democratic rights to the imperial subjects of European states.

When the war ended, these nationalists resisted European efforts to reimpose imperial rule, and a series of bloody colonial conflicts resulted. In Indonesia, war raged from 1945 to 1949 as the Dutch fought to keep hold of a region they viewed as vital to their economic survival. They lost the fight, and in 1949 the nationalist Ahmed Sukarno (1949–1966) led his country into independence. Similarly, nationalists in Indochina rose up against the return of French rule and began a lengthy war for independence.

The British, too, found much of their empire in revolt in the postwar period at precisely the moment when the economic and military demands of total war significantly weakened Britain's ability to control its far-flung possessions. To retain Britain's hold on its essential imperial territories, the first postwar prime minister, Clement Attlee, adopted a policy of jettisoning those regions that Britain no longer needed—or could no longer afford.

The British first jettisoned the Indian subcontinent. During World War II, the refusal of Indian nationalists to cooperate with the war effort made clear that Britain could no longer control India. After the war, therefore, Attlee's government opened

 Read the Document

Franz Fanon, The Wretched of the Earth

independence negotiations. Muslim nationalists led by Muhammad Ali Jinnah (1876–1948) refused to accept citizenship in a Hindu-dominated India and won from the British the creation of a separate Muslim state—Pakistan. India and Pakistan, as well as Burma (Myanmar), received independence in August 1947 (see **Map 28.2**). Just as the redrawing of boundary lines in eastern Europe resulted in mass deportations and death, so the partition of the Indian subcontinent sparked widespread devastation. More than 10 million people fled their homes and became refugees—Muslims fearing Hindu rule, Hindus fearing Muslim rule, Sikhs fearing both. Mahatma Gandhi begged for an end to the killing, but the death tolls reached 250,000—and included Gandhi himself, who was shot by an assassin just six months after India achieved independence.

In Palestine, too, British retreat led to bloodshed. After the war in Europe ended, Jewish refugees, persuaded by Hitler that a Jew could be safe only in a Jewish state, demanded that they be allowed to settle in Palestine. The British, however, sought to limit Jewish immigration to maintain regional political stability (and protect their own interests). But faced with mounting violence as well as growing international pressure to grant Jewish demands for statehood, the British announced they would leave Palestine and turned the problem over to the new United Nations. At the end of 1947, the UN announced a plan to partition Palestine into a Jewish and an Arab state. Arab leaders rejected the plan, however, and British troops left in May 1948 without transferring authority to either party. Jewish leaders proclaimed the new state of Israel, and the region erupted into war. After nine months of fighting, an uneasy peace descended, based on a partition of Palestine among Israel, Jordan, and Egypt (see Map 28.4 on page 899). Approximately 750,000 Palestinian Arabs became stateless refugees.

By withdrawing from hot spots such as India and Palestine, the British hoped to preserve what remained of the British Empire. During the 1950s, successive British governments sought to diminish the force of nationalism by diverting it down channels of constitutional reform and systems of power sharing—and stomping on nationalists who broke out of these channels. But neither compromise nor coercion stemmed the nationalist tide.

MAP **28.2** AFTER EMPIRE: ASIA Dates of national formation often give no indication of the continuing political upheaval and violence that afflicted the countries of Asia in the postwar period. Which of these newly formed states experienced prolonged warfare in the aftermath of independence?

CHRONOLOGY: THE END TO EUROPEAN EMPIRE

1946
French colonial war in Indochina begins.
1946

1947
1947
India, Pakistan, and Burma achieve independence from Britain.

1948
State of Israel established.
1948

1949
1949
Indonesia achieves independence from Dutch rule.

1952
Mau Mau rebellion begins in Kenya.
1952

1954
1954
Defeat of French forces in Indochina; partition of Vietnam; beginning of Franco-Algerian War.

1955
Bandung Conference: the "Third World" is born.
1955

1956
1956
Suez Crisis.

1957
Ghana becomes the first black-ruled African state in the British Empire to achieve independence.
1957

1960
1960
Congo, Nigeria, and most French colonies in Africa become independent.

1962
Algeria achieves independence from French rule.
1962

1963
1963
Jomo Kenyatta becomes first prime minister of Kenya.

In Kenya, for example, Britain offered a gradual process of constitutional reforms leading toward eventual self-government, but these reforms were too slow and limited to satisfy Kenyan nationalists. The result, in 1952, was the "Mau Mau" rebellion, actually a combined peasant uprising, nationalist insurgence, and civil war. Britain imposed a brutal "villagization" program, intended to cut off Mau Mau supply lines. British forces imprisoned much of the population in enclosed villages, where they were deprived of adequate food and shelter, commandeered for forced labor, and often

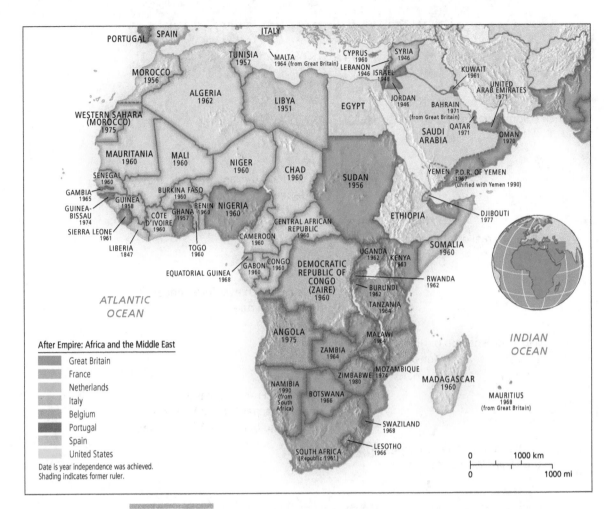

MAP **28.3** AFTER EMPIRE: AFRICA We saw in Chapter 24 that in just three decades, between 1880 and 1910, European nations divided up between them almost the entire African continent in the notorious "Scramble for Africa." African nationalists effected an even more dramatic scramble of European imperial regimes *out* of sub-Saharan Africa. Which was the first African state to become independent? How many African states became independent in the years between 1957 and 1967?

beaten and tortured. Yet all of this bloodshed did little to stop Kenyan independence. In 1963, Jomo Kenyatta (1889–1978), imprisoned for seven years because of his role in the uprising, became Kenya's first elected leader.

Many African leaders followed Kenyatta on the path from a British prison cell to a prime ministerial or presidential office (see **Map 28.3**). By the end of the 1960s, the British Empire had been reduced to an assortment of small island territories.

France, too, saw its empire disintegrate in the postwar decades despite efforts to resist nationalist movements. In Indochina, the nationalist leader Ho Chi Minh (1890–1969) adopted the U.S. Declaration of Independence for his model when he proclaimed independence in September 1945. The stirring rhetoric failed to convince the French, who fought for almost a decade to retain their hold in southeast Asia. But in 1954, the French army suffered a decisive defeat at Dien Bien Phu in Vietnam, and French rule in Indochina ended (see Map 28.2).

Humiliated by this defeat, French army officers responded ferociously to the outbreak of a nationalist revolt in Algeria that same year. Many French men and women shared the army's view that France had been pushed too far and had to stand fast. The result was the Franco-Algerian War. By the time Algeria claimed independence in 1962, approximately 200,000 Algerian nationalist fighters had been killed or imprisoned. Fifteen thousand French soldiers and auxiliary forces were dead, as were almost 23,000 Algerian and French civilians.

The Franco-Algerian War seriously divided French society, called into question the meaning of French democracy, and transformed France's political structure. Supporters of the French army in Algeria saw it as a force fighting on behalf of Western civilization against barbarism (Muslim and communist). Critics, pointing to the evidence that the French army used torture against its enemies, argued that the war threatened to corrupt French society. (See *Different Voices* in this chapter.) By 1958 France teetered on the brink of civil war, with French army officers preparing for an assault on Paris. The World War II hero Charles De Gaulle forced through a new constitution, which sharply tilted the balance of power in French domestic politics toward the president (conveniently De Gaulle himself).

The Globalization of the Cold War

The process of **decolonization** often became entangled with Cold War rivalries, and in many regions, superpower influence replaced imperial control. Despite fears of World War III and a Europe devastated by nuclear weapons, the Cold War actually turned hot only in the developing nations, at the intersection of superpower rivalries and nationalist conflicts.

THE KOREAN WAR, 1950–1953 The first such intersection occurred in Korea. Once part of the Japanese Empire, Korea, like Germany, was divided after World War II. A Soviet-linked communist regime assumed power in North Korea, and an anticommunist state propped up by the United States controlled the south (see Map 28.2, p. 890). In 1950, North

IMPERIAL SACRIFICE This poster reminded French men and women of the sacrifice made by their army at the Battle of Dien Bien Phu in Vietnam: "They sacrificed themselves for your liberty." The memory of the army's defeat at Dien Bien Phu helped strengthen French determination to hold on to Algeria.

decolonization The retreat of Western powers from their imperial territories.

Korean troops invaded South Korea in an attempt to unite the country under communist rule. This civil war, a struggle between rival groups of Korean nationalists, soon became a new theater of the Cold War. A UN-sponsored, largely American army fought alongside South Korean troops, while the Soviet Union supplied arms and Communist China provided soldiers to support North Korea.

The Korean War accelerated the globalization of the Cold War. Convinced that communism was on the march, Truman's administration supported France's struggle against the nationalists in Indochina, thus drawing the United States onto the path that would lead to its war in Vietnam. The conflict in Korea also welded Japan firmly into the Western alliance. As the U.S. army turned to the Japanese for vital military supplies, more than $3.5 billion poured into and rejuvenated the Japanese economy. (American military orders for trucks guaranteed the success of a struggling new Japanese firm called Toyota.) Transformed from an occupied enemy to a staunch ally and an economic powerhouse, Japan became the dam holding back "the red tide that threatens to engulf the world."[8] Thus, in a curious way, Japan—geographically as far "East" as one can get—became a part of the "West."

The Korean War also solidified the Cold War within Europe. The escalating costs of the war led Truman's administration to demand that its European allies strengthen their own military forces and permit the rearmament of West Germany. With the trauma of German conquest so recently behind them, many Europeans were horrified by the second demand. Britain's prime minister Attlee warned, "The policy of using Satan to defeat Sin is very dangerous." But after four years of controversy, West Germany rearmed under the NATO umbrella.

CHANGING TEMPERATURES IN THE COLD WAR, 1953–1960 In 1953, both sides in the Cold War changed leaders. Stalin died in March, just a few months after a new Republican administration headed by President Dwight Eisenhower (1890–1969) took office in the United States. This change of leadership heralded a new phase in the Cold War. When Eisenhower took office, he condemned Truman's policy of *containing* communism as defeatist, a "negative, futile and immoral policy . . . which abandons countless human beings to a despotism and Godless terrorism."[9] Instead, Eisenhower committed the United States to *roll back* communism and insisted that communist aggression would be met with massive nuclear retaliation. The term **brinkmanship** entered the Cold War vocabulary when Eisenhower's Secretary of State John Foster Dulles (1888–1959) warned, "If you try to run away from [nuclear war], if you are scared to go to the brink, you are lost."[10]

brinkmanship Style of Cold War confrontation in which each superpower endeavored to convince the other that it was willing to wage nuclear war.

CHRONOLOGY: THE COLD WAR, 1950–1968

1950
Outbreak of the Korean War. — 1950

1953 — **1953**
First American and Soviet hydrogen bomb tests; death of Joseph Stalin; end of the Korean War.

1955
First Geneva summit. — 1955

1956 — **1956**
Hungarian uprising and its repression by Soviet troops.

1957
Launch of *Sputnik*. — 1957

1959 — **1959**
Khrushchev's visit to the United States.

1961
Berlin Wall built. — 1961

1962 — **1962**
Cuban Missile Crisis.

1963
Nuclear Test Ban treaty signed. — 1963

1964 — **1964**
Khrushchev ousted; beginning of the Brezhnev era.

1965
U.S. bombing of North Vietnam begins. — 1965

Different Voices

Torture and Terrorism in the French-Algerian War

T he French-Algerian War shattered France's postwar political system and raised troubling questions about French identity. Much of the controversy aroused by the war centered on the revelations that French police and the French military routinely used torture to interrogate captured Algerian rebels. In the following excerpts we hear the voices of soldiers—the first, a high-ranking officer, the second, a volunteer paratrooper.

I. War Against Terrorism

Roger Trinquier (1908–1985) served in both World War II and Indochina before becoming commander of the 3rd Colonial Airborne Regiment in Algeria. In Modern Warfare: A French View of Counterinsurgency, *Trinquier identified terrorism—and the fight against it—as the quintessential form of modern warfare.*

The goal of modern warfare is control of the populace, and terrorism is a particularly appropriate weapon, since it aims directly at the inhabitant. . . . What characterizes modern terrorism, and makes for its basic strength, is the slaughter of generally defenseless persons. . . . The terrorist should not be considered an ordinary criminal. Actually, he fights within the framework of his organization, without personal interest, for a cause he considers noble and for a respectable ideal, the same as the soldiers in the army confronting him. On the command of his superiors, he kills without hatred individuals unknown to him, with the same indifference as the soldier on the battlefield. His victims are often women and children. . . . But during a period of history when the bombing of open cities is permitted, and when two Japanese cities were razed to hasten the end of the war in the Pacific, one cannot with good cause reproach him. The terrorist has become a soldier, like the aviator or the infantryman.

But the aviator . . . knows that anti-aircraft shells can kill or maim him. . . . It never occurs to [the infantryman] . . . to ask . . . that his enemy renounce the use of the rifle, the shell, or the bomb. . . . [The terrorist] must be made to realize that, when he is captured, he cannot be treated like an ordinary criminal. . . . No lawyer is present for such an interrogation. If the prisoner gives the information requested, the examination is quickly terminated; if not, specialists must force his secret from him. . . . The terrorist must accept this as a condition inherent in his trade and in the methods of warfare that, with full knowledge, his superiors and he himself have chosen. . . .

Interrogations in modern warfare should be conducted by specialists perfectly versed in the techniques to be employed. . . . The interrogators must always strive not to injure the physical and moral integrity of individuals. Science can easily place at the army's disposition the means for obtaining what is sought. But we must not trifle with our responsibilities. It is deceitful to permit artillery or aviation to bomb villages and slaughter women and children, while the real enemy usually escapes, and to refuse interrogation specialists the right to seize the truly guilty terrorist and spare the innocent.

If . . . our army refused to employ all the weapons of modern warfare, it could no longer fulfill its mission. We would no longer be defended. Our national independence, the civilization we hold dear, our very freedom would probably perish.

SOURCE: *Modern Warfare: A French View of Counterinsurgency* by Roger Trinquier, translated from the French by Daniel Lee; with an introduction by Bernard B. Fali; Foreword by Eliot A. Cohen (New York: Frederick Praeger, 1964), 16, 17, 20–21, 23, 115. Copyright © 1964, 2006 by Praeger Security International.

II. The Torture Room

In 1954 Pierre Leuillette enlisted in the French Army. After he finished his tour of duty in Algeria, he wrote St. Michael and the Dragon: Memoirs of a Paratrooper, *published in France in 1961.*

A volunteer paratrooper is never at the start anything but a grown-up little boy, at best an enthusiastic boy scout, dreaming of cuts and bruises, of bursts of machine-gun fire, of his parachute spread in the wind, and of the glamorous uniform, red beret, jungle-green combat suit, and commando dagger slipped into the boot. . . . He leaves everything, parents, friends, school, work, for "adventure." It's his first free act. It will be his last, too, for a long time: the enlistment is for three years. . . .

I shall speak of the torture room of the 1st Company of the 2nd R. P.C., my company. . . . Every day, the lieutenant on duty, assisted by Sergeant T., of the Signal Corps, and another sergeant, a very muscular Alsatian, spends several hours there. They have plenty to do. . . . With interrogation for a pretext, their work really amounts to torturing naked, bound prisoners, one after another, from morning to night. *[Leuillette describes the various torture methods ranging from the basic slap to simulated drowning to crushing the genitals in a vise.]* Our principal implement did not, however, exist in the Middle Ages. This refinement of civilization presents at first glance a quite innocuous appearance: simply an electric wire attached to a floor plug. . . . Besides being efficacious, [*torture by electricity*] has the added advantage of leaving no marks. . . .

Even if the great majority of those we interrogate are criminals of the most evil sort, there are also among them men only suspected—of, for example, harboring [rebels], or of collecting money for them; and there are some completely innocent, who, like most innocent people, cannot possibly prove it. . . .

(continued on next page)

(continued from previous page)

To civilians . . . I tell about what I see every day. They have always had a lofty idea of the greatness of France. They listen politely. But I sense their unbelief. They are thinking, "This isn't possible. We'd have known about it." Will they ever know about it? The German people, after the war, never stopped saying, and it was probably true, "We didn't know." . . . Have they ever realized that not knowing is also a way of being guilty?

[His tour of duty complete, Leuillette sails back to France.]
On the boat my joy is so great that all night long I whistle and sing. . . . The [ship] comes into Marseilles and my excited joy suddenly dissolves. For there on the dock several hundred soldiers are waiting to leave, just as I was three years ago. I am afraid, afraid for them. . . . For I now know that they risk more than death. They risk the loss of everything that could make them men.

SOURCE: Pierre Leuillette, *St. Michael and the Dragon: Memoirs of a Paratrooper*. Trans. John Edmonds (Boston: Houghton Mifflin, 1964), 1–2, 286–288, 298–299, 334. Originally published in French as *Saint Michel et le dragon*. Copyright © 1961 by Les Editions de Minuit. Reprinted by permission of Georges Borchardt, Inc., for Les Editions de Minuit.

For Discussion

1. Why was the French-Algerian War so divisive in France? What issues did it raise about French national identity?
2. The controversy over French police and military tactics in Algeria raised a question that is much debated today: Does the fight against terrorism demand the use of torture, or is the turn to torture as much a threat to Western values as terrorism itself? Can we use the history of the French-Algerian War to answer this question? How do we "learn from history," given the uniqueness of each historical event?

📖 Read the Document

Nikita Khrushchev, "Speech to the 22nd Congress of the Communist Party"

This newly aggressive American stance was matched on the other side of the Cold War divide. After a period of uncertainty following Stalin's death in 1953, Nikita Khrushchev (1955–1964) emerged in 1955 as the new Soviet leader. Loud and boisterous, given to off-the-cuff remarks and spontaneous displays of emotion, Khrushchev contrasted sharply with the reserved Stalin. (It is hard to imagine Stalin taking off his shoe and beating it on a table, as Khrushchev did in front of the television cameras at an assembly of the United Nations.) Khrushchev played a dangerous game of nuclear bluff, by which he convinced allies and foes alike that the Soviet Union possessed a stronger nuclear force than it actually did.

Khrushchev and Eisenhower recognized, however, that nuclear weapons made total war unwinnable. Thus, the period from 1953 until 1964 witnessed thawing superpower relations followed by the icy blasts of renewed hostilities. In 1955, for example, representatives of Britain, France, the United States, and the Soviet Union met in Geneva for the first summit of the Cold War. This initial thaw ended one year later when Khrushchev sent tanks into Hungary to crush an anti-Soviet rebellion.

The Soviets' successful launch of the first human-made satellite, *Sputnik,* in 1957 was even more chilling. Khrushchev claimed—falsely—that the Soviets possessed an advanced intercontinental ballistic missile (ICBM) force and that Soviet factories were producing rockets "like sausages from a machine."[11] *Sputnik* had ominous implications, especially for western Europeans. If the Soviets could launch a satellite into space, they seemed capable of delivering a nuclear bomb to American as well as European cities. If the Soviets invaded western Europe with conventional forces, would the Americans defend Europe—and so open their own cities to nuclear retaliation? Would the United States risk Chicago to save Paris?

Yet in the late 1950s, the Cold War ice seemed to be breaking once again. In 1958 the Soviet Union announced it would suspend nuclear testing. The United States and Britain followed suit and nuclear test ban talks opened in Geneva. The next year Khrushchev spent 12 days touring the United States. (Much to his regret, security concerns kept him from visiting Disneyland.) The communist leader impressed Americans as down-to-earth, a man rather than a monster. Khrushchev ended his U.S. visit with the promise of another four-power summit in 1960.

ON THE BRINK: THE BERLIN WALL AND THE CUBAN MISSILE CRISIS These warming relations, however, turned frosty in 1960 after the Soviet Union announced it had shot

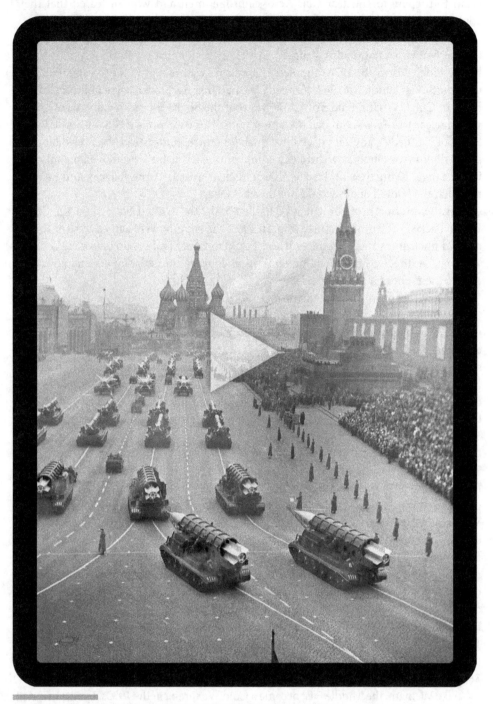

A MILITARY PARADE IN RED SQUARE, MOSCOW, NOVEMBER 7, 1963 The development of new weapons—often nuclear—became a central focus of Cold War competition between the United States and the Soviet Union. Displays such as this one, held on Revolution Day, served as a display of the Soviet Union's military might to the rest of the world.

down an American spy plane and captured its pilot. This announcement aborted the planned summit and initiated one of the most dangerous periods in the post-World War II era, one that saw the construction of the **Berlin Wall** and an escalation of the arms race. As we saw at the beginning of this chapter, the continuing outflow of East Germans to the West through Berlin led the East German communist leader Walter Ulbricht (1893–1973) and Khrushchev to erect the wall. Two weeks later, the Soviet Union resumed nuclear testing. The new American president John F. Kennedy

Berlin Wall Constructed by the East German government, a wall that physically cut the city of Berlin in two and prevented East German citizens from access to West Germany; stood from 1961 to 1989.

28.1

Watch the Video
Escaping the Berlin Wall

28.2

28.3

28.4

Watch the Video
Cold War Connections—Russia,
America, Berlin, and Cuba

Third World Term coined in 1955
to describe nations that did not
align with either the Soviet Union
or the United States; commonly
used to describe the industrially
underdeveloped nations.

Read the Document

Jawaharlal Nehru, "Why India
Is Non-Aligned"

(1917–1963) increased military spending and called for an expanded civil defense program to prepare for nuclear war. Across Europe, men and women feared that their continent would become a nuclear wasteland.

Such a war was narrowly avoided in the fall of 1962 as once again the Cold War intersected with a nationalist struggle. In 1959, a nationalist revolutionary movement led by Fidel Castro (b. 1926) toppled Cuba's pro-U.S. dictator. Castro aligned Cuba with the Soviet Union. In 1962, Kennedy learned that the Soviets were building missile bases in Cuba. What he did not know was that the Soviet forces in Cuba were armed with nuclear weapons—and had the power to use these weapons if U.S. forces attacked. Some of Kennedy's advisers urged just such an attack, but instead the president used secret diplomatic channels to broker a compromise. Khrushchev removed the missiles; in exchange, Kennedy withdrew NATO's nuclear missiles from Turkey and guaranteed that the United States would not invade Cuba.

In the aftermath of the Cuban Missile Crisis, the United States and the Soviet Union backed off from brinkmanship. In 1963, the superpowers agreed to stop aboveground nuclear testing with the Nuclear Test Ban treaty and set up between them the "hotline," a direct communications link to encourage immediate personal consultation in the event of a future crisis.

The retreat from brinkmanship did not, however, slow the globalization of the Cold War. The superpowers served as magnetic poles, attracting competing nationalist and regional forces. Many newly independent nations resisted being drawn in, as the Bandung Conference of 1955 made clear. Bandung brought together "nonaligned" states who sought to establish themselves as a collective force separate from both superpowers. French journalists at the conference gave these nations a collective label—neither the first (Western, capitalist) nor the second (Eastern, communist), but rather the **Third World**. Genuine independence, however, proved difficult to retain.

COLD WAR ARENAS: VIETNAM AND THE MIDDLE EAST The transformation of the Vietnam War from a struggle against French imperial rule into a Cold War conflict illustrates the way in which the superpowers tended to replace European empires as global powerbrokers. After the defeat of French forces at Dien Bien Phu in 1954, rival Vietnamese nationalists fought to control the Indochinese peninsula. Ho Chi Minh and his communist regime in North Vietnam relied on the Soviet Union and China for support, while American military and economic aid propped up an anticommunist (but not democratic) government in South Vietnam. Under the Kennedy presidency (1961–1963), the number of military advisers in Vietnam expanded rapidly, as did American involvement in South Vietnamese politics. When Kennedy's successor, Lyndon Johnson (1908–1973), took office, he issued a clear order, "Win the war!" In 1964, the U.S. Congress granted Johnson the authority to take "all necessary measures" to do so. By 1968, more than 500,000 American soldiers were fighting in Vietnam. About 58,000 U.S. soldiers died during the war—as did well over one million Vietnamese.

Like Vietnam, the Middle East became a Cold War arena in the 1950s. Events in Egypt proved pivotal. In 1954 the revolutionary nationalist Gamal Abdel Nasser (1918–1970) overthrew the British-dominated Egyptian monarchy. The United States immediately sought to woo Nasser to the West by offering aid to build the Aswan Dam, a huge hydroelectric project on the Nile River. But when Nasser arranged a weapons deal with Czechoslovakia, outraged American policymakers denied him funds for the dam. The Egyptian leader retaliated by aligning with the Soviet Union and by nationalizing the Suez Canal.

This series of events set off what is known as the Suez Crisis, a dramatic demonstration of the waning power of European empires and of the rising dominance of the superpowers. Angered by Nasser's seizure of the canal, the British and French governments conspired with Israel to topple him from power. Israeli forces invaded Egypt, according to plan, on October 31, 1956. Posing as peacekeepers, the British and French demanded that both sides pull back from the Canal Zone. When, as they expected,

Nasser refused, British and French troops invaded. But then the plan unraveled under superpower pressure. With the Soviet Union threatening a nuclear strike against the invading forces, President Dwight Eisenhower telephoned the British prime minister, Anthony Eden, and exploded, "Is that you, Anthony? Well, this is President Eisenhower, and I can only presume you have gone out of your mind!" Eisenhower's administration blocked Britain's IMF loan application and pushed Britain to the edge of financial collapse. Eden's government had no choice but to declare a cease fire and withdraw British troops.

While the Suez Crisis highlighted superpower dominance in the Middle East, the Six-Day War of 1967 marked a clear Cold War division of the region. In six days of fighting, Israel gained possession of the Sinai Peninsula from Egypt, the West Bank from Jordan, the Golan Heights from Syria—and one million stateless Palestinian refugees (see **Map 28.4**). In the wake of the war, American foreign policy shifted to decisive support for Israel. In turn, Egypt, Syria, Iraq, Sudan, and Libya aligned with the Soviet Union.

28.1

28.2

28.3

28.4

📖 **Read the Document**

Gamal Abdel Nasser, Speech on the Suez Canal

🔍 **View the Map**

The Formation of Modern Israel

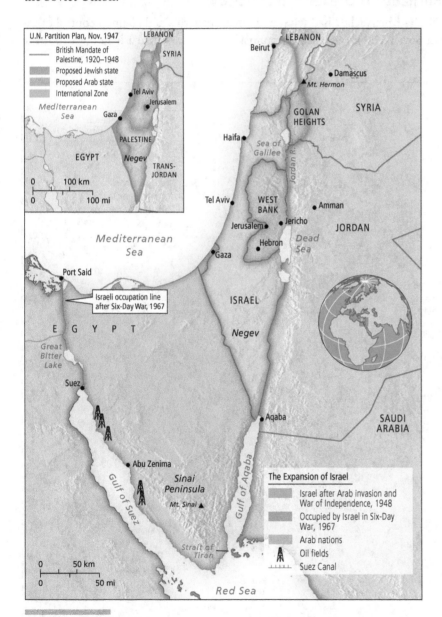

MAP **28.4** THE EXPANSION OF ISRAEL The map inset outlines the United Nations' plan to partition Palestine into Jewish and Arab states, with Jerusalem as an international zone. This plan was not implemented; instead, Israel carved out its own boundaries as a result of war with the surrounding Arab powers. What was the impact of the Six-Day War in 1967 on those boundaries?

The Soviet Union and Eastern Europe in the 1950s and 1960s

28.3 What patterns characterized the history of the Soviet Union and eastern Europe after the death of Stalin?

D ivided by the Cold War, the peoples of western and eastern Europe in the 1950s and 1960s followed separate paths (see **Map 28.5**). For the citizens of eastern Europe and the Soviet Union, Stalin's death in 1953 inaugurated a period of political reform and hope for prosperity. By the end of the 1960s, however, economic stagnation and political discontent characterized life in the Soviet bloc.

De-Stalinization Under Khrushchev

By 1955 Nikita Khrushchev had triumphed over his rivals and claimed control of the post-Stalin Soviet Union. A true communist success story, Khrushchev was born to

MAP **28.5** EUROPE IN THE COLD WAR As this map shows, during the Cold War the "West" was defined culturally and politically, rather than in geographic terms. Which "eastern" states belonged to the "West"? Which European states were neutral?

CHRONOLOGY: THE SOVIET BLOC AFTER STALIN

1953
Death of Stalin; relaxation of terror in eastern Europe and Soviet Union.

1953

1955
Khrushchev emerges as new Soviet leader.

1955

1956
Khrushchev's "Secret Speech," de-Stalinization accelerates; unrest in Poland results in new regime under Gomulka; Hungarian Revolution crushed by Soviet forces.

1956

1964
Khrushchev ousted; Brezhnev era begins.

1964

1968
Prague Spring crushed.

1968

illiterate peasants and began work as a coal miner at age 14. Recognized as a man with talent by the Communist Party, he trained as an engineer and helped build the Moscow subway system. Khrushchev owed everything to the Communist Party, and he never forgot it. Confident in the moral and material superiority of communism, Khrushchev believed that the Soviet Union would win the Cold War on the economic battlefield. But this victory would occur only if Soviet living standards substantially improved and only if the Stalinist systems of terror and rigid centralized control were dismantled. Khrushchev's accession to power thus ushered in the era of **de-Stalinization**, a time of greater openness in the Soviet bloc as governments lifted many of the controls on speech and publication. For the first time in years, dissent and debate reappeared in public life.

The most dramatic sign of de-Stalinization was the release of at least four and a half million prisoners from slave labor camps. As one Soviet citizen recalled, their return was disturbing: "In railway trains and stations, there appeared survivors of the camps, with leaden grey hair, sunken eyes, and a faded look; they choked and dragged their feet like old men."[12] These survivors often returned to find their spouses remarried, their children embarrassed by their presence, their world destroyed. Some, such as the writer Alexander Solzhenitsyn, wrote horrifying accounts of their experiences. Solzhenitsyn's books narrated the daily degradation of prison life and provided a detailed map of the network of slave labor camps that he christened "The Gulag Archipelago."

Yet in 1959, four years after the start of de-Stalinization, the Gulag still held at least one million prisoners. De-Stalinization did not end political and religious repression or artistic control. Under Khrushchev, Soviet Jews continued to suffer harassment and imprisonment while Orthodox Christians experienced an intensified anti-Christian campaign, which destroyed churches, imprisoned clergy, closed seminaries and monasteries, and in some cases removed children from Christian homes. Artists who dared challenge the standards of Socialist Realism (see Chapter 26) also suffered. An exhibition of long-hidden works by Picasso inspired many Soviet artists to experiment with abstract art; when Khrushchev saw their work on show, however, he thundered,

de-Stalinization Nikita Khrushchev's effort to decentralize political and economic control in the Soviet Union after 1956.

DE-STALINIZATION On October 31, 1956, Hungarian demonstrators pulled down a huge statue of Joseph Stalin and then dragged it two miles through the city center. Stalin's head still sits at an intersection in Budapest.

"What's hung here is simply anti-Soviet. It's immoral."[13] Within days, the artists in the show were censured, expelled, or unemployed.

De-Stalinization was also limited in its economic impact. In agriculture in particular, the Soviet Union continued to lag behind the West. Refusing to retreat from collectivization, Khrushchev instead implemented a series of poorly planned reforms, including rapid mechanization, a massive chemical fertilizer program, and the plowing of virgin lands. The fundamental productivity problem remained unsolved—and worsened in the long term because of the ecological damage inflicted on the Soviet countryside. Soil erosion increased exponentially, nitrogen runoff from fertilized fields contaminated water supplies, and soil fertility declined. The full force of these problems would not be felt until the 1980s, but as early as 1963 the Soviet Union had to import Western grain, a humiliating admission of failure for Khrushchev's regime.

Re-Stalinization and Stagnation: The Brezhnev Era

De-Stalinization unsettled many high-ranking communists who forced Khrushchev out of office in 1964. After a short period of collective leadership, Leonid Brezhnev (1906–1982) emerged as the new Soviet leader. A polite man with no interest in original ideas, Brezhnev was far more reassuring to Soviet bureaucrats than the flamboyant Khrushchev, whose boisterous embrace of ambitious schemes had proven destabilizing. Fifty-eight years old and already physically ailing when he assumed the party leadership, the increasingly decrepit Brezhnev matched his era.

Under Brezhnev the Soviet economy stagnated. Growth rates in industrial production and labor productivity slowed during the second half of the 1960s and almost disappeared in the 1970s. Improving living standards, however, masked this economic stagnation. Brezhnev continued Khrushchev's policies of free higher education and rising wages, while accelerating the expansion of consumer goods. State subsidies ensured that the cost of utilities, public transport, and rents remained far lower than in the West (although apartments were in short supply), and an extensive welfare system eased pressures on ordinary people.

By the middle of the 1960s, the Soviet Union appeared to have achieved a sort of stability. It was, however, a stability relying on repression. Judging de-Stalinization to be too risky, Brezhnev and his colleagues withdrew the limited cultural and intellectual freedoms introduced under Khrushchev. Those who expressed dissident views soon found themselves denied employment and educational opportunities, imprisoned, sent to the Gulag, or confined indefinitely in psychiatric wards.

Yet dissent did not disappear. Soviet society may have resembled a stagnant pond by the 1970s, but beneath the surface churned dangerous currents that, in the late 1980s, would engulf the entire communist system. Nationalism among the non-Russian populations served as the source of much discontent, as did resentment about political repression. Reviving a practice employed by reformers under the tsarist regime, dissidents evaded the censors by *samizdat* or "self-publishing." Novels, plays, poetry, political treatises, and historical studies were circulated privately, copied by hand, or duplicated on treasured (and often confiscated) typewriters and photocopiers and distributed more widely. Nonconformist artists, banned from official exhibitions, used private apartments to show their work.

Diversity and Dissent in Eastern Europe

Despite the uniformity imposed by Soviet-style communist systems during these decades, the nations of eastern Europe developed in different ways. De-Stalinization accelerated this diversification. In 1956, Khrushchev declared, "It is ridiculous to think that revolutions are made to order"[14] and so indicated that communist nations could follow paths diverging from the road traveled by the Soviet Union.

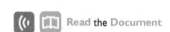

Read the Document

Henry Myers, East Berliners Rise Up Against Soviet Oppression

1956 AND AFTER But just how far from the Soviet road could those paths go? The contrasting fates of Poland and Hungary in 1956 provided the answer. In Poland, protests against Stalinist controls proved strong enough to bring back into power Wladyslaw Gomulka (1905–1982). An influential Polish communist who had been purged in the Stalinist terror in 1951, Gomulka succeeded in establishing a uniquely Polish brand of communism, one that abandoned collective farming and gave a certain amount of freedom to the Roman Catholic Church in Poland, yet remained loyal to the Warsaw Pact.

Hungary also pursued a de-Stalinizing "New Course" under the leadership of the reformist communist Imre Nagy (1896–1958). Unlike Gomulka, however, Nagy gave in to popular demands for a break with the Soviet Union. On October 31, 1956, Hungary withdrew from the Warsaw Pact—or tried to. A few days later, Khrushchev sent in the tanks. At least 4,000 Hungarians died as the Red Army crushed all resistance. Nagy was executed in 1958.

The smashing of the Hungarian revolt defined the limits of de-Stalinization in eastern Europe: The satellite states of the Soviet Union could not follow paths that led out of the Warsaw Pact. Within the confines of this structure and of the one-party state, however, the governments of eastern Europe pursued different courses. Poland held onto its small family farms, with less than one-eighth of farmland collectivized by 1960, in contrast to collectivization rates of 84 percent in Romania, and 87 percent in Czechoslovakia. In Hungary, the post-1956 government of János Kádár (1912–1989)—who had survived torture and imprisonment during the Stalinist terror of the early 1950s—instituted the New Economic Mechanism in the second half of the 1960s. This "mechanism" sharply reduced the state's control of the economy. In contrast, Romanians endured the reign of the "mini-Stalins," Gheorghe Gheorghiu-Dej (1901–1965) and Nicolae Ceauşescu (1918–1989), who imposed not only one-party but one-man control over the country through Stalinist methods of terror.

Within the diverse experiences of eastern Europeans, certain commonalities characterized the post-1956 era. Except in Romania and even more oppressive Albania, living standards improved, particularly in comparison with the hard times of the 1930s and 1940s. Educational opportunities expanded, the supply of consumer goods increased, and political repression became less overt. Even so, over-centralization, bureaucratic mismanagement, and political corruption ensured that living standards remained below those of the West. Moreover, the very consumer goods that were supposed to persuade eastern European citizens of the superiority of the communist system instead demonstrated its deficiencies. With a radio, a Hungarian teenager could tune into Radio Free Europe and hear of a livelier, more abundant society in the West. In East Germany, television watchers could view West German networks and catch a glimpse of Western prosperity.

THE PRAGUE SPRING Discontent simmered throughout the Eastern bloc during the 1960s and then, in 1968, boiled over in Czechoslovakia. During the 1960s, a reform movement emerged in the ranks of the Czechoslovakian Communist Party. It included Slovaks, who believed that the regime's centralized policies favored Czechs, and younger, university-educated managers and scientists who resented the power of uneducated party superiors. At the beginning of 1968, demands for reform fueled an intraparty revolution that brought to power the Slovakian communist Alexander Dubček (1921–1992). Dubček embarked on a program of radical reform aimed at achieving "socialism with a human face." This more humane socialism included freedom of speech, press, assembly, and travel; the removal of Communist Party controls from social and cultural life; and decentralization of the economy. Dubček's effort to reform the system from the top quickly merged with a wider popular protest movement that had arisen among intellectuals, artists, students, and workers. The result was the "**Prague Spring**"—the blossoming of political and social freedoms throughout Czechoslovakia, but especially in the capital city of Prague.

Prague Spring Short-lived popular effort in 1968 to reform Czechoslovakia's political structures; associated with the phrase "socialism with a human face."

Well aware of the fate of Hungary in 1956, Dubček reassured Brezhnev that his reforms would not lead Czechoslovakia out of the Warsaw Pact. But by the summer of 1968, word of the Prague Spring had reached other eastern European countries and the Soviet Union itself. In Ukraine, nationalist protesters looked to Prague for inspiration, while in Poland, student rioters waved placards reading "Poland is awaiting its own Dubček." Frightened communist leaders throughout the Eastern bloc demanded that Brezhnev stifle the Prague Spring.

On the night of August 20–21, 80,000 Soviet, Polish, Hungarian, and East German troops crossed the Czech border, and over the next several weeks crushed the Prague Spring. That fall, Brezhnev acknowledged that Soviet domination in eastern Europe rested on force alone when he articulated what came to be known as the "Brezhnev Doctrine." Formally a commitment to support global socialism, the Brezhnev Doctrine essentially promised to use the Red Army to destroy any effort to achieve fundamental change within the Soviet bloc.

The West: Consensus, Consumption, and Culture

28.4 What patterns characterized the history of western Europe in the 1950s and 1960s?

As in eastern Europe, in western Europe both World War II and the Cold War shaped the 1950s and 1960s. The desire to make the suffering of the war years worthwhile, and opposition to communism, fueled economic integration and strengthened political centrism. The dominant fact of the postwar years was, however, material prosperity as western European economies embarked on two decades of dramatic economic growth and consumer spending.

The Triumph of Democracy

In contrast to the interwar years, the parties in power in western Europe in the 1950s and 1960s and the voters who put them there agreed on the virtues of parliamentary democracy. The new constitutions of France, West Germany, and Italy guaranteed the protection of individual rights, and French and Italian women achieved suffrage. The democratic ideal of the universal franchise had finally been realized in most of western Europe.

Citizenship, though, meant more than the right to vote after 1945. With the triumph of *social democracy* throughout western Europe, the meaning of citizenship broadened to include the right to a decent standard of living. Through the nationalization of key industries, the establishment of public agencies to oversee and encourage investment and trade, and the manipulation of interest rates and currency supplies, governments assumed the task of ensuring full employment and material well-being for their citizens. A slogan of the German Social Democratic Party—"as much competition as possible, as much planning as necessary"—summed up an approach common to much of western Europe at this time.

Social democracy also meant the construction of comprehensive welfare states to guarantee citizens adequate incomes and medical care. By the end of the 1950s, the average western European working-class family received 63 percent of its income from wages. The substantial remaining income came from welfare benefits such as family allowances, national health services, sickness and disability insurance, and old-age pensions. In addition, state-run vaccination and inoculation programs, stricter sanitation regulation, and the development of policies to control communicable diseases all meant an improvement in the health of Europe's populations.

As we saw in Chapter 27, the victory of social democracy was rooted in the suffering of World War II, when Europeans grew determined to create a better world out of the rubble of total war. This determination remained, but wartime radicalism receded as the Cold War constricted the parameters of political debate. The mainstream political parties—Christian Democrats or Conservatives on the right, Social Democrats or Socialists on the left—agreed in refusing to allow Communist Party members to participate in governing coalitions. In France and Italy, communist parties consistently drew 20 to 30 percent of the vote, but were effectively marginalized by their exclusion from office after 1948.

With the communists isolated, and with the ideologies of the extremist Right such as fascism and Nazism discredited by the horrors of the war, western European politics became more centrist. **Christian Democracy**—which has no American or British counterpart—flourished on the European Continent. Drawing on a largely Roman Catholic base for support, Christian Democrats espoused a conservative social ideology combined with a progressive commitment to the welfare state. Christian Democrats dominated much of European politics in the 1950s and 1960s: They played significant roles in the political life of France and Belgium, governed West Germany between 1949 and 1969, and provided every prime minister except two in Italy between 1945 and 1993.

Three factors account for Christian Democracy's success. First, as anticommunists and advocates of the free market, Christian Democrats benefited from Cold War anxieties and more directly from American aid. Second, because they were based on religion (Roman Catholicism) rather than class, Christian Democratic parties appealed to middle-class and working-class voters, and particularly to women, who tended to be more religious and to vote more conservatively than men. Finally, the triumph of Christian Democracy rested on its transformation from a right-wing to a centrist political movement. In the interwar period, Christian Democracy, rooted in a religious and political tradition based on hierarchy and authoritarianism, had veered close to fascism. But during World War II, many Catholics served in the Resistance, where they absorbed progressive political ideas. The war-inspired desire to use the power

Christian Democracy Conservative and confessionally based (Roman Catholic) political parties that dominated much of western European politics after World War II.

of the state to improve the lives of ordinary people blended with traditional Catholic paternalism. After the war the Christian Democrats embraced democracy and supported the construction of comprehensive welfare states.

Prosperity in the West

These political developments unfolded against an economic backdrop of increasing prosperity. In the first half of the 1950s, Europeans moved rapidly from the austerity of the immediate postwar years to an age of affluence.

ECONOMIC INTEGRATION The greater coordination of western European economies contributed to this new prosperity. World War II provided the initial impetus for this economic integration. Fighting in conditions of unprecedented horror, Europeans looked for ways to guarantee a lasting peace. In July 1944, Resistance leaders from France, Italy, the Netherlands, and a number of other countries met in Geneva to declare their support for a federal Europe.

No such radical restructuring occurred, but Cold War concerns helped western Europeans see themselves as part of a single region with common interests. In addition, American policymakers required any state that received Marshall aid to develop transnational economic institutions. Looking back on this early stage of European economic integration, the Belgian prime minister (and ardent proponent of European union) Paul-Henri Spaak (1899–1972) wrote in the later 1960s, "Europeans, let us be modest. It is the fear of Stalin and the daring views of Marshall which led us into the right path."[15]

Efforts at European economic integration culminated with the formation of the **European Economic Community (EEC)** or Common Market in 1957. Consisting of Germany, France, Italy, and the "Benelux" states (Belgium, the Netherlands, and Luxembourg), the EEC sought to establish a free trade zone across member boundaries and to coordinate policies on wages, prices, immigration, and social security. Between 1958 and 1970, trade among its six member states increased fivefold. The rapid movement of goods, services, and even workers ensured that the economies of member states flourished. In contrast, Britain, which chose to remain outside the EEC to preserve its preferential trading relationships with its former and current colonies, struggled with growth rates below those of its continental competitors.

THE AGE OF AFFLUENCE By the mid-1950s, western Europe entered an age of consumption. After years of wartime rationing, Europeans went on a spending spree and did not stop. Climbing real wages—by 80 percent in England, for example, between 1950 and 1970—help explain why. So too does the construction of the welfare state. With full employment and comprehensive welfare services offering unprecedented financial security, Europeans shrugged off habits of thrift. Credit buying (what the British called "buying on the never-never") became commonplace and made possible even more consumption.

This spending spree transformed the interiors of European homes and their exterior environment. Housing construction boomed, and with new houses came new household goods. Items such as refrigerators and washing machines, once unaffordable luxuries, now became increasingly common in ordinary homes. In France, the stock of home appliances rose by 400 percent between 1949 and 1957. At the same time, the automobile revolutionized the rural and urban landscape. Highways, few and far between in 1950, cut across the countryside, and parking meters, unknown in Europe before 1959, dotted city streets. In 1964, the archbishop of Florence presided over a thanksgiving service in a gas station to celebrate the completion of a highway linking Milan and Naples. Out-of-town shopping centers, geared to the convenience of car owners, proliferated while city centers decayed.

European Economic Community (EEC) Originally comprising West Germany, France, Italy, Belgium, Luxembourg, and the Netherlands, the EEC was formed in 1957 to integrate its members' economic structures and so foster both economic prosperity and international peace. Also called the Common Market.

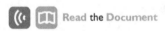

Read the Document

A Common Market and European Integration

Western Culture and Thought in the Age of Consumption

Cultural developments in Western society highlight the shift from an era structured by the austerity and suffering of World War II to an age of affluence and opportunity. By the second half of the 1950s, artists began to retreat from engagement with the horrors of war and instead produced works that commented on and reveled in the cascade of consumer abundance.

FINDING MEANING IN THE AGE OF AUSCHWITZ AND THE ATOM BOMB In the years immediately after 1945, existentialism (which first emerged in the despair of the 1930s) remained a powerful cultural force. Jean-Paul Sartre's conviction that existence has no intrinsic meaning and yet that the individual retains the freedom to act and therefore make meaning, resounded in a world that had experienced both the Holocaust and the Resistance. The existentialist emphasis on individual action as the source of meaning could lead to a life of political activism. Sartre, for example, worked with the French Resistance and became a prominent participant in left-wing political causes in the 1950s and 1960s. Yet existentialist anxiety also justified political disengagement. In the Irish-French playwright Samuel Beckett's (1906–1989) *Waiting for Godot* (1952), two tramps sit in an empty universe, waiting for someone who never comes. In this absurd void, politics has no relevance or resonance.

Existentialist themes echoed throughout the visual arts in the early 1950s. The sculptures of the Swiss artist Alberto Giacometti (1901–1966) embody existentialism—fragile, insubstantial, they appear ready to crack under the strain of being. While Giacometti's sculptures exemplify existentialist terror, the works of the preeminent British painter of the 1950s, Francis Bacon (1909–1992), evoke outright nausea. Bacon's canvases are case studies in the power of the subconscious. He painted the people he saw around him, but his perceptions were of a society disfigured by slaughter. Slabs of meat, dripping in blood, figure prominently. Bacon explained, "When you go into a butcher's shop . . . you can think of the whole horror of life, of one thing living off another."[16]

The terrors of the nuclear age also shaped cultural consciousness in this period. Because figurative painting seemed utterly incapable of capturing the power and terror of the atomic age, the Bomb reinforced the hold of abstract art over the avant-garde. But abstract art itself changed. Before the war, formal geometric compositions predominated. After the war, a type of modernism, Abstract Expressionism, displayed more spontaneous styles. The Abstract Expressionist Jackson Pollock (1912–1956), for example, invented an entirely new way of painting. Placing the canvas on the ground, he moved around and in it, dripping or pouring paint. In Pollock's works (see p. 909), the canvas has no clear center, no focal point. Instead, it disintegrates, like matter itself. As Pollock explained, "New needs need new techniques. . . . The modern painter cannot express his age, the airplane, the atom bomb . . . in the old forms."[17]

ALBERTO GIACOMETTI, *MAN POINTING* (1947) Giacometti's sculptures embodied existentialist anguish. His account of this piece's creation seems to be lifted from a Samuel Beckett play or one of Jean-Paul Sartre's novels: "Wanting to create from memory [the figures] I had seen, to my terror the sculptures became smaller and smaller, they had a likeness only when they were small, yet their dimensions revolted me, and tirelessly I began again, only to end several months later at the same point."

FRANCIS BACON, *FIGURE WITH MEAT,* 1954 Bacon's disturbing images resonated with a European public still struggling with the impact of total war. *Figure with Meat* is one of a series of paintings that Bacon modeled on Diego Velazquez's *Portrait of Pope Innocent X* (1649–1650). By replacing the draperies in Velazquez's masterpiece with slabs of meat, Bacon challenged the solace and authority of traditional religion.

Most people confronted their nuclear fears not in art galleries, but rather in movie theaters and popular fiction. In the movies, various nuclear-spawned horrors, such as giant spiders, ants, and turtles, wreaked weekly havoc on the Western world. Fittingly enough, many of these films were produced in Japan. Throughout the 1950s, nuclear war and the postnuclear struggle for survival also filled the pages of popular fiction. Probably the most important "nuclear" novel, however, confined mention of atomic bombs to a single sentence. In *Lord of the Flies* (1954), British author William Golding (1911–1993) told the simple but brutal story of a group of schoolboys stranded on an island after they flee atomic attack. Their moral deterioration poses basic questions about the meaning of civilization, a question brought to the forefront of Western society by its use of advanced science and technology to obliterate civilian populations during World War II.

CULTURE AND IDEAS IN THE WORLD OF PLENTY In the later 1950s, artists began to turn away from such big questions and to focus instead on the material stuff of everyday existence. Works such as the British artist Richard Hamilton's *Just What Is It That Makes Today's Homes So Different, So Appealing?* (1956) satirized and yet celebrated the plethora of material objects pouring off assembly lines (see p. 910). Hamilton was a leading force in the Independent Group, a loose association of British artists, designers, and architects that explored the "aesthetics of plenty"—the idea that consumer affluence had smashed the barriers between fine art and popular culture. The Independent Group, along with other movements such as "New Realism" in France and "Capitalist Realism" in West Germany, helped shape what became known as **pop art**.

pop art Effort by artists in the 1950s and 1960s both to utilize and to critique the material abundance of post-World War II popular culture.

JACKSON POLLOCK, *SHIMMERING SUBSTANCE* (1946) Many of Pollock's postwar works—huge paintings that pulse with power—show an obsession with heat and light, surely no coincidence in the dawn of the nuclear age.

Pop artists dismissed the anguish of Bacon and Giacometti as the concerns of an older generation still mired in World War II. Pop art looked outward rather than inward and focused on the material rather than the spiritual. Pop artists spoke in the vocabulary of mass materialism, relied on mass production and mass marketing, and challenged accepted ideas about the role of art and the artist in Western society. When Gerhard Richter (b. 1932) placed himself in the furniture display of a West German department store and called the resulting "piece" *Living with Pop* (1963) he turned the artist, as well as art, into a commodity, something to be bought and sold just like anything else. In the age of consumption, pop advocates declared, the individual artist's intentions were unimportant, and concepts such as artistic genius were irrelevant.

Similar themes also characterized developments in social thought. Existentialism had elevated the individual as the only source of meaning in an absurd universe. In the late 1950s, however, a new social theory, **structuralism**, pushed the individual off center stage. Structuralism, which French anthropologist Claude Lévi-Strauss

structuralism Influential post-World War II social theory that explored the common structures of language and thought.

909

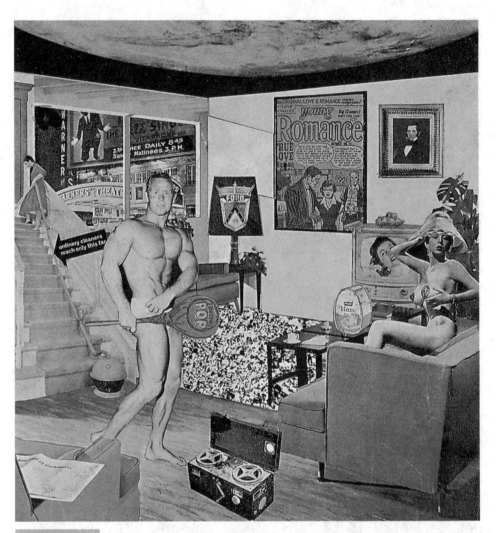

RICHARD HAMILTON, *JUST WHAT IS IT THAT MAKES TODAY'S HOMES SO DIFFERENT, SO APPEALING?*
(1956) British artist Richard Hamilton was one of the leading figures in the pop art movement of the 1950s. The
image plays with the consumerism and domesticity that marked the postwar period.

(1908–2009) first introduced to a wide audience, transformed a number of academic
disciplines, including literary criticism, political theory, sociology, and history. Lévi-
Strauss argued that the stories that people told, whether medieval French peasants or
contemporary Londoners, shared "deep structures," repeated patterns such as pair-
ings and oppositions that shape the way individuals perceive the world. The stories
themselves—and the storytellers—were unimportant.

SCIENCE AND RELIGION IN AN AGE OF MASS CONSUMPTION At the same time that
structuralists depicted the individual as stuck within a cultural and linguistic web,
breakthroughs in the biological sciences suggested that perhaps the web lay *inside* the
individual. In 1953, the British biologist Francis Crick (1916–2004) and his American
colleague James Watson (b. 1928) discovered the structure of DNA, the basic building
block of genetic material. Crick and Watson's model of the "double helix," the intertwined spirals of chemical units that, in a sense, issue the instructions for an individual's
development, caught the attention of the world. As biologists and geneticists furthered
their investigations into human genetic inheritance, they raised exciting yet disturbing
possibilities, such as the cloning of living organisms and genetic manipulation. These
possibilities added a new dimension to the perennial debate about individual freedom.

Other scientific developments assured human beings more freedom from their
physical environment than ever before. Motivated by the Cold War, the space race

launched humanity beyond the confines of Earth, culminating in 1969 with American astronaut Neil Armstrong's moon walk. Large-scale production of penicillin transformed ordinary medical care, as did rapid development of vaccines against many childhood killers such as measles. In 1953, the American doctor Jonas Salk announced the first successful clinical trial of a polio vaccine. Blood transfusions became more commonplace, along with the development of organ transplants, following the first successful kidney transplant in Chicago in 1950. Like washing machines and television sets, a long and healthy life suddenly appeared accessible to many people in the West.

While scientists were claiming more control over the physical environment, the organized churches continued to offer spiritual authority and sustenance. Church attendance, which had declined in most Western countries in the interwar period, rose during the 1950s. In the United States between 1942 and 1960, church membership per capita grew faster than at any time since the 1890s. No European nation shared this dramatic religious upsurge. Nevertheless, except in Scandinavia, western Europe experienced a gentle religious revival. In Britain during the 1950s, church membership, Sunday school enrollment, and the numbers of baptisms and religious marriages all increased. In West Germany, the rate of churchgoing rose among Protestants from 1952 until 1967. Throughout Catholic Europe, the vibrancy of Christian Democratic politics reflected the vital position of the Roman Catholic Church in society.

In the 1960s, however, the situation changed as Europeans abandoned the church sanctuary in favor of the department store, the sports stadium, and the sofa in front of the television set. Declining rates of church attendance, a growing number of civil rather than religious marriage ceremonies, and an increased reluctance to obey Church teaching on issues such as premarital sexual relations all pointed to the secularization of European society. By the 1970s, churchgoing rates in both Protestant and Catholic countries were in freefall.

Yet the churches did not remain stagnant during this time of change. A number of Protestant theologians argued that Christianity could maintain its relevance in

CHRONOLOGY: MEDICAL BREAKTHROUGHS

1950
First kidney transplant.
1950

1952
1952
First sex-change operation.

1952
Polio vaccine first produced.
1952

1953
1953
Discovery of DNA.

1957
CAT scan developed.
1957

1967
1967
First heart transplant.

Vatican II Popular term for the Second Vatican Council that convened in 1963 and introduced a series of changes within the Roman Catholic Church.

this more secular society by adapting the biblical message to a modern context. The British theologian (and Anglican bishop) John Robinson achieved great notoriety in 1963 when he proclaimed the "death of God." Most of those who jeered at or cheered for Robinson's statement missed his point—that Christians had to update the language in which they articulated their faith to make sense in the modern world.

The biggest change occurred in Roman Catholicism. In 1962 the Second Vatican Council—widely known as **Vatican II**—convened in Rome, the first Catholic council to meet since 1870. In calling the council, Pope John XXIII (r. 1958–1963) sought to modernize the Church, a process that, he recognized, would demand "a change in mentalities, ways of thinking and prejudices, all of which have a long history."[18]

John did not live to see this change in mentalities take place, but his successor Paul VI (r. 1963–1978) presided over a quiet revolution. The Church emerged from Vatican II less hierarchical, with local and regional councils sharing more power with the papacy. For ordinary Catholics, the most striking changes occurred in the worship service, where a number of reforms narrowed the gap between priest and people. The priest moved behind the altar, so that he could face the congregation; he spoke in the vernacular rather than in Latin; and all worshipers, not only the priest, received the wine at communion.

Vatican II was less revolutionary in its approach to sexual issues and gender roles. The council said nothing about homosexuality, reaffirmed the traditional doctrine of clerical celibacy, and insisted that only men could be ordained as priests. The council left open the question of birth control; three years later, however, the pope declared contraceptive use to be contrary to Catholic teaching. The issues of clerical celibacy, women's ordination, and contraceptive use would bedevil the Church for the rest of the century.

Social Encounters in the Age of Affluence

With the prosperity of the postwar years came a series of encounters—between Americans and Europeans, between immigrants and indigenous populations, between men and women, and between generations—that transformed Western cultures.

AMERICANIZATION, COCA-COLONIZATION, AND THE GAULLIST PROTEST In the postwar decades, U.S.-based corporations scattered branch offices throughout western Europe, and American-produced goods filled the shelves of European shops. The American presence in science and technology was also formidable. The United States invested more in scientific research and development, produced more graduates in the sciences and engineering than all other Western countries combined, and came out on top in terms of numbers of papers published and patents registered.

American domination of popular culture was even more striking. Immediately after World War II, the U.S. government forced European states to dismantle quotas on American film imports by threatening to withhold much-needed loans. By 1951, American productions accounted for more than 60 percent of films showing in western Europe. American television, too, quickly established a central position in European mass culture. The popular *Lone Ranger* series, for example, appeared in 24 countries. Language itself seemed subject to American takeover. Words such as *babysitter* and *comics* entered directly into German, while French children coveted *les jeans* and *le chewing-gum*.

Europeans differed in their response to this American presence. Many enthusiastically embraced American culture, equating it with openness and freedom. Others, however, feared that American products such as Coca-Cola would degrade European tastes. They spoke with alarm about the "brain drain" of scientists and academics heading to the richer universities of the United States and argued that even as Europe was losing its colonial possessions, it was itself undergoing colonization, or at least "coca-colonization."[19]

One of the most powerful voices protesting "coca-colonization" belonged to Charles De Gaulle, France's president throughout the 1960s. De Gaulle combined anticommunism and traditional social values with a commitment to a strong state and centralized direction of the economy. Perhaps most of all, **Gaullism** championed France and Frenchness. In De Gaulle's imagination, France was "like the princess in the fairy stories or the Madonna in the frescoes, as dedicated to an exalted and exceptional destiny . . . France cannot be France without greatness."[20]

De Gaulle did not sympathize with the Soviet Union, but he believed that American "coca-colonization" posed the more immediate threat to the French way of life. Taken in 1960 to view a new highway in California, De Gaulle gazed somberly at the sight of cars weaving in and out on a traffic cloverleaf and commented, "I have the impression that all this will end very badly."[21] To reduce American influence in Europe, and thus to restore France to its rightful position of grandeur and glory, De Gaulle pursued independent foreign and military policies. He extended diplomatic recognition to communist China, made a state visit to Moscow, and withdrew French forces from NATO command (although France remained formally a part of the NATO alliance). In 1960 France exploded its own atomic bomb.

Like De Gaulle, Europeans across the political spectrum feared that their countries might become secondhand versions of the United States, yet the cultural history of this era was one of reciprocal encounters rather than one-way Americanization. Europeans consumed American products with gusto, but in the process they adapted these products to suit their own needs. In the late 1950s, for example, four young working-class men from the northern British seaport of Liverpool latched on to the new American rock-and-roll music, mixed in their own regional musical styles, and transformed popular music not only in Europe, but also in the United States. The impact of the Beatles testified to the power of European culture to remake American cultural products. Even McDonald's, when it arrived in European cities in the 1960s, made subtle changes to the composition of its fast food to appeal to the differing tastes of the new markets.

IMMIGRATION AND ETHNIC DIVERSITY Rising numbers of immigrants who brought with them new and, in many cases, non-Western cultural traditions also transformed European societies during this era. Two developments—decolonization and economic prosperity—explain the upsurge in immigration. With the collapse of European imperial control, white settlers retreated to their country of origin, and colonial "losers"— indigenous groups that had allied with the colonial powers—fled because they feared persecution and discrimination. At the same time, the soaring economies of western Europe created a voracious demand for labor that governments and businesses sought to fill by recruiting outside their state borders. By the beginning of the 1970s, approximately nine million immigrants had settled in western Europe. Half of these came from the less prosperous Mediterranean states of Portugal, Spain, Italy, and Greece, and the other half from Turkey, Yugoslavia, and countries in Asia, Africa, and the Caribbean.

These workers did the dirtiest, most dangerous, least desirable jobs. They worked the night shifts, emptied the bedpans, dug the ditches, and cleaned the toilets. They lived in substandard housing, often confined to isolated dormitories or inner-city slums, and accepted low, often illegally low, pay rates. The reason they did so is starkly presented in Table 28.1. Despite racial discrimination and economic exploitation, western Europe offered greater economic opportunities than were available in the immigrants' homelands.

The majority of the early immigrants were single men. They tended to see themselves, and were seen by their host countries, as "guestworkers," temporary laborers who would earn money and then return home to their native lands. From the 1970s on, however, families began to join these men, and a second generation of "immigrants" was born. This generation changed the face of Europe.

Gaullism The political ideology associated with twentieth-century French political leader Charles De Gaulle. Gaullism combined the advocacy of a strong, centralized state with social conservatism.

TABLE **28.1** ANNUAL PER CAPITA GROSS NATIONAL PRODUCT: MID-1960s

Pakistan	$125
Jamaica	$520
Turkey	$353
Spain	$822
Italy	$1,272
Britain	$1,977
France	$2,324

SOURCE: Leslie Page Moch, *Moving Europeans: Migration in Western Europe Since 1650* (Bloomington: Indiana University Press, 1992), 177.

The emergence of urban ethnic subcultures enlivened European cultures and economies (and diets). It also complicated domestic politics and raised challenging questions about the relationship between national and ethnic identity. Racism became more overt, first, because the white settler groups who returned "home" in the wake of decolonization often brought with them hardened racist attitudes and, second, because the presence of nonwhite minority groups, clustered in certain cities, sparked resentment in societies unused to cultural diversity.

THE SECOND SEX? A third area of encounters that shaped postwar western culture was that between men and women. In 1949, the French writer Simone de Beauvoir (1908–1986) published *The Second Sex*. In this influential critique of gender divisions in Western industrial society, de Beauvoir argued that women remained the "second sex"—that despite political and legal changes, a woman's relationship to men, rather than her own actions or achievements, still defined her. Over the next two decades, the new prosperity pushed women into higher education and the labor force and so, in the long run, worked to undermine the traditional gender roles that de Beauvoir described. In the short run, however, affluence accentuated women's identity as the second sex.

Demographic changes reflected and reinforced postwar domesticity. Marriage rates rose and the marriage age dropped in the postwar years. In the United States between 1940 and 1957, the fertility rate rose by 50 percent. Europe experienced a baby "boomlet" rather than a baby boom with birth rates rising in the late 1940s but dropping in the 1950s.

By exalting women's maternal identity, both religion and popular culture provided a potent ideology for these demographic changes. The Roman Catholic Church of the 1950s placed renewed emphasis on Mary, the paragon of motherhood. Pope Pius XII (r. 1939–1958) particularly encouraged the growth of devotion to Mary. He proclaimed in 1950 that Mary had ascended bodily into heaven (the Doctrine of the Assumption) and designated 1954 as the Year of Mary. This Marian devotion encouraged women to regard motherhood as a holy calling. Popular culture reinforced this religious message, with its glossy images of what families should look like and how they should interact. In television programs and in the articles and advertisements of women's magazines, the woman stayed at home, presiding over an expanding array of household machines that, in theory, reduced her housework burden and freed her to focus on the satisfactions of motherhood.

Cold War concerns also accentuated the Western woman's domestic role. First, anticommunist propaganda hailed domesticity as a sign of Western superiority by contrasting the favorable lot of Western women to their Soviet counterparts, who combined their domestic duties with full-time outside employment, often in jobs involving heavy manual labor, and with the tiresome task of lining up for hours each day to purchase scarce goods. Second, the nuclear age made the nuclear family seem all the more important. Feeling increasingly helpless in a superpower-dominated world on the brink of nuclear annihilation, Europeans tended to withdraw for shelter to family life.

For some women, this shelter was more like a prison. In *The Feminine Mystique* (1963), the American journalist Betty Friedan (1921–2006) identified what she called "the problem that had no name," a crisis of identity and purpose among middle-class, educated women confined in the role of housewife and mother. The research of British sociologist Hannah Gavron (1936–1965) supported Friedan's argument. In *The Captive Wife* (1966), Gavron used interviews and other sociological data to explore "the conflicts of housebound mothers." She asked, "Have all the great changes in the position of women in the last one hundred and fifty years come to nothing?" A 29-year-old wife and mother of two young sons, Gavron committed suicide the year before her work was published.

Whether a nightmare or a dream, the domestic ideal remained removed from the reality of many women's lives in the postwar era. In the poorer social classes, women by necessity continued to work outside the home, as they always had. At the same time, the new culture of consumption demanded that many women, clinging precariously to middle-class status, take on waged employment to pay for the ever-expanding list of household necessities.

A new pattern of employment emerged that reconciled renewed domesticity with the needs of expanding economies and ambitious consumers. Increasingly, single women worked until they married. Many continued to do so until the first child arrived and resumed paid employment after the last child had left home or at least started school. This work was regarded, however, as secondary to their main job—the making of a home and the rearing of children. Part-time employment, with lower wages and few or no benefits, expanded accordingly. Everywhere pay rates for men and women remained unequal.

THE PROTEST ERA The unprecedented prosperity of the West in this era permitted a dramatic expansion of higher education systems. By the later 1960s, these universities became the center of powerful protests as political demonstrations exploded in almost every Western country and in the developing nations as well. In France, a student demonstration blossomed into a full-scale social revolt. Within a few days, eight million French men and women were on strike. "Paris '68" came to symbolize the political and social discontent of many in the West, particularly the youth, during these years.

Much of this discontent focused on the **New Left** argument that ordinary people, even in democratic societies, possessed little power. Appalled by the inhumanity of Stalinism, New Leftists differed from the "old" Left in their suspicion of the state. New Left thinkers such as the German philosopher Herbert Marcuse (1898–1979) warned that expanding state power threatened the individuality and independence of the ordinary citizen. They argued that debate might seem open, but that experts and elites, not ordinary people, made the actual choices. Hence, the protesters demanded "participatory" rather than parliamentary democracy, the revitalization of citizenship through active participation in decision making.

New Left Left-wing political and cultural movement that emerged in the late 1950s and early 1960s; it sought to develop a form of socialism that rejected the overcentralization, authoritarianism, and inhumanity of Stalinism.

PARIS, 1968. *La chienlit* means masquerade or carnival, a time when rules are lifted. After protests erupted in Paris and across France in 1968, General Charles De Gaulle appeared on television. In a scatological play on words, he declaimed "*La réforme, oui. La chie-en-lit, non*," literally translated as "Reform, yes, crap in bed, no." De Gaulle thus dismissed the protests as both a meaningless carnival and as something comparable to human excrement. The protesters picked up on De Gaulle's phrase, reverted back to the original *la chienlit*, and, under an image of De Gaulle's famous profile, proclaimed, "The carnival (and crap)—it's him!"

Discarding orthodox political solutions went hand-in-hand with overturning traditional social rules. In their demand for "liberation," the students focused as much on cultural as on economic and political issues. As behaviors labeled immoral or bohemian in the 1950s became commonplace—for example, couples living together before marriage or individuals engaging in sexual relationships with a variety of partners—commentators began to talk about a sexual revolution.

The protests of the later 1960s were also linked to the wider context of decolonization and the Cold War. Protesters identified their struggle for more open politics with colonial independence movements. Rejecting both Soviet-style communism and free-market capitalism, protesters turned for inspiration to the newly emerging nations of Latin America and Asia. Seeking to break free from the confines of the Cold War, they fiercely criticized American involvement in Vietnam, in which they believed the United States served not as "the leader of the free world," but rather as an imperialist oppressor.

CONCLUSION

New Definitions, New Divisions

When Soviet tanks rolled through the streets of Budapest in 1956, they flattened not only the Hungarian Revolution, but also any illusions about the democratic nature of Soviet-style communism. Yet the hope that the communist system could be reformed, that Marx's original concern for social justice and political equality could be reclaimed, remained—until 12 years later when the tanks rolled again in an eastern European city. The crushing of the Prague Spring destroyed any hope of a democratic eastern Europe under Soviet domination.

In contrast, democracy took firm root in western Europe during the postwar era, even in nations with anti-democratic cultural traditions such as West Germany and Italy. Yet in 1968, protesters in Paris and in cities throughout the world challenged the easy linkage of "the West" with democracy. They pointed out that the increasing scale and complexity of industrial society deprived ordinary people of opportunities for genuine participation in political decision making. And they pointed to the way that Cold War divisions superseded democratic commitments. Within the Cold War context, "the West" sometimes seemed to mean simply "anti-Soviet."

By the early 1970s, the sharp bipolarities of West versus East had begun to break down. Over the next three decades, economic crisis, combined with revolutionary changes in eastern European and Soviet affairs, would reshape the contemporary world. By the early 1990s, the Cold War was over and nationalist conflicts, often fueled by vicious ethnic and religious hatreds, once again played front and center after 20 years of being upstaged by superpower hostilities.

MAKING CONNECTIONS

1. Was the Cold War inevitable? If so, why? If not, what event constituted the "point of no return" and why?
2. How did consumerism structure Western economies, culture, and politics in the 1950s and 1960s?

TAKING IT FURTHER

For suggested readings, see page R-1.

Chapter Review

A Dubious Peace, 1945–1949

28.1 | Why and how did the world step from World War II to the Cold War?

A common enemy rather than shared aims cemented the alliance of the Soviet Union with the Western democracies. Differences over the political settlement of eastern and central Europe, particularly the borders of Poland and the division of Germany, strained the alliance, as did Stalin's murderous policies in the areas under Soviet control. The Truman Doctrine, the Marshall Plan, and the formation of NATO and the Warsaw Pact all marked key steps in the outbreak of the Cold War.

The West and the World: Decolonization and the Cold War

28.2 | What was the impact of decolonization and the Cold War on the global balance of power?

Although European imperial powers emerged from World War II determined to hold onto their overseas territories, the economic and political costs proved too great. Already by the late 1940s, decolonization signaled a contraction of European global power. At the same time, however, Cold War rivalries increased Soviet and American intervention around the world, as events such as the Korean War, the Suez Crisis, and the Vietnam War illustrated.

The Soviet Union and Eastern Europe in the 1950s and 1960s

28.3 | What patterns characterized the history of the Soviet Union and eastern Europe after the death of Stalin?

In an effort to stabilize political life and accelerate economic growth, Nikita Khrushchev initiated de-Stalinization, an effort at limited decentralization and the restoration of some civil liberties. Khrushchev's reform efforts shuddered to a halt in 1964, when he was removed from power. Economic stagnation and renewed political persecution characterized the Brezhnev years. In eastern Europe, the crushing of the Hungarian Revolution in 1956 signaled the sharp limits of de-Stalinization, a lesson reinforced in 1968 when the reform movement known as the Prague Spring in Czechoslovakia was defeated.

The West: Consensus, Consumption, and Culture

28.4 | What patterns characterized the history of western Europe in the 1950s and 1960s?

The artistic shift from existentialism and Abstract Expressionism to Pop Art reflected the wider western move from austerity into affluence, as consumerism became a way of life throughout western Europe and the United States. This was also a period marked by political

stability, founded on the social democratic consensus, and by efforts at European economic unification through the Common Market. Prosperity and stability attracted immigrants; by the 1970s many European societies were well on their way to becoming multi-colored, multi-cultural societies.

Chapter Time Line

1945
Potsdam Conference.

1945

1947
Truman Doctrine announced; Marshall Plan announced; India, Pakistan, and Burma achieve independence from Britain.

1947

1948
Split between Yugoslavia's communist leader Tito and Stalin, Stalinist terror throughout eastern Europe widened; Soviet blockade of West Berlin, Berlin Airlift; State of Israel established.

1948

1950
Outbreak of the Korean War.

1950

1954
Defeat of French forces in Indochina; partition of Vietnam; beginning of Franco-Algerian War.

1954

1956
Khrushchev's "Secret Speech," de-Stalinization accelerates; unrest in Poland results in new regime under Gomulka; Hungarian Revolution crushed by Soviet forces.

1956

1957
Formation of EEC (Common Market).

1957

1961
Berlin Wall built.

1961

1962
Vatican II convenes; Cuban Missile Crisis.

1962

1968
Protests in Paris; Prague Spring crushed.

1968

917

29

The West in the Contemporary Era: New Encounters and Transformations

O n the evening of November 9, 1989, East German border guards at the Berlin Wall watched nervously as thousands of East Berliners crowded in front of them and demanded to be allowed into West Berlin. This demand was extraordinary: In the 28 years that the Berlin Wall had stood, some 200 people had been shot trying to cross from east to west. But the autumn of 1989 was no ordinary time. A reformist regime had emerged in the Soviet Union and proclaimed that eastern European governments could no longer rely on the Red Army to crush domestic dissent. Poland and Hungary were in the process of replacing communist governments with pluralist parliamentary systems. And in East Germany, over one million disaffected citizens had joined illegal protest demonstrations.

In response to this overwhelming public pressure, the East German government had decided to relax the requirements for obtaining an exit visa to visit West Germany. But at a press conference on the morning of November 9, the East Berlin Communist Party boss

View the **Closer Look**   Collapse of the Berlin Wall

AND THE WALL CAME TUMBLING DOWN In the weeks after the opening of the Berlin Wall on November 9, Berliners from both East and West appropriated this once forbidden zone as their own space for celebration.

LEARNING OBJECTIVES

29.1	29.2	29.3	29.4
How did developments in the 1970s and 1980s destabilize post–World War II national and international structures?	What factors explain not only the outbreak but also the success of the revolutions of 1989–1991?	What were the consequences of the revolutions of 1989–1990 for the societies of eastern Europe?	How and why was the West redefined at the end of the twentieth century and the beginning of the twenty-first?

((Listen to Chapter 29 on MyHistoryLab

Watch the Video Series on MyHistoryLab

Learn about some key topics related to this chapter with the *MyHistoryLab Video Series: Key Topics in Western Civilization*

Gunter Schabowski stated, wrongly, that anyone who wanted to head to the West could obtain an automatic exit visa at the border. As huge crowds gathered at the checkpoints that dotted the Berlin Wall, the border guards had no idea what to do. Panicked, they opened the gates. While television cameras broadcast the scene to an astonished world, tens of thousands of East Berliners walked, ran, and danced across the border that had for so long literally and symbolically divided West from East. Elated with their new freedom and energized with a sense of power and possibility, they jumped upon the Wall. An instrument of coercion and division became a platform for partying. Within a few days, and again without any official approval, ordinary Germans, equipped with hammers and chisels, began to dismantle the Wall erected almost three decades earlier.

The fall of the Berlin Wall has come to symbolize the dramatic events that closed the twentieth century: the collapse of communist regimes throughout eastern Europe, the end of the Cold War, the disintegration of the Soviet Union, and the onset of civil war in Yugoslavia and in many formerly Soviet regions. In the subsequent decades, governments and ordinary people—not only in Europe but across the globe—struggled to build new structures to suit the transformed geopolitical landscape.

What, then, were the causes and consequences of these developments? And what were their implications for Western identity—and for the future of Western civilization?

Economic Stagnation and Political Change: The 1970s and 1980s

29.1 How did developments in the 1970s and 1980s destabilize post-World War II national and international structures?

The 1970s and 1980s saw the post-World War II political settlement, in national and international terms, begin to collapse. The stark clarity—the "Them versus Us"—of the Cold War grew more opaque at the same time that economic crisis widened divisions within Western societies and eroded the social democratic political consensus.

A More Uncertain Era

In the early 1970s, the West entered a new era. **Détente,** the effort to stabilize superpower relations through negotiations and arms control, shifted the Cold War status quo while the easy affluence of the postwar period abruptly ended. At the same time, an upsurge in terrorism unsettled western European societies. With its dramatic rejection of the processes of democratic decision making, terrorism challenged some of the most basic assumptions of the postwar order in the West.

THE ERA OF DÉTENTE West German diplomacy caused the first shift in Cold War relations. In 1969 the West Berlin mayor and Social Democratic Party (SPD) leader Willy

détente During the 1970s, a period of lessened Cold War hostilities and greater reliance on negotiation and compromise.

Brandt (1913–1992) became chancellor. For the first time in its history, West Germany had a government not led by a Christian Democrat. Brandt proceeded to implement a new *Ostpolitik* or "Eastern policy"—the opening of diplomatic and economic relations between West Germany and the Soviet Union and its satellite states. Ostpolitik reached its climax when East and West Germany recognized the legitimacy of each other's existence in 1972 and both Germanys entered the United Nations in 1973.

Economic pressures led the leaders of the superpowers to embrace a much wider version of Ostpolitik: détente. By the end of the 1960s, the Soviet and the American economies were stagnating. With both states spending colossal sums on nuclear weapons, their leaders looked for a new approach to the Cold War. Thus, in November 1969 Soviet and American negotiators began the Strategic Arms Limitation Talks (SALT). Signed in 1972, the agreement froze the existing weapons balance. SALT left the superpowers with sufficient nuclear weaponry to destroy the globe several times over, but it helped slow the armaments spiral and ease Cold War tensions.

Détente also extended to U.S. relations with the other great communist power: China. In 1971 President Richard Nixon (1913–1994) announced the lifting of travel and trade restrictions with China and then visited China himself. "East versus West" had formed a basic building block of international relations throughout the 1950s and 1960s. In the era of détente, however, the shape of international politics became more fluid.

ECONOMIC CRISIS IN THE WEST The economic outlook also blurred in this era as the 1970s brought an unprecedented combination of high inflation and high unemployment rates. Commentators labeled this new reality **stagflation**—the escalating prices of an overheated economy combined with the joblessness of economic stagnation. Between 1974 and 1976 the average annual growth rate within western European nations dropped to zero.

stagflation Term coined in the 1970s to describe an economy troubled by both high inflation and high unemployment rates.

War and oil helped create this economic crisis. In October 1973, the Yom Kippur War began when Egyptian and Syrian armies attacked Israel. In retaliation for American assistance to Israel, the oil-producing Arab states in OPEC (the Organization of Petroleum Exporting Countries) imposed an embargo on sales to the United States and quintupled the price of a barrel of oil. In 1979 political revolution in Iran doubled the price again. These two "oil crises" vastly accelerated the inflationary spiral.

Two other factors also contributed to the economic crisis. First, in 1973 President Nixon acted to defend the weakening dollar by letting it "float." Market forces rather than fixed exchange rates now determined the dollar's value against other currencies. This decision gutted the Bretton Woods Agreement, which had governed international economic affairs since World War II (see Chapter 28), and introduced a less regulated, more volatile economic era. In the two decades after the collapse of Bretton Woods, 69 countries experienced serious banking crises as currency speculators destabilized national economies and the annual economic growth rates of the developing nations fell by one-third.

A second factor in the economic crisis of the 1970s was international competition as Asian, South American, and Latin American economies industrialized. Because Western societies possessed a politicized workforce that demanded relatively high wages and extensive social services, manufacturing firms began to move south and east to take advantage of the lack of labor regulation and protection in the developing world.

CONSEQUENCES OF THE CRISIS As the economic pie appeared smaller, competition for slices increased. The 1970s saw a resurgence of industrial unrest. For example, conflict with unions brought down three successive British governments in a decade. Throughout the West images of picketing workers, often fighting with police, dominated televised news broadcasts.

Racial conflict also escalated, with the nine million immigrants residing in northern and western Europe making easy targets for those individuals and groups who sought someone to blame for their economic hardships. By 1975 West Germany, France, the Netherlands, Britain, Belgium, Sweden, and Switzerland had all banned further immigration; ironically, this legislation actually increased the size of immigrant communities. Foreign workers scrambled to get into western Europe before the doors shut, and those already established hastened to bring in family members. By 1991, 25 percent of the inhabitants of France were either immigrants or the children or grandchildren of immigrants.

The resulting encounters among peoples of different religious and cultural traditions transformed European societies. In Britain, for example, Afro-Caribbean styles of dress and music radically reshaped white working-class youth culture, while the growing southeast Asian community injected new flavors into the British diet.

Yet the European tendency, dominant since the nineteenth century, to identify "nation" not with a set of ideas (what we call "civic nationalism") but rather with race or ethnicity ("ethnic nationalism"), complicated the integration of the new residents into the wider national community. Hence, British journalists in the 1980s often described an individual born in Britain to British citizenship as a "third-generation immigrant," a label that revealed the "whiteness" of popular notions of British identity.

But at least in Britain, as well as in France, immigrants could become (or already were) legal citizens. In contrast, in West Germany, Switzerland, and the Scandinavian countries, immigrants remained "foreign," with no chance of obtaining citizenship. Thus, their children grew up in a society in which they had no political rights. These "foreigners" experienced widespread discrimination in education, housing, and employment.

THE TURN TO TERRORISM As we saw in the last chapter, the 1960s witnessed a wave of student protests across much of the world. In the 1970s, frustrated with their failure to effect real change through protest and persuasion, a minority of student activists turned to terror. The Weathermen in the United States, the Red Brigades in Italy, and Baader-Meinhof in West Germany all dived underground and resorted to bombings, assassinations, and abductions in an effort to weaken the structures of Western capitalism. In Italy, a terrorist culture emerged, with approximately 2,000 acts of terrorism committed each year during the 1970s, including the Red Brigade's dramatic kidnapping, and subsequent murder, of the Christian Democratic Party leader and former prime minister Aldo Moro in 1978.

Left-wing student groups were not the only groups to embrace the politics of the bullet and the bomb in the 1970s. Nationalism also provided fertile soil for terrorism's growth. The first confirmed killing by the Basque separatist group ETA (*Euskadi Ta Askatasuna*—"Basque Homeland and Freedom") occurred in 1968, the opening move in what became a four-decades-long campaign of terror in Spain that claimed over 800 lives. In Northern Ireland, "the Troubles" began in the early 1970s. The Irish Republican Army (IRA) sought to join the province to independent Ireland; its Unionist opponents fought to maintain the union with Britain. Both regarded innocent civilians as prime targets.

Conflict in the Middle East also bled over into western Europe in the 1970s. Palestinian nationalist groups turned to hijackings and bombings in an effort to influence international diplomacy. In 1972, at the Olympic Games in Munich, West Germany, one such group murdered 11 members of the Israeli Olympic team. The "Munich massacre" not only made an absolute mockery of Olympic internationalism, it also persuaded many of the fragility of the postwar order.

The End of Political Consensus in the West

In this new and more uncertain era, the postwar political consensus crumbled. Two off-shoots of the protests of the 1960s—new feminism and environmentalism—demanded a reorientation of social democratic politics, while New Conservatives rejected social democratic fundamentals.

29.1 **new feminism** Reemergence of the feminist movement in the 1970s.

29.2

29.3

29.4

NEW CHALLENGES AND NEW IDENTITIES: NEW FEMINISM **New feminism** (also called "Second Wave feminism") emerged directly out of the student protest movement of the 1960s, when female activists grew frustrated with their limited role—"We cook while the men talk of revolution."[1] Their efforts to liberate women from political and cultural limits gave birth to an international feminist movement.

Although new feminists worked for the election of female candidates and other such political goals, they refused to confine their efforts to parliamentary politics. Asserting that "the personal is political," new feminists attacked beauty pageants, critiqued the fashion industry, and demanded equal access for girls to sporting funds and facilities. They also sought to outlaw spousal rape and to legalize abortion. Abortions became legal first in northern Europe: in Britain in 1967, in Denmark in 1970. Catholic Europe followed: In Italy abortions became legally available in 1978, France followed suit in 1979.

New feminism extended its critique of gender inequalities to the economic and educational spheres. Feminists demanded equal pay for equal work and greater access for women to professional opportunities. They pressed for more generous parental leave policies, family allowances, and child care provisions. With women accounting for approximately half of the university students in many Western countries, feminists also began to alter the content of the curriculum. Challenging the biases that had regarded women's contributions as irrelevant and women's lives as insignificant, feminists brought to light the "hidden history" of women.

NEW CHALLENGES AND NEW IDENTITIES: ENVIRONMENTALISM Environmentalists added their voice to the political cacophony of the 1970s and 1980s. At the heart of environmentalism was the idea of natural limits, often conceptualized as "Spaceship Earth," the vision of the planet as a "single spaceship, without unlimited reservoirs of anything."[2] This vision led environmentalists to question the fundamental structures of industrial economies (capitalist and communist), particularly their inherent emphasis on "more, bigger, faster, now." The movement argued that quantitative measures of economic growth (such as the GNP) failed to factor in environmental destruction and social dislocation and that in many contexts, "small is beautiful."

📖 **Read the Document**

Marshall Sahlins, "The Original Affluent Society"

THE NEW FEMINISM In 1971, women in Paris hit the streets to demand the legalization of abortion and free access to information about contraceptives.

The environmentalist movement's concern with ecological sustainability helped create "Green" political parties. **Green politics** drew on two other sources: new feminism and the New Left. The Greens contended that the degradation of the natural environment stemmed from the same root as discrimination against women—an obsession with physical power and an unwillingness to tear down hierarchical structures. Green politics also championed the key New Leftist goal of participatory democracy (see Chapter 28) and so articulated a basic challenge to the political status quo: "We are neither left nor right; we are in front." By the late 1980s Green Parties had sprouted in 15 western European countries. The Greens were the most successful in West Germany, where they sat in the legislature from 1983 and formed an important voting bloc.

Green politics A new style of politics and set of political ideas resulting from the confluence of environmentalism, feminism, and New Left politics.

THE NEW CONSERVATIVES Discontented by the economic crisis and social unrest of the 1970s, voters throughout the West looked for new answers. In Spain, Portugal, and Greece, they turned to socialist parties. Throughout most of western Europe and in the United States, however, **New Conservatism** dominated political society. Three leaders epitomized the New Conservatism: the Republican Ronald Reagan in the United States (1911–2004), the Christian Democrat Helmut Kohl in West Germany (b. 1930), and the Conservative Margaret Thatcher in Britain (1925–2013). New Conservatives rejected the postwar emphasis on social improvement in favor of individual achievement. They argued that rising social expenditures, funded by rising taxes, bore the blame for surging inflation and declining economic growth rates. As Kohl demanded during his 1983 campaign, "Less state, more market; fewer collective burdens, more personal performance; fewer encrusted structures, more mobility, self-initiative, and competition."

New Conservatism Political ideology that emerged at the end of the 1970s combining the free market approach of nineteenth-century liberalism with social conservatism.

The New Conservative agenda included lifting regulations on business, privatizing nationalized or state-owned industries, and reining in the welfare state. Most dramatically, New Conservatives abandoned the central feature of the postwar social democratic consensus: the conviction that the state has the responsibility to ensure full employment. By imposing high interest rates on their economies, New Conservative leaders such as Thatcher lowered damaging double-digit inflation rates. But high interest rates hurt domestic manufacturing and led to rising unemployment numbers. In Britain, 13 percent of the workforce was unemployed by 1984. In West Germany, too, Kohl's policies of holding down taxes and government expenditures accompanied unemployment rates over 9 percent in the mid-1980s.

THE END OF DÉTENTE Like the emergence of New Conservatism, rising superpower tensions accelerated the breakdown of the post-World War II political consensus within Western societies. Those tensions had appeared to be receding in the early 1970s as the leaders of the superpowers embraced détente. In 1975 representatives of 32 European states, Canada, the United States, and the Soviet Union signed the **Helsinki Accords**, which ratified existing European borders, agreed to the joint notification of major military exercises (to reduce the chances of accidental nuclear war), and promised to safeguard human rights.

Helsinki Accords Signed by representatives of 32 European states, Canada, the United States, and the Soviet Union in 1975; often regarded as the apex of détente.

The Helsinki Accords came about because of détente—yet they helped destroy it. Eastern European and Soviet dissidents used the Helsinki human rights clauses to publicize the abuses committed by their governments and to demand justice. Dissident activities expanded throughout the Soviet bloc, as did efforts at repression. When U.S. president Jimmy Carter took office in 1976, he placed human rights at the center of his foreign policy. Carter's approach infuriated Soviet leaders. Détente finally died in December 1979, when Soviet troops invaded Afghanistan. Calling the invasion "the most serious threat to peace since the Second World War," Carter warned that if the Soviets moved toward the Middle East, he would use nuclear weapons.

The election of New Conservatives such as Thatcher in 1979 and Reagan in 1980 intensified the rejection of détente and the renewal of the Cold War. Reagan labeled

NEW CONSERVATIVES AT WORK British Prime Minister Margaret Thatcher and German Chancellor Helmut Kohl address the press after a meeting in London in 1988. Although they shared many New Conservative assumptions, the two leaders did not like each other, as their body language reveals.

((● [📖] Read the Document

Margaret Thatcher, The Iron Lady Speech

the Soviet Union the "Evil Empire"—a reference to the popular *Star Wars* film series released in the 1970s—and revived the anticommunist attitudes and rhetoric of the 1950s. Thatcher strongly supported Reagan's decision to accelerate the arms buildup begun by Carter. Her hard-line anticommunism won her the nickname "Iron Lady" from Soviet policymakers.

Revolution in the East

29.2 What factors explain not only the outbreak but also the success of the revolutions of 1989–1991?

Between 1989 and 1991, revolution engulfed eastern Europe and the Soviet Union and set in motion a series of breathtaking changes: Soviet control over eastern Europe ended, the Cold War came to an abrupt halt, and the Soviet Union itself ceased to exist. Mikhail Gorbachev (1931–1991), appointed Soviet Communist Party secretary in 1985, played a pivotal role in these events. But Gorbachev did not control the story. Ordinary people developed their own plot lines. What the Czech dissident (and future president) Václav Havel called "the power of the powerless" proved powerful indeed.

The Crisis of Legitimacy in the East

While Western countries in the 1970s struggled with stagflation, the Soviet Union posted record-breaking production figures. But Soviet statistics ignored the quality of goods produced, the actual demand for a product, or the cost of producing it. Soviet leaders boasted that they had completed the heavy industrial expansion planned by Khrushchev in the early 1960s; microchips now counted for more than iron ore, however, and fiber optics, not steel, buttressed the new modernity. The rigid Soviet command economy could not keep up. By the 1980s, its only growth sectors were oil and vodka—and then the bottom dropped out of the oil market. After peaking in 1981, oil prices began a steady decade-long fall—and so, too, did the Soviet economy.

The Soviet Union's satellite states in eastern Europe also lurched from apparent prosperity into economic crisis during this period. During the 1970s, two factors cushioned eastern Europe from the economic crisis in the West. First, eastern governments could purchase Soviet oil at prices below market value. (In return these states had to sell their own products to the Soviets at similar discounts.) Second, loans from Western banks helped mask fundamental problems such as overcentralization and underproductivity. But in the 1980s, the Soviet Union, struggling with its own faltering economy, began charging higher oil prices at the same time that debt loads overwhelmed eastern European economies.

THE BEGINNING OF THE END: SOLIDARITY Events in Poland indicated the fragility of the communist system and initiated the process that led to the system's collapse. Faced with negative economic growth rates, the Polish government announced in July 1980 a rise in prices for meat and other essentials. Workplace strikes protesting the price increases spread throughout Poland. Then, workers at the Lenin Shipyard in Gdansk, led by a charismatic electrician named Lech Wałęsa (b. 1943), demanded the right to form a trade union independent of communist control. One month later, they did so—**Solidarity** was born. More than a trade union, Solidarity demanded the liberation of political prisoners, an end to censorship, and a rollback of governmental power. Within just a few months, more than 11 million Poles joined Solidarity.

How could Solidarity become such a powerful political and social presence so quickly? The answer rests in the concept of **civil society**: public organizations and activities separate from the state, commerce, or the family. Ranging from church and charitable groups to sports and hobby clubs, from theater companies to rock bands to radio stations, these organizations and activities help create community life—and in such communities, an individual creates his or her own sense of independent identity. In Soviet-style communism, where the state aimed to control not only public life but even private consciousness, such a self-identity, forged outside state control, threatened the entire political system. (See *Encounters and Transformations* in this chapter.)

Solidarity Trade union and political party in Poland that led an unsuccessful effort to reform the Polish communist state in 1981; survived to lead Poland's first non-communist government since World War II in 1989.

civil society Public organizations and activities separate from the state, commerce, or the family that help to create community life and a sense of identity.

THE MOMENT OF SOLIDARITY In August 1980, Lech Walesa addressed Solidarity supporters outside the Lenin Shipyard in Gdansk. Note the picture of Pope John Paul II and the other symbols of Roman Catholicism on the wall below: Throughout the communist era, the Catholic Church served as an important non-communist focus of Polish identity and loyalty.

Encounters and Transformations

Rock and the Velvet Revolution

In September 1968, less than one month after the armies of the Soviet Union and its satellite states crushed the Prague Spring (see Chapter 28), a Czech bass player named Milan Hlavsa formed a rock band. He did not see forming a rock band as a political act. The military invasion and the subsequent political crackdown appalled Hlavsa, but it never occurred to him that he could do anything to change the harsh reality of life in the communist bloc. He simply liked Western rock music (particularly the "psychedelic" music of American rocker Frank Zappa) and wanted to play in a rock band. Yet the encounter between the communist state and the anarchic energy of rock helped undermine communist rule and so contributed to the transformation of eastern Europe.

Hlavsa and his friends called their band "The Plastic People of the Universe" (PPU), after a Frank Zappa song. PPU quickly became popular in Prague, but almost as quickly the band ran into trouble. As part of the post-1968 crackdown, the Czech communist government insisted that musical groups conform to a set of official guidelines governing how, what, and where they performed. PPU refused and, in January 1970, lost its professional license. In the communist system, the state not only controlled broadcasting and recording, but even owned the distribution of musical instruments and electrical equipment. Without a license, PPU lost access to rehearsal and recording space and their instruments as well.

But the band played on by repairing cast-off instruments and constructing amplifiers from old transistor radios. Banned in 1972 from performing in Prague, PPU moved to the countryside. Banned in 1974 from playing anywhere, PPU dove underground. Fans alerted other fans when the band would be playing at some remote farm, while recordings made in houses and garages circulated illegally.

During this period PPU became more than just a rock band. It stood at the center of what manager Ivan Jirous labeled the "Second Culture." An alternative to the official communist "First Culture," the "Second Culture" comprised musicians, fans, artists, writers, and anyone else who sought to carve out a space of individuality and integrity in a society based on conformity and lies.

On March 17, 1976, the Secret Police arrested 27 musicians, including every member of PPU. Six months later rock music went on trial. In response to international protests, the Czech government released most of the 27 rockers. But Jirous and PPU's saxophonist, Vratislav Brabenec, as well as two musicians from other bands, were found guilty of "organized disturbance of the peace" and sentenced to between 8 and 18 months in prison.

The sentence infuriated Václav Havel, a well-known playwright and an ardent Frank Zappa fan. After the trial, Havel opened his farmhouse to PPU for illegal concerts and recording sessions. More important, he decided to challenge communism openly. On January 1, 1977, Havel and other artists and intellectuals announced the formation of Charter 77 to publicize human rights abuses under communism. Over the next decade many Charter members, including Havel, spent time in prison. Yet, by calling the state to account for its crimes,

ROCKING THE BLOC In 1977, the Plastic People of the Universe play an illegal concert in Václav Havel's farmhouse.

Charter 77 helped weaken the communist regime. When revolution came in 1989, that regime toppled with astounding ease. PPU had split up two years before but one of the first individuals that President Václav Havel invited to the new free Czechoslovakia was an aging psychedelic rocker named Frank Zappa.

For Discussion

Imagine that the post-1968 Communist government in Czechoslovakia simply ignored the PPU. Would events have unfolded any differently? Why or why not?

In Poland, however, communist control had never entirely destroyed civil society, in part because of the key role of the Roman Catholic Church. Participation in the Church had long been a way for Poles to express not only their religious faith but also their Polishness—an identity not controlled by the communist government. The power of this Catholic identity became clear in 1979, when Pope John Paul II (r. 1978–2005) visited Poland. This visit marked the first time any pope traveled to a communist country—but John Paul II was not just any pope. Born Karol Wojtyla, he was the first non-Italian pope since 1523 and the first Polish pope ever. Twelve million people—one-third of the Polish population—greeted the pope during his visit. Many Solidarity members testified to the importance of this visit in empowering them to challenge the communist order.

Solidarity's growing popularity soon threatened communist control of Poland. In December 1981 Prime Minister Wojciech Jaruzelski declared martial law and arrested more than 10,000 Solidarity members (including Wałęsa). Like the Hungarian Revolution in 1956 and the Prague Spring of 1968, Solidarity seemed to be one more noble but defeated protest in eastern Europe.

But Solidarity refused to be defeated. It remained a political presence and a moral force in Polish society throughout the 1980s. Solidarity members met in small groups, published newspapers, and organized election boycotts. At the same time, activists throughout Hungary, Czechoslovakia, East Germany, and the Soviet Union itself drew on Solidarity for inspiration and practical lessons in resistance.

Before 1989 no other eastern European state experienced a protest movement as dramatic as Solidarity, yet throughout much of the region two important developments marked the later 1970s and the 1980s. First, economic hardship fed widespread political alienation and a deepening longing for radical change. And second, activists and ordinary people worked to create the structures of civil society.

 Read the Document

Lech Wałęsa, "Nobel Lecture"

ENVIRONMENTAL PROTEST For many eastern Europeans, environmental activism helped create at least the beginnings of civil society. For decades, the conquest of nature had been a key part of communist ideology: "We cannot wait for favors from nature; our task is to take from her."[3] Governments throughout the Soviet bloc ignored the most basic environmental precautions, dumping untreated sewage and nuclear waste into lakes and rivers and pumping poisons into the air. But because communist officials regarded the natural environment as insignificant, they tended to view environmentalist protest as unimportant, a "safe" outlet for popular frustration. Thus, by the later 1970s, many Soviet and eastern European citizens had joined environmentalist groups. Environmental activism worked like a termite infestation, nibbling away at communist structures. In Hungary, public outrage over a Czech-Hungarian collaboration to dam the Danube River resulted in the formation of environmentalist organizations that encouraged Hungarians to question not only the Danube project, but also the priorities and policies of the entire communist system.

Environmentalism also fueled nationalist protest among the non-Russian peoples within the Soviet Union. The various national and ethnic groups of the Soviet empire watched their forests disappear, their lakes dry up, and their ancient cities bulldozed as a result of decisions made in far-away Moscow by men they regarded as foreigners—as *Russians* rather than *comrades* or fellow Soviets. By the 1980s, for example, with schools in Latvia forced to issue gas masks as a routine safety precaution because of the dangers of chemical spills, many Latvians concluded that they would be better off in an independent Latvia.

Read the Document

"Scientists Examine Russia's Economy and Environment"

Gorbachev and Radical Reform

As these discontents simmered among the peoples of the Soviet bloc, a series of deaths ushered in an era of dramatic change. In 1982, the decrepit Leonid Brezhnev died—and so, in rapid succession, did his successors, Yuri Andropov (1914–1984) and Konstantin Chernenko (1911–1985). The time had come for a generational shift. When Mikhail Gorbachev succeeded Chernenko, he was 54 years old. Compared with his elderly colleagues on the Politburo, he looked like a teenager.

Gorbachev's biography encompassed the drama of Soviet history. Born in 1931, Gorbachev experienced Stalinism at its worst. One-third of the inhabitants of his native village in Stavropol were executed, imprisoned, or died from famine or disease in the upheavals of collectivization. Both of his grandfathers were arrested during the Great Purge. His father served in the Red Army during World War II and was wounded twice. Yet Gorbachev's family continued to believe in the communist dream. In 1948 Gorbachev and his father together won the Order of Red Banner of Labor for harvesting almost six times the average crop. This achievement, and his clear ability, won Gorbachev a university education. After earning degrees in economics and law, Gorbachev rose through the ranks of the provincial and then the national Communist Party.

Although an ardent communist, Gorbachev became convinced that the Soviet system was ailing, and that the only way to restore it to health was through radical surgery. What he did not anticipate was that such surgery would, in fact, kill the patient. Gorbachev's surgical tools were *glasnost* and *perestroika*, two Russian terms without direct English equivalents.

glasnost Loosely translated as openness or honesty; Gorbachev's effort after 1985 to break with the secrecy that had characterized Soviet political life.

GLASNOST AND PERESTROIKA **Glasnost**, sometimes translated as "openness," "publicity," or "transparency," meant abandoning the deception and censorship that had always characterized the Soviet system for a policy based on open admission of failures and problems. According to Gorbachev, "Broad, timely, and frank information is testimony of faith in people . . . and for their capacity to work things out themselves."[4]

Soviet citizens remained wary of Gorbachev's talk of glasnost—until April 1986 and the Chernobyl nuclear power plant disaster. Operator error at the Ukrainian power plant led to the most serious nuclear accident in history. In the days following the accident, 35 plant workers died. Over the next five years the cleanup effort claimed at least 7,000 lives. The accident placed more than four million inhabitants of Ukraine and Belarus at risk from excess radiation and spread a radioactive cloud that extended all the way to Scotland. When news of the accident first reached Moscow, party officials acted as they had always done: They denied it. But after monitors in Western countries recorded the radiation spewing into the atmosphere, Gorbachev dared to release accurate information to the public. In 1986, 93 percent of the Soviet population had access to a television set and what they saw on their screens convinced them that glasnost was real. A powerful change had occurred in Soviet political culture.

Through glasnost Gorbachev aimed to overcome public alienation and apathy and so convince Soviet citizens to participate in reforming political and economic life—or

perestroika Loosely translated as "restructuring"; Gorbachev's effort to decentralize, reform, and thereby strengthen Soviet economic and political structures.

perestroika, often translated as "restructuring" or "reconstruction." Gorbachev believed he could reverse Soviet economic decline by restructuring the economy through modernization, decentralization, and the introduction of a limited market. Gorbachev knew, however, that even limited economic reforms threatened the vested interests of communist bureaucrats and that these bureaucrats would block his reforms if they could. Thus, economic perestroika would not succeed without political perestroika—restructuring the political system, opening it up to limited competition to allow new leaders and new ideas to triumph. So in 1990 Gorbachev ended the Communist Party's monopoly on parliamentary power, and the Soviet Union entered the brave new world of multiparty politics.

📖 **Read the Document**

Mikhail Gorbachev, "Speech to the 27th Congress of the Communist Party of the Soviet Union"

ENDING THE COLD WAR Restructuring Soviet economics and politics led almost inevitably to restructuring international relations—and to ending the Cold War. By the 1980s, the arms race absorbed at least 18 percent of the Soviet GNP, as the Soviets

GLASNOST Mikhail Gorbachev meets with workers in Moscow in 1985.

scrambled to keep pace with the Reagan military build-up. Gorbachev concluded that the Soviet Union could not afford the Cold War. To signal to the West his desire for a new international order, Gorbachev reduced Soviet military commitments abroad and asked to resume arms control negotiations. In December 1987, Gorbachev and Reagan signed the INF (Intermediate Nuclear Forces) Treaty, agreeing to eliminate all land-based intermediate-range nuclear missiles. In 1991, the Soviets and Americans signed the Strategic Arms Reduction Treaty (START I), in which they pledged to reduce inter-continental ballistic missiles. The nuclear arms race was over.

Gorbachev also moved to restructure Soviet policies in eastern Europe. He realized, first, that western leaders would not end the Cold War as long as the Soviet Union sought to dictate eastern European affairs, and second, that the Soviet Union could no longer afford to control its satellite states. In his first informal meetings with eastern European communist leaders in 1985, Gorbachev told these aging communist stalwarts that the Red Army would no longer enforce their will on rebellious populations. By the time Gorbachev addressed the UN General Assembly at the end of 1988 and declared that the nations of eastern Europe were free to choose their own paths, dramatic changes were underway.

Revolution in Eastern Europe

Hungary and Poland were the first states to jettison communist rule. Even before Gorbachev took power, economic crisis and public discontent had driven the Polish and Hungarian governments to embrace reform. In the early 1980s Hungary moved toward a Western-oriented, market-driven economy by joining the World Bank and the International Monetary Fund (IMF) and establishing a stock market. In 1985, independent candidates for the first time appeared on Hungarian ballots—and many won. In Poland, Jaruzelski's government also experimented with restoring some measures of a market economy and with limited political reform. Once martial law ended in 1983, censorship loosened. Newspapers published criticisms of governmental policy that would never have been permitted before 1980.

Once Gorbachev came to power, the pace of reform in these two states accelerated. In January 1989, Hungary legalized noncommunist political parties and trade unions. In February, Solidarity and Polish communist officials began "roundtable talks" aimed

CHRONOLOGY: REVOLUTION IN EASTERN EUROPE

1980
Formation of Solidarity in Poland.

1980

1981

1981
Martial law declared in Poland;
Solidarity made illegal.

1983
End of martial law in Poland,
political and economic reforms
begin; political reforms liberalize
Hungarian elections.

1983

1985

1985
Independents allowed to run
for election in Hungary; Gorbachev
becomes Soviet leader.

1988
Gorbachev's address to UN: eastern
European nations free to choose
their own paths.

1988

1989
January
Noncommunist parties and unions
legalized in Hungary.
February
Roundtable talks between Polish
government and Solidarity.
June
Free elections in Poland.
September
Solidarity forms government
in Poland.
November
Fall of Berlin Wall; reformist
communists overthrow Zhivkov
in Bulgaria.
December
Collapse of communist
government in Czechoslovakia
and East Germany; execution
of Ceauşescu in Romania.

1989

1990
March
Free elections in East Germany
and Hungary.
October
Reunification of Germany.
December
Wałęsa elected president
of Poland.

1990

1993

1993
Division of Czechoslovakia into the
Czech Republic and Slovakia.

at restructuring Poland's political system. In June, Poland held the first free elections in the Soviet bloc. Solidarity swept the contest and formed the first noncommunist government in eastern Europe since 1948.

These remarkable events sparked revolutions throughout the Soviet bloc. In the fall of 1989, mass protests toppled communist governments in Czechoslovakia and East Germany. In November, as the introduction to this chapter detailed, East Berliners succeeded in tearing down the Berlin Wall. One month later the world watched in wonder as the dissident playwright Václav Havel (1936–2011) became Czechoslovakia's president.

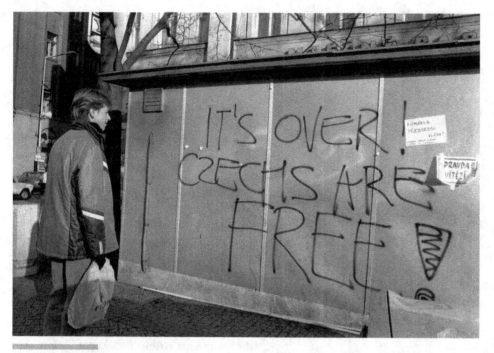

IT'S OVER! CZECHS ARE FREE! This graffiti on a bus stop in Prague sums up the revolutions of 1989.

Quickly the revolutionary fire spread to Bulgaria and Romania. There, however, communism was reformed rather than overthrown. In Bulgaria, reform-minded Communist Party members ousted the government of Todor Zhivkov, who had been in power for 35 years. The Romanian revolution was similar in outcome—but much bloodier. In December 1989, Romania's dictator Nikolae Ceaușescu ordered his army to fire on a peaceful protest and hundreds died. In a matter of days, however, the soldiers turned against Ceaușescu. He and his wife went into hiding, but on Christmas Day they were caught and executed by a firing squad. A new government formed under Ion Iliescu, a communist reformer who had attended Moscow University with Gorbachev.

View the Map

Events in Eastern Europe, 1989–1990

The final chapter of the eastern European revolutions featured a redrawing of political borders—and a corresponding shift of political identities. In October of 1990, the line dividing West and East Germany disappeared; Germany was once again a single nation-state. But three years later, the nation-state of Czechoslovakia cracked apart, as President Havel was unable to satisfy the demands of Slovakian nationalists. Out of Czechoslovakia came two new states: the Czech Republic and Slovakia.

The Disintegration of the Soviet Union

Western political leaders and ordinary people praised Gorbachev for ending the Cold War and removing the Soviet hold on eastern Europe. Gorbachev, however, regarded these changes as the international means to a domestic end—freeing the Soviet economy for prosperity and thereby saving the communist system. But prosperity eluded his grasp, and the system Gorbachev sought to save disintegrated. Economic perestroika proved a failure. By 1990, food and other essential goods were scarce, prices had risen by 20 percent since the year before, and productivity figures and incomes were falling. Dramatic increases in the number of prostitutes, abandoned babies, and the homeless population all signaled the economic and social breakdown of the Soviet Union.

MAP 29.1 THE FORMER SOVIET UNION In December 1991, the Soviet empire disintegrated. What took its place?

View the Map

Break-Up of the Soviet Union

As these problems escalated, Gorbachev faced growing opposition from hard-line communists and from reformers who wanted a thoroughly capitalist economy. These reformers found a spokesman in Boris Yeltsin (1931–2007), a charismatic, boisterous politician who became the president of Russia (as distinct from the Soviet Union) in 1991. When the hard-liners attempted to overthrow Gorbachev in August 1991, Yeltsin led the popular resistance that blocked the coup. From that point on, Yeltsin, not Gorbachev, dominated Soviet politics.

Yet nationalism rather than the hard-liners or Yeltsin's pro-capitalist movement toppled Gorbachev—and destroyed the Soviet Union. The success of eastern European nations in freeing themselves from Soviet domination encouraged separatist nationalist movements within the Soviet Union. Although Gorbachev deployed troops to quell nationalist rioting in Azerbaijan and Georgia and to counter independence movements in the Baltic states, the Soviet Union broke apart anyway. On December 25, 1991, Gorbachev resigned his office as president of a state that no longer existed (see **Map 29.1**).

In the Wake of Revolution

29.3 What were the consequences of the revolutions of 1989–1990 for the societies of eastern Europe?

The collapse of communist regimes in eastern Europe and the disintegration of the Soviet Union meant exhilarating yet exhausting change. Democracy-building proved to be a colossal task in societies burdened with the communist legacies of social division, political skepticism, and economic stagnation.

Russia After the Revolution

In contrast to states such as Poland, where the dismantling of communism came as the result of popular protests, in the Soviet Union change had been initiated from above. Moreover, unlike in eastern Europe, Russians could point with pride to at least some achievements of communism: They had created an industrial society, won World War II, and become a superpower. In the 1990s, then, Russians struggled to come to terms with their unexpected—and for some, unwanted—revolution.

RUSSIA'S ECONOMIC AND SOCIAL CRISIS As the first president of post-Soviet Russia, Boris Yeltsin promised to accelerate his nation's transformation into a prosperous capitalist democracy. But he proved unable to do so. Three interlocking developments—continuing economic crisis, widening corruption and criminality, and growing socioeconomic inequality—characterized the Yeltsin era.

In January 1992, Yeltsin applied "shock therapy" to the ailing Russian economy. He lifted price controls, abolished subsidies, and privatized state industries. But the economy did not prosper. Prices climbed dramatically, and the closure of unproductive businesses worsened unemployment; at the same time, cuts in government spending severed welfare lifelines. By 1995, 80 percent of Russians were no longer earning a living wage. Food consumption fell to the same level as the early 1950s. The economic situation worsened in 1998 when Russia effectively went bankrupt. The value of the ruble collapsed, and the state defaulted on its loans. Even Russians with jobs found it difficult to make ends meet. Many resorted to barter and the black market to survive.

This economic crisis worsened as a result of widespread corruption and crime. In the 1990s Russians suddenly had the right to own private property, but they could not count on the state to protect that property. Russia's policing and judicial systems could not keep up with the new demands placed upon them. As a result, a new force appeared in Russian life—the "Russian Mafia," crime syndicates that offered "protection" at a high price and used extortion and intimidation to seize control of large sectors of the economy.

Economic crisis, combined with criminality and corruption, meant growing inequality. By 1997, *seven* individuals controlled an estimated *50 percent* of the Russian economy. Clearly a minority of powerful and influential Russians experienced the 1990s as years of extraordinary opportunity and wealth accumulation. For many other Russians, however, the ending of the Soviet regime meant freedom of the worst kind—freedom to be hungry, homeless, and afraid. In 1999, almost 40 percent of Russians fell beneath the official poverty line.

The end of the 1990s coincided with the end of the Yeltsin era. In December of 1999 the former KGB officer Vladimir Putin (b. 1952) assumed control of Russia. Well-manicured and austere, Putin provided stable and competent government—a welcome change to the roller-coaster ride of the Yeltsin years. The economy became stronger and prosperity more widespread. By 2012, the number of Russian citizens living in poverty had fallen to 13 percent. Economic stabilization, however, came at a political price: the return to authoritarianism and the denial of civil rights. Putin centralized political power and ran roughshod over such key democratic touchstones as freedom of the press and the right to a fair trial. Demonstrations demanding greater political freedom spread across Russian cities preceding elections in the spring of 2012, but as of this writing, Putin remained firmly in control of the Russian political system.

NATIONALIST CHALLENGES IN THE FORMER SOVIET UNION The breakup of the Soviet Union did not bring an end to nationalist violence in the region. Popular nationalist movements vaulted states such as Georgia, Ukraine, and the Baltic republics to independence, but many new governments then found themselves facing their own nationalist challenges. Georgia, Armenia, and Azerbaijan all experienced civil war in the 1990s as regions within these new states sought to break away and form their own independent states.

Russia, too, faced continuing violent efforts to redraw its boundaries. Russia remained an enormous multinational federation—and not all of its national minorities wanted to remain part of Russia. The sharpest challenge came from Chechnya, one of 21 autonomous republics within the larger Russian Federation. When the Soviet Union broke up, Chechens saw no reason that Chechnya should not follow the path of Georgia or Azerbaijan toward independence. The dispute simmered until 1994 when Yeltsin sent in the Russian army to force Chechnya back within Russia's embrace. In the ensuing 20-month conflict, 80,000 died and 240,000 were wounded—80 percent of these Chechen civilians. Yeltsin negotiated a truce in the summer of 1996, but four years later Putin renewed the war. In 2009, Russia declared the successful end of its "counter-terrorism operation" in Chechnya; Chechen nationalists, however, continue to mount sporadic attacks.

Central and Eastern Europe: Toward Democracy?

Like the former Soviet Union, the states of eastern Europe found the path from communist rule to democracy strewn with obstacles. By the end of the 1990s, much of the region—but not all of it—had successfully negotiated that path and achieved political and economic stability.

STRUGGLES WITHIN THE REUNITED GERMANY Almost half the population of East Germany crossed the border into West Germany in the first week after the fall of the Berlin Wall. They returned home dazzled by the consumer delights they saw in store windows and eager for a chance to grab a piece of the capitalist pie. The West German chancellor, Helmut Kohl, recognized the power of these desires and skillfully forced the pace of reunification. When the two Germanys united at the end of 1990, Kohl became the first chancellor of the new German state.

Kohl trusted that West Germany's economy was strong enough to pull its bankrupt new partner into prosperity, but he proved overly optimistic. The residents of the former East Germany soon found their factories closing and their livelihoods gone. These economic troubles leached over into the western regions of Germany. By 1997, German unemployment stood at 12.8 percent—the highest since World War II. Economic difficulties were most concentrated in the former East Germany, where over 20 percent of the population was out of work in the later 1990s.

A wide cultural gap also divided "Wessies" (West Germans) and "Ossies" (East Germans). Women of the former East Germany, for example, often found it difficult to adjust to a culture in which more conventional gender roles and conceptions of sexual morality dominated. Ossie women expected to work full time and to have access to state-provided day care, contraceptives, and abortion. In West Germany, however, the concept of the male breadwinner/head of household was enshrined in the legal code until the end of the 1970s and prominent in West German culture for a long time after.

In the 1990s, the divide between Wessie and Ossie sometimes seemed unbridgeable. In 2005, however, the election of Angela Merkel (b. 1954) as chancellor marked an important symbolic moment for united Germany. The first woman to head the German Christian Democrats (and a Protestant in a heavily Catholic party), Merkel was also an Ossie, the first East German to hold such a prominent political office in the new Germany. Under Merkel, the divide between East and West began to wane. The economy also stabilized after the trauma of reunification. By the end of 2011, Germany's unemployment rate was the lowest it had been in two decades.

WINNERS AND LOSERS AFTER 1989 East Germany, of course, was unique among the former Soviet bloc states because of its rapid unification with West Germany, but peoples throughout the region experienced hard times immediately after 1989. Western advisers and the International Monetary Fund (IMF), which controlled access to much-needed loans, insisted that the new governments follow programs of "austerity" aimed at cutting government spending and curbing inflation. The result was economic hardship far beyond what any Western electorate would have endured.

In the second half of the 1990s, however, Poland, Hungary, the Czech Republic, and the Baltic countries saw their economies stabilize and their overall standard of living rise rapidly. In 2002, the average Pole's purchasing power was 40 percent higher than in 1989. But in countries such as Slovakia, Bulgaria, Romania, and Albania, the economies continued to flounder. In Albania, conditions were so dire that some 40 percent of Albanians of working age went abroad for jobs between 1994 and 1998. An important divide opened up in eastern Europe between the "winners" and the "losers" in the struggle to adjust to post-1989 conditions. The same divide appeared in political development. By the end of the 1990s, the "winners" had successfully negotiated the transition to stable democratic politics, while elsewhere power remained concentrated in the hands of a few.

Three factors explain this new divide between "winners" and "losers" in eastern and central Europe. First, Poland and Hungary already had begun moving toward market reforms well before 1989 and so were best prepared for the transition to capitalism, while Czechoslovakia and the Baltic states could look back to pre–World War II national independence. Second, proximity to markets in and investment from western Europe played an important role. But third and most significant of all is a factor we have already discussed: the construction of civil society. The states that floundered in the post-1989 world were those in which opposition to communist rule before 1989 had not yet coalesced in a vibrant civil society. The revolutions of 1989 in Bulgaria and Romania, for example, were carried out by reformers within the communist system, not by citizens with a sense of identity apart from—and opposed to—that system.

WHO WAS GUILTY? Many eastern Europeans wanted to draw a curtain on the communist era. Others, however, argued that those who participated in and benefited from what they regarded as a criminal regime should be punished. Yet who should be put on trial? Communism had been "normal" in eastern Europe for 40 years. Almost every citizen participated in some way or another with the communist regime just to get by.

For a solution, many of the former communist states considered **lustration**, a policy that banned anyone who had collaborated with the communist state from "public office," a category that often included jobs in state-run media and in universities. In Czechoslovakia and Germany, lustration became official policy and soon proved controversial. Lustration did not distinguish between an informer whom the communist state had brutalized into collaboration and who did her best to avoid giving any usable information, and someone who had volunteered to inform and who benefited for years because of it. Concluding that lustration constituted vengeance rather than justice, lustration's opponents argued that it threatened to undermine democratic politics. Yet the disagreements over lustration occurred in public—in parliamentary debates, newspaper columns, television and radio talk shows, and political campaigns. Dissent was not driven underground or punished. In many ways, then, the controversy bore witness to the success of democracy-building in eastern and central Europe since 1989.

lustration Implemented in many former communist states in the 1990s, this policy banned former communists and communist collaborators from public office.

The Breakup of Yugoslavia

Across eastern and central Europe in the early 1990s, many had feared that hate-based nationalist politics and policies would fill the ideological vacuum left by communism's collapse. These concerns escalated as minority populations such as the Roma became targets of discrimination and violence and as neo-Nazi movements emerged. But while racism and the treatment of minority groups remained problematic (as was the case throughout the West), fears that eastern Europe might descend once again into the whirlwind of genocidal slaughter proved unfounded—except in Yugoslavia. There the revival of nationalist hostilities led to state-sanctioned mass murder and scenes of carnage not seen in Europe since the 1940s.

When the communist guerilla leader Tito seized control of the Yugoslav state after World War II, he sought to separate Yugoslavia from the divisive battles of its recent past. To construct a united nation, Tito utilized two tools—federalism and communism. A federal political structure comprising six equal republics prevented Serbia, or any other of the republics, from dominating Yugoslavia. Communism served as a unifying ideology, a cluster of ideas that transcended divisions of ethnicity, religion, and language. Tito declared ethnic identities and rivalries unacceptable, part of the bourgeois past that Yugoslavs left behind.

Yugoslavs often said, however, that their nation consisted of "six nationalities, five languages, four religions . . . and one Tito." According to this folk wisdom, Tito—not communism, not federalism—glued together this diverse state. In 1980, Tito died. Ominously, the year after his death saw the outbreak of riots between ethnic Albanians and Serbs in the Serbian province of Kosovo. Even more ominously, Tito's death coincided with the onset of economic crisis. Rising oil prices undercut the Yugoslav economy as did its debt load. By 1987, inflation was raging at 200 percent per year; two years later it had burst through into hyperinflation—200 percent *per month*.

Under pressure from this economic crisis, the federal structure Tito built began to collapse. The wealthier Yugoslav republics such as Croatia sought to loosen their ties to poorer republics such as Serbia. Then, in 1989, the revolutions that swept through the Soviet satellite states shattered the hold of communism on Yugoslavia as well. Ethnic nationalism, long simmering under the surface of Yugoslavian political life, poured into the resulting ideological void.

In Serbia, the former communist functionary Slobodan Milošević (1941–2006) transformed himself into a popular spokesman for aggressive Serbian nationalism. To enhance Serbia's power, Milošević opposed the efforts of Croatian and other leaders to dismantle the Yugoslav federation. If Yugoslavia split apart, Serbia would be nothing but a small, poor, powerless state. As long as Yugoslavia remained intact, however, Serbia could continue to siphon the economic resources of the other, wealthier republics. Milošević also encouraged Serbs living in the other Yugoslav republics to believe that their security and prosperity depended on Yugoslav unity.

War began in 1991, when Croatia declared independence and the Serb-dominated Yugoslav army mobilized against the separatists. In 1992 the war spread to Bosnia-Herzegovina after its government, too, declared independence. Civilians endured horrendous brutality as **ethnic cleansing** became widespread during this war. To create all-Serb zones within Croatia and Bosnia, Serb paramilitary units embarked on a campaign of terror designed to force Muslims and Croats to abandon their homes and villages. They burned mosques, closed schools, vandalized houses, and imprisoned women and girls in special camps where they were subjected to regular, systematic rape. The brutality proved contagious—soon, all sides were practicing ethnic cleansing. These atrocities impelled NATO into combat for the first time in its history when, in 1994, NATO planes began bombing Serb positions. The following year, an uneasy peace settled on the now-independent Bosnia and Croatia (see **Map 29.2**).

Peace eluded Serbia during this period, however. Milošević's brand of vicious nationalism demanded a constant supply of enemies and a continuous cycle of violence. In 1998, fighting between Serbs and ethnic Albanians erupted in the province of Kosovo. Ethnic cleansing, mass rape, and a huge exodus of refugees began again. After a NATO bombing campaign in Serbia, NATO and Russian troops moved into Kosovo, which declared its independence from Serbia in 2008.

ethnic cleansing A term introduced during the wars in Yugoslavia in the 1990s; the systematic use of murder, rape, and violence by one ethnic group against members of other ethnic groups in order to establish control over a territory.

📖 Read the Document

Zlata Filipovi, *Zlata's Diary: A Child's Life in Sarajevo*

MAP **29.2** THE FORMER YUGOSLAVIA What factors impelled the breakup of Yugoslavia?

Rethinking the West

How and why was the West redefined at the end of the twentieth century and the beginning of the twenty-first?

A t the start of the 1990s, triumphalism characterized much of Western culture—at its simplest, expressed as "we won the Cold War." But who was "we"? For 40 years, the Cold War had provided a clear enemy and thus a clear identity: The West was anticommunist, anti-Soviet, anti-Warsaw Pact. The fall of communism, the disintegration of the Soviet Union, and the disappearance of the Warsaw Pact demanded that the West revise itself. But so, too, did other important social, political, and cultural changes that occurred in the wake of the tumultuous events of the later 1960s and the economic downturn of the 1970s.

The European Union

With the ending of the Cold War, the states of western Europe moved to take on a much more important role in global affairs. As **Map 29.3** shows, during the 1970s and 1980s the European Economic Community (EEC) widened its membership and became the European Community (EC), a political and cultural as well as economic organization. In 1979, Europeans voted in the first elections for the European Parliament, while the European Court of Justice gradually asserted the primacy of the European over national law.

Then, in 1991, the European Community (EC) became the **European Union (EU)**, defined by France's President François Mitterrand as "one currency, one culture, one social area, one environment." The establishment of the EU meant visible changes for ordinary Europeans. They saw their national passports replaced by a common EU document and border controls eliminated. The creation of a single EU currency—the euro, which replaced many national currencies in 2002—tore down one of the most significant economic barriers between European countries. At the same time, the powers of the European Parliament expanded and member states moved toward establishing common social policies such as labor rights.

As these developments were underway, Europeans confronted the unexpected challenge posed by the ending of the Cold War. Should the European Union (often called simply "Europe") now include East as well as West? Attracted by the EU's prosperity, the nations of the former Soviet bloc answered "Yes." Hesitant to join their countries to eastern Europe's shattered economies and divided societies, western European leaders drew up a list of qualifications for applicant nations. To belong to "Europe," nations had to meet financial requirements that demonstrated their economic stability and their commitment to market capitalism. Thus, the EU defined "Europe" first of all as capitalist. But a set of political requirements made clear that "Europe" also meant a commitment to democratic politics. Applicants' voting processes, treatment of minority groups, policing methods, and judicial systems were all scrutinized. Map 29.3 shows that in 2004 and again in 2007 the EU expanded to embrace much of central and eastern Europe.

Controversy greeted both the greater economic integration of the EU and its expansion. Britain, Denmark, and Sweden refused to adopt the euro, fearing that their economies would be dragged down by slower-performing EU states. Small traders and independent producers often felt overwhelmed by the EU bureaucracy, while many workers in western Europe feared having to compete for jobs with lower-paid eastern Europeans.

Nevertheless, during the 1990s and early 2000s, the EU seemed a resounding success. Although European unemployment rates often stood higher than in countries

European Union (EU) A successor organization to the EEC; the effort to integrate European political, economic, cultural, and military structures and policies.

📖 Read the Document

Jorg Haider, "The Freedom I Mean"

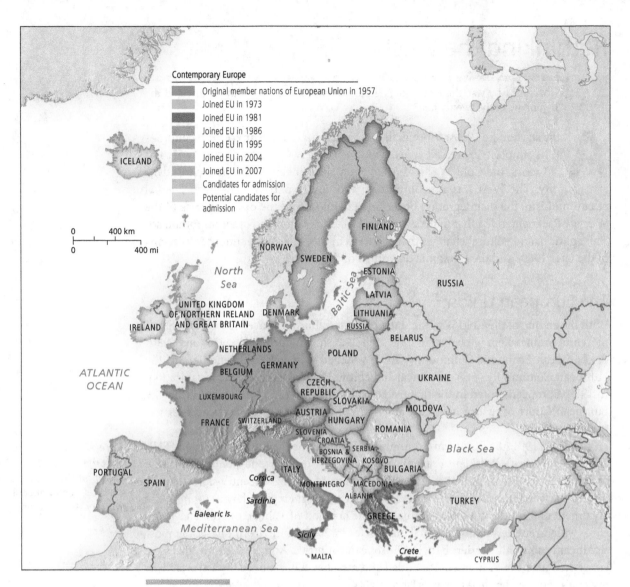

Contemporary Europe

- Original member nations of European Union in 1957
- Joined EU in 1973
- Joined EU in 1981
- Joined EU in 1986
- Joined EU in 1995
- Joined EU in 2004
- Joined EU in 2007
- Candidates for admission
- Potential candidates for admission

MAP 29.3 CONTEMPORARY EUROPE The revolutions of 1989 and their aftermath mark a clear turning point in European history, as a comparison of this map and that of Map 28.5, "Europe in the Cold War" (p. 890), shows. What significant changes in political borders have occurred? How does the widening membership of the European Union reflect a new European order?

not aligned with the EU, the Union's economies boomed. Countries like Ireland experienced unprecedented economic expansion and prosperity. Much of this boom, however, was fueled by debt, as individuals, banks, corporations—and some EU governments—amassed huge deficits.

Then, in 2008, the globalized economy sharply declined when a real estate-related financial bubble in the United States burst. The effects soon ravaged not only the American but the global economy. In the United States, unemployment rates rose sharply, housing foreclosures escalated, and millions of people saw their retirement pensions dwindle. In western Europe, government borrowing ballooned. By 2012, the EU faced a debt crisis, with the stability of the euro imperiled by the financial instability of a number of member states, including Portugal, Italy, Spain, Ireland, and Greece. The debt crisis exposed significant weaknesses in the EU structure and, for some, called into question the entire project of European unity. As the financially sound states such as Germany demanded that their weaker partners impose politically unpopular austerity programs on electorates, older nationalist hostilities resurfaced. A German magazine, for example, featured an image of the famous Greek statue of the

Venus de Milo wrapped in a tattered Greek flag and bearing the slogan, "The Frauds of Europe," while anti-austerity demonstrators in Greece burned the German flag and labeled German EU negotiators "Nazis."

Nevertheless, European leaders remained committed to the European project. Ordinary people were more ambivalent, but even after 2008, the percentages of Europeans regarding their country's membership in the EU as "a good thing" continued to outweigh those who described belonging to the Union as "a bad thing." In the Eurobarometer poll of May 2011, only the United Kingdom and Croatia showed more people who rejected rather than affirmed EU membership.

Islam and the West

At the same time that the EU struggled to integrate Europe's diverse economies, European states contended with the challenge of integrating increasingly diverse cultures within their boundaries—and, in particular, of reconciling European identity with a growing Islamic cultural and political presence. As minarets joined church steeples in the skylines of European cities, questions about the definitions of and relationships between Islamic, European, and Western identities intensified.

MUSLIM COMMUNITIES IN EUROPE In eastern European countries such as Bulgaria, Albania, and Bosnia, Muslims belonged to the indigenous nation, the descendants of those who converted to Islam during the centuries of Ottoman rule. In western Europe, by contrast, Muslim communities were relatively recent, the result of the post-World War II immigration discussed earlier in this chapter. By 1990 Muslims—drawn from many different ethnic groups and embracing a wide variety of religious practices and cultural traditions—constituted about 4 percent of Europe's population and constituted the most rapidly growing immigrant group.

In most significant ways, the Muslim experience in Europe conformed to common immigrant patterns. The Muslim struggle to adapt to new social norms reflected the usual experience of immigrants whose countries of origins are more traditional than their host societies. Like Italian Catholic or eastern European Jewish immigrants to North American cities in the 1890s, many Muslim immigrants were particularly shocked by European gender relations and sexual freedoms. Family tensions often became acute because of the conflict between immigrant parents and children, especially daughters (again, a common immigrant pattern).

ISLAMISM AND THE WEST The emergence of **Islamism** as a powerful global force complicated the integration of Islamic communities in western Europe. An umbrella term, Islamism embraces a variety of movements that call for a return to what adherents see as a purer form of Islam. As Chapter 26 discussed, movements such as Wahhabism in Saudi Arabia and the Islamic Brotherhood in Egypt emerged in the interwar period as a reaction against corrupt Western puppet regimes and a response to unsettling economic change. Explicitly anti-Western, Islamism views Western culture as a threat to Islamic identity. In its extreme form, it accepts violence, including the murder of civilians, as an acceptable means to its ends.

A number of developments fostered support for Islamism. The ongoing Palestinian-Israeli conflict played an important role, particularly given the high level of American economic and military support for Israel. (Between 1949 and 1998, Israel received more American aid than any other country.) Because more than 90 percent of Palestinians are Muslim and because the United States is widely seen as the standard-bearer of the West, Islamists framed the conflict as a battle between the West and Islam.

The Iranian Revolution of 1979 was also critical. That year a popular revolution overthrew the western-backed authoritarian regime of Shah Mohammad Reza Pahlavi

Islamism The ideology that insists that Islam demands a rejection of Western values and that violence in this struggle against the West is justified.

and vaulted the Ayatollah Khomeini (1901–1989) into power. Khomeini rapidly reversed the westernizing and modernizing policies of the Shah and condemned the United States as the "Great Satan." Under his regime Iran became a prominent supporter of violent Islamist groups, such as Hezbollah in Lebanon. Khomeini became an international Islamist hero during the "Iranian hostage crisis" of 1979–1980, when Iranian students took over the U.S. Embassy in Tehran, kidnapped 66 Americans, and held most of them for over a year. Khomeini's decision 10 years later to issue a death sentence against the British writer Salman Rushdie for what he considered to be a blasphemous portrayal of the prophet Muhammad widened the gap between his Islamist regime and the West and, once again, made him a popular hero among Islamists. (See *Justice in History* in this chapter.)

The wars in Bosnia and Chechnya in the 1990s further intensified the Islamist conviction that Muslims were under attack. The initial passivity of western Europe and the United States during the Bosnian war—while Muslim men and boys were slaughtered and Muslim women and girls raped—convinced many Muslims that Western governments had an anti-Islamic agenda. This perception grew stronger when Western states refused to back the Chechens (who are Muslim) in what many viewed as the Chechen war of independence against Russian oppression.

Finally, Islamism fed on the alienation of some Muslims, particularly young men, in immigrant communities in western Europe. Many European Muslim families lived in urban industrial areas where manufacturing jobs had been plentiful in the 1960s and 1970s but where few work opportunities were available by the 1990s. Thus, the generation coming of age in this decade saw little point in the economic aspirations that had driven their parents and grandparents. Unemployment rates in largely Muslim areas stood at double that of the national average in many western European states, and even higher among men under age 25. Moreover, while their parents and grandparents often had maintained strong ties to their country of origin, the new generation, less bound by such ties, proved more open to transnational forms of Islamic thought and practice—such as those associated with Islamism.

THE WEST AND ISLAMIST TERRORISM This textbook has traced the way in which "the West" changed meaning, often in response to places and peoples defined as "not West." With the ending of the Cold War, the West lost its main enemy, but a replacement stood readily at hand. In 1996, the American president Bill Clinton (b. 1946) identified terrorism as "the enemy of our generation." In the post–Cold War world, Islamist terrorism replaced communism as the new foe against which the West defined itself.

Because it short-circuits the democratic process by shifting decision making from the ballot box to the bomb, terrorism directly opposes what many now regard as the bedrock of Western culture—a commitment to democracy. Both this equation of the West with democracy and this definition of terrorism as "non-Western," however, conveniently ignore the history of the West and of terrorism itself: The Fenians in mid-nineteenth-century Ireland, anarchist groups throughout Europe in the 1890s, and the surge of terrorist activity throughout western Europe in the 1970s reveal that terrorism has long been part of "Western civilization." Nevertheless, as the twenty-first century opened, many in the West regarded terrorism as an outside threat, usually bearing an Arabic face and carrying a copy of the Qur'an.

This perception rested on the emergence of Islamist groups that embraced violence as a political weapon. From the 1980s on, a number of groups carried out violent attacks throughout not only the Middle East but also Africa, parts of Asia, Europe, and the United States—and, in 2001, one of the most deadly terrorist episodes yet seen. On September 11, an Islamist group called Al Qaeda hijacked four passenger planes and smashed them into the World Trade Center in New York City and the Pentagon

Justice in History
The Sentencing of Salman Rushdie

In February 1989, the Ayatollah Khomeini, political and spiritual leader of Iran, offered an award of $2.5 million to any faithful Muslim who killed the novelist Salmon Rushdie. Rushdie, a British citizen, went into hiding, where he remained for several years. His death sentence ignited the "Satanic Verses Affair," a tumultuous international crisis caused by a resounding clash of cultural assumptions and expectations.

The crisis centered on a book. In the early autumn of 1988 Viking Penguin published Rushdie's *The Satanic Verses*, a difficult novel about the complexities and contradictions of the modern immigrant experience. Born in India and raised in an Islamic home, Rushdie wrote *The Satanic Verses* to describe "migration, metamorphosis, divided selves, love, death, London, and Bombay."[5] The novel received immediate critical acclaim, with reviewers praising it as an astonishing work of postmodernist fiction.

Many Muslims, however, regarded the book as a direct attack on the foundations of their religious faith. One scene in the novel particularly horrified devout Muslims. In this episode, the central character has a psychotic breakdown and falls into a dream: The prophet Muhammad appears as a corrupt businessman, and prostitutes in a brothel take on the names of the Prophet's wives.

The novel aroused controversy from the moment of its publication. The government of India banned it almost immediately. Within a matter of weeks, several other states followed suit. Anti-Rushdie demonstrations in India and Pakistan turned violent. Bookstores received bombing and death threats. In western Europe, hostilities between Muslims and non-Muslims intensified. Then, on February 14, 1989, an announcer on Radio Tehran read aloud the text of a *fatwa,* or decree, issued by the Ayatollah Khomeini:

> I would like to inform all the intrepid Muslims of the world that the author of the book entitled *The Satanic Verses,* which has been compiled, printed and published in opposition to Islam, the Prophet and the Koran, as well as those publishers who were aware of its contents, have been

sentenced to death. I call on all zealous Muslims to execute them quickly, wherever they find them. . . . Whoever is killed on this path will be regarded as a martyr, God willing.

Western governments reacted quickly. The 12 states of the European Community, the United States, Sweden, Norway, Canada, Australia, and Brazil all condemned Khomeini's judgment, recalled their ambassadors from Tehran, and cancelled high-level diplomatic contacts with Iran.

CULTURE CLASH In 2007, Britain's Queen Elizabeth awarded Salman Rushdie a knighthood for his services to literature. The award sparked protests within the Islamic world, including this one in Lahore, Pakistan, where demonstrators burned the British flag to express their outrage.

Large numbers of Muslims, including many who spoke out against Rushdie's book, also condemned Khomeini's fatwa. Some Muslim scholars contended that the Ayatollah's fatwa was a scholarly opinion, not a legally binding judgment. Others argued that Rushdie could not be condemned without a trial or that Rushdie, who lived in a society without an Islamic government, was not bound by Islamic law.

But many ordinary Muslims ignored these theological and legal arguments and greeted the Ayatollah's fatwa with delight. The news of the Ayatollah's fatwa brought crowds of cheering Muslims into city streets across Europe. In Manchester and Bradford, young British Muslim men insisted they would kill Rushdie if given the chance. In Paris, demonstrators marched to cries of "We are all Khomeinists!"

Why did Khomeini's fatwa arouse such enthusiasm among Western Muslims? A partial answer is that many Muslims were frustrated with what they regarded as the unequal application of the laws of censorship. Faced with what they saw as a hate-filled, pornographic caricature of Islam, they had demanded that Western governments use existing laws censoring pornography and banning hate crimes to block the publication of Rushdie's book—and they had gotten nowhere. But the controversy was not simply a dispute about censorship. For some Muslims, Rushdie's *Satanic Verses* epitomized Western secular society with its scant regard for tradition or religious values. Dr. Kalim Siddiqui of the pro-Iranian Muslim Institute in Britain proclaimed, "Western

(continued on next page)

(continued from previous page)

civilization is fundamentally an immoral civilization."[6] From this perspective, Khomeini's fatwa condemned not just one book or one author, but an entire culture.

The anti-Western stance of some Muslims was mirrored by the anti-Islam position soon occupied by some Rushdie supporters. In all of his books, Rushdie condemned British racism and exposed the falsehood of Western claims to cultural superiority. Yet in an ironic twist, many of his champions now articulated precisely the sort of Western cultural chauvinism against which Rushdie had written so passionately. Many western Europeans agreed with the conclusion drawn in this letter to a British daily newspaper: "The lesson of the Rushdie affair is that it was unwise to let Muslim communities establish themselves in our midst."[7] They equated Islam with irrationalism and barbarity, while they linked the "West" to reason and civilization. At precisely the moment when the crumbling of communism and the ending of the Cold War deprived the West of one of its defining attributes, the Satanic Verses Affair offered up a new Other against which the West could define itself.

For Discussion

On what grounds are publications censored in Western societies? Given the existence of this censorship, should Rushdie's book have been banned?

Taking It Further

Bowen, David G., ed. *The Satanic Verses: Bradford Responds.* 1996. This collection of essays and documents helps explains why many British Muslims viewed the British government's failure to censor Rushdie's book as an act of injustice.

Pipes, Daniel. *The Rushdie Affair: The Novel, the Ayatollah, and the West.* 2003. An informative overview by a controversial scholar.

(the U.S. military headquarters in Washington, D.C.); the fourth plane crashed in Pennsylvania. Almost 3,000 people died.

The attacks on "9/11" opened an even more violent phase in the history of the West and Islamism. After intelligence linked Al Qaeda to the Islamist government of Afghanistan, the United States invaded Afghanistan and, with a multinational coalition, sought to destroy Al Qaeda and uproot its Afghan supporters. In March 2003, this war took a new turn when U.S. and British forces attacked Iraq. Because the Iraqi government had played no role in the attacks on 9/11, this war divided American society and proved vastly unpopular in western Europe. It also strengthened Islamist hostility toward the West, as subsequent terrorist attacks in Europe made clear. On March 11, 2004, approximately 200 people died after four bombs exploded on commuter trains during the rush hour in Madrid. Al Qaeda linked the bombing to Spain's support of the Iraq war. One year later, on July 7, 2005, a similar spate of bombings during the morning rush hour in London killed over 50 people and injured more than 700.

The men involved in the 7/7 London attacks were not only linked to Al Qaeda, they were also British. The London bombings thus revealed the power of Islamism within the West. In the wake of 9/11 and the attacks that followed, then, the question of Western identity was more troublesome than ever, as a "Them" versus "Us" mentality that ignored the long, complex history of Islam in the West became more prevalent.

EURO-ISLAM Yet the encounter between Islam and Europe was far from wholly negative. The majority of European Muslims rejected Islamism. Many, particularly those of the second and third generations of immigrant families, endeavored to create a new identity: **Euro-Islam**. Regarding themselves as fully Muslim and fully European, these individuals insisted that no contradiction existed between Islam and what many view as the core values of the West—democratic politics, respect for individual differences, and civil liberties guaranteed by law to all, regardless of race and gender.

Euro-Islam The identity and belief system being forged by European Muslims who argue that Islam does not contradict or reject European values.

Euro-Islam produced significant theological and social innovations within the Islamic community. European Muslim women fought to eradicate such traditional practices as female circumcision and the forced marriage of young girls to men from their parents' or grandparents' homelands. More generally, they claimed an equal place for women within the context of both Europe and Islam. European Muslim theologians reinforced this claim. Traditional Islamic theology cut the world into two: the "house of Islam" and the "house of war." In the "house of Islam," Islamic law prevails. In the "house of war," or societies where Islamic law is not followed, Muslims live in a state of constant spiritual battle. Euro-Islamic proponents such as the Swiss scholar Tariq Ramadan (b. 1962) argued that Muslims should not view Europe and the United States as the "house of war." Instead, these regions form a third "house," the "house of testimony," where Muslims freely profess and live their faith in community with non-Muslims.

Into the Postmodern Era

The end of the Cold War, the formation of the European Union, and the growth of significant Muslim communities within western Europe all demanded a reevaluation and redefinition of West. So, too, did a number of intellectual, artistic, and technological developments that together helped created the postmodern era. Although the term **postmodernism** covers an array of styles and stances, at its core postmodernism rejects Western cultural supremacy. More specifically, postmodernism challenges the idea that Western science and rationality have constructed a single, universally applicable form of "modernity."

THE MAKING OF THE POSTMODERN Postmodernism first took form in architecture, perhaps because the failures of modernist architecture were so obvious by the early 1970s. Motivated by their faith in human rationality and modern technology, modernist architects had erected buildings that they believed would enable people to live better, more beautiful lives. But the concrete high-rises they constructed failed to connect with the needs and emotions of their inhabitants, and many became derelict, crime-ridden, graffiti-scarred tenements.

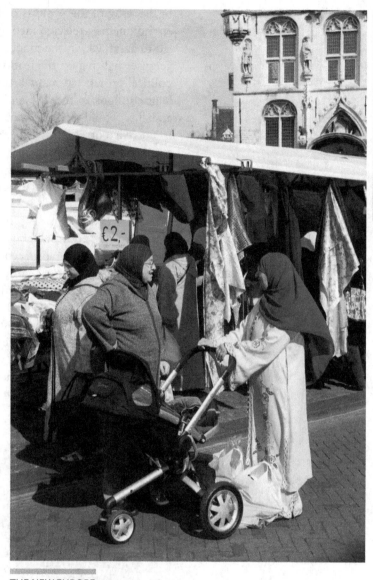

THE NEW EUROPE Muslim women exchange greetings at an outdoor market in Gouda in the Netherlands.
SOURCE: Alamy BKWKJW.

Faced with this failure, a new generation—the postmodernists—insisted that modernist architecture was too elitist. The American architect Charles Jencks (b. 1939) argued that because people tend to rely on the familiar to make sense of their world, modernism was wrong to reject traditional forms. For example, most Europeans and Americans connect domestic housing with gabled roofs (ask a child to draw a picture of a house and see if he or she draws a flat roof). Was it surprising, Jencks asked, that the concrete rectangles so typical of modernist houses alienated so many people? Postmodernist *anti-elitism* thus led to *eclecticism,* to re-creating and combining forms and styles from past eras (such as gabled roofs), and to efforts to revive local and regional styles. Why should the streets of Tokyo look like the center of London or downtown Chicago? Instead, postmodernists embraced an architecture rooted in the specifics of time and place. In addition to being anti-elitist and eclectic, then, postmodernist architecture was also *anti-universalist:* It condemned modernism for its assumption that the same modern (and Western) ideals and forms fit all individuals and all societies.

The same sorts of criticism of modernism surfaced in the art world, as the politics of the late 1960s and early 1970s transformed the visual arts in three ways. First,

 Read the Document

Justin Vaisse, "Veiled Meaning"

postmodernism Umbrella term covering a variety of artistic styles and intellectual theories and practices; in general, a rejection of a single, universal, Western style of modernity.

in the wake of the protests of 1968, artists—many coming out of left-wing activist environments—rejected ideologies based on hierarchy and authority. This rejection led to an attack on the modernist idea of the "avant-garde," the concept of artistic geniuses fighting on the frontiers of aesthetic excellence. Second, the experience of political protest led many artists to try to communicate with a wider public—and, hence, to look to the past and to popular culture for forms and material that their audience would find familiar. As the art critic Edit DeAk explained, postmodernist art relied on "the shock of recognition instead of the shock of the new."[8] Finally, feminism influenced the new art. Feminists highlighted the systematic exclusion of women from gallery and museum exhibitions. They also questioned the aesthetic hierarchy that fixed the patronizing label of "craft" to traditionally female art forms such as weaving.

By the end of the 1970s, postmodernist practices in art and architecture blended with a growing body of literary and cultural theory often called *poststructuralism*. The theory of poststructuralism centered on the work of an assorted group of French thinkers whose ideas were taken up in American universities and then filtered back into European intellectual circles. These thinkers included Roland Barthes (1915–1980) and Jacques Derrida (1930–2004) in literary studies, Michel Foucault (1926–1984) in history, and Jacques Lacan (1901–1981) in psychoanalytic theory.

Like postmodernist theories in architecture and art, poststructuralism began as an exploration into the problems of communication. Barthes declared the "Death of the Author," by which he meant that the purpose of literary study is not to ask, "What does the author mean?" but instead to explore the way in which the reader creates his or her

POSTMODERNISM AT PLAY IN THE WEST Using the "shock of recognition," Marco Ventura blends six familiar images from the Western tradition in this playful painting that he entitled "Mona Lisa Contemplating the Bust of Nefertiti as God Creates Order Out of Chaos on a Starry Night on the Island of La Grande Jatte as the Infanta Margarita Looks On" (1993).

SOURCE: Marco Ventura, "Mona Lisa Contemplating the Bust of Nefertiti as God Creates Order Out of Chaos on a Starry Night on the Island of La Grande Jatte as the Infanta Margarita Looks On," 1993, oil on gessoed paper, 10"w × 821/2"h. Painting by Marco Ventura 1993.

own meanings. Building on Barthes, Derrida argued that the world we experience is structured by language—we cannot even understand or express our very selves apart from language. But because there is no inherent match between a word (what Derrida called a "signifier") and the thing or idea to which that word refers (the "signified"), communication is never straightforward. An endless variety of meanings and interpretations results, and thus, Derrida argued, we must abandon the idea of a fixed or single truth, of ultimate or universal meaning.

This effort to challenge any single "right answer" or any center of authority (sometimes called "decentering") linked the poststructuralist concern with communication to its analysis of power. Foucault and Lacan dissected hierarchies of authority (not only in the political sphere, but also in academic disciplines, for example, or in the medical world), and the way these authorities used seemingly objective bodies of knowledge to retain their hold on power.

The blending of these poststructuralist theories of communication and power with the critique of modernism already flourishing in architecture and the arts produced postmodernism. The postmodern view of culture as a global contest for power disturbed more traditional thinkers (with "modernist" now perceived as traditional), who insisted that criteria of aesthetic excellence ("Beauty") and objective standards of knowledge ("Truth") did exist, and who warned that cultural "decentering" would destroy the social cohesion and political stability of the West. (See *Different Voices* in this chapter.)

Read the Document

Václav Havel, "The Need for Transcendence in the Postmodern World"

POSTMODERN CULTURES AND POSTINDUSTRIAL TECHNOLOGIES In many ways popular culture confirmed postmodern theories. In Britain, for example, the "Big Beat" songs that dominated the club scene in the late 1990s were produced by disc jockeys who lifted snatches from old records, played them at different speeds, and combined them with contrasting styles. Like postmodernist paintings, Big Beat contained chunks of the past, recycled in new ways.

MAKING BUILDINGS DANCE Designed by the American architect Frank Gehry and his Czech collaborator Vlado Mulunić, the "Dancing Building" fills a bomb site left vacant in central Prague since World War II. Also called "Fred and Ginger" (after the famous Hollywood dancing duo Fred Astaire and Ginger Rogers), this postmodernist piece delighted and enraged the people of Prague.

postindustrial society A service-based, rather than manufacturing-based, economy characterized by an emphasis on marketing and information and by a proliferation of communications technologies.

More generally, a series of technological developments meant that popular culture was "decentered," that a multitude of popular cultures coexisted, and that the individual consumer of culture, like Barthes's reader, was free to make meaning as he or she chose. The videocassette recorder (VCR), first marketed in 1975, and its technological successors not only transported film viewing from the public to the private sphere, they also provided the film viewer with the possibility to tailor the movie to his or her own preferences—to adjust the volume or choose another soundtrack entirely, to omit or fast-forward through certain scenes, to replay others endlessly. Similarly, the proliferation of cable and satellite television stations during the 1980s and 1990s fragmented the viewing audience and made it impossible to speak of popular culture in the singular.

Postmodernist concerns with communication, with the way in which interpretations can be endlessly modified, and with the abolition of a single center of authority certainly seemed appropriate for "the Information Age" or the **postindustrial society**. Emphasis on production characterized the industrial phase of economic development. But in the postindustrial phase, *making* things became less important than *marketing* them. If the factory symbolized industrial society, then the epitome of the postindustrial era was the home computer, with its capacity to disperse information, market products, and endlessly duplicate yet constantly alter visual and verbal images—all without any central regulating authority. Governments scrambled to impose control on the proliferating technologies of the postindustrial age, but in true postmodern fashion the centers of authority broke down. Existing laws that regulated pornography, for example, proved difficult to apply to the Internet, the vast global communications web.

Similarly, developments in medical technologies raised important questions about authority and ownership. In 1978, Louise Brown was born in Britain, the world's first "test-tube baby." Over the next 20 years, assisted fertility treatment resulted in more than one million births. As the technology grew more sophisticated, so did the ethical and political questions. Societies struggled to determine the legality of practices such as commercial surrogate motherhood, in which a woman rents her womb to a couple, and postmenopausal motherhood, in which a woman past childbearing age is implanted with a fertilized egg.

Genetic research provoked even more debate about which authorities or what principles should guide scientific research. In 1997, British scientists introduced the world to Dolly the sheep, the first mammal cloned from an adult. Many scientists assumed that the cloning of human beings, long part of science fiction and horror stories, was inevitable, even if religious leaders deemed it immoral and political authorities declared it illegal. The announcement in February 2001 that scientists had decoded the human genome—that they had mapped the set of instructions in every cell in the human body—raised such questions as, Who owns this information? Who has the authority to decide how it is to be used?

POSTMODERN PATTERNS IN RELIGIOUS LIFE Postmodern patterns—the fragmentation of cultures, the collapse of centers of authority, the supremacy of image—also characterized Western religious faith and practice after the 1970s. Christianity no longer served as a common cultural bond. In a time of increasing immigration and cultural diversity, Islam was the fastest-growing religious community in western Europe. In Britain, Muslims outnumbered Methodists by two to one. By the end of the twentieth century, regular churchgoers were a small minority of the European population—well under 20 percent in most countries. Religious faith became a private matter, the mark of subcultures (often defined by an "Us versus Them" mentality), rather than a bond tying together individuals and groups into a cohesive national culture.

Different Voices
History in a Postmodern World

In the late 1980s, postmodernist ideas penetrated the study of history. While many historians—such as Joan Wallach Scott, who wrote the first excerpt that follows—embraced postmodernist theories and methodologies, others—such as Gertrude Himmelfarb, the author of the second excerpt—condemned postmodernism as relativism run amok. This debate resonated beyond the rather small world of professional historians, as the third excerpt shows. In an effort to establish uniform standards in elementary and secondary education, Margaret Thatcher sought a national curriculum for British state schools. As her account reveals, Thatcher's ideas about history clashed with those of professional historians.

I. Joan Wallach Scott: A "New" Historian's Defense

By "history," I mean not what happened, not what "truth" is "out there" . . . but what we *know* about the past, what the rules and conventions are that govern the production and acceptance of the knowledge we designate as history. My first premise is that history is . . . constructed by historians. Written history both reflects and creates relations of power. Its standards of inclusion and exclusion, measures of importance, and rules of evaluation are not objective criteria but politically produced conventions. What we know as history is, then, the fruit of past politics. . . .

The pluralization of the subject of history challenges the notion . . . that "man" can be studied through a focus on elites. Instead, attention to women, blacks, and other Others demonstrates that history consists of many irreconcilable stories. Any master narrative—the single story of the rise of American democracy or Western civilization—is shown to be not only incomplete but impossible of completion in the terms it has been written. For those master narratives have been based on the forcible exclusion of Others' stories. They are . . . stories which in their telling legitimize the actions of those who have shaped the laws, constitutions, and governments—"official stories."

The proliferation of Others' histories . . . has raised questions about difference and power: . . . . How has the exclusion of some stories from the record of the past perpetuated inequalities based on attributions of difference? What is the connection between contemporary social hierarchy and measures of importance in historical writing? Answers to these questions . . . undermine claims by orthodox historians that . . . their history is but a transcription of how things really happened in the past. . . .

. . . [H]istory is an interpretive practice, not an objective, neutral science. To maintain this does not signal the abandonment of all standards. . . . [Historians] share a commitment to accuracy and to procedures of verification and documentation. . . . [But we see] that the meanings attributed to events of the past always vary, that the knowledge we produce is contextual, relative, open to revision and debate, and never absolute.

SOURCE: Joan Wallach Scott, "History in Crisis? The Others' Side of the Story," *American Historical Review*, 1989, 94:3, 681, 682–683,689–690. Reprinted by permission of the author.

II. Gertrude Himmelfarb: An "Old" Historian Rejects the New

Historians have always quarreled about the meaning and interpretation of facts and, indeed, about the facts themselves. But they . . . have traditionally assumed some correspondence between interpretation and fact, between language and reality. They are painfully aware of the imperfection of that correspondence—a past that always eludes them, a reality that is never fully revealed to them . . . But they have also been acutely aware of the need to try to close that gap as much as possible. . . . Today, [however,] more and more historians . . . are making the past far more indeterminate, more elusive, less real than it has ever been—thus permitting themselves to be as creative, innovative, and inventive as possible in interpreting the past. These have become the new "possibles" of history: the possibilities suggested by the historian's imagination and sensibility rather than by the contemporary experience*. . . . Contemporaries may have thought that their history was shaped by kings and statesmen, politics and diplomacy, constitutions and laws. New historians know better. . . . Race/gender/class—word-processors [early personal computers] all over the country must be programmed to print that formula with a single touch of a key. . . . The assumption that race, gender, and class are, and always have been, the basic determinants of history deconstructs the past not only as historians have known it but, in many cases, as contemporaries knew it. . . . Those benighted contemporaries, the argument goes, speak with no authority, because they were deluded by the "hegemonic culture" that was itself irredeemably sexist, racist, and elitist. Thus, all the past has to be deconstructed and constructed anew.

SOURCE: Gertrude Himmelfarb, "Some Reflections on the New History," *American Historical Review*, 1989, 94:3, 665–666, 667, 668. Reprinted by permission of the author.

III. Margaret Thatcher: A Politician Weighs In

Perhaps the hardest battle I fought on the national curriculum was about history. Though not an historian myself, I had a very clear—and I had naively imagined uncontroversial—idea of what history was. History is an account of what happened in the past. Learning history, therefore, requires knowledge of events . . . [and] knowing dates. No amount of imaginative sympathy for historical characters or situations can be a substitute for the initially tedious but ultimately rewarding business of memorizing what actually happened. . . .

In July 1989 the History Working Group produced its interim report. I was appalled. It put the emphasis on interpretation and enquiry as against content and knowledge. There

*Here and throughout this essay, Himmelfarb uses the term contemporary to mean the period in the past that the historian is studying.

(continued on next page)

(continued from previous page)

was insufficient weight given to British history. There was not enough emphasis on history as chronological study. . . .

[The *final report arrived in March 1990. Thatcher was not pleased.*] The attainment targets it set out did not specifically include knowledge of historical facts, which seemed to me extraordinary [and] the coverage of some subjects—for example, twentieth-century British history—was too skewed to social, religious, cultural and aesthetic matters rather than political events. . . . By now I had become thoroughly exasperated. . . .

SOURCE: Margaret Thatcher, *The Downing Street Years*, 1993, 595–596. Copyright © 1993 by Margaret Thatcher. Reprinted by permission of HarperCollins Publishers.

For Discussion

1. What does Scott mean when she argues that "what we know as history" is actually "the fruit of past politics"? How would Thatcher have replied?
2. Himmelfarb argues that an overemphasis on race, gender, and class characterizes postmodernist interpretations of history. Why might postmodernists emphasize these three categories? Why does Himmelfarb object? Would Thatcher have sympathized with Himmelfarb's argument?
3. Imagine that you are present *in 1989* at a debate featuring Scott, Himmelfarb, and Thatcher. Each woman has been asked to define "the West." How do you think each might have responded?

CHRONOLOGY: MEDICAL CHALLENGES AND ACHIEVEMENTS

1977
First diagnosed case of AIDS. — 1977

1978 — **1978**
First test-tube baby.

1980
Worldwide eradication of smallpox. — 1980

1982 — **1982**
First use of genetic engineering (insulin manufactured from bacteria).

1983
First artificially created chromosome. — 1983

1984 — **1984**
HIV identified.

1985
First use of laser surgery to clear blocked arteries. — 1985

1997 — **1997**
Successful cloning of sheep.

2001
Human genome decoded. — 2001

But at the same time, the long-reigning Pope John Paul II experienced unprecedented popularity. The most well-traveled and populist-oriented of twentieth-century popes, John Paul II became a media star, greeted with the same sort of cheering crowds and tee-shirt vendors that accompanied famous rock bands. Much of his popularity rested on his intimate connection with Poland's Solidarity and, therefore, with an image of liberation. But the pope's support for Solidarity did not mean he supported other forms of rebellion against authority. He adopted a firmly centralized approach to church government and opposed birth control, married clergy, and the ordination of women. Confronted with the postmodernist message that authority had fragmented and that no universal truth existed, many Christians found the pope's uncompromising stand a source of great comfort.

Yet throughout the West the pope's flock moved out of his control. In the United States, millions turned out to cheer John Paul II waving from an open car (the "popemobile"), yet the percentage of American Catholics using birth control—in direct violation of papal teachings—mirrored that of the population at large. Catholic Italy boasted the second-lowest birth rate in the world (after China), with the one-child family becoming the norm. It was hard to avoid the conclusion that in much of Western Roman Catholicism, as in much of postmodern society, image ruled while authority dissipated.

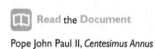 Read the Document

Pope John Paul II, *Centesimus Annus*

SEXUAL PRACTICE AND IDENTITY IN A POSTMODERN WORLD The postmodern rejection of a single "right" answer or central authoritative voice was also apparent in sexual behaviors and the debates this behavior provoked. As many in the West abandoned traditional moral codes, rates of extramarital sex and divorce soared, the age at which individuals became sexually active tumbled, and sexual imagery in films, advertising, and publishing became more explicit.

Three developments contributed to this sexual revolution. First, the declining rates of religious belief and observance meant that religious-backed codes of sexual behavior carried less weight. At the same time, the rebellions of the 1960s and early 1970s glorified resistance to traditional conventions and rules. Second, breaking those rules seemed less risky for women as oral and barrier contraceptives and—particularly in eastern Europe—abortion became widely available. Third, feminism played an important role in encouraging women to see themselves as sexual beings.

The sexual revolution also meant greater visibility for sexual identities that did not conform to the dominant heterosexual pattern. Denmark became the first European state to legalize homosexual acts in 1933, but most European countries moved toward equalizing the legal treatment of homosexuality and heterosexuality during or after the 1960s. In England, for example, homosexual acts became legal in 1967, in Scotland in 1980. Denmark moved to the forefront once again in 1989 when it became the first state to legalize registered partnerships (also called civil unions) between couples of the same sex. By 2006, 20 European countries had done so. In the Netherlands, Belgium, Spain, Portugal, Norway, Sweden, Iceland, Canada, and South Africa, gays and lesbians can legally marry on the same basis as heterosexuals.

The ongoing sexual revolution differentiated the West from much of the rest of the world, where more traditional sexual cultures remained strong. It also escalated the continuing debate within Western societies over what the "West" really means. Many Europeans and Americans, for example, saw the legalization of homosexual marriage as a logical and just extension of the concept of human rights—a central aspect of Western identity. Their opponents emphasized a different definition of the West when they argued that such a step violated the foundational Judeo-Christian values of Western culture. The growing numbers of Western citizens who were not Jewish or Christian but who adhered to religiously sanctioned sexual codes and roles—Muslim, Hindu, Sikh, and many others—intensified the debate still further.

The West in the Twenty-First Century

At the beginning of the twenty-first century, a worldwide environmental crisis raised significant questions about the ecological sustainability of Western habits of consumption. Environmental issues revealed the permeability of national borders and the limits of traditional political responses. As early as 1985, 257 multilateral treaties mandated some form of environmental protection—restrictions on trade in endangered species, wetlands preservation, forest conservation, or regulation of industrial emissions. Yet the degradation of the planet proceeded apace. By 2000, half of the world's rivers were polluted or running dry, the number of people displaced by water crises stood at 25 million (versus 21 million war-related refugees), and the potential catastrophe of global warming loomed. Faced with this potential catastrophe, representatives of 192 countries from around the world gathered in Copenhagen for a United Nations-sponsored conference on climate change in December 2009.

Environmental issues such as climate change underlined the fact that global systems of production, distribution, and consumption linked the peoples of the world. Technological developments accelerated this **globalization.** Fiber-optic cables that transmitted signals 4,000 times faster than their copper predecessors made instant communication across national boundaries a reality. In this global economy, multinational corporations, with quick access to cheap Third World labor and raw materials, possessed significant economic—and political—power. So, too, did the World Bank and the IMF, the institutions that directed the flow of aid and loans throughout much of the world. The IMF, for example, insisted that governments receiving loans cut government spending on social and welfare programs and restrict the money supply to reduce inflation. Thus, economists or investors in offices far away, not elected leaders, called the shots in much of the world.

Multinational corporations, the World Bank, and the IMF embodied the characteristic Western confidence of the post-World War II era. Expert economists and agronomists taught that an infusion of Western capital and expertise would set the rest of the world on the path to economic growth. The growing gap between "North" and "South," however, called into question the reliability of Western economic models. Beginning in the 1990s, anti-globalization campaigners disrupted meetings of the World Bank, the IMF, and the "G8" (Japan, the United States, Britain, Canada, France, Germany, Italy, and Russia). These protesters sought to highlight the social costs of global capitalism and challenged the sustainability of Western models of economic growth.

CONCLUSION

Where Is the West Now?

In England, the most popular fast food is not fish and chips, long the quintessential English national supper, nor is it the Big Mac, as opponents of economic globalization might predict. Instead it is curry, the gift of the minority South Asian immigrant community. In the twenty-first century, "the West" may no longer serve as an important conceptual border marker. By many of the criteria explored in this textbook—economic, technological, political, and cultural—Tokyo would be defined as a Western city. So, too, would Melbourne—or Budapest or Shanghai. Nevertheless, the economic and social trauma that afflicted Russia and the poorer nations of the former Soviet bloc such as Romania and Bulgaria after 1989 demonstrates that the "West" retains its distinct identity, for the gap between it and the "East" remains wide. The admittedly hesitant, still incomplete spread of the Western ideal of democracy has thrown a fragile bridge across that gap. But perhaps the real divide for the twenty-first century stretches between "North" and "South"—the huge and growing difference between the global Haves and the Have-Nots. Whether any bridge can stretch across that span remains to be seen.

globalization The process by which global systems of production, distribution, and communication link together the peoples of the world.

MAKING CONNECTIONS

1. What do historians mean when they talk about the "postwar political consensus"? When did this consensus break apart and why?
2. How does the Hungarian uprising of 1956 and the Prague Spring (see Chapter 28) compare with Solidarity? Why did Solidarity succeed when the two earlier popular risings failed?
3. How can Western technological, religious, and sexual developments since 1980 be described as "postmodern"? How have these developments shaped the relationship between the West and the rest of the world?

TAKING IT FURTHER

For suggested readings, see page R-1.

On MyHistoryLab

☑ Take the Study Plan for Chapter 29,
The West in the Contemporary Era:
New Encounters and Transformations,
on MyHistoryLab

Chapter Review

Economic Stagnation and Political Change: The 1970s and 1980s

29.1 How did developments in the 1970s and 1980s destabilize post-World War II national and international structures?

As the superpowers attempted to stabilize relations through negotiation and arms control, rising tensions due to economic crisis escalated industrial unrest and political conflict, eroding the social democratic political consensus and leading to the crumbling of détente.

Revolution in the East

29.2 What factors explain not only the outbreak but also the success of the revolutions of 1989–1991?

Economic hardship contributed to a longing for radical change, while activists and ordinary people worked to create the structures of civil society that were crucial for the successful revolutions that tore through the Soviet bloc.

In the Wake of Revolution

29.3 What were the consequences of the revolutions of 1989–1990 for the societies of eastern Europe?

The complicated and exhausting process of building new nations divided eastern Europe into "winners," states that were able to stabilize their economies and establish democratic governments, and "losers," those with economies that continued to flounder and where power was concentrated with just a few.

Rethinking the West

29.4 How and why was the West redefined at the end of the twentieth century and the beginning of the twenty-first?

Islamist terrorism replaced communism as the new foe of the West, and intellectual, artistic, and technological developments contributed to a postmodernism rejection of Western cultural supremacy. The struggle to integrate diverse economies within the European Union, as well as increasingly diverse cultures within societies, continues to redefine the West.

Chapter Time Line

1969 Ostpolitik and SALT talks inaugurate détente. — 1969

1973 — **1973** Yom Kippur War; era of stagflation begins.

1977 Formation of Charter 77 in Czechoslovakia. — 1977

1979 — **1979** Iranian Revolution; Margaret Thatcher elected prime minister in Britain.

1980 Birth of Solidarity in Poland. — 1980

1985 — **1985** Gorbachev becomes Soviet leader.

1989 Revolutions in eastern Europe. — 1989

1991 — **1991** End of Soviet Union; war begins in the former Yugoslavia; EC becomes the EU.

2001 Islamist terrorist attacks in U.S. — 2001

2008 — **2008** Global recession underway.

GLOSSARY

absolutism (p. 493)   A theory and form of government in the seventeenth and eighteenth centuries in which a ruler claimed unrivaled power.

acropolis (p. 80)   The defensible hilltop around which a polis grew. In classical Athens, the Acropolis was the site of the Parthenon (Temple of Athena).

agora (p. 81)   An open area in the town center of a Greek polis that served as a market and a place for informal discussion.

agricultural revolution (p. 298)   Refers to technological innovations that began to appear during the eleventh century, making possible a dramatic growth in population. The agricultural revolution came about through harnessing new sources of power with water and windmills, improving the pulling power of animals with better collars, using heavy plows to better exploit the soils of northern Europe, and employing a three-field crop rotation system that increased the amount and quality of food available.

alchemy (p. 531)   The practice, rooted in a philosophical tradition, of attempting to turn base metals into precious ones. It also involved the identification of natural substances for medical purposes. Alchemy was influential in the development of chemistry and medicine in the sixteenth and seventeenth centuries.

aldeias (p. 412)   Settlements for natives who had converted to Christianity in Brazil. In these settlements the Jesuit fathers protected the natives from enslavement.

Alexandrianism (p. 131)   A style of Hellenistic poetry that demonstrated a command of meter and language and appealed more to the intellect than the emotions.

Allies (p. 779)   During World War I, the states allied against the Central Powers of Germany and Austria-Hungary. During World War II, the states allied against the regimes of Nazi Germany, fascist Italy, and imperial Japan.

Anabaptism (p. 447)   Meaning "to rebaptize"; refers to those Protestant radicals of the sixteenth century who rejected infant baptism and adopted adult baptism. Anabaptists treated the Bible as a blueprint for reforming not just the church but all of society, a tendency that led them to reject the authority of the state, to live in self-governing "holy communities," and in some cases to practice a primitive form of communism.

anarchism (p. 732)   Ideology that views the state as unnecessary and repressive and rejects participation in parliamentary politics in favor of direct, usually violent, action.

anticlericalism (p. 759)   Opposition to the political influence of the Roman Catholic Church.

Antonine Age (p. 172)   Almost one hundred years of political stability in the Roman Empire, inaugurated when Nerva adopted Trajan as his son and heir.

Antonine Decree (p. 180)   In 212 C.E. the emperor Aurelius Antoninus, called Caracalla, issued a decree that granted citizenship to all the free inhabitants of the Roman Empire. The decree enabled Roman law to embrace the entire population of the empire.

Apocalypse (p. 439)   In the language of the Bible, the end times which would lead into Christ's Second Coming.

appeasement (p. 849)   British diplomatic and financial efforts to stabilize Germany in the 1920s and 1930s and so avoid a second world war.

Arians (p. 212)   Christians who believe that God the Father is superior to Jesus Christ his Son. Most of the Germanic settlers in western Europe in the fifth century were Arians.

aristocracy (p. 587)   A term that originally applied to those who were considered the most fit to rule and later identified the wealthiest members of society, especially those who owned land.

asceticism (p. 214)   The Christian practice of severely suppressing physical needs and daily desires in an effort to achieve a spiritual union with God. Asceticism is the practice that underlies the monastic movement.

auto-da-fé (p. 468)   Meaning literally a "theater of faith," an *auto* was practiced by the Catholic Church in early modern Spain and Portugal as an extended public ritual of penance designed to cause physical pain among the sinful and promote fear of God's judgment among those who witnessed it.

auxiliary (p. 176)   Soldiers in the Roman imperial army who were drawn from subject peoples. Auxiliaries received Roman citizenship after their term of service.

Babylonian Captivity of the Church (p. 352)   Between 1305 and 1378, seven consecutive popes voluntarily chose to reside in Avignon, France, in order to escape anarchy in the streets of Rome. During this period the popes became subservient to the kings of France.

Babylonian Exile (p. 69)   The period of Jewish history between the destruction of Solomon's temple in Jerusalem by Babylonian armies in 587 B.C.E., and 538 B.C.E, when Cyrus of Persia permitted Jews to return to Palestine and rebuild the temple.

balance of power (p. 501)   An arrangement in which various countries form alliances to prevent any one state from dominating the others.

Balfour Declaration (p. 809)   Declaration of 1917 that affirmed British support of a Jewish state in Palestine.

barbarians (p. 112)   A term used by Greeks to describe people who did not speak Greek and who were therefore considered uncivilized.

baroque (pp. 129, 498)   A dynamic style in art, architecture, and music that was intended to elicit an emotional response.

Baroque buildings were massive, imposing structures with sweeping façades. The baroque style represented a development of Greek classicism in the Hellenistic period. In the seventeenth century the baroque style was closely associated with royal absolutism.

Berlin Wall (p. 897)   Constructed by the East German government, the wall physically cut the city of Berlin in two and prevented East German citizens from access to West Germany; stood from 1961 to 1989.

Big Three (p. 883)   Term applied to the British, Soviet, and U.S. leaders during World War II: until 1945, Winston Churchill, Joseph Stalin, and Franklin Roosevelt; by the summer of 1945, Clement Attlee, Joseph Stalin, and Harry Truman.

Black Death (p. 330)   An epidemic disease, possibly Bubonic plague, that struck Europe between 1348 and the 1350s, killing at least one-third of the total population.

blitzkrieg (p. 851)   "Lightning war"; offensive military tactic making use of airplanes, tanks, and motorized infantry to punch through enemy defenses and secure key territory. First demonstrated by the German army in World War II.

boers (p. 557)   Dutch settlers, most of them farmers, who settled in the Dutch colony established at the Cape of Good Hope in southern Africa.

Bolsheviks (p. 803)   Minority group of Russian socialists, headed by Vladimir Lenin, who espoused an immediate transition to a socialist state. It became the Communist Party in the Soviet Union.

boule (p. 85)   A council of 400 male citizens established by Solon in Greece in the sixth century B.C.E. It served as an advisory body for the general assembly of all male citizens.

Bourbon reforms (p. 559)   Measures introduced by the Bourbon kings of Spain in the eighteenth century to make the Spanish Empire more manageable and profitable.

bourgeoisie (p. 594)   A social group, technically consisting of those who were untitled people living in the towns, that included prosperous merchants and financiers, members of the professions, and some skilled craftsmen known as "petty bourgeoisie." In later centuries, synonymous with "middle class."

boyars (p. 487)   Upper-level nobles who dominated Russian society until the tsars began to supplant them in the fifteenth and sixteenth centuries.

Bretton Woods Agreement (p. 884)   Agreement signed in 1944 that established the post–World War II economic framework in which the U.S. dollar served as the world's reserve currency.

brinkmanship (p. 894)   Style of Cold War confrontation in which each superpower endeavored to convince the other that it was willing to wage nuclear war.

Byzantine Empire (p. 225)   The eastern half of the Roman Empire, which lasted from the founding of Constantinople in 324 to its conquest by the Ottoman Turks in 1453.

caliphate (p. 248)   The Islamic imperial government that evolved under the leadership of Abu Bakr (r. 632–634), the successor of the prophet Muhammad. The sectarian division within Islam between the Shi'ites and Sunni derived from a disagreement over how to determine the hereditary succession from Muhammad to the caliphate, which combined governmental and some religious responsibilities.

calling (p. 443)   The Calvinist doctrine that God calls the Elect to perform his will on Earth. God's calling gave Calvinists a powerful sense of personal direction.

canon law (p. 276)   The collected laws of the Roman Catholic Church. Canon law applied to cases involving the clergy, disputes about church property, and donations to the Church. It also applied to the laity for annulling marriages, legitimating bastards, prosecuting bigamy, protecting widows and orphans, and resolving inheritance disputes.

capital (p. 661)   All the physical assets used in production, including fixed capital, such as machinery, and circulating capital, such as raw materials; more generally, the cost of these physical assets.

caravels (p. 397)   Hybrid three-masted ships developed about 1450 in the Iberian peninsula by combining the rigging of square with triangular lateen sails. These ships could be sailed in a variety of winds, carry large cargoes, be managed by a small crew, and be defended by guns mounted in the castle superstructure.

Carolingian Renaissance (p. 275)   The "rebirth" of interest in ancient Greek and Latin literature and language during the reign of the Frankish emperor Charlemagne (r. 768–814). Charlemagne promoted the intensive study of Latin to promote governmental efficiency and to propagate the Christian faith.

Catholic Reformation (p. 451)   A series of efforts during the sixteenth century to purify the Church that evolved out of late medieval spirituality and that included the creation of new religious orders, especially the Society of Jesus.

Central Powers (p. 779)   Germany and Austria-Hungary in World War I.

Chalcedonians (p. 213)   Christians who followed the doctrinal decisions and definitions of the Council of Chalcedon in 451 C.E. stating that Christ's human and divine natures were equal, but entirely distinct and united in one person "without confusion, division, separation, or change." Chalcedonian Christianity came to be associated with the Byzantine Empire and is called Greek Orthodoxy. In western Europe it is known as Roman Catholicism.

Chartists (p. 698)   A British group of workers and middle-class radicals who drafted a People's Charter in 1837 demanding universal male suffrage and other political reforms.

chinoiserie (p. 576)   A French word for an eighteenth-century decorative art that combined Chinese and European motifs.

Christian Democracy, Christian Democratic parties (p. 905)   Conservative and confessionally based (Roman Catholic) political parties that dominated much of western European politics after World War II.

Christian humanists (p. 429)   During the fifteenth and sixteenth centuries these experts in Greek, Latin, and Hebrew subjected the Bible to philological study in an attempt to understand the precise meaning of the founding text of Christianity.

Church Fathers (p. 219)   Writers in late antiquity from both the Greek- and Latin-speaking worlds who sought to reconcile Christianity with classical learning.

circuit court (p. 317)   Established by King Henry II (r. 1154–1189) to make royal justice available to virtually anyone in England. Circuit court judges visited every shire in England four times a year.

civic humanism (p. 376)   A branch of humanism introduced by the Florentine chancellor Leonardo Bruni, who defended the republican institutions and values of the city. Civic humanism promoted the ethic of responsible citizenship.

civic virtue (p. 167)   The belief that the success of a republic depended on its citizens' possession of personal traits that contributed to the common good.

civilization (p. 11)   The term used by archaeologists to describe a society differentiated by levels of wealth and power, and in which religious, economic, and political control are based in cities.

civil society (p. 925)   Public organizations and activities separate from the state, commerce, or the family that help to create community life and a sense of identity.

clans or kin groups (p. 267)   The basic social and political unit of Germanic society consisting of blood relatives obliged to defend one another and take vengeance for crimes against the group and its members.

class (p. 588)   A social group with similar economic and political interests.

class consciousness (p. 670)   The awareness of people from different occupations that they belonged to a class.

classicism (p. 591)   A style in art, architecture, music, and literature that emphasizes proportion, adherence to traditional forms, and a rejection of emotion and enthusiasm.

Cluny (p. 304)   A monastery founded in Burgundy in 910 that became the center of a far-reaching movement to reform the Church that was sustained in more than 1,500 Cluniac monasteries, modeled after the original in Cluny.

Cold War (p. 883)   Struggle for global supremacy between the United States and the Soviet Union, waged from the end of World War II until 1990.

collectivization (p. 828)   The replacement of private and village farms with large cooperative agricultural enterprises run by state-employed managers. Collectivization was a key part of Joseph Stalin's plans for modernizing the Soviet economy and destroying peasant opposition to communist rule.

Columbian exchange (p. 417)   The trade of peoples, plants, animals, microbes, and ideas between the Old and New Worlds that began with Columbus.

Columbian question (p. 420)   The debate among historians and epidemiologists about whether syphilis or its ancestor disease originated in the Americas and was brought to the Old World after Columbus's voyages.

communes (p. 301)   Sworn defensive associations of merchants and workers that appeared in north-central Italy after 1070 and that became the effective government of more than a hundred cities. The communes evolved into city-states by seizing control of the surrounding countryside.

communism (p. 686)   The revolutionary form of socialism developed by Karl Marx and Friedrich Engels that promoted the overthrow of bourgeois or capitalist institutions and the establishment of a dictatorship of the proletariat.

Companions (p. 113)   Elite regiments of cavalrymen armed with heavy lances formed by Philip of Macedon in the fourth century B.C.E.

Concert of Europe (p. 693)   The joint efforts made by Austria, Prussia, Russia, Britain, and France during the years following the Congress of Vienna to suppress liberal and nationalist movements throughout Europe.

Conciliar Movement (p. 352)   A fifteenth-century movement that advocated ending the Great Schism and reforming church government by calling a general meeting or council of the bishops, who would exercise authority over the rival popes.

confessions (p. 460)   The formal sixteenth-century statements of religious doctrine: the Confession of Augsburg for Lutherans, the Helvetic Confessions for Calvinists, the Thirty-Nine Articles for Anglicans, and the decrees of the Council of Trent for Catholics.

Congress of Vienna (p. 647)   A conference of the major powers of Europe in 1814–1815 to establish a new balance of power at the end of the Napoleonic Wars.

conquistadores (p. 407)   Spanish adventurers in the Americas who explored and conquered the lands of indigenous peoples, sometimes without legal authority but usually with a legal privilege granted by the king of Spain who required that one-fifth of all things of value be turned over to the crown. The conquistadores extended Spanish sovereignty over new lands.

conservatism (p. 683)   A nineteenth-century ideology intended to prevent a recurrence of the revolutionary changes of the 1790s and the implementation of liberal policies.

corporatism (p. 819)   The practice by which committees (or "corporations") made up of representatives of workers, employers, and the state direct the economy.

Cortes (p. 494)   Legislative assemblies in the Spanish kingdoms.

cosmology (p. 134)   A theory concerning the structure and nature of the universe such as those proposed by Aristotle in the fourth century B.C.E. and Copernicus in the sixteenth century.

counties (p. 275)   Territorial units devised by the Carolingian dynasty during the eighth and ninth centuries for the administration of the empire. Each county was administered by a count who was rewarded with lands and sent to areas where he had no family ties to serve as a combined provincial governor, judge, military commander, and representative of the king.

courtly love (p. 323)   An ethic first found in the poems of the late twelfth- and thirteenth-century troubadours that portrayed the ennobling possibilities of the love between a man and a woman. Courtly love formed the basis for the modern idea of romantic love.

creoles (p. 559)   People of Spanish descent who had been born in Spanish America.

Crusades (p. 287)   Between 1095 and 1291, Latin Christians heeding the call of the pope launched eight major expeditions and many smaller ones against Muslim armies in an attempt to gain control of and hold Jerusalem.

Cubism (p. 756)   Modernist artistic movement of the early twentieth century that emphasized the fragmentation of human perception through visual experiments with geometric forms.

Cubists (p. 756)   Followers of the early twentieth century modernist artistic movement that emphasized the fragmentation of human perception through visual experiments with geometric forms.

cultural relativism (p. 421)   A mode of thought first explored during the sixteenth century to explain why the peoples of the New World did not appear in the Bible. Cultural relativism recognized that many (but not necessarily all) standards of judgment are specific to particular cultures rather than the fixed truths established by natural or divine law.

culture (p. 11)   The knowledge and adaptive behavior created by communities that helps them to mediate between themselves and the natural world through time.

cuneiform (p. 24)   A kind of writing in which wedge-shaped symbols are pressed into clay tablets to indicate words and ideas. Cuneiform writing originated in ancient Sumer.

curia (p. 307)   The administrative bureaucracy of the Roman Catholic Church.

Cynics (p. 133)   Followers of the teachings of Antisthenes (ca. 445–360 B.C.E.) who rejected pleasures, possessions, and social conventions to find peace of mind.

Darwinian theory of evolution (p. 747)   Scientific theory associated with the nineteenth-century scientist Charles Darwin that highlights the role of variation and natural selection in the evolution of species.

D-Day (p. 861)   Common term for June 6, 1944, when 150,000 Allied troops landed on the shores of northern France to open an effective second front against German-occupied Europe.

Decembrists (p. 694)   Russian liberals who staged a revolt against Tsar Nicholas I on the first day of his reign in December 1825.

de-Christianization (p. 633)   A program inaugurated in France in 1793 by the radical Jacobin and former priest Joseph Fouché that closed churches, eliminated religious symbols, and attempted to establish a purely civic religion.

decolonization (p. 893)   The retreat of Western powers from their imperial territories.

deduction, deductive reasoning (p. 533)   The logical process by which ideas and laws are derived from basic truths or principles.

Defenders (p. 581)   Irish Catholic peasants who joined the United Irishmen in the rebellion against Britain in 1798.

deism (p. 597)   The belief that God created the universe and established immutable laws of nature but did not subsequently intervene in the operation of nature or in human affairs.

deists (p. 543)   Seventeenth- and eighteenth-century thinkers who believed that God created the universe and established immutable laws of nature but did not subsequently intervene in the operation of nature or in human affairs.

Delian League (p. 94)   The alliance among many Greek cities organized by Athens in 478 B.C.E. in order to fight Persian forces in the eastern Aegean Sea. The Athenians gradually turned the Delian League into the Athenian Empire.

demand (p. 662)   The desire of consumers to acquire goods and the need of producers to acquire raw materials and machinery.

democracy (p. 84)   A form of government in which citizens devise their own governing institutions and choose their leaders; began in Athens, Greece, in the fifth century B.C.E.

de-Stalinization (p. 901)   Nikita Khrushchev's effort to decentralize political and economic control in the Soviet Union after 1956.

détente (p. 919)   During the 1970s, a period of lessened Cold War hostilities and greater reliance on negotiation and compromise.

dialectic (p. 686)   The theory that history advanced in stages as the result of the conflict between different ideas or social groups.

dialectical materialism (p. 686)   The socialist philosophy of Karl Marx according to which history advanced as the result of material or economic forces and would lead to the creation of a classless society.

Diaspora (p. 195)   Literally "dispersion of population"; usually used to refer to the dispersion of the Jewish population after the Roman destruction of the Temple in Jerusalem in 70 C.E.

diets (p. 494)   Legislative assemblies in German territories.

divination (p. 23)   The practice of discerning the future by looking for messages imprinted in nature.

divine right (p. 494)   The theory that rulers received their power directly from God.

division of labor (p. 657)   The assignment of one stage of production to a single worker or group of workers to increase efficiency and productive output.

domestic system (p. 656)   An economic arrangement developed in the sixteenth century in which capitalist entrepreneurs employed families in rural areas to spin and weave cloth and make nails and cutlery.

Dreyfus Affair (p. 725)   The trials of Captain Alfred Dreyfus on treason charges, which dominated French political life in the decade after 1894 and revealed fundamental divisions in French society.

dualistic (pp. 88, 534)   A term used to describe a philosophy or a religion in which a rigid distinction is made between body and mind, good and evil, or the material and the immaterial world.

Dutch Revolt (p. 479)   The rebellion against Spanish rule of the seven northern provinces of the Netherlands between 1579 and 1648, which resulted in the independence of the Republic of the United Provinces.

Edict of Nantes (p. 476)   Promulgated by King Henry IV in 1598, the edict allowed the Huguenots to build a quasi-independent state within the kingdom of France, giving them the right to have their own troops, church organization, and political autonomy within their walled towns, but banning them from the royal court and the city of Paris. King Louis XIV revoked the edict in 1685.

empires (pp. 19, 554)   Large political formations consisting of different kingdoms or territories outside the boundaries of the states that control them.

empiricism (p. 532)   The practice of testing scientific theories by observation and experiment.

enclosure (p. 660)   The consolidation of scattered agricultural holdings into large, compact fields which were then closed off by hedges, bushes, or walls, giving farmers complete control over the uses of their land.

encomienda (p. 409)   The basic form of economic and social organization in early Spanish America, based on a royal grant awarded to a Spaniard for military or other services that gave the grantee and his successors the right to gather tribute from the Indians in a defined area.

English Parliament (p. 318)   King Edward I (r. 1272–1307) began to call the English Parliament in order to raise sums of money for his foreign wars. The English Parliament differed from similar assemblies in Europe. It usually included representatives of the "commons," which consisted of townsmen and prosperous farmers who lacked titles of nobility, but whom the king summoned because he needed their money. As a result, a broader spectrum of the population joined Parliament than in most other medieval kingdoms.

enlightened despots (p. 611)   The term assigned to absolute monarchs who initiated a series of legal and political reforms in an effort to realize the goals of the Enlightenment.

Enlightenment (p. 595)   An international intellectual movement of the eighteenth century that emphasized the use of reason and the application of the laws of nature to human society.

Epicureans (p. 132)   Followers of the teachings of the philosopher Epicurus (341–271 B.C.E.). Epicureans tried to gain peace of mind by choosing pleasures rationally.

Estates General (p. 494)   The legislative assembly of France in the Old Regime.

ethnic cleansing (p. 936)   A term introduced during the wars in Yugoslavia in the 1990s; the systematic use of murder, rape, and violence by one ethnic group against members of other ethnic groups in order to establish control over a territory.

Eucharist (p. 313)   Also known as Holy Communion or the Lord's Supper, the Eucharistic rite of the Mass celebrates Jesus's last meal with his apostles when the priest-celebrant consecrates wafers of bread and a chalice of wine as the body and blood of Christ. In the Middle Ages the wafers of bread were distributed for the congregation to eat, but drinking from the chalice was a special privilege of the priesthood. Protestants in the sixteenth century and Catholics in the late twentieth century began to allow the laity to drink from the chalice.

eugenics (p. 835)   The effort to improve the physical and intellectual capacities of the population by encouraging individuals with "desirable" traits to reproduce and/or by discouraging those individuals designated as "undesirable" from reproducing.

Euro-Islam (p. 942)   The identity and belief system being forged by European Muslims who argue that Islam does not contradict or reject European values.

European Economic Community (EEC) (p. 906)   Originally comprising West Germany, France, Italy, Belgium, Luxembourg, and the Netherlands, the EEC was formed in 1957 to integrate its members' economic structures and so foster both economic prosperity and international peace. Also called the Common Market.

European Union (EU) (p. 937)   A successor organization to the EEC; the effort to integrate European political, economic, cultural, and military structures and policies.

excommunication (p. 306)   A decree by the pope or a bishop prohibiting a sinner from participating in the sacraments of the Church and forbidding any social contact whatsoever with the surrounding community.

existentialism (p. 814)   Twentieth-century philosophy that emerged in the interwar era and influenced many thinkers and artists after World War II. Existentialism emphasizes individual freedom in a world devoid of meaning or coherence.

Expressionism (p. 756)   Modernist artistic movement of the early twentieth century that used bold colors and experimental forms to express emotional realities.

factories (p. 415)   Trading posts established by European powers in foreign lands.

fanatic (p. 474)   Originally referring to someone possessed by a demon, during the sixteenth century a fanatic came to mean a person who expressed immoderate enthusiasm in religious matters or who pursued a supposedly divine mission, often to violent ends.

fascism (p. 818)   Twentieth-century political ideology that rejected the existing alternatives of conservatism, communism, socialism, and liberalism. Fascists stressed the authoritarian power of the state, the efficacy of violent action, the need to build a national community, and the use of new technologies of influence and control.

feminism, feminist movement (p. 737)   International movement that emerged in the second half of the nineteenth century and demanded broader political, legal, and economic rights for women.

Fertile Crescent (p. 13)   Also known as the Levantine Corridor, this 25-mile-wide arc of land stretching from the Jordan River to the Euphrates River was the place where food production and settled communities first appeared in southwest Asia (the Middle East).

feudalism (p. 281)   A term historians use to describe a social system common during the Middle Ages in which lords granted fiefs (tracts of land or some other form of income) to dependents, known as vassals, who owed their lords personal services in exchange. Feudalism refers to a society governed through personal ties of dependency rather than public political institutions.

fief (p. 281) During the Middle Ages a fief was a grant of land or some other form of income that a lord gave to a vassal in exchange for loyalty and certain services (usually military assistance).

Final Solution (p. 868) Nazi term for the effort to murder every Jew in Europe during World War II.

fin-de-siecle (p. 751) French term for the "turn of the century"; used to refer to the cultural crisis of the late nineteenth century.

firestorm (p. 864) Human-made catastrophe: incendiary bombs cause fires, which combine with winds to suck the oxygen out of the air and raise temperatures to combustible levels. First experienced during the British bombing of the German city of Hamburg in World War II.

First Triumvirate (p. 163) The informal political alliance made by Julius Caesar, Pompey, and Crassus in 60 B.C.E. to share power in the Roman Republic. It led directly to the collapse of the Republic.

Forms (p. 103) In the philosophical teachings of Plato, these are eternal, unchanging absolutes such as Truth, Justice, and Beauty that represent true reality, as opposed to the approximations of reality that humans encounter in everyday life.

Fourteen Points (p. 806) The principles outlined by U.S. President Woodrow Wilson as the basis for a new world order after World War I.

freemasons (p. 609) Members of secret societies of men and women that flourished during the Enlightenment, dedicated to the creation of a society based on reason and virtue and committed to the principles of liberty and equality.

French Wars of Religion (p. 475) A series of political assassinations, massacres, and military engagements between French Catholics and Calvinists from 1560 to 1598.

friars (p. 312) "Brothers" who wandered from city to city and throughout the countryside begging for alms. Unlike monks who remained in a cloister, friars tried to help ordinary laypeople with their problems by preaching and administering to the sick and poor.

Gaullism (p. 913) The political ideology associated with twentieth-century French political leader Charles de Gaulle. Gaullism combined the advocacy of a strong, centralized state with social conservatism.

general strike (p. 732) Syndicalist tactic that called for every worker to go on strike and thus disrupt the capitalist economy and force a political revolution.

genocide (p. 800) The murder of an entire people.

German-Soviet Non-Aggression Pact (p. 849) Signed by Joseph Stalin and Adolf Hitler in 1939, the agreement publicly pledged Germany and the Soviet Union not to attack each other and secretly divided up Poland and the Baltic states between the two powers.

Girondins (p. 625) The more conservative members of the Jacobin party who favored greater economic freedom and opposed further centralization of state power during the French Revolution.

glasnost (p. 928) Loosely translated as openness or honesty; Gorbachev's effort after 1985 to break with the secrecy that had characterized Soviet political life.

globalization (p. 950) The process by which global systems of production, distribution, and communication link together the peoples of the world.

Gnostic (p. 197) Religious doctrine that emphasizes the importance of *gnosis*, or hidden truth, as a way of releasing spiritual reality from the prison of the essentially unreal or evil material world.

Gothic (p. 325) A style in architecture in western Europe from the late twelfth and thirteenth centuries, characterized by ribbed vaults and pointed arches, which drew the eyes of worshipers upward toward God. Flying buttresses, which redistributed the weight of the roof, made possible thin walls pierced by large expanses of stained glass.

grand jury (p. 318) In medieval England after the judicial reforms of King Henry II (r. 1154–1189), grand juries were called when the circuit court judge arrived in a shire. The sheriff assembled a group of men familiar with local affairs who constituted the grand jury and who reported to the judge the major crimes that had been committed since the judge's last visit.

Great Depression (p. 819) Calamitous drop in prices, reduction in trade, and rise in unemployment that devastated the global economy in 1929.

Great Persecution (p. 206) An attack on Christians in the Roman Empire begun by the emperor Galerius in 303 C.E. on the grounds that their worship was endangering the empire. Several thousand Christians were executed.

Great Purge (p. 831) Period of mass arrests and executions particularly aimed at Communist Party members in the Soviet Union.

Great Schism (p. 352) The division of the Catholic Church (1378–1417) between rival Italian and French claimants to the papal throne.

Green movement, Green politics (p. 923) A new style of politics and set of political ideas resulting from the confluence of environmentalism, feminism, and anti-nuclear protests of the 1970s.

guilds (p. 343) Professional associations devoted to protecting the special interests of a particular trade or craft and to monopolizing production and trade in the goods the guild produced.

Gulag (p. 829) Term for the network of forced labor and prison camps in the Soviet Union.

habiru (p. 55) Peasants who existed outside the palace system of the Late Bronze Age; often seen as bandits.

haciendas (p. 409) Large landed estates that began to be established in the seventeenth century and replaced encomiendas throughout much of Spanish America.

Hallstatt culture (p. 124) The first Celtic civilization in central Europe; from about 750 to about 450 B.C.E., Hallstatt Celts spread throughout Europe.

Hellenistic (p. 112) The word used to describe the civilization, based on that of Greece, that developed in the wake of the conquests of Alexander the Great.

helots (p. 84)   The brutally oppressed subject peoples of the Spartans. Tied to the land they farmed for Spartan masters, they were treated little better than beasts of burden.

Helsinki Accords (p. 923)   Signed by representatives of 32 European states, Canada, the United States, and the Soviet Union in 1975; often regarded as the apex of détente.

heresy (p. 196)   A teaching or belief not considered orthodox.

hetairai (p. 98)   Elite courtesans in ancient Greece who provided intellectual as well as sexual companionship.

hieroglyphs (p. 31)   Ancient Egyptian system of writing that represented both sounds and objects.

Holocaust (p. 867)   Adolf Hitler's effort to murder all the Jews in Europe during World War II.

Homo sapiens sapiens (p. 12)   Scientific term meaning "most intelligent people"; applied to physically and intellectually modern human beings that first appeared between 200,000 and 100,000 years ago in Africa.

hoplites (p. 82)   Greek soldiers in the Archaic Age who could afford their own weapons. Hoplite tactics made soldiers fighting as a group dependent on one another. This contributed to the internal cohesion of the polis and eventually to the rise of democracy.

Huguenots (p. 474)   The term for French Calvinists, who constituted some 10 percent of the population by 1560.

humanists (p. 374)   During the Renaissance, writers and orators who studied ancient Latin and sometimes Greek texts. Their principal interests were grammar, rhetoric, poetry, history, and ethics.

Hundred Years' War (p. 345)   A series of engagements (1337–1453) between England and France over England's attempts to assert its claims to territories in France.

hyperinflation (p. 821)   Catastrophic price increases and currency devaluation, such as that which occurred in Germany in 1923.

iconoclasm (p. 241)   The destruction of religious images in the Byzantine Empire in the eighth century.

icons (p. 240)   The Christian images of God and saints found in Byzantine art.

ideologies (p. 682)   Theories of society and government that form the basis of political programs.

Indo-European (p. 45)   Parent language of a majority of modern European languages as well as modern Armenian and Persian; sometimes used to refer to the people who spoke this language.

induction (pp. 24, 532)   The process of reasoning that formulates general hypotheses and theories on the basis of specific observation and the accumulation of data.

indulgences (p. 352)   Certificates that allowed penitents to atone for their sins and reduce their time in purgatory. Usually these were issued for going on a pilgrimage or performing a pious act; however, during the Babylonian Captivity of the Church (1305–1378) popes began to sell them, a practice Martin Luther protested in 1517 in an act that brought on the Protestant Reformation.

industrial capitalism (p. 669)   A form of capitalism characterized by the ownership of factories by private individuals and the employment of wage labor.

inheritance of acquired characteristics (p. 749)   Now discredited scientific theory of evolutionary change, which was powerful in the nineteenth century.

intendants (p. 496)   French royal officials who became the main agents of French provincial administration in the seventeenth century.

interdict (p. 307)   A papal decree prohibiting the celebration of the sacraments in an entire city or kingdom.

Investiture Controversy (p. 306)   A dispute that began in 1076 between the popes and the German emperors over the right to invest bishops with their offices. The most famous episode was the conflict between Pope Gregory VII and Emperor Henry IV. The controversy was resolved by the Concordat of Worms in 1122.

Iron Age (p. 57)   Historical period following the Bronze Age; marked by the prevalent use of iron.

Iron Curtain (p. 883)   Metaphor for the Cold War division of Europe after World War II.

Islamism (p. 939)   Ideology that insists that Islam demands a rejection of Western values and that violence in this struggle against the West is justified.

Jacobins (p. 621)   A French political party supporting a democratic republic that found support in political clubs throughout the country and dominated the National Convention from 1792 until 1794.

Jim Crow (p. 770)   Series of laws mandating racial segregation throughout the American South.

Julio-Claudian dynasty (p. 172)   Established by Octavian Augustus, this hereditary monarchy drawn from members of his extended family ruled Rome until 68 C.E.

Junkers (p. 508)   The traditional nobility of Prussia.

justification by faith (p. 432)   Refers to Martin Luther's insight that humanity is incapable of performing enough religious good works to earn eternal salvation. Salvation is an unmerited gift from God called grace. Those who receive grace are called the Elect.

Keynesian economics (p. 833)   Economic theories associated with the British economist John Maynard Keynes that advocate using the power of the democratic state to ensure economic prosperity.

knight (p. 281)   During the Middle Ages a knight was a soldier who fought on horseback. A knight was a vassal or dependent of a lord, who usually financed the knight's expenses of armor and weapons and of raising and feeding horses with a grant of land known as a fief.

Koine (p. 127)   The standard version of the Greek language spoken throughout the Hellenistic world.

kulak (p. 828)   Russian term for a peasant who was relatively prosperous.

laissez-faire (p. 683)   The principle that governments should not regulate or otherwise intervene in the economy unless it is necessary to protect property rights and public order.

late antiquity (p. 202) The period between about 250 and 600, which bridged the classical world and the Middle Ages.

Late Bronze Age (p. 44) The period from 1500 to 1100 B.C.E., characterized by an unprecedented degree of international trade and diplomatic exchange.

La Tène culture (p. 125) A phase of Celtic civilization that lasted from about 450 to 200 B.C.E. La Tène culture became strong especially in the regions of the Rhine and Danube Rivers.

Latin Christendom (p. 214) The parts of medieval Europe, including all of western Europe, united by Christianity and the use of Latin in worship and intellectual life. Latin served as an international language among the ruling elites in western Europe, even though they spoke different languages in their daily lives.

Latin War (p. 145) A war that the Latin peoples of Italy waged against the Roman Republic between 340 and 338 B.C.E.

Law of the Twelve Tables (p. 142) A body of written law inscribed on 12 bronze tablets and published in 451 B.C.E. This written summary of existing law was the first body of written law in Rome.

lay investiture (p. 305) The practice of nobles, kings, or emperors installing churchmen and giving them the symbols of office.

League of Nations (p. 806) Association of states set up after World War I to resolve international conflicts through open and peaceful negotiation.

Lend-Lease Act (p. 858) Passed in March 1941, the act gave Britain and later the Soviet Union access to U.S. industrial products during World War II, with payment postponed for the duration of the war.

Levantine Corridor (p. 13) Also known as the Fertile Crescent, this arc of land stretching from the Jordan River to the Euphrates River was the place where food production and settled communities first appeared in southwest Asia (the Middle East).

liberalism (p. 682) An ideology based on the conviction that individual freedom is of supreme importance and the main responsibility of government is to protect that freedom.

"Linear B" (p. 49) The earliest written form of Greek, used by the Mycenaeans.

linear perspective (p. 382) In the arts, the use of geometrical principles to depict a three-dimensional space on a flat, two-dimensional surface.

liturgy (p. 263) The forms of Christian worship, including the prayers, chants, and rituals to be said, sung, or performed throughout the year.

lord (p. 280) During the Middle Ages, a lord was someone who offered protection to dependents, known as vassals, who took an oath of loyalty to him. Most lords demanded military services from their vassals and sometimes granted them tracts of land known as fiefs.

lustration (p. 935) Implemented in many former communist states in the 1990s, this policy banned former communists and communist collaborators from public office.

ma'at (p. 30) Ancient Egyptian concept of the fundamental order established by the gods.

Macedonian Renaissance (p. 242) During the Macedonian dynasty's rule of Byzantium (867–1056), aristocratic families, the Church, and monasteries devoted their immense riches to embellishing Constantinople with new buildings, mosaics, and icons. The emperors sponsored historical, philosophical, and religious writing.

Mafia (p. 706) Organizations of armed men who took control of local politics and the economy in late nineteenth-century Sicily.

magic (p. 470) Learned opinion described two kinds of magic: natural magic, which involved the manipulation of occult forces believed to exist in nature, and demonic magic, which called upon evil spirits to gain access to power. This was widely accepted as a reality until the middle of the seventeenth century.

Magisterial Reformation (p. 440) Refers to Protestant churches that received official government sanction.

Magna Carta (p. 318) In 1215 some English barons forced King John to sign the "great charter," in which the king pledged to respect the traditional feudal privileges of the nobility, towns, and clergy. Subsequent kings swore to uphold it, thereby accepting the fundamental principle that even the king was obliged to respect the law.

Malthusian population trap (p. 668) The theory of Thomas Malthus (1766–1834) that the natural tendency of population to grow faster than the food supply would eventually drive the size of populations back to sustainable levels and end periods of economic expansion that usually accompany the growth of population.

Manhattan Project (p. 864) Code name given to the secret Anglo-American project that resulted in the construction of the atom bomb during World War II.

manor (p. 299) A medieval unit of agricultural management in which a lord managed and served as the presiding judge over peasants who worked the land.

marches (p. 275) Territorial units of the Carolingian Empire for the administration of frontier regions. Each march was ruled by a margrave who had special powers necessary to defend vulnerable borders.

Marshall Plan (p. 886) The use of U.S. economic aid to restore stability to Europe after World War II and so undercut the appeal of communist ideology.

martyr (p. 199) In Christian tradition, believers who chose to die rather than to renounce or deny their Christian beliefs.

mass politics (p. 717) A political culture characterized by the participation of non-elites.

matriarchy/matriarchal (p. 48) A social or cultural system in which family lineage is traced through the mother and/or in which women hold significant power.

mechanical philosophy (p. 534) The seventeenth-century philosophy of nature, championed by René Descartes, holding that nature operated in a mechanical way, just like a machine made by a human being.

megalith (p. 16) A very large stone used in prehistoric European monuments between 5000 and 1500 B.C.E.

mercantilism (p. 499)   The theory that the wealth of a state depended on its ability to import fewer commodities than it exported and thus acquire the largest possible share of the world's monetary supply. The theory encouraged state intervention in the economy and the regulation of trade.

meritocracy (p. 640)   The practice of appointing people to office solely on the basis of ability and performance rather than social or economic status.

mesmerism (p. 610)   A pseudoscience developed by Franz Anton Mesmer in the eighteenth century that treated sickness by massaging or hypnotizing the patient to produce a crisis that restored health.

mestizos (p. 573)   People of mixed white and Indian ancestry.

metropolis (p. 553)   The parent country of a colony or imperial possession; the "mother state" that controlled an empire.

Middle Kingdom (p. 32)   In ancient Near Eastern history, refers to the period of Egyptian history from 2040 to 1720 B.C.E.

Middle Passage (p. 569)   The journey taken by European ships bringing slaves from Africa to the Americas.

Mishnah (p. 195)   Completed around 220, a collection of homilies and decisions to explain Jewish law.

Modern Devotion (p. 354)   A fifteenth-century religious movement that stressed individual piety, ethical behavior, and intense religious education. The Modern Devotion was promoted by the Brothers of the Common Life, a religious order whose influence was broadly felt through its extensive network of schools.

modernism, modernist (pp. 752, 754)   Term applied to artistic and literary movements from the late nineteenth century through the 1950s. Modernists sought to create new aesthetic forms and values.

monastic movement (p. 215)   In late antiquity, Christian ascetics organized communities where men and women could pursue a life of spirituality through work, prayer, and asceticism. Called the monastic movement, this spiritual quest spread quickly throughout Christian lands.

Monophysites (p. 214)   Christians who do not accept the Council of Chalcedon (see Chalcedonians). Monophysites believe that Jesus Christ has only one nature, equally divine and human.

monotheism (p. 39)   The belief in only one god, first attributed to the ancient Hebrews. Monotheism is the foundation of Judaism, Christianity, Islam, and Zoroastrianism.

mosque (p. 246)   A place of Muslim worship.

Mountain, the (p. 625)   Members of the radical faction within the Jacobin party during the French Revolution who advocated the centralization of state power and instituted the Reign of Terror.

mulattos (p. 565)   People of mixed white and black race.

Munich Agreement (p. 849)   The agreement in 1939 between the governments of Nazi Germany, Britain, and France that granted Germany sovereignty over the Sudetenland; part of the effort to appease the Nazi government and avoid a second total war in Europe.

nabobs (p. 575)   Members of the British East India Company who made fortunes in India and returned to Britain, flaunting their wealth.

Napoleonic Code (p. 639)   The name eventually given to the Civil Code of 1804, promulgated by Napoleon, which gave France a uniform and authoritative code of law.

nation (p. 687)   A large community of people who possess a sense of unity based on a belief that they have a common homeland and share a similar culture.

national consciousness (p. 688)   The awareness or belief of people that they belong to a nation.

nationalism (p. 687)   The belief that the people who form a nation should have their own political institutions and that the interests of the nation should be defended and promoted at all costs.

nationalist-racist politics (p. 732)   Anti-liberal politics that appeal to race-based identities and fears.

national self-determination (p. 687)   The doctrine advanced by nationalists that any group that considers itself a nation has the right to be ruled only by the members of their own nation and to have all members of the nation included in that state.

nation-state (p. 687)   A political structure sought by nationalists in which the boundaries of the state and the nation are identical, so that all the members of a nation are governed by the same political authorities.

natural law (p. 144)   A law that is believed to be inherent in nature rather than established by human beings.

nawabs (p. 573)   Native provincial governors in eighteenth-century India.

Nazism (p. 820)   Twentieth-century political ideology associated with Adolf Hitler that adopted many fascist ideas but with a central focus on racism and particularly anti-Semitism.

neoclassicism (p. 591)   The revival of the classical art and architecture of ancient Greece and Rome in the eighteenth century.

Neolithic Age (p. 11)   The New Stone Age, characterized by the development of agriculture and the use of stone tools.

Neoplatonism (pp. 221, 536)   A philosophy based on the teachings of Plato and his successors that flourished in late antiquity, especially in the teachings of Plotinus. Neoplatonism influenced Christianity in late antiquity. During the Renaissance Neoplatonism was linked to the belief that the natural world was charged with occult forces that could be used in the practice of magic.

New Conservatism (p. 923)   Political ideology that emerged at the end of the 1970s combining the free market approach of nineteenth-century liberalism with social conservatism.

New Economic Policy (NEP) (p. 827)   Vladimir Lenin's economic turnaround in 1921 that allowed and even encouraged small private businesses and farms in the Soviet Union.

new feminism (p. 922)   Reemergence of the feminist movement in the 1970s.

new imperialism (p. 760)   The third phase of modern European imperialism, which occurred in the late nineteenth and early twentieth centuries and extended Western control over almost all of Africa and much of Asia.

New Kingdom (p. 35)   In ancient Near Eastern history, the period in Egyptian history from 1550 to 1150 B.C.E. During the New Kingdom, Egyptian kings first took the title of pharaoh and established an empire that reached to the Euphrates River.

New Left (p. 915)   Left-wing political and cultural movement that emerged in the late 1950s and early 1960s; sought to develop a form of socialism that rejected the overcentralization, authoritarianism, and inhumanity of Stalinism.

New Testament (p. 196)   The collection of texts that together with the Hebrew Bible, or Old Testament, comprise the Christian Bible. New Testament texts include the Epistles (letters of Paul of Tarsus to early Christians), the Gospels (stories of Jesus Christ's life, death, and resurrection), and other early Christian documents.

95 theses (p. 434)   Propositions about indulgences Martin Luther announced he was willing to defend in debate. The publication of the 95 theses in 1517 started the Protestant Reformation.

nobility (p. 588)   Members of the aristocracy who received official recognition of their hereditary status, including their titles of honor and legal privileges.

nobility of the robe (p. 588)   French noblemen whose families acquired their status by appointment to office.

no-man's-land (p. 786)   The area between the combatants' trenches on the Western Front during World War I.

North Atlantic Treaty Organization (NATO) (p. 889)   Defensive anti-Soviet alliance of the United States, Canada, and the nations of western Europe established in 1949.

northern Renaissance (p. 430)   A movement in northern Europe that built on the foundations of the Italian Renaissance, especially to subject the Bible and the sources of Christianity to critical scrutiny.

Nuremberg trials (p. 870)   Post-World War II trials of members of the Nazi Party and German military; conducted by an international tribunal.

Old Kingdom (p. 29)   In ancient Near Eastern history, the period in Egyptian history from ca. 2680–2200 B.C.E., formed by the unification of the kingdoms of Upper Egypt and Lower Egypt.

Old Regime (p. 611)   The political order of eighteenth-century France, dominated by an absolute monarch and a privileged nobility and clergy.

oligarchy (p. 84)   A government consisting of only a few people rather than the entire community.

Olympic Games (p. 81)   Greek athletic contests held in Olympia every four years between 776 B.C.E and 217 C.E.

orthodox, orthodoxy (p. 196)   In Christianity, the term indicates doctrinally correct belief.

Ottonian Renaissance (p. 284)   Under the patronage of the Saxon Emperor Otto I (936–973) and his brother Bruno, learned monks, Greek philosophers from Byzantium, and Italian scholars gathered at the imperial court, stimulating a cultural revival in literature and the arts. The writers and artists enhanced the reputation of Otto.

pagan (p. 210)   The Christian term for polytheist worship (worshiping more than one god). In the course of late antiquity, the Christian Church suppressed paganism, the traditional religions of the Roman Empire.

palace system (p. 53)   Late Bronze Age social system that concentrated religious, economic, political, and military power in the hands of an elite, who lived apart from most people in monumental fortified compounds.

pan-Arabism (p. 839)   Nationalist ideology that called for the political unification of all Arabs, regardless of religious affiliation.

papacy (p. 209)   The bishop of the city of Rome, sometimes referred to as "Father." The papacy refers to the administrative and political institutions controlled by the Pope. The papacy began to gain strength in the sixth century in the absence of Roman imperial government in Italy.

papal infallibility (p. 759)   The doctrine of the Roman Catholic Church proclaimed at the First Vatican Council in 1870 that the pope could not err when making solemn declarations regarding faith or morals.

paradigm (p. 536)   A conceptual model or intellectual framework within which scientists conduct their research and experimentation.

parlements (p. 496)   The highest provincial courts in France, the most important of which was the Parlement of Paris.

patriarchy (p. 28)   A social or cultural system in which men occupy the positions of power; in a family system, a father-centered household.

patricians (p. 141)   In ancient Rome, patricians were aristocratic clans with the highest status and the most political influence.

patrons and clients (p. 156)   In ancient Roman society, a system in which a powerful man (the patron) would exercise influence on behalf of a social subordinate (the client) in anticipation of future support or assistance.

Pax Romana (p. 170)   Latin for "Roman Peace," this term refers to the Roman Empire established by Augustus that lasted until the early third century C.E.

Pentateuch (p. 73)   The first five books of the Hebrew Bible.

perestroika (p. 928)   Loosely translated as "restructuring"; Gorbachev's effort to decentralize, reform, and thereby strengthen Soviet economic and political structures.

personal rule (p. 515)   The period from 1629 to 1640 in England when King Charles I ruled without Parliament.

phalanx (p. 82)   The military formation favored by hoplite soldiers. Standing shoulder-to-shoulder in ranks often eight men deep, hoplites moved in unison and depended on one another for protection.

pharaoh (p. 35)   Title for the Egyptian king, used during the New Kingdom period.

philology (p. 374)   A method reintroduced by the humanists during the Italian Renaissance devoted to the comparative study of language, especially to understanding the meaning of a word in a particular historical context.

philosophes (p. 596)   The writers and thinkers of the Enlightenment, especially in France.

pilgrimages (p. 217)   Religious journeys made to holy sites in order to encounter relics.

Pillars of Islam (p. 248)   The five basic principles of Islam as taught by Muhammad.

plantation colony (p. 398)   First appearing in the Cape Verde Islands and later in the tropical parts of the Americas, these colonies were established by Europeans who used African slave labor to cultivate cash crops such as sugar, indigo, cotton, coffee, and tobacco.

plebeians (p. 141)   The general body of Roman citizens.

plebiscite (p. 631)   A popular vote for or against a form of government or rule by a particular person.

pogroms (p. 735)   An organized and often officially encouraged riot or attack to persecute a particular ethnic or religious group, especially associated with eastern European attacks against Jews.

polis (p. 80)   A self-governing Greek city-state.

polytheistic (p. 23)   The belief in many gods.

pop art (p. 908)   Effort by artists in the 1950s and 1960s both to utilize and to critique the material abundance of post-World War II popular culture.

Popular Front (p. 833)   A political coalition of liberals, socialists, and communists designed to defeat fascist and racist-nationalist political rivals.

positivism (p. 689)   The philosophy developed by August Comte in the nineteenth century according to which human society passed through a series of stages, leading to the final positive stage in which the accumulation of scientific data would enable thinkers to discover the laws of human behavior and bring about the improvement of society.

positivist (p. 751)   The emphasis on the use of the scientific method to reach truth; a stress on observable fact.

postindustrialism, postindustrial society (p. 946)   A service-based, rather than manufacturing-based, economy characterized by an emphasis on marketing and information and by a proliferation of communications technologies.

postmodernism (p. 943)   Umbrella term covering a variety of artistic styles and intellectual theories and practices; in general, a rejection of a single, universal, Western style of modernity.

Potsdam Conference (p. 885)   The meeting in July 1945 of the Allied leaders of Britain, the Soviet Union, and the United States in the German city of Potsdam.

Pragmatic Sanction of Bourges (p. 387)   An agreement in 1438 that guaranteed the virtual autonomy of the French Church from papal control, enabling the French king to interfere in religious affairs and exploit Church revenues for government purposes.

Prague Spring (p. 904)   Short-lived popular effort in 1968 to reform Czechoslovakia's political structures; associated with the phrase "socialism with a human face."

predestination (p. 442)   The doctrine promoted by John Calvin that since God, the all-knowing and all-powerful being, knew everything in advance and caused everything to happen, then the salvation of any individual was predetermined.

prerogative (p. 515)   The set of powers exercised by the English monarch alone, rather than in conjunction with Parliament.

Price Revolution (p. 464)   The period between about 1540 and 1640 in which Europe, after a long period of falling or stable prices that stretched back to the fourteenth century, experienced sustained price increases. This caused widespread social and economic turmoil.

priesthood of all believers (p. 435)   Martin Luther's doctrine that all those of pure faith were themselves priests, a doctrine that undermined the authority of the Catholic clergy over the laity.

primogeniture (p. 513)   The legal arrangement by which the eldest son inherits the entire estate upon the death of the father.

proletariat (p. 686)   The word used by Karl Marx and Friedrich Engels to identify the class of workers who received their income from wages.

prophetic movement (p. 72)   An important phase in the development of what became Judaism. In the ninth century B.C.E., Hebrew religious reformers, or prophets, demanded the transformation of religious and economic practices to reflect ideals of social justice and religious purity.

protectionism (p. 561)   The policy of shielding domestic industries from foreign competition through a policy of levying tariffs on imported goods.

Protestant Reformation (p. 427)   Period that dominated European affairs between 1517 and 1560 when the movement for religious reform begun by Martin Luther led Germany, Britain, and most of northern Europe to break away from the Catholic Church.

Radical Reformation (p. 440)   Refers to Protestant movements that failed to gain official government recognition and were at best tolerated, at worst persecuted, during the sixteenth century.

Radical Right (p. 820)   Refers to extremist ideologies on the far right of the political spectrum, such as fascism and Nazism.

rationalism (p. 533)   The theory that the mind contains rational categories independent of sensory observation; more generally that reason is the primary source of truth.

Realpolitik (p. 707)   The adoption of political tactics based solely on their realistic chances of success.

redistributive economies (p. 19)   Type of economic system characteristic of ancient Mesopotamian societies. The central political authority controls all agricultural resources and their redistribution.

regency (p. 496)   Rule by relative of a monarch during a period when the monarch was too young to rule or otherwise incapacitated.

Reign of Terror (p. 627)   A purging of alleged enemies of the French state between 1793 and 1794, superintended by the Committee of Public Safety, that resulted in the execution of 17,000 people.

relativity, theory of (p. 750)   Albert Einstein's revolutionary model of the physical universe as four-dimensional.

relics (p. 217)   In Christian belief, relics are sacred objects that have miraculous powers. They are associated with saints, biblical figures, or some object associated with them. They served as contacts between Earth and Heaven and were verified by miracles.

Religious Peace of Augsburg (p. 440)   In 1555 this peace between Lutherans and Catholics within the Holy Roman Empire established the principle of *cuius regio, eius religio*, which means "he who rules determines the religion of the land." Protestant princes in the Empire were permitted to retain all church lands seized before 1552 and to enforce Protestant worship, but Catholic princes were also allowed to enforce Catholic worship in their territories.

Renaissance (p. 365)   A term meaning "rebirth" used by historians to describe a movement that sought to imitate and understand the culture of antiquity. The Renaissance generally refers to a movement that began in Italy and then spread throughout Europe from about 1350 to 1550.

reparations (p. 807)   Payments imposed upon Germany after World War I by the Versailles Treaty to cover the costs of the war.

republic (p. 141)   A state in which political power resides in the people or their representatives rather than in a monarch.

republicanism (p. 366)   A political theory first developed by the ancient Greeks, especially the philosopher Plato, but elaborated by the ancient Romans and rediscovered during the Italian Renaissance. The fundamental principle of republicanism as developed during the Italian Renaissance was that government officials should be elected by the people or a portion of the people.

Republic of Letters (p. 596)   An international community of Enlightenment writers and thinkers in the eighteenth century.

Republic of Virtue (p. 625)   The ideal form of government proposed by Maximilien Robespierre and other Jacobins during the French Revolution. Its proponents wished to make the republic established in 1792 more egalitarian and secular and inspire civic pride and patriotism in the people.

requerimiento (p. 407)   A document read by conquistadores to the natives of the Americas before making war on them. The document briefly explained the principles of Christianity and commanded the natives to accept them immediately along with the authority of the pope and the sovereignty of the king of Spain. If the natives refused, they were warned they would be forced to accept Christian conversion and subjected to Spain anyway.

Resistance, the (p. 870)   Label given to the many different underground political and partisan movements directed against Nazi rule in German-occupied Europe during World War II.

revisionism, socialist revisionism (p. 731)   The belief that an equal society can be built through participation in parliamentary politics rather than through violent revolution.

rhetoric (p. 374)   The art of persuasive or emotive speaking and writing, which was especially valued by the Renaissance humanists.

Romanesque (p. 324)   A style in architecture that spread throughout western Europe during the eleventh and the first half of the twelfth centuries and was characterized by arched stone roofs supported by rounded arches, massive stone pillars, and thick walls.

Romanization (p. 177)   The process by which conquered peoples absorbed aspects of Roman culture, especially the Latin language, city life, and religion.

romanticism (p. 690)   An artistic and literary movement of the late eighteenth and nineteenth centuries that involved a protest against classicism, appealed to the passions rather than the intellect, and emphasized the beauty and power of nature.

Rome-Berlin Axis (p. 848)   Alliance between Benito Mussolini's Italy and Adolf Hitler's Germany formed in 1936.

Russification (p. 727)   Tsarist policy from the 1890s until the outbreak of World War I that imposed the use of Russian language and emphasized Russian Orthodox religious and cultural practices.

salons (p. 609)   Private sitting rooms or parlors of aristocratic French women where discussions of philosophy, science, literature, and politics took place in the eighteenth century.

sans-culottes (p. 621)   The militant citizens of Paris who refused to wear the pants worn by noblemen and provided support for the Jacobins during the French Revolution; literally, those without breeches.

satraps (p. 117)   Persian provincial governors who collected taxes and oversaw the bureaucracy.

Schlieffen Plan (p. 783)   German military plan devised in 1905 that called for a sweeping attack on France through Belgium and the Netherlands.

scholasticism (p. 320)   A term referring to a broad philosophical and theological movement that dominated medieval thought and university training. Scholasticism used logic learned from Aristotle to interpret the meaning of the Bible and the writings of the Church Fathers, who created Christian theology in its first centuries.

Scramble for Africa (p. 765)   The frenzied imposition of European control over most of Africa that occurred between 1870 and 1914.

scriptorium (p. 271)   The room in a monastery where monks copied books and manuscripts.

Sea Peoples (p. 55)   Name given by the Egyptians to the diverse groups of migrants whose attacks helped bring the International Bronze Age to an end.

Second Industrial Revolution (p. 718)   A new phase in the industrialization of the processes of production and consumption, which was underway in Europe in the 1870s.

Second Triumvirate (p. 166)   In 43 B.C.E. Octavian (later called Caesar Augustus), Mark Antony, and Lepidus made an informal alliance to share power in Rome while they jockeyed for control. Octavian emerged as the sole ruler of Rome in 31 B.C.E.

secularization (p. 545)   The reduction of the importance of religion in society and culture.

seigneur (p. 593)   The lord of a French estate who received payments from the peasants who lived on his land.

separate spheres (p. 607)   The theory that men and women should conduct their lives in different social and political environments, confining women to the domestic sphere and excluding them from the public sphere of political involvement.

sepoys (p. 574)   Indian troops serving in the armed forces of the British East India Company.

Septuagint (p. 127)   The Greek translation of the Hebrew Bible (Old Testament).

serfs (p. 299)   During the Middle Ages serfs were agricultural laborers who worked and lived on a plot of land granted them by a lord to whom they owed a certain portion of their crops. They could not leave the land, but they had certain legal rights that were denied to slaves.

settler colony (p. 398)   A colony authorized when a private person obtained a license from a king to seize an island or parcel of land and occupied it with settlers from Europe who exported their own culture to the new lands. Settler colonies first appeared among the islands of the eastern Atlantic and portions of the Americas.

simony (p. 305)   The practice of buying and selling church offices.

skepticism (p. 541)   A tendency to doubt what one has been taught or is expected to believe.

Social Darwinism (p. 748)   The later-nineteenth-century application of the theory of evolution to entire human societies.

social democracy (p. 831)   Political system in which a democratically elected parliamentary government endeavors to ensure a decent standard of living for its citizens through both economic regulation and the maintenance of a welfare state.

socialism (p. 684)   An ideology calling for the ownership of the means of production by the community with the purpose of reducing inequalities of income, wealth, opportunity, and economic power.

socialist revisionism (p. 731)   The belief that an equal society can be built through participation in parliamentary politics rather than through violent revolution.

Social War (p. 160)   The revolt of Rome's allies against the Republic in 90 B.C.E. demanding full Roman citizenship.

Solidarity (p. 925)   Trade union and political party in Poland that led an unsuccessful effort to reform the Polish communist state in 1981; survived to lead Poland's first non-communist government since World War II in 1989.

Sophists (p. 103)   Professional educators who traveled throughout the ancient Greek world, teaching many subjects. Their goal was to teach people the best ways to lead better lives.

soviets (p. 801)   Workers' and soldiers' councils formed in Russia during the Revolution of 1917.

Spanish Armada (p. 478)   A fleet of 132 ships, which sailed from Portugal to rendezvous with the Spanish army stationed in the Netherlands and launch an invasion of England in 1588. The English defeated the Armada as it passed through the English Channel. The defeat marked a shift in the power balance from Spain to England.

Spanish Reconquest (p. 259)   Refers to the numerous military campaigns by the Christian kingdoms of northern Spain to capture the Muslim-controlled cities and kingdoms of southern Spain. This long, intermittent struggle began with the capture of Toledo in 1085 and lasted until Granada fell to Christian armies in 1492.

spiritualists (p. 448)   A tendency within Protestantism, especially Lutheranism, to emphasize the power of personal spiritual illumination, called the "inner Word," a living form of the Scriptures written directly on the believer's soul by the hand of God.

stagflation (p. 920)   Term coined in the 1970s to describe an economy troubled by both high inflation and high unemployment rates.

standing armies (p. 494)   Trained and equipped military forces that were not disbanded after the conclusion of war. Standing armies often helped maintain order and enforce governmental policy at home.

states (p. 553)   Consolidated territorial areas that have their own political institutions and recognize no higher political authority.

Stoics (p. 133)   Followers of the philosophy developed by Zeno of Citium (ca. 335–ca. 263 B.C.E.) that urged acceptance of fate while participating fully in everyday life.

structuralism (p. 909)   Influential post-World War II social theory that explored the common structures of language and thought.

Struggle of the Orders (p. 142)   The political strife between patrician and plebeian Romans beginning in the fifth century B.C.E. The plebeians gradually won political rights and influence as a result of the struggle.

suffragettes (p. 742)   Feminist movement that emerged in Britain in the early twentieth century. Unlike the suffragists, who sought to achieve the national vote for women through rational persuasion, the suffragettes adopted the tactics of violent protest.

suffragists (p. 742)   Feminists who sought to achieve the national vote for women through rational persuasion and parliamentary politics.

supply (p. 662)   The amounts of capital, labor, and food that are needed to produce goods for the market as well as the quantities of those goods themselves.

syncretism (p. 70)   The practice of blending foreign religious beliefs with an indigenous religious system; a common practice throughout the Roman Empire.

syndicalism (p. 732)   Ideology of the late nineteenth and early twentieth century that sought to achieve a working-class revolution through economic action, particularly through mass labor strikes.

Talmud (p. 216)   Commentaries on Jewish law. Rabbis completed the Babylonian Talmud and the Jerusalem Talmud by the end of the fifth century C.E.

tetrarchy (p. 204)   The government by four rulers established by the Roman emperor Diocletian in 293 C.E. that lasted until 312. During the tetrarchy many administrative and military reforms altered the fabric of Roman society.

Third Estate (p. 618)   The component of the Estates General in Old Regime France that technically represented all the commoners in the kingdom.

Third Reich (p. 854)   Term for Adolf Hitler's Germany; articulates the Nazi aim of extending German rule across Europe.

Third World (p. 898)   Term coined in 1955 to describe nations that did not align with either the Soviet Union or the United States; commonly used to describe the industrially underdeveloped nations.

Thomism (p. 322)   A branch of medieval philosophy associated with the work of the Dominican thinker, Thomas Aquinas (1225–1274), who wrote encyclopedic summaries of human knowledge that confirmed Christian faith.

Time of Troubles (p. 489)   The period from 1604 to 1613 when Russia fell into chaos, which ended when the national assembly elected Tsar Michael Romanov, whose descendants ruled Russia until they were deposed in 1917.

Torah (p. 73)   Most commonly, the first five books of the Hebrew Bible; also used to refer to the whole body of Jewish sacred writings and tradition.

total war (p. 779)   A war that demands extensive state regulation of economic production, distribution, and consumption; a war that blurs (or erases entirely) the distinction between civilian and soldier.

trading posts (p. 400)   Areas built by European traders along the coasts of Africa and Asia as a base for trade with the interior. Trading posts or factories were islands of European law and sovereignty, but European authority seldom extended very far beyond the fortified post.

transubstantiation (p. 313)   A doctrine promulgated at the Fourth Lateran Council in 1215 that distinguished the difference between the outward appearances and the inner substance of how the Eucharistic bread and wine changed into the body and blood of Christ.

Treaty of Brest-Litovsk (p. 791)   Treaty between Germany and Bolshevik-controlled Russia, signed in March 1918, that ceded to Germany all of Russia's western territories.

trial by jury (p. 318)   When disputes about the possession of land arose after the late twelfth century in England, sheriffs assembled a group of 12 local men who testified under oath about the claims of the plaintiffs; the circuit court judge then made his decision on the basis of their testimony. The system was later extended to criminal cases.

Triple Alliance (p. 781)   Defensive alliance of Germany, Austria-Hungary, and Italy, signed in 1882.

Triple Entente (p. 781)   Informal defensive agreement linking France, Great Britain, and Russia before World War I.

triremes (p. 91)   Greek warships with three banks of oars. Triremes manned by the poorest people of Athenian society became the backbone of the Athenian Empire.

troubadours (p. 323)   Poets from the late twelfth and thirteenth centuries who wrote love poems, meant to be sung to music, which reflected a new sensibility, called courtly love, about the ennobling possibilities of the love between a man and a woman.

Truman Doctrine (p. 886)   Named after U.S. president Harry Truman, the doctrine that in 1947 inaugurated the Cold War policy of resisting the expansion of communist control.

Twelfth-Century Renaissance (p. 321)   An intellectual revival of interest in ancient Greek philosophy and science and in Roman law in western Europe during the twelfth and early thirteenth centuries. The term also refers to a flowering of vernacular literature and the Romanesque and Gothic styles in architecture.

tyrants (p. 83)   Rulers in Greek city-states, usually members of the aristocracy, who seized power illegitimately rather than acquiring it by heredity or election. Tyrants often gained political support from the hoplites and the poor.

Unitarians (p. 449)   A religious reform movement that began in the sixteenth century and rejected the Christian doctrine of the Trinity. Unitarians (also called Arians, Socinians, and Anti-Trinitarians) taught a rationalist interpretation of the Scriptures and argued that Jesus was a divinely inspired man, not God who became a man, as other Christians believed.

United Kingdom (p. 688)   The name of the British state formed by the union of England and Scotland in 1707. In 1801 Ireland became part of the United Kingdom, but after the establishment of the Irish Free State in 1922, only the six Irish counties in the northern province of Ulster remained united to Britain.

universal law of gravitation (p. 530)   A law of nature established by Isaac Newton in 1687 holding that any two bodies attract each other with a force that is directly proportional to the product of their masses and indirectly proportional to the square of the distance between them. The law was presented in mathematical terms.

universal male suffrage (p. 624)   The granting of the right to vote to all adult males.

vassals (p. 280)   During the Middle Ages, men voluntarily submitted themselves to a lord by taking an oath of loyalty. Vassals owed the lord certain services—usually military assistance—and sometimes received in exchange a grant of land known as a fief.

Vatican II (p. 912)   Popular term for the Second Vatican Council that convened in 1963 and introduced a series of changes within the Roman Catholic Church.

vernacular languages (p. 480)   The native spoken languages of Europe, which became literary languages and began to replace Latin as the dominant form of learned expression during the sixteenth century.

Versailles Treaty (p. 807)   Treaty between Germany and the victorious Allies after World War I.

Vichy, Vichy regime, Vichy government (p. 852)   Authoritarian state established in France after its defeat by the German army in 1940.

vizier (p. 36)   The chief minister of state in New Kingdom Egypt, the vizier supervised the administration of the entire kingdom.

Vulgate (p. 213)   The Latin translation of the Bible produced about 410 by the monk Jerome. It was the standard Bible in western Christian churches until the sixteenth century.

Wahhabism (p. 840)   A religious reform and revival movement founded by Muhammad Abd al-Wahhab (1703–1787) in the eighteenth century to purify Islam by returning to a strict interpretation of the *Sharia,* or Islamic law. Revived during the 1920s in Saudi Arabia.

Warsaw Pact (p. 889)   Military alliance of the Soviet Union and its eastern European satellite states in the Cold War era.

Weimar Republic (p. 820)   The democratic German state constructed after defeat in World War I and destroyed by the Nazis in 1933.

wergild (p. 267)   In Germanic societies, the term referred to what an individual was worth in case he or she suffered an injury. It was the amount of compensation in gold that the wrongdoer's family had to pay to the victim's family.

witch-hunt (p. 470)   Refers to the dramatic increase in the judicial prosecution of alleged witches in either church or secular courts from the middle of the sixteenth to the middle of the seventeenth centuries.

Yahwism (p. 70)   The worship of Yahweh ("Jehovah"); the form of early Israelite religious belief.

Yalta Conference (p. 884)   Meeting in 1945 of the leaders of the Allied states of Britain, the Soviet Union, and the United States to devise plans for postwar Europe.

ziggurat (p. 23)   Monumental tiered or terraced temple characteristic of ancient Mesopotamia.

Zionism (p. 736)   Nationalist movement that emerged in the late nineteenth century and sought to establish a Jewish political state in Palestine (the Biblical Zion).

Zoroastrianism (p. 88)   The monotheistic religion of Persia founded by Zoroaster that became the official religion of the Persian Empire.

SUGGESTIONS FOR FURTHER READING

CHAPTER 20   THE AGE OF THE FRENCH REVOLUTION, 1789–1815

Andress, David. *The French Revolution and the People.* 2004. Focuses on the role played by the common people of France—the peasants, craftsmen, and those living on the margins of society—in the revolution.

Blanning, T. C. W. *The French Revolutionary Wars, 1787–1802.* 1996. An authoritative political and military narrative that assesses the impact of the wars on French politics.

Chartier, Roger. *The Cultural Origins of the French Revolution.* 1991. Explores the connections between the culture of the Enlightenment and the cultural transformations of the revolutionary period.

Cobban, Alfred. *The Social Interpretation of the French Revolution.* 1964. Challenges the Marxist interpretation of the causes and effects of the revolution.

Doyle, William. *The Oxford History of the French Revolution.* 1989. An excellent synthesis.

Ellis, Geoffrey. *Napoleon.* 1997. A study of the nature and mechanics of Napoleon's power and an analysis of his imperial policy.

Furet, François. *The French Revolution, 1770–1814.* 1992. A provocative narrative that sees Napoleon as the architect of a second, authoritarian revolution that reversed the gains of the first.

Hardman, John. *Louis XVI: The Silent King.* 2000. A reassessment of the king that mixes sympathy with criticism.

Higonnet, Patrice. *Goodness Beyond Virtue: Jacobins During the French Revolution.* 1998. Explores the contradictions of Jacobin ideology and its descent into the Terror.

Hunt, Lynn. *Politics, Culture and Class in the French Revolution.* 1984. Analyzes the formation of a revolutionary political culture.

Kennedy, Emmet. *The Culture of the French Revolution.* 1989. A comprehensive study of all cultural developments before and during the revolution.

Landes, Joan B. *Women and the Public Sphere in the Age of the French Revolution.* 1988. Explores how the new political culture of the revolution changed the position of women in society.

Lefebvre, Georges. *The Great Fear of 1789: Rural Panic in Revolutionary France.* 1973. Shows the importance of the rural unrest of July 1789 that provided the backdrop of the legislation of August 1789.

Schama, Simon. *Citizens: A Chronicle of the French Revolution.* 1989. Depicts the tragic unraveling of a vision of liberty and happiness into a scenario of hunger, anger, violence, and death.

Scurr, Ruth. *Fatal Purity: Robespierre and the French Revolution.* 2006. A judicious assessment of this controversial revolutionary figure.

CHAPTER 21   THE INDUSTRIAL REVOLUTION

Ashton, T. A. *The Industrial Revolution,* reprint edition with preface by P. Hudson. 1992. The classic statement of the optimist position, identifying the benefits of the revolution.

Berg, Maxine. *The Age of Manufactures, 1700–1820: Industry, Innovation and Work in Britain.* 1994. A study of the process and character of specific industries, especially those employing women.

Brinley, Thomas. *The Industrial Revolution and the Atlantic Economy: Selected Essays.* 1993. Essays challenging the view that Britain's Industrial Revolution was a gradual process.

Deane, Phyllis. *The First Industrial Revolution.* 1967. The best study of technological innovation in Britain.

Gutmann, Myron. *Toward the Modern Economy: Early Industry in Europe, 1500–1800.* 1988. A study of cottage industry, especially in France.

Hobsbawm, E. J. *Industry and Empire.* 1968. A general economic history of Britain from 1750 to 1970 that analyzes the position of Britain in the world economy.

Jacob, Margaret. *Scientific Culture and the Making of the Industrial West.* 1997. An exploration of the spread of scientific knowledge and its connection with industrialization.

Morris, Charles. *The Dawn of Innovation: The First American Industrial Revolution.* 2012. Empasizes industrial competition between Britain and the United States in the early nineteenth century.

Morris, R. J. *Class and Class Consciousness in the Industrial Revolution, 1780–1850.* 1979. A balanced treatment of the link between industrialization and class formation.

Pollard, Sidney. *Peaceful Conquest: The Industrialization of Europe, 1760–1970.* 1981. Links coal supplies to economic development.

Rule, John. *The Vital Century: England's Developing Economy, 1714–1815.* 1992. A general economic history establishing the importance of early eighteenth-century developments.

Stearns, Peter. *The Industrial Revolution in World History,* 2nd ed. 1998. The best study of industrialization in a global context.

Teich, Mikulas, and Roy Porter, eds. *The Industrial Revolution in National Context: Europe and the USA.* 1981. Essays illustrating similarities as well as national differences in the process of industrialization.

Wrigley, E. A. *Continuity, Chance and Change: The Character of the Industrial Revolution in Britain.* 1988. Includes the best discussion of the transition from an advanced organic economy to one based on minerals.

CHAPTER 22   IDEOLOGICAL CONFLICT AND NATIONAL UNIFICATION, 1815–1871

Anderson, Benedict. *Imagined Communities: Reflections on the Origin and Spread of Nationalism.* 1991. A discussion of the ways in which people conceptualize the nation.

Clark, Martin. *The Italian Risorgimento.* 1999. A comprehensive study of the social, economic, and religious context of Italian unification as well as its political and diplomatic dimensions.

Figes, Orlando. *The Crimean War: A History.* 2010. A fascinating narrative history of a brutal global war involving four empires.

Gellner, Ernest. *Nations and Nationalism.* 1983. An interpretive study that emphasizes the social roots of nationalism.

Hamerow, Theodore S. *Restoration, Revolution, Reaction: Economics and Politics in Germany, 1815–1871.* 1966. An investigation of the social basis of ideological encounters in Germany.

Holmes, Richard. *The Age of Wonder: How the Romantic Generation Discovered the Beauty and Terror of Nature.* 2009. Argues that science inspired the romantic imagination.

Honour, Hugh. *Romanticism.* 1979. A comprehensive study of romantic painting.

Hunczak, Tara, ed. *Russian Imperialism from Ivan the Great to the Revolution.* 1974. A collection of essays that illuminate Russian nationalism as well as imperialism over a long period of time.

Lichtheim, George. *A Short History of Socialism.* 1970. A good general treatment of the subject.

Nipperdey, Thomas. *Germany from Napoleon to Bismarck, 1800–1866.* 1996. An exploration of the creation of German nationalism as well as the failure of liberalism.

Onuf, Peter S. *Jefferson's Empire: The Language of American Nationhood.* 2000. A study of Jefferson's expansionary nationalism.

Pflanze, Otto. *Bismarck and the Development of Germany: The Period of Unification, 1815–1871.* 1963. The classic study of Bismarck and German unification.

Pinckney, David. *The French Revolution of 1830.* 1972. The best treatment of this revolution.

Seton-Watson, Hugh. *Nations and States.* 1977. A clearly written study of the nation-state.

Sperber, Jonathan. *The European Revolutions, 1848–1851.* 1994. The best study of the revolutions of 1848.

Steinberg, Jonathan. *Bismarck: A Life.* 2011. A critical portrait of the "Iron Chancellor" that exposes the deep flaws in his personality.

Tombs, Robert. *The War Against Paris, 1871.* 1981. A narrative history of the Paris Commune.

CHAPTER 23   THE COMING OF MASS POLITICS, 1870–1914

Bayly, C. A. *The Birth of the Modern World, 1780–1914: Global Connections and Comparisons.* 2004. Places the emergence of the modern West within a global perspective.

Clyman, Toby W., and Judith Vowles, eds. *Russia Through Women's Eyes: Autobiographies from Tsarist Russia.* 1999. Fascinating collection that allows us to see both women's history and Russian history in new ways.

Geraci, Robert. *Window on the East: National and Imperial Identities in Late Tsarist Russia.* 2001. Explores the effort to Russify the various peoples of "the East" in the empire.

Hoerder, Dirk. *Cultures in Contact: World Migrations in the Second Millennium.* 2002. Wide-ranging study of the causes and consequences of human migration.

Kern, Stephen. *The Culture of Time and Space, 1880–1918.* 1983. An important work that explores the cultural impact of technological change.

Lazarski, Christopher. *Power Tends to Corrupt: Lord Acton's Study of Liberty.* 2012. An examination of the role of the ideal of liberty in Western culture.

Lidtke, Vernon. *The Alternative Culture: Socialist Labor in Imperial Germany.* 1985. Looks beyond the world of parliamentary politics to assess the meaning and impact of working-class socialism.

Lindemann, Albert. *Esau's Tears: Modern Anti-Semitism and the Rise of the Jews.* 1997. A comprehensive and detailed survey that challenges many assumptions about the roots and nature of modern anti-Semitism.

Mayer, Arno. *The Persistence of the Old Regime: Europe to the Great War.* 1981. Argues that landed elites maintained a considerable amount of economic and political power throughout the nineteenth century.

Maynes, Mary Jo. *Taking the Hard Road: Life Course in French and German Workers' Autobiographies in the Era of Industrialization.* 1995. Fascinating study of the "life course" of industrial workers.

Nord, Philip. *The Republican Moment: Struggles for Democracy in Nineteenth-Century France.* 1996. Illuminates the struggle to define and redefine France.

Offen, Karen. *European Feminisms, 1700–1950: A Political History.* 1999. Comprehensive overview.

Pilbeam, Pamela. *The Middle Classes in Europe, 1789–1914: France, Germany, Italy, and Russia.* 1990. A comparative approach that helps clarify the patterns of social change.

Rappaport, Erica. *Shopping for Pleasure: Women in the Making of London's West End.* 2000. Important study of women and consumerism.

Richards, Thomas. *The Commodity Culture of Victorian England: Advertising and Spectacle, 1851–1914.* 1990. Fascinating study of the manufacturing of desire.

Slezkine, Yuri. *The Jewish Century.* 2004. A good companion volume to Lindemann's *Esau's Tears.*

Steenson, Gary P. *After Marx, Before Lenin: Marxism and Socialist Working-Class Parties in Europe, 1884–1914.* 1991. Examines both ideology and political practice within Europe's socialist parties.

Weber, Eugen. *Peasants into Frenchmen: The Modernization of Rural France, 1870–1914.* 1976. A very important work that helped shape the way historians think about "nation making."

CHAPTER 24   THE WEST AND THE WORLD: CULTURAL CRISIS AND THE NEW IMPERIALISM, 1870–1914

Adas, Michael. *Machines as the Measure of Men: Science, Technology, and Ideologies of Western Dominance.* 1989. A superb study of the way in which the ideology of empire was inextricably connected with cultural and intellectual developments within the West.

Barnes, David S. *The Great Stink of Paris and the Nineteenth-Century Struggle Against Filth and Germs.* 2005. Important study of developing attitudes toward public health.

Butler, Christopher. *Early Modernism: Literature, Music, and Painting in Europe, 1900–1916.* 1994. Wide-ranging and nicely illustrated.

Crews, Robert. *For Prophet and Tsar: Islam and Empire in Russia and Central Asia.* 2006. Important study of an often-overlooked aspect of imperialism.

Dijkstra, Bram. *Idols of Perversity: Fantasies of Feminine Evil in* Fin-de-Siècle *Culture.* 1986. This richly illustrated work shows how anxiety over the changing role of women permeated artistic production at the end of the nineteenth century.

Ellis, John. *The Social History of the Machine Gun.* 1975. Lively, nicely illustrated, and informative.

Gould, Stephen Jay. *The Mismeasure of Man.* 1996. A compelling look at the manipulation of scientific data and statistics to provide "proof" for racist and elitist assumptions.

Headrick, Daniel R. *The Tools of Empire: Technology and European Imperialism in the Nineteenth Century.* 1981. Highlights the important role played by technology in determining both the timing and success of Western imperialism.

Hochschild, Adam. *King Leopold's Ghost.* 1998. Blistering account of Leopold's imperialist rule in the Congo.

Hull, Isabel. *Absolute Destruction: Military Culture and the Practices of War in Imperial Germany.* 2005. Argues that a distinctive German military culture emerged in the late nineteenth century.

Pick, Daniel. *Faces of Degeneration: A European Disorder, c. 1848–1918.* 1993. Argues that concern over degeneration formed a central theme in European culture in the second half of the nineteenth century.

Showalter, Elaine. *Sexual Anarchy: Gender and Culture at the* Fin de Siècle. 1990. An illuminating look at the turbulence that characterized gender relations in the *fin-de-siècle*.

Sperber, Jonathan. *Popular Catholicism in Nineteenth-Century Germany.* 1984. A look at the religious dimensions of popular culture.

Vandervort, Bruce. *Wars of Imperial Conquest in Africa, 1830–1914.* 1998. Clearly presented study by a military historian.

Weeks, Theodore. *Nation and State in Late Imperial Russia: Nationalism and Russification on the Western Frontier.* 1966. Important study of Russian imperialism and nation-making.

Weiner, Jonathan. *The Beak of the Finch: The Story of Evolution in Our Time.* 1994. Prize-winning study of Darwin's theory and its impact.

Wesseling, H. L. *Divide and Rule: The Partition of Africa, 1880–1914.* 1996. A solid survey of complex developments.

CHAPTER 25   THE FIRST WORLD WAR

Barry, John M. *The Great Influenza: The Epic Story of the Deadliest Plague in History.* 2004. Riveting account of an often overlooked story.

Cooper, John Milton. *Breaking the Heart of the World: Woodrow Wilson and the Fight for the League of Nations.* 2001. Examines the failure of Wilson's new world order.

Cork, Richard. *A Bitter Truth: Avant-Garde Art and the Great War.* 1994. A beautifully illustrated work that looks at the cultural impact of the war.

Davis, Belinda. *Home Fires Burning: Food, Politics, and Everyday Life in World War I Berlin.* 2000. An important look at the German home front.

Ferguson, Niall. *The Pity of War.* 1999. Controversial reconsideration of many accepted interpretations of the origins and experience of the war.

Figes, Orlando. *A People's Tragedy: A History of the Russian Revolution.* 1997. Award-winning, gripping account of the revolutionary years.

Fitzpatrick, Sheila. *The Russian Revolution, 1917–1932.* 1994. As the title indicates, Fitzpatrick sees the revolutions of 1917 as the opening battle in a more than 10-year struggle to shape the new Russia.

Gatrell, Peter. *Russia's First World War: A Social and Economic History.* 2005. Comprehensive survey.

Healy, Maureen. *Vienna and the Fall of the Habsburg Empire: Total War and Everyday Life in World War I.* 2004. Explores the civilian conflict on the home front.

Higonnet, Margaret. *Lines of Fire: Women's Visions of World War I.* 1998. An important study of women's experiences.

Joll, James. *The Origins of the First World War.* 1984. One of the best and most carefully balanced studies of this complicated question.

Keegan, John. *The First World War.* 1999. Military history at its best.

Liulevicius, Vejas Gabriel. *War Land on the Eastern Front: Culture, National Identity, and German Occupation in World War I.* 2000. Path-breaking study of the German occupation of Russia.

Steinberg, M. D. *Voices of Revolution, 1917.* 2001. The Russian Revolution in the words of the ordinary people who made and experienced it.

Zuckerman, Larry. *The Rape of Belgium: The Untold Story of World War I.* 2004. Corrective account that takes a hard look at German atrocities.

CHAPTER 26 RECONSTRUCTION, REACTION, AND CONTINUING REVOLUTION—THE 1920s AND 1930s

Balderston, Theo, ed. *The World Economy and National Economics in the Interwar Slump.* 2003. Collections of essays exploring the impact of the Great Depression.

Berend, Ivan T. *Decades of Crisis: Central and Eastern Europe Before World War II.* 2001. Surveys the complex history of these crucial regions.

Blinkhorn, Martin. *Fascism and the Right in Europe 1919–1945.* 2000. A clear and concise historical and historiographical survey, with a selection of key primary documents.

Bookbinder, Paul. *Weimar Germany: The Republic of the Reasonable.* 1996. An innovative interpretation.

Bosworth, R. J. B. *Mussolini's Italy: Life under the Fascist Dictatorship.* 2007. Crucial study of a crucial place and time.

Brendon, Piers. *The Dark Valley: A Panorama of the 1930s.* 2000. Fast-paced but carefully researched and comprehensive overview of the histories of the United States, Germany, Italy, France, Britain, Japan, Russia, and Spain.

Brown, Kate. *A Biography of No Place: From Ethnic Borderland to Soviet Heartland.* 2004. Innovative and thought-provoking exploration of "no place," the borderlands between historic Poland and Russia.

Fitzpatrick, Sheila. *Everyday Stalinism. Ordinary Life in Extraordinary Times: Soviet Russia in the 1930s.* 1999. Explores the daily life of the ordinary urban worker in Stalinist Russia.

Fitzpatrick, Sheila. *Stalin's Peasants: Resistance and Survival in the Russian Village After Collectivization.* 1995. A superb history from the bottom up.

Getty, J. Arch, and Oleg V. Naumov. *The Road to Terror: Stalin and the Self-Destruction of the Bolsheviks, 1932–1939.* 1999. Interweaves recently discovered documents with an up-to-date interpretation of the Great Purge.

Gilbert, Bentley Brinkerhoff. *Britain 1914–1945: The Aftermath of Power.* 1996. Short, readable overview, designed for beginning students.

Jackson, Julian. *The Popular Front in France: Defending Democracy, 1934–1938.* 1988. A political and cultural history.

Kitchen, Martin. *Nazi Germany: A Critical Introduction.* 2004. Short, clearly written introduction and overview.

Mack Smith, Denis. *Mussolini: A Biography.* 1983. An engaging read and a now-classic account.

Marks, Sally. *The Ebbing of European Ascendancy: An International History of the World, 1914–1945.* 2002. Uses a global approach to examine the way in which the United States replaced Europe as the ascendant power in the world.

Pedersen, Susan. *Family, Dependence, and the Origins of the Welfare State: Britain and France, 1914–1945.* 1993. Shows how welfare policy was inextricably linked to demographic and eugenic concerns.

Seidman, Michael. *Republic of Egos: A Social History of the Spanish Civil War.* 2002. Examines the experiences of ordinary people in an extraordinary time.

Ward, Alan J. *The Easter Rising: Revolution and Irish Nationalism.* 2003. Short, nuanced, clear.

Wolpert, Stanley. *Gandhi's Passion: The Life and Legacy of Mahatma Gandhi.* 2001. An intellectual and spiritual biography by one of the foremost historians of modern India.

CHAPTER 27 WORLD WAR II

Alperovitz, Gar. *Atomic Diplomacy: Hiroshima and Potsdam. The Use of the Atomic Bomb and the American Confrontation with Soviet Power.* 1994. The first edition of this book, published in 1965, sparked an ongoing scholarly debate over whether or not U.S. fears about Soviet power influenced the decision to use the atomic bombs against Japan.

Browning, Christopher. *Ordinary Men: Reserve Police Battalion 101 and the Final Solution in Poland.* 1992. A powerful account of the participation of a group of "ordinary men" in mass murder.

Browning, Christopher. *The Origins of the Final Solution: The Evolution of Nazi Jewish Policy, September 1939–March 1942.* 2004. Highly recommended study of the origins of the Holocaust.

Calder, Angus. *The People's War: Britain, 1939–1945.* 1969. Lengthy—but worth the effort for students wishing to explore the war's impact on British society. (Those who want a shorter account can turn to Robert Mackay, *The Test of War: Inside Britain 1939–45* [1999].)

Frayn, Michael. *Copenhagen.* 1998. A remarkable play in which Frayn dramatizes a meeting (that actually did occur) between the German atomic physicist Werner Heisenberg and his Danish anti-Nazi colleague Niels Bohr. Contains both extremely clear explanations of the workings of atomic physics and a provocative exploration of the moral issues involved in the making of the atom bomb.

Friedlander, Saul. *Nazi Germany and the Jews, 1933–1939.* 1998. An important study of the evolution of Nazi anti-Semitic policy before the war.

Hilberg, Raul. *Perpetrators, Victims, Bystanders: The Jewish Catastrophe, 1933–1945.* 1992. As his title indicates, Hilberg looks at the three principal sets of participants in the Holocaust.

Iriye, Akira. *The Origins of the Second World War in Asia and the Pacific.* 1987. Part of Longman's "Origins of Modern Wars" series aimed at university students, this short and readable study highlights the major issues and events.

Keegan, John. *The Second World War.* 1989. Provides clear explanations of military technologies and techniques; packed with useful maps and vivid illustrations.

Kitchen, Martin. *Nazi Germany at War.* 1995. A short and nicely organized survey of the German home front.

Maudsley, Evan. *Thunder in the East: The Nazi-Soviet War 1941–1945*. 2005. A wide-ranging account that looks at social and political contexts as well as military strategy and technology.

Mazower, Mark. *Hitler's Empire: How the Nazis Ruled Europe*. 2008. Impressively wide-ranging account that challenges many assumptions.

Merridale, Catherine. *Ivan's War: Life and Death in the Red Army, 1939–1945*. 2007. "From-the-bottom-up" military history, this account looks at the often harrowing experiences of ordinary soldiers.

Moore, Bob, ed. *Resistance in Western Europe*. 2000. A collection of essays that explores recent research on this controversial topic.

Overy, Richard. *Russia's War: A History of the Soviet War Effort, 1941–1945*. 1997. A compelling account, written to accompany the television documentary *Russia's War*.

Paxton, Robert. *Vichy France: Old Guard and New Order, 1940–1944*. 1972. A now-classic study of the aims and evolution of France's collaborationist government.

Rees, Laurence. *WWII Behind Closed Doors: Stalin, the Nazis and the West*. 2008. Winner of the British Book Award for History and companion volume to the BBC Television series, this account uses recently revealed archival documents and interviews to explore the morally complex issues involved in the strange alliance between Stalin and Western democracy.

Rhodes, Richard. *The Making of the Atomic Bomb*. 1986. A lengthy but very readable account; very good at explaining the complicated science involved.

Snyder, Timothy. *Bloodlands: Europe Between Hitler and Stalin*. 2010. One of the most important works to be published in recent years.

Weinberg, Gerhard. *A World at Arms: A Global History of World War II*. 1994. Places the war within a global rather than simply a European context.

CHAPTER 28 REDEFINING THE WEST AFTER WORLD WAR II

Ansprenger, Franz. *The Dissolution of Colonial Empires*. 1989. A clear and comprehensive account (that unfortunately includes no maps).

Applebaum, Anne. *Iron Curtain. The Crushing of Eastern Europe, 1944–1956*. 2012. Now the definitive account of the origins of the Cold War.

Castles, Stephen, et al. *Here for Good: Western Europe's New Ethnic Minorities*. 1984. A useful exploration of the impact of postwar immigration, despite the rather rigid Marxist analysis.

Crampton, R. J. *Eastern Europe in the Twentieth Century—And After*. 1997. Detailed chapters on the 1950s and 1960s, including a substantial discussion of the Prague Spring.

De Grazia, Victoria. *Irresistible Empire: America's Advance Through Twentieth-Century Europe*. 2005. A study of the Americanization of Europe.

Elkins, Caroline. *Imperial Reckoning: The Untold Story of Britain's Gulag in Kenya*. 2005. This controversial work won the Pulitzer Prize for Nonfiction.

Fineberg, Jonathan. *Art Since 1940: Strategies of Being*. 1995. A big, bold, lavishly illustrated volume that makes the unfashionable argument that individuals matter.

Fink, Carole, et al. *1968: The World Transformed*. 1998. A collection of essays that explores both the international and the domestic political context for the turmoil of 1968.

Gaddis, John Lewis. *The Cold War: A New History*. 2005. A comprehensive overview by a prominent Cold War historian.

Gillingham, John. *European Integration, 1950–2003: Superstate or New Market Economy?* 2003. An important interpretive history of the European Union.

Gross, Jan T., ed. *The Politics of Retribution in Europe: World War II and Its Aftermath*. 2000. This series of essays makes clear that war did not end in Europe in May 1945.

Judge, Edward, and John Langdon. *A Hard and Bitter Peace: A Global History of the Cold War*. 1999. An extremely useful survey for students. Excellent maps.

Judt, Tony. *Postwar: A History of Europe Since 1945*. 2005. An important interpretive survey.

Judt, Tony, and Timothy Snyder. *Thinking the Twentieth Century*. 2012. Exciting survey of 20th-century intellectual history.

Keep, John. *Last of the Empires: A History of the Soviet Union, 1945–1991*. 1995. Looks beyond the Kremlin to explore social, cultural, and economic developments.

Madaraz, Jeannette. *Working in East Germany: Normality in a Socialist Dictatorship, 1961–1979*. 2006. Examines ordinary life in an extraordinary society.

Poiger, Uta. *Jazz, Rock, and Rebels: Cold War Politics and American Culture in a Divided Germany*. 2000. Explores the interplay among youth culture, Americanization, and political protest.

Rees, Laurence. *WWII Behind Closed Doors: Stalin, the Nazis and the West*. 2008. Winner of the British Book Award for History and companion volume to the BBC Television series, this account uses recently revealed archival documents and interviews to explore the compromises that created Cold War Europe.

Shepard, Todd. *The Invention of Decolonization: The Algerian War and the Remaking of France*. 2006. Explores not only the history but also the continuing impact of the Algerian fight for independence from France.

Steege, Paul. *Black Market Cold War: Everyday Life in Berlin, 1946–1949*. 2007. History "from the bottom up" that explores the ways Berlin became the symbolic center of the Cold War and its impact on the people of Berlin.

Taubman, William. *Khrushchev: The Man and His Era*. 2003. The first biography of Khrushchev to make use of sources made available since the end of the Cold War.

Taylor, Frederick. *The Berlin Wall: A World Divided, 1961–1989*. 2007. Uses the dramatic history of the Berlin Wall to explore the global impact of the Cold War.

Westad, Odd Arne. *The Global Cold War: Third World Interventions and the Making of Our Time*. 2007. Highly recommended study of the Cold War's globalization.

Wyman, Mark. *DPs: Europe's Displaced Persons, 1945–1951.* 1989. An important study of an often-neglected topic.

CHAPTER 29   THE WEST IN THE CONTEMPORARY ERA: NEW ENCOUNTERS AND TRANSFORMATIONS

NOTE: Many of the readings recommended for Chapter 28 supplement this chapter as well.

Ardagh, John. *Germany and the Germans: The United Germany in the Mid-1990s.* 1996. A snapshot of a society in the midst of social and economic change.

Jenkins, Philip. *God's Continent: Christianity, Islam, and Europe's Religious Crisis.* 2007. Balanced, sensible, historically informed; an important book.

Kenney, Padraic. *The Burdens of Freedom: Eastern Europe Since 1989.* 2006. In only 160 pages, Kenney offers a lucid and very helpful account of postrevolutionary developments.

Kotkin, Stephen. *Armageddon Averted: The Soviet Collapse, 1970–2000.* 2001. Clear and compelling account.

Lebovics, Herman. *Bringing the Empire Back Home: France in the Global Age.* 2004. Cultural history of the contemporary struggle to define French identity.

Lewis, Jane, ed. *Women and Social Policies in Europe: Work, Family and the State.* 1993. A series of essays exploring the position of women in western Europe. Packed with statistics and useful tables.

Lovell, Stephen. *Destination in Doubt: Russia Since 1989.* 2006. A clear and succinct account.

McNeill, John. *Something New Under the Sun: An Environmental History of the Twentieth Century.* 2000. Argues that twentieth-century human economic activity has transformed the ecology of the globe—an ongoing experiment with a potentially devastating outcome.

Ost, David. *The Defeat of Solidarity: Anger and Politics in Postcommunist Europe.* 2005. Fascinating and sometimes disturbing account of Polish developments since the victory of Solidarity over communism.

Rogel, Carole. *The Breakup of Yugoslavia and the War in Bosnia.* 1998. Designed for undergraduates, this work includes a short but detailed historical narrative, biographies of the main personalities, and a set of primary documents.

Rosenberg, Tina. *The Haunted Land: Facing Europe's Ghosts After Communism.* 1995. Winner of the Pulitzer Prize, this disturbing account focuses on the fundamental moral issues facing postcommunist political cultures.

Sandler, Irving. *Art of the Postmodern Era: From the Late 1960s to the Early 1980s.* 1996. Much more broad-ranging than the title suggests, this well-written, blessedly jargon-free work sets both contemporary art and the theories of the postmodern within the wider historical context.

Stokes, Gale. *The Walls Came Tumbling Down: The Collapse of Communism in Eastern Europe.* 1993. A superb account, firmly embedded in history.

Taylor-Gooby, Peter. *Reframing Social Citizenship.* 2008. An analysis of the impact of welfare reforms since the rise of New Conservatism.

Veldman, Meredith. *Margaret Thatcher: Shaping the New Conservatism.* 2014. Part of Westview Press's *On the World Stage: Biographies of Important Individuals in World History* series.

NOTES

CHAPTER 20

1. H. Wallon, *Histoire du tribunal révolutionnaire de Paris*, vol. 4 (1880–1882), 511.

CHAPTER 21

1. Lord Ashley's Commission on Mines, *Parliamentary Papers*, vols. 15–17 (1842), Appendix 1, Note 26.
2. Sir James Kay-Shuttleworth (1832), quoted in John Rule, *The Labouring Classes in Early Industrial England* (1986).
3. John Richardson, *The Friend: A Religious and Literary Journal*, 30 (1856), 97.
4. "Report of the Select Committee on the Factories Bill," *Parliamentary Papers*, vol. 20 (1833).
5. John O'Rourke, *The History of the Great Irish Famine of 1847* (1902).
6. David Gillard, ed., *British Documents on Foreign Affairs*, vol. 1: *The Ottoman Empire in the Balkans, 1856–1875* (1984–1985), 20.

CHAPTER 23

1. Leslie Moch, *Moving Europeans: Migration in Western Europe Since 1650* (1992), 147.
2. Quoted in Eugen Weber, *Peasants into Frenchmen: The Modernization of Rural France, 1870–1914* (1976), 332–333.
3. Norman Kleeblatt, *The Dreyfus Affair: Art, Truth, and Justice* (1987), 96.
4. Quoted in Eric Cahm, *The Dreyfus Affair in French Society and Politics* (1994), 167.
5. Quoted in Robert Gildea, *Barricades and Borders: Europe, 1800–1914* (1987), 317.
6. Eugen Weber, *France, Fin-de-Siècle* (1986), 126.
7. Albert Lindemann, *Esau's Tears: Modern Anti-Semitism and the Rise of the Jews* (1997).
8. Maria Desraismes, "La Femme et Le Droit," *Eve dans l'humanite* (1891), 16–17.

CHAPTER 24

1. Winston Churchill, *The River War: An Account of the Re-Conquest of the Sudan* (1933); quoted in Daniel Headrick, *The Tools of Empire: Technology and European Imperialism in the Nineteenth Century* (1981), 118.
2. Quoted in Anne McClintock, *Imperial Leather: Race, Gender, and Sexuality in the Colonial Contest* (1995), 50.
3. From Rider Haggard, *She* (1887).

4. Quoted in H. Stuart Hughes, *Consciousness and Society* (1958), 296.
5. Quoted in Shearer West, *Fin de Siècle* (1993), 24.
6. Stephen Kern, *The Culture of Time and Space, 1880–1918* (1983), 195.
7. From *Elementary Forms*, quoted in Hughes, *Consciousness and Society*, 284–285.
8. Quoted in William Schneider, *An Empire for the Masses: The French Popular Image of Africa, 1870–1900* (1982), 72.
9. Heinrich von Treitschke, *Politics* (1897).
10. Yves-Alain Bois, "Painting as Trauma," in Christopher Green, *Picasso's* Les Demoiselles d'Avignon (2001), 49.
11. Quoted in Catherine Hall, *Cultures of Empire: Colonizers in Britain and the Empire in the Nineteenth and Twentieth Centuries* (2000), p. 299.
12. Brassaï, *Conversations with Picasso*, translated by Jane Marie Todd (1999), 32.
13. John Golding, "*Les Demoiselles D'Avignon* and the Exhibition of 1988," in Green, *Picasso's* Les Demoiselles, 29.
14. Mary Kingsley, in *West African Studies* (1901), 329–330.
15. Rudyard Kipling, *Verse* (1920).
16. Headrick, *The Tools of Empire*, 101. Headrick is the historian who identified the crucial role of the steamship, the quinine prophylaxis, and the breech-loading, repeating rifle in the conquest of Africa.
17. Quoted in Thomas Pakenham, *The Scramble for Africa, 1876–1912* (1991), 22.
18. Quoted in F. K. Crowley (ed.), *A New History of Australia* (1974), 6.
19. Ibid., 207.
20. Quoted in W. G. Beasley, *Japanese Imperialism, 1894–1945* (1987), 31–33.

CHAPTER 25

1. Quoted in Niall Ferguson, *The Pity of War* (1999), 152.
2. Quoted in Eric Leeds, *No Man's Land: Combat and Identity in World War I* (1979), 17.
3. Allister Horne, *The Price of Glory: Verdun, 1916* (1967), 27.
4. Siegfried Sassoon, *Memoirs of an Infantry Officer* (1937), 228.
5. Peter Gatrell, *A Whole Empire Walking: Refugees in Russia During World War I* (2000).
6. Ernst Lissauer, "Hymn of Hate" (1914), in *Jugend* (1914), translated by Barbara Henderson, *New York Times*, October 15, 1914.
7. Quoted in W. Bruce Lincoln, *Red Victory: A History of the Russian Civil War* (1989), 32.

8. Quoted in Edvard Radzinsky, *The Last Tsar*, translated by Marian Schwartz (1993), 336.

9. From the written account of Yakov Yurovsky, quoted in Radzinsky, *The Last Tsar*, 355.

10. Quoted in William Henry Chamberlin, *The Russian Revolution, 1917-1921, vol. 2: From the Civil War to the Consolidation of Power* (1987), 91.

11. Quoted in Lincoln, *Red Victory*, 151.

12. Ibid., 155.

13. Quoted in Radzinsky, *The Last Tsar*, 326.

14. Richard Pipes et al. (eds.), *The Unknown Lenin* (1999), 6.

15. Ibid., Document 59.

CHAPTER 26

1. Quoted in Peter Gay, *Weimar Culture* (1970), 99.

2. Martin J. Sherwin, *A World Destroyed: Hiroshima and the Origins of the Arms Race* (1987), 17.

3. Quoted in Michael Burleigh, *The Third Reich: A New History* (2000), 36.

4. Quoted in Ibid., 52.

5. Quoted in Joachim Fest, *Hitler* (1973), 190-193.

6. Ibid., 192, 218.

7. Quoted in Claudia Koonz, *Mothers in the Fatherland* (1987), 130.

8. Quoted in Fest, *Hitler*, 445.

9. Quoted in Koonz, *Mothers in the Fatherland*, 194.

10. Quoted in Mark Mazower, *Dark Continent: Europe's Twentieth Century* (1998), 123.

11. Quoted in Sheila Fitzpatrick, *Everyday Stalinism* (1999), 68.

12. Quoted in Koonz, *Mothers in the Fatherland*, 178.

13. Ibid., 56; Victoria DeGrazia, *How Fascism Ruled Women: Italy, 1922-1945* (1992), 234.

14. Quoted in Wendy Goldman, *Women, the State, and Revolution: Soviet Family Policy and Social Life, 1917-1936* (1993), 5.

15. Quoted in Felix Gilbert, *The End of the European Era* (1991), 162.

16. Mohandas K. Gandhi, *An Autobiography: The Story of My Experiments with Truth* (1957), 120.

17. Quoted in Tyler Stovall, *Paris Noir: African Americans in the City of Light* (1996), 32.

CHAPTER 27

1. Quoted in Robert H. Abzug, *Inside the Vicious Heart: Americans and the Liberation of Nazi Concentration Camps* (1985), 19.

2. Quoted in Gordon Horwitz, *In the Shadow of Death: Living Outside the Gates of Mauthausen* (1991), 167.

3. Quoted in Piers Brendon, *The Dark Valley: A Panorama of the 1930s* (2000), 282.

4. Quoted in Richard Overy, *Russia's War* (1998), 95.

5. Quoted in Mark Mazower, *Dark Continent: Europe's Twentieth Century* (1999), 157.

6. Quoted in Peter Clarke, *Hope and Glory: Britain, 1900-1990* (1996), 204.

7. Quoted in Joachim Fest, *Hitler* (1973), 665.

8. Mark Mazower, *Hitler's Empire: How the Nazis Ruled Europe* (2008), 522.

9. Ibid., 523.

10. Quoted in Richard Rhodes, *The Making of the Atomic Bomb* (1988), 474.

11. Timothy Snyder, *Bloodlands: Europe Between Hitler and Stalin* (2010).

12. Elie Wiesel, *Night* (1960), 39.

13. Gideon Hausner, *Justice in Jerusalem* (1966), 291.

14. Ibid., 323-324.

15. From Hausner's opening statement; quoted in Moshe Pearlman, *The Capture and Trial of Adolf Eichmann* (1963), 149.

16. Ibid., 463-465.

17. Ibid., 603; Hausner, *Justice in Jerusalem*, 422.

18. Kate Brown, *Biography of No Place: From Ethnic Borderlands to Soviet Heartland* (2004), 221.

19. Quoted in Ulrich Herbert, *Hitler's Foreign Workers* (1997), 306.

CHAPTER 28

1. Stalin to Maxim Litvinov, cited in Vladislav Zubok and Constantine Pleshakov, *Inside the Kremlin's Cold War: From Stalin to Khrushchev* (Cambridge, 1996), 37-38.

2. Leo Crowley, director of the Foreign Economic Administration under Roosevelt and Truman; quoted in William Appleman Williams, *The Tragedy of American Diplomacy* (New York, 1972), 241.

3. Lawrence Rees, *World War II Behind Closed Doors: Stalin, the Nazis, and the West* (2008), 221, 236.

4. Quoted in William Hardy McNeill, *America, Britain, and Russia: Their Cooperation and Conflict 1941-1946* (New York, 1970), 700, note 2.

5. Quoted in Karel Kaplan, *Report on the Murder of the General Secretary* (1990), 159.

6. Ibid., 242.

7. Quoted in John Hargreaves, *Decolonization in Africa* (1996), 113.

8. Quotation from *Time* magazine, 1950; quoted in Martin Walker, *The Cold War and the Making of the Modern World* (1993), 66-67.

9. Quoted in Walker, *The Cold War*, 83.

10. Quoted in Stephen Ambrose, *Rise to Globalism* (1971), 225.

11. Quoted in Donald White, *The American Century* (1999), 286.

12. Quoted in John L. H. Keep, *Last of the Empires: A History of the Soviet Union, 1945-1991* (1995), 79.

13. Quoted in Michael Scammell, *From Gulag to Glasnost: Nonconformist Art in the Soviet Union*, eds. Alla Rosenfeld and Norton T. Dodge (1995), 61.

14. Quoted in Walker, *The Cold War*, 105.

15. Quoted in Robert Paxton, *Europe in the Twentieth Century* (1997), 578.

16. Quoted in Jonathan Fineberg, *Art Since 1940: Strategies of Being* (1995), 144.

17. Ibid., 89.

18. Quoted in Adrian Hastings, *Modern Catholicism: Vatican II and After* (1991), 29.

19. Reinhold Wagnleitner, *Coca-Colonization and the Cold War: The Cultural Mission of the United States in Austria After the Second World War* (1994).

20. Quoted in Felix Gilbert, *The End of the European Era, 1890 to the Present* (1991), 429.

21. Quoted in Richard Kuisel, *Seducing the French: The Dilemma of Americanization* (1993), 147.

CHAPTER 29

1. Quoted in Robert Paxton, *Europe in the Twentieth Century* (1997), 613.

2. Kenneth Boulding, "The Economics of the Coming Spaceship Earth," first published in 1966, reprinted in *Toward a Steady-State Economy*, ed. Herman Daly (1973).

3. Quoted in D. J. Peterson, *Troubled Lands: The Legacy of Soviet Environmental Destruction* (1993), 12.

4. Quoted in Archie Brown, *The Gorbachev Factor* (1996), 125.

5. Salman Rushdie, "Please, Read *Satanic Verses* Before Condemning It," *Illustrated Weekly of India* (October 1988). Reprinted in M. M. Ahsan and A. R. Kidwai, *Sacrilege Versus Civility: Muslim Perspectives on The Satanic Verses Affair* (1991), 63.

6. Quoted in Malise Ruthven, *A Satanic Affair: Salman Rushdie and the Wrath of Islam* (1991), 100.

7. *The Sunday Telegraph* (June 24, 1990), quoted in Ahsan and Kidwai, *Sacrilege Versus Civility*, 80.

8. Quoted in Irving Sandler, *Art of the Postmodern Era* (1996), 4.

PHOTO CREDITS

INDEX

Amenemhet (Egypt), 33

Amenhotep III (Egypt), 36, 38–39. *See also* Akhenaten (Egypt)

Amenhotep IV (Egypt), 38–39. *See also* Akhenaten (Egypt)

America. *See also* England (Britain); *specific countries and regions*

American Indians, 422

Americas, Europeans in, 400–414

Ammon, 59, 69

Amorites, 21

Amos (Hebrew prophet), 72

Amphitheaters, *179* (illus)

Amsterdam, stock exchange in, 521, *521* (illus)

Amun, temple of (Karnak), 36

Anabaptists, 447–448

Anasazi people, 400

Anatolia (Turkey). *See also* Turkey
    in Byzantine Empire, *237* (map)
    Cyrus conquering of, 87
    economic hardship and political fragmentation, 40
    Egypt and, 36, 40
    fall of, 60
    food production in, 13, 15
    Hittite Empire in, 45–47
    International Bronze Age and, 50, 54
    Medes and, 87
    Ottomans in, 337–339, *339* (map)
    Pergamum in, *111* (illus), *120* (map), *129*, *129* (illus)
    Troy/Wilusa, 50

Anatomy
    chronology of publication, 380
    dissection and, *533* (illus)
    first handbook on, 134
    Vesalius and, 379

Anaximander, 102

Anaximenes, 102

Andes Mountains regions, Inca Empire in, 402

Anglo-Saxon Chronicle, 285

Anglo-Saxons
    conversion to Christianity, 270–271
    in England, 284–285

Angra Mainyu (god), 88

Anguissola, Sofonisba, 383

Animals
    agriculture and, 42
    in Columbian Exchange, 420
    domestication of, 42

Annals of Assurbanipal II, 70

Anne of Austria, 497

Anti-Chalcedonian (Monophysite) Christians, 214, 254

Antigone (Sophocles), 101

Antigonus, 119

Antioch, Syria
    Christianity in, 208
    Persia and, 228
    sack of, 228

Antiochus IV Epiphanes and Jews, 124

Antiquity and Renaissance arts, 380–383

Anti-semitism. *See also* Jews and Judaism

Antisthenes, 133

Antonine Age (Rome), 172

Antonine Decree, 180

Antonius, Marcus (Mark Antony), 181

Antwerp, 462, 479

Anu (god), 23, 26

Anubis (god), *193* (illus)

Anxiety, Price Revolution and, 464–465

Aphrodite (goddess), 154

Aphrodite, Temple of, *130* (illus)

Aphrodite of Melos (statue), *128* (illus)

Apocalypse, 439

Apopis (god), 30

Apuleius (writer), 193

Aquinas, Thomas, 322

Aquitaine and Hundred Years' War, 345, *346* (maps)

Arab world: Islamic caliphates in, 250, 252–255

Arabian Nights, 256

Arabian Peninsula, Midian and, 70

Arabs
    Arameans and, 57
    before Islam, 245
    in Sicily, 256–259

Aragon
    Castile joined with, 389–390
    Castile united with, 502–503

Aramaic language, 57

Aram-Damasus, 57

Arameans, 57

Arch of Titus (Rome), *195* (illus)

Archaic Age, in Greece, 79–86

Archbishops, in Western church, 208

Archers, *347* (illus)

Archimedes, 536

Archimedes of Syracuse, 134

Architecture
    Brunelleschi and, 381
    of Egyptian pyramids, 30–31

Gothic, *324* (illus)

Hellenistic, 128–129

in Rome, 153

of St. Petersburg, 514

Sumerian, 23

Arcimboldo, Giuseppe, *484* (illus)

Ares (god), 154

Arian Christianity, 212
    of Germanic tribes, 224

Aristarchus of Samos, 134, 535

Aristides, Aelius (writer), 169–170

Aristocracy. *See also* Nobility

Aristocrats, 26

Aristophanes of Athens, 101

Aristotelianism and education, 540–541

Aristotle, 106
    geocentric theories of, 134, 526–527
    impetus theory and, 535
    on physics, 527, 535

Ark of the Covenant, 72

Armada, Spanish, 478

Armed forces
    charioteers in, 20–21, 35, 49, 52
    of Mongols, 337
    in Sparta, 84, 85
    standing armies and, 494–495

Armenian language, 211, 213

Arminius (Germany), 186

Armor and military revolution, 349–350, 372

Art of Dying, 356, *357* (illus)

"Art of Love, The" (Ovid), 191

Artemis (goddess), 154

Arthur (legendary English king), 223–224

Art(s)
    in Carolingian Renaissance, 275–276, *276* (illus)
    in Classical Greece, 100–101
    in Egypt, 32
    Greek, 80
    in Hellenistic cities, 128–129
    icons and, 240
    Minoan, 48
    in Rome, 153

Asceticism and Antony, 214–215

Asherah (goddess), 60

Ashtart (goddess), 60

Ashurbanipal (Neo-Assyrian Empire), library of, 62–63

Ashurbanipal III (Neo-Assyrian Empire), cavalry, *62* (illus)

Ashurnasirpal II (Neo-Assyria Empire), 61